On Board RMS Titanic

On Board RMS Titanic

Memories of the Maiden Voyage

George Behe

For my mother

By the same author

Titanic: Psychic Forewarnings of a Tragedy (Patrick Stephens, 1988)
Lost at Sea: Ghost Ships and Other Mysteries [with Michael Goss] (Prometheus Books, 1994)
Titanic: Safety, Speed and Sacrifice (Transportation Trails, 1997)
'Archie': The Life of Major Archibald Butt from Georgia to the Titanic (Lulu.com Press, 2010)
A Death on the Titanic: The Loss of Major Archibald Butt (Lulu.com Press, 2011)
The Carpathia and the Titanic: Rescue at Sea (Lulu.com Press, 2011)

First published 2012
This paperback edition 2017

The History Press
The Mill, Brimscombe Port
Stroud, Gloucestershire, GL5 2QG
www.thehistorypress.co.uk

British Library Cataloguing in Publication Data.
A catalogue record for this book is available from the British Library.

ISBN 978 0 7509 8268 9

Typesetting and origination by The History Press
Printed and bound by CPI Group (UK) Ltd

TABLE OF CONTENTS

	Acknowledgements	7
	Introduction	9
1	Prelude: 31 May 1911	15
2	Pre-Sailing Days	17
3	10 April 1912: *Titanic* at Southampton	25
4	10 April 1912: *Titanic* Sails from Southampton for Cherbourg	31
5	11 April 1912: *Titanic* Arrives at Queenstown and Sails Onward	45
6	12 April 1912: *Titanic* at Sea	69
7	13 April 1912: *Titanic* at Sea	73
8	14 April 1912: *Titanic* at Sea	75
9	15 April 1912: Disaster	77
10	16 April 1912: On board the *Carpathia*	79
11	17 April 1912: On board the *Carpathia*	91
12	18 April 1912: On board the *Carpathia*	103
13	19 April 1912 and Afterwards	139
14	Passenger and Crew Biographies	407
	Notes	499
	Index	507

Acknowledgements

Although the present author was responsible for discovering the texts of many *Titanic*-related letters and documents during the course of his own research, a large number of friends and fellow researchers were kind enough to donate the texts of additional letters, postcards and memoirs that form a part of their own collections. I am extremely grateful to all of these people, but several of them went so far above and beyond the call of duty in making contributions to this volume that I feel they deserve special recognition:

Don Lynch, for sharing rare documents from his collection and for contributing valuable biographical information regarding the *Titanic*'s passengers and crewmen.

The Titanic Historical Society and Titanic Museum, for granting me permission to publish the texts of numerous documents from their collection.

Kalman Tanito, for providing the texts of numerous foreign documents, including articles from the Finnish newspaper *Karjalan Sanomat*, and for his tireless efforts to translate those documents on my behalf.

Geoff Whitfield, for providing me with numerous documents and for connecting me with other collectors who own additional documents of interest.

Brian Ticehurst, for alerting me to the existence of the 1912 newspaper that published the marvellous letters written by Kate Buss and for providing the texts of several other letters. (Note: Brian published the Buss letters himself in his booklet, *Titanic Passenger Miss Kate Buss of Sittingbourne, Kent.*)

Patrick Bogue of Onslows, for generously granting me permission to quote the published texts of documents that have appeared in his firm's auction catalogues.

Randy Bryan Bigham, for sharing a number of rare documents related to Lucy Duff Gordon and Archibald Gracie.

Per Kristian Sebak, for providing numerous foreign documents and for kindly translating those documents into English.

Steve Rigby, for his invaluable assistance in providing me with the texts of a number of important documents.

Craig Stringer, for his marvellous CD index 'Titanic People, 1912' which provided me with passenger and crew biographical information on those rare occasions when I was unable to uncover much information through my own efforts.

Steve Hall, for his unfailing friendship and support during the many years we have exchanged information about the *Titanic* disaster.

Amy Rigg, for her kindness and willingness to help this project come to fruition.

Other friends who helped me by generously providing *Titanic* documents from their personal collections are: Lady Flavia Anderson, Nelson Arnstein, Stephen Bottomore, Rustie Brown, Frederica Burgess, Robert Burr, Malcolm Cheape, Julia Collyer, Pat Cook, John Cowart, John Creamer, Nestor Diaz, Enrique Dick, Klaus Egvang, Richard Faber, Lynne Farr, Alfonso Carbone Garbuci, Joan Kilgannon-Glunk, Christina Gorch, Jacque Gorch, Andy Gronberg, Holger Gronberg, Jim Harper, Roland Hauser, Priscilla Hibbard, Ben Holme, Vera Jones, Daniel Klistorner, Roy Kristiansen, John Lamoreau, Lady Clair Lindsay, Ken Marschall, Elizabeth Jean Martin, Wanda Martin, Steve Maynard, Melissa McClone, Jim McDonald, Olivier Mendez, Linda Messenger, Steve Miller, Arne Mjåland, Sheila Pierce, Eric Porch, Tony Probst, Dinah Quilter, Trudy Ransome, Carl Sagan, Richard de Roussy de Sales, Eric Sauder, Brigitte Schwartzenbach, Hermann Söldner, Craig Sopin, Rebecca Stares, Susan Stares, Robert Thompson, Gladys Weaver and Quincy Williams.

And finally, the author would like to thank the following *Titanic* survivors, who offered me their friendship and shared their personal memories of the disaster: Frank Aks, Ruth Becker Blanchard, Bertram Dean, Millvina Dean, Edith Brown Haisman, Eva Hart, Edwina Troutt MacKenzie, Bertha Watt Marshall, Michel Navratil, Nan Harper Pont, Louise Kink Pope, Marjorie Newell Robb, Maude Sincock Roberts, Eleanor Johnson Shuman, Nelle Snyder, George Thomas, and Winnifred Quick Van Tongerloo. All of these survivors are now deceased, but I will never forget them and will always owe them a debt of gratitude that I will never be able to repay.

INTRODUCTION

The basic facts of the story are well known. The White Star liner *Titanic* – the largest ship in the world – was scheduled to leave Southampton on 10 April 1912 on the first leg of her maiden voyage. The *Titanic* was described as being 'practically unsinkable,' and an oral tradition arose that ignored the qualifier 'practically' and promoted the belief among the general public that the ship was *absolutely* unsinkable. In addition to her own passengers and crewmen, the *Titanic* was scheduled to carry a large number of passengers from other liners whose sailings had been cancelled due to a coal strike, and most of the people who were scheduled to sail on the brand new ship eagerly let their friends and loved ones know about their travel plans; many letters and postcards describing these travel plans were written and mailed to people living in many widely scattered locations.

At noon on 10 April the *Titanic* was gently eased away from the White Star dock in Southampton and gradually began making her way down the channel toward the open sea. As the ship moved abreast of the moored liners *Oceanic* and *New York*, however, the sudden displacement of water caused by the *Titanic*'s passing caused the *New York* to strain at her moorings; the lines that connected the *New York* to the *Oceanic* snapped like twine, and the helpless vessel drifted out into the channel and was pulled relentlessly toward the huge passenger liner that was moving through the water nearby. The *New York*'s stern narrowly missed striking the *Titanic*'s port quarter, and several tugs wrestled with the helpless vessel as she drifted forward along the *Titanic*'s port side and cleared the big liner's bows by a matter of feet. Despite this close call, the *Titanic* remained unscathed, and after a brief delay she resumed her run for the open sea.

That evening the *Titanic* stopped briefly at Cherbourg, and the following noon she stopped at Queenstown, Ireland; at both locations the vessel picked up additional passengers and mail, and the letters that had been written on board the great vessel during the previous twenty-four hours were carried ashore and entrusted to the postal systems of France and Ireland for delivery to their ultimate destinations. Many of these communications contained descriptions of the previous day's voyage and the close call that the *Titanic* had had during her near-collision with the *New York*.

After leaving Queenstown on 11 April the *Titanic* turned her bows westward and headed out onto the vast expanse of the North Atlantic as she proceeded toward New York. Her passengers included some of the wealthiest and best-known personages in England and the United States, but – in addition to these luminaries – the great vessel carried a full complement of business and pleasure travellers as well as a large number of European, Irish and Middle Eastern immigrants who were leaving their homelands in order to create new lives for themselves in the New World. The passengers travelling on board the *Titanic* totalled 1,318, a number that was augmented by the vessel's 891 crewmen – most of whom hailed from the Southampton area and left families whose livelihood depended upon the payslips that the crewmen would receive from the White Star Line when they returned to England.

For the next three days the *Titanic*'s maiden voyage proceeded normally, and with each passing day the ship's officers gradually increased her speed with the intention of bettering the crossing time that had been achieved by her sister ship *Olympic* during that vessel's own maiden voyage the previous year. The *Titanic*'s passengers enjoyed their brief respite from everyday life on shore and took advantage of this golden opportunity to socialise with friends and acquaintances, listen to the ship's orchestra and partake of the excellent food and drink served in the ship's spacious dining rooms.

During these idyllic days at sea the *Titanic*'s passengers and crewmen continued to write letters and postcards to their friends and loved ones at home; most (but not all) of these communications were deposited in the ship's mailboxes and were collected and sorted every day by the mail clerks, who placed them in the appropriate mail bags for offloading and delivery once the *Titanic* arrived in New York.

With the arrival of Sunday 14 April the *Titanic* began to receive wireless messages from other vessels warning of icebergs and masses of field ice that stretched diagonally across the southern steamer track – the track that the *Titanic* was traversing during her maiden trip to New York. The icefield in question lay ahead of the *Titanic* in a position that her officers calculated she would reach sometime around 11 p.m. that same evening. Weather conditions and visibility remained ideal throughout the day, though, and at 7 p.m. three additional boilers were connected to the *Titanic*'s engines, an action that increased the vessel's speed to 22½ knots – the fastest speed she had achieved during the entire voyage.

Darkness came, and the *Titanic* steamed through the night, her speed undiminished despite the presence of the icefield that was known to lie directly in her path. 11 p.m came and went, and the *Titanic*'s lookouts were later heard to allege that they reported several iceberg sightings to the ship's officers during the next half-hour – but that the officers did not slow the vessel down or taken any other action to minimise the chances of a possible collision. Whether or not these allegations were true, at 11.40 p.m. the officers' lack of prudent action caught up with the *Titanic* when she collided with an iceberg that opened six of her forward compartments to the sea.

The *Titanic*'s officers began evacuating passengers from the vessel despite an insufficient number of lifeboats, but two hours and forty minutes later the ship upended, broke in half and sank beneath the waves, taking with her two-thirds of the passengers and crewmen who had entrusted their lives to the White Star Line. The 712 people who were lucky enough to find places in lifeboats that night were picked up by the Cunard liner *Carpathia*, which landed them in New York three days later.

To the best of this author's knowledge the story of the *Titanic*'s maiden voyage and tragic end has never been told entirely from the perspective of the passengers and crewmen *themselves*. Aside from the use of occasional direct quotes, the story is usually told in paraphrased form by authors who were not even alive when the *Titanic* set sail on her maiden voyage. A few researchers who were luckier than most were able to speak in person with living *Titanic* survivors who described their experiences in vivid detail, but the last of those survivors is gone now and – aside from recordings – the sound of their voices has been stilled forever.

But only the *sound* of their voices has been silenced ...

One source of information about the *Titanic* disaster that has often been overlooked by historians is the large number of postcards, letters and diary entries that were written by passengers and crewmen before and during the *Titanic*'s maiden voyage itself, as well as letters and memoirs that were written by survivors during the tragic days that followed the sinking – a period when memories were still fresh and the horror of the disaster was a raw, open wound that had not yet had a chance to heal. The texts of these personal documents serve as windows into their writers' souls, but – despite the fact that these documents are widely scattered and difficult to track down – finding them is the only way a researcher can glimpse the emotions that were experienced by the passengers and crewmen at various periods during the *Titanic*'s maiden voyage and its tragic aftermath.

The letters and postcards that were written by passengers and crewmen prior to the *Titanic*'s maiden voyage are commonplace in nature and are similar to written documents that any human being – past or present – might write prior to starting on a long journey. There were announcements of travel plans, words of farewell, words of advice to loved ones, last minute requests, expressions of excitement regarding the upcoming voyage and expressions of pleasure at the traveller's impending reunion with friends and loved ones in the United States.

The documents that were written during the five days of the *Titanic*'s maiden voyage are similarly prosaic and describe the day-to-day activities of each traveller on board the ship herself. Again, these are commonplace documents describing routine shipboard events that could easily have occurred to the present reader or to any other traveller who finds himself bound from one port of call to another.

But the banal nature of the passenger and crew communications changes dramatically after the sinking of the *Titanic* on 15 April, and the horrifying content of subsequent written documents bursts upon us unexpectedly like a bolt from the blue. No longer do we read about everyday happenings experienced by ordinary people under routine circumstances; instead, we suddenly find ourselves reading about heart-shaking events that spelled the difference between life and death to 2,209 people who just happened to find themselves on board the 'unsinkable' *Titanic* during her last hours of existence.

It is hoped that the letters, postcards and other documents that we will be examining in this book will become a convenient resource for future historians who wish to use primary source material to shed light on *Titanic* topics both major and minor – from documenting the activities of specific passengers and crewmen to shedding light on esoteric topics like the kind of weather the *Titanic* experienced right up to the hour she vanished beneath the surface of the sea. The documents in this book represent a rich haul of primary source material that will spare future historians from the many thousands of hours it would take them to track down each of these documents individually – assuming they knew where to look.

Although most of the documents in this book describe incidents that the writers witnessed at first hand, the reader should be forewarned that not every word contained in these documents can necessarily be taken as absolute gospel. It should be noted that occasionally passengers wrote about incidents that they only *heard* about from other passengers but did not see with their own eyes – although that of course doesn't mean that at least *some* of the controversial incidents mentioned in those letters did not happen exactly as described. For instance, one or two documents contain hints about the lookouts' alleged sightings of nearby icebergs prior to their documented sighting of the fatal 'berg that the *Titanic* actually struck. Other letters describe incidents that the writers claimed to have witnessed with their own eyes but which some modern researchers have difficulty accepting as being true. For instance, survivor George Rheims wrote a letter claiming that he personally witnessed the suicide of one of the *Titanic*'s officers, and survivor Charlotte Collyer stated that she was present in Fifth Officer Harold Lowe's lifeboat when Lowe took that boat back to the scene of the sinking to rescue swimmers from the water. (Even though Lowe and other crewmen later claimed that no passengers accompanied them during this rescue attempt, Mrs Collyer's claim is supported by survivor Edith Brown Haisman, who told the present author that she was *also* present in Lowe's lifeboat during that officer's attempted rescue of swimmers.)

Although many of the documents in this book describe selfless acts of heroism that were displayed by a number of passengers and crewmen during the sinking of the *Titanic*, other documents contain occasional whispers of unsavoury behaviour that was displayed by several people both before and after the ship went down. Human beings are sometimes contradictory in nature and can display dramatically different characteristics in different situations, and a person who behaves honourably and heroically at one moment in time can behave cruelly and unfeelingly in another – a dichotomy that is clearly demonstrated in the documents that highlight the altering moods and behaviour of Fifth Officer Harold Lowe. Despite the fact that a number of accounts attest to the fact that Lowe was an undoubted hero who saved a number of lives that night, it is disturbing to read an allegation about that officer's reluctance to rescue a swimming passenger based solely on that passenger's race, and it is equally disturbing to read Lowe's proud boast to another survivor that he deliberately prevented some of the *Titanic*'s rich passengers from entering lifeboats solely because of his egalitarian desire to make those rich 'nabobs' remain on the sinking ship with 'good men'. (Interestingly, Lowe's subsequent admission that he would have committed suicide if he wasn't saddled with a lifeboat full of survivors should give modern-day researchers pause when they consider the fact that First Officer William Murdoch is said to have done that very thing and taken his own life right before the ship went down – an allegation that Murdoch's modern-day admirers do not wish to believe.)

The letters and memoirs contained in this book are undoubtedly of great importance in a historical sense, but it is important for us to remember that they were written by human beings who were living lives of their own prior to the day when they set foot on the *Titanic*. With this thought in mind, the present author has concluded this volume by including brief biographical sketches of all of the people whose letters and memoirs appear in the book. Before reading each individual letter, the reader might find it informative to read about the person who wrote the letter in question and find out why that person was sailing on the largest ship in the world in the spring of 1912.

The present author has spent almost forty years visiting various archives and libraries in England, Canada and the United States in search of the texts of passenger and crew letters and memoirs that – in many cases – have been forgotten since the day they were written. The texts of many of these documents were originally gathered by newspaper reporters who covered the disaster itself in 1912, and the present author has discovered that microfilms of newspapers of the period are a gold mine for the discovery of such texts. However, the texts of many of the other written documents that appear in this book have been generously donated by descendants of the writers themselves as well as by some of the world's foremost historians who have devoted themselves to researching the sinking of the *Titanic*.

Many of the *Titanic* passengers and crewmen whose letters are contained in this book are represented by an embarrassment of written riches, but the reader will immediately notice that many other passengers and crewmen only whisper to us with one or two handwritten lines. The poignancy of this fact strikes home when we remember that these quiet whispers often represent the last recorded thoughts of people whose lives were about to be cut short and who were destined never to see or be seen by their loved ones – or anyone else – ever again.

The letters, postcards and memoirs that appear in this book are only a small fraction of the similar communications that are known to still exist. Rather than lament the absence of the documents that have been excluded from this work, though, the present author rejoices in the fact that so many generous people throughout the world have been willing to share the texts of the fascinating historical material of which they are the current guardians. These people have asked for nothing except to be acknowledged as the contributors of the documents in question, and the author has been truly humbled by the generosity and many kindnesses that these outstanding people have extended to him over the years. Thank you, my friends.

George Behe
Mount Clemens, Michigan

PRELUDE: 31 MAY 1911

JOHN KIRKWOOD **Toronto Businessman**

In 1912 Mr Kirkwood, the manager of Toronto's Walter Thompson Advertising Agency, wrote a letter describing the launch of the *Titanic*, an event he witnessed on 31 May 1911:

> When the *Titanic* was launched at Belfast last May, I saw the event from the vantage point of the harbour master's boat.
>
> The occasion was tense with interest and expectation. Countless thousands were gathered to witness the immense hull slip from its steel cage into the sea. A year or so before the *Olympic* had been similarly launched but no multitudes of citizens and workmen thronged the nearby wharves, for it was feared that these would be submerged by the wave arising from the plunge into the water of so vast a vessel. But there was no wave – only an 18-inch ripple, so gently did the *Olympic* slide from the slips.
>
> The signal for the liberation of the *Titanic* was the explosion of a rocket. Almost imperceptibly the black monster began its first short voyage, its easy descent being assured by the use of £300 worth of soap.
>
> Some of us expected to see the huge hull take the water heavily, with splash and foam, but she breasted her element so lightly that we felt no swell, and she was pulled up in her own length. The journey down the slips took only

62 seconds. Without a minute's delay tugs were hauling the *Titanic* to her berth to be completely fitted up before a year should pass.

Three days previously the *Olympic* had occupied the place to which the *Titanic* was being shifted. Before she left Belfast the public were given an opportunity of inspecting the largest and most magnificent ship ever built up to that time. I remember seeing Lord Pirrie, the distinguished head of Harland and Wolff shipbuilders, guiding a little company of friends over the noble vessel. I was told that his firm was given the contracts for the building of the *Olympic* and *Titanic* without submitting a tender, only an estimate so implicit is the reliance of the White Star authorities in the integrity of Lord Pirrie's firm and in the thoroughness of their work. I was told also that on the very day named for delivery the *Titanic*, ready for her maiden voyage, would surely be handed over to her owners.

At the launching of the *Titanic* there were no forebodings of catastrophe. The skies were blue. The hearts of all were gay, enthusiasm was unbounded. The pride of every citizen of Belfast was at its zenith. Today, less than a year afterwards, on its first brave venturing the great ship shattered and a sepulchre lies two thousand fathoms deep on the ocean's bed.[1]

PRE-SAILING DAYS

THE *TITANIC'S* PASSENGERS AND CREWMEN MAKE PREPARATIONS FOR THEIR UPCOMING VOYAGE TO AMERICA

THOMAS ANDREWS **First Class Passenger**

On 2 April, after the *Titanic* completed her trials at Belfast, Ireland and was being delivered to Southampton, Mr Andrews, her chief designer, wrote a letter to his wife in Belfast:

> Just a line to let you know that we got away this morning in fine style and have had a very satisfactory trial. We are getting more ship-shape every hour, but there is still a great deal to be done.

After the *Titanic* arrived at Southampton, on 4 April Mr Andrews wrote a letter to his wife which contained the following statements:

> I wired you this morning of our safe arrival after a very satisfactory trip. The weather was good and everyone most pleasant. I think the ship will clean up all right before sailing on Wednesday.

(Andrews also mentioned that Lord Pirrie's doctors refused to allow him to sail on the maiden voyage.)

Mr Andrews inspected the *Titanic* and wrote two subsequent letters, one of which recorded serious trouble with the vessel's restaurant galley hot press and directed attention to a design for reducing the number of screws in stateroom hat hooks. The other letter agreed with the *Titanic*'s owners that the hue of the pebble dashing on the private promenade decks was too dark, and he noted a plan for staining green the wicker furniture on one side of the vessel. On 9 April Mr Andrews wrote another letter to his wife and stated:

> The *Titanic* is now about complete and will I think do the old Firm credit to-morrow when we sail.[2]

ROGER BRICOUX **Crew (Bandsman)**

On 17 March 1912, while serving on board the *Carpathia*, Mr Bricoux wrote the following letter to his parents in Monaco:

> On Board the Cunard RMS *Carpathia*
> 17/3/12.
>
> Dear Parents, Just a few quick words as the ship is about to reach Gibraltar and I had no time to write from Naples as we left for a tour of the city. You can tell Vissotty that I accept what he proposed me. As for Dad being ill, you told me in your letter your father is slightly ill, but you never told me he was suffering from an illness that could prove grave. As for sending postcards I no longer can. We are going to New-York where I will board the *Mauretania*, the biggest ship in the world 32,000 tons and when in Liverpool, I will head for Southampton, where I will board the *Titanic* which will be launched on 10 April and will be the biggest ship in the world 50,000 tons it is a city: Turkish baths, bicycle (yeah, there's a bike on board), gymnasium, a swimming pool that is 100 metres long the ship is 945 metres long (English yard, which means over a French kilometre and only New York harbour can welcome us). I like this life a lot but I will be with you with great pleasure as for marrying, I will only marry a girl who will have money, in order to fit my tastes ... I'd better drown myself. I imagine love in silk linen or at least nothing less than a 'comfortable home' and not in an attic, with fear of starving the day after. Ambitious? maybe and why not and something tells me I ought to be for it is the only way to success. I send you my heart and I kiss you. Roger. Send me your letter on board the *Carpathia*, New-York (America).[3]

After transferring to the *Mauretania*, Mr Bricoux sent the following undated letter to his parents:

The Cunard Steamship Company Limited
RMS *Mauretania*.

Dear Dad, You will certainly think that I took too much time to send this letter but this is not my fault as I've been on the *Mauretania* for ten days and had no opportunity to post this letter. Well, this is why I'm writing: I want to kiss you very warmly and wish you all my best wishes and wish you good health. Vissotty wrote me that you were a little feeble at the moment but I hope it is nothing important and that my letter will find you in good health or else may it help you recover quickly.

The ship's vibrations are so irritating that I cannot write. Can you imagine, we run 400 miles a day, it is the world's record, one mile is 1837 metres, 5 days from New-York to Liverpool. Well, I'll send you a long letter from the *Titanic*. Please kiss mom for me and give her all my love. Roger, on board the *Titanic*, Southampton, England, I expect a letter from you in New York.[4]

HARRY BRISTOW	**Crew (Saloon Steward)**

On 9 April Mr Bristow wrote the following wife to his wife Ethel:

Titanic
Southampton 9-4-12

Dearest Et

I have earned my first day's pay on the *Titanic* and been paid and I may say spent it. Do you know dearie I forgot about towels, also cloth brush so I've to buy two. My uniform will cost £1-17-6, coat plus waistcoat and cap and Star regulation collars and paper front (don't laugh dearie it's quite true) two white jackets etc. so it won't leave me very much to take up. My pay is £3-15s plus tips. I'm in the first class saloon so I may pick up a bit. I've been scrubbing the floor today in saloon, about a dozen of us. I lost myself a time or two, she is such an enormous size I expect it will take me a couple of trips before I know my way about here. I believe we're due back here again about the 4th next month. I am not sure though ... I've to be aboard tomorrow morning 6 o/c sharp, means turning out at 5am. You might send a letter to me addressed as envelope enclosed a day before we're expected in so that I could have it directly I come ashore, now dearie with fondest love to boy and self & be brave as you always are, your ever loving Harry[5]

ARCHIBALD BUTT **First Class Passenger**

On 2 March 1912, while sailing to Italy with Frank Millet on the liner *Berlin*, Major Butt wrote the following letter to presidential secretary Charles Hilles:

> Dear Hilles,
> I want to come back by the *Titanic* of the White Star Line which sails from Southampton on the 10th of April. I have splendid rates offered me by the other lines. Could not you or Forster take this up with the White Star people in New York and get them to send me a letter, care of the American Ambassador at Rome, reserving for me good accommodation at same minimum rate.
> To my horror I learned from old Kill Joy Cosby last night that when one is on sick leave he has to give up his commutation of quarters [illegible] & fuel allowance and everything that makes one [illegible] a livable allowance. Hence these letters or this note.
> Love to all, Mrs Henry Taft is on board. It is beautiful today, cloudy, but I hope it will clear up later. I miss the President badly. It seems so funny to be away from him and all of you. Good bye now, best wishes.
> Archie W. Butt[6]

Shortly before he sailed on the *Titanic*, Major Butt wrote a letter to a relative in Atlanta that contained the following sentence:

> My ambition is to die leaving a name that will reflect credit on my family.[7]

Major Butt experienced a premonition of impending disaster throughout his travels in Europe, and not long before he boarded the *Titanic* he wrote a final letter to President Taft that began with the following phrase:

> For fear I may never have an opportunity to report in person, I am committing this to writing ...[8]

SIDNEY COLLETT **Second Class Passenger**

On 9 April, before leaving London, Mr Collett mailed an envelope to his parents which contained a smaller envelope addressed to 'Sidney Stuart Collett'. This smaller envelope contained insurance papers and an accompanying letter to his parents which read as follows:

> Dear Father and Mother,
> In the event of anything unforeseen happening to me in my journey to you,

please open the enclosed letter addressed to me. With love from son,
Sidney[9]

MARY DAVISON **Third Class Passenger**

While preparing to leave her home in Chippenham, England, Mrs Davison wrote the following note to her sister, Mrs Fred Baillis of Marion, Ohio:

> We are sailing on the *Titanic* April 10, so by the time you get this letter we will be well upon our way. We have just finished packing and will get to New York about April 17. So please God we shall soon see you again.
> Your loving brother and sister,
> Harry and Mary[10]

JACQUES FUTRELLE **First Class Passenger**

While in London in late March 1912, Jacques Futrelle and his wife May wrote a letter to Mrs Futrelle's brother, John Peele of Atlanta, Georgia. The Futrelles gave Mr Peele power of attorney for the administration of their estates should anything befall them during their travels, and they included a list of banking houses where they had money and securities. Directions were given as to the future care of the couple's children, and Mr Futrelle continued:

> You can never tell what will happen. May and I want everything straight for the kiddies if anything should happen.[11]

ARCHIBALD GRACIE **First Class Passenger**

On 14 March 1912, while travelling from the United States to Europe, Colonel Gracie sent the following postcard to his wife and daughter in Washington, D.C.:

Blessings on my dear ones. I beg you constantly to pray for me and my safety during this our first extended separation. Do not neglect any opportunity in church or elsewhere to pray for me.[12]

HENRY FORBES JULIAN **First Class Passenger**

On 10 April Mr Julian wrote a letter to his wife, and posted it before the *Titanic* sailed:

Southampton
On board RMS *Titanic*
10th April, 1912

I have just been over the ship and seen all the sitting- and saloon-rooms. It is all most luxurious ... The decks are magnificent, and the enclosed ones are fitted up more like smoking-rooms. My cabin is not the one shown ... on the *Olympic* plan ... It is, however, more like a small bedroom than a ship's cabin ... If only you could have got safely to the ship, I know you would love to have the voyage ... So far there are very few people on board, but the London train has not yet arrived ... I left the hotel at 10 o'clock and walked to the ship, a matter of only ten minutes. My trunks were taken charge of by the South-Western man, who sent them to the ship and put them into my cabin. I want you to take great care of yourself ... Do everything that is possible to get rid of the influenza, and then I shall feel happier about leaving you ...[13]

ALICE PHILLIPS **Second Class Passenger**

On the evening of 9 April Miss Phillips wrote a letter to her grandmother which contained the following statement:

Dad and I have been to look at the *Titanic*. It is a monstrous great boat as high as the Clarence Hotel, and I cannot tell you how long! We are going to embark tomorrow morning soon after breakfast.[14]

EDWARD J. SMITH **Crew (Captain)**

On 14 February 1912 the *Titanic*'s Captain Smith wrote the following letter to his nephew Frank Hancock:

On Board RMS *Olympic*
14th February 1912

My dear Frank,

Yours of the 24th December and the one introducing Miss Brookfield came to hand and I owe you an apology for not answering promptly but I seemed to be kept in a perfect whirl and the days passed so quickly. When I thought of your letter it was somewhere where it was not convenient to write and then it would slip from my memory, so there you are, it was not want of appreciation I assure you. I am pleased to hear you are hopeful of success in your undertakings. Sinclair is in Florida at present but when I meet him again I will just mention you and sound him. You have no doubt heard we are appealing the case [the verdict against the White Star Line in regard to the *Olympic–Hawke* collision]. I have not much hope as it is hard to upset a verdict in England; however it will let them see we are not going to take it lying down.

The Mallocks crossed with me last trip. We had a poor trip as far as weather was concerned but enjoyed one or two chats at the table. I did all I could for Miss Brookfield's comfort. I had her placed at my table but found she was in the Second Class, so could not have the pleasure of her company, however she was well looked after and I think was comfortable on the trip.

We had disagreeable weather and I had no opportunity of seeing her. We have not had pictures taken for years, you shall have one of the first.

I leave this ship after another voyage and bring out *Titanic* on April 10 from Southampton. Give my regards to the Gordons and Churchill if you see any of them. With Kindest and best wishes,

Your Affectionate Uncle
Edw. J. Smith[15]

WILLIAM T. STEAD **First Class Passenger**

On 9 April Mr Stead sent the following letter to Mr R. Penny, a psychic who had written to Mr Stead warning him of possible misfortune in his future:

Dear Penny,

Thank you very much for your kind letter, which reached me just as I am starting for America. I sincerely hope that none of the misfortunes which you seem to think may happen to myself or my wife will happen, but I will keep your letter, and will write to you when I come back.

I am, yours truly,
W.T. Stead [16]

EMIL TAUSSIG **First Class Passenger**

In 1908 and 1909 Mr Taussig wrote letters to the United States Steamship Inspection Service urging the enforcement of regulations that would compel steamships to carry enough lifeboats to accommodate every passenger and crewmember in case of accident. Mr Taussig wrote:

> It will certainly be calamitous if at the next disaster, which may occur, any of the passengers have lost their lives simply because there were not lifeboats enough for them to get into. That is a responsibility that nobody would be willing to shoulder.
>
> In lieu of all these matters brought before you and your experience in the service, is the board willing to take the responsibility that in case of an accident to a vessel that a large number of people lose their lives due to the fact that there were lifeboats carried by the ship to save only a small portion of the passengers?
>
> Do you want to take the responsibility in view of the added facilities in the direction of enabling steamships to carry a sufficient number of lifeboats to enable any one to say these people lost their lives owing to the fact that the board of steamship supervising inspectors did not prescribe or compel steamships to carry more boats?
>
> Just as sure as you are living and just as sure as there is a sun above us, this thing will come to pass sooner or later, unless the rules are amended compelling steamships to carry more boats.[17]

10 April 1912: *Titanic* at Southampton

ERNEST TOWNLEY **A London Citizen**

Mr Townley recorded his memories of his tour of the *Titanic* at Southampton on 10 April:

> On Wednesday last I sat in the wireless room of the great *Titanic* as she lay alongside the quay in Southampton docks, and one of the operators, a young enthusiast of the new electric age, proudly told me of the wonders which he controlled.
>
> We were in a small operating office on the immensely high boat deck next to the ship's officers' quarters, and away from the bustle of the general life of the mammoth ship. You entered by a cool, white passage, closed the white door behind you, and there you sat in a quiet, white enamelled Marconi cell, seemingly as much cut off from the rush of the world as if you were in a Trappist monastery.
>
> Then the young operator placed his hand affectionately on a mysterious apparatus, and said, 'This will send a message five hundred miles across the Atlantic in daytime and fifteen hundred miles at night.' He opened another white enamelled door and showed me the dark inner room where the marvellous

boxes of Marconi wizardry were compactly arranged. He had some new piece of wonder-working mechanism which, I think he said, the *Titanic* alone among ships possessed.

He pulled a handle, and the bluish sparks cracked and spat fire.

'At night,' he said, 'we shall only be out of touch of land for a few hours. Soon after we lose touch with Europe we shall gain touch with America.'

I wondered then what messages of fate those uncanny boxes were destined to send and to receive, but little did I imagine that the first marconigram from the *Titanic* I should read would be the one I have just read. And yet, when I turned away from the quay on Wednesday last, as the great vessel moved in slow majesty down Southampton Water, I felt a touch of unbidden disquiet of mind, and I asked myself again and again, 'Can anything go wrong with this mighty ship?'

I regretted that I could not follow her down the Solent, and see her safely on the great sea, for to a landsman she looked too huge a body to move in those narrow waters. She reminded me of a whale in the shallows. And yet it is in the deeps that she has met disaster.

No doubt it was the strange, almost incredible, circumstance which marked the very beginning of the voyage that roused vague, unwelcome wonderings as to what the rest of the voyage would bring forth. I spent nearly a couple of hours in a rapid tour of the great liner and saw her move away from her berth. I then turned with many others to leave the docks, but when I had gone a hundred yards the magic of the *Titanic* made me stop. 'Is she all right now?' I thought, and so I turned again, and walked to the far end of the quay.

There, with great amazement, I saw how the suction of the water caused by the octopus liner's triple propellers had dragged the 10,000-ton liner *New York* from the quay-side, where she was moored with half a dozen stout hawsers, which snapped like string under the strain.

The thing was astounding. It gave one an eerie fear of the greatest steamer in the world. Yet on board the *Titanic* one felt as safe as if one were sitting in the Savoy or the Cecil Hotel, with thousands of tons of concrete for foundations. She was so much larger than one even expected; she looked so solidly constructed, as one knew she must be, and her interior arrangements and appointments were so palatial that one forgot now and then that she was a ship at all. She seemed to be a spacious regal home of princes.

I sat in the big carved mahogany settee, with deep, wide springy leather upholstering, and toasted my feet at the big coal fire that blazed in a fireplace worthy of a king's palace. Over the fireplace was a beautiful sea picture by Mr Norman Wilkinson. The settee formed two horns on either side of the fire, and a dozen folk could sit in this settee in comfort.

The apartment was a lounge where a couple of hundred guests might rest at ease in cosy chairs. Its walls were panelled with a rich, dark wood, exquisitely inlaid with mother-of-pearl. It spoke of wealth, refinement, luxury. It was a place for millionaires of taste and millionaires of beauty.

Some of the passengers came in to sample it. There were women in beautiful clothes, who moved with a conquering air of possession, but the *Titanic* was too vast a thing to take in in a two-hours round. There was the great first-class dining-room, where I think they said six hundred persons could dine at once. There were scores of tables for parties of from two to eight. I recall a sensation of thick pile carpets, spotless napery, glittering silver, and countless flowers; and you entered by wide door-ways from the large crush room where the guests gathered before and after meals.

Then there was the large library and reading room, with its many shelves of calf-bound, gilt-edged volumes, and its comfortable armchairs, and the spacious writing-room, where some of the passengers were already writing letters on the ship's notepaper, headed 'RMS *Titanic*, at Sea'. I wonder whether those letters will ever be read?

I toured five storeys of the *Titanic*, going up and down in swift electric lifts. The public apartments of the second class were equal to those of many first-class hotels in roominess and comfort. The degree of comfort in the third-class quarters was as surprising as were the more luxurious surroundings of the millionaires. Most of the third-class passengers I saw on board were fair-haired, happy looking Scandinavians. The first and second-class seemed all to be English or Americans, and I was told that many more Americans would be picked up at Cherbourg.

The *Titanic* was assuredly the last thing in comfort and luxury afloat. The 'cabins' of the first-class were not cabins but rooms furnished in lavish richness by Maple's. There were Marie Antoinette bedrooms, bedrooms with lovely, old-fashioned English four-poster wooden bedsteads, with old rose canopies and valences, and bedrooms done in the old Dutch style. There were family suites with beautiful sitting-rooms and servants quarters. One wondered how even in so huge a ship room could be found for so much; and to go up on the boat deck – a mighty open-air promenade, ninety feet above the keel – and look down on the old *Majestic* and the *Philadelphia* lying down there below, 10,000-ton Atlantic liners that by comparison looked like ferry-boats, made one feel how mighty a stride in shipbuilding the *Titanic* represented.

Her size suggested rock-like safety, while at the same time it made one think how great might be the disaster if something unforeseen went wrong. Her height out of the water looked immense, and I wondered how she would behave in a gale.

The vision of the great liner as she moved away from Southampton quay forms an imperishable memory. She looked so colossal and so queenly. Passengers waved fare-wells from her decks and windows – she has large, square windows high up, as well as port-holes lower down – and a mob of jolly stokers yelled from the forecastle side. One of these – he must have been a Cockney – played a mouth organ and waved his old cap. He seemed a merry soul then; I wonder what happened to him and his mouth organ when the *Titanic* struck?[18]

UNKNOWN NEWSPAPER CORRESPONDENT

On 10 April an anonymous Irish newspaper correspondent toured the *Titanic* at Southampton and wrote the following description of that tour after the great vessel departed the city on the first leg of her maiden voyage:

> There were but 1,470 passengers, besides the 800 members of the crew and scores of attendants on board today, so that there was no crowding in any part of the vessel. Fully an hour before she sailed the gymnasium, in charge of a professional gymnast, was in working. On one side a lady was having a camel ride and recalling the delights of the Pyramids; in another corner there was a bicycle race; many passengers took their own weights on the automatic chairs, and some had a spin on the mechanical rowing machines. In the squash racquets court two Americans were 'fighting the battle of their lives' – it might have been at the Bath Club, so thoroughly at home did they look.
>
> In the third class, or steerage, departments the loveliest linen, glass, cutlery were displayed ready for luncheon, while the easy chairs, card tables, pianos and settees reminded one of the first class accommodation on many liners twenty years ago.
>
> But the most fascinating feature, perhaps, of the *Titanic* today was the trips of 'discovery.' Men and women set out to explore. They were shot into the depths by splendidly equipped electric lifts. They called at the post office for a chat with the post-master on the sorting arrangements. They wandered to the swimming baths and the luxurious Turkish saloons.
>
> They examined the kitchens, with their thousands of dishes and plates, tons of silver and cutlery, and acres of glass and linen. They touched the pianos on every deck in every corner of advantage, or listened to the band; scanned the array of novels and more serious works in the libraries, and learned all sorts of wonderful things about the electric buttons which control this 47,000 ton vessel, command its engines, and its little army of services alike.
>
> At 11.45 the bells clanged. The visitors wandered down the gangways. Hatchways were closed. The tugs snorted, and the *Titanic* set out on her maiden trip. But scarcely had she moved 600 yards into the bay when it was evident that something unlooked for had occurred.
>
> Among the crowds still waving handkerchiefs there was a sudden silence. The gigantic triple expansion engines had begun to work. Nearby were the *Oceanic* and the *New York* – great vessels in their day – now dwarfed to comparative insignificance. Directly the huge screws of the *Titanic* began to revolve the suction caused the seven great stern ropes of the *New York* to part, and the American liner's stern swung round into mid stream.
>
> Only the stoppage of the *Titanic*'s engines and the prompt action of a tug prevented a collision between the two big vessels, and ultimately the *New York* was towed clear.[19]

WHITE STAR LINE

This standard form letter advocating safe and prudent navigation practices was issued by the White Star Line to each of its captains:

Liverpool
Captain [Edward J. Smith]
Liverpool

Dear Sir,

In placing the steamer [*Titanic*] temporarily under your command, we desire to direct your attention to the company's regulations for the safe and efficient navigation of its vessels and also to impress upon you in the most forcible manner, the paramount and vital importance of exercising the utmost caution in the navigation of the ships and that the safety of the passengers and crew weighs with us above and before all other considerations.

You are to dismiss all idea of competitive passages with other vessels, and to concentrate your attention upon a cautious, prudent and ever watchful system of navigation which shall lose time or suffer any other temporary inconvenience rather than incur the slightest risk which can be avoided.

We request you to make an invariable practice of being yourself on deck and in full charge when the weather is thick or obscure, in all narrow waters and whenever the ship is within sixty miles of land, also that you will give a wide berth to all Headlands, Shoals and other positions involving peril, that where possible you will take cross bearings when approaching any coast, and that you will keep the lead going when approaching the land in thick or doubtful weather, as the only really reliable proof of the safety of the ship's position.

The most rigid discipline on the part of your officers must be observed and you will require them to avoid at all times convivial intercourse with passengers or each other, the crew also must be kept under judicious control and the lookout men carefully selected and zealously watched when on duty, and you are to report to us promptly all instances of inattention, incapacity or irregularity on the part of your officers or any others under your control.

Whilst we have confidence in your sobriety of habit and demeanour we exhort you to use your best endeavours to imbue your officers and all those about you with a due sense of the advantage which will accrue not only to the Company but to themselves by being strictly temperate, as this quality will weigh with us in an especial degree when giving promotion. The consumption of coals, water, provisions and other stores, together with the prevention of waste in any of the departments, should engage your daily and most careful attention, in order that you may be forewarned of any deficiency that may be impending, that waste may be avoided, and a limitation in quantity determined on, in case you should deem such a step necessary, in the interest of prudence.

Should you at any time have any suggestion to make bearing upon the improvement of the steamers, their arrangement, equipment or any other matter connected with the service on which they are engaged, we shall always be glad to receive and consider same.

In the event of a collision, stranding or other accident of a serious nature happening to one of the Company's steamers, necessitating the holding of an Enquiry by the Managers, written notice of the same will be given to the Commander, who shall immediately on receipt of such notice hand in a letter tendering the resignation of his position in the Company's Services, which letter will be retained pending the result of the Enquiry.

We have alluded, generally, to the subject of safe and watchful navigation, and we desire earnestly to impress on you how deeply these considerations affect not only the well-being, but the very existence of this Company itself, and the injury which it would sustain in the event of any misfortune attending the management of your vessel, first from the blow which would be inflicted to the reputation of the Line, secondly from the pecuniary loss that would accrue, (the Company being their own insurers), and thirdly from the interruption of a regular service upon which the success of the present organisation must necessarily depend.

We request your co-operation in achieving those satisfactory results which can only be obtained by unremitting care and prudence at all times, whether in the presence of danger or when by its absence you may be lured into a false sense of security; where there is least apparent peril the greatest danger often exists, a well-founded truism which cannot be too prominently born in mind.

We are,

Yours truly

[White Star Line][20]

10 April 1912: *Titanic* Sails from Southampton for Cherbourg

THOMAS ANDREWS **First Class Passenger**

Mr Andrews wrote several letters to his wife after the *Titanic* left Southampton. One letter mentioned the *Titanic*'s near-collision with the *New York* and said that the danger was soon past 'but the situation was decidedly unpleasant'. Mr Andrews wrote another letter to his wife after the *Titanic* arrived at Cherbourg:

> We reached here in nice time and took on board quite a number of passengers. The two little tenders looked well, you will remember we built them about a year ago. We expect to arrive at Queenstown about 10.30 a.m. tomorrow. The weather is fine and everything shaping for a good voyage. I have a seat at the Doctor's table.[21]

ROBERT BATEMAN **Second Class Passenger**

On 10 April, while the *Titanic* was headed for Cherbourg, the Revd Bateman sent a letter-card to his friend J.C. Stevens in Essex:

April 10

Dear Josiah,

We have started and as I near France I drop this to thank you for your kind attention to matters, for one I will soon let you hear from me.

Ada is sitting outside wrapped in her shawl thinking of home but I shall do my best for her and all of them and leave the rest with my Heavenly Father.

Give my love to mother, Laura and Maggie and all the dear ones and believe me your affectionate brother.

Robert Bateman

Mail now closing[22]

Revd Bateman also wrote a letter to his wife in Jacksonville, Florida:

On Board RMS *Titanic*
April 10

My Dear Wife:

I am now on my way home. Ada is with me, and I feel that my trip has not been in vain. God has singularly blessed me. We had a glorious revival, and when I came away all Staplehill and Kingswood came with a brass band to the depot and bade me farewell. It was the time of my life. Your sister was wonderfully surprised at the love the people had in their hearts for me, but so it was. Shall be at home in about twelve days from this writing. Kindly remember me to all the children and friends with much love.

Your Loving Husband,

Robert J. Bateman[23]

EDITH BROWN **Second Class Passenger**

On 10 April Miss Brown wrote the following postcard to her stepsister in South Africa. (She neglected to mail the card, and it remained in her coat pocket throughout the *Titanic*'s maiden voyage.)

We are just sailing today by this boat for New York – 4,000 tons – all well. With love to all, Your loving Sis. EB.[24]

EWART BURR **Crew (Saloon Steward)**

On 10 April Mr Burr wrote the following letter-card to his wife Ethel in Southampton:

On Board RMS *Titanic*
April 10, 1912

My Own Darling Wife,

Here we are again at sea. It seems strange after so long ashore. Well, dear, I have had my first day in the saloon and it has proved a success.

I know, darling, you will be glad to know this. I have got a five table, one being the Countess of Rothes, nice and young and very nice to run. I think if I keep this table I shall have a good show.

We have just finished work and you can bet I am tired, 10:36 p.m. This is all the paper I could get, dear, so you must excuse shortness of letter.

The fellows in the saloon are a jolly nice lot and I am sure we shall get on well together. It is so different from third class and second.

Dearest Ethel I need not mention to you to take care of our little son as I know you love him as much as I do. Give him my love and kiss him each night for daddy.

Give my love to all at home.

Well, dearest, I shall say Au Revoir for a little while.

Fondest love and kisses. Always your loving and true

Ewart[25]

KATE BUSS **Second Class Passenger**

As the *Titanic* was approaching Cherbourg on the afternoon of 10 April, Kate Buss wrote the following letter to Percy James:

On Board RMS *Titanic*
April 10 1912

Dr Percy,

I received yours on vessel today, have posted mother & Mrs Lingham from Cherbourg. This I think will go out from Queenstown tomorrow. I've been quite allright – but now I feel dead tired & more fit for bed than anything – Have to go to dinner – tea in half an hour. Percy W. [illegible] spent about an hour on the vessel & They might easily have spent another without waste of time. The first class apartments are really magnificent & unless you had first seen them you would think the second were the same. We were due to reach Cherbourg at 5 pm but not there yet, altho the mail is cleared. I think I'd best try & get some post cards of the vessel.

My fellow passenger hasn't turned up yet, so if she is coming it will be from Cherbourg or Queenstown.

I was advised to eat well so had a good lunch. Two clergymen opposite me at table.

No sign of sea sickness yet but mustn't crow.

Hedley & PW both kissed me 'Good Bye' so I wasn't made to feel too lonely. HP set PW the example tho it was done quite as a matter of course without a word. I've only sent Mr Lingham a kiss. I'm so fearfully tired I do not feel I can write more tonight or I would write Elsie – The only thing I object to is new paint so far – Must clear & have a wash now. Will pop this in the box in case I'm sea sick tomorrow. PW bought a box of chocolates. Shouldn't wonder if I'm like Jim Buss & get it the other way.

Give my love to all enquirers – must go.

Much love, Katie[26]

CHARLES CLARKE **Second Class Passenger**

Mr Clarke wrote the following letter to his parents after the *Titanic* picked up additional passengers at Cherbourg on the evening of 10 April:

On board RMS *Titanic*
April 10, 1912

Dear father and mother,

Just a line to let you know we are both well and are doing justice to what we have paid for. I hope everything in the business is going on all right. What sort of time did you have at Easter – plenty to do, as you had the races extra? We are well on the way to Queenstown, which we expect to reach about noon tomorrow. We spent quite a long time at Cherbourg. A tender brought all the passengers to our ship. We nearly had a collision on leaving Southampton, which I will tell you about in my next letter if we reach New York. We had a roll before we got into Cherbourg. We are just going to bed now, as the time is getting on. Kind regards from us both, I remain your loving son,

Charl[27]

REGINALD COLERIDGE **Second Class Passenger**

On the afternoon of 10 April Mr Coleridge wrote the following postcard to Miss E. Coleridge of Wisbech, England:

Wed. aft.

Writing this in Mid Channel to thank you for your letter. Glad you enjoyed yourselves. All right so far – smooth & comfy. Just nearing Cherbourg after a jolly cruise down the Channel along the South Coast.

RCC[28]

CHARLES DAVIES **Second Class Passenger**

Mr Davies wrote the following postcard on 10 April while the *Titanic* was on her way to Cherbourg:

My Dear Bertha,

I thought I would just send you a card on the way out, we are having a fine time on board the *Titanic*, arrives in France about 6 tonight. It's a lovely ship, this is her first trip out to America, as you will see by the card. Will write & let you know all about Canada when I get there. Much Love.

Yours very sincerely,

C. Davies[29]

THOMAS FRANKLIN **First Class Passenger**

After the *Titanic* left Cherbourg on the evening of 10 April, Mr Franklin wrote the following postcard to his sister, Grace, in Essex:

Titanic
April 10th, 1912

We have just left Cherbourg. Plenty of wind and very cold. This is a lovely boat. Just like a town. I spent about an hour in the gym this afternoon.

Love to all.

Tom[30]

ARTHUR GEE **First Class Passenger**

Mr Gee wrote the following letter after the *Titanic* left Southampton on 10 April:

On board RMS *Titanic*
April 10, 1912

My dear —,

In the language of the poet, 'This is a knock-out.' I have never seen anything so magnificent, even in a first class hotel. I might be living in a palace. It is, indeed, an experience. We seem to be miles above the water, and there are certainly miles of promenade deck. The lobbies are so long that they appear to come to a point in the distance. Just finished dinner. They call us up to dress by bugle. It reminded me of some Russian villages where they call the cattle home from the fields by horn made from the bark of a tree. Such a dinner!!! My gracious!!![31]

GEORGE GRAHAM **First Class Passenger**

On 10 April, while the *Titanic* was bound for Cherbourg, Mr Graham wrote the following letter to his friends Wes Herod and Gordon Stanley in Stoke-on-Trent:

On Board RMS *Titanic*
April 10, 1912

Dear Wes and Gordon,

I received your kind message this morning and I thank you. I hope that you will both enjoy the best of health and that you will find lots of new goods. I meet Dennis, Van Camp, Shaw, Fortons and Mr C. Booth in London. I understand that Mr Booth is sailing about the end of this month.

Dennis, Shaw and Van Camp are all sailing Saturday of this week from Liverpool so if you want to see them you had better motor over there Saturday.

I saw a wire from Dressel that they had sent your dolls to London the middle of March so if you will ask Fortlock about the message I am sure he will be able to locate your dolls. I have met a number of boys I knew so I am not going to be alone after all although I would have liked to have had some of our own boys along.

We had quite a time getting out of Southampton this morning as a boat called the *New York* broke away from the dock and we nearly ran into her, however it did not happen and we are now on our way to Cherbourg.

I hope that you have a real good time in England, give my kindest regard to Rhodes, Harry and Frielding and tell them that will often think of the good time we had together.

Weather is very fine but a bit cold. There is not a very big passenger list, about four hundred.

It is a beautiful boat and I have a very fine state room on C deck right in the middle of the boat.

Now I think I have told you all the news. Hoping to see you in England again and that we will make another trip together.

I remain your friend,

Geo. E. Graham

Give Till Harding my kindest regard and tell her to see that you go to bed early.

G.[32]

HENRY HODGES **Second Class Passenger**

On 10 April Mr Hodges wrote two communications while the *Titanic* was headed for Cherbourg. The first was a postcard that he sent to John Young in Southampton:

> Everything very fine up to now. No sickness anywhere. The ship is wonderful. Wished you could have come. H.P.[33]

Mr Hodges' second communication was a letter addressed to Hector Young in Southampton:

> We've had a fine time up to now. You do not notice anything of the movement of this ship, but the weather is very fine.
>
> On the top deck there are about 20 boys, from 20 upwards, marching round and singing. Others are playing dominoes and cards in the saloons. Some are reading, some writing.
>
> Everything is quite different from what you would expect to see at sea ... I am going to bed early for I feel as tired as a dead dog.[34]

HENRY JULIAN **First Class Passenger**

Mr Julian wrote the following letter to his wife on the evening of 10 April after the *Titanic* picked up additional passengers at Cherbourg:

On board RMS *Titanic*
10th April, 1912

I was delighted to get your nice long letter and the telegram just after leaving the dock. Our ship had some trouble in getting away. There are a great many large steamers lying in the docks on account of the Coal Strike, among them being the four American liners and the *Oceanic*. The *New York*, which was secured to the *Oceanic*, broke loose, due to the back-rush of water from the *Titanic* as she was moving past. Tugs rushed to the assistance and succeeded in holding the *New York*, which was moored to another part of the dock in order that we might move away without doing damage to other boats. This delayed us, and we did not reach Cherbourg until 7 instead of 6. There were great crowds watching us leave, but very few strangers were allowed on board.

I have now explored the ship, except the Turkish bath and the swimming-bath. The Parisian café is quite a novelty and looks very real. I do not know to what extent it is patronised, but it will, no doubt, become popular amongst rich Americans ... There are two bands, one in the lounge and the other in the café. I also visited the gymnasium, which is full of the most wonderful machines, which cure all the aches that flesh is heir to. There are over three hundred first-saloon passengers on board – a large proportion being Americans.

The weather has been fine, but cool and more or less cloudy. I expect we shall reach Queenstown about 7 in the morning, and I don't suppose they will give us time to write in answer to yours, so I am writing this evening ...[35]

THOMAS MUDD **Second Class Passenger**

On 10 April Mr Mudd sent the following postcard to members of his family in London:

Dear Willie + Nellie, Hadel Muriel + Cyril,
I arrived at Shampton [*sic*] safe. I think the Titanic a most lovely boat + you hardly know you are moving. Will write more later. With love to all,
Tom [36]

EMILE RICHARD **Second Class Passenger**

On 10 April, prior to boarding the tender that ferried him from Cherbourg out to the *Titanic*, Mr Richard wrote a postcard to Mr F. Santif:

Goodbye to France and all my best wishes to everybody.
Milou
I feel a little bit excited anyway. [37]

Mr Richard also wrote a postcard to his mother, Madame Achille Richard:

Cherbourg, 10 April, 4 PM

Dear Mom,
We are boarding, the *Titanic* is at anchor. I am in good health, and as the weather is fine, certainly nice trip ahead. I kiss you all very strongly, and if possible, I kiss you more than the others.
Your affectionate kid
Milou[38]

RICHARD ROUSE **Third Class Passenger**

After sailing on the *Titanic*, Mr Rouse wrote the following postcard to his wife:

Don't worry – everything is fine. It's a wonderful ship. I'll wire you as soon as we reach New York.[39]

ADOLPHE SAALFELD **First Class Passenger**

On 10 April Mr Saalfeld wrote two letters to his wife. The first was written on board the *Titanic* before the ship left Southampton:

On Board RMS *Titanic*
10 / 4 1912

Dear Wifey,
Thanks for your letter. I just had an hour's roaming about on this wonderful boat together with Paul. I like my cabin very much it is like a bed-sitting room and rather large. I am the first man to write a letter on board. Au revoir in Whit-week please God! Love to you all! and a kiss for you!
Adolphe[40]

Mr Saalfeld began writing a second letter to his wife at 3 p.m. on 10 April, and he concluded the letter with a final instalment at 10 p.m. that evening:

On Board RMS *Titanic*
April 10, 1912 3 p.m.

Dear Wifey,

After leaving at noon we had quite a little excitement, as the tremendous suction of our steamer made all the hausers of the SS *New York* snap as we passed her and she drifted on to our boat, a collision being only averted by our stopping and our tugs coming to the rescue of the *New York*. You will probably have read of the accounts in the papers. Thanks for your wire, Baur & Burfy and Smee also sent telegrams. The weather is calm and fine, the sky overcast. There are only 370 1st Class Passengers. So far the boat does not move and goes very steady. It is not nice to travel alone and leave you behind. I think you will have to come next time. I had quite an appetite for luncheon – soup, fillet of plaice, a loin chop with cauliflower and fried potatoes, apple Manhattan & Roquefort cheese washed down with a large spaten beer iced, so you see I am not faring badly. 10.00 pm I had a long promenade and a doze for an hour up to 5 o'cl. The band played in the afternoon for tea, but I savour a café with bread and butter in the verandah café and quite thought I should have to pay, but anything and everything in the eating line is gratis. At 6 o'clock we anchored outside Cherbourg and two tugs with passengers came alongside. Owing to our little mishap at Southampton we were all one hour late. I had dinner only at 7-30 instead of 7-00 o'clock as usual. The name of my friend, the White Star Manager in London, works wonders and I have a small table for two to myself. I had a very good dinner and to finish had two cigars in the smoke room and shall now go to bed as I am tired. But for a slight vibration, you would not know that you were at sea. My cabin is very nice, hot and cold water laid on, an electric heating stove which you can turn on and off, a nice couch with an oval table in front and of course everything is new. So far, apart from occasional remarks I have not spoken to anyone. I want to keep quiet and have a thorough rest. As I do not know whether I will be up in time for the mail at Queenstown, I am posting this letter tonight. A kiss for you and love to all from your loving husband,

Adolphe[41]

JOHN PILLSBURY SNYDER **First Class Passenger**

On 10 April Mr Snyder wrote the following note to a friend who sent him a box of cigars as a farewell gift:

On Board RMS *Titanic*
April 10, 1912

My dear Mr Miles,

While I sit here at the writing desk peacefully and complacently smoking 'one of your best,' I just want to thank you ever and ever so much.

Everything reached me in perfect order at the hotel, and my one real regret upon leaving London was that I was unable to get down to Great Deacon Street so as to bid you good-bye.

If you can come to America try and come to Minneapolis where I shall be only too glad to try and make your visit pleasant as well as interesting.

Thanking you again for your remembrance,

Yours very sincerely,

John P. Snyder[42]

WILLIAM T. STEAD **First Class Passenger**

Mr Stead wrote the following letter-card to Edwin Stout, editor of the *Review of Reviews*:

On board RMS *Titanic*
April 10, 1912

Dear Mr Stout,

I got off safely and am writing in a room as comfortable as any in town. Please see that Strong supplies the better paper for the advert this month. Last month he pleaded off because of the coal strike. I hope that the Thursday tea consultation may be kept up in my absence and let me have minutes of the deliberations suggestions etc. I also want the staff replies to the Enquiry Paper for the New *Review*. The *American Review* I see reaches London before we publish the *English Review*. We shall have to sacrifice the latter magazine. Hoping that all may go well in my absence I am yours truly W.T. Stead [43]

ROSALIE IDA STRAUS **First Class Passenger**

Mrs Straus wrote the following letter to a friend after the *Titanic* left Southampton on 10 April:

On board RMS *Titanic*
Wednesday 1912

Dear Mrs Burbidge,

You cannot imagine how pleased I was to find your exquisite basket of flowers in our sitting-room on the steamer. The roses and carnations are all so beautiful in colour and so fresh as though they had just been cut. Thank you so much for your sweet attention which we both appreciate very much.

But what a ship! So huge and so magnificently appointed. Our rooms are furnished in the best of taste and most luxuriously, and they are really rooms, not cabins.

But size seems to bring its troubles – Mr Straus, who was on deck when the start was made said that at one time it looked painfully near to the repetition of the *Olympic*'s experience on her first trip out of the harbour, but the danger was soon averted and we are now well on to our course across the channel to Cherbourg.

Again thanking you and Mr Burbidge for your lovely attention and good wishes and in the pleasant satisfaction of seeing you with us next summer, I am with cordial greetings in which Mr Straus heartily joins,

Very sincerely yours,
Ida R. Straus[44]

ELIZABETH WATT — Second Class Passenger

On 10 April 1912 Mrs Watt wrote the following letter after the *Titanic* left Cherbourg and headed for Queenstown:

W.S.L. *Titanic*
Wednesday, April 10, 7:05 P.M.

At last you will see we have started to cross the Atlantic. We have just taken on passengers at Cherbourg (France) and tomorrow we go to Queenstown (Ireland). Oh, Dear. The style is awful. It seems it is not a fast boat, it is built for comfort, not speed, and they say we won't be in till Wednesday night (the 17th).

There are two other ladies in our stateroom, but it is nice and big; two wardrobes in one, with a large mirror door and four drawers, two wash basins, besides the lavatory and bathroom.[45]

RICHARD WILLIAMS **First Class Passenger**

On the evening of 10 April, immediately after boarding the *Titanic* at Cherbourg, Mr Williams wrote the following letter to his mother and posted it before the tender left the ship:

> Dear Good Things:
>
> Father is writing to you just opposite me but as he will not tell you any news I shall just tell you what this boat looks like.
>
> The room in which we are is about as big as the national dining room and it is not the biggest on the boat. We have beautiful room nearly as big as my work room in Geneva.
>
> Of course there is room after room – smoking-reading-lounge-palm room; you can imagine that there are many other rooms but as we have only been on board about 10 minutes, really not more, we have not been able to see everything.
>
> Father says I must stop as the letter must go.
>
> Au revoir, good things[46]

11 April 1912: *Titanic* Arrives at Queenstown and Sails Onward

RAMON ARTAGAVEYTIA **First Class Passenger**

On 11 April 1912 Mr Artagaveytia wrote the following letter to his brother Adolfo:

On Board RMS *Titanic*
April 11, 1912

My dear Adolfo:

On the 9th at night I wrote from Paris to Elisa and Manuel, departing with the feeling I had not written that letter. From Manuel I have received nothing since the 24th of February, he who would write to me every week. Could he be having trouble with his eyesight or could it be something else?

I depart on this voyage thinking that one of them could be sick, in what part angers me because I do not know.

Yesterday from Cherbourg I sent a postcard to Elisa and what is left at New York, I will send by telegram to Manuel, if they don't take it to you, since I only put Artagaveytia.

The desire is to see North America, even though at full steam and attracted by the size of these 45 000 tons that will make its first journey, I closed my eyes and embarked.

Everything I say about it [the *Titanic*] is little. When we approached it yesterday surrounded by the steam it seemed like 'Rio de la Plata' and to look up at it it gave me the effect of a 5 storey house. At the entrance there were like 50 butlers. One of them took my luggage and through the elevator (there were 3) we went up to my floor B. The dining room on D and more floors below.

The room is very good, with an electric heater, which I had on all night because it was cold. Today there is sun, but we are going to N.N.E., to Queenstown, Ireland, to collect our correspondence, which will probably cause us to delay our journey, of which I will take advantage of to write.

The dining room is like for 500 and something people. Yesterday we were only 340, being left with the width of 30 metres. The steamer is even wider, because there are hallways on its sides. The food is very good with an abundance of dishes. Last night we were a Mexican, congressman and Doctor friend of Diaz, still young, a Spaniard and a Misses and a Miss of English background who were very serious.

I visited what I could of the steamer, its different rooms, and today to find this room to write in, there must be more than two, it cost me to know. The dining rooms are painted in white and some rooms like this one, have carved wood, I think it's oak, with lounges and chairs covered in rich and elegant jade green velvet.

The walkway has on one side 647 feet, you reach a free space that today was full of sun and on the other, something smaller, so one can go without having to walk around in circles for 340 metres. Also from the bow to the stern of this steamer is 260 metres in length. The dining room has 30 metres in width so including the hallways the steamer would have 40 or 45 metres.

For description of the steamer which attracts attention, I enclose these brochures. But I see to do that and I see land close by, Ireland, so I end this letter leaving you all my memories and hugs.

Your brother
Ramon[47]

HENRY BEAUCHAMP **Second Class Passenger**

On 11 April Mr Beauchamp wrote the following letter to a friend while the *Titanic* was bound for Queenstown, Ireland:

Dear Mr Streeton,

My letter will no doubt give rise to alarm but my hasty departure from London I trust will not be so to you. I will write to you from New York and detail matters concerning myself. I am going to Toronto to a berth and I trust my new venture will clean the past which I have created by my own folly. My wife is in England do not write to her the parting has been bitter but she has submitted to this for our future welfare. I shall pen you my desires and intentions in the week and post at New York. Do not refer to my wife my letter to you in the chance of you meeting her. Yours still faithfully,

H Beauchamp[48]

JACOB BIRNBAUM **First Class Passenger**

Mr Birnbaum wrote the following letter to Willie Alford, a young Canadian acquaintance, while the *Titanic* was headed for Queenstown:

On Board RMS *Titanic*
April 11, 1912

Dear Willie,

Going back to America. I remind myself of the promise I gave you to send you some Belgian money with holes.

As I spent a whole lot of money in Europe I cannot send you more than the amount you will find enclosed.

I am on the *Titanic* an entirely new steamer. They are just closing the mail box and I have to hurry up. Give my best regards to your father. Write me whether you were seasick on your return trip.

Best regards,

J. Birnbaum

704 Market St. San Francisco, Cal.[49]

ELIZABETH BONNELL **First Class Passenger**

Miss Bonnell wrote the following letter to her sisters while the *Titanic* was approaching Queenstown, Ireland:

On board RMS *Titanic*
April 9th, 1912

My dear Sisters,

I have just five minutes before the letter box closes. I had a good night. Bath at 7.30. I waited till after nine for my breakfast. Hollie said George wanted his at 5.30 so thought I would be ready. I find it was from 21 Welhech Road the (telegr) P.C. came. No signature. It is ten & Caroline has just said good morning to me. It is simply glorious this morning. The sun shining. It was most interesting seeing the people come on board at Cherbourg. I changed for dinner last night & was nearly frozen. Shall wear a jacket tonight.

There is not much news. The net slips I sent you were very cheap but they looked good over either black or white. I hope the curtain rods will go through the holes. It has the nicest pattern. I got thirteen yards as twelve leaves just a little piece. Don't make them any smaller than the others. Will write again before we land. Much love to you both from us all.

Your loving sister,
Elzth Bonnell[50]

KATE BUSS **Second Class Passenger**

On 11 April Miss Buss began writing a long letter to her parents; the letter was written in daily instalments, with the following being the first:

On board RMS *Titanic*
April 11th, 1912.

Dear all.

It is about 11 pm by your time, but we have to put our watches back about an hour, or nearly so, each day. We didn't reach Queenstown until mid-day and I hear we arrive at New York on Tuesday night, and land Wednesday morning. I wrote to Percy, but left the letters in my bag by mistake when we were at Queenstown, and I posted my cards. I'm having a good time.

Wednesday. – After Percy and Mr Peters left I went down to luncheon. It took me a long time to exchange my ticket for a table ticket, but I pushed my way in and got it done. Then, as there are eight persons at each table, I found myself opposite two clergy, one quite a young foreigner and the other very ugly. I have an end seat. On my left is a mere boy; next him a man whose acquaintance I have since made. He is, I should say, somewhat reduced in circumstance and tells me has left a wife and two children for two years, as things were bad in England. He is bound for Toronto. Tonight I noticed he wore a dress coat. Next him is a lady; opposite her is a Kentucky doctor. He is a regular traveller, and makes himself very agreeable. The first man that we (that is the girl I've chummed up with and myself) call 'Mr Sad Man'. The other, our 'doctor man' – I know he is a doctor because this morning some soot got into my eye. Although he was standing behind me he saw it at once, and came forward and took it out, remarking 'I happen to be an eye doctor.' Well I had a good lunch yesterday, and felt somewhat lonely. I gained courage and went on deck. While standing there this said young lady (Miss Wright) offered to share her rug. I accepted. We asked questions of each other. She is going to Oregon, but her fiancé is meeting and marrying her in New York. She, like me, has her wedding presents.

I'm quite the centre of attraction to a few who know I'm undertaking the journey alone and the doctor man thinks he should be a grand man who would lead me to make the sacrifice of home and country and take such a journey. He found out some folk on board who are going to Sacramento, and introduced me, but my rail ticket is not quite right. I expect a little trouble in New York. They only gave me an emigrant's ticket at Southampton, and they all say I really must not travel by that. I've spoken to the Purser, and he has made a note of it, and says he'll cause enquiries to be made.

Well, I came to bed last night about 10.30. I couldn't sleep at first, owing to the vibration. There is a good deal of it, and I fancy they travelled at a pretty good speed last night to make up for lost time. I have eaten anything and everything. We are living very well. So far, although the vibration makes me wakeful, I do not feel the least bit sick. I wrote letters last night, and some again this morning. We've been up on deck a good deal. We have three promenade decks, one above the other. Each one has a sort of hall lounge, and on the one above my cabin the band plays every afternoon and evening.

The cello man is a favourite of mine, every time he finishes a piece he looks at me and we smile. It's a real Liberty Hall. Everyone seems to be as happy as sandboys for the time being. Miss W. was given an introduction to a youth on board. He is a nephew of one of the old Huntleys, of Huntley Palmer. He was known to her people in Reading years ago. In fact her own mother was a Huntley. The young man in question (Stuart Collett) tries to teach us all religion.

There is a clergyman and his wife on our deck from St Jude's, Whitechapel, going to Kansas. They have been visiting Maidstone, and the surrounding districts. She tells me I must admire everything that is American for a start, or I shall not be well received. Tonight, after dinner, we first listened to the band, and then went up by lift to the top deck. It was glorious. The doctor man said he had half-a-day to spare in New York, and would show me around if I liked. Of course, I declined with thanks. One woman, a Southerner, told me they charge two-and-a-half dollars a meal on the train, and 25 cents if your ask for a quart of boiling water. She advises me to pack a hamper. I shall ask the Clergyman who is meeting me. I shall begin collecting from the table. Well now I think I will go to bed. I want to try and get to sleep before I know everyone else has gone. I have my cabin to myself. That makes me extremely comfortable, a wardrobe and a couch all to myself. Miss W. has one to herself, too, for which she paid 10/0 extra; but it isn't quite so large as mine. We are rolling a bit now. You ought to see my face, such a colour I have. We are going to try and get up in time for a run on deck before breakfast tomorrow.

I shall be glad when my journey is done, because of what I hear about New York charges, but the people I've met may arrange to go on my line, only I have to wait and see what happens at New York.

Such a noise by the many youths aboard. The second-class is very mixed. Some very ordinary, and some very nice. One can really walk miles a day going around the decks. It is a mixed-up assembly, Japs, French, Germans, Americans and English.

Good-night, will write more to-morrow, all very well.[51]

JACK BUTTERWORTH **Crew (Saloon Steward)**

Mr Butterworth wrote the following letter while the *Titanic* was on her way to Queenstown:

RMS TIATANIC. [*sic*]
Queenstown
12th Apl 1912

My Darling Girl,

We have been having a very fierce time in this steamer. I suppose you heard of the accident that occurred to the *New York* as we sailed this ship carried so much water between the *Oceanic* & *New York* that the *York* broke all her ropes & sailed all on her own, you could have tossed a penny from our ship to her she was so close, it was a good job she did not hit us as it would have been another case of *Hawke* colis[ion] – Well dearest how do you feel, pretty lonely I guess after me being home for so long, but still we cannot grumble my dear as we have had a real good & happy time & I am so happy to think everything is alright. Well there is one consolation about it I shall soon be with you again all being well. We do really enjoy ourselves when I am home. Well I do not see why we should not anyhow & again I think it does us both good for me to go away for a little stretch don't you dear?

There are quite a lot of American Line men here so it is a little better for us to see a few old faces. Our shore stwd. was aboard yes'day before we sailed & he saw me, so he said 'hello have you signed here', so I said yes & then he said 'see & come back in time for your own ship', so of course I thanked him & said yes, which I may do if things do not turn out good here. Will now close sweetheart take care of yourself dear love to all at home & fondest love to yourself dearest.

Yours Always

Jack

Don't forget Plymouth & a football paper.[52]

JOHN AND SARAH CHAPMAN **Second Class Passengers**

On the morning of 11 April, while the *Titanic* was approaching Queenstown, Mr Chapman wrote the following postcard to Miss Maud Chapman in Cornwall:

My Dear Maud,

With love to you from Uncle Jack and Aunt Lizzie XXX[53]

On that same morning Mrs Chapman wrote the following postcard to Maud Chapman's sister Sidonia:

My Dear S,

We shall be into Queenstown in about an hour. Hope you are all well, with love from Auntie XXX[54]

HARVEY COLLYER **Second Class Passenger**

On 11 April 1912, as the *Titanic* approached Queenstown, Mr Collyer wrote the following letter to his parents:

Titanic
April 11th

My dear Mum and Dad

It don't seem possible we are out on the briny writing to you. Well dears so far we are having a delightful trip the weather is beautiful and the ship magnificent. We can't describe the tables it's like a floating town. I can tell you we do swank we shall miss it on the trains as we go third on them. You would not imagine you were on a ship. There is hardly any motion she is so large we have not felt sick yet we expect to get to Queenstown today so thought I would drop this with the mails.

We had a fine send off from Southampton and Mrs S and the boys with others saw us off. We will post again at New York then when we get to Payette.

Lots of love don't worry about us.

Ever your loving children

Harvey, Lot & Madge[55]

SELINA ROGERS COOK **Second Class Passenger**

Mrs Cook wrote the following postcard to her husband while the *Titanic* was bound for Queenstown, Ireland:

Dearest Arthur,

Just a PC today. I went to bed at 10 oc & slept well. Got up at 7.30 & eat a good breakfast have been sitting on deck with Millie am close to Queenstown now. 200 are to embark there. Just going up to watch there. Am very happy & am not sick. With love,

from Nin[56]

EVA DEAN **Third Class Passenger**

On 11 April Mrs Dean wrote the following postcard to her mother:

Dear Mother,

Just a card to say we are enjoying ourselves fine up to now. Little baby was very restless.

With best love,

Etty[57]

ALBERT ERVINE **Crew (Assistant Electrician)**

On 11 April 1912 Mr Ervine posted the following letter to his mother while the *Titanic* was approaching Queenstown, Ireland:

> Yours received in Cherbourg, France yesterday evening. We have had everything working nicely so far, except when leaving Southampton.
>
> As soon as the *Titanic* began to move out of the dock, the suction caused the *Oceanic*, which was alongside her berth, to swing outwards, while another liner broke loose altogether and bumped into the *Oceanic*. The gangway of the *Oceanic* simply dissolved.
>
> Middleton and myself were on top of the after funnel, so we saw everything quite distinctly. I thought there was going to be a proper smash up owing to the high wind; but I don't think anyone was hurt.
>
> Well, we were at Cherbourg last night. It was just a mass of fortifications. We are on our way to County Cork. The next call then is New York...
>
> I am on duty morning and evening from 8 to 12; that is four hours work and eight hours off ... (Have just been away attending the alarm bell.)
>
> This morning we had a full dress rehearsal of an emergency. The alarm bells all rang for ten seconds, then about 50 doors, all steel, gradually slid down into their places, so that water could not escape from any one section into the next.
>
> So you see it would be impossible for the ship to be sunk in collision with another ...[58]

THOMAS EVERETT **Third Class Passenger**

Mr Everett wrote a letter to his wife while the *Titanic* was headed for Queenstown. He stated that he was enjoying the journey and continued:

> I do wish you were all here. Fred and I are in a berth with four young fellows, two from Bristol and two from Southampton – all Englishmen. We expect to arrive in New York next Tuesday evening. Will write from New York. With love to Harry, Harold, and all, not forgetting yourself.[59]

ERNEST FARRENDEN **Crew (Confectioner)**

Mr Farrenden wrote a picture postcard of the *Titanic* to his mother while the vessel was bound for Queenstown:

Queenstown, April 11th

Hope you and father are well. Did you see the ship which ran into H.M.S. *Hawke* in the Solent. It might have been serious. Don't you think this a fine ship. Give my kind regards to all. Much love,

Ern[60]

MARGARETHA FROLICHER-STEHLI **First Class Passenger**

Mrs Frolicher-Stehli wrote the following letter to her son Willy while the *Titanic* was headed for Queenstown:

11 April 1912
10 o'clock, Thursday morning

Dear Willy,

We left Cherbourg yesterday with some delay, as the *Titanic* was late (You know the *Titanic* took us aboard within the harbour). It is interesting how you can get from one ship to another. On the side of the *Titanic* they made an opening and used a bridge to connect the two ships. The ship will land one more time (11 a.m. tomorrow) on the Irish coast at Queenstown (you can look it up on the map). From there we will send you greetings from this side of the globe.

We all slept well and do not feel seasick. The weather is nice although not cloudless. The sea is mostly calm.

Now, dear Willy, God be with you. Don't forget to pray. Keep us in your thoughts and let us all hope that we will dock next Tuesday well and happy in New York. With God's will we hope for a happy arrival and we will send the grandparents a telegram. Give our greetings to the minister. With all our love for you,

from your Papa, Madi, and Mama[61]

JOHN HARPER **Second Class Passenger**

On 11 April, while the *Titanic* was headed for Queenstown, Revd Harper wrote the following letter to a married couple who were mourning the death of their child:

On Board RMS *Titanic*
11th April 1912

My dear Brother & Sister,

I am in this spare moment writing you these few lines to convey to you both my deepest sympathy. Although you have not heard from me earlier I have not forgotten you and my prayer has been that our gracious Lord may sustain and comfort you in your deep sorrow. I know how your hearts feel and yet I know you both know that you have both lost your little lamb. That which Jesus keeps for us in his own bright upper fold is not lost. It is but a link into heaven and home. Through all this He is preparing you both for larger service. The measure of our service is the measure of our sympathy and the measure of our sympathy is that of our experience.

May His grace be more & more magnified in you & through you.

Ever remembering with deep gratitude to God our sweet fellowship together recommending you both to His grace with Christian love. Ever your loving Pastor,

John Harper

P.S. A little note any time to the Moody Church. I shall be so glad to hear from you in Chicago [illegible].[62]

Revd Harper also wrote a letter to a friend:

On board RMS *Titanic*
11 April 1912

My dear brother Young,

I am penning you this line just before we get in to Queenstown to assure you that I have not forgotten you, and especially all your kindness while we were North. I intended sending on Miss Pratt's train fares just before I left but in the rush which was exceptional having had 11 or 12 services for the weekend I was unable to get it done. I will send it on from Chicago. We had a great season of blessing during the last few days in Walworth.

I don't know how I am to thank dear Aunt Mary and yourself for all your kindness. The Lord will repay you for it all.

Trust things are going well at Paisley Road. The warriors are with me here and are doing well so far on the journey.

Very kindest love
Your loving auld Pastor
J H[63]

WALLACE HARTLEY **Crew (Bandsman)**

On 11 April, while the *Titanic* was bound for Queenstown, Mr Hartley sent the following letter to his parents in England:

> ... the ship got away all right. This is a fine ship and there ought to be plenty of money around. We have a fine band and the boys seem very nice.
>
> I've missed coming home very much and it would have been nice to have seen you all, if only for an hour or two, but I could not manage it.[64]

(Hartley also informed his parents that he had sent some washing home by post and that he expected to be home on the Sunday morning after the *Titanic*'s return to Southampton.)

SAMUEL JAMES HOCKING **Second Class Passenger**

On 11 April Mr Hocking wrote the following letter to his wife:

> On Board RMS *Titanic*
> April 11, 1912
>
> My Dear Ada,
>
> Just a few lines as I hear we are calling for passengers at Queenstown Ireland & they will also take letters & we are just off there now 7.30 a.m. It is a lovely morning with high wind but no heavy seas in fact it has been like a mill pond so far but I expect we shall get it a bit stiffer in the Bay of Biscay if this wind continues. This will be the ship for you, you can hardly realise you are on board except for the jolting of the engines that is why it is such bad writing. I am longing when you can come out ... I turned in at ten o'clock last night but could get no sleep owing to the rattle of water bottles, glasses and other things too numerous to mention so I was glad to get up at six o'clock ... Already for you to have a trip I wish it had been possible for us to have all come together. It would have been a treat. I have fallen in with a young couple on Liskeard named Chapman. He has been home for six months holiday and got married and they are now going out together. He like myself worked for his father but could not get on with him ... In fact you don't meet anyone rough second class. I have a bunk to myself which is pretty lovely but I still would rather be alone than have a foreigner who I could not talk to. There are two beds in a bunk and a couch ... I must draw to a close as we are getting pretty close to Queenstown and I'm afraid of missing the post ...
>
> Your ever loving husband,
>
> Jim

Everybody tells me I shall not regret the step I have taken, so buck up and we shan't be long.[65]

JAKOB JOHANSSON **Third Class Passenger**

Mr Johansson wrote the following diary entry on 11 April after the *Titanic* left Queenstown, Ireland:

April 11: At 12 o'clock was in Ireland where many passengers came onboard.[66]

ELIZABETH JOHNSTON **Third Class Passenger**

Mrs Johnston wrote the following postcard to her father while the *Titanic* was bound for Queenstown:

Dear Father,

We are just arriving at Queenstown. We are all feeling A1. The kids are skipping about like skylarks. Love from us all.

Eliza[67]

HENRY JULIAN **First Class Passenger**

Mr Julian wrote the following letter to his wife Hester while the *Titanic* was bound for Queenstown:

On board RMS *Titanic*
11th April, 1912

We do not arrive at Queenstown until about noon, which gives me an opportunity of writing again. I had a good night and was very comfortable. The ship is so steady that it is almost the same as being on land. More than half the officers and stewards on board are familiar faces to me, as they are taken from the *Adriatic* and *Oceanic*. The two deck-stewards remembered me quite well, and allotted me a chair in a select part of the deck.

This is a brilliant morning and quite warm ... I think if you could only have reached the ship safely you would have been all right, for there are practically no draughts. Revolving doors are much in use, which prevent any through currents of air. In the smoking room there is a big fireplace, which makes it cosy. The other rooms also have fireplaces, but have imitation fires heated by electricity; they are poor things compared with the real article ... The bands are unusually good ... I will feel happy with the thought that you are taking care of yourself at 'Redholme' ...[68]

JULIETTE LAROCHE **Second Class Passenger**

On 11 April, while the *Titanic* was bound for Queenstown, Mrs Laroche wrote the following letter to her father in Seine, France:

On Board RMS *Titanic*
11 April 1912

My dear Papa,

I have just been told that we are going to stop in a moment, so I take this opportunity to drop you a few lines and tell you about us.

We boarded the *Titanic* last evening at 7:00. If you could see this monster, our tender looked like a fly compared to her. The arrangements could not be more comfortable. We have two bunks in our cabin, and the two babies sleep on a sofa that converts into a bed. One is at the head, the other at the bottom. A board put before them prevents them from falling. They're as well, if not better, than in their beds. The boat set out when we were eating and we could not believe she was moving: we are less shaken than in a train. We just feel a slight trepidation. The girls ate well last night. They only took a nap in the whole night and the chime of the bell announcing breakfast woke them up. Louise laughed a lot at it. At the moment, they are strolling on the enclosed deck with Joseph, Louise is in her pram, and Simonne is pushing her. They already have become acquainted with people: we made the trip from Paris with a gentleman and his lady, and their little boy too, who is the same age as Louise. I think they are the only French people on the boat, so we sat at the same table so that we could chat together. Simonne was so funny a moment ago, she was playing with a young English girl who had lent her her doll. My Simonne was having a great conversation with her, but the girl did not understand a single word. People on board are very nice. Yesterday, they both were running after a gentleman who had given them chocolates. This morning I tried to count all the children on the boat. In second class only, I am sure that there are more than twenty. There is a small family with four children, they remind me of my Uncle's. The youngest child looks very much like fat Marcelle. I am writing from the reading room: there is a concert in here, near me, one violin, two cellos, one piano.

Up to now I have not felt seasick. I hope it will go on this way. The sea is very smooth, the weather is magnificent. If you could see how big this ship is! One can hardly find the way back to one's cabin in the number of corridors.

I will stop here now for I believe we are going to put in and I wouldn't like to miss the next mail. Once again, thank you my dear papa for all your marks of bounty towards us, and receive all the warmest kisses from your loving daughter,

Juliette

Warmly kiss for us all our dear good Grandmother, Maurice, Marguerite, and Madeleine. Little Simonne and Louise kiss their good grandfather. They had just their dresses on this morning when they wanted to go and see you.[69]

BERTHE LEROY **First Class Passenger**

Miss Leroy wrote the following postcard to her mother in Pas de Calais while the *Titanic* was approaching Queenstown:

Dear mother,

Calm down, I am most happy on this lovely ship and I wish you could visit it.

Berthe.[70]

MARION MEANWELL **Third Class Passenger**

Before the *Titanic* arrived at Queenstown, Mrs Meanwell wrote a letter to her friend Mrs Beck, and after declaring herself 'delighted' with the *Titanic*, added:

> In my view, nothing approaching the accommodation has been experienced in any of the previous journeys and nothing but a pleasant voyage is anticipated.[71]

FRANCIS MILLET — First Class Passenger

Mr Millet wrote the following letter to his friend Alfred Parsons while the *Titanic* was bound for Queenstown:

On Board RMS *Titanic*
April 11, 1912

Dear Alfred,

I got yours this morning and was glad to hear from you. I thought I told you my ship was the *Titanic*. She has everything but taxicabs and theatres. Table d'hote, restaurant a la carte, gymnasium, Turkish bath, squash court, palm gardens, smoking rooms for 'ladies and gents', intended I fancy to keep the women out of the men's smoking room which they infest in the German and French steamers. The fittings are in the order of Haddon Hall and are exceedingly agreeable in design and colour. As for the rooms they are larger than the ordinary hotel room and much more luxurious with wooden bedsteads, dressing tables, hot and cold water, etc. etc., electric fans, electric heater and all. The suites with their damask hangings and mahogany oak furniture are really very sumptuous and tasteful. I have the best room I ever had in a ship and it isn't one of the best either, a great long corridor in which to hang my clothes and a square window as big as the one in the studio alongside the large light. No end of furniture cupboards, wardrobe, dressing table, couch etc. etc. Not a bit like going to sea. You can have no idea of the spaciousness of this ship and the extent and size of the decks. The boat deck has an uninterrupted space as long as our tennis court almost, and the chair decks are nearly as wide as our large courtyard, or quite, 500 people don't make a show on the decks. Queer lot of people on this ship. Looking over the list I only find three or four I know but there are a good many of 'our people' I think and a number of obnoxious ostentatious American women, the scourge of any place they infest and worse on shipboard than anywhere. Many of them carry tiny dogs and lead husbands around like pet lambs. I tell you when she starts out the American woman is a buster. She should be put in a harem and kept there.

Yes I had the Devil of a time in Rome and if this sort of thing goes on I shall chuck it. I won't lose my time and my temper too. I think Mead will resign. Lily will tell you about her, the b... she makes trouble everywhere and he, poor wretch, has to dangle about her day and night. I pity him. I wrote from Paris the day we arrived. I couldn't tell where we should stop because I didn't know whether Lily would go to the Grand or not. We found it excellent.

Yours always,
Frank[72]

THOMAS MUDD **Second Class Passenger**

While the *Titanic* was approaching Queenstown, Mr Mudd wrote the following letter to his mother:

On board RMS *Titanic*
April 11, 1912

Dear Mother and all at home,

I am now taking the opportunity of sending you a few lines about how we started from Southampton. The express train quickly brought us from Waterloo, Edie saw me off at that place. We have been having very rough weather but the ship is so steady you would hardly know it was moving was it not for the throbbing of the engines. We are now nearing Queenstown. The ship is like a magnificent palace. The lounge and dining hall are very beautiful and we are having excellent food. I have made friends with a young English gentleman and he is very nice indeed. The beds are very nice also with plenty of covering to keep warm also they have spring mattresses. Please dear mother next time you write put in Edie's address as I must write to her, as she has been so kind. Cousin W and N treated us like kings. I think them all very nice people. Excuse writing as the ship is rolling a bit. Now I must close with love to all I remain your loving son,

Tom[73]

HENRY OLSEN **Third Class Passenger**

On 11 April Mr Olsen wrote the following postcard to his wife Sina:

S/S *Titanic*

Dear Sina,

On the way to New York. A very nice boat to travel with, you can imagine. Don't feel anything of the sea. Will most likely arrive in New York next Tuesday. Love to everyone at home. Love, your Henry.[74]

WILLIAM ROGERS **Third Class Passenger**

On 11 April Mr Rogers wrote the following postcard to his friend James Day in Swansea, Wales:

> Dear Friend,
> Just a line to show that I am alive & kicking going grand. It's a treat.
> Yours
> W J R[75]

ADOLPHE SAALFELD **First Class Passenger**

Mr Saalfeld sent the following letter-card to his wife in Manchester, England while the *Titanic* was bound for Queenstown:

> On Board RMS *Titanic*
> Thursday morning
>
> Dear Wifey,
> After a fair night's rest and an excellent breakfast I am enjoying a promenade in glorious weather. The wind is fresh and the sea 'moderate' but on this big boat one hardly notices any movement.
> I write these lines just before we are getting into Queenstown so that you can get them tomorrow morning.
> I shall not be able to write to you again before getting to New York.
> Fondest love to all.
> Adolphe
> * Shall write to office on arrival
> + Eric will no doubt phone you at once.[76]

STELLA SAGE — Third Class Passenger

Miss Sage wrote the following postcard to her friend Mrs Todd while the *Titanic* was bound for Queenstown:

> Dear Mrs Todd, Just a postcard of the boat. I am not seasick yet and hope I shall not be. Will write a long letter while on the boat. Cheer up, I'm coming back soon. With love Stella.[77]

ANNA SALKJELSVIK — Third Class Passenger

On 11 April Miss Salkjelsvik wrote the following postcard to her father:

> All is well with me. When I come ashore in America I will write more to you. On board Titanig [*sic*] on 11th April 1912.
> Love from Anna[78]

RICHARD SMITH — First Class Passenger

On 11 April 1912 Mr Smith wrote the following postcard just before the *Titanic* left Queenstown:

> Have had a fine run round to Queenstown, just leaving for the land of Stars and Stripes.
> Hope you are all well at home.
> Kind regards.
> R W S[79]

Mr Smith also wrote the following postcard to Miss Eva Roberts:

> You'll be pleased to hear I am now looking on dear Ireland once more & she certainly looks as if she could rule herself: had a nice blow round: would have just suited George and plenty of room for another. Kindest Regards –
> R W S[80]

WILLIAM T. STEAD **First Class Passenger**

Mr Stead wrote two letters to his daughter Estelle while the *Titanic* was bound for Queenstown. The first letter included the following lines:

> By the time you get this I shall be half-way across the Atlantic. At present the sky is beautifully blue and the sea as smooth as a mill pond.
>
> I am somewhat curious as to the work in front of me. I know my speech will be an important speech. But that is only one, and possibly not the most important work before me.[81]

Stead's second letter to his daughter reported:

> I am going to America to deliver one speech. But I feel as if that were but the Asses which Saul went forth to seek when he was crowned King of Israel. What else I am to do I do not know. Something is awaiting me, some important work the nature of which will be disclosed to me in good time. But what it is, whether journalistic, spiritual, social, or political, I know not. I await my marching orders, being assured that He who has called me will make clear His good will and pleasure in due season.[82]

Mr Stead wrote a third letter, this one to his secretary Edith Harper:

> Off Queenstown, April 11, 1912
>
> ... The ship is as firm as a rock, and the sea is like a mill-pond. If it lasts I shall be able to work better here than at home, for there are no telephones to worry me, and no callers ...[83]

EDWINA TROUTT **Second Class Passenger**

Miss Troutt wrote the following letter while the *Titanic* was bound for Queenstown:

> On board RMS *Titanic*
> April 11, 1912
>
> My Dear Gladys,
>
> I only wish you were enjoying yourself on a floating 'Palace' (like me). I am sure your Mother will fill you all up with 'Titanic.'
>
> She was very much taken up with everything on the boat. You cannot realise what it is like. She must look lovely out in mid ocean & is as firm as a rock. Did you read in the paper how we just escaped an accident. I was beginning to regret

being upon her, but she seems alright now. We were in Cherbourg 1½ hours & we are due at Queenstown at 11 today.

I must send you a long letter when my voyage is over.

So give my love to everyone & Good Bye from your

Loving Aunt Winnie[84]

UNKNOWN PASSENGER

The following account of the *Titanic*'s voyage between Southampton and Queenstown was written by an unnamed newspaper correspondent who apparently disembarked at Queenstown:

'Look at how that ship is rolling. I never thought it was so rough.'

The voice was a lady's, and the place was the sun deck of the *Titanic*. We had just got well clear of the eastern end of the Isle of Wight, and were shaping our course down the English Channel towards Cherbourg.

The ship that had elicited the remark was a large three-masted sailing vessel, which rolled and pitched so heavily that over her bow the seas were constantly breaking. But up where we were – some 60 feet above the water line – there was no indication of the strength of tossing swell below. This indeed is the one great impression I received from my first trip on the *Titanic* – and everyone with whom I spoke shared it – her wonderful steadiness. Were it not for the brisk breeze blowing along the decks, one would have scarcely imagined that every hour found us some 20 knots farther upon our course. And then this morning, when the full Atlantic swell came upon our port side, so stately and measured was the roll of the mighty ship that one needed to compare the moving of the side with the steady line of the clear horizon.

After a windy night on the Irish Sea, when the sturdy Packet boat tossed and tumbled to her heart's content – by the way; have ships a heart? – the lordly contempt of the *Titanic* for anything less than a hurricane seemed most marvellous and comforting. But other things besides her steadiness filled us with wonder. Deck over deck and apartment after apartment lent their deceitful aid to persuade us that instead of being on the sea we were still on *terra firma*. It is useless for me to attempt a description of the wonders of the saloon – the smoking room with its inlaid mother-of-pearl – the lounge with its green velvet and dull polished oak – the reading-room, with its marble fire place and deep soft chairs and rich carpet of old rose hue – all these things have been told over and over again, and only lose in the telling. So vast was it all that after several hours on board some of us were still uncertain of our way about – though we must state that – with commendable alacrity and accuracy some 325 found their way to the great dining saloon at 7.30 when the bugle sounded the call to dinner. After dinner as we sat in the beautiful lounge listening to the White Star orchestra playing the 'Tales of Hoffman' and

'Cavalleria Rusticana' selections more than once we heard the remark: 'You would never imagine you were on board a ship.' Still harder was it to believe that up on the top deck it was blowing a gale, but we had to go to bed, and this reminds me that on the *Titanic* the expression is literally accurate. Nowhere were the berths of other days seen, and everywhere comfortable oaken bedsteads gave place to furniture in the famous suites beloved by millionaires. Then the morning plunge in the great swimming bath, where the ceaseless ripple of the tepid seawater was almost the only indication that somewhere in the distance 72,000 horses in the guise of steam engines fretted and strained under the skilful guidance of the engineers, and after the plunge a half-hour in the gymnasium helped to send one's blood coursing freely, and created a big appetite for the morning meal.

But if the saloon of the *Titanic* is wonderful no less so is the second-class and in its degree the third-class. A word from the genial purser acted as the open sesame of the Arabian Nights, and secured us an English officer and his son, whose acquaintance I had made at lunch, and myself a free passage through all this floating wonder. Lifts and lounges and libraries are not generally associated in the public mind with second class, yet in the *Titanic* all are found. It needed the assurance of our guide that we had left the saloon and were really in the second class.

On the crowded third-class deck were hundreds of English, Dutch, Italian and French mingling in happy fellowship, and when we wandered down among them we found that for them, too, the *Titanic* was a wonder. No more general cabins, but hundreds of comfortable rooms, with two, four or six berths each, beautifully covered in red and white coverlets. Here, too, are lounges and smoking rooms, less magnificent than those amidships to be sure, but none the less comfortable, and which, with the swivel chairs and separate tables in the dining-rooms, struck me as not quite fitting in with my previous notion of steerage accommodation.[85]

UNKNOWN PASSENGER

An unknown passenger sent the following postcard to Master Tom Richmond of Lothian, England:

Dear Tom,

I am having a good time on this big ship and run about with a nice little girl. Wish you had come with us. We are coming to the Irish coast the last port of call till we arrive at Chicago ... [illegible].[86]

FREDERICK WRIGHT **Crew (Racquet Steward)**

On 11 April Mr Wright wrote the following letter to his sister:

> On Board RMS *Titanic*
> Thursday 11th 1912
> My Dearest Ida,
> I have been worrying my heart out thinking I shouldent [*sic*] have time to drop you a line. I left it till this morning and have been busy since first thing and the last one [i.e. racquets partner] has just gone, and we expect to arrive [at Queenstown] any minute. I must say I am fairly well except my usual cold and my finger is a little painful, but you need not worry it will be alright. Of course I can't tell you much news as I want to drop Tom and co a line, there is not much difference in the ships of course this is the best. I am looking forward to your letter to hear how you all are and how you got on on Mon night, I do hope you will write at New York, give my best love to Dad and all and see those things go back safely to Aunt Lucy for me, heeps of love in haste
> Fred xxxx
> PS Must tell you I landed home 11.15, what a blessing I didn't wait for that 10 o'clock [train] there was eighteen in our carriage when we reached Willesden one woman fainted it was terrible. [87]

POSTSCRIPT

UNKNOWN SOUTHAMPTON RESIDENT

On 11 April an unknown resident of Southampton purchased a postcard featuring the *Titanic* and posted it to Mayor Gaynor of New York City, along with the following message:

> Guess you had better chain up the Statue of Liberty to a skyscraper in Fifth Avenue. Or to the ramparts of Fort Pitt. As I 'reckon and calculate' that the foundations are liable to be swallowed up by the wash of this 'octopus' from the other side, which sucked up from its moorings, like a barnacle, the 'Yankee Doodle' liner *New York* yesterday in Southampton docks.
> Better instruct the United States fleet to tow her in, or I guess New York will be wiped off the map.
> SEXTON BLAKE[88]

(Note: Sexton Blake was a fictional British detective of the time, whose name was appropriated by the sender of the postcard.)

12 April 1912: *Titanic* at Sea

KATE BUSS **Second Class Passenger**

While on board the *Titanic* Miss Buss began writing a long letter to her parents describing her voyage; the second instalment of her letter was written on 12 April:

> Friday Morning, April 12/12 – Dressed at 7 a.m. – had a good night. Promised to go on deck before breakfast, but I hear so many men about outside I'm afraid to go on the deck below and fetch Miss W. Shall wait until I hear the dressing gong. My face is as red as possible. Wish I had some grease, but it's no good. There are two of the finest little Jap baby girls about three or four years old, who look like dolls running about. I hear a baby screaming now, two or three are on board, but nothing particularly classy 2nd class, that I've seen, but some seem to turn up only at meal times.
>
> I cannot get on with work or reading. Yesterday, we seemed to do nothing but walk about and when one gets back into the deck chair sleep seems the only possible thing, with an occasional wink or blink at some apparently interested passer-by.

Now I've got my cabin to myself I feel A1. I can move about and do as I like. Feel quite important in fact. We dress a bit for dinner; and am going to wear my grey frock on Sunday.

Noon. – We had our blow. Met Mr 'Sad man' up on deck. Spent the morning first on upper deck. Then down in one of the inner decks to hear the band.

At breakfast this morning we received a book containing list of passengers (we each ticked our own names) and of our destination. The Doctor is a proper Yankee, a most interesting fellow traveller, as he explains things so well. The parsons are Roman Catholics, but we've had a long chat this morning with some people we met yesterday. He is the Vicar or Rector of Whitechapel. They are going to Kansas to visit friends, just for the Easter vacation, I presume. It is much more choppy than yesterday. Several folk have been sick.

Luncheon. – My companion, especially Dr R., chips me about getting nearer to California. Why don't I go to Kentucky?

After luncheon we spent most of our time on deck reading. Saw Doctor just after dinner, and reminded him of his promise to ask our cello man to play a solo. Says he would if I'd go to Kentucky. He waited for us, and we took our seats on the stairs. Too late to arrange, so going to ask for it tomorrow. Cello man quite nice. Very superior bandsman, and he always smiles his parting to us.

Been pacing the deck with Doctor R. right until nine o'clock. I'm writing now in my berth, on the sofa. There is every possible convenience on ship. For instance, when you go into the lavatories and bedrooms they are in darkness until you close the door, which is connected with a clip to the electric light, you open the door and the light goes off.

I have two clips to the one light in my cabin, one at the head of my bed and the other at the door.

A very odd company of second-class passengers; so many transferred from other vessels. Certainly we are not full. Guess folks were scared. They tell me that when we left Southampton Docks we drew the *New York* from her moorings, and nearly as possible ran into her. The tugs that should have pulled us out had to rush to her assistance and drag her away. I understand that the captain was a very interested spectator, but I saw nothing of it myself. I'm getting all sorts of advice as to my rail journey.

I do hope I shall get through all right, but they tell me prices are ruinous for food, etc. Doctor says he'll get as much information as is possible tomorrow. He lost his wife there by shock in that railway accident on the London Brighton and South Coast Railway. Don't you remember that Christmas Eve? He says he never recovered from the shock; he is jolly, but quite straight, and a Southerner. They are the people Sam says are the best. I've discovered I forgot to post to Percy at Queenstown. This must do for you all, everyone. Retiring now.[89]

JAKOB JOHANSSON **Third Class Passenger**

Mr Johansson wrote the following diary entry on 12 April 1912:

> April 12: Beautiful weather no wind we have an excellent accommodation everything is clean and tidy big promenade deck and light and fresh roe.[90]

13 April 1912: *Titanic* at Sea

JEREMIAH BURKE **Third Class Passenger**

On 13 April – two days after the *Titanic* left Queenstown – Mr Burke sealed the following note inside a small bottle and cast it into the sea. The bottle and message washed ashore near Cork Harbour in May 1913.

13/4/1912
From *Titanic*

Goodbye all
Burke of Glanmire
Cork[91]

KATE BUSS **Second Class Passenger**

On 13 April Miss Buss wrote the third instalment of her long letter to her parents:

> Saturday, 13/4/12 – Morning; just missed Miss W. on the staircase; there are two to each deck. Just think, all these hundreds, of miles from land, and cocks can be heard crowing now at this time of night. Just had a bath, so will write a little of today's doings. Bless those cockerels! Well, I got through my paces at breakfast, and had a little run on deck. Arranged to meet the Doctor and go and hear the band. Couldn't get near to ask our cello man for solo. Went up and had a walk with Doctor; then down on deck. Oh, for soup. Back to the chairs on covered deck. After luncheon we went with a French lady to hear her sing. We had previously met the cello man and asked if he would play a solo. He is quite gentlemanly. He agreed, and we chatted, amongst other things about the *Olympic*. He was on her when the accident happened. She was struck just where their berths were, and he said that had they been in there, they must have been killed. We have the *Olympic* captain on board. The French lady's husband will not allow her to sing before a lot of folk, unless it's at a concert for charity; so we went with a few to the dining saloon.
>
> There is to be a concert on Monday, and anyone willing to assist are asked to put their names down. Miss W. put hers down, but I haven't. I find Mr 'Sad man' talks different languages, and the Doctor talks four or five. This morning Miss W. discovered another gentleman who was asked to look out for her – a Dr P., Canadian. Quite a young fellow, rather nice, too, but, as I've said, young; he takes everything one says very seriously. I must go to bed now, eye neuralgia coming bad. That means a bad day tomorrow, I'm afraid.
>
> I tell them all that I smiled at the young person, and he bolted as if he'd been shot. He was ill today and had to leave the table. Doctor asked if I'd been at my old tricks again. I'm just beginning to know quite a few, and wish I could get all the way by water.
>
> Goodbye. Hope you won't worry. I've got a declaration sheet to fill in. Don't know however I shall do it: it's a beastly nuisance. Tomorrow is Sunday. Hope it will keep fine.[92]

JAKOB JOHANSSON **Third Class Passenger**

On 13 April Mr Johansson made the following entry in his diary:

> April 13: The weather is beautiful but still the women are sick great many are still staying up.[93]

14 APRIL 1912: *TITANIC* AT SEA

ESTHER HART **Second Class Passenger**

On 14 April 1912 Mrs Hart wrote the following letter to Mrs Bloomfield of Essex, England and placed it in her pocket. It was never posted:

On board RMS *Titanic*
Sunday afternoon

My dear ones all,

As you see it is Sunday afternoon & we are reading in the Library after luncheon. I was very bad all day yesterday. Could not eat or drink, & sick all the while, but today I have got over it. This morning Eva & I went to church & she was so pleased they sang Oh God Our Help in Ages Past; that is her Hymn she sang so nicely, so she sang out loud. She is very bonny. She has had a nice ball & a box of toffee and a photo of the ship bought her today. Everybody takes notice of her through the Teddy Bear. There is to be a concert on Board tomorrow night in aid of the Sailors Home & she is going to sing so am I.

Well the sailors say we have had a wonderful passage up to now. There has been no tempest, but God knows what it must be [like] when there is one. This mighty expanse of water, no land in sight & the ship rolling from side to side is very wonderful tho they say this ship does not roll on account of its size. Any how it rolls enough for me. I shall never forget it. It is nice weather but awfully windy & cold. They say we may get into New York Tuesday night, but we are really due early on Wednesday morning. Shall write as soon as we get there. This letter won't leave the ship but will remain & come back to England where she is due again on the 26th. Where you see the letter all of a screw is when she rolls & shakes my arm. I am sending you on a [illegible] to show you how we live. I shall be looking forward to a line from somebody to cheer me up a bit. I am always shutting my eyes & I see everything as I left it. I hope you are all quite well. Let this be an all round letter as I can't write properly to all till I can set my foot on shore again.

We have met some nice people on Board [illegible] & so it has been nice so far, but oh the long long days & nights – it's the longest week I ever spent in my life.

I must close now with all our fondest love to all of you

From your loving Esther

heaps of love and kisses to all from

Eva X X X X X X X X X X X X X X X X[94]

JAKOB JOHANSSON **Third Class Passenger**

On 14 April 1912 Mr Johansson wrote the following entry in his diary:

April 14: Sunday today it is raining and everybody must stay inside. There are all kinds of nationalities here among others Turks and Japanese.[95]

15 April 1912: Disaster

UNITED STATES HYDROGRAPHIC OFFICE **Washington, D.C.**

On 15 April 1912 Captain J.J. Knapp wrote the following daily report summarising recent sightings of floating hazards in the North Atlantic shipping lanes:

Hydrographic Office
Washington, D.C.

DAILY MEMORANDUM

No.1013 April 15, 1912.
NORTH ATLANTIC OCEAN

OBSTRUCTIONS OFF THE AMERICAN COAST

Mar. 28 – Lat 24 degrees 20', lon 80 degrees 02', passed a broken spar projecting about 3 feet out of water, apparently attached to sunken wreckage. – EVELYN (SS) Wright.

OBSTRUCTIONS ALONG THE OVER-SEA ROUTES

Apr 7 – Lat 35 degrees 20', lon 59 degrees 40', saw a lowermast covered with marine growth. – ADRIATICO (It ss), Cevascu.

ICE REPORTS

Apr 7 – Lat 45 degrees 10', lon 56 degrees 40', ran into a strip of field ice about 3 or 4 miles wide extending north and south as far as could be seen. Some very heavy pans were seen. – ROSALIND (Br ss), Williams.
Apr 10 – Lat 41 degrees 50', lon 50 degrees 25', passed a large ice field a few hundred feet wide and 15 miles long extending in a NNE direction. – EXCELSIOR (Ger ss). (*New York Herald*)
COLLISION WITH ICEBERG – Apr 14 – Lat 41 degrees 46', lon 50 degrees 14', the British steamer TITANIC collided with an iceberg seriously damaging her bow; extent not definitely known.
Apr 14 – The German steamer AMERIKA reported by radio telegraph passing two large icebergs in lat 41 degrees 27', lon 50 degrees 08', – *Titanic* (Br ss).
Apr 14 – Lat 42 degrees 06', lon 49 degrees 43', encountered extensive field ice and saw seven icebergs of considerable size. – PISA (Ger ss).
J. J. Knapp
Captain, U. S. Navy
Hydrographer[96]

A. JOHNSON — Southampton Resident

On the afternoon of 15 April 1912 Mr Johnson purchased a *Titanic* picture postcard in Southampton and used it to write the following message:

> This is the ship which is supposed to be sinking. It is sad. Soton is all astir this afternoon. I hope it is not so bad as they think.
> A. Johnson[97]

16 April 1912: On Board the *Carpathia*

NELLIE BECKER **Second Class Passenger**

On 16 April Mrs Becker wrote the following letter to her husband in India:

> Sunday night I was awakened by a jolt, and the engines stopped. I heard people running about and went out into the hall to see what the matter was. A man said, 'Nothing;' so I went back into the room and lay down again. Then I heard people rushing again, and I looked out the door and there stood our cabin Steward. I asked: 'What is the trouble?' He said, 'Tie on your life-belt and go on deck at once.' I said: 'Have we time to dress?' He said: 'No, Madame, you have time for nothing.' But I did put on the children's shoes and stockings and then their coats and caps over their night clothes. I carried Sonny with his heavy coat on, wrapped in a blanket. Up there, there was perfect order. An Officer came and said to me: 'Get into this life boat.' They were putting women and children in as fast as possible. They threw Marion and Sonny in, and were lowing the boat, when I said: 'Oh, please let me go with my children,' and while the boat was being lowered, an Officer picked me up and threw me into the boat, but I could not find the children. At last I saw them. One sailor had Sonny and was kissing him and trying to

comfort him. I took him and he went to sleep. I stood up and he leaned against one side of me and Marion the other. They put Ruth in another boat, but I did not feel anxious, for I saw her being put in another boat.

We had struck the iceberg at 11:30 and got off 12:30. We had a perfectly calm sea, but cold. It was bitterly cold. I forgot to mention that when we got on deck they were sending up rockets. When we got away from the boat we saw that the bow up to the first deck had already sunk and she was going fast. Our boatmen were fine. One Officer stood in the end and gave orders, and although the boatmen demurred, he never answered a word, but made them obey him. But the current was against us and we could hardly get away from the *Titanic*, and we were all so afraid of the suction. It was about half an hour from the time we got off till the *Titanic* sank. She seemed to break right in the middle, and the middle to fall in. It was terrible beyond words. I shall never forget that sound. And then the awful cries that went up – moaning and groaning, and crying and praying. No words can tell how awful it was. Then broken pieces of the ship came floating about and dead bodies, and men half alive. Oh! it was horrible, horrible, horrible. The Officers stood with revolvers and said they would shoot the first man who tried to get into the boats, and one did shoot, but I do not think he really shot anyone.

Well, we thought all had been saved except a few sailors. The Officers so told us. There were fifty people in our boat. After drifting about till daylight, all but frozen, and not knowing whether the wireless messages had been received, we saw a large boat in the distance and then the rockets from her to tell us she had come to our rescue. Never can anyone know how we felt when we knew we were saved, and we went with light hearts to her, thinking that very few were lost. We were so numb with cold when we came to the boat that we could not get out. The Officers of the *Carpathia* had to come and get us out. The children they lifted in gunny sacks. Then they took us and tied us into a sort of swing and lifted us up. When they got us up, the Stewards lifted us up and carried us into the saloon, gave us brandy and wrapped us up in blankets. Many children were almost dead, and they worked with them all day. When we got into the *Carpathia* women were shrieking, crying, fainting, for we then first knew that two lifeboats had capsized and that the men could not get into lifeboats for there were no more. There is one woman in the second class who has her husband: all the rest are widows. You simply cannot imagine the sadness here. Only two Stewardesses out of fourteen were saved; almost all the Stewards gone; only one or two left. About a dozen little orphaned children are here. Of course nobody saved a thing. Many have not a cent. Some tried to take handbags, but the officers just took them and threw them into the sea. On the *Carpathia* we stay at day in the saloon and at night in the Officers' quarters, for the boat is full up.[98]

KATE BUSS **Second Class Passenger**

On 16 April, after being rescued by the *Carpathia*, Miss Buss continued writing the long letter that she had begun while on board the *Titanic* and which was still in her coat pocket:

> Before you get this you will have heard of the awful experience I have had. I had been pitying Nance when I saw how beautiful our ship was. Sunday morning we paced the deck with the Rector or Vicar of St Jude's, Whitechapel, and his wife. After luncheon she insisted on my having a good rest in her husband's chair, as I looked so tired. Such a splendid character; and now she is gone. We had a very short morning service by the Purser, but no address. Strange to say after that, although we didn't quite realise it, every prayer and hymn seemed to be preparing us for that awful experience. I shall never forget the splendid lives that were lost, one seemed as if they had known them for years: and I am still grieving now much more for them than myself.
>
> Sunday evening we had a hymn singing congregation; no set service; it was lovely. We met the Dr P. who was told off by his friend to look out for my ship friend, Miss W., and took him in with us. Another acquaintance, a young fellow, so nice, Mr N. (Edinburgh) played the piano.
>
> We all four took supper together, and, strange to say, met on deck as the ship struck. I cannot bear to think of how we had to leave them to get into the lifeboats, so strong as they were for us. I'd give so much to meet them again; one couldn't ever forget them, living or dead. If you see either of those names mentioned as living, be sure and let me know; also of the Rev. and Mrs Carter, who, I believe, went down on the vessel. Heaps died of exposure, and some have died in hospital. Try to remember that I am one of the very few, and that I'd willingly have waited if I had realised how few lifeboats there were, and have let some poor creatures have their husbands with them. It's too cruel to know of such reckless waste of lives.
>
> Had there been more boats nearly all might have been saved: and until we reached the *Carpathia* we quite expected that at least nearly all the passengers were saved. The lifeboats had no lights, and some no oars; there were not half enough seamen, and I hear they estimate the loss at nearly 2,000.
>
> One poor fellow on our deck I saw some hours after we came aboard; he is the only one I knew to speak to that is saved; quite a lad. I was so delighted that I felt I must kiss him. He had an awful time, and is aching with bruises from floating wreckage. He had six hours in the water before he was picked up, and he told me there were 50 in the boat who died, but he didn't know who they were, it was so dark.
>
> Thank God we fared wonderfully well, considering. At one time we thought the icebergs would have overtaken us. It was a toss-up between those and the ship, at one time, when we were rowing against the tide toward the *Carpathia*. We drifted after we got beyond reach of the suction of the *Titanic* for four or five hours. I've lost everything of course. I was talking in my cabin to Miss W., and had just jumped into my berth, when the crash came. Nobody seemed to be moving, so I

calmly put on my dressing gown and slippers and went down to her. She was just coming to me. We went on deck and met Mr N., who had seen the iceberg. All he regretted was that he had not got his camera.

We decided to stay up for a time in case of emergencies, so went down for a bit more clothing. I went down, put on my stockings, the woollen petticoat, and my long coat. As a last thought I picked up my rug and went up again. Then the stewards came to tell us (oh so quietly) that it was the Captain's rule to make people wear lifebelts in case of emergencies; and so we went down to get them. I snatched up my bag with my papers, but alas, no money. The Purser had the majority, with my pendant, chain, watch chain, and bracelet. My purse I forgot, and I was struggling with my lifebelt.

On deck I saw Mr N. again, and Dr P. was looking out for Miss W.; neither wore lifebelts, thinking it was unnecessary. With such a big ship and Marconi communication, they thought we should have had relief before she sank. We didn't realise that a lot of passengers were off the vessel, and it seemed quite by chance that we went round to the other side of the ship and heard them call, 'Any more ladies on deck?' and 'Ladies first.'

I suppose we drifted some miles, for several hours elapsed before we sighted the steamer. Then we had to row those miles back again against the tide. But what was worst of all was climbing the rigging. The first woman lost her footing, and was hanging mid-way while our boat left the side of the vessel, and so she had nothing to fall into if she fell. They attempted to let them climb with the rope, and orders were shouted down that one rope was to be used in every case. I was willingly the last woman to climb, I felt I would almost rather the boat turn upside down than attempt it. But I made myself climb calmly, as if it were an ordinary ladder. They hauled me up the last few steps, and waiting at the top was someone with a rug, who wrapped it around me, and half carried me into the saloon. There all the stewards were busy making hot brandy and water for each person as they came up.

They have looked after us wonderfully well, and I am fortunate in sharing a berth with a nurse, given up by a gentleman, when I preferred to sleep on the deck than going right below steerage in the sailors' berths: I felt I should smother if I did.

I have had neuralgia in my head fearfully, but then I cried so much when I knew we had lost our friends, and it's simply awful to see the distressed widows and distracted parents.

Never as long as I live shall I forget it nor the brave souls who, I know, have perished.

I wonder if you got the cables I sent? They told me I could send without money and charge to the White Star Company. But I believe it was really to rally us. I hear they haven't gone. Well, I haven't a farthing, so I must trust that the Reverend Mr Watkins will meet and assist me for the time being. Everything has gone, every single thing but my life.

The musicians were such nice men. I asked one night for a cello solo, and got it at once. Mr N. told me on Sunday night that the last thing they played was at his request, and I hear that they were playing 'Nearer My God to Thee'. That night the pianist had asked me if I would mind taking round the subscription, as I had appreciated the music. At supper I talked Mr N. and Dr P. into promising to do it for me, and as a joke the former rehearsed a possible speech, and then said 'Meet me on the upper deck at six in the morning. I will talk it over.'

I saw the pianist as I was going to bed, and promised. That is the last I saw of them. I met Dr N. on the upper deck, but it was before six o'clock. The ship struck at 11.45, and I think it was about 6.30 when we were hauled upon the deck.

She sank at 12.45. We had just got beyond the reach of the suction. It was a grand sight at sea, and with every light on she was a picture. She parted right in halves, the forward part went down first, and the aft seemed to stand upright. There was a terrific explosion; the cries of the souls on board were awful to hear, but there was absolutely nothing to be seen. I heard one sailor say to another, 'We must get still farther away'; and so they rowed out for a bit. But we were near the Gulf Stream, and had it been at all rough or foggy, no boats could have stood it.

Many were overturned. Men and women died of exhaustion and exposure. We had the burial service read by a Roman Catholic priest. Those brought in dead were buried yesterday afternoon.

I was blind with neuralgia. A gentleman gave me a chair in the sun, and a lady brought me a cup of tea. No lounge and beautiful sitting room, it's just an emigrants' ship, and a cruise to Naples.[99]

ALICE LEADER **First Class Passenger**

On 16 April Dr Leader wrote the following letter to her friend, Mrs Sarah Babcock of Philadelphia:

My Dear Mrs Babcock,

We have been through a most terrible experience – the *Titanic* and above a thousand souls sunk on Monday about 3 o'clock in the morning. Margaret and I are safe, although we have lost everything. One of our party also. Mr Kenyon was lost. He was such a charming man, so honourable and good. I sat talking to him a little before the accident and a little later he was dead. His wife is crushed by the blow. I can say one thing, nothing could part me from my husband in time of danger. After floating about for four hours we were taken on board the steamer that was bound for Naples but she is now taking us to New York.

It is terrible to see the people who have lost their families and friends – one lady has lost $15,000 worth of clothing, and no one has saved anything. Many of the passengers have only their night clothes with coats over them. I shall never forget the sight of that beautiful boat as she went down, the orchestra playing to the last, the lights burning until they were extinguished by the waves. It sounds so unreal, like a scene on the stage. We were hit by an iceberg. We were in the midst of a field of ice, towers of ice: fantastic shapes of ice. It is all photographed on my mind. There was no panic. Every one met death with composure – as one said, the passengers were a set of thoroughbreds.

We are moving slowly toward New York. Everyone on this boat is so kind to us. Clothing and all the necessaries are at our convenience. I am attired in my old blue serge & steamer hat; truth to tell I am a sorry looking object to land in New York. This is rather a mixed up epistle, but please pardon lack of clearness of expression. If you want me, some time I will come to Philadelphia for a day or two in the future.

With dear love,
Alice F. Leader[100]

MARY LINES **First Class Passenger**

On 16 April Miss Lines wrote the following letter to her friend, Miss Helen Iselin:

On Board the Cunard RMS *Carpathia*
Wednesday April 16

My dearest;

God has been so good to us. My mother and I have been saved. I'm writing to you from the ship that picked us up. Oh, my darling, it was a horrible night, and I hope you never have to pass one like it.

I'm going to try to tell you everything. First at a quarter to midnight my mother felt that the ship had received a terrible blow. She jumps from her bed and wakes me up, for I was still asleep. Then we hear the sound of steam escaping with a frightful hissing. We ring for the steward who reassures us and tells us to go to bed. Then our next-door neighbours (Hilga and Ragnhild's uncle and cousin) come down again and the father tells us there's no danger at all. Then we go to bed. Ten minutes later we hear Mr White who comes down and shouts to his son: 'Richard! Lifeboats!' You can imagine that we hurried to get up, we quickly grabbed some coats, then we rushed to the deck. As I'm leaving our cabin I hear Mr White's son (he was just 21) shouting 'Lifebelts!' I go back to look for them and there we are on deck. They tell us to go back down for a little while and since we weren't dressed, my mother runs to look for our things. Since she was slow in returning I got worried and rushed to our cabin. I beg her to come and we roll up all our things in a blanket. Then as were going up again we see everybody hurrying, hurrying. We arrive on deck and jump into a small rowing boat. They lower the boat on ropes down to the water; and there we are, away. Meanwhile I'd thrown away all our clothing, since the bundle was too big to bring along in the little boat. We pull away from the *Titanic* as fast as possible, and a half-hour later it has sunk. Oh! my darling, what a horrible thing, this enormous ship engulfed in the little space of two hours. And the cries of the dying as it sank!!! For there are only 700 saved out of two thousand, I believe. Finally we drifted on the sea, which by the grace of God was calm like your pond at Brion, for three hours and a half. At four o'clock we made out a ship in the distance, and the men started to row with all their might; and soon we were picked up by this ship. I'll never forget this sunrise; the sky clear as a glass of water, the sea calm as a mirror, and the enormous icebergs surrounding us, white as swans. Then all of a sudden on the horizon these two stars, but steady stars that didn't fade and that soon appeared as ship's lights. How happy we were. You can't imagine it. God has shown miraculous clemency and mercy towards us.

There are still lots of details of this frightful night that would interest you, but I'll write them to you later or I'll tell you about them when I see you again, if God grants that I see you again. We are now surrounded by a thick, thick fog, and I don't know when we'll see New York.

Oh! my darling, help me to thank God for his inexpressible goodness!

My mother isn't very well today. She's beginning to feel the fatigues of the other night.

Naturally we've lost everything. My dresses, my hats, everything is at the bottom of the sea.

Au revoir, my dear, write me soon. Our address will be:

158 Archer Avenue
Mount Vernon
New York.

With heaps of love

Yours as ever – Mary [101]

OLGA LUNDIN **Second Class Passenger**

On 16 April Miss Lundin wrote the following letter to her family in Sweden:

On the waves of the Atlantic 16th

Dear Mother and Sister,

I will now briefly write a few words to you to let you know that I am alive after great suffering and difficulties. You have probably read in the newspaper that the ship we travelled on sank. Oh great God what I have suffered on this voyage. Imagine that on Sunday night we woke up to a dangerous noise, the ship hit an iceberg. We all got up, imagine the panic, but still we didn't think that she would go down. She was the biggest steamship in the world. I feel so strange I can hardly write, I can't collect my thoughts. I am so nervous and weak that I can't do anything. I have bad news to tell, Nils, Albert and Paul have found a grave in the waves of the Atlantic. Oh merciful God so sad, the thought is such that I can't describe it with the pen, I had Nils in one arm and Kalle in the other, we read and prayed as long as we could and so we decided not to separate but to die together, we saw no other way out. Albert and Paul went after, we five [Olga Lundin, Pal Andreasson, Albert Augustsson, Nils Johansson and Carl Jonsson] were like brothers and sisters, and would so be separated on the waves of the Atlantic.

It was 12 o'clock when this happened and within an hour the whole of the big ship was in the deep with 3,000, there has probably never been a bigger disaster at sea. Oh how I mourn after Nils who as his other, his last word said when we had prayed that he didn't pray only for himself but for his parents and sisters. There we stood on the deck and saw nothing else but death in front of us. They were lowering lifeboats and I was thrown into one of them. I held on to Nils with one hand and wanted to take him along, but they held him, being afraid that there would be too many of us. I screamed as loud as I could and wanted to go back, but at the same time I was lowered. There I sat in a small fishing boat in the middle of the Atlantic and expected nothing else but death, at any moment. But now my time is a little longer and that is probably why I stayed alive. I don't know how many have been saved, but certainly not more that 100 out of the 3,000. Kalle [Carl Jonsson] didn't get in any lifeboat until at last he lay on a door in the water for six hours so he was almost dead when he came up on this ship that we now sit in. But good Lord we are like pigs here, there are but Japanese and Gypsies here. It smells so that one is about to die and nothing can be eaten.[102]

ELIZABETH NYE **Second Class Passenger**

On 16 April Mrs Nye wrote the following letter to her parents while the *Carpathia* was returning to New York:

Royal Mail Steamship *Carpathia*
Tuesday, April 16th 1912

My dear mother and dad,

I expect you have been wondering whether you would ever hear from me again. You have seen by the papers the wreck of the *Titanic*, but after the most terrible time of my life, I am safe. My nerves are very shattered, I look and feel about ten years older, but I will get over it again after a time.

You will like to hear the truth of the wreck from me, for the papers never tell the right news. We were all in bed on Sunday night at about 11.30, when we felt an awful jerk, and the boat grazed something along its side, and the sea seemed to splash right over the deck. The men in the next cabin slipped on their coats and ran up to see what it was, and came and told us the ship had run into an iceberg nearly as large as herself.

Most of the people went back to bed again, but then came an order 'get up and put something warm on, put on a lifebelt and come on deck.' So I got one underskirt on and a skirt, and stockings, and shoes and coat, and ran up to find a lifebelt, because there were only three in our berth for four of us. A boy from the next cabin stole one from ours, but he went down with it poor boy. We did not have time to go back to our cabins again to get anything, and we did not dream it was serious. I thought I should get back to get more clothes on and get a few other things, but we were put into the lifeboats, and pushed off at once. They put all ladies and children in first. I guess there were 30 or 40 in our boat. It seemed to be the last one lowered with women in it.

When we got away from the ship we could understand the hurry and the order to get half a mile away as soon as possible. For the *Titanic* was half in the water. We watched the port holes go under until half the ship, only the back half, stuck up. Then the lights went out, and the boilers burst and blew up. There was a sickening roar like hundreds of lions, and we heard no more but THE MOANING AND SHOUTING for help from the hundreds of men and a few women who went down with her.

There were not enough boats for so many people. Twenty lifeboats were lowered, and only fourteen boats were picked up. Several men were on a raft that was thrown out, and their cries for help were so pitiful for so long. Only one fellow, about 21 years old, is alive from the raft. He says the men were pushed off to make it lighter. This man was on it for six hours and then saved.

Just before the ship went down the Captain, the same Captain Smith of the twin ship *Olympic*, jumped into the sea and picked up a little girl who was hanging to the ship, and put her on the raft. They pulled him on, too, but he would not stay. He said 'Good-bye boys, I must go with the ship.' He swam back through the icy waters and died at his post ... [missing text probably said that the only light present in her lifeboat was] ... only a lighted rope end. We had no drink or provisions. The only thing in our favour was the clear starlight night and fairly smooth sea.

This boat, the *Carpathia*, of the Cunard line, was going from Halifax to Berlin. She was the only ship near enough to catch the wireless message for help from the *Titanic*, and then the operators says he was just leaving and closing the door, when he heard the clicking of the wireless. So it was taken just in time, for they never sent another message, and it was an hour and quarter after that before the first lifeboat got to the ship. Of course, she stood still, and waited for us all to come up. They were all in but two when we got in.

We were in the little boat for just five hours and a half before being rescued. They lowered bags for the babies to pull them up, and we sat on a kind of swing and were drawn up by a rope to safety. They have been most kind to us. Led us one by one to the dining room, and gave us brandy. I drank half a glass of brandy down without water. We were all perished, and it put life into us. The ship is, of course, filled with its own passengers, but they found places for us all to sleep, but none of us slept well after going through such A HORRIBLE NIGHTMARE. This ship stood right over the place where the *Titanic* went down, and picked us up. Two small boats were picked up later. They were floating. One had seven dead bodies in it, and the other just a dead boatman. They sewed them up in canvas here, weighted them, and gave them a Christian burial at sea. Two small boats filled with passengers capsized. They all went down but two or three, who clung to the upturned boat, and were saved.

We are told that the SS *Baltic* picked up about fifty men, and the poor women here are hoping their husbands are among the fifty. It is supposed there are 160 more widows through this wreck, and most of them have children. It was so heart breaking to see and hear them crying for their husbands.

We were all gathered together, and our names taken for the newspapers. Of course, they cannot tell how many are dead, but we have on this ship only two hundred crew out of 910 and 500 passengers out of 2,000. I am amongst the fortunate, for God has spared my life when I was so near death again. I have lost everything I had on board. The only thing I saved was my watch Dad gave me eleven years ago. But all my treasures and clothes and some money have gone. I have only the scanty clothes that I stand up in, including my big coat, which has been a blessing.

We expect to land on Wednesday night, or next morning. I shall be so thankful, for I feel so ill on this boat. The boat is not so nice, and we have to sleep in the bottom of the boat. But still, I thank God I am alive.

I could tell you much more of the horrors of Sunday night, but will write again later on land. I can't bear to think of it all now. Will you let Auntie and Edie see this letter, and tell my friends I am safe. You must have all been anxious.

With fondest love to all, from Lizzie[103]

ELIZABETH SHUTE **First Class Passenger**

On 16 April Miss Shute wrote a letter in which she described:

> ... seeing that great helpless vessel 'Titantic' [*sic*] disappear before my eyes ... [and] the moans of those left to drown.[104]

EDWINA TROUTT **Second Class Passenger**

On 16 April Miss Troutt began writing a letter to her parents in England:

On board the Cunard RMS *Carpathia*

My dear Mother, Father and all,

You will be pleased to know that I am safe on the *Carpathia*, after a 'thrilling yet safe experience.' But I am very much afraid all the men have lost their lives; they were very brave. It was the greatest surprise to everyone. We were all in bed, and told to remain there, as it was only an 'Iceberg,' so we were only in our night attire. Everything is lost, money, pictures and all. We were launched in the lifeboats at 1.15 a.m. and picked up at 6.15. The *Titanic* was cut in two and was sunk to the second deck when I reached a lifeboat. I saved a baby in arms, and we had to sing for our lives at such a perilous time. The sailors were singing 'Pull for the shore, sailors' and rowing, half dressed in frozen garments. The conduct of all the passengers was really wonderful. 'Babies and ladies first' was the order. I think there were only sixteen boats. We were fortunate to have calm seas and a good nerve.

We could not any of us realise the peril until we were safe on this boat. Then the pathetic scenes occurred. Women were looking for their husbands and mothers for their babies. The band was playing until the last.

I cannot write any more just now, but please don't worry. I will try and get along the best I can. Trusting you are getting over the shock.

From your loving daughter,

Winnie[105]

ELIZABETH WATT **Second Class Passenger**

On 16 April Mrs Watt wrote the following letter while the *Carpathia* was bound for New York:

I was in bed, but I could not sleep, and at quarter to 12 there was such a bump, and then the engine stopped dead. I got up out of bed and threw on my dressing gown and ran up the stairs, but they kept on saying it was nothing.

When we went on deck a young fellow from Edinburgh told me it was an iceberg, but, of course, the officers said there was nothing wrong. I went downstairs and put my heavy coat on, and went on top again with Miss Wright, who is to live in Cottage Grove. (I think I told you about her in my last letter. She is to marry a fruit grower there. He is to meet her in New York to marry her. She is such a nice girl. I will see her married, and it will be someone to know when we get out).

I will be glad to get on land. Bertha is quite off food, being upset with the shock. I suppose she will soon be all right again. We fared, I think, better than any of the boats, as we were only in the small boat about six hours. Of course it was very cold, and we had so little on. I have made a skirt for Bertha out of one of the blue blankets on this boat (the *Carpathia*), so you may guess how swell we will be to land!

The people on board have been very kind, but, of course, it is not fitted for so many passengers, and we are sleeping in the sailors' quarters. Some have to lie on deck, and some have suffered awfully. I believe the saved are: 220 first, 120 second, 160 third, 210 crew, out of 3500 in all. But I suppose you have got all this in the papers long before now.

The ocean was like a lake when we left the *Titanic*, but oh, so cold. But there had not been such a calm night since we started. I have often read about icebergs, but I never thought to see one.[106]

17 April 1912: On Board the *Carpathia*

KORNELIA ANDREWS **First Class Passenger**

While the *Carpathia* was bound for New York, Miss Andrews wrote the following letter to a friend in Hudson, New York:

> It was about midnight when the crash came and we were all in bed. I rushed to my door and met Gretchen coming from hers, and ice crystals were all over her, having come in the port hole, so I knew at once we had struck an iceberg. They told us there was no danger, and as we had no moment's suspicion that such a magnificent ship could be sunk we all went back to our beds without a fear. After a half hour we heard a little commotion in our corridor and they told us to put on life preservers at once, and to be on deck in five minutes and this gave us time to do little. We put on our fur coats and didn't even wait for hats. When we reached the deck they were commencing to fill a lifeboat, and there was such a great crowd before us that we waited until the fourth boat. They called out for men who could row to jump in. One man was a Chinese and the other an Armenian. They didn't know how to row and both became seasick. So Gretchen took an oar on one side with one sailor and two or three women on the other.

We saw the *Titanic* slowly but surely sinking before our eyes, and as we feared the suction we rowed out about a mile and as we left the ship there stood that unbroken line of splendid Americans, not allowed to get into the boats before the women and children were off. It would make you proud of your countrymen. There was Mr Thayer, president of the Philadelphia Railroad; Col. Astor waving a farewell to his beautiful young wife; Major Archibald Butt, Taft's first aide; Mr Case, president of the Vacuum Oil Co., all multi-millionaires, and hundreds of other men, all standing without complaint or murmur, not making one attempt to save themselves, but happy to think wives and relatives were in the boats, and they must have known there was no hope. Was that not chivalry for you?

Think of it, no boats for a third of the passengers. We watched the ship go down. At last came a mighty crash, the boilers had exploded, and then in a moment the ship seemed to break in pieces or rather in half; the bow going down first and then all the lights went out and in a short time nothing more was to be seen and then the shrieks and screams as that one thousand in the steerage went down. The crew and officers and captain and all the other first class passengers must have gone down at the same time.

Some probably jumped just before and one of our boats picked up seventeen, all sailors, two died almost immediately, one went mad. No one could have lived an hour in that icy water. We were in a whole field of icebergs. We were all so bitterly cold. We were in a lifeboat from before 12 to 9 in the morning, and all that saved us was the calm night.

About dawn a wind arose and the waves grew large and we were afraid of shipping water. Gretchen rowed until her hands were nearly frozen and she was nearly exhausted. You see it was nearly ten long hours, and each hour seemed like twenty-four. About dawn we saw a ship in the dim distance, but it was miles away. The *Carpathia*, which had come sixty miles and out of her course to find us in answer to a Marconi. It commenced to pick up the boats as soon as they reached her, but it was nearly 9 o'clock before we could reach her, and in the meantime such sights and sounds! A dead baby floated past. In the distance some saw two boats full of women and children capsize. They had no men to man their boats and no one could rescue them.

Some of the ice fields we passed seemed to be a mile long. The iceberg we struck was only 50 feet high above the water, and they had not put on their searchlight for this trip and icebergs are hard to see at night because they are the same colour as the water. The ship was not really equipped; they expected to do it later. The discipline was good, probably because none of us appreciated the danger. They told us the *Olympic* would pick us up in two hours and that the ship would stand for hours without sinking.

With stiff, frozen fingers we climbed up rope ladders of the *Carpathia*, but they put a rope around our waists so that we could be caught if our feet slipped, and we had stood on our feet ten hours and our feet with thin slippers were frozen with no feeling in them. There was no room to sit down.

The people on the *Carpathia* were kind, indeed. Three ladies offered their staterooms, but there were so many others who needed them more than we, so we are sleeping on floor of library and dining room.

Seventeen lifeboats have brought these passengers on *Carpathia*, making just 660.[107]

ETHEL BEANE **Second Class Passenger**

While on board the *Carpathia*, Mrs Beane wrote the following letter to her father, Mr G. Clarke:

> Thank God! We are both saved together. There are 130 widows on this boat. We were on a small boat all Sunday night around the ice. I have not even got a hair pin to call my own. But we must be thankful we were saved together, as they were shooting down the men who came into the ladies' boats. We were not far from the liner when it went down, and the screaming and the shouting were dreadful. We were rescued at five o'clock in the morning, and were hauled up by ladders and big ropes, as none could help ourselves. We were put to hot rooms, blankets, and had plenty of brandy, but a great many have died since they were rescued.[108]

AMELIA BROWN **Second Class Passenger**

Miss Brown wrote the following letter to her mother while the *Carpathia* was returning to New York:

On board the *Carpathia*
April 17th, 1912

My Dear Mother,

At last I have made myself sit down to write to you. I don't know how the time has gone since the wreck but I can't help thinking how lucky I am to be amongst the rescued. There were 2,000 people – about that – on board and only about 700 saved.

It happened at 11.30 on Sunday night. Our ship ran into an iceberg and within 1½ hours the vessel had sunk. I couldn't believe it was serious and wouldn't get up until Swane came and made me, that was the last I saw of him poor fellow.

No sooner was I on deck than I was bustled to the first class deck and pushed into one of the boats, and I found nurse and the baby there, it was awful to put the life belt on, it seemed as if you really were gone. Then came the lowering of the boat. I shut my eyes and hoped I should wake and find it a dream.

Then came the awful suspense of waiting till a vessel should pass our way. The wireless telegraph had been used and this vessel which was southward bound came miles out of its way to pick us up.

By the time we had got out of reach of the suction we stopped to watch her go down, and you could watch her go too it went in the front until it was standing like this: \ and all the lights went out, shortly after we heard the engines explode and then the cries of the people for help. Never shall I forget it as long as I live. I dare not let myself think of it.

We were on the water from 12 till 6 in this small boat. Thank goodness it was a clear calm night or I don't know what would have happened. We were nearly frozen as there were icebergs all round us, ever since I've been here I've felt in a stupor, everything seems too much trouble and I can't bother what happens to one.

I found Sallie had got on alright but poor girl she keeps worrying about her things, of course we have lost everything but what we stand up in. I had my watch on my arm, in fact it has never left it since we sailed, and my money was in my pocket.

I have not seen Mr & Mrs Allison or Loraine so I suppose they have gone under, but there is just the chance they may have been picked up by another ship. I'm not going to worry about it, and they have several friends on board, and then there are the partners of the firm. We have been offered a home until something is found for us.

This vessel has turned back to New York with us. I have slept on the dining room floor both nights, and we had a most awful thunder storm last night and today it's that foggy I shall be glad to be on terra firma again.

We had a bad start. The *New York* broke adrift and ran into us at Southampton. Well I won't write any more now. Will you let Aunt Em and Nell, or anyone you think read this as I don't feel like going all over it again, and don't worry about me as I shall be well looked after and I've made several well to do friends on board.

lots of love to all
from your loving daughter
Millie[109]

DANIEL BUCKLEY **Third Class Passenger**

Mr Buckley wrote the following letter to his mother in Ireland:

> Our ship struck an iceberg. I went on deck and met a sailor who asked me to help him lower the boats. The sailor said, 'Take a chance yourself.' I did, as did my friend, but the officers came along and ordered us off the boat. A woman said, 'Lay down, lad, you are somebody's child.' She put a rug over me and the boat went out, so I was saved. I'll write you a note when I get to New York.[110]

KATE BUSS **Second Class Passenger**

On 17 April Miss Buss wrote the next instalment of her lengthy letter to her parents:

> Wednesday – I'm still here, but I shall be, oh so thankful to get to land. I never closed my eyes last night. There was a thunderstorm, and I expected to hear the call to lower the boats again. I felt worse than I did when we were wrecked.
>
> Another passenger buried this morning; it's too awful. Yet how fortunate I am. However, I shall cross again I don't know. At times I wish we were sailing back to England.
>
> This vessel (the *Carpathia*) is so slow, and we have to live another two nights. Everyone is good, but, some of those excitable foreigners. The stewardess of our cabin is a French Jewess, and there are Hungarians, French and Germans all around us.
>
> Last night there was a greater noise over a lost pillow by one of them than I heard all the time in the *Titanic*. Not being able to understand them and the sea being so high, I thought there was great danger. But afterwards I heard, in broken English, that is [*sic*] was my own pillow. I felt a little more pacified, but unable to sleep.
>
> Did I tell you that on board as the boat went down all who were left, lined up on deck, and knelt down in prayer before they jumped overboard, or sank with her.
>
> If I reach New York safely you will get this letter, if I get any cash, so that you may know what I am doing. I hope you will not have worried too much before you see my name among the saved.
>
> I've been thinking if you get this and know I'm all right, that I should like to return thanks in Halling Church as Mrs Lingham said they prayed for a safe voyage.
>
> We hope to reach New York about 8 pm, and I shall be very glad, if only to be anchored. I lie awake at night expecting to be called up at every little sound. I hear that there has been a lot of fog for days, and we hear noises on this vessel that we never heard on the *Titanic*. We have some awfully kind-hearted folks on board. Yesterday we stated our case before a committee of ladies and gentlemen, who intend to get as much as possible from the White Star Company.

There is friction with the millionaires. They are raising a subscription for crews, both rescued and rescuers, and they will see they take care of us until we return or continue our journey. I have lost every penny, and I have to depend on a friend to buy a cap and hairpins. I brought the rug with me and my shawl. I have to carry them with me every time I move.

You dare not turn your head two minutes. I lent my rug in the lifeboat to a child who had no frock on, and today the poor child, who drifted so long, and is so queer.

I've seen two first class passengers who drifted and the tales become more harrowing. But there you'll get it in the papers. They saved 320 first class passengers, 220 second-class and 170 third class.[111]

ALBERT CALDWELL **Second Class Passenger**

Mr Caldwell wrote the following letter to Dr C. Walker in Siam (now Thailand):

Royal Mail Steamship *Carpathia*

Dear Folks,

Here we are safe. We were one of few families who kept together when the *Titanic* went down.

Hundreds of lives were lost, mostly men. Nearly all the women and children were saved. The trouble was, no one realised the danger, and thought this 'largest boat in the world' would not sink, and if she did it would take many hours.

She struck the iceberg at midnight and in a little over two hours she was at the bottom.

We were picked up by this boat at daylight. The ocean was as calm as a lake, while we were in the life boats.

As the people did not realise how quick she would go down, there was no hurry and the life boats were not full enough. Some of the boats went down with the ship and there were not enough boats in the first place. The *Titanic* was considered a 'non-sinkable' boat.

We were about 1500 miles from New York. This boat was bound for Gibraltar when she picked us up, but she turned around and is taking us to New York.

I understand that about 700 were saved. There are many, many wives who have lost their husbands.

We are very very thankful to God for his 'Goodness' to us and know that it was the prayers of our loved ones and friends that saved us.

It was a sad sight to see that beautiful ship go down and awful to hear the shrieks of the hundreds who were dying.

It was a terrible night and one that I will never forget.

The names of the survivors were sent to N.Y. so we hope that our folks have heard of our safety, as they knew we were on the *Titanic*.

Address us
c/o Rev. W. E. Caldwell
Biggsville,
Ill.

Sylvia and Alden are well and we are <u>so</u> happy & thankful.

Yours Sincerely,
A. E. Caldwell[112]

GLADYS CHERRY **First Class Passenger**

On 17 April Miss Cherry wrote the following letter to her mother while the *Carpathia* was bound for New York:

On board the *Carpathia*
Wednesday, 17th April, 1912 4.15.

You have heard by this time that we are quite safe, (officially). I also hope you have got my Marconi, but the official messages had to be got off first, there were such dozens of these that they had to go in turn.

We have been on here since Monday at 8.30 A.M., when we were picked up, and I have not been able to write a line before, it has been too ghastly, and I still seem dazed.

Sunday night on the *Titanic*, it got very, very cold, icy, and I asked the Steward why it was so cold, and he said it was icebergs, but we did not slow down at all and were going 22 knots per hour.

Noel and I went to bed at 10 p.m. very gay we felt that night, and at a quarter to 12 we were awakened by an awful sort of bang and the engines stopping suddenly, we had an extraordinary feeling that something dreadful had happened, as when the engine stopped there was a terrible silence, then the awful noise of steam being let off, then we heard one or two people walking up and down the passage, so we got up and asked the steward what had happened, he said we had struck an iceberg, so this rather excited us and we put on our dressing gowns and fur coats, and went up on deck, and went forward and saw the bow of the ship covered in ice – but we could not see the berg; we watched a bit on deck and talked and then wondered if we should go back to bed or not, when suddenly the Captain appeared and said: 'I don't want to frighten anyone, but will you all go quietly and put on your life belts and go up on the top deck?' we all dispersed very calmly and slowly, and got to our own stateroom but could find no life belts; an awfully nice man came with us and hunted, and then a steward came. I did not even know that the order for life belts had been given he said but he got them for us from under the bed and we were told there was time to dress which we did, and put on life belts and calmly and quietly went to the top boat-deck; you see by this the perfect confidence the people had in that great boat, no one could believe there was danger – then the boats began to be filled with women, we were about the fourth to be lowered 75 feet from the top deck – we had a terrible scene with a little Spanish lady, who would cling to her husband and at last he threw her in our arms and asked us to take care of her – we were only 24 women in our boat, with one Able Seaman and two stewards who could not row!

As I try to write this as I know you will want to know, it seems as if I can't for it's all too terrible: the lowering of that boat 75 feet into the darkness seemed too awful, when we reached the water I felt we had done a foolish thing to leave that big safe boat, but when we had rowed a few yards, we saw that great ship with her bows right down in the water, (before we began to dress the water was pouring into the Racquet Court and Baggage rooms). The Captain gave us orders to row to a light he saw, and come back to the boat to get others – we were only twenty-four women and three men, and we could have held 50. It was the stillest night possible, not a ripple on the water and the stars wonderful; that icy air and the stars I never want to see or feel again.

Four of us and the seaman wanted to go back and get more people into our boat, but the other women and two stewards would have killed us rather than go back, and we started to row to that awful light that never got nearer.

I was at the tiller, steering the boat all night, and the women in our boat who rowed were magnificent, we rowed with the seamen for five hours.

The terror of seeing that boat go down in and the fearful screams and shrieks of the Steerage passengers who were left was too awful – Then the awful noise of all the air-tight compartments going, going, and then like an earthquake or a distant battle and then the whole ship went under, we had to row away as fast as we could because of the suction.

We were in that boat till dawn, following the light that never got nearer, then suddenly we saw the lights of this steamer, and we turned and began to row towards her; that awful time until we got to her I shall never forget, we got there about 8.30, and it was beginning to get rough and very difficult to steer, I was numb from the waist downwards – when we got here we were pulled up in a hoist – like a swing.

Noel went up just before me, I could not walk when I got up as my legs had got numb, they took us all into the Saloon. I could not find Noel at first and then found that she had fainted directly she got off the hoist, the strain had been too much – then all the women came in some unconscious, some hysterical and all more or less collapsed, they had brandy for us and hot coffee, and they were wonderful all they did for us; there are about 150 young widows, and to see all these poor women is too terrible – they have managed accommodation for us all here, with lots sleeping on the floor in the dining saloon; we have a cabin with four of us in, but are so thankful to be in anything.

My nerves are all to pieces, and we are in a dense fog at present, we ought to get to New York tomorrow ... it's all been too ghastly, I can't blame anyone and they say the Captain shot himself; but there seemed no discipline on the boat, as there ought to have been an officer in each boat – there were only 16 lifeboats and 2 canvas ones for 2,600 passengers, there are 490 passengers and 210 crew saved 700 altogether out of nearly 3,000, isn't it awful? Why did we go at that pace when they knew we were near ice bergs.

The separating of husbands and wives was ghastly. Noel and I are so thankful we had no man with us ... our women some of them here are wonderful – Mrs Tyrrell Cavendish is here but the husband gone.[113]

BERTHA MULVIHILL **Third Class Passenger**

Miss Mulvihill wrote the following letter to her sister while the *Carpathia* was bound for New York:

On board the RMS *Carpathia*

Dear Maud,

Experience is great – I am fine and dandy – never better. What time did you hear of the disaster?

I AM SO GLAD I WAS IN IT. I shall never forget it. We are just [about] in New York. Having a jolly time. Don't worry. How is father? Nothing like a bit of life. Don't worry for me. I am O.K. We lost 2472 passengers and saved 710. I was a hero to the last. We were picked up after eight hours by a ship bound for Naples, everyone was very good to us, and then transferred to the *Carpathia*.

The passengers on the *Carpathia* gave us clothes. I had a prayer book, a watch and a little money in my pocket. All the rest lost. I never saw such a sight as when the dear old *Titanic* sank. She broke in two pieces. The scene was awful. Don't think me mad for being so happy to witness the sight ... I am with a jolly crowd in this old ship (the *Carpathia*) ... I am awfully happy – like the night I was born – never felt happier in my life. I have nothing to worry ... I can imagine, mother dear, that when you heard the news you felt for your lost daughter, but she is the safest one you have got. I shall be a millionaire when I arrive in New York. I shall go back this summer, it may be on my honeymoon, but let's keep that quiet. My watch was saved but a picture I had of Robert Emmet has gone down. 'Good-bye, Robert,' said I as the ship went down. Poor lad he was drowned. Sarah Curran, I am sure, felt terribly sorry at being left alone ... Pray for me, I am so happy; console all my friends. There is no place like the sea ... I am writing this in a hurry, for I want my supper ... The little Summerhill girl went down unless she is picked up by another ship that we don't know of ... We struck the iceberg at 10 minutes to 12 and the ship sunk at 2. We were launched in small boats at 1 ... I am a d—il or an angel I don't know which ... Tell Pat I had his pen in my petticoats and that it gave me fifty sticks in my legs. [114]

(Note: Bertha Mulvihill had taken the part of Sarah Curran in an amateur performance of the play *Robert Emmet* some months previous to this in Athlone, Ireland.)

MAUDE SINCOCK **Second Class Passenger**

Miss Sincock wrote the following letter to her mother in St Ives, England:

> Dear Mother,
>
> I am saved, but I have lost everything. I must, however, be thankful for my life. I have not a penny and no clothes. I was thrown on board a little boat in my nightdress and boots. I had no stockings on. We were in this little boat in the middle of the ocean for six hours, and I was nearly frozen when we were picked up. I shall be a pretty sight when I land. We were rescued by a passing ship, the *Carpathia*. The *Titanic* struck just before midnight, and was under water about 2 o'clock. There were over 1000 persons on board when she foundered. Mrs Davis and her son John Morgan are saved, but we have not seen anything of Joe. We think he is drowned. We have not seen anything of the other 'boys' who left St Ives. We could hear the screams from the men as the *Titanic* was sinking. I think there are hundreds drowned. Mrs Davis told me to ask you to send a message to Balnoon to tell her aunt she was saved, but that we don't know anything about Joe. I don't know what I shall do when I get to New York ... I am frightened to death nearly, and I am afraid I shall catch my death of cold by the time I get to Hancock. I will write again as soon as possible and tell you more news. I don't know where they are going to put us when we get to NY.
>
> Your loving daughter,
>
> Maud[115]

EDWINA TROUTT **Second Class Passenger**

On 17 April Miss Troutt continued writing her letter to her parents in England:

> Wednesday, *Carpathia*
>
> Just another line to say I am very well and getting quite used to things now. We are encountering lots of strange things here, thunder, and lightning, fog and rain; but I suppose eventually I shall reach my destination. I believe this boat has picked up 700, and we think that is all that are saved. We have had several

burials, people dying from the exposure. This boat was on her Mediterranean cruise, but is good enough to go to New York. We were 150 miles out of our course and going at 25 knots an hour. They say the captain was so proud of the record and was trying to make a record trip. The iceberg was three times the size of the *Titanic*. We were on the North Ocean and surrounded with icebergs, and when we reached this ship we could see nothing but fields of ice. It was a beautiful picture; and then the trails of the whales was another sight. I saw about seven. I escaped in my nightdress and coat and petticoats; everything else has gone. We were going to hold a concert on Monday night. There was a priest on board, who celebrated Mass on Sunday. I never in all my life met such devoted people, and I often think we were all too happy to live long. I should very much like to see the account of it in the papers. We are sleeping like a lot of dead things all over the floors of the ship ... I dare say you all have lots of sympathy for me, but believe me, I am one of the lucky ones. My life is saved, my health is not impaired, and I have not lost anyone belonging to me. I tell you I have lots to be thankful for. I was ready to go down with the ship, but they forced me into the lifeboat. I think it wicked to save the single girls, but now that I saved a baby whose mother was in another boat I don't mind. We are still very fog bound, which makes all very anxious to arrive at New York.

W[116]

Miss Troutt also began writing a diary on 17 April, and her first entry was a brief summary of the events she had experienced during the sinking of the *Titanic*:

... The distress signal was repeatedly going off while we were on board deck & when we reached the water t'was then only we could believe that the *Titanic* was sinking. In sight of all of us she sank within a half hour of departure. The men acted magnificently. Our seamen were singing Pull for the Shore Sailors & rowing for their life. We had a lamp, no oil in it, but managed to catch another life boat with a light. The men tied them together & let them drift until we could see the lights of the *Carpathia*. Then they turned around & made for her which was in readiness. Reached her 6:30. Blankets, hot drinks, & nothing spared us. The passengers of the *Carpathia* helped to clothe us, but the cries of the women for their husbands & lost sons was terrible. Boats were being emptied on both sides of the ship. Special prayers were read & all pleasures were stopped.

On Board 'Carpathia.' The captain informed us that all private messages only would be sent & that no p[rivate] messages were sent to press & the demand was too great.[117]

18 April 1912: On board the *Carpathia*

KORNELIA ANDREWS **First Class Passenger**

On 18 April Miss Andrews wrote the following letter to her niece, Mathilde Weiant, of Newark, New Jersey:

My Dear:

You have seen everything by this time in the papers, but I want you to have a single word from me about our terrible experience, now when I have a moment.

Oh, my dear, may you never have to pass through such frightful hours. It was 12 midnight when the crash came and we were all in bed. I rushed to my door and saw the ice crystals all over, they having come in through the porthole next to mine and I knew it was an iceberg, but they told us immediately that there was no danger and of course it never entered our heads for one moment that a magnificent ship like the *Titanic* could sink, so we foolishly all went to bed without a fear. After a while we heard a commotion in the corridor and went out to inquire, and then they told us to put on life preservers and come out in five minutes. That was every moment we had to get ready. Gretchen put on stockings and slippers and not a single article of underclothing, but a cloth skirt and waist, and we had very little more, but we put on our fur coats. I did not wait to even put on a hat, but I did rescue three hair pins, and we went upstairs, not even then frightened. We finally got in the fourth boat. There was no panic, but no discipline. We had one sailor, and then any man who could row was allowed to get in and so a Chinese and an Armenian got in, saying they could row, but they could not, so Gretchen assisted the sailor on one side and two or three women on the other, until her hands were frozen stiff. We pulled away from the ship so that we would not be drawn in with the suction should the ship go down. All women and children in the boats, and these ignorant men put in our boats while those splendid Americans stood and were not allowed to come with us. Oh, it would have broken your heart to have seen them standing there so bravely and waving farewell to their wives and daughters. It would have made you proud of your countrymen. There was Mr Thayer, president of the Pennsylvania Railroad, Mr John Jacob Astor, having to wave farewell to his beautiful wife, Major Butt and hundreds of others, who probably knew there was no hope for them. We have never seen them since. We rowed off a ways and in less than an hour there was a mighty explosion. The boilers had exploded and the ship was broken right in two, and then, my dear, the screams and the shrieks as 1000 of the steerage went down, and I suppose, the crew and the officers and all the Americans. All my life I will hear those shrieks. We were in the safety of the boat from 12 o'clock until 9 the next morning, and all that saved us was the calmness and beauty of the night. About dawn a wind came up and great waves commenced to appear, and then we almost despaired. The one man who could row was almost exhausted, and Gretchen stuck to it until her strength was gone. Then, as it seemed a hundred miles away, we saw a ship, the *Carpathia*, and it commenced to pick up boats as soon as it could, but this was only dawn, and it was not until 9 or 9:30 o'clock that we were pulled up over the sides on a rope ladder. But such sights and sounds! The boat next to us put a lot of their passengers in our lifeboat, and then they picked up 17 out of the water. Two died almost immediately and one went mad. A little baby floated past us. Two boats of women and children capsized and were lost. No one could rescue them.

And all this, my dear, was most wickedly criminal. We were in a sea of ice, some of the fields over a mile long, and no one, apparently was watching for them. We cannot hear that anyone saw this ice until the collision, and the night was clear and cold. The captain had attended a dinner given for him, and perhaps one officer was on the bridge, but we were going too fast to stop suddenly, and there was no one to command the boats.

Here on the *Carpathia* we see, my dear, such sad things. Nearly every other woman is weeping for her husband or child and it is all past description. They are kind, so kind. I have had three staterooms offered me, but there are others who need them so much more, and so we slept on the floor in the library with 25 or 30 others, babies crying because both parents were lost, and others because their mothers were gone. And to think it was all so unnecessary. No lifeboats for half the passengers. Every passenger will unite with me in this fearful condition of things. Of course we are so thankful for our escape, but the sorrow everywhere saddens you, so you can think of nothing else. We carried everything we possessed with us, so we haven't a stitch or anything to crawl into when we get home. And we bought beautiful furs and each two or three dresses. But we don't think of that – that all amounts to nothing. One lady gave me a handkerchief, and oh, what a joy to have one. A man, Mr Mauro, gave me a toothbrush. He had bought ten to take to Italy. He has a beautiful villa out of Genoa; and is most charming. Another lady gave me some hairpins, and Gretchen found an old school friend here who has fitted her out with some clothes and a hat, so you see, they are all most kind. I don't believe I can ever write again all these things, and I shall not be in Hudson for a week or two. I must buy a few things to wear. Haven't even a pair of shoes, and if they had only notified us in time, I could at least have saved a few things to wear. If we had known when the crash came that there was danger, we could at least have dressed properly, but we were not notified until the last moment. The thing for which the line should be censured the most is, of course that only one-third of the passengers had any arrangements made for their safety. Only 22 boats and sixty could not have taken in more than two-thirds. Is that not a perfect crime.

We did not have enough clothing, by half, to keep warm, for it was so bitterly cold. The icebergs all around made the water and air intensely cold, and those long, long hours of agony, nearly 10 hours in mid-ocean, women crying all around because they felt so sure their husbands and brothers would not be saved. One woman had two little ones. Her husband and three others were not with us and we have never heard of them. Of course we are hoping some may be picked up by other steamers, but we cannot tell. I wonder, can you read this. All my glasses are gone. I had three pairs and I cannot see without them. And now, I could not tell you in weeks the sad, sad stories around us. Mrs Astor is, they say, very calm, but does not leave her stateroom. One of the officers gave his up to her. Goodbye. We hope to land tomorrow.[118]

EDWARD BEANE — Second Class Passenger

On the evening of 18 April Mr Beane jotted down the following notes regarding his experiences on board the *Titanic*:

The iceberg that the *Titanic* struck towered seventy feet above the water. The *Titanic* was going at the rate of about eighteen knots at the time.

My wife had retired. I was in the smoking room. There was a sudden jolt. I ran on deck. No one seemed to be greatly excited. Apparently the captain and crew thought the *Titanic* was unsinkable.

However, the officers were getting the lifeboats ready. It was a splendid crew – a brave crew. As they worked at the lifeboats they did not seem to be worried.

I questioned one of them. He laughed at the idea that the *Titanic* was in great danger and said the boats were being made ready simply as a precautionary measure. I concluded that it would be best to bring my wife on deck. So I went to our stateroom and called her. She came up on deck with me. All of the men where I was agreed that we would see the women and children into the boats first, and afterward the married men. My wife remained with me until there was room in a boat for both of us.

An hour and a half after we had put away from the *Titanic* there was an explosion. We could see bodies blown into the air. We suffered severely from the cold until the *Carpathia* came along and picked us up.[119]

LAWRENCE BEESLEY **Second Class Passenger**

While on board the *Carpathia*, Mr Beesley wrote the following account of his experiences on the *Titanic*:

The voyage from Queenstown had been quite uneventful; very fine weather was experienced and the sea was quite calm. The wind had been westerly to southwesterly the whole way, but very cold, particularly the last day; in fact, after dinner on Sunday evening it was almost too cold to be out on deck.

I had been in my berth for about ten minutes when, at about 11:46 p.m., I felt a slight jar, and then soon after a second one, but not sufficiently large to cause any anxiety to anyone, however nervous they may have been. However, the engines stopped immediately afterwards and my first thought was 'She has lost a propeller.'

I went up on the top deck in a dressing gown and found only a few people there who had come up similarly to enquire why we had stopped, but there was no sort of anxiety in the minds of anyone. We saw through the smoking room window a game of cards going on and went in to enquire if they knew anything; it seems they felt more of the jar, and, looking through the window had seen a huge iceberg go by close by the side of the boat. They thought we had grazed it with a glancing blow, and that the engines had been stopped to see if any damage had been done. No one, of course, had any conception that she had been pierced below by part of the submerged iceberg.

The game went on without any thought of disaster, and I retired to my cabin to read until we went on again. I never saw any of the players or the onlookers again. A little later, hearing people going upstairs, I went out again and found everyone wanting to know why the engines had stopped. No doubt many were awakened from sleep by the sudden stopping of a vibration to which they had become accustomed during the four days we had been on board. Naturally, with such powerful engines as the *Titanic* carried, the vibration was very noticeable all the time, and the sudden stopping had something the same effect as the stopping of a loud ticking grandfather's clock in a room.

On going on deck again I saw that there was an undoubted list downwards from stern to bow, but, knowing nothing of what happened, concluded some of the front compartments had been filled and weighed her down. I went down again to put on warmer clothing, and as I dressed heard an order shouted, 'All passengers on deck with lifebelts on.'

We all walked slowly up with them tied on over our clothing, but even then presumed this was a wise precaution the captain was taking and that we should return in a short time and retire to bed. There was a total absence of any panic or any expressions of alarm, and I suppose this can be accounted for by the exceedingly calm night and the absence of any sign of the accident.

The ship was absolutely still and, except for a gentle tilt downwards, which I don't think one person in ten would have noticed at that time, no signs of the approaching disaster were visible. She lay just as if she were waiting the order to go on again when some trifling matter had been adjusted. But in a few moments we saw the covers lifted from the boats and the crew allotted to them standing by and curling up the ropes which were to lower them by the pulley blocks into the water.

We then began to realise that it was more serious than had been supposed, and my first thought was to go down and get more clothing and some money, but seeing people pouring up the stairs, decided it was better to cause no confusion to people coming up by doing so. Presently we heard the order, 'All men stand back away from the boats and all ladies retire to next deck below' – the smoking room deck, or 'B' deck. The men all stood away and remained in absolute silence leaning against the end railings of the deck or pacing slowly up and down. The boats were swung out and lowered from 'A' deck.

When they were down to the level of 'B' deck, where all the ladies were collected, the ladies got in quietly, with the exception of some who refused to leave their husbands. In some cases they were torn from them and pushed into the boats, but in many instances they were allowed to remain because there was no one to insist they should go.

Looking over the side, one saw boats from aft already in the water, slipping quietly away into the darkness, and presently the boats near to me were lowered and with much creaking as the new ropes slipped through the pulley blocks down the 90 feet which separated them from the water. An officer in uniform came up as one boat went down and shouted: 'When you are afloat row around to the companion ladder and stand by with the other boats for orders.'

'Aye, aye, sir,' came the reply, but I don't think any boat was able to obey the order. When they were afloat and had the oars at work the condition of the rapidly settling boat was so much more a sight for alarm for those in the boats than those on board that in common prudence the sailors saw they could do nothing but row from the sinking ship to save, at any rate, some lives. They no doubt anticipated that suction from such an enormous vessel would be more than usually dangerous to a crowded boat, mostly filled with women.

All this time there was no trace of any disorder; no panic or rush to the boats, and no scenes of women sobbing hysterically such as one generally pictures happening at such times.

Everyone seemed to realise so slowly that there was imminent danger. When it was realised that we might all be presently in the sea with nothing but our life-belts to support us until we were picked up by passing steamers, it was extraordinary how calm everyone was and how completely self-controlled.

One by one the boats were filled with women and children lowered and rowed away into the night. Presently the word went around among the men: 'The men are to be put in boats on the starboard side.' I was on the port side, and most of the men walked across the deck to see if this was so. I remained where I was and presently heard the call: 'Any more ladies?'

Looking over the side of the ship, I saw the boat, No.13, swinging level with B deck, half full of ladies. Again the call was repeated: 'Any more ladies?'

I saw none come on, and then one of the crew looked up and said: 'Any ladies on your deck, sir?'

'No,' I replied. 'Then you had better jump.' I dropped in and fell in the bottom as they cried: 'Lower away.' As the boat began to descend, two ladies were pushed hurriedly through the crowd on B deck, and heaved over into the boat, and a baby of 10 months passed down after them.

Down we went, the crew calling to those lowering which end to keep her level. 'Aft,' 'stern,' 'both together,' until we were some ten feet from the water, and here occurred the only anxious moment we had during the whole of our experience, from leaving the deck to reaching the Carpathia. Immediately below our boat was the exhaust of the condensers, a huge stream of water pouring all the time from the ship's side just above the water line. It was plain we ought to be smart away from this not to be swamped by it when we touched water. We had no officer aboard, no petty officer or member of the crew to take charge. So one of the stokers shouted: 'Find the pin which releases the boat from the ropes and pull it up.' No one knew where it was. We felt as well as we could on the floor and sides but found nothing, and it was hard to move among so many people – we had sixty or seventy on board.

Down we went and presently floated with our ropes still holding us, the exhaust washing us away from the side of the vessel and the swell of the sea urging us back against the side again. The resultant of all these forces was an impetus which carried us parallel to the ship's side and directly under boat No.14, which had filled rapidly with men and was coming down on us in a way that threatened to submerge our boat.

'Stop lowering 14,' our crew shouted, and the crew of No.14, now only twenty feet above, shouted the same. But the distance to the top was some seventy feet and the creaking pulleys must have deadened all sound to those above, for down she came- 15 feet, 10 feet, 5 feet, and a stoker and I reached up and touched her swinging above our heads, but just before she dropped another stoker sprang to the ropes with his knife.

'One,' I heard him say. 'Two,' as his knife cut through the pulley ropes, and the next moment the exhaust stream had carried us clear while boat No.14 dropped into the water into the space we had the moment before occupied, our gunwales almost touching.

We drifted away easily as the oars were got out and headed directly away from the ship. The crew seemed to me to be mostly cooks in white jackets, two to an oar, with a stoker at the tiller. There was a certain amount of shouting from one end of the boat to the other and discussion as to which way we should go, but finally it was decided to elect the stoker, who was steering, captain, and for all to obey his orders. He went to work at once to get into touch with the other boats, calling to them and getting as close as seemed wise, so that when the search-boats came in the morning to look for us, there would be more chance for all to be rescued by keeping together.

It was now about 1 a.m.; a beautiful night, with no moon and so not very light. The sea was as calm as a pond, just a gentle heave as the boat dipped up and down in the swell; an ideal night, except for the bitter cold, for anyone who had to be out in the middle of the Atlantic Ocean in an open boat, and if ever there was a time when such a night was needed, surely it was now with hundreds of people, mostly women and children, afloat hundreds of miles from land.

The captain stoker told us that he had been at sea 26 years and had never yet seen such a calm night on the Atlantic. As we rowed away from the *Titanic*, we looked back from time to time to watch her, and a more striking spectacle it as not possible for anyone to see.

Only the evening before at dinner I remarked to my neighbour that when we arrived at New York, I should take an opportunity to get a look at her from a distance to realise something of her dimensions. We did not think our desire was so soon to be gratified. In the distance she looked an enormous length, her great bulk outlined in black against the starry sky. Every porthole and saloon blazing with light. It was impossible to think anything could be wrong with such a leviathan, were it not for that ominous tilt downwards in the bows, where the water was by now up to the lowest row of port holes.

We were now about two miles from her, and all the crew insisted that such a tremendous wave would be formed by suction as she went down that we ought to get as far away as possible. The captain agreed and they lay on their oars and widened the distance between us and the sinking vessel.

Presently, about 2 a.m., as near as I can remember, we observed her settling very rapidly, with the bows and the bridge completely under water and concluded it was now only a question of minutes before she went down, and so it proved. She slowly tilted straight on end with the stern vertically upwards, and as she did, the lights in the cabins and saloons which had not yet flickered for a moment since we left, died out, came on again for a single flash, and finally went out altogether. At the same time the machinery roared down through the vessel with a rattle and a groaning that could be heard for miles, the weirdest sound surely that could be heard in the middle of the ocean, a thousand miles away from land. But this was not yet quite the end.

To our amazement she remained in that upright position for a time which I estimate at five minutes, others in the boat less, but it was certainly some minutes

– while we watched at least 150 feet of the *Titanic* towering up above the level of the sea and looming black against the sky.

Then with a quick dive she disappeared beneath the waters and our eyes had looked for the last time upon the gigantic vessel in which we set out from Southampton last Wednesday, and there was left to us the gently heaving sea, the boat filled to standing room with men and women in every conceivable condition of dress and undress, above the powerful sky of brilliant stars and with not a cloud in the sky, all tempered with a bitter cold – a curious, deadening, bitter cold, unlike anything we had felt before.

And then with all these, there fell on the ear the most appalling noise that human being ever listened to – the cries of hundreds of our fellow beings struggling in the icy cold water, crying for help – a cry that we knew could not be answered. We longed to return and pick up some of those swimming, but this would have meant swamping our boat and further loss of the lives of all of us.

We tried to sing to keep the women from hearing the cries and rowed hard to get away from the scene of the wreck, but I think the memory of those sounds will be one of the things the rescued will find it hard to efface from memory. We are all trying hard not to think of it.

We kept a lookout for lights and several times it was shouted that steamers' lights were seen, but they turned out to be a light from another boat or a star down on the horizon. About 3 a.m. we saw faint lights showing on the sky and all rejoiced to see what we expected was the coming dawn, but after watching for half an hour and seeing no change in the intensity of the light, realised it was the Northern Lights.

Presently, low down on the horizon, we saw a light which slowly resolved itself into a double light, and we watched eagerly to see if the two lights would separate and so prove to be only two of our boats, or whether they would remain together, in which case we should expect them to be the masthead light and a deck light below of a rescuing steamer.

To our joy they moved as one, and round we swung the boat and headed for her. The steersman shouted: 'Now, boys, sing,' and for the first time the boat broke into song with 'Row For the Shore, Boys,' and for the first time tears came to the eyes of us all as we realised that safety was at hand. The song was sung, but it was a very poor imitation of the real thing, for quavering voices make poor song. A cheer was given next, and that was better; you needn't keep in time for a cheer.

Our rescuer showed up rapidly and as she swung round we saw her cabins all alight and knew she must be a large steamer. She was now motionless and we had to row to her. Just then day broke, a beautiful quiet dawn with faint pink clouds just above the horizon and a new moon whose crescent just touched the horizon.

'Turn over your money, boys,' said our cheery steersman. 'That is, if you have any,' he added. We laughed at him for his superstition at such a time, but he countered very neatly by adding: 'Well, I shall never say again that 13 is an unlucky number. Boat 13 has been the best friend we ever had.' Certainly the 13 superstition is killed forever in the minds of those who escaped from the *Titanic* in boat 13.

As we neared the *Carpathia* we saw in the dawning light what we thought was a full rigged schooner standing up near her and presently behind her another, all sails set, and we said: 'They are the fisher boats from the Newfoundland banks and have seen the steamer lying to and are standing by to help.'

But in another five minutes the light showed pink on them and we saw they were icebergs towering many feet in the air, huge glistening masses, deadly white, still, and peaked in a way that had easily suggested a schooner. We glanced round the horizon, and there were others wherever the eye could reach. The steamer we had to reach was surrounded by them and we had to make a detour to reach her, for between her and us lay another huge berg. We rowed up to the *Carpathia* about 4:30 a.m., and were hoisted or climbed up the ship's sides with very grateful hearts.

We were received with a welcome that was overwhelming in its warmth, and I should like to say that there is not a member of the *Titanic* on board who feels capable of expressing in adequate terms his gratitude for the attentions showered upon us by the captain, officers, crew and passengers on board the *Carpathia*. They were called upon suddenly in mid-ocean to receive, they thought, 3000 passengers and crew and, although this was not to be, they made every arrangement for so doing. Hot meals, blankets and berths were provided for each as they came on board. Clothing and money were supplied individually by passengers. Berths were given up by men who slept on the smoke room floor or anywhere else that a corner could be found.

The ship has sent off hundreds of Marconigrams free of charge to anxious relatives. The catering arrangements in charge of the purser and stewards have been so admirably organised that it would not be possible to be better served had we been regular passengers aboard our own ship.

The captain has placed all private messages to friends in front of press messages – in fact, he has refused to send any press messages beyond a bare 20 words to a press association and the names of all those saved, placing the needs of the private passengers of the *Titanic* in front of any copy for the press; this morning (April 18) a Marconigram from Marconi was on the screen saying no press news was coming through and asking that some be sent by navy boats or Siasconset.[120]

While on board the *Carpathia*, Mr Beesley wrote the following letter to the editor of *The Times* of London which he planned to transmit to the newspaper after the *Carpathia* reached New York:

To the Editor of the *Times*,

Sirs – As one of the few surviving Englishmen from the steamship *Titanic* which sank in mid-Atlantic on Monday morning last, I am asking you to lay before your readers a few facts concerning the disaster in the hope that something may be done in the near future to ensure the safety of that portion of the travelling public who use the Atlantic highway for business or pleasure.

I wish to dissociate myself entirely from any report that would seek to fix the responsibility on any person or persons or body of people, and by simply calling attention to matters of fact, the authenticity of which is I think, beyond question and can be established in any court of inquiry, to allow your readers to draw their own conclusions as to the responsibility for the collision.

First, that it was known to those in charge of the *Titanic* that we were in the iceberg region; that the atmosphere and temperature conditions suggested the near presence of icebergs, that a wireless message was received from a ship ahead of use warning us that they had seen in the locality of which latitude and longitude were given.

Second, that at the time of the collision the *Titanic* was running at a high rate of speed.

Third, that the accommodation for saving passengers and crew was totally inadequate being sufficient only for a total of 950. This gave with the highest possible complement of 3,400 a less than one in three chance of being saved in the case of an accident.

Fourth, that the number landed in the *Carpathia*, approximate 700 is a high percentage of the possible 950, and bears excellent testimony to the courage, resource and devotion to duty of the officers and crew of the vessel; many instances of their nobility and personal self sacrifice are within our possession, and we know that they did all they could do with the means at their disposal.

Fifth, that practice of running mail and passenger vessels through fog and iceberg regions at a high rate of speed is a common one; they are timed to run almost as an express train is run, and they cannot, therefore, slow down more than a few knots in time of possible danger. I have neither knowledge nor experience to say what remedies I consider should be applied; but, perhaps the following suggestion may serve as a help:

First, that no vessel should be allowed to leave a British port without sufficient lifeboats and other accommodations to allow each passenger and member of the crew a seat; and that at the time of booking this fact should be pointed out to a passenger and the number of the seat in the particular boat allotted to him then.

Second, that as soon as it is practical after sailing each passenger should go through a boat drill in company with the crew assigned to his boat.

Third, that each passenger boat engaged in the transatlantic service should be instructed to slow down to a few knots when in the iceberg region, and should be fitted with sufficient searchlights.

I am, Sir, yours faithfully,
Lawrence Beesley
Cornell University Club
New York
April 19, 1912[121]

DANIEL BUCKLEY **Third Class Passenger**

Mr Buckley wrote the following letter to his mother in Ireland:

On board the *Carpathia*
18th April, 1912

Dear Mother,

I am writing these few lines on board the *Carpathia*, the ship that saved our lives. As I might not have much time when I get to New York I mean to give you an account of the terrible shipwreck we had. At 11.40 p.m. on the 14th our ship *Titanic* struck an iceberg, and sank to the deep at 2.22 a.m. on the 15th. The present estimation is 1,500 lost, 710 saved. Thank God some of us are amongst the number saved. Hannah Riordan, Bridgie Bradley, Nonie O'Leary, and the Shine girl from Lisrobin are all right. There is no account of Patie O'Connell, Michael Linehan, from Freeholds, or Jim Connor, Hugh's son, from Tureenavonsoane. However, I hope they were taken into some other ship. There were four of us sleeping in the same apartment. We had a bed of our own and in every apartment there were four lifebelts, one for each person. At the time when the ship got struck I heard a terrible noise. I jumped out of bed and told my comrades there was something wrong, but they only laughed. I turned on the gas, and to my surprise there was a small stream of water running along the floor. I had only just dressed myself when the sailors came along shouting, 'All up on deck unless you want to get drowned.' We all ran up on deck. I thought to go down again to my room for a lifebelt and my little bag. When I was going down the last flight of stairs the water was up three steps of the stairs, so I did not go any further. I just thought of Dan Ring's saying – 'Stick to your lifebelts, and face a tearing ocean.' We were not long on deck when the lifeboats were prepared. There were only sixteen boats, and that amount was only enough to carry a tenth of the passengers. The third boat that was let down I went on it; there were about forty men in it. An officer came along and said half the men should come out of the boat, and let some ladies in. When I heard this I hid in the lower part of the boat. We were only fifteen minutes in the boat when the big ship went down. It was a terrible sight. It would make the stones cry to hear those on board shrieking. It made a terrible noise, like thunder when it was sinking. There were a great many Irish boys and girls drowned. I got out without any wound. There were a lot of men and women got wounded getting off the steamer. A good many died coming out on the lifeboats and after getting on the *Carpathia*. It was a great change to us to get on this strange steamer as we had a grand time on the *Titanic*. We got very good diet and we had a very jolly time dancing and singing. We had every kind of an instrument on board to amuse us, but all the amusement sank in the deep. I have no more to say at present. I will write a note when I get to New York. Goodbye at present.

Dannie[122]

GLADYS CHERRY — First Class Passenger

On 18 April Miss Cherry wrote the following letter while the *Carpathia* was headed toward New York:

On board the *Carpathia*
Thursday, 18th April, 1912

I think we all feel a little better this morning, We, that are so fortunate, having lost no one; but all the poor women's faces are piteous to see; yesterday morning I was very busy with a Ship's Bosun, cutting out garments for the Steerage and Second Class children, some of whom had no clothes at all, we made little coats and leggings out of the blankets.

Then I went round the Steerage and Hospitals with the Doctor, who is a charming man, and he said a cheery face and word did so much for them, our *Titanic* men most of them with legs and feet frozen are wonderful when you think what they have been through ... We are supposed to get into New York tonight, but we are still in fog; under ordinary circumstances they would not land us at night, but perhaps now they will, if you could only imagine how we long for land – This water all round is terrible, and one's nerves now seem worse than on that dreadful night. The Doctor gave me a little Bromide last night and I slept a little better, but one wakens terrified, which is very silly, as we have nothing to grumble at in comparison with the poor widows, Oh it is too dreadful to see them, Noel and I have helped in seeing after these poor distressed souls, and it has helped us so much ...

One girl has just come up and given me stockings and gloves to land in, as my stockings were all ripped up that night in the boat, people are so good – one lady who has her husband (only about five of them have), is an American and she is going to ask a friend of hers to take us round in her car in New York to buy some things, as we have nothing but what we stand up in, we could have taken so much in our pockets if we had realised, but the only thing I took up was the little photograph of you, then I thought 'how silly' we shall soon be back here and I put it down again; it is all such a horrible nightmare, one don't think of it at all and the nights are so awful.

I dread the voyage back again, I am afraid this fog will prevent us getting in tonight, and I can't stand another night on the sea; all the crew, Captain, passengers, and stewards are perfectly sweet to us; there are two little French children 3 years and 20 months old, who have lost their father and I take one of them every day for a bit while the mother rests.

I love to do something, as it stops one thinking. I hope we shan't have another accident in this fog – Noel's poor maid is very sick, she was sick all the way from Cherbourg but she behaved splendidly in the boat that night.[123]

GERSHON COHEN **Third Class Passenger**

On 18 April, after the *Carpathia* reached New York, Mr Cohen wrote the following letter:

On Board the Cunard RMS *Carpathia*
101 Cook St., Brooklyn
New York, 18/4/12

Dear Hettie,

I've arrived, rescued and myself safe at New York. I suppose you heard about the *Titanic* and I suppose you thought I was drowned but thank God I just managed to escape.

I will explain how the accident happened. At 10.30 we were all sent to bed, lively shouting and singing and doing everything. At 11.45 we were awakened, as about a dozen crewmen came by our decks. We did not take the slightest notice and went to bed again, but we were awakened by the sailors to put on lifebelts. I did not have any because I could not find one, and still I was making a lark of it, and people were singing and playing the piano, the band was also playing. When I went on deck I saw tons of ice which the boat had struck, then I saw that we were in danger. The order was given to man the lifeboats for women and children first. Of course I was left out, so I walked about the deck and in wandering along I saw men & women praying and all the Officers saying good bye to each. It was a sight enough to make you go mad. I went to the berth I was sleeping but I saw it was under water, and saw it was time to act. I climbed to the first-class deck to look for a life belt and after ½ hour I found one. I had just put it on when the boat tilted right over and a lot of people fell in the water and were drowned. I clung to the railings of the deck for dear life, and I was about 200 feet above the level of the water. Whilst holding the last lifeboat was manned and I and about 3 or 400 people were left on deck. As we were holding the boatswain of the last lifeboat shouted out that there was just enough room for 3 or 4 men. When I heard this I stood up, but saw to get in the boat I had to jump about 200 or 300 feet [illegible]. The only thing I saw was a beam of iron jutting out from the deck and a rope hanging from it. I climbed on to the beam but some stokers who wanted to save their own lives threw me on deck again, but still I climbed again, but I saw that I had to jump 5 feet horizontally in mid air above water to reach the rope. I took my chance and jumped but I missed the rope and as I was falling I clutched hold of the rope. [illegible] gloves on and that really saved me because if I would not have those I would have cut my hands very much. As it is the rope cut through the gloves and cut my hands, and it made a cut about a inch in my forehead. My troubles were not over because I fell in the water and was kept up by my lifebelt. After being five minutes in the water (it seemed hours) I was dragged in the last lifeboat. There was nearly all women and children and 3 men. I was given one of the oars to pull the boat. We had to pull very hard because the *Titanic* was sinking and the suction would pull us all down. We rowed for dear life and when were a safe distance from the ship the first explosion occurred. Then came the second explosion and then it sank.[124]

LAURA CRIBB **Third Class Passenger**

On 18 April Miss Cribb purportedly wrote the following account for publication after she left St Vincent's Hospital for the home of her friend, Mrs L.R. Keafer:

My father and I were travelling third class in order to save as much money as possible so that he would have sufficient means to go into business when we reached this country. However, we were very comfortable. The first few days of the voyage were glorious, and we made many friends among the passengers who were coming to this country to start their lives new in what my father had always termed the Land of Promise. He was a highly educated man, and for years he had been desirous of coming to America, but it was only a month ago that we decided to leave our home in Dorset.

I was in my berth early Sunday night and was thrown violently to the floor by the impact of the boat when it struck the iceberg. It was then about 11:30 o'clock, and for a moment I was so stunned that I was unable to imagine what had occurred until I heard one of the officers of the ship shouting that the boat had struck an iceberg. He gave hurried instructions that we should dress and go up on the second deck.

Ah, the courage and bravery of those officers was glorious to see. They seemed to be everywhere at once, shouting instructions, giving advice, quieting those who were terrified and lending aid and assistance to those who were too frightened to help themselves.

Why, I saw one officer who stood on the second deck with his revolver in his hand and threatened to shoot any man who attempted to enter a boat before every woman was cared for.

And he shot three.

It would have been a horrible sight at any other time, but in that hour of chaos and excitement I don't think there was a single person who didn't, inwardly at least, glory in his deed.

Shortly after we left the third deck we were lowered in a lifeboat, all women and children except six members of the crew, and we pushed away far enough to be out of the suction zone. We were so fascinated by the sights on the *Titanic*, however, that we could not keep our eyes off her until the last lights went out and the final notes of the band were drowned in the hiss and roar that came with the final plunge of the great ship as she sank bow first.

Each of us knew that with the sinking we had lost some dear one – my father went down with those other brave men who stuck to their posts and gave their lives that we women and children might be saved – but each of us was glad and proud, I think, to know that they were real men, the kind of men who are heroes.

We were in the boat for nearly four hours before we were picked up by the four sailing vessels from the *Titanic*, which had been lashed together for greater safety. It was then some time before we reached the *Carpathia* – I don't know how long, for I had become so benumbed by then that I was unable to correctly keep track. We saw the *Carpathia* for a great distance, but it seemed hours and hours before we reached her and were finally hauled over her side to safety.[125]

HEDWIG MARGARITHA FROLICHER **First Class Passenger**

On 18 April Miss Frolicher wrote the following letter to her brother:

On board the *Carpathia*
18. April 1912

Dearest Willy,

Today for the first time we are pulling ourselves together to write some letters, as there is a good possibility of reaching at least the entrance to the New York harbour tonight, and so we are shaking off the gloomy atmosphere that has been hanging over us since the 14th.

Papa is writing an extensive report to Grandpa, so I don't have to write you all the details, and anyway the papers will give a better report than we can, as when one has lived through it, there are many things one would rather not talk about.

Well, I enjoyed the beauty of the *Titanic* (God bless and keep her!) for only one day. After that I took to my cabin and for three days was unbearably seasick, although the weather was beautiful and the sea calm.

On Sunday I was so miserable that I said to Papa, 'If only the (darn) ship would sink!' Papa laughed at me and went to play Skat with Mr Simonius and Dr Staehelin from Basel till eleven that night. Suddenly at four minutes to 12, I woke up and for a moment even forgot my seasickness. Without thinking, I dressed warmly and ran with Papa to the upper deck to try and find out what the jolt was all about.

On deck we met up with barely 10 people, amongst them by coincidence both our Basel friends who made fun of me, saying that it seemed to take an iceberg to bring me back on deck. We all looked down on the water rather sheepishly, and then decided to go back to bed as there was no one around that showed any signs of fear. Then we met a gentleman below who was putting on his lifevest, but I was feeling so seasick, that although the engines had stopped, I lay down again and just left the cabin door open. I relaxed somewhat thinking back on a conversation that I had had with our steward the day before, when I had asked him if the lifevests, lying on top of my closet, were good for anything. He had told me the

Titanic could never sink, that even the greatest leak would do no harm because of the watertight walls that would be let down in case of an emergency.

Within half a minute Papa was back in the doorway and said that the steward was helping Mama into a lifevest. Papa helped me buckle up the contraption, and because of the extreme cold, I put my evening coat on over it, and then the three of us went back up to the upper deck, where to our amazement we saw about 30 people standing around a lifeboat. 'Oh dear me, this is it!' that's all I thought. I saw two men lift Mama into it, and immediately it was my turn to be shoved inside, and I hoped Papa would follow. Then I heard that cursed 'Ladies first,' and was so terrified that Papa would not get a seat, that I screamed at the top of my lungs, 'Come, otherwise I'm getting back out!' although of course I most certainly could not have gotten out again. Mama was as upset as I was, as were all the other women who were sitting in the lifeboat with us. Then the sailors let a few men in, but Papa, instead of coming, kept on calling 'Goodbye.' He still wanted to wait. Thank God there were no more women there, and so Papa came too. Then we were told to hold very still, and now we were lowered rather quickly the 30 metres from the upper deck. Everything was handled with the utmost order and calm by the crew, and we the passengers also barely spoke a word.

Actually, no one seemed scared, although we told ourselves it was most likely hopeless, as what good is a lifeboat in the middle of the Atlantic Ocean midway between Europe and America? But we were unbelievably lucky in every way. First of all, the sea was like the Lake of Zurich in good weather, and then there was that darling of a Marconi man, who from his station sent the two emergency telegrams 'Utmost need, sinking rapidly' which saved our lives.

Actually we did not know this as we sat huddled together in the boat, in the beautiful starlit night, holding our breath, and watching the beautiful *Titanic* slowly, slowly begin to sink. We were afraid that we might be sucked into the whirlpool, and so we rowed away from the ship for a while as fast as we could. We saw then how the many rows of electric lights sank lower and lower down to the water level, but only when we heard the anguished cries of many hundreds of people did we realise what a terrible tragedy we were witnessing. Then a horrid sound and again undefined moans which slowly diminished, and then we were alone with a few other boats, drifting with the waves. We spent the next 3½ hours like this, but it only seemed like about ten minutes, as we were in constant suspense and expectation due to the various lights that appeared and disappeared on the horizon, till finally one light turned into a real rescue light, hanging on the mast of the *Carpathia*, and this gave us new courage.

Never had a morning appeared to me to be more beautiful than that of April 15th, and all the sadness of the last few hours was forgotten as we rowed towards the steamer in the icy morning wind. We raced the other lifeboats and ours was number two or three to arrive. You should have seen our Mother, how well she managed to climb the ten metre high rope ladder!! Within a quarter of an hour Mr Simonius and his friend also arrived, and we were greatly relieved.

Now I am too lazy to write any more, and the rest I will have to tell you some other time. I want to enjoy the sea a little more, also the life on board ship, which in spite of all the terrible experiences, was really very lovely.

Affectionately,

Your sister Madi[126]

ANNA HAMALAINEN — Second Class Passenger

On 18 April Mrs Hamalainen wrote the following letter to a friend in Finland:

> You have probably already seen in the newspapers that the *Titanic*, the greatest ship in the world, sank on Monday morning at around 2.15. Words cannot describe the horror that prevailed on the ship at that time. One side of the ship was caught on a lump of ice and the ship was broken in two before sinking. One had to run on deck in their underwear and leave everything at the mercy of the sea. I gave my handbag to Martta and said to her: take care of it and follow me. But many people have been so scared in such a situation that they don't understand anything and this happened to Martta as well, she stayed on the deck looking around and probably drowned. We were saved with Viljo in one of the lifeboats and in about five minutes the *Titanic* sank to the bottom. Two or three rescue ships arrived, most, about 900 people, being rescued by this ship. Today we shall arrive in New York.[127]

CHARLES LIGHTOLLER — Crew (Second Officer)

Second Officer Lightoller wrote the following note at the request of survivor Arthur Peuchen; the purpose of the note was to document the fact that Major Peuchen had entered a lifeboat 'honourably' and that he had not saved his own life at the expense of women and children:

> Major Arthur Peuchen was ordered into the boat by me, owing to the fact that I required a seaman, which he proved himself to be, as well as a brave man.
>
> C.H. Lightoller
>
> Second Officer late S.S. *Titanic*[128]

ALFRED PUGH **Crew (Steward)**

On 18 April Mr Pugh wrote the following letter-card to his father, R.J. Pugh, in Newport News, Virginia:

On Board the Cunard RMS *Carpathia*
Thursday, Ap 18

Dear Dad,

Am sending a line to Newport also Bahia in case you have already left for the latter port. I was on the *Titanic* in the 1st Saloon for the voyage & intended to rejoin the *Oceanic* on our return. Of the 110 stewards we had in the Saloon alone only 5 or 6 were saved. She struck at 11 PM. I was asleep but woke at once of course – we were ordered to the boats about 12 & she sank at 1.30. We were picked up at 5 AM by the *Carpathia* outward to Gibraltar etc & she is landing us at NY tonight where we hope to be transferred to the *Cedric* & home on Sat week. The total number of stewards saved out of 400 is just 46 as near as we know. There were not sufficient boats to accommodate more than were saved.

Total saved Passengers & crew 710 out of 3,000.

Names of survivors went home by wireless.

Trusting you are well.

Yours very affectionately, Alfie[129]

EMMA SCHABERT **First Class Passenger**

Mrs Schabert wrote the following letter to her sister:

On board the *Carpathia*

My darling sister,

While on the *Titanic* I wrote you four or five pages every day, telling you of the marvellous ship, with its wonderful restaurants, lounge and reception rooms, of our large cabin, of the fashionable, well dressed people who gathered in the hall after dinner. All my impressions are at the bottom of the sea now, dearest, and I am just trying to give you a faint idea of the sinking of the mightiest craft on the ocean.

Boy [Philip Mock] and I had gone to bed early. At a little before twelve there was a mighty crash which awoke me. Boy and I had spoken of how we should be able to die as stoics if the ship went down, so when I heard the crash I immediately thought of how we might be called upon to verify our words. Boy came into my cabin and said it was an iceberg, and that it would be well to dress and go upstairs to find out particulars. I dressed warmly without a blouse, however, just wearing a knitted jacket and a scarf on my head. On deck women were walking about in evening gowns, talking the matter over. We went forward quite alone in the dark, and watched the sailors working and to see the ice on the lower decks. Suddenly a tall dark figure loomed up and said: 'Get on your life preservers right away.'

We were quite surprised and started downstairs, where pale-looking, silent stewards were putting life preservers on passengers. Everybody was so quiet and collected it was marvellous. On deck the first lifeboats were being let down. They had to be dropped 60 feet, and it was gruesome to see them being let down. Boy and I had resolved to stay together. As the boat was rapidly sinking the order soon came: 'Ladies only into the life boats.' So one boat after the other left with women who were leaving their husbands behind. The great Mr Ismay tried to make me enter the last boat on the upper deck; when I refused and it had gone, he said, 'You made a great mistake not to get into that boat.' I answered: 'It does not matter. I prefer staying with my brother.' Meanwhile the boat was sinking lower. Then someone said there was a boat on the lower deck and we went down to find it nearly crowded. There were just a few women left on deck so I risked it and went in, and after the other women were put in there was room for one man and Boy was allowed to enter. The officers had pistols to shoot any man who entered without permission. Can you realise my joy when we were both in the lifeboat? Then we were lowered in the lifeboat jerk after jerk, and so unevenly that we expected to be thrown into the water. But the sea was calm and we were soon rapidly rowing away from the sinking vessel, to avoid the suction. She was still brilliantly lighted and looked very mighty in the starlit night.

We had been out about half an hour when the bow of the boat disappeared, the stern rose high into the air and then the tremendous craft slid rapidly into the bottomless ocean. Then we heard explosion after explosion and dreadful cries of help in the darkness. I must not forget to tell you how, before we left the steamer, tremendous rockets were sent into the night for help. They sounded like cannons, and looked like wonderful fireworks. But it gave us a sensation of awe. All the women were really wonderful, no crying or wailing, no pushing. While I was on board there was no panic. But there were men who stayed till the last and were hurled into the icy water, where they swam for hours and finally were picked up into a lifeboat. These men tell harrowing tales of the last moments of men and women. But we were drifting in the darkness without even a light, wondering whether we should be rescued. If a storm came we should be lost and starve or freeze. We were in the boat with a stewardess, 'second class' women and children. No one complained of any discomfort or the cold. Boy helped to row. We could discern the outlines of great icebergs and now and then the light of another lifeboat.

As we drifted hour after hour, I thought of many things, Martha dear, of destiny which had fitted me to face death without fear. I did not like the idea of the icy water but I knew it could not last very long. And I thought of you my darling and of many other things. And then we saw the light of a steamer and hoped we might reach her, and after two hours we were hauled on this steamer with ropes. There were 660 saved and over 2100 drowned. There are countless widows on board whose husbands went down, mostly young brides. It was a mistake to separate them. If I had not insisted on staying on with Boy he would have been lost too. Even Mr John Jacob Astor with his one hundred million dollars was pushed back from a boat and left to drown while his young bride is rescued. She expects a baby and they say she is very ill. People were so heroic. As we went down to our life boats the orchestra was playing in the drawing room. The men who played knew they must sink any minute. That was real heroism.

The steamer had been bound for Gibraltar but the captain is taking us back to New York. It must be hard on the people who were going to Italy. The ship is dreadfully crowded. We have not been out of our clothes, sleeping in the smoking room or library. Last night a young lady let me sleep on her sofa. Everyone has been so kind. Some women had come on board in their nightgowns, and ladies of the *Carpathia* have given up clothes and their berths to others. It is pitiful to see so many young widows sitting about weeping. I am landing without a hat. I just bought a cap off the barber and a funny looking blouse. I have saved my fur coat and sable scarf and most of my jewellery. I lost my bracelets, two little diamond pins and the collar of sapphires and diamonds you used to like. I also lost my gold purse, pencil, etc. and many new things I had bought in Paris. But my pearls and best jewels are safe. Boy lost everything he owns. I do hope I shall hear from you soon. Are my babies well? It is pitiful to see little babies here who have been saved while their mothers and fathers were drowned. Dearest Martha, you may let any of my friends see this letter if you think it best.

I hope you and mother did not worry too much about me, when you heard my news. The Marconi boy on the *Titanic* must have been very heroic. He kept telegraphing to the steamer 'sinking fast. No hope for me,' he said to the Marconi boy on this boat. This steamer was 60 miles distant when they heard the message for help and the captain sailed for our ship at top speed through the region of icebergs. It looked like the North Pole to me. Miles and miles of ice white and silvery in the sun. Give my love to mother. I shall write soon. We may be landed tonight or tomorrow. Paul sent me a very sweet wireless yesterday.

With all my love,
your devoted sister[130]

WILLIAM SLOPER — First Class Passenger

Mr Sloper wrote the following account on 18 April while the *Carpathia* was approaching New York:

While it is still fresh in my mind I shall try to set down here for the benefit of my friends and those interested, as clearly as I can, what I saw and experienced as a passenger on the ill-fated ship *Titanic*.

I did not book passage on this ship until the day before she sailed, and I should not have done so had I not met friends who came over with me in January and with whom I had been more or less in Egypt during the winter. There were fourteen of us who were on the *Titanic*, who had been in Egypt together, and as I write this there are only seven survivors.

On Sunday evening a gentleman who I had not met previously, asked me if I would make a fourth at bridge. A mother and her daughter from New York and himself. I accepted his invitation, and to this fact I feel that I owe my life, as I had been going to bed early every night previously and I should probably have been in bed when the accident happened.

We played in the 'Lounge', and at 11:30 the steward asked us to finish our game, as everyone else had gone to bed and the lights were going to be put out in the room. We finished the game, and at 11:40 I said good-night to the ladies and was on the stairway going down to my cabin. Suddenly there was a lurch and a creaking crash; the boat seemed to shiver and keel over to port.

A half-dozen room stewards and I rushed out onto the promenade deck and peered into the starlit darkness. We could see what appeared to be a sail or something white standing out off our starboard side, astern. It was very cold, and we soon went back into the companionway, where it was warmer.

Meanwhile the engines had stopped and frightened faced people commenced to appear, many scantily attired, inquiring anxiously as to what had happened. They told them that the ship had struck an iceberg, but as it was apparently a glancing blow that it could not have done much damage and that there was no danger.

I was not so sure, however, about there being no danger, and when the ladies, with whom I had been playing cards, appeared I told them to go to their cabins and change their evening clothes for heavier ones. It being Sunday night I had not dressed for dinner, so that I had on a very heavy sack suit. I went for my sweater and heavy overcoat and took my pocket-book from another coat pocket – this was all that I saved, but I'm not complaining.

When I left my cabin, which was in the bow of the ship, I noticed that the floor seemed uneven and that the ship was listing toward the starboard bow. Meeting the ladies again on the stairs and the gentleman who had been playing cards with us, we went out on deck together and took a turn about the deck. As we started forward from the stern my heart sank to see that there was really quite a pitch downward of the deck under our feet. Many more people had appeared on deck, some clad only in night clothes and dressing gowns.

There was no confusion, however, or anything resembling a panic. The stewards assured everyone who asked them that the water tight bulkheads were closed and that while there was a hole in her, she could not possibly sink, and many who had got out of bed to ascertain the trouble returned satisfied. All this time the steam from the boilers was blowing off furiously overhead, and the noise on the deck was deafening. We went back into the companionway, and Miss —, who had only just recovered from an attack of nervous prostration, and was greatly alarmed and excited, stopped everyone as they came out from the lower deck and asked them if there was any danger. The designer of the *Titanic*, who was aboard, came rushing up from below at this minute, and although he said nothing about the seriousness of the trouble, one look at his face convinced me he was worried.

Someone else appeared at this moment and said that the water was rushing in through the squash court wall, and that she was filling rapidly. We were now ordered by the stewards to put on life preservers in case anything should happen that should make it necessary for us to leave the ship. We returned to our staterooms for our life preservers and assembled on the upper stairway leading out on the top deck. The feeling which came over me as I stood in the companionway with these people while we tied on our life preservers cannot be put down adequately on paper. As long as I live I shall never forget that feeling. I had read many stories and accounts of just this thing, and here I was going through the terrible experience myself.

I could only think that I must be asleep and in an awful dream. As a man, I was bound to cheer up the ladies and act as calm as I could, but to say that I felt that was underneath would be untrue. All this time there was no sign of panic or distress among passengers or crew. Everyone behaved wonderfully calm and cheerful. I felt as certain as anyone could feel that we had come to the end, and that many, if not all, would soon be gone. All of the people who were there in this companionway at this time, passed out quietly onto the deck where the lifeboats were. I remember distinctly that there was no crowding through the doorway – everyone was over polite.

The covers had been taken off the lifeboats and they were quickly swung off on the davits and lowered to the level of the deck. From this deck, we were, if I remember correctly, somewhere about eighty feet above the water, and to leave a well-lighted ship that at the time seemed to have listed slightly, and step into a small boat that might plunge down into the darkness below, or, if it reached the sea safely, be capsized by the water, was a question which made some people hold back.

Miss G[ibson], who was now in a state of high nervous excitement, made toward the first boat, and for fear that she might misstep or jump, I kept hold of her arm, and I remember tried to quiet her by saying 'Keep a stiff upper lip.' When the officers in charge of the first boat motioned for us to step in she stepped forward with her mother and the gentleman who had been playing cards with us, and I helped them into the boat and followed after them. People sort of hung back at this time. Many men wouldn't leave the ship or let their friends, as they couldn't believe that the ship could really go down.

Colonel Astor was directly behind me, with Mrs Astor, and he suddenly drew back and pulled his wife back with him. Someone spoke to him, but I did not overhear what was said. At any rate they did not follow us into the boat. When twenty-nine people, including three of the crew, were in the boat, and as nobody else seemed ready to follow, the officer on the deck gave word to 'lower away.'

We might have taken a few more people and managed somehow, although the boat was pretty well filled. While we were being lowered I expected one end of the boat would drop faster than the other and that we should be thrown out into the sea, but we were finally in the water without any mishap. Cutting loose from the ship we pulled away as quickly as we could, as other boats were being lowered overhead and we wished to get out of the way of them. When the people above on the *Titanic* saw the first two or three lifeboats get away safely they eventually decided to come, too, for the rest of the boats on our side quickly filled and were lowered.

Fortunately, the sea was as smooth as a mill pond, and for the time being I felt that we were safe. It was very cold and I was glad to take an oar and help row. As we left the deck somebody had thrown in a number of steamer rugs which were wrapped around the women. The people in our boat were evenly divided, as half were men and half women. Most of the boats that followed afterward had only two or three men in them and had a hard time making headway with so few to manage the boat. One of the three sailors took our tiller and the command of the boat. After we had rowed 200 yards or so we rested on our oars and waited to see what should happen.

The *Titanic* was settling rapidly in the bow and it was evident that it was only a question of a few minutes when the largest and finest ship in the world would go down. Every one began to question the three sailors in our boat as to whether there were boats for everyone to get off in, whether the wireless operator had been at his post and whether he had been in communication with other ships when we struck the iceberg. When we realised that there were at least 2,200 souls and that the lifeboats filled with the same number as ours would only accommodate 800, we began to realise the awfulness of the situation. The sailors told us that there were rafts and collapsible boats enough to take nearly every one, but that in the confusion and at the rate that the *Titanic* was filling they were afraid that these rafts and boats would not be gotten ready in time.

We were rapidly drifting away from the ship and we could dimly see other lifeboats around us full of people. I looked at my watch at this time and it was a quarter of two in the morning. As we sat there on the calm sea with the stars overhead and watched the big ship's bow sinking lower and lower, suddenly the lights dimmed and we knew that the end was near. In a minute the lights went out entirely and then the stern seemed to rise up perpendicularly in the air.

There were two loud explosions, a grinding crash, and the big ship plunged down out of sight. Then followed the most awful thing that I have ever listened to – the screams and cries of all of the hundreds of poor people who were not instantly killed by the explosion, and who were struggling in the water. The ship's barber (whom I didn't know had been saved for two days afterwards, as he was quite badly injured) told me that he was on the upper deck trying to unfasten one of the collapsible boats when the plunge came, which preceded the two explosions. He was thrown off the ship and fell onto several deck chairs which were floating in the sea. He lay there on his stomach and when the explosions came he was badly injured by something heavy falling on his back and across his legs.

Just before he was pitched off the ship he saw hundreds of the third class passengers and some of the officers, with the ship's two doctors, standing on the top deck near the stern of the vessel. When the stern stood up perpendicularly these people were flung helter skelter against a barrier which divided first class from the second class portion of the deck. Then when the explosions came many of these people were blown up into the air along with a lot of debris. The barber was picked up in one of the last boats which left the ship just before the end and brought to the *Carpathia*.

I might tell here of many other thrilling escapes from death, such as the barber had, but I will not take the space to do so, as this account is supposed to be just my own experience. We made fast to another lifeboat full of people which drew alongside of our boat and waited for what should follow. Except for a ground swell the sea was motionless and we sat there anxiously scanning the horizon for the lights of a ship which should come to rescue us from our perilous position. As the other lifeboat had thirty-five people we took three people and a baby over into our boat. We had no lights and we sat there in darkness and silence, wondering if the wireless operator had succeeded in reaching anybody before the *Titanic* went down.

One of the lifeboats kept burning green fire, which I afterward learned one of the stewards had brought in his pocket, he having been shipwrecked once before. We kept close behind this boat and just before dawn we saw the mast lights of a ship on the horizon, and we felt sure that they must have seen the green fire or the rockets that were sent up from the *Titanic*'s bridge just before she sank. At any rate we felt pretty sure that we should be rescued.

Casting off from the other boat we each rowed with renewed strength for the ship which we could see more and more clearly with every passing moment. As the dawn approached we could see that the sea around us was dotted here and there with icebergs and in one direction there seemed to be an ice field of some miles in length. Here and there was a lifeboat, all headed toward the ship; a breeze sprang up with the rising sun, making the sea rougher, and it was very difficult for landlubbers like myself to manage the long heavy oars with which we were trying to row the boat. As lifeboats were approaching the ship from all directions she lay to and waited for us to row alongside. We finally pulled up under the lee of the vessel, which proved to be the *Carpathia*, and after waiting for half an hour for our turn we were at last safely on board.

All of the harrowing details will have been told by others, so that I need go into them only briefly. Just to say that the two gentlemen who sat with me at the small table in the dining-room, a Mr W.C. Dulles from Goshen, N.Y., and a Mr Hoyt of New York City were not saved. The horror of it all is forced upon one by the sight of these poor people who such a short time ago were so happy on board that splendid ship, but who are now mourning the loss of people dear to them. Most of the lifeboats were filled with women, as when it became apparent that the ship was really sinking, and people were anxious to leave, the officers stood by the lifeboats with revolvers, I am told, and would let only enough men get in each boat to row it.

I feel that I owe my life to the fact that the young lady lost control of herself and went into that first boat, pulling me after her. There is also the fact that at first when we left the ship people hung back and they had difficulty in filling the first two or three lifeboats. My inclination was to stay aboard and wait a while until we saw whether there really was danger of the ship sinking. Later on when they wouldn't let the men go I could not have left. Many husbands and sons were separated from their women folks by this rule. One young lad whom I knew was with his father on the ship to the last. They were both thrown into the sea by the plunge which preceded the explosion. They clung to a collapsible boat to which fifty or sixty others were trying to cling until his father's strength gave out and he was forced to let go, leaving his son to be rescued some time later. One family of Canadians from Winnipeg, whom I knew – three girls and a mother – are here, but the father and son are gone, held back at pistol point.

A poor little lady in the next room to me on the *Carpathia* last night was hysterical all night and between her sobs I could hear her say: 'He said he would shoot him if he followed me.' She lost her husband and I think they had not been long married. The heartbroken people, as they leaned over the rail of the *Carpathia* looking down into each lifeboat as it came alongside to see if their missing dear ones were aboard, were pitiful objects to behold. It was terrible to look down into these boats as they came alongside, into the upturned faces of these women, in some cases standing in water up to their ankles with dead men lying in the bottom of the boat anxiously scanning our faces at the rail to see if their dear ones were safe on board.

Some of the rescued people who were the last to leave the ship told me that when they left the orchestra was playing in the 'Lounge,' and that it was brave but ghastly to hear them. The stewards and crew were wonderful, and I didn't hear of anyone who lost his head or nerve. Only those who have been as near to death in a shipwreck as we were can realise the awfulness of some of the scenes which the rescued witnessed, or how thankful they feel to have been saved.

I can hardly realise now that the great ship and all those brave ladies and gentlemen have really gone down while I am here alive. It was a beautiful night and the sunrise the next morning from our small boat was the most glorious sunrise I have ever seen. Truly the ways of the Almighty are beyond our feeble understanding.

In finishing this account I wish to give testimony to the kindness and sympathy of the passengers and crew of the Cunard steamship *Carpathia*, which rescued us. In ten minutes the wireless operator on this ship would have gone to bed and our message would not have reached this vessel. We might still have been on the sea in small boats or swamped and drowned. The stewards and crew have worked ceaselessly to make us comfortable and feed us while the passengers have given up their berths and submitted without a murmur to having their trip terminate in New York when they expected to be in Naples at that time.

William T. Sloper[131]

MARGARETTA SPEDDEN **First Class Passenger**

On 18 April Mrs Spedden wrote the following letter to a friend in Madeira:

On Board SS *Carpathia*
April 18th, -12

I know you will be anxious to hear from us and as I shall be too busy to write after we land, I will send you a line today. We had hoped to get in at noon, but the fog which we have had off and on for two days has delayed us and we may not reach the dock till tonight or tomorrow a.m.

We are still in a dazed state from the effects of the disaster and in spite of all the horrors around us, I don't think we will realise its enormity till we reach shore. The ship struck the iceberg at 11.55 Sunday night and we immediately got partly dressed and went up on deck but it was so dark that we couldn't see anything except ice on the forward deck and that the ship was listing a little bit, so we decided to go down and finish dressing.

There was no panic then, for a number of people hadn't even gotten up, and some who had, had been reassured by some stewards and sent back to bed. I met our stewardess, however, who said the water was already in the baggage room, so we hurried to get all our warm clothes on, I grabbed my jewellery, and we five kept close together and went up on the boat deck where 2 boats were being lowered. We got in the 3rd, and F[red] said goodbye to us, but even then we simply could not realise that anything serious was going to happen and I felt that F. would be in the next boat, so you may imagine my joy when I suddenly saw him near me. There were no other women on deck at the time so he and about 20 other men were ordered to jump in and the boat was lowered from an enormous height, and many times it looked as if it would upset but no one moved or spoke and we finally reached the water and rowed off.

Luckily the sea was as smooth as glass (otherwise not a soul would have been saved), and we had the stars to guide us. We tied up to another boat once, but the rope broke and we also lost 2 oars, and got pretty well separated from the others. Then some of them lighted their lanterns after awhile and we kept track of them.

It was so dark that we couldn't find our light, and the bow of our boat was so packed we couldn't move. Altogether there were 32 of us, 10 of them being stokers and sailors, but we had no officer with us. We told Douglas we were taking a trip to see the stars, a statement which he accepted (though he told us afterwards he thought it was a very silly thing to do when we were so comfortable on the *Titanic* and peacefully went to sleep.)

I shall never forget the sight of that wonderful ship going slowly down, nor the cries of the poor people who couldn't get off. It was too dreadful and yet almost impossible to realise.

Many times we were deceived into thinking that the stars on the horizon were the lights of a ship, so we could hardly believe our eyes when we saw the mast-light of the *Carpathia* and her rockets.

It was a curious fact that none of us expressed any fear of death, but it was perhaps because none of us gave up hope, for on Sunday we were in communication with 8 ships. We had sent a wireless to Capt. Barr and, by the way, I had written to you. We helped at the oars in rowing towards the *Carpathia* which had stopped near the scene of the wreck and it was soon after dawn when we reached her. I never saw a more wonderful sunrise and the glow on the huge ice bergs and the ice floes around us was awe-inspiring. We could see different life-boats coming in and we were about the fourth to reach the ship. One fat woman in our boat had been dreadful all along for she never stopped talking and telling the sailors what to do, and she imbibed from her brandy flask frequently, never offering a drop to anyone else. It was very cold too just before dawn, when a breeze came up and a chilly blast from the ice berg struck us. As we approached the ship, 'our' woman promptly sprang up in order to get off first, when she had been warned to sit still, and it gave me the greatest satisfaction to grab her by her life belt and drag her down.

She fell flat in the bottom of the boat with her heels in the air and was furious because we held her there till we were alongside the *Carpathia* when we were all charmed to let her go up in the sling first. D[ouglas] was so good when he was put in alone and told to keep perfectly quiet and when I greeted him at the top with the officers who were almost devouring him, he remarked, 'My, what a fuss.' The discipline on this ship is remarkable and the welcome they gave us and the care that was taken of the sick and injured at once, no-one will ever forget. We were taken into the dining-room and the scenes which followed as the poor bereaved creatures came in were frightfully harrowing. One poor woman who lost her baby went out of her mind and her screams were appalling to hear. Fortunately we who were fortunate enough to escape together could help a lot and it was the greatest blessing to be able to keep busy. Burns is splendid and her knowledge of nursing has helped tremendously, but I am worried about a cough which she has developed.

Yesterday we spent in cutting up blankets and making garments for the women and children and loads of clothes have been ordered by wireless from the N.Y. Stores. I feel so sorry for the five officers rescued from our ship, for people are questioning them to death and criticising everything that was done, but the more sane passengers are going to do their utmost to contradict any statements derogatory to the officers and crew, for they are a noble lot and did their very best.

One really shouldn't blame anyone for the tragedy, for every man was at his post and the ship had slowed down, but in spite of the star-light it was impossible to see anything. Of course there weren't enough lifeboats, but that was not the fault of any one on the ship.

I have met a Tuxedo couple on board who have been lovely to us and in fact the passengers have done everything in their power to make people comfortable giving them their clothes, their cabins &c. The Drs look done up, for they have hardly slept in three days, a number of those rescued have died of exposure and pneumonia and so many who had to be thrown into the boats are suffering from broken arms and legs. The number of widows is pitiful, to say nothing of the motherless and fatherless children. We had two friends on board, Archie Gracie who clung to an upturned boat as the ship went down, and Jim Smith, a dear man, who missed his hold on the same boat and was lost. Poor young Mrs Astor who is expecting her baby very soon, is in a pretty bad state, and Mr Ismay who was in the last boat, is just beginning to recover from shock. People calmed down a bit yesterday, but today the poor things are very excited and running about crying and wondering what is to become of them. We spend our time sitting on people who are cruel enough to say that no steerage should have been saved, as if they weren't human beings! F. has just been up with Mr Ismay and all the officers helping in making up a clear and just statement of facts, which everyone hopes will be accepted as true. We dread the many lies that will be printed about the poor men who did their duty to the last, and also dread the ordeal of landing and meeting all the poor creatures who will be looking for their friends and relatives. It is hard enough to keep up on the ship, but we have managed to do it as we have kept so busy, somehow the idea of seeing land makes one feel weak in the knees.

We thought of you all as we were out in the boat and hated to think of the anxiety our friends would feel for us.[132]

HUGH WOOLNER **First Class Passenger**

While on board the *Carpathia*, Mr Woolner wrote the following letter to his family:

We were sitting, a party of about six, drinking hot whiskey and water. On Sunday night I noticed that everyone was drinking hot drinks. On the previous night iced drinks had been the favourites, but on Sunday night everyone seemed to be drinking grog. It had suddenly become deadly cold in the lounge and restaurant and the lady of our party had gone off to her room.

Then we men strolled up just above to the smoking room and had been seated only a few minutes when there came a heavy grinding sort of shock beginning far ahead of us in the bows and rapidly passing along the ship and away under our feet. Everyone sprang up and ran out through the swing doors astern.

A man in front of me called out that he had seen an iceberg towering fifty feet above the deck, which was 100ft above the sea, and passing away astern. This was the explanation.

I went with a Swedish friend whose acquaintance I made on board, Björnström Steffanson of the Swedish Embassy in Washington. We sought out the lady who had been recommended to my care, Mrs Churchill Candee, who was returning from Paris to see her only son who had met with a serious aeroplane accident in America.

We found her and I took her up on to the A deck to see how things were going. We found the engines stopped and the officers and crew making preparations to lower the boats. The officers were assuring everyone that there was no danger to life, but that the ladies were to be put into the boats as a precautionary measure.

We continued our walk awhile, and then I saw passengers coming up with life belts on. I got Mrs Candee's tied on to her and then went off to my room and got on mine and brought away an extra one which I soon gave to some scared person who had none. Bjornstrom and I took Mrs Candee up to the upper A deck where the boats were hung and we put her safely with a rug into the first boat, which gradually was filled with women and children and a few of the crew were put in, three I think, and a youth with a broken arm.

Not enough men were put into the first boats really. We then bade her a cheery good-bye and told her we should help her onboard again when the ship had steadied herself. She wanted us to come too but we laughed this off.

We then went and helped with several more life boats, bundling in the women and children. Meanwhile several gentlemen were standing calmly by and looking on. Several men crept into these few boats, as it came out, and they give fatuous explanations how they came to do so. They were forced in by zealous friends against their own wish, and so on.

The calm courage of the passengers was most inspiring. Many women refused to leave without their husbands. Björnström and I look many of them at their husbands' desire and bodily chucked them into the boats. Eventually all the lifeboats on the port side were launched, and while the crew were putting a big Berthon collapsible boat on the davits he and I went down to the lower deck and around to look for stray women.

We found three ladies close together and then we rushed them into a boat on the starboard side by sheer bluff. We shouted our way through the press; 'Make way for ladies!' and then we hoisted them up, one of us on each side, and giving them a final heave in they had to go, head over heels. We then turned our attention to a boat ready on the starboard side, where there was shouting going on.

We saw the first officer twice fire a pistol in the air ordering a crowd of the crew out of the boat. We ran in and helped bundle the men out onto the deck and then we got a lot, about ten, Italian and other foreign women into that boat and when we saw it was being safely lowered we went away and made a final search on the deck below.

The electric lights were beginning to turn red and not a soul was to be seen on the whole deck of 160 yards. The thick glass windows were all closed and Björnström said to me: 'I think we may now make a try for ourselves.' I replied: 'All right.'

We walked along through an open door beyond the glass windows, where there was an open gunwale. Looking out we saw the sea pouring over the bows and through the captain's bridge. Just opposite us was the collapsible boat which we had seen being hooked onto the last davits on the port side. She was being lowered into the sea and hung about nine feet away from us. I said: 'Let's make a jump for it! There is plenty of room in her bows!' Björnström replied 'Right you are!'

We skipped on the gunwale, balanced ourselves for a moment and leaped into the air. He landed fair and square into the boat. I landed on my chest and caught hold with my hands on the gunwale and slipped off backward. I hauled myself up with my arms and got my right foot over the gunwale.

Björnström said, 'All right, I've got you,' and levered me up by my right foot. But that time my left leg was in the sea, so it was a near thing.

The water was pouring in through the door we had just walked through. It rose so rapidly that if we had waited another minute we should have been pinned between the deck and its roof. We first hauled in another man passenger who was in the sea, and then I climbed over a number of women and children and got out two oars. Björnström took one, I took another, a steward got another and another man took the fourth.

I handed him a rowlock so that he could steer and we began to pull like the deuce to get clear of the ship, which I knew was doomed; but I was anxious to get away from the suction when the big ship when under. I never pulled harder in my life. About thirty women and children were in the boat, with only three oars to pull. However we got away from her and got clear, but only about 150 yards, when I saw the monster take a huge tilt forward and her stern came clean out of the water at least eighty feet.

Lights were still burning and she settled forward still further, then stopped for about thirty seconds. Suddenly, with a terrific roar, like thousands of tons of rocks rumbling down a metal chute, she plunged bodily down, head first. Every light went out and the roaring went on for about a minute.

Then arose the most fearful and bloodcurdling wail. It was awful. One thousand seven hundred men in the dark, going down amid that ghastly turmoil! I can never forget it.

We continued our course, for it would have been sheer madness to have returned and tried to pick up any more. It would have meant all of us perishing.

The sea was as smooth as a pond or none of us would be alive. The *Titanic* struck at 11.45 p.m. on a starry, clear night. She sank finally at 2.22 a.m. I believe seventeen boats got away. I was in the seventeenth.

It got colder and colder. Fortunately I had on my fur coat and under that my dress clothes. The only thing I saved was my money. I worked all through the excitement with Björnström at my side. We spoke with strong authority and people simply stood aside and made way for us when we came up with women in tow. It was remarkable!

There were scenes of magnificent unselfishness and devotion; women who absolutely refused to go without their husbands; dozens of husbands who simply obeyed orders and remained silent and quiet on deck while their wives were put into safety. In particular a very handsome old gentleman, Mr Isidor Straus, and his wife were there and declined to be separated and when we suggested that so old a man was justified in going into the boat that was waiting, Mr Straus said: 'Not before the other men.'

His wife tightened her grasp on his arm and patted it and smiled up at him and then smiled at us.

In our boat we floated around for a long time in the dark, the cries getting fainter and fewer in the distance. Then a boat with an officer came along and he gave us orders for us to form a string by making fast our painter's head and tail, so as to make a more conspicuous mark on the ocean for a passing ship to see. This we did and it gave us something to do.

After a while orders were given to lighten the officer's boat, so that he could go and help some poor wretches on an upturned boat, which by now was faintly visible in the distance. We got seven more into our already pretty full boat, but we could stand them upright. Other boats got others, and the officer went away with his sail up and got in about twenty shivering men who had been balancing themselves for over three hours up to their ankles on an upturned collapsible boat. Think of it!

Faint streaks of light began in the east by this time and I saw a breeze coming towards us, which was a serious matter in our heavily loaded condition. I advised throwing off the painter and keeping her head into the sea. This was done. The wind continued to freshen.

Looking around, I saw about twenty icebergs that looked like photographs of the Antarctic expedition. The whole horizon was snow – the edge of a floe, which turned out to be at least forty miles long and yet our lookout on the *Titanic* had seen nothing and we had been going full speed ahead all through the night.

Then I saw a rocket and a little later the lights of a steamer coming our way. This cheered us mightily, as you may imagine. Very slowly she seemed to come on, picking her way through the ice. Eventually she slowed down and then stopped and we saw boats about her sides and I understood that our first boatloads were being taken aboard.

The officer in the sailboat bore down on us and seeing we were being rather roughly knocked about by the sea, gave us a tow, but started away from the steamer and we then saw he was making for another set of unfortunates, who were standing up, apparently in the water. They were a party of fourteen or so, among them a black haired woman and two corpses.

The living having been taken aboard, we wore around and made for the ship, the breeze freshening all the while. It seemed a very long time, but eventually we came alongside the *Carpathia* on her way with a crowd of tourists on their way to Gibraltar. Getting under the lee side, we made fast and soon had the women hoisted in a sling, and then we men clambered stiffly up the rope ladders.

Stewards steered us to the dining saloon, where hot brandy and water and biscuits awaited us. Seven hundred, about, were saved out of, I believe, 2,500.

Everything possible has been done on board to make us comfortable, and nothing could exceed the kindness the passengers on the *Carpathia* showed to the shivering people who came up out of the sea. I was given a sofa in the first officer's cabin. We had fogs nearly all the time since we were rescued and our speed was therefore moderate.

This general description will serve to show that the behaviour of the American and English passengers and of the whole crew was admirable with very few exceptions.

Hugh Woolner[133]

MARIE YOUNG **First Class Passenger**

On the afternoon of 18 April Miss Young wrote the following account while seated in the *Carpathia*'s library:

On Board the Cunard Steamship *Carpathia*

April 18

The survivors of the *Titanic* are gathered this afternoon in the library of the *Carpathia*. In our midst are heartbroken wives, mourning for husbands who forced them into lifeboats; here also are motherless and fatherless babies, for whom busy fingers are eagerly fashioning garments cut from clothing furnished by generous women of the *Carpathia*. Mothers and sisters are crying for lost sons and brothers. Men are here, too, with frozen, bandaged feet and hands. From these tragic surroundings, while words of despair, of cheer, of hope, and of solace pass and re-pass. I send my recollections of a night of horror that language can never adequately describe.

The steamship *Titanic* was moving swiftly over a quiet sea, under a sky brilliant with stars. I had just switched off the light over my bed, when the ship struck with a grinding, wrenching force, followed by several violent bumps. My friend, Mrs White, and I thought we had struck a small boat, and she urged me to go with her immediately to Deck A, where the promenade deck was situated. Since sailing from Cherbourg, Mrs White had been confined to her bed with a sprained ankle and wrist, but had she not made the effort to leave her stateroom immediately, our lives might have been lost, for it seems certain many passengers perished in their staterooms, as very few report being called.

We put on our wrappers and fur coats, and went up from Deck C to Deck A, where a steward told the gathering passengers that we had grazed an iceberg but the ship was in no danger.

Consequently, we lost valuable time, sitting in the corridors watching the young girls and men come in from the deck, carrying pieces of ice which had fallen on the deck (70 feet above the sea) when we struck. In this time we might have collected valuables, and dressed warmly for the undreamed-of exit into the icy night. The engines were letting off steam, all headway being stopped.

Suddenly Captain Smith ran downstairs, calling out, 'Put on your lifebelts!'

It seemed impossible we could have really understood his words, so full of tragic import, and spoken on such a gigantic, 'unsinkable' boat as the *Titanic*.

I ran down to our room, took a life preserver from the rack on the ceiling, and finding the second one caught in the hinge, I took another from the top of the wardrobe. Then catching up some money lying near, and a sweater and extra coat, I ran to Deck A again, in time to hear the order given for all women to go to the boat deck.

There was no hurry, no confusion, no crowding. The ship was so large the passengers had not gathered together.

We heard that chivalrous and gallant command, 'Women first.'

One boat had already been lowered from the port side when we were lifted into Boat No.8. The captain was beside us, and from a hamper nearby he threw a huge loaf of bread into the boat. To a group of waiting seamen and stewards we heard the question put, 'Can you row?'

No sailor had any station assigned him for any boat, and this 'scratch' crew had known no boat drills.

Eagerly, four men entered our boat as oarsmen, and with only 22 souls aboard we were lowered away from the height of 80 feet into the sea. Our stern lowered at such a start it seemed certain we would ship water, but finally we slipped gently from the hawsers and rested on the ocean, whose calmness was our salvation.

Capt. Smith called to us to pull for a green light seen in the distance to unload passengers and return to the boat at once. We left above us weeping wives who refused to leave their husbands, and young mothers who had come up to place nurses and babies in a boat. They went below to save other children, but they were not seen again. Our boat was rowed a short distance, then rested, as opinions were divided between following the captain's orders and staying to pick up possible survivors.

How we hoped and prayed that the *Titanic* would staunchly bear up, with her waiting hundreds, until succouring ships had completed the work of rescue. Finally, we started in pursuit of the low-lying, distant light pointed out, but again and again our horrified eyes were held by the lighted, sinking steamer.

Slowly, deck after deck sunk out of sight, the water covering the bow port holes, and as she crouched lower, she seemed a gigantic kneeling animal.

It was more like a nightmare than reality, to watch the death struggle of the ship whose warm and superlative luxury had so recently enfolded us. What bitter regret one felt at the thought of the millions spent in palm gardens, Turkish baths, squash court, tapestried walls and inlaid woods, when the great essential of sufficient lifeboats was lacking.

All aboard her had such faith in her staunchness that they waited by preference aboard her after her deathblow, believing her unsinkable. Her wireless call rent the sky, rockets blazed, illuminating the huge iceberg on the starboard side, and her cannon boomed again and again for succour.

The incredible sound of music reached us, and with disappearing lights, the roar of explosions and the wail of 1,600 agonising souls, was mingled the heroic music played by what trembling hands God only knows.

Horror and grief stunned us. How could we witness it and live?

One seaman said over and over again, 'I'd rather go back and drown with them than save myself.'

Yet we were in the hands of men who had lighted their cigarettes with calm indifference before we left the steamer's deck. A steward near me, trying to row, said, 'I never held an oar before.' No officer was at our helm. We depended on girls to steer us, and all night the women rowed, standing facing the men, so four hands were throwing all bodily strength into each pull of the oars.

Mrs Swift, of Brooklyn, rowed throughout the entire night.

Often the lantern was lifted and waved. It burned badly, and we lost time trimming it. The sea stretched so smoothly before us that the stars were reflected. Twinkling about us were the lights of other *Titanic* boats. Those that were launched without lanterns burned rope and hats as signals.

A seaman broke the silence.

'Will one of the ladies have my coat?'

'Where is your coat?'

'Oh! I have it on, but you are welcome to it,' he answered.

Slowly dawn came.

Never had our eyes watched so eagerly for the creeping light that turned from black to grey, then flushed to pink on low-lying clouds. Then what a joyous cry went up. Far away from the elusive light we had vainly followed, shone a light, too high to be anything but a mast light. What salvation lay in its existence, could we but reach it, or call it to us!

Soon it showed deck lights, as it swung its side toward us, and from the fear of death awaiting us our hearts surged to the belief that help, relief and life itself reached out glad, welcoming hands.

'Courage, now,' we cried, as the sea grew rough, as the wind rose with the approaching dawn.

How desirable life looked!

Freezing hands laboured at the oars, and the first gleams of the sun displayed a horizon with fifteen icebergs white against it. Seagulls flew over our boat, returning to hover over the crew of straining women and men at the oars.

As far as eye could see, were small white boats struggling toward the rescuers called by the miracle of the wireless message. Boat after boat gathered close to that waiting ship. Would such joy ever be ours, to become one of them, and feel a line of safety thrown to hold us to her side?

We saw her black hull, the swinging rope ladders, and men waiting on her decks. Whirling ropes flew toward us, oars were shipped, and just as safety seemed certain, we crashed against the hull of the *Carpathia*, in the wild wash of the roughening sea.

A voice called, 'Any children aboard?'

Up went a shout, 'No!'

Secured at bow and stern, a 'bos'n's seat' was lowered, looking like a stout wooden swing. It worked on a pulley, and many hands held it. The thought of being seated in it was terrifying, as it swayed dizzily between sky and sea, but strength and assurance of safety rang in the voices above.

Life preservers were discarded, and the passenger nearest the bow was pulled upward in a series of vigorous leaps.

Outstretched arms secured each one in turn, and the deck of the good ship *Carpathia* was a haven of safety.

Never, while life lasts, will I forget my fear when my friend, Mrs White, who had cheered and consoled us all the night was drawn upward, clinging to that rope.

Kind hands wrapped us in blankets and helped us to the library on the deck above, in whosc warmth we were glad indeed to rest.

How the *Carpathia* rushed to the *Titanic*'s aid is another story – it is a record of a captain's supreme command of his own brain and hand and heart, and of those under his command. Fame everlasting should emblazon his name in American history, and of his officers' and crew's efficiency hundreds of grateful hearts will testify.[134]

POSTSCRIPT

COMMISSIONER OF IMMIGRATION

On the afternoon of 18 April 1912 William Williams, the United States Commissioner of Immigration, wrote the following letter to Secretary of Commerce, Charles Nagel:

Department of Commerce and Labor
Immigration Service

Office of Commissioner of Immigration
Ellis Island, New York Harbour, N.Y.
April 18, 1912

Dear Mr Secretary:

The information now is that the *Carpathia* will arrive very much earlier than it was supposed she would this morning when I talked with you over the telephone. She is expected to dock between 8 and 9. I have planned to be on hand to receive the immigrants and supervise the work of caring for them, and shall, therefore, be unable to dine with you. I enclose a Custom House pass to the pier (foot of West 14th Street or thereabouts) should you care to come. This is likely to be a terrible night there.

Yours very truly,
William Williams[135]

19 April 1912 and Afterwards

After the *Carpathia*'s Arrival in New York

KAREN ABELSETH **Third Class Passenger**

After the *Carpathia* arrived in New York, Miss Abelseth wrote the following letter to her father in Norway:

St Vincent's Hospital
New York City,

Well, now I must try to write some words to you, so that you can hear that I am alive. Oh, it has been a terrible time. The experience that I have had since I left you. If I had only known, I never would have travelled. Suppose I must tell you something about what happened. Sunday evening we went to bed at about 10. At 12 o'clock they came down to wake us up. I didn't know what it meant when Adolph Humblen stood in front of my bed and said that I must hurry up because we hit an iceberg. When we had come out of the corridor, many people had already got up and were dragging their suitcases along. Dear you at home, had you only known how terrible it was. I hardly managed to stand. Sigurd had to stand and hold me. Oh, Sigurd! He isn't here, he who was so kind to me. I have almost cried to pieces, but it doesn't help at all.

When we came upstairs and went over the railing, the ship was tilting heavily. After a while people began to enter the lifeboats. Olaus, Sigurd and Peter followed me up to the lifeboat. Just think how hard it was when I was to enter the boat, and they had to stay behind. I didn't want to enter, but Sigurd said 'just be strong. It will all end well.' That was the last he said to me. I was the last who went in that lifeboat, and there was only one lifeboat left. If I had waited any longer, you would have never heard from me anymore.

Then we were lowered. The others had to stay behind. I wish that I was there, and that somebody else could be saved.

When we had come to a short distance away from the ship, we saw how it started to sink. At the end, we heard a terrible noise, and *Titanic* went under with over 2,000 people. As soon as it sank there was a terrible scream. Oh, if you could have only heard it. I will in my life never forget it. I thought I was going to lose my mind, the way they cried. Imagine when so many people start to call for help, and no one can give them assistance. First *Titanic* sank, then she resurfaced close to where we were and overturned twice. We heard the cries for many hours. Those were the worst hours I've ever experienced and I hope I will never experience such a thing again. Imagine those cries, those cries.

At 6 o'clock we saw a ship far away, and then we were very glad as you can imagine. We came alongside the ship at 7 o'clock. There we got blankets around us. But it didn't matter, I thought, because I didn't see any of my company, except Anna, the girl who joined us in Aalesund. After awhile we went through a corridor. There was Olaus. You can imagine there was joy. I wouldn't have had an oar if he was not saved. But Sigurd and Peter were not there. I have hardly tasted any food since I was on board the *Titanic*.

Now there was a nice young lady here and she took me on her lap and she was so kind to me. We are at a hospital. Here everything is so sad. They are only speaking English, every one. Anna is sitting and writing, and Olaus is ill. It was so hard for him that Sigurd was not to be saved. 'Oh, had it only been me who died in his place,' he says. You should have seen how much he is crying sometimes. Just imagine what would have happened to me and Anna if he had drowned as well.

Anna has also lost her companion. That was Adolph Humblen, brother of our schoolteacher. He was so kind, so kind. Everybody was kind. One day we were ill, so we could not go downstairs to eat. They then first came with food, and then with all kinds of fruit and we had such a nice time. Then the dreadful thing was going to happen.

Many tears have fallen down on this paper. It isn't easy making sense of what I am writing today, because I have a terrible headache. I have difficulties writing to the others but will make up for it when I arrive.[136]

OLAUS ABELSETH **Third Class Passenger**

On 19 April Mr Abelseth wrote the following letter to his father and uncle:

> At 12 o'clock at night on the 15th April we struck an iceberg. A man from Langevag and I were in the same cabin. We went up on deck, where there were already a lot of people. I asked one of the crew if there was any danger. He answered: 'No, you are quite safe.' I then went down to Peter and Sigurd who were sharing a cabin, and told them what had happened and that it would be wise to get up. They did so, and we went up on deck. It was so dark that we couldn't see much. After standing there for a while, I said it was best we went down to get life jackets. Peter and I went below. Sigurd stayed behind.
>
> When we came back again, we became aware of a light out in the ocean. One of the crew came and said we could be at ease, because it was a light from an approaching ship. We thought we saw the light and ship, but that was a mistake. He probably meant the ship that brought us to New York, but it was 6 o'clock in the morning before she arrived.
>
> When we had waited on deck for a while, it was said that all women had to go in the lifeboats. Karen went in one of them and was saved. We also went up to the top deck, where the boats were, but we couldn't get into any of them.
>
> We just stood there and watched. I asked Peter if he could swim. 'No', he said. 'If we had a rope, we could have tied ourselves together', he added. Those were the last words between us.
>
> Some of the people cried, others prayed. All told, everyone was very quiet. Peter stood on one side of me and Sigurd on the other. About half of the ship was submerged when we jumped overboard. Sigurd held my hand. But as I hit the water, I became tangled up in a rope, so I had to let go to be able to get loose. That was the last I saw of them.
>
> I swam around in the water for about twenty minutes, but did not see them again. Eventually, I came to a boat which was full of water and people. Some tried to stand up, but they were so very cold that they couldn't manage it. I got up in the boat and stood up. Cold as ice, I stood there for 4 hours with my feet in water. Then a boat came and took us aboard the Cunard Line's steamer *Carpathia*. My clothes were wet, but I didn't get dry ones before we arrived in New York and that took three days. We arrived here yesterday evening at 10 o'clock and we are now in a hospital. I am well, but have got a slight cold.[137]

ELIZABETH ALLEN **First Class Passenger**

Following the disaster, Miss Allen wrote a letter to survivor Archibald Gracie and gave him the following description of her experiences on the *Titanic*:

My aunt's maid came to my door and asked if she could speak to me. I went into the corridor and she said, 'Miss Allen, the baggage room is full of water.' I replied that she needn't worry because the watertight compartments would be shut and it would be all right for her to go back to her cabin. She went back and returned to us immediately to say her cabin, which was forward on Deck E, was flooded.

We were on the boat deck some minutes before being ordered into the lifeboat. Neither my aunt, Mrs Robert, my cousin, Miss Madill, nor myself ever saw or heard the band. As we stood there we saw a line of men file by and get into the boat – some 16 or 18 stokers. An officer came along and shouted to them, 'Get out, you damned cowards; I'd like to see everyone of you overboard.' They all got out and the officer said 'Women and children into this boat' and we got in and were lowered.

With the exception of two very harrowing leave-takings, we saw nothing but perfect order and quiet on board the *Titanic*. We were rowed around the stern to the starboard side and away from the ship, as our boat was a small one and Boxhall feared the suction. Mrs Cornell helped to row all the time.

As the *Titanic* plunged deeper and deeper, we could see her stern rising higher and higher until her lights began to go out. As the last lights on the stern went out we saw her plunge distinctively, bow first and intact. Then the screams began and seemed to last eternally. We rowed back after the *Titanic* sank but we saw no one in the water, nor were we near enough to any lifeboats to see them. When [Fourth Officer] Boxhall lit his first light the screams grew louder and then died down.

We could hear the lapping of the water on the icebergs, but saw none, even when Boxhall lit his green lights, which he did at regular intervals, till we sighted the *Carpathia*. Our boat was the first one picked up by the *Carpathia*. I happened to be the first one up the ladder, as the others seemed afraid to start up, and when the officer who received me asked where the *Titanic* was, I told him she had gone down.[138]

RUTH BECKER **Second Class Passenger**

Miss Becker wrote the following letter to *St. Nicholas Magazine* in 1913:

Dear St. Nicholas:

I am a girl thirteen years of age and have lived in India with my mother and father for ten years. My brother, sister, mother and myself came to America and were passengers on the *Titanic*. My father stayed in India for another year. I am going to tell you about the *Titanic* disaster.

We started from India, March 7, on the steamer *City of Benares*. We had a very nice voyage to Port Said, the sea was very calm. While in the Suez Canal, we saw camels and many other interesting objects. When we left Port Said, it began getting cooler and the sea was getting a little rougher.

We went between the two islands, Corsica and Sardinia to Marseilles. There, nearly everybody got off to go shopping. When we left Marseilles, we got into the Gulf of Lyon and it was very rough there. The waves just dashed over the highest deck. When we got through the Strait of Gibraltar, we did not see the rock because it was night. It was rough when we went into the Bay of Biscay too, but those were the only places.

We got to London on the fifth of April, Good Friday. We were never so glad to get off anything, I think, as that boat. We had been on it twenty-nine days, almost a month. We stayed in London five days so as to make the connection with the steamship *Titanic* which was sailing on the 10th of April from Southampton.

During those five days, we went to the places of interest like St Paul's Cathedral, the Zoological Gardens, and Westminster Abbey. We also saw the largest clock in the world which was called Big Ben.

`On the 10th we left London for Southampton on the train. We got on the *Titanic* about 10 o'clock and sailed about twelve. We were thinking about getting to New York in about six or seven days.

When we got on the *Titanic*, we heard people say we were going to get there in about 4 or 5 days, that Captain Smith was going to make his maiden voyage a record one.

We were just dazzled when we got on this big lovely boat. Our cabin was just like a hotel room, it was so big. The dining room was beautiful with the linen and silver. There was an elevator, so we didn't have to walk up or down.

We had been in the *Titanic* for three or four days when we found it was beginning to get bitterly cold. On Sunday, we all crowded to the inner decks especially made for winter.

On Sunday night, my mother had just gone to bed it seemed, when she was awakened by the engines stopping. Then she heard a pounding noise above our cabin and she got up and asked a steward what the matter was, but he said, 'Nothing' and she should go back to bed. She went back to the cabin but then our own cabin steward came and she asked him and he said to tie on her lifebelt and come as the ship was sinking. So she awakened me and we put on our clothes, stockings and our coats over our nightclothes and went to the upper deck.

We heard them sending off rockets for help and the band was playing. Soon, an officer came and told us all to come and get into the lifeboats. We went. My mother, brother and sister got into one lifeboat and then they said it was all for this boat. So mother told me to get into the next one. I got into another boat and when they were lowering it, another one nearly came down on top of us.

We finally did get to the surface of the water with much difficulty. The *Titanic* was sinking lower and lower. We could see the port lights go under one by one until there was an awful explosion of the boilers bursting. And then the ship seemed to break right down the middle ... and after a bit, go down. When it did go down, we heard terrible screams and cries from the people who were going down with the boat.

We rowed for quite a while and then the oarsmen on our boat began singing songs to cheer us up. Sometimes we would think we saw a light, but it would only be a star on the horizon. It was bitterly cold and we did not have anything on except our coats over our nightclothes. None of our family had on any lifebelts at all.

Suddenly, in the early morning, we saw a faint green light. It came nearer and nearer. It proved to be the lights of the rescue ship *Carpathia*, which was sending off rockets to notify us that it had come to save us. We rowed as fast as we could to it and we were one of the first boats to get there.

I was the first to be taken off and a steward came and took me to the First Class Dining Saloon and gave me brandy and hot coffee. But I could not drink anything, I was so worried about my mother. After a while, though, I found her in the Second Class Dining Saloon trying to find me with my sister and brother. My, but I was glad to see her!

The women were hunting for their husbands and when they could not find them, they knew they had gone down with the *Titanic*. It was an awful sight.

Then, before we sailed for New York, they sent four lifeboats afloat so they could get anyone that was drowning. We had fog all the way to New York and got there in the pouring rain. We went right to a hotel and the next day we went on to Michigan.

I have taken *St. Nicholas Magazine* for a year now and like it very much. I can hardly wait until the time for the next one to come.

Your most interested reader,
Ruth E. Becker[139]

RICHARD BECKWITH — First Class Passenger

When the *Carpathia* arrived in New York, Mr and Mrs Beckwith were met at the dock by Mrs Beckwith's brother, Peris Monypeny, who wrote down their story for publication:

> The bottles on the dressing table in the cabin were not knocked over [by the collision]. So light was the shock that no one realised there was any danger. We went on deck, more out of curiosity than anything else. Most of the people on deck were on the starboard side, but they went to port.

(Monypeny's own paraphrased account of Beckwith's story continued:)

> A mate stood close by them and Bruce Ismay was near the mate. Both of them gave orders for families to keep together and said that everyone could go as there was room for all. The Beckwiths were placed in the second boat, which was lowered from the ship. There were hardly enough people to man the boat and Mr Beckwith and [Karl] Behr took oars and rowed all night.

When the first boats left but few, if any, realised the danger and many refused to go into the boats. For this reason many were lost who might have been saved. The passengers were confident the big liner could not sink.

When the Beckwiths' boat reached the water the people in it had the same trouble that others report concerning casting loose. They found patent tackle blocks that no one knew how to work. Mr Beckwith happened to have a small gold pocket knife in his evening clothes, and with this he cut the ropes. There was no light on the lifeboat, but those with oars pushed away from the sinking ship as rapidly as possible.

The horrifying part of the experience came with the sinking of the boat. Over the waters came the music of the band as the big liner went down. This was followed by shrieks of persons who had been thrown into the waters, but had succeeded in keeping afloat for a time. For an hour these wild cries came over the water, growing fainter and fainter until finally all was quiet.[140]

LAWRENCE BEESLEY **Second Class Passenger**

After the *Carpathia* arrived in New York, Mr Beesley was requested by the editor of the *New York Times* to record his impressions regarding the ultimate cause of the *Titanic* disaster:

I have been asked by the editor of *The Times* to review the whole circumstances of the sinking of the *Titanic* from the point of view of a survivor as well as from that of the ordinary reader who has followed the evidence given before the Senate Committee. The only reason that makes me think I am fitted to accede to the request is that I have absolutely no bias in the matter. I was alone on board and have lost no friends by the disaster; the few belongings I had were of no value beyond their immediate utility, with the exception of money locked in the purser's safe, and this, by the way, the White Star Line has mostly refunded on my bare statement as to the amount. I knew no officer on board the *Titanic*, and the only official of the line I spoke to was Second Officer Lightoller on the *Carpathia*, and under the following circumstances:

While on board the *Carpathia* I had written a letter to *The London Times*, urging the taking of immediate steps to insure safety of passengers and pointing out as dispassionately as possible the reasons for the disaster, without seeking to apportion the blame for it. This letter appeared in *The London Times* on Saturday last, and I understand they were glad to have it as the opinion of a survivor. It became known on the *Carpathia* that such a letter was in preparation, and Lightoller came to me with Mr Ismay's compliments to ask if he could take the letter to Mr Ismay. I have never seen Mr Ismay.

I hesitated, knowing that while it did not seek to affix blame, the deduction would be that there was blame attachable somewhere – where I did not know and I did not wish Mr Ismay to think we were planning to criticise either his officers or his company. However, I knew every statement in the letter was absolutely justifiable and likely to help forward the question of passenger safety, and so I sent the letter to Mr Ismay. He returned it without raising the slightest objection to it. I asked Lightoller to read it. He did so, and said it was calculated to help all concerned – the officers and crew no less than the passengers.

I mention these details only to make it quite clear that my connection with officials of the line is limited to a few moments' conversation, and that I know no motive that induces me to either criticise or defend their actions.

Now, the facts of the disaster are briefly these: The *Titanic*, with a lifeboat provision for saving less than one in three of its passengers, proceeded at full speed through an iceberg region, in which, moreover, it was definitely known that icebergs had been seen and might be expected. An awful indictment! An unbelievable accusation, were it not that we know every detail is attested to by scores of responsible witnesses.

But let us analyse the whole circumstances in a just manner. Let us not form hasty judgments or make rash statements. The power of correct analysis is unfortunately sadly lacking in the average man and woman, and most people are prone to rush to rapid conclusions on totally insufficient evidence. Now, I take it what the editor of *The Times* wishes me to do is analyse as closely as possible the reasons, motives, and aims of those concerned in the disaster, and as far as in me lies I will do so.

I take it there are two main questions to be considered: (1) At whose door should the blame for this overwhelming disaster be placed, and, (2) What are the precautions to be adopted in the future against the repetition of such a disaster?

Now, I think the first of these questions is not by any means the more important; in fact, it should be considered only as a means to aid the efficiency of the methods suggested in the second question. Our motive in fixing responsibility should not be that some person or corporation shall be pilloried and punished; that helps neither them nor the public safety. No one dreams that the ship was lost with deliberate intent. If it be proved that any one has been guilty of criminal negligence, let it be brought home to him or to them and let punishment be meted out if it is thought well; but criminal negligence will be found a difficult thing to prove, and the travelling public that denounces the officials concerned may find the charge a possible boomerang that returns to wound themselves.

It will, therefore, be better to take the second question first and consider what are the precautions to be adopted in the future against the repetition of such a disaster. The general public cannot attempt to discuss such technical questions as bulkhead compartments and double bottoms: they are for the expert in ship construction: but is not the main question after all one of ordinary common sense which the general public is quite as capable of using as the trained official? Perhaps by his very ignorance of technical construction details the average man is not so apt to lose sight of the simpler precautions. The following points will, I think, occur to everyone as being eminently sane and rational. The fact that they have not been attended to in the past seems unbelievable, but several factors, some of which I hope to discuss shortly, have tended to eliminate these safeguards from the policy of sailing mail passenger vessels.

The route fixed by agreement among the steamship lines is normally a safe one, but apparently we are faced this year with an exceptionally large icefield, extending much further south than is usual. It is normally safe, however, only with due precautions: it can never be safe at full speed in the dark when icebergs are a possibility.

But if safety is assured by fixing the steamship lane further south, even much further south, so that an extra day is taken for the passage, let it be done. Only the speed maniac will grumble, and public opinion will soon rise up and tell such a man he is a public offence and a danger to all who travel, whether by sea or by land. We must not forget the effect, largely unconscious, no doubt, which this demand for saving an extra day or hour has on the policy of those engaged in catering to the travelling public.

The protection of a searchlight is two-fold – the ability to sweep the sea for many hundreds of yards ahead and discern anything afloat and the utility of searchlight flashes as signals to other ships. The vessel that was only five miles away when the *Titanic* struck could not fail to have returned when a powerful searchlight lighted her up and so made known the *Titanic*'s distressed condition.

I do not say, however, that an iceberg is an easy thing to detect, even with a searchlight, but it would seem quite possible to see a berg quite far ahead to avoid it. I suppose no one has any doubt that the *Titanic* would be safe now had there been a searchlight fitted on her. The conditions for its use were ideal that night.

The provision of sufficient boats to enable each passenger to claim a seat is an elementary precaution. It should be compulsory on the steamship companies to assign a numbered place in a particular boat to each passenger. Passenger drills with the crew assigned to each boat should also be compulsory. There would be no necessity for the enforcement of the unwritten law of 'women and children first,' for all would have a place. The forcing apart of wife from husband, the painful scenes of parting such as the *Titanic* witnessed, would not be possible.

But the provision of lifeboats is not alone a remedy. In some conditions it would be the poorest of safeguards. Remember that when we embarked from the *Titanic* the climatic conditions were such as are found only in many years, perhaps – an absolutely calm sea. No wind, an unclouded sky – ideal conditions for transferring closely packed boatloads of people from one vessel to another. Given a rough sea, combined with the lack of knowledge of seamanship evident in the crew of most of the boats that were afloat, and the number who handed in their names on board the *Carpathia* would have to be halved or divided by even a larger figure than two.

Is the increase in the size of a ship in itself any precaution against sinking? I venture to think not, except in a sinister way – that in the event of collision with a smaller ship the larger one is more likely to come off the better. On the other hand, I think it may be a positive danger. Every student of mechanics knows that the striking impact of a moving body is determined by its momentum, and the formula M = m x v is a statement of the principle that the momentum of a body is equal to the product of the mass into the velocity. Now the larger 'm' is, the greater the momentum, even if 'v' remains the same, or even if 'v' is sensibly reduced and 'm' is large the momentum may still be enormous.

It is related that in the early days of the Peninsular wars English soldiers would see spent cannon balls rolling comparatively slowly toward them, and, stopping down to stop them, would find themselves deprived of their hands. What they could do with a cricket ball could not be done with a cannon ball rolling at perhaps a much less speed.

When the *Titanic* struck 'm' was the highest yet attained in any age, and 'v' was very high, although not the highest known; but, undoubtedly, m multiplied by v for the *Titanic* at the moment of striking, was the greatest possible for any of them afloat on the sea. Could any form of construction provide against such a force of impact? Could any plates be made strong enough to resist that terrific shock? I think not.

We are told that it would have been better had we headed straight for the berg and collided head on instead of having the side cut open. Probably it would, but even then would anything stand the shattering destruction behind that mass of 60,000 tons moving at 25 miles an hour? I do not know, but I think not. Certainly not unless passengers' boats are to be built as ironclads are, with protective armour.

Would it be possible to have a cruising lightship in iceberg regions, fitted with every possible signal apparatus – Marconi system, searchlight and flashlight, submarine signalling, to give warning to every ship approaching such regions of the position of icebergs, their probable direction and amount of daily drift. It might at least be worth considering, at the iceberg season and be paid for internationally.

But each of these precautions is useless if our other precaution be avoided – that of reducing speed in dangerous conditions. Look at the formula again – when 'v' is zero, M = m x o, which is M = o; the striking impact is nil; 'm x o' is the only real safeguard there is: the other things are good, but they are not even necessary in dangerous conditions. M x v = o for every ship afloat. You cannot eliminate 'm' from the formula – that is constant – but you can make 'v' anything you like from the highest speed your boilers are capable of down to zero. I wonder how it would be to display on the bridge of every ship the following notice: 'M = m x v. Where 'v' is 25 knots the force of impact of this vessel is ___ thousands foot-tons. Where 'v' is zero, the force of impact is nil.' Not that every officer does not know this, but the remainder might be useful.

Having considered the precautions that may be adopted for the future, let us now consider the conditions in which the *Titanic* and her passengers and crew were found from the moment no collision until they were picked up by the *Carpathia* or perished in the icy, cold water of the mid-Atlantic. If there is any responsibility to be fixed, let us see if we can discover where. It will help every

Captain and officer and passenger in the future to know who or what is to blame for the *Titanic* sinking on her maiden voyage.

Now in analysing the facts as presented to us, it must, of necessity, be that some questions to which we would like a reply cannot at this time be answered. Some of those who could answer are, alas, no longer here, and some are silent because officialdom sets a seal on their lips. But I do not think there are many such questions. The facts are too well known and public opinion is too much aroused to permit retention of much information that will be for the common good.

Let us take the officials one by one – the order of taking them is purely for convenience, and see what circumstances, if any, point to the fixing of responsibility for the disaster.

First Officer Murdoch. – He was on duty on the bridge at the time of collision and had been for some time previously. He was not responsible either for the speed of the ship nor for the course that it was taking. The lookout says he warned him of icebergs some time before the collision but got no reply; if so, this was negligence, but he is not here to give evidence on his own behalf.

Is the lookout an unbiased witness? I think not. Is it conceivable that any officer who was not mad or intoxicated (and this is ample evidence that the chief officer was active in getting away lifeboats subsequently – I saw him doing so – and he was neither of these) would disregard such a warning? Suppose the chief officer were here and said 'I never had the slightest warning from the crow's nest of any iceberg until just before the collision.'

His statement would be at least as reliable as that of the lookout. It is said: 'No wonder he shot himself.' But did he? And if he did, was it because he had deliberately neglected a precaution that would endanger his own life and that of thousands of others. I cannot think it possible.

It is said, too, that when he did see the berg he should have headed for her; that the glancing blow cut her open in the most vulnerable place. But what a choice to have to make! How many men would have the courage to head for the berg when every instinct told them to turn the ship away – even supposing it was not the best thing to turn her away! I cannot see how he is to blame.

As commander the Captain is responsible directly for the course and the speed. Whoever else is on board and however much other officers might tender their advice to him, he alone is responsible for the conditions under which the ship is running, and at first sight it seems difficult to see how he can escape responsibility for the disaster. But here we must be cautious.

Did he do anything which was in defiance of all custom in running his ship at full speed through the iceberg region? Did he do anything that has not been done by many Captains for years past? (I do not say every Captain, but many Captains of fast mail-passenger steamers.) Did he defy and outrage all precedent in not slowing down? I think the answer to all these is 'No.'

I suppose it is difficult for a landsman to estimate the probabilities of collision with an iceberg in mid-ocean. He is apt to magnify them far too much. The sea is wide, the ship is small in comparison, and the chances of collision with anything but the largest iceberg (which ours was probably not) are very small. I do not wish to seem to take away any responsibility that should be laid on Captain Smith, but as he is not here to defend himself, let us all see that no undeserved censure be meted out to him. He took the risk which many other Captains have taken. What the chances were in taking the risk no man can say, but in his case the awful thing happened that should never have happened. In the case of all other Captains who have taken a similar risk it did not happen. If he is to be blamed it seems they are all equally blamable for the disaster, for he took the same risk as they did – no more or no less. Remember how the fastest boats are timed to run: 'Leave New York Wednesday, dine in London the following Monday,' and it is done.

Now there must be times when fog and icebergs are dangerous factors, but do the vessels slow down much? My information is that they do not, but if I am wrong, then it will be very easy to give particulars that such and such a boat on a certain date was so many hours or days late because of reduced speed through fog and icebergs. Extracts from ships' logs can be cited, &c. The following was told me by an experienced traveller:

We left Southampton by a boat timed to do the journey to New York in seven days. From the moment of leaving Queenstown to docking at New York there was fog except for the brief space of half an hour, and they did the journey in some hours over the seven days.

If such experiences are uncommon, and if the best boats do not take risks, then let us hear that it is so, and the public will rejoice to know. It will not be so in the future, I am convinced, but for the sake of Captain Smith it seems important to know what the custom has been, for if he has taken a risk many take, the responsibility for such loss of life is fixed on a common system, to which many owners and Captains have agreed, perhaps unconsciously. If he took an uncommon and extraordinary risk, then it seems he is largely to blame.

From another point of view, do not let us magnify the seeming enormity of running full speed in iceberg regions. I am informed by a very experienced officer that the movements of icebergs are most unaccountable. A ship will hear that bergs are ahead in a certain latitude and longitude, and on reaching the position no trace of them can be seen. Perhaps a warm current has swept around them and melted them. Again, news will be heard of a ship ahead with no mention of icebergs, and presently in the same position the ship following will sight numbers of them. I am told there is no question concerning navigation so uncertain as the diagnosis of the presence of icebergs. Cold air is a factor, but cold winds blow across from Labrador, and, on the other hand, a single berg large enough to sink a ship does not necessarily create a cold atmosphere.

Low temperature is another factor, but here again an uncertain one. Look at the map and see how the cold current running down from Labrador meets the warm Gulf Stream; as they meet they do not mingle, nor do the run necessarily side by side; it is a common thing for them to interlace and run in streaks. Interlace the fingers of the hands, and it gives an elementary idea of how the temperature of the water may vary. The thermometer may read something like this as the vessel runs across these streaks: Thirty-five degrees, 60 degrees, 34 degrees, 59 degrees, and so on, all within a few miles.

From what has been said in some sections of the press, it would seem as if the boat was deliberately run through a locality in which it was certain an iceberg was floating in a particular position and no precautions were taken to avoid such a position – in fact, that the utmost criminal negligence was observed; but to say so is to become hysterical. What seems likely is that the risk was taken which it is a frequent custom to take, and the unusually southern position of the field and bergs as well as the large number of the latter, united to increase enormously the probabilities of collision.

So that if you blame Captain Smith you must blame a large number of other people. Shall you blame Captain Rostron of the *Carpathia*, who 'knew icebergs were there but went ahead at full speed, stopped at 4:10 because of iceberg ahead,' and when the day dawned icebergs were around his ship and on every part of the horizon? He must have been near them many times in the night. He took the risk in a splendid cause, and no one is more grateful to him than I am that he did so, and never did a day dawn with greater rejoicing for me than when I climbed aboard his ship. But he did take the risk. I admit there is no comparison between the reasons why he took the risk and why Captain Smith took his, but after all Captain Rostron had his own ship and passengers to consider, and he could not take too great a risk; the fact that he took it at all means it was not considered to be such a danger as we, who have known only the abnormal and not the normal result of taking the risk, might suppose.

I do not think anyone can say Capt. Smith can be held solely responsible.

Not many men have had to undergo such a castigation at the hands of the press as Mr Ismay. He has been called an arrant coward for leaving at all. He should have sunk with the boat in company with the Captain and Chief Officer. He was responsible for the speed, the course, the whole accident, in fact – and then in a moment of danger he ran away. The equipment was faulty and the White Star Line is responsible for criminal negligence and damages can be recovered from it. The Captain was apparently completely under Mr Ismay's thumb and had to do as Mr Ismay told him.

All this and more has been levelled at Mr Ismay. It may be true in part, but is not very likely to be true *in toto*; it may not be true at all. He says he left in a boat when there were no other women passengers near. This is corroborated by witnesses and is extremely probable. The dimensions of the ship were huge. The number on the first-class deck at any time would be small compared with the deck space, and it is exceedingly probable it was as he said. The evidence of Mr Lightoller is that the Chief Officer bundled Mr Ismay into a boat. It seems a very natural act for an officer of the line to perform toward the head of the line. The officer would have a natural anxiety to save his chief, the one who directed mainly the policy of the line.

I left in boat 13, when a call for ladies had been made three times and not answered and no ladies were visible, and was then invited to enter the boat. Mr Ismay left under very similar circumstances. It is said that as managing director he should have remained and gone down, but I think it is quite a debatable point. If he had interfered in the navigation, control and conduct of the ship. Yes. If he had insisted on certain conditions of speed. Yes. If he had insisted on any other rights than those of any other passenger. Yes. But did he do all these things? He says he did not, and I do not know that any strong evidence has been brought forward to disprove his statement.

After all, what are the probabilities? He says he had the information which the Captain and all other officers had about the icebergs, and adds he would not dream of suggesting to an officer of Captain Smith's experience what should be done. That sounds reasonable. He was not a navigator, and he could not suggest. He might express a wish to go fast and Captain Smith in the relation of an official to a managing director might desire to comply with such a wish, and might be unconsciously – or even consciously – swayed to take a greater risk than he would have done if Ismay were not there. But here we are on the delicate ground of surmise as to what passed in Captain Smith's mind – and that we shall never know.

In weighing Mr Ismay's responsibility, the difficult question has to be considered as to how far a managing director who knew nothing of navigation could influence a Captain of the line whose duty it was to know everything about navigation and thereby to control absolutely the lives of the thousands of people committed to his care without a suggestion of advice from anyone not a navigator. It does not seem likely Capt. Smith would be so influenced, but I admit the possibility and there it must be left. It is no more than a possibility, and should there be no evidence to the contrary, we ought to assume that the course and speed were controlled by Capt. Smith. There is Mrs Ryerson's testimony, but this Mr Ismay denies absolutely.

Let us remember Mr Ismay as being questioned not by marine experts, but by men who know nothing of the sea, – and less than nothing, when he is asked whether the watertight compartments were a refuge for passengers. One rather gets the impression that Mr Ismay was prejudged before he went to the inquiry. If so, he has not been fairly treated and we must give him absolute justice.

The *Cedric* messages again have been read as showing an attempt on the part of Mr Ismay to escape inquiry, but this can be dismissed on two grounds – first, that Mr Lightoller now accepts responsibility for sending them and would not have dreamed of sending them had he known there was to be an inquiry in America; and, secondly, Mr Ismay knew it was quite impossible to avoid an inquiry. He knew perfectly well that he would have to stand up before marine and other experts in London and be subject to the most rigid cross-examination, and he knows today that he will still have to do it.

The White Star Line has been criticised for not planning the boat equipment properly or for sending her to sea before her full equipment was on board.

As regards the boat accommodation it was entirely insufficient to accommodate the people on board, but let us bear in mind that the White Star Line set out to build an absolutely unsinkable boat, and in their opinion they had done so. They knew, they said, that the *Titanic* could not be sunk, and from the evidence before them they were quite justified in that knowledge. So that lifeboats were a superfluity from one point of view, but they carried them because they had to do so by Board of Trade regulations; and, again, the ship might always be called upon to rescue lives of other people at sea. But if the theory of the unsinkable boat deluded them into not providing lifeboat accommodation for all on board it helped in another way. When the *Titanic* struck everyone said:

'Well, we are all right; this boat cannot sink. We shall have to wait here until another ship comes along to take us off.'

This, I have little doubt, stopped panic and prevented those rushes for boats which might have taken place had the theory not been so widely and firmly held.

But here, again, if you blame the White Star, you must blame other lines similarly. The *Titanic* was at any rate better equipped than other boats, i.e. on the unsinkable theory plus sixteen lifeboats and four rafts.

Naturally, I do not wish to criticise the Cunard Line and their ship the *Carpathia*; but because I noticed her equipment posted up on the public screen, I noted it mentally and think the figures are as follows: Highest possible total of crew and passengers, 2,864; boat equipment, 20 boats with accommodation for 800 passengers – (I think this is perhaps higher than the accommodation, but I have put it as high as possible) – and no rafts or collapsible boats. This would be a lower accommodation per head than the *Titanic*, and I don't think the *Carpathia* was built as an unsinkable boat. Now, the Cunard's record is that of not having lost a life, and a record that they are justly proud of; but judged from this question of boat accommodation alone, the *Titanic* was better equipped than the *Carpathia*.

Again, the Board of Trade had subjected the *Titanic* to a rigid inspection and had passed her. The White Star had complied to the full with the law of the land. The system again, and not this one particular steamship line! 'They ought to have foreseen the danger.' Well, so ought the Board of Trade: they employ the best experts, presumably. And then the French government and the American government have the right of veto on the entry of any ship into their ports.

If the White Star had been so negligent, why did not these Governments stop their entry? The French, and particularly the American experts must share the responsibility with the Board of Trade and the White Star Line. The American particularly, because the traffic is greater with America, and the Government had only to say the word and lifeboats would have been on board the next day. The responsibility is with the system to which three Governments have agreed.

Again. Let anyone read the standing instructions of the White Star Line to its Captains. They are to 'run no risks': 'the safety of lives of passengers is the ruling principle' to insure 'a reputation for safety.' This is a clear and definite statement of policy, and if the instructions are disobeyed the company's rules are broken, and it cannot be held responsible.

On the other hand, custom establishes many unwritten laws, and may override printed instructions. It seems it did in this case.

Did the White Star know its printed instructions were regularly disobeyed, or did it think the risks taken were negligible? I think the question should be answered.

I would like to give here a personal experience of the Marconi apparatus on board the *Titanic*. It would seem to show the apparatus was not the best obtainable.

I coded a message (which I still have) on the day before the collision, to my friends in London, and took it to the purser for transmission. To my surprise he said:

'We cannot accept this, because our apparatus has only a range of 200 miles. We shall be in touch with Cape Race tomorrow, and can send it then, but I will ring up the operating room.'

He did so, and was told there was no one in communication with us, and so the message was returned with the remark again that we reached only 200 miles. He may have been wrong in his estimate of the distance, but in any case it had not apparently a very long range.

The glasses for the lookout seem to have been an omission, but whether they would have helped to avert the disaster is problematical. The ship was nearly a sixth of a mile long, and at the speed she was travelling it is doubtful whether she could be turned away from an object half a mile away without some part of her touching, and with the peculiarly dark atmosphere of the night, I don't suppose the lookout could have seen icebergs half a mile away. He says he could have seen them in time to avert the disaster, but perhaps he has not considered the tremendous length of the ship, and the room required to take her out of her course.

The number of practical seamen seems to have been too small. I heard of several boats without one. Ours had none, and a stoker took command. This same stoker told me there were only 30 seamen among a crew of 800, but I have no means of checking his statement. If true it seems far too small.

In many boats there was no food, water or lights, either coloured or white. This was the case in mine, and yet No.13 was not launched until over an hour after the collision. There should have been time to put these bare necessities in.

I hope I am not criticising unduly here. Perhaps the organisation was not developed, or perhaps it broke down under the strain. But in a boat these things are essentials and should always be available. The drills would have insured their proper provision.

The method of embarking passengers seems to be open to some criticism. The boats I saw were loaded to standing room – 65 in mine – and then lowered some 70 feet into the water. Neither tackle nor boats are meant to stand such a strain. They did stand it, fortunately. Again, is not the risk of upsetting such a boatload very great? These are the reasons why the officers thought it better that the first boats should be only partially filled and sent away. They might have stood by and taken more aboard from rope ladders, &c., had the crew been organised. I suppose the correct way is to lower the boat and then embark passengers, but was the *Titanic* arranged for that? I am told it was not possible in the way she was built.

There is one more person whose responsibility should be considered, and I have purposely left him to the last, because he is the most important. He is the average man who travels. Columbus took ninety days in a forty-ton ship. A friend of mine crossed fifty years ago in a paddle steamer that took six weeks. And now we cross in something over four days. And all the time 'm' and 'v' in the formula are increasing and their product 'M' is raised day by day until one shudders at the craze for speed and luxury, for in ships size spells luxury. The public demand it and the lines supply it, and that is why the Titanic sank.

You cannot have both 'm' and 'v' high in the formula, and until we sacrifice one or both to some extent the danger will always be the same. No bulkheads or double bottoms or extra lifeboats or searchlights are of lasting value while 'm' and 'v' leap upward!

I think no responsibility will ever be fixed on an individual or on individuals for this disaster. All those who have cried for speed – you and I and our neighbour – have to share it among ourselves in so far as we have expressed a wish to travel faster and in greater comfort, for the expression of such a desire and the discontent with what we call slow travel (a very relative consideration when we remember Columbus!) are the seed sown in the minds of men which presently bear fruit in an insistence on greater speed and size. You and I may not have done it directly, but we may have talked about it and thought about it and after all, no action begins without thought.

I said at the commencement that accusations sometimes come back to wound the accuser; let every man who has ever grumbled to a ship's officer about the slow speed, take it to heart. He had, perhaps, something to do with the sinking of the *Titanic*.

And now to consider one or two other matters arising out of the disaster. I should like to ask readers of *The New York Times* a question that has occurred to me in studying the lists of the rescued. It is this: What is the relative value of the lives of a first-class passenger and a steerage passenger? I have worked out the percentage of the saved of the four classes, and find it as follows: First-class, 63.6 percent; second-class, 39 per cent; steerage, 26.7 per cent; officers and crew, 22.3 per cent. They are instructive, those figures. The payment of about £15 excess of first over third, gives you more than twice the chance of your life being saved! Who can say that a first-class passenger's life is of more value to the community than that of a steerage passenger? It may be that it is so actually, at this present time, but perhaps not potentially so. But the possession of a few more pieces of a particular metal determines the value of a life and not the relative merits of such a life.

John Ericsson, from Sweden, may come in the steerage to America with infinitely greater means of blessings to the community in himself and his family than the millionaire in the first saloon, but the percentages of those saved show that he is not allowed the same opportunity of expressing such blessing.

Again, Major Butt and Col. Astor and Mr Straus died as brave men died, but did not John Brown and Wilhelm Klein and Karl Johanssen? And yet they are not chronicled, and no newspaper has columns on their self-sacrifice and personal courage. But we know these things were true, and we can bear testimony now to every brave man who perished in the steerage, even if we know not his name.

But with sufficient boat accommodation these distinctions would never have had to be drawn. Think of it! A few more boats, only a few more pieces of wood nailed together, and many brave men and women for whom this country and the whole world mourns would be here and these words would not be written.

One incident has occurred to me during the week that has elapsed since we landed in New York that may be of interest, especially to those who had friends on board. Among the passengers were the Rev. and Mrs Carter, who were on their way to Canada. Mr Carter was instrumental in arranging on the Sunday evening, a few hours before we struck, what he called a 'hymn sing-song.'

There was no evening service, and he invited to the saloon such passengers as cared to come to sing hymns. Any one was allowed to choose a hymn, and, as many were present and were thoroughly enjoying the quite informal gathering, the singing went on to quite a late hour.

Mr Carter was apparently well acquainted with the history of many of the hymns, their authors, where they were written and in what circumstances, and he interested all present with his remarks on each hymn before it was sung. I recollect that many chose hymns dealing with safety at sea. 'For Those in Peril on the Sea' was sung by all with no hint of the peril that lay but a very few miles ahead.

Mr Carter closed with a few words of thanks to the purser for allowing him to use the saloon, made a few remarks as to the happy voyage we had had on a maiden trip and the safety there was in this vessel; and then the meeting closed with an impromptu prayer by him. This cannot have been more than two hours before the *Titanic* struck.

My motive in mentioning this is that some of those who have lost relatives may like to know that their friends must have been helped and cheered at the last by the words that they had sung but a short time before; the sound of singing voices must have been still a conscious one to many as they stood on the deck faced with the 'peril on the sea.'

I will finish with a few purely personal remarks. My only excuse for putting them on record is that to me they are absolutely true. I do not make them with any intention of asking a single person to believe in them or to agree with me in what I say, but, having been face to face with the possibility of death and having seen its shadow rather near, I may perhaps not be trespassing on the columns of *The Times* in saying how I consider I was saved.

I have been a Christian Scientist in England for the last six years, and was on my way to America to study the greater work in New York, Boston and the West. The moment I realised there was any danger I turned at once to the method and habit of thought which are incumbent on a Christian Scientist – the attempt to eliminate fear from the human mind. After dressing and before going on deck I read quietly, and then went upstairs with a knowledge that fear was almost entirely eliminated and that opportunity to escape from the peril that threatened was a right we ought all to be able to claim. This condition of mind enabled me to stand quietly on the deck and watch boats being lowered until the moment came when I was able to get a place in a boat without depriving any one of room. I was asked to go by one of the crew in a perfectly natural manner. There were only a few men standing near, and they all came away, leaving the deck quite clear.

I think it certain that I should have walked about seeking every available opportunity to escape had I not been taught by Christian Science to wait quietly and get rid of fear. Had I gone about seeking opportunities, I do not imagine I should now be writing these words. I need hardly add that my gratitude to Christian Science and its founder, Mrs Eddy, is unbounded.

Lawrence Beesley[141]

A few days later Mr Beesley wrote the following letter to the editor of the *New York Times*:

> May I trespass on your space in order to correct a statement I made in an article that appeared in your issue of April 29? I said that the *Titanic* lifeboats were not supplied with bread and water, and so far as I was aware this was correct; none could be found in the lifeboat I came in, and several passengers from other lifeboats related a similar experience. I have, however, received from Second Officer Lightoller a letter in which he says:
>
> 'One statement only (in the article) is not correct, namely; that bread and water were lacking in the boats. Mr Pitman and myself examined every boat from the *Titanic* on board the *Carpathia* and found ample supply of fresh biscuits and two casks (beakers) of water in every lifeboat.'
>
> I am sure you will allow me through your columns to make this correction. I can explain the mistake only by saying we could not find these necessities in the dark night and with a crowded boat. I know your readers will be glad to have this additional evidence of preparation on the part of the owners and officers of the *Titanic*.
>
> Lawrence Beesley
> Roxbury, Mass.
> May 6, 1912[142]

In the autumn of 1912 Mr Beesley wrote the following account for publication in the *Christian Science Sentinel*:

> It would be impossible within a limited space to do more than enumerate the profound changes of thought which Christian Science has wrought in me during the seven years I have known of it. When I first saw the text-book, 'Science and Health with Key to the Scriptures' by Mrs Eddy, I was numbered among that negative class of people called agnostics, a name which I suppose all its advocates recognise as eminently unsatisfactory and indicative of a waiting frame of mind, a waiting for more definite knowledge than the creeds and dogmas of centuries are able to supply. I had studied natural science for many years, having graduated from Cambridge University in the departments of chemistry, physics, and the biological sciences, and had subsequently engaged in research work there, publishing the results of that work. During the time between leaving Cambridge and my first introduction to Christian Science, I had taught and lectured on natural science in one of England's largest schools, where the principal part of my work consisted in laying the foundation of a future medical career for the boys who attended my classes.
>
> When Christian Science was first presented to me, it was essentially a new theory, which required the proof of application and derived result before it could be accepted as true, just as any other theory required to be tested. During these seven years it has been shown day by day, in thousands of instances, to be not a mere theory, but a statement of definite, unchangeable law, which is susceptible

of proof at any time and in any place, and which in its application has been at tended by entirely satisfactory and successful results in the exact proportion to my faithfulness in obeying the law.

Among the many proofs of the law of demand and supply which Christian Science offers, from the point of view that it will supply what is needed, I wish to return my deepest gratitude for one which came to me. I was a passenger on the steamship *Titanic* which collided with an iceberg and sank in mid-ocean on April 14, 1912, and I am convinced that if it had not been for the knowledge of Christian Science, and the application of such knowledge to overcome conditions of fear and danger, my name would now be on the list of the missing. We know, as Christian Scientists, that we are learning day by day to rely on God absolutely for our help in every condition of human life, and are content to accept the innumerable blessings which come to us as a result of such reliance, without seeking or wishing to know the intermediate steps that come between our faith and its results. But in this case the way in which a small knowledge of Christian Science protected me, and led me out of danger, is so unmistakable that it may be helpful to relate it.

At the first sign of danger, after the collision occurred, I went to my cabin and read the ninety-first psalm through carefully three times. I had just turned from this study to the interpretation of the twenty-third psalm as given in Science and Health (p.578), beginning, '[Divine Love] is my shepherd,' when the final call on deck was made. I put the Bible and Science and Health in my pockets and responded to the call, armed with the knowledge which Christian Science reads into the ninety-first psalm, known as it is to every Christian Scientist as a refuge in time of danger. In this mental condition I was able to remain quietly in the position where I first placed myself, on the starboard side, and watch the boats, which had been lowered to the deck below, fill with the women and children collected there, descend to the sea, and row away into the darkness. While doing so, a rumour went around among the men on the top deck that they would be taken off on the port side, and although subsequent events proved it had no official origin, this report seemed at the time to be authentic, and was accordingly acted upon by nearly every one. But it seemed more in harmony with the spiritual sense of the ninety-first psalm, more in tune with the teaching of Christian Science, to 'be still, and know that I am God,' to avoid the crowd and remain quietly on the starboard side until some opportunity of escape presented itself.

Some little time later there were repeated calls for women on the deck below, where the boats were being filled, and looking over the edge of the top deck I saw a life-boat almost full. No more women were to be found, and one of the crew, seeing me looking over, first inquired if any women were to be found on the top deck, and on my replying that they had all been sent down half an hour before, he told me to jump in. I did so, and the boat was presently lowered to the sea. After some hours of wandering about in the darkness we reached the *Carpathia* safely, where all the passengers landed in perfect health and without any untoward incident.

From the moment of being picked up from the lifeboat I was free from any sense of strain or shock, and during the four days on the *Carpathia* I found the knowledge of Christian Science sufficient to meet every condition that presented, itself. When finally landed on the dock at New York, there was an insistent sense of loss, since all my baggage, clothing, and money had gone down with the ship. But here again the knowledge that Christian Science gives was able to destroy this thought and prove that every human need is supplied by reliance on God as the source of all supply. I had insured my baggage, a few minutes before embarking at Southampton, for a sum that covered the whole cost of new trunks and clothing. My money, which had been entrusted to the purser of the *Titanic* and locked up in his safe, was in the form of a letter of credit and bank-notes. The amount of the former was easily made good to me, and the numbers of the latter had been noted by my bankers, so that the value of these notes was returned to me by the Bank of England in due course.

There can be no reasonable doubt that Christian Science was the means by which I escaped from the wreck of the *Titanic*, and it is equally certain that any knowledge which I had of the material laws of natural science was useless on such an occasion. It would never have occurred to me to turn to the latter for help in such conditions of danger, but it was quite a natural and almost unconscious act to resort at once to the Bible and the interpretation which Christian Science gives. Equally natural was it to bring away from the wreck the Bible and the Christian Science textbook as the most important things with which to face the embarkation in boats and the drifting about on the sea. Something of the true value of Christian Science was revealed to me that night, and the way its students come to appreciate their reliance upon it.

The debt which we as Christian Scientists owe to our Leader, Mrs Eddy, the Discoverer and Founder of Christian Science, is brought home to one by an experience of this kind, I have realised more than ever before that such results are attributable directly to her purity of insight, her unconquerable determination to learn the exact truth about God in the face of every obstacle, and the spiritual nature which enabled her to place on record the availability of divine laws for humanity in every conceivable circumstance.

Lawrence Beesley
London, England[143]

On 1 October 1912, after the publication of his book about the *Titanic* disaster, Mr Beesley wrote the following letter to *Carpathia* passengers Mr and Mrs Fenwick:

46 Pembroke House
Oxford St. N
Oct. 1st, 1912

Dear Mr Fenwick & Mrs Fenwick,

Many thanks for your letter enclosing photograph taken on board the *Carpathia*. Your letter was forwarded to England by Houghton, Mifflin and followed me around for some time, so that, while I have a certain feeling of shame for not replying before to thank you for it, there are some excuses to be made for me!

I found such a mass of correspondence from friends and relatives of those lost on the *Titanic* that it has taken me until now to begin other correspondence.

I am so glad to have the picture you enclosed, it takes me back to the *Carpathia* and your kindness to me when I landed cold and partly dressed – which reminds me I still have a stud of yours. I will keep it as a remembrance of you and the occasion.

I am glad you liked my book and found it of interest. I think it had already done something towards convincing the public that reforms are necessary but there is much more to be done – at any rate, this side of the water. There is a tendency for the shipping interest to decry any reform on the grounds that this was an unusual accident which would never occur again. We shall have to see that they are all educated of out such a callous state of mind.

I should be delighted to have other snapshots taken on the *Carpathia*. I should treasure them in memory of the hospitable time we all had – from the officials and passengers alike.

So glad to hear you liked dear old London. Next time you come don't fail to see Derbyshire and Devonshire, as representing some of our most beautiful country scenery.

I had a very happy time in America. I went to New York – Boston – New York – Boston – Cornish (New Hampshire) – Toronto – Buffalo – Cleveland – Chicago – Cleveland (I must've been near Columbus when you were home, I wish I had known) Lake George – Champlain – Rutland – Boston – & sailed on the *Laconia* home. I met with nothing but hospitality & kindness at every turn & retain the happiest memories of America & its inhabitants. Thank you for your addresses; I will certainly keep them. Don't fail to look me up when you are here again.

With most kindest regards,
Yours sincerely,
Lawrence Beesley[144]

KARL BEHR **First Class Passenger**

Following the *Carpathia*'s arrival in New York, Mr Behr dictated the following account of his experiences on board the *Titanic*:

We were a party of four, Mr and Mrs R.L. Beckwith, their daughter, Miss Helen W. Newsom, and myself. I had a stateroom on C deck, they two on D deck near where the actual blow was struck.

Mr Beckwith and myself had stayed up in the card room while the women had retired at [illegible]. We left the smoking room just before the closing for the night and I started to undress in my cabin. I felt a distinct jar, followed by a quivering of the boat. It was distinct enough to know we hit something. I dressed and immediately went after my party, having clearly in mind what course I would pursue. I met Miss Newsom in the passage, she having been awakened by the thud. We went together to the very upper deck, and found it bitterly cold. The ship noticeably listed to starboard, the side which had been hit. I knew the boat was dangerously injured, although I could not then believe she was doomed. Together we went to the cabin of the Beckwiths, telling them to dress. Everybody put on warm clothing.

When we were proceeding along the passage someone told us orders were issued to don life belts, which we did very calmly. We met Captain Smith on the main stairways and he was telling everyone to put on life belts. Knowing exactly where the lifeboats were, I led my party to the uppermost deck. We waited quietly while one boat was filled. It appeared to be comfortably occupied. We then went to the second boat, which had about forty in it. Mr Ismay himself directed the launching splendidly. Before getting in, however, Mrs Beckwith turned to him and asked if the men-folks could come too, and he said: 'Why certainly.' We got into the boat and then Mr Ismay asked if there was anybody else to get in and there was no one at all left around there.

Fully three minutes he waited, for others to come along, before he gave orders to launch the boat, having sent in two petty officers and two or three seamen. The latter were under perfect control. We were evidently the last passengers on the top deck. This was later explained by the fact that passengers were ordered to go to A deck, while we had gone above that. There were other lifeboats on our side, but they must have been filled later from the lower decks. Our boat being lowered into the water, we rowed immediately away from the ship. We could only work four oars at a time on account of the somewhat cramped positions. We made good progress, however, and were soon a safe distance from the ship, which we still did not believe was going to sink. We stopped rowing when far enough out and transferred some of our passengers to another boat, probably the first one launched. The night was perfectly clear and all we could do was to sit and wait. We had no idea of the number of lifeboats, and although it seemed only a few minutes, it was two hours before the boat actually sank. The officer in charge of our boat, seeing the men swimming in the water, refused to go back, and I guess he was right, for he claimed we surely would have been swamped by the hundreds in the water. Fortunately for us, when we left the ship, everything was handled in the most perfect manner and discipline, thanks to Mr Ismay. He made sure that our crew was complete.

What happened actually on board, of course, I saw little of. No panic was evident and I heard no pistol shots. We floated around until dawn, when we saw the lights of the Carpathia, and started to row in her direction, as did all of the lifeboats. The people aboard the Carpathia were fine, and officers, men and passengers cannot be praised too highly. They had made every preparation for our comfort. Quarters and clothes were generously distributed. Personally I am a little unnerved, but otherwise none the worse for the experience.[145]

CAROLINE BONNELL **First Class Passenger**

Miss Bonnell began writing the following account while the *Carpathia* was steaming toward New York; she completed it after landing in New York on the evening of 18 April:

'Well, thank goodness, Natalie, we are going to see our iceberg at last.'

That, that foolish little sentence, was the one thing of all things that I said to my cousin as the great, beautiful *Titanic* was shivering beneath her death-blow.

And yet it was the most natural thing in the world for me to say that Sunday midnight at the very minute when the hand of death began putting down its terrible cargo of souls. For, though the world has not come to realise it, that was a hidden hand – a hand so hidden that none of us suspected it for an instant, or how strong or how cruel it was until less than two hours afterward, it gave a quick, final jerk and the titan of vessels sank beneath the swells.

My cousin, Natalie Wick, and I were lying in our berth half asleep when the blow came. It was terrific. For a second the whole boat just stood stock still in its swift track and then gave a great shiver all through.

After that everything was quiet for a minute.

Then, 'Oh, she's hit an iceberg!' came singing through the window in a shrill woman's voice.

For ten minutes after the blow Natalie and I lay in bed and discussed whether or not we would get up to view the blow. Natalie was pretty sleepy, but I had been up to fill a hot water bottle and was wide awake enough for anything. Finally we decided to 'go up', as we had been waiting to see an iceberg all the way over, but had been told that it was probably too late in the season.

We just slipped on our shoes and stockings and put on some heavy outside wraps and went up. When we got out on the decks everything was as calm as an August afternoon. The sea was as smooth as glass. There wasn't a berg or an ice floe in sight, and the sky was just thick with stars. I never saw so many stars in the heavens in my life as there were that night. The water itself glittered with their glow.

We had just decided to go back to bed when an officer came up to us and another group of people who had gotten up to find out what was the matter.

'Go below and get on your life belts,' he said. 'You may need them later.'

We went down at once and told my aunt and uncle, Mr and Mrs George Wick, what we had been told. Uncle George just laughed at us.

'Why, that's nonsense, girls,' he said. 'This boat is all right. She's going along finely. She just got a glancing blow, I guess.'

That's the way every one seemed to think, and we went into our stateroom; but in a minute or so an officer knocked at the door and told us to go up on the 'A' deck. He said there was really no danger and that it was just a precautionary measure. We got a few clothes on and went up. I picked up my eye glasses in my excitement and left my watch lying on the dresser. Natalie hung her watch around her neck. We both wore two or three coats, it was so cold outside.

When we got on the deck uncle and aunt both were there, and I went down to another part of the steamer and got my Aunt Elizabeth. When I got back crowds of people were standing about. No one seemed excited. Everyone was talking and it seemed the general idea that we would soon be ordered back to bed.

Just then an officer came up to us and explained we should go up to the next deck, the boat deck. By that time nearly everyone was up. Mrs John Jacob Astor was there sitting in a steamer chair. Her husband was beside her and her maid was helping her to finish dressing. There was no confusion here even yet, although we noticed that the boat was beginning to list toward the starboard. The men who had been in the smoking room at the time the ship struck said that they had seen the berg when it passed, and that most of it was under water. Whatever damage was done the vessel was done beneath the water line we knew, for above she was in perfect condition. She had hit the berg alongside and not in front.

After we had been on the top deck for awhile, considerably more than an hour, the women were told to stand by in a group by themselves and to be ready to get into the lifeboats. The men drew back and the women stood at the railing.

This was the condition which prevailed on our side of the boat, on the other side the men and women were not told to separate and that accounts for the men who were saved. Mr Ismay, director of the line, was on that side of the boat and so of course got in one of the lifeboats with the other men.

There was very little excitement. In fact, there was practically none. People had to be begged to get into the lifeboats. No one thought the *Titanic* was going to sink and passengers didn't feel like trusting themselves to tiny rowboats when they were on the biggest liner in the world. At least so they argued with the officers.

As soon as the men withdrew the women were told to get into the lifeboats. Most of them who did so were urged to do so by their relatives, the officers taking little part in it. We never once saw the captain.

The boat we were in was the second to be let down over the side, but the first to strike the water. In it, though it would have held more, were but twenty women, two sailors and a steward. The latter were to do the rowing. As we took to the oars, the officers shouted to us to row over to a distant light and to land there, sending the boat back for others.

We watched the other boats being lowered as we got under way, and then we noticed in a few minutes that the *Titanic* began to list more heavily. After a while when we were a considerable distance away, a whole deck of lights, the lowest deck, was suddenly snuffed out. At the same time the mast light dropped a little further down in the star pointed sky. After this the tragedy moved with a relentless swiftness. Deck by deck we watched the lights go out as the boat dropped lower and lower into the sea.

At last but four rows of lights were left. Then the water reached the portholes and as it rushed in there was one great explosion and then another and then the ship left the horizon unbroken.

And those that were in the life boat that was close to the vessel say that the orchestra played to the very last and that the men went down singing 'Nearer, My God, to Thee.'

As soon as the ship sank, we started to row in good earnest. All night long we made those three men keep to the oars. They wanted to stop but we told them that we had been told to get to that light and we were going to do so, but the light never seemed to come nearer.

As the dawn crept out over the silent whole sea the light seemed only a very little larger than it had when we started for it.

In the lifeboat it was terrible. Some of the women had scarcely any clothes on at all and they suffered greatly with the cold. One woman had white satin slippers and an evening dress on. I don't know whether she had that attire on when we struck or whether in the excitement she put it on by mistake.

We were provided with the most miserable oil lamp I ever saw. I guess it didn't have any kerosene in it for it kept going out as fast as we lighted it with the matches which the steward happened to bring along. We couldn't have been seen at all or signalled at all had it not been for the fact that some woman had a cane with a little electric light in the end of it.

As far as I know there was no food or water in the craft but I will not complain of that for we were the luckiest I guess of all the survivors. The other boats all leaked, and the women told us afterwards that the water was up to their knees. And that water was below freezing point – thirty one degrees to be exact.

For nearly eight hours the sixteen boat-loads of hysterical, cold, wet, hungry women and men were at the mercy of the elements. During the darkness it was bad enough, but the dawn brought a fresh danger. It disclosed the fact that we were beset by vast fields of ice and icebergs. Those gloomy mountains of ice were everywhere. We were almost afraid to move and to add to our distress a stiff breeze was coming up, churning the sea to a nasty choppiness. Still we kept on rowing.

The men were exhausted so we women took a hand. But those oars – they were the heaviest I have ever seen. I am a good oarsman but with the aid of another woman I could scarcely swing one of them. There were three sets of them and they all had to be used to make any progress.

Toward 6 o'clock we gave up hope of ever reaching that light. It had got a trifle larger, but it absolutely was no nearer and we had no food, very little clothing, no heat and nearly every lifeboat was shipping water to an alarming extent.

And on top of all that these women didn't know whether they were able ever to see their husbands in this world or not.

It was terrible and to say that they were the most wonderful women to keep their minds in balance is putting it too mildly by far.

And then somebody looked back – and there – there was a big search light shining on the bow of a great liner. That light was the most beautiful sight I shall ever see. Distress was turned to hope as we put directly about and rowed hard for an hour toward the vessel. At the end of that time we were alongside of the *Carpathia*. It wasn't long until they let down a little wooden seat about two feet long and a foot wide. Men on deck held the end of a cable to which this seat was attached. The lifeboat was bobbling up and down on the waves and it was pretty hard to stand up in it long enough to climb on the seat but you can wager we all did it.

As soon as we were on deck we were rolled in blankets and given brandy and water. And nothing I have ever tasted was quite as good as that brandy and water. By 10 o'clock the *Carpathia* had picked up all the sixteen life boats containing the survivors. In addition to the people who had gotten into the life boats in the first place there were several others in them. These men had been picked up as they were swimming. They were weakened from the exposure and four of them died on the *Carpathia*. These men were W.H. White [Hoyt] and Abraham Hornner [Harmer], passengers, and S.C. Sievert [Siebert], steward and T. Lyons, sailor. They were wrapped in the stars and stripes and buried off the *Carpathia* Monday, returning to the sea from which they had been so vainly rescued.

After we had picked up all lifeboats, we steamed again to the scene of the disaster. In among the glassy peaks of ice, we threaded our way seeing a bit of wreckage here and a baby's bonnet or a man's glove there. But no more boats, and we turned toward Ambrose lightship and home.

'Oh, if I only knew whether my husband had been saved or not,' was the all night cry of more than one sorrow stricken wife. Oft-times they fell upon their knees and prayed for the safe recovery of their loved ones. And it was only the hope that they would finally find them here on land when they arrived that most of the women are as sane as they are. What will they do now that they know that as they watched the *Titanic*'s life being blotted out they watched also the life of their own loved ones being snuffed out by the same hard sea?

The distress of the *Titanic*'s survivors secured for them every concession from the passengers of the *Carpathia*. Women and men alike gave up their staterooms to us and slept on floors of the library and smoking room. Mrs John Jacob Astor was given one of the best rooms in the cabin and she never emerged from it during the trip. It is said that she is ill from grief and exposure.

Every one on the *Carpathia* was kindness itself. Captain Rostron, the surgeon, the stewards, everyone could not do enough for us. The final shock was given us Thursday night as we came up the bay. It was then that we learned how very near we all came to not being rescued at all.

The wireless operator on the *Carpathia* told us during the evening that he had closed his instruments Sunday night and had started to go to bed when something came over him telling him to open it again. The moment he did he gathered in the cry for help with which the *Titanic* was rendering the sea and of course the *Carpathia* began her rush to our side. And she made that sixty intervening miles, her captain told me with his own lips, in faster time than on her speed-breaking voyage, and through the ice fields too.

'And it is a great wonder to me,' said Captain Rostron, 'that we ourselves didn't split on one of them – those most treacherous, most deadly enemies of those who go down to the sea in ships.'

And to think that Natalie and I wished to see an iceberg all the way over![146]

HAROLD BRIDE **Crew (Junior Wireless Operator)**

On 27 April 1912, Mr Bride wrote the following letter to Mr W. Cross, the traffic manager of the Marconi Co.:

No.294 WEST NINETY-SECOND STREET
New York City, N.Y.
April 27, 1912.
W.R. Cross, Esq.,

Dear Sir:

Hearing of the conflicting reports concerning the loss of the *Titanic*, which are being spread around, I think it is advisable for me to give you, to the best of my ability, a true account of the disaster, so that the Marconi Co. may be in full possession of all the facts.

I regret to say my memory fails me with regard to the time of the occurrence or any of the preceding incidents; but otherwise I am sure of all my statements.

The night before the disaster Mr Phillips and myself had had a deal of trouble, owing to the leads from the secondary of the transformer having burnt through inside the casing and make contact with certain iron bolts holding the woodwork and frame together, thereby earthing the power to a great extent.

After binding these leads with rubber tape, we once more had the apparatus in perfect working order, but not before we had put in nearly six hours' work, Mr Phillips being of the opinion that, in the first place, it was the condensers which had broken, and these we had had out and examined before locating the damage in the transformer.

Owing to this trouble, I had promised to relieve Mr Phillips on the following night at midnight instead of the usual time, 2 o'clock, as he seemed very tired.

During Sunday afternoon, toward 5 o'clock, I was called by the *Californian* (call letters MWL) with an ice report, but I did not immediately answer, as I was writing up the abstracts; and also it used to take us some considerable time to start up the motor and alternator, it not being advisable to leave them working, as the alternator was liable to run hot.

I, however, acknowledged the receipt of the report when 'MWL' transmitted it to the *Baltic*, and took it myself to the officer on watch on the bridge.

Neither Mr Phillips nor I, to my knowledge, received any further ice reports.

About 9 p.m. I turned in and woke on my own accord just about midnight, relieving Mr Phillips, who had just finished sending a large batch of telegrams to Cape Race.

Mr Phillips told me that apparently we had struck something, as previous to my turning out he had felt the ship tremble and stop, and expressed an opinion that we should have to return to Belfast.

I took over the telephone from him, and he was preparing to retire when Capt. Smith entered the cabin and told us to get assistance immediately.

Mr Phillips resumed the phones, after asking the captain if he should use the regulation distress call 'CQD.'

The captain said 'Yes,' and Mr Phillips started in with 'CQD,' having obtained the latitude and longitude of the *Titanic*.

The *Frankfurt* was the first to answer. We gave him the ships position, which he acknowledged by 'OK, stdbi.'

The second answer was from the *Carpathia* who immediately responded with his position and informed us he was coming to our assistance as fast as possible.

These communications I reported myself to the captain, who was, when I found him, engaging in superintending the filling and lowering of the lifeboats.

The noise of escaping steam directly over our cabin caused a deal of trouble to Mr Phillips in reading the replies to our distress call, and this I also reported to Capt. Smith, who by some means managed to get it abated.

The *Olympic* next answered our call, but as far as I know, Mr Phillips did not go to much trouble with her, as we now realised the awful state of affairs, the ship listing heavily to port and forward.

The captain also came in and told us she was sinking fast and could not last longer than half an hour.

Mr Phillips then went outside to see how things were progressing, and meanwhile I established communication with the *Baltic*, telling him we were in urgent need of assistance.

This I reported to Mr Phillips on his return, but suggested 'MBC' was too far away to be of any use.

Mr Phillips told me the forward well deck was under water, and we got our lifebelts out and tied on each other, after putting on additional clothing.

Again Mr Phillips called 'CQD' and 'SOS' and for nearly five minutes got no reply, and then both the *Carpathia* and the *Frankfurt* called.

Just at this moment the captain came into the cabin and said, 'You can do nothing more; look out for yourselves.'

Mr Phillips again resumed the phones and after listening a few seconds jumped up and fairly screamed, 'The — fool. He says, 'What's up old man?' I asked 'Who?' Mr Phillips replied the *Frankfurt* and at that time it seemed perfectly clear to us that the *Frankfurt*'s operator had taken no notice or misunderstood our first call for help.

Mr Phillips reply to this was 'You fool, stdbi and keep out.'

Undoubtedly both Mr Phillips and I were under a great strain at this time, but though the committee inquiring into the facts on this side are inclined to censure that reply, I am still of the opinion that Mr Phillips was justified in sending it.

Leaving Mr Phillips operating, I went to our sleeping cabin, and got all our money together, returning to find a fireman or coal trimmer gently relieving Mr Phillips of his life belt.

There immediately followed a general scrimmage with the three of us.

I regret to say that we left too hurriedly to take the man in question with us, and without a doubt he sank with the ship in the Marconi cabin as we left him.

I had up to this time kept the PV entered up, intending when we left the ship to tear out the lot and each to take a copy, but now we could hear the water washing over the boat deck, and Mr Phillips said, 'Come, let's clear out.'

We had nearly the whole time been in possession of full power from the ship's dynamo, though toward the end the lights sank, and we were ready to stand by with emergency apparatus and candles, but there was no necessity to use them.

Leaving the cabin, we climbed on top of the houses comprising the officers' quarters and our own, and here I saw the last of Mr Phillips, for he disappeared walking aft.

I now assisted in pushing off a collapsible lifeboat, which was on the port side of the forward funnel, onto the boat deck. Just as the boat fell I noticed Capt. Smith dive from the bridge into the sea.

Then followed a general scramble down on the boat deck, but no sooner had we got there than the sea washed over. I managed to catch hold of the boat we had previously fixed up and was swept overboard with her.

I then experienced the most exciting three or four hours anyone could reasonably wish for, and was in due course, with the rest of the survivors, picked up by the *Carpathia*.

As you have probably heard, I got on the collapsible boat a second time, which was, as I had left it, upturned. I called Phillips several times, but got no response, but learned later from several sources that he was on this boat and expired even before we were picked off by the *Titanic*'s boat.

I am told fright and exposure was the cause of his death.

As far as I can find out, he was taken on board the *Carpathia* and buried at sea from her, though for some reason the bodies of those who had died were not identified before burial from the *Carpathia*, and so I cannot vouch for the truth of this.

After a short stay in the hospital of the *Carpathia* I was asked to assist Mr Cottam, the operator, who seemed fairly worn out with work.

Hundreds of telegrams from survivors were waiting to go as soon as we could get communication with shore stations.

Regarding the working of the *Carpathia*. The list of survivors, Mr Cottam told me, had been sent to the *Minnewaska* and the *Olympic*.

When we established communication with the various coast stations, all of which had heavy traffic for us, in some cases running into hundreds of messages, we told them we would only accept service and urgent messages, as we knew the remainder would be press and messages inquiring after someone on the *Titanic*.

It is easy to see we might have spent hours receiving messages inquiring after some survivor, while we had messages waiting from that survivor for transmission.

News was not withheld by Mr Cottam or myself with the idea of making money, but because, as far as I know, the captain of the *Carpathia* was advising Mr Cottam to get off the survivors' traffic first.

Quite 75 percent of this we got off.

On arrival in New York Mr Marconi came on board with a reporter of the *New York Times*. Also Mr Sammis was present, and I received $500 for my story, which both Mr Marconi and Mr Sammis authorised me to tell.

I have forgotten to mention that the United States Government sent out a ship, as they said, to assist us named the *Chester*.

Several messages passed between the commander of that vessel and the *Carpathia*, and resulted in the captain telling us to transmit the names of the third-class passengers to the *Chester*.

Though it has since been reported that the most expert operator in the United States Navy was on board the *Chester*, I had to repeat these names, nearly 300 in all, several times to him, taking up nearly a couple of hours of valuable time, though I sent them in the first place slowly and carefully.

I am now staying with relatives and waiting orders from the Marconi Co. here, who have been most considerate and kind, buying me much needed clothes and looking after me generally.

I am glad to say I can now walk around, the sprain in my left foot being much better, though my right foot remains numbed from the exposure and cold, but causes me no pain or inconvenience whatever.

I greatly appreciate the cable the company so kindly sent me and thank them for the same.

Trusting this report will be satisfactory until my return to England, I beg to remain.

Yours, obediently,
Harold S. Bride[147]

AMELIA BROWN **Second Class Passenger**

After arriving in New York, Miss Brown sent the following letter to her mother:

We landed in an awful thunderstorm when we were met by the Allison relations. Such a number of them – and by the way, Mr and Mrs and Loraine are really drowned – so we are staying at Mr Allison's brother's house. They all had a whimper and made a fuss about the baby. We caught the 8:40 train from New York to Montreal where we arrived twelve hours later. I must say I thoroughly enjoyed the ride, as the scenery was grand. We followed the Hudson River for quite a distance and the mountains on each side were splendid ... it reminded me very much of *Ivanhoe* or *The Deerslayer*. When we arrived at the station, Mr Allison's partners met us. Then we had a taxi to a hotel where we stayed the night (The Windsor). There were 14 storeys and we were on the 8th. By the way this was the first time I had slept in a bed since the Saturday night. I gave vent to my feelings and had a good 'laugh' you know. I had had to keep it in so long. We had been travelling with the others and had to keep ourselves in.[148]

MARGARET BROWN **First Class Passenger**

Following the disaster, Mrs Brown wrote the following account of the disaster for the *Newport Herald*:

> A special boat train (train deluxe) from Paris reached Cherbourg at 5 p.m. April 10th. When we arrived, no steamer in sight. She was late, having met with some difficulty in leaving the docks at Liverpool. We all boarded the tender that was waiting to convey the hundreds of passengers to the master palace of the sea, that proved later to be the tomb of many of them.
>
> After an hour or more of waiting in the cold, grey atmosphere, the funnels of the *Titanic*, the world's greatest masterpiece of modern ocean liners appeared over the other side of the breakwater.
>
> In a few minutes more this wonderful floating palace hove in sight around the curve of the dyke and dropped anchor. The tender put on steam, and after half an hour in a running sea we were alongside the keel of the *Titanic*. The tossing of the small craft in the choppy sea caused most of the passengers to be uncomfortable and actively ill. All were chilled through.
>
> On boarding the vessel, the greater number of passengers immediately sought their staterooms. The bugle for dinner sounded a half-hour later, but it was unsuccessful in calling forth many to its magnificent dining room. The electric heater and warm covering were found too comfortable to be deserted even for the many-course dinner, even at the craving of the inner man.
>
> The second day out broke clearer and less crisp, and half after twelve found most of the passengers promenading the deck or basking in the warm sun outside the Palm Garden. There were long benches on the long bow of the boat for those who found the sway-back steamer chairs uncomfortable.
>
> The last half-hour lapsing between the first and second gongs, when all take their exercise before descending to the dining hall, most of the passengers are to be found walking enveloped in heavy wraps. The women were in luxurious furs, and the men in heavy overcoats buttoned closely around their necks and partly disguised in steamer caps. In passing to and fro they discovered old friends on board, and some made new ones. Small groups were standing here and there, discussing the ship and its marvels, its possibility for speed and all its wonderful advantages over anything of its kind heretofore put afloat. Each and all seemed to have consulted the log as to the distance covered that day and each successive day. The number of knots covered was registered there each day at noon, and was the topic of conversation on deck and at the table at the luncheon hour.
>
> After luncheon, or about two-thirty, the favourite and popular place was the reading room, where the passengers settled themselves comfortably with some chosen book from the well-equipped library on the ship. Others were taking a quiet siesta on the deck, wrapped in heavy steamer rugs. Few remained in their staterooms, for the sea was perfectly calm and no vibration was felt. Consequently, there was little or no mal-de-mer.
>
> Thus Thursday, Friday and Saturday were passed.

Sunday services were held at ten-thirty, quite one-half of the passengers attending. Later the passengers went outside to promenade on deck, but much more briskly as the temperature had dropped perceptibly lower. After luncheon a few remained on deck, but all were restlessly searching for a warm place. The comfortable chairs in the lounge held but few, as a shaft of cold air seemed to penetrate every nook and corner, and chill the marrow. Heavy furs and warm clothing were donned.

Dinner time found few inclined to shed their warm clothing for dinner dress. Even the innumerable brides, who on various occasions appeared in a different Paris creation each night, could not be induced to change. Though the board groaned with viands, the passengers found it uncomfortable to sit through the many-course dinner. Many sought their staterooms immediately afterwards.

The writer sought some exceedingly intellectual and much travelled acquaintances, a Mrs Bucknell, whose husband has founded the Bucknell University of Philadelphia, and Dr Brewe of Philadelphia, who had done much in scientific research. During our conversation that I had with her on the tender while waiting for the *Titanic*, she said she feared boarding the ship, she had evil forebodings that something might happen. We laughed at her premonitions, and shortly afterwards sought our quarters.

Anxious to finish a book, I stretched on the brass bed at the side of which was a lamp. So completely absorbed in my reading, I gave little thought to the crash that struck at my window overhead and threw me to the floor. Picking myself up I proceeded to see what the steamer had struck. On emerging from the stateroom, I found many men in the gangway in their pajamas, whom I had overheard a few moments before entering their staterooms saying that they were nearly frozen and had to leave the smoking-rooms. They, while standing, were chaffing each other, one of them remarked, 'Are you prepared to swim in those things?' referring to the pajamas. Women were standing along the corridors in their kimonos. All seemed to be quietly listening, thinking nothing serious had occurred, though realising at the time that the engines had stopped immediately after the crash and the boat was at a standstill, and as there was no confusion of any kind, the book was again picked up.

On overhearing the occupants of the adjoining stateroom say, 'We will go on deck and see what has happened,' I again arose and saw six or more stewards and one officer in the corridor forcing an auger through a hole in the floor, while treating the whole thing with levity. Again returning to my book, presently I saw the curtains moving, but no-one was visible.

I again looked out and saw a man whose face was blanched, his eyes protruding, wearing the look of a haunted creature. He was gasping for breath, and in an undertone he gasped, 'Get your life-saver.' I immediately reached above and dragged all out, as I thought some others might need them. Snatching up furs and placing a silk capote on my head, I hurriedly mounted the stairs to A deck, and there I found possibly fifty passengers, all putting on their life-belts. Strapping myself into mine, I afterwards was told to go up on the storm deck.

My party that I was travelling with had already gone up. On reaching A deck, Mrs Bucknell approached and whispered to me, 'Didn't I tell you something was going to happen?' On reaching the storm deck we found a number of men trying to unravel the tackle of the boats to let them down, which seemed at the time very difficult. We were approached by an officer and told to descend to the deck below. We found the lifeboats there were being lowered from the falls and were at that time flush with the deck. Madame DeVallier [de Villiers; i.e. Berthe Mayne], of Paris, appeared from below in a night dress and evening slippers with no stockings, over which she wore a woollen motor coat. She clutched at my arm and in a terrified voice said she was going below for her money and jewels. After much persuasion I prevailed upon her not to go down but to get into the boat. As she hesitated and became very excited, I told her it was all only a precaution and she would be able to return to the then-sinking steamer later. After she got on, I turned and found the lady of my party in a lowering boat. I was walking away eager to see what was being done with the boats on the other side, not fearing any immediate danger, thinking if the worst should happen I could swim out. Suddenly I saw a shadow, and a few seconds later I was taken hold of, and with the words, 'You are going, too,' I was dropped fully four feet into the lowering lifeboat. When I got in, on looking around I saw but one man, who was in charge of the boat.

While being lowered by jerks by an officer from above, I discovered that a great gush of water was spouting through the porthole from D deck, and our lifeboat was in grave danger of being submerged. I immediately grasped an oar and held the lifeboat away from the ship. While being lowered we were conscious of strains of music being wafted on the night air. As we reached a sea as smooth as glass, we looked up and saw the benign, resigned countenance, the venerable white hair, and the Chesterfieldian bearing of our beloved Captain (with whom I had crossed twice before – only three months previous, on the *Olympic*, our party sat at his table), as he peered down upon us like a solicitous father, directing us to row to the light in the distance, and all boats keep together. With but one man in the boat, and possibly fourteen women, I saw that it was necessary for someone to bend to the oars. I placed mine in the rowlocks and asked a young woman near me to hold one while I placed the other one on the further side. To my surprise she immediately began to row like a galley-slave, every stroke counting. Myself on the other side we managed to pull out from the steamer. All the time while rowing we were facing the starboard side of the sinking vessel. By that time E & C decks were completely submerged, and the strains of music became fainter, as though the instruments were filling up with water. Suddenly all ceased when the heroic musicians could play no more.

The only seaman in our boat was the quartermaster. He was at the rudder, and standing much higher than we were. He was shivering like an aspen. As we pulled away from the boat, we heard sounds of firing, and were told later that it was officers shooting as they were letting down the boats from the steamer, trying to prevent those from the lower decks jumping into the lifeboats. Others said it was the boilers.

The quartermaster in command of our boat burst out in a frightened voice and warned us of the fate that awaited us, telling us our task in rowing away from the sinking ship was futile, as she was so large that in sinking she would draw everything for miles around down with her suction, and if we escaped that the boilers would burst and rip up the bottom of the sea, tearing the icebergs asunder and completely submerge us. We were truly doomed either way. He dwelt on the dire fate awaiting us, narrating at great length the incidents that happened at Liverpool – how two large steamers, the *New York* and one other, were drawn under and almost capsized, we all the while bending to the oars with a vengeance, tugging on. All occupants of the lifeboats remained as mute as the dead, all standing erect clustered in the middle of the boat.

Presently we heard shouts and cries of terror from the fast sinking ship. We were told the shouts were from the trunk men on the collapsible boats. Our quartermaster haggled long and loud. The splash of the oars partly drowned the voices of the perishing men on the doomed steamer. The ladies all seemed terrified. Those having husbands, sons or fathers buried their heads on the shoulders of those near them, and moaned and groaned only.

While my eyes were glued on the fast disappearing ship, I particularly watched the broad promenade deck. It was fully lighted but not one moving object was visible. Suddenly a rift in the water, the sea opened up and the surface foamed like giant arms spread around the ship, and the vessel disappeared from sight, and not a sound was heard.

When none of the calamities that were predicted by our terrified boatman was experienced, we asked him to return and pick up those in the water. Again we were admonished and told how the frantic drowning victims would grapple the sides of our boat and capsize us. He not yielding to our entreaties, we pulled away vigorously toward the faintly glimmering light on the horizon. After three hours of pulling at the oars, the light grew fainter and then completely disappeared. Then our quartermaster, who stood on his pinnacle trembling, with an attitude like someone preaching to the multitude, fanning the air with his hands, recommenced the tirade of evil foreboding, telling us we were likely to drift for days, all the while reminding us that we were surrounded by icebergs, pointing to a pyramid of ice looming up in the distance, possibly seventy feet high reflected by the myriad stars in the sky, that looked like a black shaft. He most forcibly impressed upon us that there was no water in the casks in the lifeboats and no bread, no compass and no chart. No one answered him. They all seemed to be stricken dumb.

One of the ladies in the boat had had the presence of mind to procure her silver brandy flask. As she held it in her hand, the silver glittered and he being attracted to it implored her to give it to him, saying he was frozen. She refused the brandy, but removed the steamer blanket and put it around his shoulders, while another lady wrapped a second blanket around his head and limbs, he looking 'as snug as a bug in a rug.'

We asked him to relieve one or the other at the oars, saying to him that we would manage the rudder. He flatly refused and continued to rampoon us at the oars, bursting out, 'Here, you fellow on the starboard side, your oar is not being put in the water at the right angle!' No one made any protest to his outbursts, as he broke the monotony, but we continued to pull at the oars, with no goal in sight. Presently he raised his voice, shouting to another lifeboat to pull near and lash to, commanding some of the other ladies to take the light and signal to the other lifeboats. His command was immediately obeyed. That and one other command – that we drop the oars and lie fallow until we were rescued. Some time later, after hearing shouts, a lifeboat hove to and obeyed his orders to throw a rope and be tied to ours. Alongside she dropped oars, and on the cross-seat of that boat stood a man in white pajamas. He looked like a snowman in that icy region. His teeth were chattering, and he appeared quite numb. Seeing his predicament, I told him he had better get to rowing to keep his blood in circulation, which was met with forcible protest from our quartermaster.

We, after the exercise, felt the bluest from the icy fields and demanded that we be allowed to keep warm. Immediately over into our boat jumped a half-frozen stoker, black and covered with coal dust, dressed as he was in thin jumpers. I picked up a large sable stole that I had dropped in the boat, and from his waist down wrapped it around his limbs, tying the tails around his ankles. I handed him an oar and then told the pajama man to cut loose, and a howl arose from our seaman. He moved to prevent it, and I said if he did he would be thrown overboard. Then I felt a hand laid on my shoulder to stay my threats, knowing it would not be necessary to push him over, had I only moved in his direction he would have tumbled into the sea, so paralysed was he with fright. He had by this time worked himself up to such a pitch of sheer despair, fearing that a scramble of any kind would remove the plug from the bottom of the boat (that it had taken three of us some length of time to feel around, find it and place it in the hole), and if it were displaced the water would sweep in and there was grave danger of filling the boat. The quartermaster became very impertinent and our fur-enveloped stoker, in as broad a cockney as one hears in the Haymarket, shouted, 'Soy, don't you know you are talking to a loidy?'

For the time being the seaman was silenced, and we again set at our task.

Two other ladies came to the rescue of those rowing and caught hold of the oars and backed the water. Thus we aimlessly tugged on over the vast waste of water. Lights were flashed from other lifeboats miles away.

While glancing around, watching the edge of the horizon, the beautiful modulated voice of the young English woman at the oar exclaimed, 'There is a flash of light!' All looked in the direction pointed out, and our pessimistic seaman said, 'That is a falling star.' It became brighter and later was multiplied by those on the lighted deck. He was convinced then that it was a ship (or said it was the *Olympic*, as she had to have passed after midnight; the *Olympic* passed two days later.) Then he gave a sigh of relief and again ordered us to drop the oars.

We saw this steamer approaching the small lifeboats near her, while we were then possibly six or eight miles off. However, the distance seemed interminable. We saw she was anchored.

Again a declaration was made that we, regardless of what our quartermaster said, would row toward her. Again the young Englishwoman from the Thames got to work, accompanying her strokes with cheerful words to the wilted occupants of the boat.

A little while later dawn disclosed our awful situation. There were fields of ice on which, like points on the landscape, rested innumerable pyramids of icy peaks. Seemingly half an hour later the sun, like a ball of molten lead, appeared at its background. The hand of Nature portrayed a scenic effect beyond the ken of the human mind. The heretofore smooth sea became choppy, which seemed to retard our progress. All the while we saw the small lifeboats being hauled aboard.

By the time we reached the *Carpathia* a heavy sea was running. Our boat being the last to approach, we found it difficult to get close. Three or four unsuccessful attempts were made. Each time we were dashed against the keel and bounded off like a rubber ball. A rope was then thrown to us, which was spliced in four at the bottom, where a wide board was held in four large knots. Feet first, we got on and sat on the seat that formed a swing. Catching hold of the one thick rope, we were hoisted up to where a dozen of the crew and officers and doctors were waiting. Stimulants were given those who needed them and hot coffee was provided for all the survivors.

Everything was done for our comfort, the *Carpathia* passengers sharing their staterooms, clothes and toilet articles, they, then retiring to the far corner of the ship where their deck chairs were placed, giving the lounge up completely to the survivors, and the two succeeding foggy murky days, when the deck was too damp to sit out, they remained in their stuffy staterooms rather than use up the space there.

After picking up the lifeboats, only half filled, the ship reconnoitred for hours around the place where the *Titanic* had sunk. In doing so they passed fifty miles of icefields, so I was told, endangering their own safety in their endeavour to rescue more.

On entering the dining salon, I saw in one corner our brave and heroic quartermaster with a cluster of people around him. He was wildly gesticulating, trying to impress upon them what difficulty he had had in disciplining the occupants of his boat. On seeing a few of us near, he did not tarry long but made a hasty retreat.

On the swivel chairs in the dining salon were seated the *Titanic* survivors. They were speechless, half-clad, their eyes protruding, hair streaming down those who, only twelve hours before, were immaculately groomed and richly gowned and furred – evidence of 'Vanity, vanity, all is vanity.' Here they sat, shaven and shorn and in utter hopelessness and despair, almost all bereft of husbands and sons, fathers and brothers. Unable to grasp the situation, they sat moist, not being able to realise in the one short hour between a quarter of twelve, when the boat struck, and somewhat after one, when she sank, that their dear ones were swallowed up in the jaws of death.

Sprinkled among the affluent were our sisters of the second class, and for a time there was that social levelling caused only by the close proximity of death.

While getting the addresses from many of the survivors of their relatives that they might be apprised by Marconi of their safety, I was grappled by a poor woman of the second class, who held in her closed hand long strands of hair she had pulled from her head. Holding them on high, as though measuring them with her eyes, she frantically shouted to me to find her baby. I promised her I would. Seeing she was mentally unbalanced, a doctor was called and she was put under opiates. When she had gotten into the boat her baby was being handed to her and somehow was dropped into the sea and drowned.

Fortunately the *Carpathia* was carrying something more than half she usually accommodates so the second morning found a greater number of the *Titanic* survivors provided for. The overflow beds were made on the couches in the lounge, and pallets of blankets were made on the floor. The first night many of the men slept on the deck in steamer chairs, others slept in the smoking room and dining salon. The Captain gave up his stateroom, it accommodating four of the socially representative ladies.

The barber, fortunately, had in stock a few dozen toothbrushes, combs and other toilet articles. The *Carpathia*'s objective points being ports on the Mediterranean, she was carrying on an extra large supply of food. In that line there was nothing left to be desired.

On reaching the *Carpathia* the first thing found necessary to be done was to relieve the anxiety of relatives of the survivors. Immediately on obtaining the addresses, I visited the Marconi quarters and left the written messages that had to be paid before sending, though there were many who had little or no funds.

The system was so glutted in sending messages of the wreck and names of surviving passengers, it was the third day before the private ones could be sent, their Marconi system being limited, so I was told, to 250 miles.

The kindly spirit and tender solicitation of officers, crew and passengers elicited the thought that we, the survivors, should in some substantial way express our gratitude to the Captain to the form of a loving-cup and to compensate the crew for their efficiency and double hours of labour on our behalf.

At breakfast the second morning, when I suggested to the gentlemen at the table that immediate action should be taken, I found they were eager to express gratitude but made a protest at funds being collected. A committee was later formed, and a typed notice was tacked up that a meeting of the survivors would be held in the dining salon at three in the afternoon. Almost the full list of survivors were present. Resolutions of gratitude, first to God, and then to the captain and officers, were framed and read.

A subscription list was immediately started, and about $4,000 was subscribed in money and checks. The names and amounts subscribed were typed and tacked on the wall at the foot of the stairs and an open list for those not having yet given in their names and amounts. The day before reaching New York the fund was augmented to the extent of $10,000, so I was informed by the Secretary.

The gravity of the situation was there and then relieved, if the expression on faces was any criterion. The tense mental anxiety was perceptibly mitigated.

A large number of the passengers living out of New York were momentarily embarrassed for funds and only needed enough to tide them over. The Committee waited upon the owner; the survivors' demands being made known, he conceded all. The demand was that the White Star Line furnish transportation and other necessities to their destination.

The second officer, who acted as spokesman for the crew of the *Titanic*, stated that their services were at an end when the *Titanic* sank, and upon reaching New York they would be set adrift. It was immediately seen to that their transportation to England would be given, and also employment on reaching there.

The three succeeding days were spent among the passengers, listing their needs and making provision in the way of clothes, as many escaped in their night-clothing, over which was drawn a cloak. A number who were in our boat had only sandals on and no stockings.

The day before landing three Irish girls were found in the steerage, they having kept their berths since the rescue, having no clothes and refusing to rise with blankets only to wrap around them, they were among the passengers going to New York.

As the *Carpathia* was nearing the harbour, it was surrounded by smaller boats that went out to meet it, in which were newspaper men and photographers to take flashlights. They impeded the progress of the *Carpathia*. The excitement of this and the Captain calling through a megaphone to the pilot to disperse the drafts or he would be unable to reach the dock, and the seeing and hearing of the multitude of humanity on the wharf so frightened these women that they refused to quit the ship and go with the ladies of the Travellers Aid Society, who came on to take them to a place of safety until friends were found and arrangements were made for them to either return to their homes in Europe, or other destinations in America. Feeling it a duty to remain with those, and after the army of Red Cross doctors and nurses, White Star Line officials and general Aid Corps, had taken leave of the ship, we found it was necessary to improvise beds in the lounge, so I remained with them on board all night. There were many who had friends on the dock but did not know them, so with each one was sent an escort and the names called out, and there, finding their friends, would return to the ship and report, and we kept a list of their whereabouts. For some of those remaining, telegrams were sent that night and the next morning. Friends of many came aboard, and the others, less fortunate, consented to go with the ladies of the Travellers Aid conditionally that they would be allowed to see me at the Ritz-Carlton, where I would be, and I promised to have their various consuls there and we would try to find their friends, whose addresses their husbands had when the ship sank. This took some days afterwards.

The next morning, on the ship, I was joined with five members of the committee, who brought on $5,000 so they said, in funds to be distributed among the much overworked crew of the *Carpathia*. This being done, an order was given for the loving-cup to be presented to the captain on the return of his ship from Naples. Having taken a list of those of the survivors who were to be assisted, a copy was made and given to the White Star agents who came on the boat.

The further work of the committee of the survivors of the *Titanic* was to see, by keeping check, that the company were keeping their promise and that all were cared for.

The only comment that could be made was that the *Carpathia* did not follow the customary procedure on boats. Where there is death on board, they usually bury them at night in place of adding to the horror of passengers by burying the men who died on board after being rescued from the collapsible boat at the hour of four in the afternoon when the passengers were around. They possibly may have had a good and sufficient reason for such a departure from the usual procedure. The men who died were rescued by the lifeboat in which were the four prominent lady personages.

In rescuing these, the plug in their lifeboat was dislodged and a foot of water covered the bottom of their boat, which, to prevent the filling of the boat, it was needful that they bail it out with a large dipper hanging from the seat. In the boat two of the men rescued, I was told, died and lay for hours in the bottom of the boat during the six hours on the open sea before the passengers were rescued by the *Carpathia*.

It was very apparent that the consideration and solicitation shown toward the unfortunate survivors had been taken exception to from some sources. On one occasion, when ladies of the committee stopped to inquire the way to reach the second and third class, they were intercepted by the doctor as he emerged from the quarters of the secluded plutocrat. He approached one of the ladies and said, 'Madam, we have the situation under perfect control. Blankets have been cut up and we are having clothes made. Cutting up blankets would not soothe their tortured minds.' Then and there we were more determined, and a notice was posted that the hours of eleven to one and three to six the committee would be in the dining salon. During those hours the survivors came in twos and fours and poured out their grief and story of distress. Between flows of tears they unburdened their sorrows that lay like a weight upon their breasts. The gratitude shown by these people and the evidence that the great mental strain they were under was partly relieved when they knew that someone was interested in their welfare, was proof conclusive to the committee that they were working along the right lines regardless of how the doctor felt in the matter, feeling that he was voicing only the sentiment of the secluded autocrat, as a number of these foreign women of the first and second class were told that now they had no funds, their arrival in America would be under the Allen Law. They were terrified at their being subject to such humiliation. They were fully convinced that such was not the case that they would be provided with means and transportation. They arose and said their lodestone was then and there lifted and their minds were very much relieved.

Another instance when the ladies were made to feel that they were overstepping their bounds in their endeavour to relieve the situation for those people was when the resolutions were read. They were told emphatically it was an absolute affront to the owners and manager who was on board. We replied we were only compelled to do what he had neglected as his duty. If this interest had been shown by him, it would have placed him in a very different light than that of doing as he did, concealing himself behind closed doors to the exclusion of everyone. The contrast was extremely noticeable, as he was the most conspicuous figure on the *Titanic* before she went down. He was six feet tall and of the oriental type, with manner of pacing the deck with an expression of intensity of purpose and determination, he had always been in extreme evidence. Assuming this attitude at this time was extremely ridiculous.

In passing up the stairs at noon on the day we were rescued, two tall men stood aside for me to pass. Looking up, I saw the face of the man and his friend who had told me to get my life-preserver and who later put me into the boat when I was walking away on the *Titanic*. Putting out my hand, it is needless to say how profuse I was in expressing my gratitude. I asked to whom I was indebted for my life and safety. He handed me their cards, reading 'Calderhead and Bough, buyers for Kimball Brothers, New York.' They stated that, in seeing the distress of many women who were bereft of their husbands and some who had perished, it made them feel extremely embarrassed, and their attitude in keeping out of sight other than when they came to the dining salon for meals, was that of men feeling that their lives being saved was somewhat of a stigma, and the worn expression of their faces, as though they continually asked themselves the question, what woman's place in the lifeboat did they fill, and in an apologetic manner they told how inadvertently they caught the last boat being lowered half-empty. They told me of the navigation laws restricting men from the boats when women and children were on board. I replied that such must have been the ancient law, and now that equal rights existed, truly all should be relieved, as I chance; that their conscience on that score should be relieved, as I was a living evidence of their thoughtfulness to womankind, as at the time they placed me in the boat I had no intention of getting off, but was most concerned in knowing what was taking place on the other side of the steamer, and marvelling all the while at the clumsiness of the crew in letting down the lifeboats, comparing the discipline of what I had seen in my travels on German liners, where a daily drill of military tactics in handling lifeboats took place. It was truly shown at the time that the crew of the *Titanic* were amateurs in comparison to what I had seen on a German ship on the China seas, when we encountered the outer forces of a typhoon that set us aground until the tide took us out to the rescue of those floating around in the wreckage of a submerged tramp steamer. The comparison seemed crude indeed, as there was no organisation or discipline shown at the time, though it was known, as soon as she struck the high iceberg and when riding over the submerged one, the bottom of the boat was ripped off, as immediately trunks began to float about in the hold and an officer was seen dragging the mailbags a few minutes after she struck, giving them time to realise the worst had happened and for the crew to be at their posts.

On the contrary, it was plain to be seen that of the seventy stewards who were saved, none attempted to warn those in the staterooms of their danger.

One of the heroes on board was the eighteen-year-old son of the Thayers of Philadelphia. He and his father, after having taken an affectionate farewell of his mother after placing her in the lifeboat, while walking on the deck of the *Titanic* plunged off. While swimming, he was drawn twice under the keel by the suction. In his struggles he grasped hold of the collapsible boat and was among those who were rescued. He was on board the *Carpathia* when his mother was hoisted from the lifeboat. She was under the impression that both her husband and son had perished on the *Titanic*, but, to her supreme joy, she was clasped in her son's arms. In her great thankfulness in having one spared her, for the rest of the voyage not more than a few minutes at a time would she permit him to be separate from her.

The attitude of the men who were rescued was indeed pathetic. Each and all seemed as though they were trying to efface themselves when they were encountered passing to and fro. It was noticed how they all tried to explain how it came about like a miracle that their lives were saved, with an expression of apology as though it were a blight on their manhood. One man displaying an order he had demanded from the officer when asked to get into the lifeboat half-filled with women that he might row, all stating that they took the boats when there was no one around to get in.

The third day on the *Carpathia* I talked at great length with one of the officers of the *Titanic* [Fifth Officer Lowe] who had had in his command five lifeboats, he having the one that went back and rescued those on the collapsible. In talking it over, he stated that they saw to it that, among those who were saved would not be any of the rich nabobs, again reiterating the same, adding, 'We saw to it that they would take their chances with good men.' While preening his feathers over this fact, he stated that there was one who got through without the officers knowing it. He later displayed his weapon and told how with that, he made one who persistently attempted to get in the boat with his wife, was told in the strong expletive of the masculine lexicon to 'chase himself around the deck.' He stated the only thing he regretted was the oaths he had used towards the ladies in the boats.[149]

DAGMAR BRYHL — Second Class Passenger

After arriving in New York, Miss Bryhl wrote the following letter to her uncle in Rockford, Illinois:

Dearest Uncle,

As uncle has, of course, read in the newspaper, the *Titanic* has gone down. I don't know whether my fiancé or my brother, Kurt, are saved. Evidently they are not for most of the men went under. I was saved and have been taken in charge by good people.

I am at a hospital, but am not sick, although very feeble. I have lost everything. I have no clothes, and so cannot get up, but must lay in bed for present.

I would have been glad if I had been permitted to die, because life no longer has any value for me since I lost my beloved. I feel myself so dreadfully alone in this land.

These people are certainly good, but nevertheless do not understand me.

Could uncle possibly come here, if it would not be too difficult or expensive? I would rather wish uncle to come, because father has spoken so much of you that I feel I know you best. I need someone to help me to rights. Perhaps uncle thinks I ask too much but I feel myself so bewildered and lonely. With the heartiest greetings to all relatives.

Uncle's affectionate,

Dagmar[150]

KATE BUSS **Second Class Passenger**

On 23 April 1912 Miss Buss wrote the following letter to her parents:

My Dear Father and Mother,

I can just imagine the state you have all been in, and I've done all that was possible to relieve your anxiety by cablegram, but I know how unsatisfactory it has all been to you, though now you have heard that I've reached the house of Mrs Dalziel, you will be feeling better. In the docks at New York I posted the long letter I had written on my journey.

The details of being conveyed to the Junior League's House are not at all pleasant, but for the kindness of the American women in our distress I cannot speak too highly. All the red tape and formalities were most fearfully trying, and especially to English folk. The disgraceful use of cameras and the knowledge of our own fearfully rough condition seemed hard to bear, but of course we can better see now the reason for our having to give some dozens of times and to various people, our names and destinations, our father's names etc. We felt, or I did, like one of a pen of sheep. At the Junior League's we were conveyed in motor cars. There we were provided with food and with what was far more necessary, a bath. How delighted I was to get the latter, no-one knows but myself. I shudder now when I think of the way we had to walk about on the *Carpathia*. When I saw some ladies fully dressed and wearing their jewellery I wondered how it was possible for them to dress so coolly, although, perhaps, while they were doing that I was just as calmly staying on deck with the idea of seeing the wonderful iceberg.

Well, at Junior League House we met with very great kindness, although we were practically prisoners. It didn't hurt me much to be that, but beyond my dressing gown I had nothing in which to appear, either to receive visitors or to go to the dining room.

The Rev. Mr Halstead Watkins found me the next afternoon. I was also invited by the two deaconesses, who knew him, and they wanted me to go away with them. However, it seemed to me that everyone wanted to do the most, so I was not allowed to go. This Junior League House is an hotel for girls and women who work in the city. They can rent a room from four to seven dollars a week, with breakfast, and 6 pm dinner inclusive, so that they need not go abroad for temptation. For recreation there is a room, provided with electric piano for dancing, etc., and they are able to invite, I presume, at a nominal charge, their own lady or gentleman friends to dinners or a chat. It is really a splendid institution, and just the place for friendless girls. Its only fault is that it is built in an Italian quarter of the city, and five miles from the docks. We had to give all particulars to the manageress, Mrs Ball, to send on to the Customs, as they waived the usual formalities when we landed, in order that we might go somewhere for the night.

There was so much secrecy and trouble at our landing that no-one knew if they would be allowed to land that night or not, until the last minute. Mr Dalziel and Mr A. were searching for me two whole days. When the former, after much trouble, got a pass for the boat, he found me gone. What I should have done I do not know without him. The Relief Committee have been awfully good. In England there could not have been so much assistance given, I should imagine, as there is not the wealth in the country. It broke me up entirely to be forced to wear my soiled clothes until I was able to go and buy more at the stores yesterday. They gave me 150 dollars as a beginning, but Mr A. is going to try and get me more. Oh! dear me. I now know that £200 would not have bought my things here. The prices are fearful.

I've been preserved from reporters. Have heard since coming here that they have all been trying to find me, and because they could not see me, have put most ridiculous accounts of my health and distress in the papers. I have saved some cuttings. Mr A. has made one paper contradict a report today, and says, if they want a correct account they must pay for it. Both he and Mr and Mrs Dalziel must have spent quite a lot of money looking for me.

I've spent nearly all the 150 dollars in clothes, and then I know you would be scared if you saw the quality. I've placed a claim for my money and jewellery, of course. Whatever I get short of £300 will never repay me in my actual loss, and will never bring back the associations. I cannot help grieving when I think of all my personal belongings, my photographs and nice presents. Well it is useless and wicked to complain, since I have been spared. For all that, one cannot help thinking that but for men thirsting for gold this terrible calamity would never have happened. And it should be a lesson to all who put their faith in gold.

I hope the reports of my serious illness haven't reached you. I am reported as being under the care of physicians, and the chief drawback to my recovery is that I cannot get news from 'the man I love, who is doubtless crossing the Continent to meet his bride.' The funniest part is they describe me as 'a pretty young English girl.' It's positive proof they never saw me.

Oh, that *Carpathia*! The officers, crew, and passengers were awfully good, but oh, the dirt. It was like going from a palace to a pig sty. I thought at first I must return to England. But I must wait. At one time I thought I would never cross the ocean again. But I guess I will when I get over this a bit. America has its charms already, but I will never be satisfied until I have been home to see you all again.

I never felt the slightest bit sea-sick, but my nerves on the *Carpathia* were awful. The first night we had a thunderstorm, and when I heard the crash and saw the lightning through my port-holes, I was terrified because I thought the vessel had struck. I never closed my eyes for more than an hour all the three nights. I should have been all right if I could have been on deck and seen it was only a storm. It's the uncertainty of being down below that makes one feel so bad. I'll never trust anyone again when they tell me there is no danger, until I have satisfied myself.

America they say has been in a panic since she got the news. Every vessel's flag is half mast and the crowds when we landed were indescribable. I can never describe things properly in a letter, my mind wanders from one thing to another; it is like a long and horrible dream. Every morning now when I waken I am going up and down and the whole house is moving and even now I feel the vibration of the ship. On the whole and considering all things I've been wonderfully well. If it had not been for the shocking loss of lives it wouldn't have been so bad. But it is impossible to help grieving for the noble hearts that stayed behind, even although we knew them only for a few days.

You will get all the paper talk, but no-one will ever know the exact truth, the reports are so twisted: and when I read them, of my own and Miss Wright's experiences, it seems to be reading accounts utterly absurd. They gave it that she went up on deck and saw the iceberg, and came for me, whereas I was up first (not on the deck), went down for her, and we went on deck together. We saw no iceberg, but talked to a gentleman who did. We were, I believe, the first ladies on deck, because I remember now saying, 'Well if there are no other ladies up here we had better retire, or at least get some more clothing.' I would not knowingly give any information concerning the wreck to reporters in America.

We certainly struck about 11.45, and I should say the ship sank somewhere about two, but although I looked at my watch at the time I could hardly tell exactly, because I couldn't remember if I had altered my watch, as is necessary, to get right with New York time that night. Such a sight as met us when dawn broke, I've never seen before, only in pictures. But, after all, it was very beautiful. I think I must have felt far more calm on the ocean than most, for I never suffered as some of them, except for cold. I knew that no man could save me. I was alone with God, and whatever happened must be for the best. I felt as I have felt before when death has stared me in the face, that I had to do nothing but wait God's will.

We just rowed out beyond the suction of the *Titanic*, and then the men rested on their oars while we watched her sink. Soon the tide came in, and we drifted for hours near the Gulf Stream. We heard sometimes shouts and sometimes singing from the other boats, but they had no lights, half of them, neither had we, but we lighted matches and reserved the torch possessed by someone, with about half-an-hour's store of light, until we could sight a ship. We had no compass either, and it was some time before they could find a rudder, yet ours was the most comfortable experience. We had no water in the boat, we only had 35 passengers, and when we were lowered in the water, a distance of 75 to 90 feet, we touched it almost without a splash, unless indeed I was past all feeling. There are so many accounts that one wonders if they can depend upon themselves. One woman, a Frenchwoman, made a good deal of noise. I shouted out once for silence myself, because the poor seamen got worried. They have reported the women as being far braver than the men, and I think they were. One big fellow, near me, fidgeted a sailor so, that he said to me, 'He hasn't been on the water ten minutes, and is worrying like a baby.' I lent my rug to a little girl, as she had no skirt on. The seaman lent me his coat, and I returned it just before I climbed the ladder. After an hour or two I found my own rug on the back of this said man, so I claimed it, and kept it until the night before I landed; then, as the steamer rugs seemed to be used by all sorts, I lent it to the poor fellow who was knocked about so on the raft. During the night they carried him to a first-class cabin given up by a gentleman to him. He said he saw the rug there, but when I went for it, it had gone, so I had to do without it. I saved my little bag (not a farthing in cash) with my bank book and papers, needlework, etc.

You would like to see these American wooden houses, with a large garden. But it is so funny to leave life and come out here to death. What I mean is, that I left the trees in full bloom, and out here the ground is covered with dead leaves.[151]

ALBERT CALDWELL — Second Class Passenger

Mr Caldwell wrote the following letter to his college alumni newspaper in May 1912:

Biggsville, Ill.
April 30th, 1912

Dear Mr Buchanan:

Have at hand your letter dated April 29th. In answer to your request for us to send pictures, I beg to state that every picture or anything looking like a picture that we ever possessed, is in the bottom of the Atlantic Ocean.

With reference to our recent experience, you wrote that you did not want a detailed account but a few facts concerning our rescue.

As the Alumni have all seen the accounts in the papers, I will only give a few personal incidents.

I owe my life to my baby boy or rather to God who used him to save me. The fact that I had him in my arms gave me the precedence to take a vacant place in the lifeboat after the women and children were loaded.

We were in boat number 13 (not unlucky this time as we were among the first to reach the *Carpathia*.) I saw none of the famous people as I was too busy looking after my wife and baby to see anyone.

The most exciting and perilous moment we had was at the time the lifeboat was being lowered. We thought that at any moment we would all be spilled out (two boat loads of women and children were lost that way.) Boat number 15 came down on top of us while we were trying to loose the 'block and tackle' and we thought we would be crushed.

There was no officer in our boat, which numbered about fifty women and children and fifteen men, so we elected a 'stoker' to be in command of the boat. We were about half a mile from the *Titanic* when she sank and I will never forget the shrieks of those people in the water. We supposed at the time that there were 40 or 50, never dreaming that over 1,600 would lose their lives that night.

The sea was as calm as a lake, which was nothing less than a miracle.

The baby slept through it all and is none the worse for this experience. He was pulled up in a sack onto the *Carpathia*.

Mrs Caldwell and the baby slept in a corner on the floor of the dining saloon of the *Carpathia* but we were all thankful to have any place at all to sleep.

I attribute the wreck to nothing but carelessness.

We all thought the boat non-sinkable and I believe that the poor fellows who were lost had hope to the last that she would not sink for many hours.

I think that the real heroes were the officers who stayed at their posts, knowing that the boat would soon sink, and the sailors who helped others into the boats and let them down one by one, never thinking of taking a place themselves which they could have so easily done, and yet realising all the time that their only means of escape was the lifeboats which were leaving without them.

It was an awful experience and one that I can never forget, but I am so thankful to God that we were one of the very few families who were saved together.

We are all well with the exception that Mrs Caldwell is still suffering from the nervous shock, but we are grateful and happy here with our loved ones.

We will go to Colorado Springs next week for a visit with Mrs Caldwell's mother and sisters. I expect to be at Park the last of this week and stay over Sunday.

Yours sincerely,

Albert Caldwell, '09[152]

SYLVIA CALDWELL **Second Class Passenger**

In the weeks following the disaster, Sylvia Caldwell wrote the following tribute to the women who sailed on the *Titanic*:

I have been sitting in the dusk, rocking to sleep the precious young life that was spared to me from the last great disaster and my heart goes out to the heart broken mothers whose babies have been snatched from their arms. Babes? Yes and husbands, breadwinners for the little ones. It brings tears to the eyes of you, who can comprehend in a tiny degree the sorrow and suffering of the broken circles. How much more are our hearts weighed down, who witnessed the direful scene.

I am not a writer, far from it. But I thought it was due the world of women to set forth some of the incidents of the fortitude and bravery of their sisters.

There was no screaming, hysteria or violent sobbing. Here and there were little groups chatting, little knowing that at that moment the great vessel was gradually sinking.

When the women were ordered to enter the lifeboats, they quietly did as they were bid. I speak of English-speaking women, eliminating all the foreign element. Some stayed back to leave with their husbands or to die with them, if need be.

The huge, almost defying work of man had dived to its grave. There was no sound but the dip of the oars in the water. When suddenly there arose upon the stillness, the weirdest, most appalling, heart rending noise that ever mortal might hear – the cry of hundreds of human souls for help. Pity them who could not be saved; aye and pity those who heard them and could not save them. Some man said the cries were people singing; but who could be deceived? Another said, 'Start a song.' A poor woman in a weak and trembling voice sang thru one verse of a hymn. Was that bravery? Yes. In her effort to comfort and keep from our ears those pitiful cries, she offered her a mite of cheer.

Can you picture the scene? In the middle of the Atlantic ocean, in the darkness of the night, out in that mighty deep, in a boat that a wave could crush; one woman's voice going up in song while the poor quavering voice was almost drowned by the voice of the perishing. In another boat sat a mother with her eight year old daughter by her side. There was a great deal of confusion and jumping into the life boats by the men who were steerage passengers. This greatly endangered the lives of the women and children already in the boats. 'Stop it or I'll fire,' shouted the officer. His threat was of no avail. The officer shot and the dear little child walked up, touched his sleeve and said, 'Oh mister officer please don't shoot again.' And he didn't. She in her simple plea probably saved a life. The officer told me later that he would never forget that little plea.

The same little girl, her name is Marjorie [Collyer], leaned over to her mother and said, 'Mother, do you think daddy is alright? Do you think he is safe in a boat?' And the mother answered, 'I don't know, darling, but I hope so.'

'Mother,' said Marjorie, 'do you think that if I would pray to Jesus it would help daddy?' And the trembling lips of the mother said, 'Yes, dear, I am sure it would.' She put up her dear little hands and asked God to save her daddy. Her prayer was not answered on earth, but I feel sure that she will find her father saved in that bright Beyond. A great many of my incidents centre around this mother and her child, for I learned to know and love them well.

Never was dawn more welcome, and as we neared the rescuing ship our stoker oarsman broke into song, 'Pull for the shore, sailors, pull for the shore.' Tears rolled down the faces of men and women alike, tears of joy mingled with tears of sorrow.

A tired crew waited to help us up the side of the ship. They had been up all night waiting for us, and their watch was rewarded. The sea was beginning to get rough and our boat seemed longing to leave the side of the ship. Helpless infants, mine among them, were pulled up in a sack, but women were as brave as men as they mounted the rope ladders, the mighty ocean lapping ominously beneath them. I, chilled to the bone, my teeth chattering as I tried to talk, turned to the two men who had helped me into the ship and said, 'Oh thank you.'

'Don't stop for that, we are only too happy to be here to do it,' was the answer, and with that I was carried to the dining room and given brandy and hot coffee.

The dining room. Yes. That brings back a sorry sight. Sitting all around the table were women, wild eyed and haggard, silently weeping. Most of them were clad in their night apparel, hair streaming down their backs. A lifeboat would come up and the eager, half frozen wives and mothers stood and scanned the faces of those entering; another boat and those poor, wild eyes, never tiring, searched in vain. One foreign woman was crying, 'Baby, baby, baby.' Aside from that, there was no noise save the silent sobbing which was a Godsend to many.

Few women had any money and the few who did had but little. Nevertheless, I saw women who had but five dollars themselves, all they owned in the world, going around and buying for those who had not a cent.

We had been up all night in the life boats, and the next night women with their babies went to bed on the floor, with a blanket for a mattress. Here many of us slept for three nights and in the mornings were compelled, because of breakfast, to arise at five thirty. Always I saw the tired, heavy hearted rise, most of them with a smile.

The mother of little Marjorie, as we called her, told the child, with tears in her eyes, that daddy was in heaven and the little girl, seeing her mother weeping, said, 'Never mind, mother dear, I am sure he will be waiting for us in New York.'

This dear child watched her mother and when she saw tears trickling down her face, she would say, 'Let me tell you a story, mother. What shall it be, about the robins or the bears?' And then she would tell the poor, brave, suffering mother a story the daddy had taught her.

Just a word about this broken family. They were comfortably settled in England. The mother was not strong and the husband decided that they would come to America and live among the mountains, where they had a friend. They sold their home and all and were coming to this country to make them a new home. They sat at our table in the dining room of the *Titanic* and here I knew them, a family unbroken. The husband is gone, the money saved through ten years of married life is gone and the widow with her fatherless child arrived in New York, penniless and in a strange country. 'I will go out West and work for my child,' she said. 'I think that that is what my husband would want me to do. If I go back to England, my relatives would take us but if I have my child to work for, then I have something to live for.'

I call that heroism. Yes, greater than that of the wife dying with her husband. She saved herself and was willing to live and suffer for the sake of her child. How much easier it would have been to have died in his arms. She said, 'I cannot think of life without him, but if he could speak I know he would be pleased to know I have stayed with Marjorie.' I was proud to welcome such a heroine to my country. This bereaved woman would go about comforting others and then come back saying, 'How much I have to be thankful for. I feel it when I see so many worse off than I.' In her great trouble, she still could think of others. Her attitude was Christ-like.

Women passengers on the *Carpathia* gave away all the clothing they could spare and more too. One young lady tore up her flannelette night dresses to provide for the needs of the babies. She would give soap here, hair pins there and find the mother with the suckling child and to her she would give fruit and milk. The hearts of humanity were opened. God was working in a mysterious way.

A few hours after we were taken on the *Carpathia* I was sitting, holding my child, when one of the *Titanic* stewards came up, picked up my baby and held him close. He did not say a word but the tears came to his eyes. He put my babe in his arms, sat down by my side and said, 'I have a son at home just the age of this little fellow, and I never saw two babies more alike.' What a comfort a dear cuddling babe is.

The rumour started that another ship had picked up seventy men and then hope arose in the hearts of all. Women who had lost their husbands longed for the arrival in New York where they would, they prayed, have word awaiting them. We were given our telegrams as the ship was entering the harbour, and as the names of some were called they rushed eagerly forward, hoping, yes sure, that it was a message from their lost. I can see a woman now, as her name was called, press her hands together and raise her hands to heaven and say, 'My God' in a tone as though already she was giving thanks that her husband had been saved. It was but another disappointment.

Most of the women were coming to America for the first time. Huddled together in the corners on the floor and on the dining room chairs, I could hear a great deal of their conversation. One afternoon (I think I was never so proud that I was an American as then) one said, 'I have nothing in the world and I have no place to go since my husband is lost. But I am not afraid. I have always heard that the Americans were the kindest people in the world.' This remark made me sit up a few inches straighter. Another lady said to me, 'Now I am not saying this because you are an American; but somehow I feel as if I were going to friends. I have never been to America but I would rather it was America I was going to in this condition than any other country in the world.' One lady said to another who was wondering what would become of her, 'Never mind, I never saw an American who didn't have a big heart. I am sure they will take good care of us.' And the one who said this had never before crossed the Atlantic.

These are a few of many similar remarks I heard. Why should I not be proud of my country. And before I draw this to a close, I wish to say that I was not disappointed in my countrymen. The best of everything was provided to us. We were all clad in new and pretty clothing. My baby who only had a nightie and a coat made out of a steamer rug, was given a complete outfit. In hotels, on trains and everywhere donations were made. I am sure no survivor is now penniless.

An amusing but pitiful incident occurred when the officers came on the steamer when we first arrived in New York. We all had tried to fix up as best we could. I had the little coat made of the steamer rug on my baby and a dirty blanket over his head.

Poor darling, he looked like a little Italian immigrant. I had a few things tied up in a coloured shawl, and with this in my hand I looked as though I might well be the mother of an Italian baby. Two steamship inspectors came into the second cabin dining room, looked around, scowled and said, 'Is this steerage?' I laughed as best I could, it was so hard to laugh, and said, 'I don't blame you for asking that.'

You will be interested to know that I read in a paper that Marjorie and her mother were offered a home in California. I am sure all their wants were supplied and comfort and sympathy for the aching heart was not lacking in the Americans of New York, even though strangers.

I have never seen such self-possessed women. I have never seen such unselfishness among women. I have never seen such bravery among women.

You, oh sorrowing women of the disaster, have caused the name of women to be raised to a higher pedestal.

You, oh ministering women, who have so bountifully and tenderly cared for the suffering, I say may God in His richest fullness bless you.[153]

LUCILE CARTER **First Class Passenger**

On 24 May 1912 Lucile Carter wrote the following letter to survivor Bruce Ismay, chairman of the White Star Line:

May 24th
Gwenda
Bryn Mawr
Pennsylvania

Dear Mr Ismay,

I want to write to you how glad I am that you are home safely, and also how pleased we were to read of the great ovation you had in England when you landed for no one realised more than Billy and I did how much you had been through, and how wonderful you were through it all. The notoriety we all got, and the dreadful things our own press is allowed to say in this country is certainly revolting, and makes us sometimes ashamed that we live here, but fortunately when they go to extremes, it is quickly over, and how completely it has died out, and no one even mentions it, and they are now criticising something else. I am enclosing a letter to you which Billy received in behalf our chauffeur's widow (Mrs Aldworth) he was with us. Would you send her name into the fund, it seems ridiculous to bother you about such a trifle, but I really don't exactly know how to keep her here, there was quite a sum raised at our home, Rotherty Leicester because the chauffeur was the only one lost from there. I hope you are well and that your nerves haven't suffered. We are all quite well. I send you many kind wishes, and I hope to see you next winter when we go to Melton to hunt.

Sincerely yours,

Lucile Carter

Mrs Thayer is very well, and the boy splendid, you will be pleased to hear.[154]

ELEANOR CASSEBEER **First Class Passenger**

On 7 May Mrs Cassebeer issued the following statement for publication in her home town newspaper:

In the first place I wish to absolutely deny the report which appeared in a morning paper that I had given out for publication any story of the happenings on the *Titanic*. The story as it appeared this morning was absolutely false. There was no champagne in evidence on the *Titanic* nor was there any sign of drunkenness on the part of any of the officers. The story this morning also quotes me as saying that the discipline on board was not what could be expected is a lie. The discipline on board the *Titanic* was perfect. Everything was done in perfect order and the crew worked like a company of soldiers in preparing and launching the lifeboats. There was no 'spirit of recklessness predominant.' I never made a statement blaming Officer Murdoch for not being on the bridge.

My being aboard the *Titanic* was merely a matter of chance. I was visiting in Paris and being desirous of coming to America, I took the first available steamer, which, as luck would have it, happened to be the *Titanic*.

I have travelled considerably and this was the 10th time that I have crossed the Atlantic Ocean. My cabin was situated on D deck on the starboard side of the boat, and I felt the full impact of the iceberg when we struck it.

I was reclining on a couch in my room at the time and I had summoned a stewardess to inquire if it would be safe for me to allow the electric grate to burn throughout the night. She assured me that it would and immediately after she had left my cabin the shock of the cabin came. It sounded as if something were grinding and tearing away the very entrails of the monster liner. I knew immediately that there was something radically wrong and slipping on a kimono and slippers, I hurried on deck where I met Harry Anderson, a fellow passenger, and together we made our way to the bow of the boat where we found a litter of small particles of ice which was torn from the iceberg by force of the impact. We could see the berg towering some 75 to 100 feet out of the sea, and, as I afterwards learned only one-fifth of the iceberg shows above the water you can imagine the enormous size of that mountain of ice. Here we also met Thomas Andrews, who I understand was the designer of the *Titanic*. In answer to many questions he assured everybody that we were absolutely safe and that the *Titanic* was absolutely unsinkable. He said that she could break in three separate and distinct parts and that each part would stay afloat indefinitely.

It was not long after this, however, that the pursers started to go among the passengers ordering them to go below and put on warm clothing and be prepared to embark in the lifeboats. I hurried below and dressed and when I came on deck again I found that the deck had started to list in a very alarming manner. I had already donned a life preserver which I found with some difficulty, and when I reached the deck I met Mr Andrews again and he took me by the arm and led me to the lifeboat.

I could not hear just what he said to me at the time on account of the din, but I saw him motion to me to get into the boat, which was about to be swung over the rail 90 feet above the water. I asked him why he did not get in also, and he said: 'No, women and children first.'

Right here I wish to say that Bruce Ismay was there also, helping to load the women and children into the boat. He was dressed in pajamas in slippers with a coat thrown over his shoulders and as the boat I was in the sixth to leave the ship you can see that reports that he was in one of the first boats are absolutely false.

There was absolutely no panic. The discipline was excellent. I was in the boat commanded by Third Officer H.J. Pitman. There were 37 people in the boat, five of them being seamen. The boat could not hold any more at the time, as it would have been foolhardy to attempt to overload it, inasmuch as it would have buckled and broken in two from the extra weight the moment it was swung from the davits.

We saw the *Titanic* when it made its final plunge. The lights were burning until the very last moment and it was a spectacular as well as awesome sight. After the *Titanic* had sunk there were thousands of people struggling in the water crying piteously for help. Three times Officer Pitman ordered his men to turn about so that he could pick up some of them, but each time they were prevented from doing so by some of the passengers in the lifeboat who called upon the seamen frantically to go ahead and when they grasped the oars and interfered with the proper handling of the boat so that the seamen were finally forced to give up their efforts of turning back to rescue any of the unfortunates.

We were all wrapped warmly in rugs which the stewards and pursers had pinned about our waists before we got into the boat. When we were picked up by the *Carpathia* we were treated beautifully by both officers and the passengers. Many of whom gave up their quarters for our accommodation.

Aboard the *Titanic* I sat at the same table with Dr O'Loughlin, the ship's surgeon and Thomas Andrews of the Holland and Wolf [*sic*] Building Company, I believe the name of the firm is. Mr Andrews is said to have designed the *Titanic*. Harry Anderson was also a member of our party.

When the boat first started to list so alarmingly I immediately started to make my way to where the men were assembled because I knew that there I would assuredly be safe. I am a staunch admirer in American and British manhood.

A fact that is not generally known is that it was very hard for the men to coax the women into the lifeboats and it became necessary for some of them men to get into the lifeboats first before the women would venture into them, so confident were they that the big steamship was absolutely unsinkable. Then again some of the women absolutely refused to leave their husband's sides and it almost became necessary for Mr Ismay and Mr Andrews to use force in making some of the men get into the boats with the womenfolk so that they might be saved.

Another thing that is not generally known is that the *Titanic* was not ready to sail at the time she did. Mr Andrews told me himself and said that the only reason they allowed her to go when they did was that the sailing date had already been fixed and they just simply had to start. While the ship was fitted up most sumptuously once could not help but notice that she was not prepared to sail.

There were none of the usual printed notices in the cabins. The frames for them were on the walls, but the notices themselves were not there and when I tried to find a life preserver I did not know where to look for it and was compelled to inquire of some stewards who showed me where to find it.

While I knew matters were very serious I did not realise just how badly we were off until I came up on deck the last time and stumbled over the ropes with which they were preparing to lower the lifeboats. My boat was the third to leave the starboard side and the sixth to leave the ship.[155]

NORMAN CHAMBERS — First Class Passenger

In October 1912 Mr Chambers wrote the following account for his college alumni newspaper:

Little did we think when we reached Southampton the Saturday before the monster *Titanic* was to make her maiden trip, that we should be on her: still less did we realise as we steamed into Southampton harbour on the *Aragon*, a relatively little, but comfortable ship in every way, and on some seas a large one, that the gigantic *Titanic* which towered above everything in sight, would, in a brief eight days, have disappeared from the face of the sea forever. On boarding this great ship the keynote of the subsequent disaster was apparent at once: she could not sink; it was utterly impossible for this steamer with her five passenger decks, which made elevators not a comfort but a necessity; with a promenade deck which was so long that one really did not care how long it was; with her splendid equipment and just from the builders – she could not sink!

Even the evil omen of our breaking the hawsers of the *New York* as we were leaving port seemed helpless in the face of this great ship. Here also one of the causes of the disaster became at once apparent. The crew were inexperienced with the ship. No one knew where anything was. Discipline existed to a degree, but of organisation there were the barest rudiments only, and this held throughout the entire time she continued to float after the accident Sunday night.

Up to the time of our leaving the ship, never was there the slightest evidence of fear on the part of any of the men, either passengers or crew; and it is said that up to the last, orders were given and obeyed in a soldierly manner.

We had just retired before the accident and I was reading when the shock came. It was so slight, as if we had run into floating timber, that I should not have been disturbed about it at all, even tho the shock was immediately followed by a jangling as that of chains being dragged along the side of the ship. As our engines stopped immediately, I assumed that an accident had occurred to our starboard propeller, and would have continued reading, had not my wife, who was awakened by the shock, became frightened and insisted on getting up. Leaving her dressing, I slipped on my clothes and an overcoat, and went up on the A-deck to investigate. On going out on the promenade deck I found nothing visible, but the air was extremely cold. I then returned to the stateroom, passing on the way at each deck groups of passengers not at all frightened, but rather merely interested in what had occurred – even one man who laughingly exhibited a piece of ice which had come thru the porthole of his stateroom.

My wife and I then returned to the A-deck, which was the uppermost berth deck and also the promenade, and made a thorough circuit in search of information. On looking over the side I could not find any lights which had been lowered to determine the extent of the damage above the waterline. The only sound audible (our engines having been stopped for some time) was that of exhausting steam; this appeared to be coming from the bow of the ship and gave the idea that we had become imbedded in an iceberg and were thawing our way out.

Upon finding nothing after a thorough search, we were about to go below again and retire, when I noticed that the ship had a slight list to starboard in place of the list to port which had prevailed all day, while the ship seemed to be down by the head just sufficiently to bring the forward part of the deck level with mid-ships.

When we reached the E-deck again and started for our stateroom, we noticed that at the forward end of the alley-way there was a small group of uniformed men with a few passengers. It was here that the companion led to the next deck where the mail clerks were quartered, and then another companion led to the deck below where the trunk-room was situated on the other side of the forward bulkhead. On joining this group at the head of the companion, we found that it included two mail clerks who were wet to the knees, and had a pouch of registered mail on each side of them. They said they had gotten away just in time to save a small part of the registered mail.

On looking down the companion we saw that the trunk-room two decks below was filled with water to within eighteen inches or two feet of the deck above, and on this water were floating innumerable letters. The fact of the water being so near caused us no alarm as a bulkhead intervened at the existing level of the water, and we assumed that the ship was undamaged aft of the bulkhead.

While we stood there joking about the accident, three of the ship's officers, whose rating and department I did not distinguish, passed down the first companion, and looked carefully in the baggage-room; returning upward again, one of them, in a tone of voice which we could all hear, said: 'She is not gaining on us.'

We then returned to our stateroom to dress more fully as, in spite of appearances, we had decided to remain up the rest of the night. On our way to the stateroom our steward passed us and said: 'Everything is all right now, sir, you may turn in.' While I was finishing dressing, my wife went into the alleyway again to obtain the latest news, and came rushing back saying that orders had been given to put on lifebelts and go on the boat deck. I immediately ran out and found our steward, who verified this order.

We started for the upper deck and coming out on the port side of the A-deck, went aft where I found the deck steward, who opened his office and gave us our steamer rugs. We then ascended to the boat deck by the outside port companion and found no passengers on this side of the ship, although the crew were busy clearing away the forward group of lifeboats. At this time it was utterly impossible to hear any spoken word as the sound of exhausting steam which had appeared to us to be coming from the bow of the ship, was in reality from the forward exhaust pipe, and was well-nigh deafening.

Thinking that perhaps the lifeboats would lower more easily from the starboard side, to which the ship was now listing more noticeably, we passed over the raised central deck and down on the starboard side. Here we found a number of passengers assembled and, joining them, stood and waited for orders.

There was no confusion noticeable, even on the part of the passengers. Such of us as were standing there were shouting jokes in each other's ears and borrowing matches, waiting. We noticed a line of men who appeared to have come from the bakery, going up the deck toward the lifeboats, with white, wooden cases on their shoulders; this seemed quite natural to us and we assumed that they were carrying provisions. Apparently no trace has since been found of any provisions in any of the lifeboats, the majority of which were also equipped with water breakers, which, however, were empty.

By that time more passengers began coming out of the deck house and we decided to go forward where the lifeboats were and see what was being done.

On trying to pass the deck house entrance from which the passengers were now appearing, we were instructed by a steward stationed there to go aft. Instead of doing this we stayed behind the vestibule of the entrance and waited until the passengers ceased coming. When we went forward to the lifeboats, there appeared to be few passengers left, although the men were coiling up ropes from the falls, and the first boat in our line of vision, the after one of the forward group, was swung away from the side of the ship. It had passengers in it and appeared to be crowded, and I should not have entered it but my wife insisted that she was going and jumped in, calling me to follow. Knowing that she would not remain if I did not go also, I finally joined her and was followed by two more men who had come to join their wives at the last minute, as there appeared to be no more women in sight. Just then a tall, young officer ordered another in our boat to take charge of the boats on the starboard side, telling him to hold onto the painter when we were in the water and to pull up alongside the gangway. This in itself was a very peculiar order, as I was certain that none of the doors in the ship's side had been opened and had seen no activities in that direction.

They lowered away very calmly in union, so that we descended with the boat level. Shortly before reaching the water it occurred to someone to enquire regarding the plug, and several people shouted; the mate finally blew his whistle, calling up for them to stop lowering, that we wished to see if the plug were in, and received a cheering reply from someone on the upper deck: 'It is your own blooming business to see that the plug is in.'

When we were finally in the water, the passengers were so tightly packed in a standing position that the little quartermaster had great difficulty in crawling between our legs to reach the trigger amidships for releasing the falls simultaneously.

We then put out a few straggling oars and, no gangway being visible, dropped our painter; and Mr Pitman, finally giving in to the insistence of the majority of the passengers, who were shouting to pull away from the ship, rowed off 300 or 400 yards where we took in our oars and waited, very shortly picking up another boat which was not so heavily loaded as our own, and to which we remained lashed during the night. On taking count we found that there were in the neighbourhood of thirty-eight passengers in our boat, while the other had but some thirty, so that we transferred three of our people into the emptier boat, as it happened, reuniting a family.

We lay in this position for some time without anything noteworthy occurring. There were practically no sounds from the steamer, the water was nearly dead calm, and she merely continued to go down by the head, slowly but surely.

After a long interval the rockets suddenly arose from the ship; it appeared to me that they put off two forward and two aft.

Then only did the realisation come to us that the ship was doomed. Up to that moment we had thought that our leaving the ship was a mere precaution which the Captain considered advisable to take, and that we should return for breakfast in the morning.

In what must actually have been a very short time after the rockets had been sent up, although it appeared to us interminable, a series of explosions commenced; these were dull booms, one following the other in rapid succession, accompanied by the slow sinking of the ship by the head. She continued to go down until she was practically in a vertical position, when the explosions ceased for a brief instant. They then became more frequent than before, and the *Titanic* sank out of sight.

Immediately the ship sank, there arose from the spot where she had last been see loud cries of such power and volume as to make it appear incredible that they came from people floating in the water. Most of us landsmen thought the cries came from the steerage passengers who were on the life-rafts and wished to be taken into the boats; we never for a moment doubted that the ship had more than sufficient accommodation for all on board.

Such of the crew as were in our boat, as well as Mr Pitman, the third officer, were very insistent that we return and pick up such people as might be in the water; they apparently realised the true state of affairs, but this the passengers would not permit, and the officer, again giving in to the consensus of opinion, ordered his men to take in their oars, which they had started to put out, and stand by.

The shouting continued for about an hour from the time the ship sank, until all was quiet again.

Our boats were entirely unprovided with lights and, in fact, the only light visible from time to time was that of some coloured lights burned in a boat lying nearby, but not close enough for us to see her outlines.

The night was calm with no wind, and an oily swell; and to those of us who were properly clothed, not excessively cold.

After the *Titanic* sank, we realised that it was a question of waiting, and all made themselves as comfortable as possible.

Up to the time of the sinking, most of the men had been standing up, the women sitting on the benches around the edge of the boat. Later, when we had arranged ourselves as best we could, we were, with the exception of some three or four men, comfortably seated, but crowded.

It is worthy of note that there were but thirty-five of us in a lifeboat which the Board of Trade registers as having a capacity of sixty people, and we were crowded, the boat being just manageable!

During the long wait that followed there were many rumours of lights on the horizon, and as far as we could see they were false. Our seamen and the officers did not at any time admit the possibility of these lights being real. We lay there quietly waiting. Finally, shortly before the light of dawn began to show in the west, we thought we saw a light, then two lights, and finally after a longer wait the port lights of a steamer! By this time it was light and we could see this welcome ship coming towards us. While she was yet a long distance off, she stopped. We separated from the boat which had been our companion through the night, and both of us put out our oars and started to row for the rescue ship.

With the coming of the dawn we could see that only a miracle would have saved the *Titanic*. In every direction were icebergs! The majority of them, it is true, appeared small, but nevertheless they were icebergs, and many of them. Also, as it became light, the morning breeze sprang up bitterly cold and added to the discomforts of the many who were insufficiently clothed.

After about an hour's rowing we had reached the vicinity of the ship and found that a number of boats had already come alongside and been emptied of their freight. One boat had been cast adrift and was floating astern of the *Carpathia*. The *Carpathia*, as we then found her to be, had stopped some distance from an iceberg toward which she kept drifting, for, as we came alongside, she was compelled to turn over her propellers several times to get a safer distance from the berg.

All available doors in the side of the ship were open, and ladders were hanging from them to the water line. We pulled alongside, as directed, and the women were sent up the side with a rope under their arms and climbed as best they could.

Small children were pulled up the side in coal bags.

On reaching the deck of the *Carpathia* the relief from the feeling of being saved was increased by the comfortable sensation of being where every possible care would be given. As the survivors came aboard, one man, stationed at the head of a ladder, quickly removed the life preservers; another was provided with a pile of steerage blankets for those who needed them, and round whose shoulders they were instantly thrown; while a third relay of stewards almost thrust us into the saloon where, once seated, brandy and coffee were forced upon us.

At the time of our arrival the saloon presented a sight which is best left undescribed. There were women of every rank and many countries, and some few men. The majority of the women were weeping and in hysterics, while the men appeared dazed.

I hastened from the saloon as quickly as possible, to join my wife who had left the lifeboat among the first of the women, and there from the deck watched the arrival of the remaining boats. We saw one collapsible come alongside in perfect condition, thoroughly dry and containing a pitiful handful of women, with, perhaps three men; a group, which hardly sufficed to cover the centre part of the space. In all the boats which came alongside, there was a predominance of women. Some boats appeared to have no men at all.

Finally a short distance off we noticed a pretty sight. One of the lifeboats, as we later learned, under command of the second officer, Mr Lightoller, had stepped her mast and was coming up under sail, towing behind a collapsible lifeboat fully loaded. This, after the terrible tragedy which we could then, as yet, but faintly appreciate, came like a refreshing draft, creating a great desire to cheer for the Anglo-Saxon coolness and determination of one of the heroes of that terrible night.

At last there were no more boats in sight.

The crew of the *Carpathia*, who had swung the ship's own boats in on their chocks, lowered the falls and picked up as many of the *Titanic*'s boats as there was space for; more were taken on deck forward and aft until the deck space was filled.

Just then a ship appeared in the distance and slowly approached us; this we finally made out to be the *California* [*Californian*] with whom our captain conversed briefly by semaphore, which appeared strange, as both vessels were strung for wireless. We started ahead slowly, very slowly made a large circle, and then started on our return to New York, leaving the *California* moving slowly and looking for further survivors or wreckage. At the time there was a doubt as to the number of boats missing. While some said that all had been accounted for, it appeared best to console the widows with the statement that one boat was missing.

Of our treatment on the *Carpathia* I cannot speak too highly. The discipline was the usual perfect Cunard discipline, and this was backed up by warm hearts and willing hands. There was not the slightest thing which they could have done for our comfort which was not done almost before it was thought of. Arrangements were made for the accommodation of the different classes of passengers with their respective classes on the *Carpathia*. All the ladies in the first cabin were provided with a place to sleep, although a great many preferred not to be in a stateroom. The men turned in where they could find a place.

The passengers of the *Carpathia* fell into the spirit of the occasion and many gave up their staterooms and doubled up with others, in order to provide sufficient accommodations for the survivors. Had it not been for the terrible tragedy which occurred, the reality of which was brought closer to us every moment by the many widows, some of the sights would have been amusing. Some women spent the night in the smoking room up forward, and as many men as could fit in there; in this room were three tables with sofas on three sides. In the morning it was quite usual to find a man asleep on each of the lateral sofas, two men on the cross portion and a man on the table. The last was usually of such height that his feet hung over onto the stomach of the man sleeping on the lateral. Another man would be sleeping under the table. This position was often occupied by Karl Behr, who escaped on the same boat with us.

The trip into New York was a quiet one, but seemed interminable. We were, of course, crowded for space, and the stewards of the *Carpathia* obtained very little sleep, as they were up day and night, even though assisted by such of the *Titanic*'s stewards as survived the disaster. As far as the survivors knew, we were out of wireless communication with the shore most of the time, and we did not know whether those on shore knew who had survived and who had gone down. While we all had a more or less strong realisation of the magnitude of the catastrophe and an accurate knowledge of the number of lives lost, it had not come home to us as strongly as to those on shore, and we were astounded to learn of the effect the disaster had had on the general public in the country.[156]

JOSEPH CHAPMAN — Crew (Boots Steward)

In September 1912 Mr Chapman wrote the following letter to fellow survivor Kate Buss Willis:

On board RMS *Olympic*
Sept. 26th, 1912, New York

Dear Miss Willis,

Thanks for kind letter which I received last time home. I was very pleased to hear from you, you are the only person I have heard anything about since that awful calamity and I have often wondered what became of the survivors and to what parts of the world they scattered. Well I am pleased to be able to tell you some of my experiences since we parted. When we were landed at New York we were sent to the s/s *Lapland* and sent home on Saturday we had a pleasant voyage under the circumstances and landed at Plymouth then we were detained for 2 days by the government for witnesses for the inquiry into the affair, then we were allowed to go home and the scenes at Southampton when we met were heartrending. I heard my wife had been seriously ill but thank goodness she was able to meet me the children luckily were too young to understand the only thing they missed was my box in which I was in the habit of taking them some toys & they could not understand why I did not bring it home that time. Shortly after I was sent to London as witness & I was up there for 2 weeks. After that I went back to the *Olympic* where I have been ever since but she is always having accidents every trip something happens. We are now running with one broken propeller & a damaged one, only yesterday in a storm a large wave broke 3 ports in the saloon just as we were going to lunch and washed the saloon clean out and raced down to two decks below. I am afraid she will have a serious accident some day but I am not nervous as we are laying up for 6 months when we get back for her to have a new shell inside which will cost a quarter million pounds. I am pleased to say everything is going quite well at home now. The company has not paid any compensation to the crew as they say we are not entitled to it so before we could come away again we had to get another complete outfit which was rather expensive but never mind all's well that ends well I have been trying to call you to mind but up to the present I have not been able to but if ever I should see you again I think I should remember you. I hope & trust you are quite well and will never have such another experience again once in a lifetime is quite sufficient.

With best wishes
I Remain
Yours Sincerely
J. Chapman

[*Handwritten note by Mrs Willis*] Unless I made an error this was a member of the crew who lent me a coat on lifeboat 2 to whom I mailed a little money after landing in New York.[157]

GLADYS CHERRY **First Class Passenger**

Miss Cherry wrote at least two letters after arriving in New York. The first was to an unknown recipient:

19th April, 1912.

At last we are here safe and sound; now that it is all over one feels full of gratitude and thankfulness for the deliverance from the dangers we have been brought through.

... It all seems like an ugly dream ... We got into the dock last night at 9.30, after a dreadful time coming up the river, with all the newspaper tugs that wanted to put Pressmen on board, but of course, our captain would allow no one on board but the Pilot.

All these people meeting the boat stood under their names, all the officials standing in lines to keep back the crowds; motors by the million were waiting.

The reports about the condition of the passengers that had got about were terrible, it was quite upsetting.

Friday, April 19, 1912 – 1:15
New York

I am here with Charlie and am all right – am resting I am so tired. Thank God I am here![158]

Miss Cherry's second letter was to Tom Jones, the *Titanic* crewman who had taken charge of her lifeboat during the sinking:

Great Northern Hotel
New York

I feel I must write you and tell you how splendidly you took charge of our boat on the fatal night. There were only four English people in it – my cousin, Lady Rothes, her maid, you, and myself, and I think you were wonderful.

The dreadful regret I shall always have, and I know you share with me, is that we ought to have gone back to see whom we could pick up. But if you remember, there was only an American lady, my cousin, self, and you who wanted to return. I could not hear the discussion very clearly, as I was at the tiller, but everyone forward and the three men refused. But I shall always remember your words: 'Ladies, if any of us are saved, remember I wanted to go back. I would rather drown with them than leave them.' You did all you could, and being my own countryman I wanted to tell you this.

Yours very truly,
Gladys Cherry[159]

SIDNEY COLLETT **Second Class Passenger**

Mr Collett wrote the following letter to a church newspaper regarding Revd John Harper, who lost his life on the *Titanic*:

Lost? No, never! for death to him was simply the entrance into the gateway of life. Our loss! Yes, indeed! But his eternal gain.

Just briefly and simply, I desire to relate just how our beloved friend in Christ spent some of the last hours on earth.

On Sunday morning at Divine Service, I thought I recognised him, the face being so familiar, and assuring myself of our meeting somewhere I made myself known to him, he remembering me as an evangelist of The Evangelization Society, London.

One in faith, hope and doctrine, our interest deepened and acquaintance was renewed. He gave me his card, then requested me to return it for him to write the name of his church upon it. We enjoyed a real time of fellowship together. I read to him the story of Colgate giving his tithe to God's work as related by the late Dr A.T. Pierson. Then having just finished reading his autobiography, I left the book upon his deck chair with a booklet entitled 'One of God's Choicest Ones,' little thinking that in a short time he would be one among the many choicest in being translated. During the morning, word was sent down to our now departed friend to say, 'Photographs are being taken, will you join us?' The reply was to the effect, 'Sorry, unable, it is the Lord's day.'

He was a man of principle. Later on in the afternoon while walking with a friend on deck, I stopped just near Mr Harper, and if ever a young man received a Gospel talk my friend did – a Gospel address, quite informal, with a lad on deck at sea, after Christ's style of preaching. On deciding that we would have a service of hymn singing, I went down to our dear one's cabin to invite him to attend, but he had retired to rest early. Soon after the accident, I saw him on deck. It was the last I saw of him, calm in spirit, with a firm trust in God.

Only asleep and yet to wake
On that bright morning fair,
Together to be just caught up
To meet Him in the air.[160]

CHARLOTTE COLLYER **Second Class Passenger**

On 21 April Mrs Collyer wrote the following letter to her mother:

Sun April 21st

My dear dear Mother & all,

I don't know how to write to you or what to say I feel I should go mad sometimes, but dear, as much as my heart aches it aches for you too for he is your son and the best that ever lived. I had not given up hope till today that he might be found, but I am told all boats are accounted for. Oh mother, how can I live without him. I wish I had gone with him. If they had not wrenched Madge from me I should have stayed and gone with him, but they threw her into a boat and pulled me in, too, but he was so calm and I know he would rather I lived for her little sake, otherwise she would have been an orphan. The agony of that night can never be told. Poor mite

> was frozen. I have been ill but have been taken care of by a rich New York Doctor and feel better now. They are giving us every comfort and have collected quite a few pounds for us and loaded us with clothes, and a gentleman on Monday is taking us to the White Star office and also to another office to get us some more from the Fund that is being raised here. Oh mother, there are some good kind hearts in New York. Some want me to go back to England, but I can't. I could never, at least not yet, go over the ground where my all is sleeping. Sometimes I feel we lived too much for each other; that is why I've lost him, but mother, we shall meet him in heaven. When that band played Nearer My God to Thee I know he thought of you and me, for we both loved that Hymn and I feel that if I go to Payette I am doing what he would wish me to, so I hope to go West the end of next week where I shall have friends and work and I will work for his darling as long as she needs me. Oh, she is a comfort but she don't realise yet that her daddy is in heaven. There are some dear children here who have loaded her with lovely toys, but it's when I'm alone with her she will miss him. Oh mother, I haven't a thing in the world that was his, only his rings. Everything we had went down. Will you, dear mother, send me on a last Photo of us? Get it copied. I will pay you later on. Mrs Hallen's brother from Chicago is doing all he can for us; in fact, the night we landed in New York in our nightgowns he had engaged a room at a big hotel with food and every comfort waiting us. He has been a father to us. I will send his address on a card (Mr Horder). Perhaps you might like to write to him at some time. God bless you, dear mother, and help comfort you in this awful sorrow. Your loving child, Lot[161]

Shortly after the disaster, Mrs Collyer wrote the following account of her experiences on board the *Titanic*:

> Of the many shocking things that I remember in connection with the lost *Titanic*, there is one impression that will never leave me. It is the irony of the faith that I had in the big ship. 'She is unsinkable,' I had been told; 'she is the safest boat afloat.' I had never been on an ocean voyage, and I was afraid of the sea. But I listened to the people who said: 'Take the new *Titanic*. She can never come to any harm. New inventions have made her safe; and then, the officers will be extra careful on her first trip.' That sounded as if it must be true; and so Harvey, my husband, and our eight-year-old daughter, Marjorie, and I decided to go to America that way. Marjorie and I are here, safe; but we are alone. For my husband was drowned, and with the *Titanic* there went to the bottom of the Atlantic all that we had in the world.
>
> I must first tell how we came to leave England. We lived in Bishopstoke, a little village near Southampton, Hampshire. My husband kept a grocery store; in fact, although only thirty-five years old, he was the principal grocer in the village, and was liked by all the neighbours. He was clerk of the parish, by which I mean that he was that member of the church vestry who helped the vicar to keep his accounts, to fill out marriage licences, birth certificates, and so forth. He was also in charge of our chime of bells, which are more than one hundred years old, and are thought to be among the best in England.

Some friends had gone a few years before to the Payette Valley, in Idaho. They had bought a fruit farm, and had made a success of it. They wrote us wonderful accounts of the climate, and advised us to join them. We did not think that we would go; but last year my health began to get very poor – my lungs are weak – and in the end we made up our minds to sell our business, and to buy a farm in the same valley where our friends had settled. I can never forget that it was for my sake, and for the sake of Marjorie, that my dead husband decided to do this. He would have been better off in England.

The day before we were to sail, our neighbours in Bishopstoke made much of us. It seems as if there must have been hundreds who called to bid us good-bye; and in the afternoon the members of the church arranged a surprise for my husband. They led him to a seat under an old tree in the churchyard; then, some of them went up into the belfry, and in his honour they rang all the chimes that they knew. It took more than an hour, and he was very pleased. But, somehow, it made me a little sad. They gave the solemn old tunes, as well as the gay ones, and to me it was too much of a farewell ceremony. Why cannot people help those who are going away to forget that they are leaving behind the things that they hold dear? It is a question I often ask myself.

The next morning, we went to Southampton; and there my husband drew from the bank all his money, including the sum we had received for our store. It came to several thousand dollars in American money, and he took it all in bank notes. The clerk asked him if he did not want a draft; but he shook his head and put the notes in a wallet which he kept, to the end, in the inside breast pocket of his coat. We had already sent forward the few personal treasures that we had kept from our old home; so that, when we went on board the *Titanic*, our every earthly possession was with us.

We were travelling second cabin, and from our deck, which was situated well forward, we saw the great send-off that was given to the boat. I do not think there had ever been so large a crowd in Southampton, and I am not surprised that it should have come together. The *Titanic* was wonderful, far more splendid and huge than I had dreamed of. The other craft in the harbour were like cockle-shells beside here, and they, mind you, were the boats of the American and other lines that a few years ago were thought enormous. I remember a friend said to me, just before visitors were ordered ashore: 'Aren't you afraid to venture on the sea?' But now it was I who was confident. 'What, on this boat!' I answered. 'Even the worst storm couldn't harm her.' Before we left the harbour, I saw the accident to the *New York*, the liner that was dragged from her moorings and swept against us in the channel. It did not frighten anyone, as it only seemed to prove how powerful the *Titanic* was.

I don't remember very much about the first few days of the voyage. I was a bit sea-sick, and kept to my cabin most of the time. But on Sunday, April 14, I was up and about. At dinner-time I was at my place in the saloon, and enjoyed the meal, though I thought it too heavy and rich. No effort had been spared to serve even to the second cabin passengers on that Sunday the best dinner that money could buy. After I had eaten, I listened to the orchestra for a while; then, at perhaps nine o'clock, or half-past nine, I went to my cabin.

I had just climbed into my berth when a stewardess came in. She was a sweet woman, who had been very kind to me. I take this opportunity to thank her; for I shall never see her again. She went down with the *Titanic*.

'Do you know where we are?' she said pleasantly. 'We are in what is called The Devil's Hole.'

'What does that mean?' I asked.

'That it is a dangerous part of the Ocean,' she answered. 'Many accidents have happened near here. They say that icebergs drift down as far as this. It's getting to be very cold on deck, so perhaps there's ice around us now!'

She left the cabin, and I soon dropped off to sleep. Her talk about icebergs had not frightened me; but it shows that the crew were awake to the danger. As far as I can tell, we had not slackened our speed in the least.

It must have been a little after ten o'clock when my husband came in, and woke me up. He sat about and talked to me, for how long I do not know, before he began to make ready to go to bed.

And then, the crash!

The sensation, to me, was as if the ship had been seized by a giant hand and shaken once, twice; then stopped dead in its course. That is to say, there was a long backward jerk, followed by a shorter forward one. I was not thrown out of my berth, and my husband staggered on his feet only slightly. We heard no strange sounds, no rending of plates and woodwork; but we noticed that the engines had ceased running. They tried to restart the engines a few minutes later; but, after some coughing and rumbling, there was silence once more. Our cabin was so situated that we could follow this clearly.

My husband and I were not alarmed. He said that there must have been some slight accident in the engine room, and at first he did not intend to go on deck. Then he changed his mind, put on his coat and left me. I lay quietly in my berth with my little girl and almost fell asleep again.

In what seemed like a very few moments my husband returned. He was a bit excited then. 'What do you think?' he exclaimed. 'We have struck an iceberg, a big one; but there is no danger. An officer just told me so.'

I could hear the footsteps of people on the deck above my head. There was some stamping, and queer noises as if the ship's tackle was being pulled about.

'Are the people frightened?' I asked quietly.

'No,' he replied; 'I don't think the shock waked up many in the second cabin, and few of those in the saloons have troubled to go on deck. I saw five professional gamblers playing with some of the passengers, as I went by. Their cards had been jerked off the table when the boat struck; but they were gathering them up and had started their game again before I left the saloon.'

The story reassured me. If those people at their cards were not worried, why should I be? I think my husband would have retired to his berth without asking any more questions about the accident; but suddenly we heard hundreds of people running along the passage-way in front of our door. They did not cry out, but the pattering of their feet reminded me of rats scurrying through an empty room.

I could see my face in a mirror opposite, and it had grown very white. My husband, too, was pale, and he stammered when he spoke to me.

'We had better go on deck and see what's wrong,' he said.

I jumped out of bed and put over my night dress a dressing gown and then an ulster. My hair was down, but I hurriedly tied it back with a ribbon. By this time, although the boat had not made any progress, it seemed to have tilted forward a little. I caught up my daughter, Marjorie, just as she was, in her night gown, wrapped a White Star cabin blanket around her and started out of the door. My husband followed immediately behind. Neither of us took any of our belongings from the cabin, and I remember that he even left his watch lying on his pillow. We did not doubt instant that we would return.

When we reached the second-cabin promenade deck, we found a great many people there. Some officers were walking up and down and shouting: 'There is no danger, no danger whatever!' It was a clear starlight night, but very cold. There was not a ripple on the sea. A few of the passengers were standing by the rail and looking down, but I want to say that, at that time, no one was frightened.

My husband stepped over to an officer – it was either Fifth Officer Harold Lowe or First Officer Murdoch – and asked him a question. I heard him shout back:

'No, we have no searchlight, but we have a few rockets on board. Keep calm! There is no danger!'

Our party of three stood close together. I did not recognise any of the other faces about me, probably because of the excitement. I never went near the first-cabin promenade deck, so I did not see any of the prominent people on board.

Suddenly there was a commotion near one of the gangways, and we saw a stoker climbing up from below. He stopped a few feet away from us. All of the fingers of one hand had been cut off. Blood was running from the stumps, and blood was spattered over his face and over his clothes. The red marks showed very clearly against the coal dust with which he was covered.

I started over and spoke to him. I asked him if there was any danger.

'Dynger!' he screamed at the top of his voice. 'I should just sye so! It's 'ell down below. Look at me! This boat'll sink like a log in ten minutes.'

He staggered away and lay down, fainting, with his head on a coil of rope. And at that moment I got my first grip of fear – awful, sickening fear. That poor man, with his bleeding hand and his speckled face, brought up a picture of smashed engines and mangled human bodies. I hung onto my husband's arm, and although he was very brave and was not trembling, I saw that his face was as white as paper. We realised that the accident was much worse than we had supposed, but even then I, and all the others about me of whom I have any knowledge, did not believe that the *Titanic* could go down.

The officers now were running to and fro and shouting orders. I have no clear idea of what happened during the next quarter of an hour. The time seemed much shorter, but it must have been between ten and fifteen minutes. I saw First Officer Murdoch place guards by the gangways to prevent others like the wounded stoker from coming on deck. How many unhappy men were shut off in that way from their one chance of safety I do not know, but Mr Murdoch was probably right. He was a masterful man, astoundingly brave and cool. I had met him the day before, when he was inspecting the second cabin quarters and thought him a bull-dog of a man who would not be afraid of anything. This proved to be true; he kept order to the last, and died at his post. They say he shot himself. I do not know.

Those in charge must have herded us toward the nearest boat deck, for that is where I presently found myself, still clinging to my husband's arm and with little Marjorie beside me. Many women were standing with their husbands, and there was no confusion.

Then, above the clamour of people asking questions of each other, there came the terrible cry: 'Lower the boats! Women and children first!' Someone was shouting those last four words over and over again: 'Women and children first! Women and children first!' They struck utter terror into my heart, and now they will ring in my ears until I die. They meant my own safety; but they also meant the greatest loss I have ever suffered – the life of my husband.

The first lifeboat was quickly filled and lowered away. Very few men went in her, only five or six members of the crew, I should say. The male passengers made no attempt to save themselves. I never saw such courage or believed it possible. How the people in the first cabin and the steerage may have acted, I do not know, but our second-cabin men were heroes. I want to tell that to every reader of the article.

The lowering of the second boat took more time. I think all those women who were really afraid and eager to go had got into the first. Those who remained were wives who did not want to leave their husbands, or daughters who would not leave their parents. The officer in charge was Harold Lowe; First Officer Murdoch had moved to the other end of the deck. I was never close to him again.

Mr Lowe was very young and boyish-looking, but somehow he compelled people to obey him. He rushed among the passengers and ordered the women into the boat. Many of them followed him in a dazed kind of way, but others stayed by their men. I could have had a seat in that second boat, but I refused to go. It was filled at last and disappeared over the side with a rush.

There were two more lifeboats at that part of the deck. A man in plain clothes was fussing about them and screaming out instructions. I saw Fifth Officer Lowe order him away. I did not recognise him, but from what I have read in the newspapers it must have been Mr J. Bruce Ismay, the managing director of the line.

The third boat was about half full when a sailor caught Marjorie, my daughter, in his arms, tore her away from me and threw her into the boat. She was not even given a chance to tell her father good-bye!

'You, too!' a man yelled close to my ear. 'You're a woman. Take a seat in that boat, or it will be too late.'

The deck seemed to be slipping under my feet. It was leaning at a sharp angle, for the ship was then sinking fast, bows down. I clung desperately to my husband. I do not know what I said, but I shall always be glad to think that I did not want to leave him.

A man seized me by the arm. Then, another threw both his arms about my waist and dragged me away by main strength. I heard my husband say: 'Go, Lotty! For God's sake be brave and go! I'll get a seat in another boat.' The men who held me rushed me across the deck and hurled me bodily into the lifeboat. I landed on one shoulder and bruised it badly. Other women were crowding behind me, but I stumbled to my feet and saw over their heads my husband's back as he walked steadily down the deck and disappeared among the men. His face was turned away, so that I never saw it again, but I know that he went unafraid to his death.

His last words, when he said that he would get a seat in another boat, buoyed me up until every vestige of hope was gone. Many women were strengthened by the same promise or they must have gone mad and leaped into the sea. I let myself be saved because I believed that he, too, would escape, but I sometimes envy those whom no earthly power could tear from their husbands' arms. There were several such among those brave second-cabin passengers. I saw them standing beside their loved ones to the last, and when the roll was called the next day on board the *Carpathia*, they did not answer.

The boat was practically full, and no more women were anywhere near it when Fifth Officer Lowe jumped in and ordered it lowered. The sailors on deck had started to obey him when a very sad thing happened. A young lad, hardly more than a school boy, a pink-cheeked lad almost small enough to be counted as a child, was standing close to the rail. He had made no attempt to force his way into the boat, though his eyes had been fixed piteously on the officer. Now, when he realised that he was really to be left behind, his courage failed him. With a cry, he climbed upon the rail and leaped down into the boat. He fell among us women and crawled under a seat. I and another woman covered him up with our skirts. We wanted to give the poor lad a chance, but the officer dragged him to his feet and ordered him back upon the ship.

He begged for his life. I remember him saying that he would not take up much room, but the officer drew his revolver and thrust it into his face. 'I'll give you just ten seconds to get back on to that ship before I blow your brains out!' he shouted. The lad only begged the harder, and I thought I should see him shot as he stood. But the officer suddenly changed his tone. He lowered his revolver and looked the boy squarely in the eyes. 'For God's sake, be a man!' he said gently. 'We've got women and children to save. We must stop at the decks lower down and take on women and children.'

The little lad turned round and climbed back over the rail without a word. He took a few uncertain steps, then lay face down upon the deck, his head beside a coil of rope. He was not saved.

All the women about me were sobbing, and I saw my little Marjorie take the officer's hand. 'Oh, Mr Man, don't shoot, please don't shoot the poor man!' she was saying, and he spared the time to shake his head and smile.

He screamed another order for the boat to be lowered, but just as we were getting away a steerage passenger, an Italian, I think, came running the whole length of the deck and hurled himself into the boat. He fell upon a young child,

I found out afterward, and injured her internally. The officer seized him by the collar and by sheer brute strength pushed him back on to the *Titanic*. As we shot down toward the sea, I caught a last glimpse of this coward. He was in the hands of about a dozen men of the second cabin. They were driving their fists into his face, and he was bleeding from the nose and mouth.

As a matter of fact, we did not stop at any other deck to take on other women and children. It would have been impossible, I suppose. The bottom of our boat slapped the ocean, as we came down, with a force that I thought must shock us all overboard. We were drenched with ice-cold spray, but we hung on and the men at the oars rowed us rapidly away from the wreck.

It was then that I saw for the first time the iceberg that had done such terrible damage. It loomed up in the clear starlight, a bluish-white mountain quite near to us. Two other icebergs lay close together, like twin peaks. Later I thought I saw three or four more, but I cannot be sure. Loose ice was floating in the water. It was very cold.

We had gone perhaps half a mile when the officer ordered the men to cease rowing. No other boats were in sight, and we did not even have a lantern to signal with. We lay there in silence and darkness on that utterly calm sea.

I shall never forget the terrible beauty of the *Titanic* at that moment. She was tilted forward, head down, with her first funnel partly under water. To me she looked like an enormous glow worm, for she was alight from the rising water line clear to her stern – electric lights blazing in every cabin on all the decks and lights at her mast heads. No sound reached us except the music of the band, which I seemed, strange to say, to be aware of for the first time. Oh, those brave musicians! How wonderful they were! They were playing lively tunes, ragtime, and they kept it up to the very end. Only the engulfing ocean had power to drown them into silence.

At that distance it was impossible to recognise any one on board. But I could make out groups of men on every deck. They were standing with arms crossed upon their chests, and with lowered heads. I am sure that they were in prayer. On the boat deck that I had just left, perhaps fifty men had come together. In the midst of them was a tall figure. This man had climbed upon a chair, or a coil of rope, so that he was raised far above the rest. His hands were stretched out as if he were pronouncing a blessing. During the day a priest, a certain Father Byles, had held services in the second cabin saloon, and I think it must have been he who stood there leading those doomed men in prayer. The band was playing 'Nearer My God to Thee'; I could hear it distinctly. The end was very close.

It came with a deafening roar that stunned me. Something in the very bowels of the *Titanic* exploded, and millions of sparks shot up to the sky, like rockets in a park on the night of a summer holiday. This red spurt was fan-shaped as it went up, but the sparks descended in every direction in the shape of a fountain of fire. Two other explosions followed, dull and heavy, as if below the surface. The *Titanic* broke in two before my eyes. The fore part was already partly under the water. It wallowed over and disappeared instantly. The stern reared straight on end and stood poised on the ocean for many seconds – they seemed minutes to me.

It was only then that the electric lights on board went out. Before the darkness came, I saw hundreds of human bodies clinging to the wreck or leaping into the water. The *Titanic* was like a swarming bee-hive, but the bees were men, and they had broken their silence now. Cries more terrible than I had ever heard rang in my ears. I turned my face away, but looked round the next instant and saw the second half of the great boat slip below the surface as casually as a pebble in a pond. I shall always remember that last moment as the most hideous of the whole disaster.

Many calls for help came from the floating wreckage, but Fifth Officer Lowe told some women who asked him to go back that it would certainly result in our being swamped. I believe that some of the boats picked up survivors at this time, and I was told afterward by more than one trustworthy person that Captain E.J. Smith was washed against a collapsible boat and held onto it for a few moments. A member of the crew assured me that he tried to pull the captain on board, but that he shook his head, cast himself off and sunk out of sight.

For our part, we went in search of other lifeboats that had escaped. We found four or five, and Mr Lowe took command of the little fleet. He ordered that the boats should be linked together with ropes so as to prevent any one of them from drifting away and losing itself in the darkness. This proved to be a very good plan and made our rescue all the more certain when the *Carpathia* came.

He then, with great difficulty, distributed most of the women in our boat among the other craft. This took perhaps half-an-hour. It gave him an almost empty boat, and as soon as possible he cut loose and we went in search of survivors.

I have no idea of the passage of time during the balance of that awful night. Someone gave me a ship's blanket, which served to protect me from the bitter cold, and Marjorie had the cabin blanket that I had wrapped around her. But we were sitting with our feet in several inches of icy water. The salt spray had made us terribly thirsty, and there was no fresh water and certainly no food of any kind on board the boat. The sufferings of most of the women, from these various causes, was beyond belief. The worst thing that happened to me was when I fell over, half fainting, against one of the men at the oars. My loose hair was caught in the rowlock, and half of it was torn out by the roots.

I know that we rescued a large number of men from the wreckage, but I can clearly recall only two incidents.

Not far from where the *Titanic* went down we found a lifeboat floating bottom up. Along its keel were lying about twenty men. They were packed closely together and were hanging on desperately, but even the strongest were so badly frozen that, in a few moments more, they must have slipped into the ocean. We took them on board, one by one, and found that of the number four were already corpses. The dead men were cast into the sea. The living grovelled in the bottom of our boat, some of them babbling like maniacs.

A little farther on we saw a floating door that must have been torn loose when the ship went down. Lying upon it, face downward, was a small Japanese. He had lashed himself with a rope to his frail raft, using the broken hinges to make the knots secure. As far as we could see, he was dead. The sea washed over him every time the door bobbed up and down, and he was frozen stiff. He did not answer when he was hailed, and the officer hesitated about trying to save him.

'What's the use?' said Mr Lowe. 'He's dead, likely, and if he isn't there's others better worth saving than a Jap!'

He had actually turned our boat around, but he changed his mind and went back. The Japanese was hauled on board, and one of the women rubbed his chest, while others chafed his hands and feet. In less time than it takes to tell, he opened his eyes. He spoke to us in his own tongue; then, seeing that we did not understand, he struggled to his feet, stretched his arms above his head, stamped his feet, and in five minutes or so had almost recovered his strength. One of the sailors near to him was so tired that he could hardly pull his oar. The Japanese hustled over, pushed him from his seat, took the oar and worked like a hero until we were finally picked up. I saw Mr Lowe watching him in open-mouthed surprise.

'By Jove!' muttered the officer. 'I'm ashamed of what I said about the little blighter. I'd save the likes of him six times over if I got the chance.'

After this rescue all my memories are hazy until the *Carpathia* arrived at dawn. She stopped maybe four miles away from us, and the task of rowing over to her was one of the hardest that our poor frozen men, and women, too, had to face. Many women helped at the oars, and one by one the boats crawled over the ocean to the side of the waiting liner. They let down rope ladders to us, but the women were so weak that it is a marvel that some of them did not lose their hold and drop back into the water.

When it came to saving the babies and young children, the difficulty was even greater, as no one was strong enough to risk carrying a live burden. One of the mail clerks on the *Carpathia* solved the problem. He let down empty United States mail bags. The little mites were tumbled in, the bags locked, and so they were hauled up to safety.

We all stood at last upon the deck of the *Carpathia*, more than six hundred and seventy of us, and the tragedy of the scene that followed is too deep for words. There was scarcely any one who had not been separated from husband, child or friend. Was the lost one among this handful of saved? We could only rush frantically from group to group, searching the haggard faces, crying out names and endless questions.

No survivor knows better than I the bitter cruelty of disappointment and despair. I had a husband to search for, a husband whom, in the greatness of my faith, I had believed would be found in one of the boats.

He was not there; and it is with these words that I can best end my story of the *Titanic*. There are hundreds of others who can tell, and have already told, of that sad journey on the *Carpathia* to New York.

Friends in America have been good to us, and I intend to follow out our original plan. I shall go to Idaho and make a home in the new world of the West. For a while I thought of returning to England, but I can never face the sea again. And besides that, I must take my little Marjorie to the place where her father would have taken us both. That is all I care about – to do what he would have had me do.[162]

On 8 June 1912 the widowed Mrs Collyer wrote an open letter to the American people thanking them for their generosity in providing financial assistance to her and her little daughter Marjorie:

My Dear American Friends,

My heart is too full of gratitude for all the kindness and sympathy and generous help you have showered at me and my little daughter, for me to begin to tell you even a part of what I feel. The greatest comfort to me in my sorrow, my greatest support in the struggle I have made to carry out my husband's wishes and to make a home for myself and Marjorie in this wonderful land, have been the way that God's love for us has been revealed to me in the loving letters and aid received from all the dear friends my story has made for us.

I do not feel able to tell you in detail how I was at last compelled to give up my cherished plans and to return to England. I must leave that task to another. But I could not bear to have any of you feel that I am ungrateful or unappreciative of your goodness.

It is only that the experiences I have been through have left me without the necessary strength to make the fight alone. In my dead husband's name, and Marjorie's, and from my heart, I thank you all.

Charlotte Collyer

New York, June 8, 1912[163]

MARY COUTTS — Third Class Passenger

Following the disaster, Mrs Coutts wrote the following letter to a friend in England:

143 Fourth Avenue, Brooklyn,
New York City, U.S.A.
April 26th, 1912

Dear Mrs —,

Just a few lines to let you know that we are well, except Neville. He got whooping cough. Caught it on the *Titanic*. There were two young children there suffering from it; both got drowned, and their mother as well. I can scarcely believe that it is little more than a fortnight since we left London, so many unexpected things have happened since then. Shortly after Mr — said good-bye to us at Waterloo, two men came into the compartment: both were going to New York. It was from them I first heard of it being the *Titanic*'s maiden voyage. One was about 40 years; a great traveller; had been to China, Japan and almost every country. The other was quite a young fellow, and very nervous; he was afraid of accidents, sea-sickness, and whatnot. His mother told him to stuff cotton-wool in his ears and it would prevent sea-sickness. We all laughed, and the older man promised the boy's mother that he would look after him. I was speaking to them both several times on the *Titanic* and later on I met the young man on board the *Carpathia*. He had jumped into the sea and got picked up. The other man was drowned. The accommodation on the *Titanic* – food, &c. – was everything that could be desired. None of us were sea-sick; and one could hear on all sides people remarking what a splendid steamer she was and looking forward to joining their friends in New York. I was asleep when the ship struck. The crash was so slight that I thought little of it. I lay awake for fully 15 minutes. Presently I could hear people opening their cabin doors and inquiring what was the matter, and some of the stewards assuring them that there was no danger – she would start again in a little while. However, I got up just to find out all about it. I was surprised to see foreigners carrying all their belongings – rugs, blankets, and even small trunks – up on deck. The women were excited – that is, the foreigners – children were crying; but in a short time they were all up on deck, and everything was quiet again. The deck being two storeys up, we could not hear what they were doing. I was standing in the corridor quite a long time, trying to find out what really had happened, but everybody said there was no danger, and I never felt the least bit frightened. I thought it better not to go up on deck in case that I might not be able to get down again. Then I woke Willie and told him there had been an accident; not to be afraid, and on no account to cry, even if we did get drowned. I let Neville sleep as long as possible. It was only when I heard the order for life-preservers that I pulled Neville out of bed, put on his knickers and coat over his sleeping suit, and put on his boots; no time to lace them up. There were only two life-belts in my cabin, and I put one on Willie and the other on Neville. By this time some people were getting excited and running from one cabin to another looking for life-belts. I mentioned to an officer that I had not got one, and he said he was afraid there weren't any more. I asked several other people if they knew of any to spare, but there weren't any. Nearly everybody was on deck now, and we were just going when I saw the same officer. I said to him again that I had not got a life-preserver. He told me to follow him, and ordered the few people still in the corridors up on deck. He took us through quite a number of corridors and passages right into the first-class saloons to his own quarters. There he got his own life-belt and tied it on me, saying at the same time, 'There, my child; if the boat goes down you'll remember me.' I asked him if there really was danger, and he said he was afraid there was. He then told us to go out a certain way, but when I got there neither Willie or I could open the door. We felt that we were trapped; but strange as it may appear, I was not a bit afraid. I made Willie promise that if I should be drowned he would look after Neville and not let anyone take him away. Willie was very good. He never cried, although he was very near it. Presently we saw a sailor, and he showed us the way to the first-class deck.

So you will see that it was only by great good luck we were saved. If I had had a life-belt I should have been on the third-class deck, and ten to one we would not have got near where the lifeboats were at all, there was such a great crowd, and us being so late in getting on deck would have made the chances even less. Even when Neville was in the small boat and I was just getting in, Willie was nearly being left behind, but I would not go in without him, and wanted Neville out again, and that we would wait on the next boat. In the end they put him in.

We saw the ship go down, and heard the cries, groans, and shouts. It was terrible; I shall never forget it. We were in one of the small collapsible boats; seventeen in it. Neville cried with the cold. I had to threaten to drown him to keep him quiet. Too bad after what he had just come through. We were the first boat picked up by the *Carpathia* about 4 a.m., I should think. I know it was not light. We had a great reception in New York, and everybody was very kind, offering to lend clothes, &c.

And now I will conclude. Did not mean to write so much when I started. Will write you soon again – Yours sincerely,

Minnie Coutts[164]

CATHERINE CROSBY — First Class Passenger

On 17 May Mrs Crosby made the following deposition for the Senate *Titanic* inquiry:

CATHERINE E. CROSBY, being first duly sworn, upon her oath says that she is the widow of Capt. Edward Gifford Crosby, deceased; that she resides at 474 Marshall Street, city of Milwaukee, which is her home.

Deponent further says that, on the 10th day of April, 1912, at Southampton, England, she embarked as a passenger on the steamer *Titanic* for the port of New York; that her husband, Edward G. Crosby, and her daughter, Harriette H. Crosby, were with her on said steamer; that she and her husband occupied stateroom No.22 and her daughter occupied stateroom No.26, they being first-class passengers on said steamer. Deponent noticed nothing unusual or out of the ordinary, either in the equipment of the vessel or in the handling of her, and nothing unusual occurred until Sunday, the 14th day of April, 1912, when deponent noticed that the seamen on board the *Titanic* were taking the temperature of the water on the afternoon of that day, and it was stated by those engaged in doing this that the temperature of the water was colder and indicated that the boat was in the vicinity of ice fields; this was about the middle of the afternoon, as I recollect it.

At that time my husband and I were walking up and down the promenade deck, which, as I recollect it, was the deck below the hurricane deck, and it was while we were walking up and down this deck that I first noticed these seamen taking the temperature of the water. My husband was a sailor all his lifetime, and he told me all about it, and it was from that that I knew what they were doing. I could see what they were doing. My husband retired at about 9 o'clock that evening, and I retired about 10.30. Elmer Taylor, one of the passengers who went over with us on the steamer, told me afterwards, when we were on the *Carpathia*, that at the time I retired that night he noticed the boat was going full speed. I had not retired long when I was suddenly awakened by the thumping of the boat. The engines stopped suddenly. This was about 11.30. Capt. Crosby got up, dressed, and went out, and came back again and said to me, 'You will lie there and drown,' and went out again. He said to my daughter, 'The boat is badly damaged; but I think the watertight compartments will hold her up.' I then got up and dressed, and my daughter dressed, and followed my husband on deck, and she got up on deck, and the officer told her to go back and get on her life preserver and come back on deck as soon as possible. She reported that to me, and we both went out on deck where the officer told us to come. I think it was the first or second boat that we got into. I do not recollect other boats being lowered at that time. I did not see them. This was on the left-hand side where the officer told us to come, and it was the deck above the one on which our staterooms were located; our staterooms were located on the B deck, and we went to the A deck where the officer and lifeboat were. We got into the lifeboat that was hanging over the rail alongside the deck; we got in and men and women, with their families, got in the boat with us; there was no discrimination between men and women. About 36 persons got in the boat with us. There were only two officers in the boat, and the rest were all first-class passengers. My husband did not come back again after he left me, and I don't know what became of him, except that his body was found and brought to Milwaukee and buried.

There were absolutely no lights in the lifeboats, and they did not even know whether the plug was in the bottom of the boat to prevent the boat from sinking; there were no lanterns, no provisions, no lights, nothing at all in these boats but the oars. One of the officers asked one of the passengers for a match with which to light up the bottom of the boat to see if the plug was in place; the officers rowed the boat a short distance from the *Titanic*, and I was unable to see the lowering of any other boats, and we must have rowed quite a distance, but could see the steamer very plainly; saw them firing rockets, and heard a gun fired as distress signals to indicate that the steamer was in danger; we continued a safe distance away from the steamer, probably a quarter of a mile at least, and finally saw the steamer go down very distinctly; we did not see nor hear about any trouble on the steamer that is reported to have taken place afterwards; we got away first, and got away a safe distance, so that we could not see nor hear what took place, until the steamer went down, which was about 2.20 a.m. on the morning of the 15th; I heard the terrible cries of the people that were on board when the boat went down, and heard repeated explosions, as though the boilers had exploded, and we then knew that the steamer had gone down, as her lights were out, and the cries of the people and the explosions were terrible; our boat drifted around in that vicinity until about daybreak, when the *Carpathia* was sighted and were taken on board; we had to row quite a long time and quite a distance before we were taken on board the *Carpathia*; I was suffering from the cold while I was drifting around, and one of the officers put a sail around me and over my head to keep me warm, and I was hindered from seeing any of the other lifeboats drifting in the vicinity or observe anything that took place while we were drifting around until the *Carpathia* took us on board; we received very good treatment on the *Carpathia*, and finally arrived in New York; it was reported on the *Carpathia* by passengers, whose names I do not recollect, that the lookout who was on duty at the time the *Titanic* struck the iceberg had said: 'I know they will blame me for it, because I was on duty, but it was not my fault; I had warned the officers three or four times before striking the iceberg that we were in the vicinity of icebergs, but the officer on the bridge paid no attention to my signals.' I cannot give the name of any passenger who made that statement, but it was common talk on the *Carpathia* that that is what the lookout said.

I don't know anything about workmen being on the boat, and that the boat was not finished, and that the water-tight compartments refused to work: I have read it in the papers, but I personally know nothing about it; I also heard that there were no glasses on board the vessel; they were loaned from a vessel to be used on the voyage from Liverpool to Southampton and then returned to the vessel, and the *Titanic* proceeded without any glasses; Mr Elmer Taylor informed me after we got on the *Carpathia* that a dinner was in progress at the time the boat struck; this banquet was given for the captain, and the wine flowed freely; personally I know nothing about this; I do not recollect anything of importance that occurred any more than I have stated. – Catherine E. Crosby[165]

CHARLES DAHL — **Third Class Passenger**

Mr T.P. Shaver of Toronto was travelling by train between Toronto and Winnipeg when he fell in with four *Titanic* survivors, among whom was Charles Dahl; Mr Dahl related the following story to Shaver, who recorded it for publication:

> From the time we left Southampton on Wednesday afternoon until Sunday evening our voyage was uneventful. I was walking on the deck with other friends at 9:30 Sunday evening. I remarked to a lady and her husband that we must be very close to icebergs as the weather had turned so cold. We all went into the saloon. I had a smoke and returned to my cabin and retired.
>
> I was awakened by the ship crashing into the ice. I got up very much confused. I did not know where I was for the moment, as I had been awakened from a very sound sleep. I went up on the deck and saw a great quantity of ice scattered everywhere over the ship, but I could see no iceberg. I went back to my cabin to get some more clothes, as the air was very cold. I returned to the deck, and on being told that the water was pouring into 'C' compartment I went back for a lifebelt. After getting it I went up on the steerage deck aft. I saw the first class passengers putting on their lifebelts, so I put on mine and went up to the first class deck. When I got there I saw them getting ready to put out the lifeboats. I went to the port side and waited for half an hour or more, but no one was allowed into the boats. Some of the passengers came from the starboard side and said that all the lifeboats had left that side. There were hundreds of people waiting on the port

side, and when I saw that, I thought there was no chance of being saved on that side of the boat. I ran over to the starboard side and to my surprise saw a boat half lowered nearly full of people. I asked the chief officer if I could not go into the boat. He said, 'No, the boat is too far down, you cannot get to it.' I said, 'I will manage that if you give me the permission.' He said, 'All right, then. Go on.' I went down on the tackle, hand under hand, until I got to the lifeboat.

One officer and two sailors were putting out the boats. Just after getting into the boat, I heard a terrible scream beneath us. I looked over the edge of ours and saw that there was a lifeboat of women and children that had not yet been cleared. Had our boat been lowered instantly it would have swamped theirs. They saw their danger, hence this scream. I reached over and got hold of the stern of the lower boat and kept it clear of ours, then we were lowered down. We had hard work to get the tackle off our boat, as we could not get the lever to work. I got a knife and cut away the ropes, thus getting clear of the ship. There were 82 people in our lifeboat, number 15. Seven were children, eight women and the rest men.

These men were mostly stewards, firemen, trimmers, and the balance passengers. After getting clear, we rowed about three-quarters of a mile from the ship. By this time the water was up to the bridge of the doomed vessel. The bow settled long before the stern. Suddenly we heard an explosion, and in about two minutes a second followed.

All the lights then went out. She seemed to break in two. The stern went down. There was no trouble for us to see it. There seemed to be a black cloud come up as the head went down. There were terrible noises as of the crushing of timber. The passengers from the stern of the top deck screamed horribly. Every few minutes we could hear it. The cries of the people on the doomed ship sounded very much to me like the bleating of the sheep and lambs when in great fear or distress.

We were in the lifeboat until about 6 o'clock, with one of the firemen in charge. I do not know that anyone appointed him as officer. I think he took it on himself, as he seemed to know but little about it anyway. Our sufferings were very great. We were out on a sea packed with ice, with no water, no food, no lights and many of us with but scant clothing.

We were finally picked up by the *Carpathia* with all our members safe. We received every kindness possible. We landed in New York on Thursday evening, and 30 of us were sent to St Vincent's hospital. The sisters and all connected with that institution were extremely kind to us. As I had lost my money and most of my clothing, about $600 in all, the Ladies' society furnished me with some extra clothing and gave me $100. I left New York on Monday night, and I am now on my ay to see my mother, who lives in Fingal, North Dakota.

After the boat struck, everyone was quiet, as no one believed that she could possibly go down. When it became known, however, that there was danger, there was an attempt made to rush the boats. I heard no revolver shots, although I was told by others when we got on the *Carpathia* that two Italians were shot. I heard one of the officers on the port side say, 'If anyone does not obey orders – lay him out.' The people were told to stand back or no one could get a chance. I did not see Captain Smith after the ship struck, but I heard his voice on the bridge giving orders as I was going down to No.15.

I believe there was a ship near us. I saw a light low down on the water and said, 'That is the light of a ship.' Others thought it was a star, but I still believe that I was correct. I was the first in our boat to see the light of the *Carpathia*, and when I saw it and told the rest that a ship was coming, they again argued that I saw only a star. But the lights in both instances were the same, and that convinced me that there was a ship which could have seen our signals of distress.

I have little to say regarding the management. I do think, though, that they waited too long before lowering the lifeboats on the port side. Had there been sufficient lifeboats the greater part of the people would have been saved. Certainly there were not half enough boats.[166]

EUGENE DALY **Third Class Passenger**

Mr Daly wrote the following letter to his family in Ireland:

I was in compartment 23, Deck C, steerage. Two other men were with me. I was in my bunk asleep on the Sunday night (the night of the disaster). A crash waked me up. It nearly threw me from my bed. I got up and went to the door. I put on my trousers and shoes. I met the steward in the gangway. He said there was nothing serious and that I might go back. I went back for a little while. Then I went up on deck as I heard a noise there. People were running around. Then I went down and went to the room where Maggie Daly and Bertha Mulvihill were ... I went for a life buoy in the stern and Maggie and Bertha came with me. I had a scuffle with a man for a life buoy. He would not give it to me but he gave it to Maggie Daly ... A boat was lowered then. It was being filled with women. Maggie and Bertha got in and I got in. The officer called to me to go back but I got in. Life was sweet to me and I wanted to save myself. They told me to get out but I didn't stir. Then they got hold of me and pulled me out ... The officer in charge pointed a revolver and waved his hand and said that if any man tried to get in he would shoot him on the spot. Two men tried to break through and he shot them both. I saw him shoot them ... I tried to get to the boat also but was afraid I would be shot and stayed back. Afterwards there was another shot and I saw the officer himself lying on the deck. They told me that he shot himself but I did not see him ... Everyone was rushing round but there were no boats. Then I dived overboard. When I struck the water I swam for the boat that had been washed over. When I got to her she was upside down. I pulled myself up on her. About fifteen or more got upon her the same way. At the time I jumped there were a lot of people jumping overboard.

As I stood on the craft I saw the ship go down. Her stern went up and she gradually sunk forward. Her stern stuck up high. I thought she would fall on us

> as she seemed to be swinging around, but she did not. There was no suction at all that we felt. Our craft was not drawn in at all.[167]

Mr Daly also wrote the following note to his mother after the *Carpathia* arrived in New York:

> Dear Mother,
> Got here safe. Had a narrow escape, but, please God, am safe; also Maggie. I think the disaster caused you to fret, but things could be much worse than what they were.[168]

MARGARET DALY — Third Class Passenger

Miss Daly wrote the following letter to a friend or relative in Ireland:

> I am sure you think by this time I must be in the bottom of the sea. Well I must say I am one of the lucky ones. I and Eugene [Daly] and Bertha Mulvihill are all that remain. That little girl from Summerhill and the boy [Michael] Connaughton and I think Mrs Rice and her five boys perished. It was a sight I shall never forget – twenty people out of two hundred Irish saved ... All I have to regret is that I lost all my clothes. I thought I had a hard fight but I would never have been saved only for Eugene. He fought very hard for our lives ... In the present deplorable disaster he appears to have upheld the tradition of the Gael and one can well imagine that when the Captain seized the megaphone and roared 'Be British' Daly thought of the Pipers Club in the old Border Town and determined to be Irish as he ever has been ...[169]

THEODOOR DE MULDER — Third Class Passenger

On 1 May Mr de Mulder wrote the following letter to his family:

> Dear Parents, wife and children,
> You are probably waiting with fear and impatience the news of my way to America that I write, thank to God, with my own hands.
> Happily and gladly I let you know that I have been saved from a certain death and I am in good health. However, my trip went on awfully and no pen will ever be able to describe the fear and the horrible events I saw.

It was around midnight that our ship collided with the iceberg; we jumped out of our beds and, oh my God ... the water was already 4 feet high in our cabin. We went up with fear and scare, and of the group of twenty Flemish, only we three survived.

Look here how I was rescued:

When the boat seemed to sink to the bottom, I took a chair of the 1st class, threw it into the sea and jumped after it. I tried to hold it under my body the best I could and after half an hour of swimming around, I found a boat which I could get on. I just arrived 'on board' when three Arabs swam to the boat and tried to get in, all three on the same side. And we were again the prey of the waves. Then I took my chair and realised once again, more dead than alive, that it is the only means to be saved. And my dear parents, wife and children, no pen will ever be able to describe what I experienced during those 3 hours; holding my breath, seeing death in front of my eyes, the heart-rending cries of hundreds of people who are not among the living any more, the cries for help and the lamenting sounds echoing on the immeasurably huge water, the constant motion of hundreds of people struggling for life in the water, everything shivering and terrifying me, and I will always see that terrible play in front of my eyes.

After 3 hours of fighting against death, I began to lose my power, when I was picked up by the 'Cunard', together with some Belgians; one from Haaltert and one from West-Flanders.

We were picked up and a nurse put all his effort to save us, but in spite of this five more persons died (luckily none of the Belgians). I myself was also very far gone, but thanks to the nurse I was saved from death, but still! All that was left were my trousers and my shirt; everything else; my suitcase, my money, my clothes, my gun, everything I had, to a value of 450 fr was senselessly lost. Only the things listed in my insurance booklet will be compensated for by the company. Please inform the agent of this.

Now you are probably curious to know where I am.

After arrival in New York, we were provided with some clothes, trousers, a jacket, a suit and 30 fr; with this we had at least something, and sometimes we had the opportunity to get into circuses and theatres that we took advantage of.

We got a contract for 8 months for 5 dollars a day to be seen and heard for 4 hours a day; as you can see, it is already a beautiful little sum for not too much work. And if we stayed in Detroit, we could get 25 dollars for one occasion to be seen and heard together with my friend, but we chose the best, the one we have now.

With this, dear parents, wife and children, I will close my letter and give you some more news later on.

Regards,
your affectionate son, husband and father
Polydoor De Mulder
Nee Aspelare[170]

VERA DICK **First Class Passenger**

Mrs Dick wrote the following account of her experiences for publication in a newspaper:

> The night on which the big steamship *Titanic* crushed out its life against the iceberg juggernaut was very clear, and there was a tang in the air. I was on deck and was almost thrown from my feet by the shock of the collision. I have heard it said that the sinking of the *Titanic* was caused by an explosion in the engine room. This is untrue.
>
> I saw the iceberg that brought down the *Titanic*. The ship officers saw it, too, and the bells were rung to reverse the course. The boat actually escaped the exposed part of the berg, but grounded on the unexposed part.
>
> There were terrified screams from all parts of the boat. Women came rushing upon deck with hardly any clothes upon them. Half a score were in their night gowns, and many were in their bare feet. Capt. Smith and a man who was said to be the personal aide to the President of the United States were among the coolest men on board.
>
> They ordered the men into line, and then the women were called to one side. I saw a number of immigrants rushing up the stairs, yelling and screaming and fighting to get to the boats. Officers drew guns and told them that if they moved toward the boats they would be shot dead.
>
> There were some terrible scenes. I saw fathers parting from their children and giving them an encouraging pat on the shoulders. I saw men kissing their wives and telling them that they would be with them shortly.
>
> One man said there was absolutely no danger, that the boat was the finest ever built, with water-tight compartments, and that it could not sink. That seemed to be the general impression.
>
> One of the most interesting sidelights on the whole tragedy is the way some of the women in evening dress faced the tragedy. It was evident that they did not appreciate the danger.
>
> One man handed a life-saver to a woman with the remark, 'We are wearing these this season. They are most becoming.'
>
> One woman had a fox terrier in her arms, and the man told her to try a life-saver on the dog.
>
> 'Everybody is wearing them now,' he laughed.
>
> It was evident that many people thought that there was too much agitation, and that for a boat of that kind to sink was absolutely impossible.
>
> Some of the people on the boat have said I was brave because I wanted to remain on board until the last, and refused to take a seat in the first boat when the captain wanted to put me in. As a matter of fact, there were women older and more nervous than I, and I thought they should have the first chance. I realised the danger, but I am young and felt equal to the situation.
>
> Capt. Smith, or maybe it was Mr Moore – I don't know which – finally insisted that I leave. 'This is no place for a woman, and you will have to go in the next

boat,' they told me. I then allowed myself to be put off the *Titanic*, although I would like to have stayed until the last. I could have jumped overboard as some of the men did.

A band was playing on the *Titanic* when it went down. The captain had ordered the band to play, and to play continuously, so that the women would not feel that they were in danger. The bandsmen were loyal. They kept on playing jolly, happy tunes. They were playing some American air when the guards shot the jaw off an immigrant who tried to crowd into one of the boats, brushing the women aside.

They played, and their airs were mingled with the shrieks of terrified women. And as I went over the side, they were still playing – discordantly it seemed – and I guess they kept on until the *Titanic* was swallowed up by the ocean.

The boat in which I was placed was rowed quickly away from the *Titanic*. We kept looking back, like Lot's wife. It might have cost us our lives, or it might have delayed us, but still we looked back at the great *Titanic*, with its lines of light indicating the floors like a skyscraper when the occupants are at work.

It was about 11:45 when we struck the iceberg, and it was 2:20 when the boat went down.

As we looked back, we saw the lowest floor of lights wiped out by the waterline. Then another floor went out, then another, and another, one floor of lights after another, as the *Titanic* settled. There was no suddenness about it. It was rhythmic – tragically, heart-rendingly rhythmic.

In the boat in which I was there were women in their night gowns and bare feet. The night was very clear, starlight, but very, very cold. Many of them shivered horribly. Some of them talked of suicide – those who had lost loved ones. We drifted about all that night, subsisting on bread and water – that was all we had – and then were picked up by the *Carpathia*. When we took an account of the people who were saved, we found 44 deck hands, 73 engineers, 210 first-class passengers, 125 second-class, 144 third class, 16 stewardesses, and 38 stewards.

Some of the rescued passengers died afterward on the *Carpathia*, and were buried at sea. There were none of the usual formalities. It was desired that no attention be directed to the occurrences. The rescued passengers were frantic enough already.[171]

WASHINGTON DODGE **First Class Passenger**

After the *Carpathia*'s arrival in New York, Mr Dodge presented the following address to San Francisco's Commonwealth Club describing his experiences on the *Titanic*:

A few days since I was approached by the chairman of the Committee on Program, Dr Giannini, who requested me to make a few remarks to the Club on the subject of the wreck of the *Titanic*. To this request I demurred. The doctor, however, was quite insistent and stated that, owing to the widespread interest in this catastrophe, and owing to the many conflicting reports of the same which had been published, he hoped I would grant his request. I knew what the doctor stated to be true, for on my return to San Francisco I had seen numerous interviews, both with myself and my wife, which purported interviews had been wired from New York and published in our local papers. My wife had never given an interview, and had made none of the statements attributed to her. With one exception, all of the interviews attributed to me were wholly unfounded. On reconsideration, I decided to comply with the doctor's request. Having little time to give to the preparation of these remarks, and desiring in the short space of time allotted to me to cover the matter as fully as possible, I decided this could best be done by me, with the assistance of my stenographer. This is my reason for reading this narrative.

In the past ten days following the first uncertain and contradictory reports in the press of the disaster, the actual occurrences connected with the same have been positively established. The full evidence given under oath before the congressional committee has been published in several of the New York papers, as well as in several weekly publications. I presume that most of those present have had an opportunity to read some such authentic report, and for that reason I have, in compliance with Dr Giannini's request, based my narrative of events, largely on my personal experiences and observations.

I will first state briefly the facts of the wreck. On April 10th the White Star liner *Titanic* started from Southampton on her maiden trip across the Atlantic. She was the largest vessel afloat – a little less than nine hundred feet, or over one-sixth of a mile in length – and was heralded by her builders and owners as an unsinkable ship, having, in addition to a double bottom, fifteen water-tight compartments. She carried 2,340 persons. Five days later she was at the bottom of the ocean and through her loss over two-thirds of those on board, or 1,635 people, had perished.

The voyage, up to the time of the disaster, had been a perfect one. The weather was fine and the sea calm. At all times one might walk the decks, with the same security as if walking down Market Street, so little motion was there to the vessel. It was hard to realise, when dining in the spacious dining saloon, that one was not in some large and sumptuous hotel.

The Sunday evening of the night of the disaster was a clear cold night. The temperature had fallen rapidly after sundown until it had reached thirty-one degrees. This was undoubtedly due to our close proximity to the immense ice field, and to the numerous icebergs, which were revealed the nest morning. The temperature of the water had been taken every two hours throughout the day and evening, but had failed to show our close proximity to the icefield. The great vessel was ploughing ahead at a speed of approximately 21½ knots an hour. The ship's officers had been warned by wireless of their proximity to icebergs, and the orders had been given to the lookout in the 'Crow's Nest' to keep a sharp watch for small icebergs.

According to the evidence given at the congressional investigation, Chief Officer Murdoch relieved Second Officer Lightoller on the bridge at ten o'clock. The men discussed the icebergs, which the ship was known to be approaching, and decided that they would probably encounter them within about an hour.

At about twenty minutes to twelve, the lookout in the 'Crow's Nest' rang a signal on the bridge of three bells, meaning, 'Danger ahead.' A few seconds thereafter he telephoned to the bridge, 'Large iceberg right ahead.' An order was given to the man at the wheel to throw the vessel to port. This was done and the engines reversed, but in an instant later the ship had been struck beneath the water-line by the iceberg. The lever was then thrown, which from the bridge, closes all the water-tight compartments in thirty seconds.

These facts were related to me on the *Carpathia* by Quartermaster Hichens, who was at the wheel on the *Titanic*. It was he who received the signals from the 'Crow's Nest', and he to whom the order was given by the chief officer to throw the vessel to port.

The shock to the steamer was so slight, that many of the passengers, who had already retired, were not awakened thereby. My wife and I, however, were both awakened by the shock to the vessel. Listening for a moment, I became aware of the fact that the engines had been stopped, and shortly afterwards hearing hurried footsteps on the boat decks which was directly over our stateroom, I concluded that I would go out and inquire what had occurred. Partially dressing I slipped out of our room into the forward companionway, there to find possibly half a dozen men, all speculating as to what had happened. While we stood there an officer passed by somewhat hurriedly, and I asked him what was the trouble; he replied that he thought something had gone wrong with the propeller, but that it was nothing serious.

Leaving the few passengers that I had observed, still laughing and chatting, I returned to my stateroom. My wife being somewhat uneasy desired to arise and dress. I assured her that nothing had occurred which would harm the ship, and persuaded her to remain in bed. I informed my wife what the officer had told me, that something had gone wrong with the propeller. We both agreed, however, judging from the nature of the shock, that something had struck the vessel on its side. This however, owing to the slight jar to the vessel, and to our knowledge of her immense size, and unsinkable construction, did not alarm us. I decided, nevertheless, to again go out and investigate further.

This time I went from the companionway out onto the promenade deck, where I found a group of possibly six or eight men, who were gaily conversing about the incident. I heard one man say that the impact was due to ice. Upon one of his listeners questioning the authority of this, he replied: 'Go up forward and look down on the poop deck, and you can see for yourself.' I at once walked forward to the end of the promenade deck, and looking down could see, just within the starboard rail, small fragments of broken ice, amounting possibly to several cartloads. As I stood there an incident occurred which made me take a more serious view of the situation, than I otherwise would.

Two stokers, who had slipped up onto the promenade deck unobserved, said to me: 'Do you think there is any danger, sir?' I replied: 'If there is any danger it would be due to the vessel having sprung a leak, and you ought to know more about it than I.' They replied, in what appeared to me, to be an alarmed tone: 'Well, sir, the water was pouring into the stoke 'old when we came up, sir.' At this time I observed quite a number of steerage passengers, who were amusing themselves by walking over the ice, and kicking it about the deck. No ice or iceberg was to be seen in the ocean.

Not observing any sign of apprehension on the part of any one, nor seeing any unusual number of persons on any part of the ship, I again returned to my cabin and told my wife what I had seen and heard.

As the vessel was still stationary, I again stepped out into the companionway, and observing our steward standing in the centre of the same, I asked him if he had heard anything. He replied that the order had just come down, for all passengers to put on life-preservers. Asking him if he really meant it, and being convinced from his manner and answer, that the command had actually been given, I at once sprang to my stateroom door, which was but a few steps from where I was standing, and hurriedly told my wife to throw on something warm and come with me. While she partly dressed herself and our child, I pulled down the three life-preservers which were in the stateroom, and threw them over my arm. We then quickly made our way to the boat deck. In order to reach this we had to ascend only one short flight of stairs, and passing onto the boat deck on the starboard side, we were at once next to the forward lifeboats. I learned afterwards that the order was given by the officers, for the women and children to go to the port side of the vessel. It was on this side that the captain had taken charge of the launching of the lifeboats. At the time that we reached the boat deck, the first boat on the starboard side, No.1, was hanging over the side of the vessel from the davits, and a few persons, men and women, were seated therein. The officer in charge was calling for women and children to fill the boat, but seemed to have difficulty in finding those who were willing to enter. I myself hesitated to place my wife and child in this boat, being unable to decide whether it would be safer to keep them on the steamer, or to entrust them to this frail boat which was the first to be launched, and which hung over eighty feet above the water. In the meantime I busied myself with strapping on their life-preservers, and heard the officer give the command to 'Lower away'. This boat was launched with but twenty-six persons in it, although its capacity was over fifty, and about one-third were male passengers.

As I observed this boat lowered without accident, I placed my wife and child in the next boat, No.3, – boats on the starboard side having the odd numbers. This boat was ordered lowered when it contained less than thirty-five persons. In neither case were additional women to be found. Each of these boats contained at least ten male passengers. As I saw this boat lowered, containing my wife and child, I was overwhelmed with doubts, as to whether or not I was exposing them to greater danger, than if they had remained on board the ship.

During the ensuing half or three-quarters of an hour, I watched the boats on the starboard side as they were successively filled and lowered away. At no time during this period was there any panic, or evidence of fears or unusual alarm. I saw no women nor children weep, nor were there any evidences of hysteria observed by me.

Many expressed their determination to take their chances with the steamer rather than embark in the lifeboats. This unusual circumstance may be accounted for by the fact that the officers had insisted that under the worst conditions possible, the *Titanic* could not sink in less than eight or ten hours, and that a number of steamers had been communicated with by wireless, and would be standing by to offer relief within an hour or two.

I watched all boats on the starboard side, comprising the odd numbers from one to thirteen, as they were launched. Not a boat was launched which would not have held from ten to twenty-five more persons. Never were there enough women or children present to fill any boat before it was launched. In all cases, as soon as those who responded to the officers' call were in the boats, the order was given to 'Lower away'.

At no time were there many people on the starboard side that night. Why was that? The most reasonable explanation that I can give is that the captain was in charge of the launching of the boats on port side. Now, in times of danger the captain always draws a crowd. The more notable men on board, who were known by sight to the other passengers, knew Captain Smith personally and remained near him. These men attracted others. In this way the crowd grew on the port side, while at no time was there anything like a crowd on the starboard side. Again, the orders for women and children to go to the port side greatly increased the number there.

Now this condition may explain many things. It may explain why the boats were launched from the starboard side so much more quickly and successfully, and why when the last boats on this side were reached, Nos. 13 and 15, there were practically no women around, and not many men. When the order to launch the boats was given, Captain Smith took command of the port side and never left there. Chief Officer Murdoch took command on the starboard side.

What the conditions were on the port side of the vessel I had no means of observing. We were in semi-darkness on the boat deck, and owing to the immense length and breadth of the vessel, and the fact that between the port and starboard side of the boat deck, there were officers' cabins, staterooms for passengers, a gymnasium, and innumerable immense ventilators, it would have been impossible, even in daylight, to have obtained a view of but a limited portion of this boat deck. We only knew what was going on about us within a radius of possibly forty feet.

Boats Nos. 13 and 15 were swung from the davits at about the same moment. I heard the officer in charge of No.13 say, 'We'll lower this boat to deck A.' Observing a group of possibly fifty or sixty about boat 15, a small proportion of which number were women, I descended by means of a stairway close at hand to the deck below, deck 'A.' Here, as the boat was lowered even with the deck, the women, about eight in number, were assisted by several of us over the rail of the steamer into the boat. The officer in charge then held the boat, and called repeatedly for more women. None appearing, and there being none visible on the deck, which was then brightly illuminated, the men were told to tumble in. Along with those present I entered the boat.

As there seems to be in the minds of a few of the people in this community, a question as to why any of the eighty men saved from the first class passengers should have been, when later events disclosed the fact that there were women remaining on board, I would like to quote here from an article of *The New York Times* of recent date, by Mr Lawrence Beesley. This article was sent to me a few days since by Mr Leahey of this city.

Mr Beesley, a very intelligent man, and a close observer evidently, also wrote a review of the disaster for the *London Times*. On reading this article I ascertained that Mr Beesley had left the steamer in the same boat that I had. His words on the subject were as follows:

'I will finish with a few purely personal remarks. My only excuse for putting them on record is that to me they are absolutely true. I do not make them with any intention of asking a single person to believe in them, or to agree with me in what I say, but, having been face to face with the possibility of death, and having seen its shadow rather near, I may perhaps not be trespassing on the columns of the *Times* in saying how I consider I was saved.

'I left in boat 13, when a call for ladies had been made three times and not answered, and no ladies were visible, and was then invited to enter the boat. I had stood quietly on the deck watching boats being launched, until the moment arrived when I was able to get a seat in a boat without depriving any one of room. I was asked to go by one of the crew, and when the boat was lowered, the deck was left quite clear.'

This statement of facts by Mr Beesley coincides exactly with my observations. Mr Ismay, who left in the next boat, No.15, which was being launched about the same time, testified, under oath, before the Congressional Committee, to exactly the same conditions.

Curiously enough another newspaper record of the experiences of a survivor who escaped in my boat, came into my possession a few days since. This paper was handed to me by Mr Madison Kirby, of this city, with the remark that he had just received it from his old home in Illinois, and he thought the account referred to might interest me. To my surprise I again found that the narrative was given by an occupant of the boat 13. This article appeared in the *Roseville Times-Citizen*, printed under date of April 26th in Roseville, Illinois. The article, which is rather lengthy, gives a detailed account written by the Rev. A.F. Caldwell of the escape of himself, wife, and little son from the *Titanic*. Mr Caldwell, it appears gave this interview on arriving at his home in Roseville. He describes in this article the incidents connected with the filling and launching of boat No.13, and the narrow escape of the boat from being swamped, which I will relate presently.

He relates that after being awakened by the shock he dressed and went out on the deck, and was told by an officer that the vessel has struck an iceberg, but he not being conscious of the real peril and seeing so few scenes of serious danger, returned to bed. When awakened later by the shouting of orders for all to go on the deck, he and his family dressed fully and went to A deck. He then proceeds: 'As we joined the group gathered there, lifeboat No.13 was about to be lowered and Mrs Caldwell was put into it. She was the last woman left in the group, and I was about to lower the baby down to her when she said, 'can't my husband come too?' There being ample room, I was put into the boat and other men followed and the work of lowering away began.'

Mr Caldwell also states in his account that just before he left the steamer, the passengers were repeatedly assured that there was no danger; that the *Olympic* was near and would take off the passengers and crew. He believed, when he embarked in the lifeboat, that it could be more prudent to stay on the steamer. In common with others he felt that the *Titanic* was so big, and so strongly constructed, that her sinking was unbelievable, and he remarks that it was this belief that resigned so many to stay on board, as they thought that no matter how seriously she was injured she would certainly keep afloat for hours, and perhaps days.

At the Congressional investigation Fifth Officer Lowe testified as follows:

Q. Did you have any difficulty in filling No.3?
A. Yes, sir; I had difficulty all along. I could not get enough people.
Q. Did any women attempt to get in either of these boats (3 or 5) and did not succeed in getting in?
A. No, sir.
Q. Did any men so attempt and fail to get in?
A. No, not one.
Q. What did you do about it yourself; did you arbitrarily select from the deck?
A. You say 'select'. There was no such thing as selecting. It was simply the first woman, either first class, second class, third class, or sixty-seventh class; it was all the same – women and children were first.
Q. Do you mean that there was a procession of women?
A. The first woman was first into the boat; the second woman was second into the boat, no matter whether she was a first-class passenger or another class.
Q. Now as they came along, you would pass them one at a time into the lifeboat? What order did you have – 'to pass women and children?'
A. I simply shouted, 'Women and children first; men stand back.'
Q. How did it happen that you did not put more people into lifeboat No.3 than forty-five?
A. There did not seem to be any people there.
Q. You did not find anybody that wanted to go?
A. Those that were there did not seem to want to go. I hallooed out: 'Who's next for the boat?' And there was no response.

In view of these conditions the query arises, why were any women lost? The list of survivors shows that of the first class women passengers only fifteen were lost. Of these nine were ladies' maids travelling with their ladies. What follows may account for so many of these latter being lost! It was related to me by a woman in my lifeboat, that just before she came on deck and got into the boat, she saw the purser's office surrounded by a crowd demanding their valuables, which the purser and his assistant were endeavouring to hand out as quickly as possible. In this crowd were many women. I believe further, that there were some women, on some of the lower decks, who were not awakened at all. One of the crew of the *Titanic*, the head baker, testified at the official investigation in London, that some women had to be carried from the lower decks up to the lifeboats. That many refused to get into the boats under any consideration. In this connection your attention is drawn to the fact that the *Titanic* had twelve steel decks, and that passengers had rooms on decks which were seven and eight decks below the boat deck.

The boat in which I embarked was rapidly lowered, and as it approached the water I observed, as I looked over the edge of the boat, that the bow, near which I was seated, was being lowered directly into an enormous stream of water, three or four feet in diameter, which was being thrown with great force from the side of the vessel. This was the water thrown out by the condenser pumps. Had our boat been lowered into the same it would have been swamped in an instant. The loud cries which were raised by the occupants of the boat, caused those who were sixty or seventy feet above us to cease lowering our boat. Securing an oar with considerable difficulty, as the oars had been firmly lashed together by means of heavy tarred twine, and as in addition they were on the seat running parallel with the side of the lifeboat, with no less than eight or ten occupants of the boat sitting on them, none of whom showed any tendency to disturb themselves – we pushed the bow of the lifeboat, by means of the oar, a sufficient distance away from the side of the *Titanic* to clear this great stream of water which was gushing forth. We were then safely lowered to the water. During the few moments occupied by these occurrences I felt for the only time a sense of impending danger.

We were directed to pull our lifeboat from the steamer, and to follow a light which was carried in one of the other lifeboats, which had been launched prior to ours. Our lifeboat was found to contain no lantern, as the regulations require; nor was there a single sailor, or officer in the boat. Those who undertook to handle the oars were poor oarsmen, almost without exception, and our progress was extremely slow. Together with two or three other lifeboats which were in the vicinity, we endeavoured to overtake the lifeboat which carried the light, in order that we might not drift away and possibly become lost. This light appeared to be a quarter of a mile distant, but in spite of our best endeavours, we were never enabled to approach any nearer to it, although we must have rowed at least a mile.

When I left the steamer, which, as near as I can fix the time, must have been from an hour to an hour and a half after the collision, I was not conscious that the *Titanic* showed any list or displacement whatever.

After we had been afloat possibly half an hour I observed, on looking at the steamer, that the line of lights from the portholes, showed that the vessel had settled forward into the water, but to no great extent. This was a matter of considerable surprise to me at the moment. Watching the vessel closely, it was seen from time to time that this submergence forward was increasing. No one in our boat, however, had any idea that the ship was in any danger of sinking. In spite of the intense cold, a cheerful atmosphere pervaded those present and they indulged, from time to time, in jesting and even singing, 'Pull for the shore, sailor.'

The gradual submersion of the vessel forward increased, and in about an hour was suddenly followed by the extinguishment of all the lights, which had been burning brightly, illuminating every deck and gleaming forth from innumerable portholes. We saw the vessel then clearly outlined as a great dark shadow on the water, probably at a distance of about a mile. It was remarked by several, that if the vessel should sink, fortunately there had been plenty of time for everyone aboard to get off. I had the same feeling, believing that if events subsequent to our departure had shown that the ship was liable to sink, all those on board would have had an opportunity to leave her.

Suddenly, while I was looking at the dark outline of the steamer, I saw her stern rise high from the water, and then the vessel was seen to completely disappear from sight with startling rapidity. A series of loud explosions, three or four in number, were then heard, due, as we all believed, to bursting boilers.

Any impression which I had had that there were no survivors aboard, was speedily removed from my mind by the faint, yet distinct, cries which were wafted across the waters. Some there were in our boat, who insisted that these cries came from occupants of the different lifeboats, which were nearer the scene of the wreck than we were, as they called one to another. To my ear, however they had but one meaning – and the awful fact was borne in upon me that many lives were perishing in those icy waters.

With the disappearance of the steamer, a great sense of loneliness and depression seemed to take possession of those in our boat. Few words were then spoken. I heard the remark: 'This is no joke, we may knock about here days before we are picked up, if at all.' And the hours between this and daylight were spent, in ceaselessly scanning the ocean for some sign of a steamer's light. It was recalled how we had been told, that four or five steamers would be standing by within an hour or two, and every pair of eyes were strained to the utmost, to discover the first sign of approaching help.

Out of the sixteen lifeboats there were probably four or five that carried lanterns. The occupants of the other boats were, from time to time, apparently burning a piece of paper, as were we in our boat. These facts led several in our boat to assert many times, that they saw a new light, which certainly must be a steamer's light. With each disappointment, added gloom seemed to settle upon our little company, as they began to realise the seriousness of our situation.

About this time, quite a breeze began to spring up, and the ocean became more rough. It was apparent that we were drifting with the wind, being only partially able to keep the bow of the boat headed into the wind.

Shortly before dawn, one of the occupants announced that he was sure that he saw a new light on the horizon. No one, however, placed any credence in his statement, although all could see dimly a light, which appeared to be similar to those that we had seen repeatedly in the different lifeboats. It was not many minutes, nevertheless, before the same person declared that he could now see two lights, where formerly there was but one: Personally, I was unable to distinguish but one light. Five minutes later, however, two lights were plainly discerned, one above the other, appearing to be close together. The conviction grew that help was approaching. This was made a certainty a very few moments later, when the lights of a large steamer could be plainly discerned. The steamer was bearing directly down upon our lifeboat, when suddenly she was seen to change her course, and steam off in the direction of a lifeboat which had been, from time to time, displaying coloured lights.

Just about this time, day began to dawn, and we could see the steamer come to rest, where we knew this lifeboat to be located. At this time, the man who was pulling the oar next to the one which I handled turned to me and said: 'Doctor, are your wife and baby safe?' I told him that I had placed them in one of the first boats to be launched. Recognising the speaker as our table steward, I said to him: 'I had no idea that you were here.' To which he replied: 'Why, I was right behind you as we left the steamer, and called to you to get in.'

We now began to pull towards the vessel, but although it was not more than two miles distant, we did not reach her until long after sunrise, notwithstanding that the wind was directly astern of us. We could now see numerous other lifeboats coming from all points and rowing towards the *Carpathia*, for such our rescuing steamer proved to be. We could also see numerous icebergs, and an ice field to the north of us, which proved to be over fifty miles long.

When our boat reached the ship's side we passed in front of her bow, to reach the port side, where we would have the shelter from the wind, and a smoother sea to disembark. An officer of the *Carpathia* called to us to come up on the starboard side. The vessel was then unloading lifeboats on each side. Those of us who were rowing endeavoured for five minutes to pull back across the bow of the ship, but so ineffective were our efforts, that we were unable against the wind to make any progress. We finally had to disembark on the port side.

As the *Carpathia* had taken aboard the occupants of four or five lifeboats before ours arrived, I was naturally consumed with anxiety to ascertain whether my wife and child were aboard. After a short search I found them in the dining room, where the women and children were being tenderly cared for, and being revived by the administration of warm drinks and the application of warm wraps.

The *Carpathia* lay to for several hours, while the occupants of the various lifeboats were being taken aboard as they rowed up, one by one. Several of those who were passengers on the *Carpathia* busied themselves by taking photographs of the lifeboats, as they drew alongside of the steamer. These photographs have been reproduced in many of the newspapers and magazines of the country, and show many of the lifeboats to have been but half filled. None of them were properly manned, there being few seamen in any of them.

There were taken aboard the *Carpathia* 705 persons. A number of the lifeboats contained the bodies of men who had been rescued from the icy waters but who had died before the boats reached the *Carpathia* from the cold and exposure incident to their immersion. Several men were brought aboard in a condition of collapse, these being some of those who had jumped from the steamer as she sank, and who had been immersed in the water for from two to three hours. I helped to resuscitate several of these men, and on the following days, before the *Carpathia* reached New York, learned from them the conditions which prevailed aboard the *Titanic* after my departure, and the events which immediately preceded her sinking. This information thus obtained at first hand I will set forth later.

Scarcely had I set foot on the *Carpathia* when I was I greeted by Mr Wallace Bradford, of the firm of Hulse-Bradford Company of this city, who was a passenger on the *Carpathia* bound for Trieste. He insisted upon putting his stateroom at the disposal of my wife and child, which offer I gladly accepted.

The *Carpathia*, being comfortably well filled by her own passengers, was extremely overcrowded by our 700 additional persons. All, however, were comfortably cared for. The male passengers aboard, and in many instances the ladies, surrendered their cabins to women and children of the *Titanic*. So able and tenderly were the survivors cared for by the captain and crew of the *Carpathia*, that the former subscribed to a purse of several thousand dollars to be given to the officers and crew, and to purchase a loving cup suitably inscribed for the captain.

In the preceding remarks I have set forth the facts connected with the loss of the *Titanic* as observed by myself. My knowledge of subsequent events, as stated, is derived from extended conversation held with several of the men who swam off the *Titanic* as she sank. By observing, and noting the points in their narratives, in which there was no conflict, I was enabled to form, I think, a fairly accurate opinion of the events connected with and preceding the sinking of the ship.

The lifeboats on the starboard side were all launched a considerable length of time, possibly three quarters of an hour, before those on the port side were launched. There had been some trouble in launching the boats on the port side. The fact that orders had been given for the women and children to assemble on the port side, where the captain was, caused a greater congestion on this side of the vessel. The boats, however, on that side were all successfully launched and no panic, or great fear, was manifested among the passengers. Shortly after the launching of the last lifeboat, however, when there was still left four collapsible boats unlaunched, the male steerage passengers swarmed upon the boat deck. Many of these carried drawn daggers and knives in their hands, and others were armed with clubs of wood. They began to fight their way desperately to the collapsible boats, and try to gain possession of the same.

About this time the steamer suddenly settled to a very much greater degree forward, so that the waters at the forward end of the boat deck approached to within eight or ten feet of the same. With these conditions prevailing, panic ensued. Those fighting their way to the lifeboats attempted to jump into the same, and several were shot down by officers.

Only one collapsible boat was successfully launched, another was hanging from the davits ready to be launched, and a third was hastily pushed over the side of the steamer into the waters below, but unfortunately fell upside down and drifted from the ship. A number of the men then jumped from the steamer and swam to this overturned collapsible boat, which, by the way, was a flat-bottomed boat. They managed to climb upon the same, using it as a raft.

At this time, one of the survivors, who related the incident to me, was endeavouring to cut the ropes that bound the remaining collapsible boat to the deck. He had about half of these severed, when the bow of the *Titanic* was suddenly submerged, and the rush of waters tore the remaining fastenings loose. He, being flung into the water, saved himself by clinging to the boat. At this instant, many of those who were on the forward end of the boat deck were either washed off or jumped into the water clinging to wreckage.

Captain Smith, so I was told by an eye witness, called out, 'Now it's every man for himself,' and sprang into the water. Three of those who were at this time in the water, told me the same story of the succeeding events. They stated that as the *Titanic*'s bow sunk deeper and deeper into the water, they heard a series of two or three reports following each other at intervals, apparently from the hold of the vessel toward the bow. These reports, they stated, resembled those of a gun. Following the last, and the loudest report, they stated that an immense volume of water rushed upward within the vessel, above the level of the ocean, bursting the windows and doors outward. These reports, they went on to state, were, in their opinion, caused by the successive giving away of the submerged bulkheads, constituting the water-tight compartments forward. With the last report, connected with the upward rush of the water within the steamer, the bow of the vessel disappeared beneath the level of the sea, and her whole stern was lifted high into the air. As one who was then in the ocean expressed it: 'It looked like a great mountain hanging directly over my head, which I expected would instantly fall back upon me.' Following this the vessel was seen to buckle close to the water line, and immediately she took her final plunge into the ocean depths. All of these latter events transpired in the space of a very few moments.

My idea is, that when the stern of the ship was lifted high out of the water by the bursting of the water-tight compartments, in the forward end of the vessel, that the vast weight of the machinery caused the framework and the plates of the ship to give way, thus allowing the great inrush of waters to complete her destruction.

From the preceding narrative it is seen that those who escaped in the lifeboats, had little or no knowledge of the terrible events which transpired with the sinking of the ship. As near as I can fix the lapse of time, an hour or an hour and a quarter elapsed, after the lifeboat, in which I left the vessel, was launched, up to the time of the sinking of the steamer.

The tales told me, however, by these men who were on board the vessel, or in the water, as she sunk, are almost too harrowing for repetition. These men, for hours after their arrival on the *Carpathia* would burst forth in tears, lamenting the terrible scenes through which they passed.

With some of these men, there clambered onto the bottom of the collapsible boat, other survivors, until it held in the neighbourhood of forty persons. So many, however, climbed upon the same, that it was constantly submerged from six inches to three feet, and there they stood shoulder to shoulder, endeavouring to balance and prevent the raft from overturning. Numbers died on this raft, chilled by the icy waters to the point where they succumbed, when their bodies were cast into the sea by the survivors. Several times the raft was capsized, and always some would be lost in their attempt to clamber back upon it. When the survivors were taken off the raft, but sixteen remained of the original forty. (The preceding was all given me in detail by several who were on the raft.)

Following the collision the band which had earlier in the evening given the usual Sunday evening concert, continued to play. They played ragtime and other lively music. But a few moments before the steamer sank, when the danger was apparent to all, they were playing 'Lead Kindly Light.' There were five musicians, all of whom were lost.

When all of the survivors were gathered aboard the *Carpathia*, word was circulated requesting that all first class and second-class passengers give their names to the purser, in order that a list of the rescued might be sent ashore by means of the Marconi wireless. The purser had a book in which the survivors wrote their names. I wrote in this book distinctly the name of myself, with that of my wife and that of my little son. Unfortunately somewhere in the repetition of this list, after it had left the *Carpathia*, by the vessel relaying the same, or the operator ashore, the error was made of reporting my name as 'Mr Washington,' the 'Dodge' being omitted. My proof of the fact that my name was correctly sent off the day of the disaster, by the Marconi operator of the *Carpathia*, is proven by what, to me, is a most interesting incident.

I received, only three days since, a letter written on board the steamship *Olympic*, which was the sister ship to the *Titanic*, and which at the time of the disaster was on her way to England from New York. This letter is as follows:

'On Board RMS *Olympic*, at sea,
April 15th

Dr Washington Dodge.

Dear Sir: I want to congratulate you, Mrs Dodge, and your little child, on your escape from the awful disaster. We, on the sister ship have been rushing to your aid all day, but alas, to no effect. We have positively no news of the disaster, except a partial list of survivors, among whom I was very happy to see your names.

Hoping that your family suffers no ill effects, I remain,

Yours very truly,
B.M. JOSEPH,
With Raphael, Weill & Co.'

Mr Joseph, a buyer for the White House, was on his annual trip to Europe, and on reaching Southampton mailed this letter which, as stated, only reached me a few day since. Had this error not been made my relatives, and friends, would have been spared the two days of suspense which I learned of after reaching New York. The *Olympic*, on which Mr Joseph was a passenger, received our first wireless call for help. Later in the day she received a wireless from the *Carpathia* informing her of the *Titanic*'s loss and giving a list of those rescued.

A question frequently asked me has been whether following the collision, the passengers believed that they were in any immediate danger. I think that what I have narrated shows that up to the time following the launching of the last lifeboat, little apprehension existed in the minds of most of the passengers. This, to some, may seem almost incredible. When one rejects, however, that the *Titanic* was considered by all, in itself, a life boat, and an unsinkable vessel, and that no one had any idea of the terrible injury to the ship, caused by a shock so slight, as that given by the impact with the iceberg: – when she was seen to be afloat with apparently no displacement, on a calm sea, with no ice in sight, it can readily be conceived that the idea of the vessel sinking did not impress itself on the minds of the passengers. When, to these facts, there was added the assurance of the officers that under no conditions could the ship sink in less than eight or ten hours, and that within an hour or two, not one, but three or four, steamers would be alongside – they having been signalled by wireless – it can readily be seen how this confidence grew.

Perhaps a few incidents which came to my knowledge will serve to illustrate these facts more forcibly. Mr Carter and Mr Widener were two prominent Philadelphians aboard the steamer. Mr Carter was saved. Mr Widener was lost. Mr Carter related the following circumstances: 'We had been together on the port side of the steamer, and had seen a number of boats launched. I said to my friend: 'Harry, let's go around on the starboard side, as we might have a chance to get aboard a boat there.' He replied, 'You go ahead, old man, if you want to, I am going to take my chance with the steamer.' Mr Carter related that he then went to the starboard side, and there entered the last boat on that side which was then being launched. This was boat 15 in which Mr Ismay embarked, and which boat I saw launched.

Another incident. Myself and wife were acquainted with a couple residing in Los Angeles, who were passengers on the *Titanic*. On the *Carpathia*, the morning after the disaster, we found the wife, but the husband was missing. The wife related the following: At the time of the collision her husband was on the upper deck (deck A) in the card room, engaged with some friends, in a game of cards. She was on one of the lower decks (C deck, I think) preparing to retire, being partially disrobed. Being conscious of the jar, and noticing that the engines had stopped, she put on her clothing, and went up two decks above, to her husband in the card room. He assured her that there was nothing to be alarmed at, that he had been so told by one of the officers, and told her to return to her stateroom, where he would join her presently. This she did; he continuing in the game of cards. As she reached her stateroom door, she saw a man with a life preserver on, hurrying along the corridor. She laughed at him, and said, 'Well, you must be a pretty nervous man.' He then told her that the order had been given for all passengers to put on life preservers. She again went up to 'A' deck, and informed her husband of what she had been told. They then went down to their stateroom, put on warmer underclothing, and dressed in the warmest clothing that they had. After this they proceeded to the boat deck, where they were joined by another couple they knew, and there watched the boats being launched. The ladies refused to enter the lifeboats, stating that they would wait and go with their husbands later. Eventually, after several of the boats were launched, the officers insisted that they get into a boat, their husbands adding their request, and assisting them into the boat. After this neither of them ever saw or heard anything of her husband. But as this lady in narrating the circumstances stated: 'Neither of us thought that there was any danger of our not meeting again. My husband handed me some money saying: 'We may be separated, and you might need this.' But he did not kiss me good bye, nor did he even say goodbye. I know he had no more idea of the possibility of his being lost than had I.'

Those who swam from the sinking steamer at the last moment had no idea that the vessel was in danger of sinking, until her body suddenly sank deeper in the waters a few moments before she sank. As they stated, had they believed the vessel was in any danger of sinking they would have had sufficient time, following the launching of the lifeboats, to have prepared temporary life rafts sufficient, in that calm sea, to have saved the lives of hundreds. There were on the decks stacked against the cabins, over 800 folding steamer chairs made of heavy oak frames. A few of these lashed together would have formed an emergency raft capable of sustaining one or more persons indefinitely. Hundreds of heavy wooden doors, and dining room tables and other material, were easily available for the same purpose.

These survivors stated, however, that until the sudden downward dip of the vessel forward, coincident with the rush onto the boat deck of the steerage passengers, they did not apprehend that there was and danger of the vessel sinking for hours or days, if at all. I quote again from the very able review published in the London papers, and in the *New York Times*, by Mr Lawrence Beesley, a passenger to whom reference has already been made:

'When the *Titanic* struck every one said, 'We are all right, this boat cannot sink. We will only have to wait around until another ship comes along to take us off.' This, he states, no doubt stopped the panic, and prevented those rushes after boats which probably would have occurred had this theory not been so widely and firmly held.'

There are a few matters relating to this disaster which have caused widespread criticism and discussion, which I will briefly touch upon. I am aware, however, that there are probably many present who are far better qualified than I to express an opinion on these matters.

The criticism has been made that gross carelessness was displayed, in driving the steamship at such a rate of speed after warnings of icebergs ahead had been given. The charge is also made that the steamer was equipped with lifeboats sufficient to carry less than one-third of those aboard. Also, that not enough seamen to properly launch and man the lifeboats were at hand, and that the steamer was not provided with a searchlight.

There can be no question of the fact that the steamer was running at an unwarranted rate of speed after it had received the warning it had. Neither can there be any question of the fact that the lifeboats were not sufficient to carry all of those aboard. The number of seamen was positively insufficient. Owing to this great insufficiency, there being but sixteen seamen to launch and man twenty lifeboats, the lifeboats appeared to be filled and lowered consecutively, rather than simultaneously. The seriousness of this point is apparent when we consider that when the ship sank, nearly three hours after she struck, there still remained three collapsible boats, each capable of holding thirty or more persons, unlaunched. As to the searchlight, it is not disputed that the steamer was without one.

In answer to these criticisms the only excuse that can be offered is the following. Many steamship companies undoubtedly endeavour to meet the requirements of the public for rapid transit. The fast liners that advertise to leave New York on Mondays and take dinner in London on Saturday, seldom fail to arrive on schedule time. As the craze on the part of the public for speed, and the incident saving of time is manifested on the water, so we see the same evidenced on shore by the 'cannon-ball express,' and '20th century limited' trains. Sleet, snow, and even fog are often disregarded in the running of these trains and boats, no matter how great the menace, if only the time schedule can be lived up to. As was done by the captain of the *Titanic*, so, many captains for years past have done, that is, to run at full speed through the iceberg region. While this is not done by every captain, yet it is not an uncommon occurrence for captains of fast passenger-mail steamers to do so. Considering the vastness of the ocean, and the small size of an iceberg, the chance of striking one are about as remote as the finding of the proverbial needle in a haystack. These chances of disaster have been taken thousands of times previous to the disaster of the *Titanic*, but unfortunately here the chance was taken once too often. The *Titanic* encountered the only thing in the ocean which was capable, in my opinion, of sinking her.

There is, to my mind, no excuse for such a catastrophe, but it is difficult to free the travelling public from all responsibility for such disasters.

As to the insufficiency of lifeboats, taking into consideration the unsinkable qualities of the *Titanic*, and the fact, as Captain Rostron of the *Carpathia* stated it: 'She was herself a lifeboat,' she was probably better equipped than are the majority of passenger steamers today.

Very similar conditions prevail on other steamers regarding the insufficiency of seamen. The crews are made up principally of engineers, oilers, stokers, and stewards. When a catastrophe such as this occurs, the lack of seamen to man the lifeboats is a serious matter. Had the sea not been unusually calm, not one-fourth of those saved would have been rescued.

The absence of a searchlight seems inexcusable. The fact that passenger steamers at this time of the year, when icebergs are a menace take the northern route, rather than a more southern and safer route, simply because this northern route is shorter, and entails less expense and time in making the trip, seems positively unwarranted.

In conclusion, I will state that I hope this narrative has given you a clearer understanding of the events connected with this great disaster. There is no doubt that the catastrophe will result in the adoption of rules, regarding the equipment of ocean-going steamers, and their navigation which will make the repetition of such a disaster less liable.[172]

MAHALA DOUGLAS **First Class Passenger**

Following the disaster, Mrs Douglas wrote the following brief statement for publication in a newspaper:

> Even the passengers knew that we were getting among the icebergs early on Sunday – hours before the crash came we felt the temperature drop and realised the truth.
>
> That this fact was well known to Bruce Ismay was evidenced from his own actions and statements. I told Senator Smith of the Senate Inquiry Committee of an incident that confirmed this.
>
> Sunday evening I was walking the deck with Mrs Ryerson when she told me that Mr Ismay had exhibited a wireless message that told of the presence of the dangerous icebergs.
>
> 'What does the message say?' Mrs Ryerson asked.
>
> 'That we are among the icebergs,' was his reply.
>
> 'Of course you are going to slow down?' Mrs Ryerson asked him.
>
> 'Certainly not, we are going to put on more steam and run away from them,' said Mr Ismay.
>
> One of the seamen lowered a bucket into the ocean, but drew it back before it had touched the water. Then he drew the water from the ship's tanks to take temperature.
>
> I called the attention of my husband to this fact, but he belittled it and told me it would not be necessary to tell the ship's officers of the incident.[173]

On 2 May 1912 Mrs Douglas made the following affidavit for the Senate *Titanic* inquiry:

> We left Cherbourg late on account of trouble at Southampton, but once off, everything seemed to go perfectly. The boat was so luxurious, so steady, so immense, and such a marvel of mechanism that one could not believe he was on a boat – and there the danger lay. We had smooth seas, clear, starlit nights, fresh favouring winds; nothing to mar our pleasure.
>
> On Saturday, as Mr Douglas and I were walking forward, we saw a seaman taking the temperature of the water. The deck seemed so high above the sea I was interested to know if the tiny pail could reach it. There was quite a breeze, and although the pail was weighted, it did not. This I watched from the open window of the covered deck. Drawing up the pail the seaman filled it with water from the stand pipe, placed the thermometer in it, and went with it to the officer in charge.
>
> On Sunday we had a delightful day; everyone in the best of spirits; the time the boat was making was considered very good, and all were interested in getting into New York early. We dined in the restaurant, going in about 8 o'clock. We found the people dining, as follows: (See sketch of dining room.)
>
> As far as I have been able to learn, not a man in that room [was saved]; all those who served, from the head steward down, including Mr Gatti, in charge; the musicians who played in the corridor outside, and all the guests were lost

except Sir Cosmo Duff Gordon, Mr Carter, and Mr Ismay. All stories of excessive gaiety are, to my mind, absolutely unfounded. We did not leave the tables until most of the others had left, including Mr Ismay, Mr and Mrs Widener, and their guests, and the evening was passed very quietly. As we went to our stateroom – C-86 – we both remarked that the boat was going faster than she ever had. The vibration as one passed the stairway in the centre was very noticeable. The shock of the collision was not great to us; the engines stopped, then went on for a few moments, then stopped again. We waited some little time, Mr Douglas reassuring me that there was no danger before going out of the cabin. But later Mr Douglas went out to see what had happened, and I put on my heavy boots and fur coat to go up on deck later. I waited in the corridor to see or hear what I could. We received no orders; no one knocked at our door; we saw no officers nor stewards – no one to give an order or answer our questions. As I waited for Mr Douglas to return I went back to speak to my maid, who was in the same cabin as Mrs Carter's maid. Now people commenced to appear with life preservers, and I heard from someone that the order had been given to put them on. I took three from our cabin, gave one to the maid, telling her to get off in the small boat when her turn came. Mr Douglas met me as I was going up to find him and asked, jestingly, what I was doing with those life preservers. He did not think even then that the accident was serious. We both put them on, however, and went up on the boat deck. Mr Douglas told me if I waited we might both go together, and we stood there waiting. We heard that the boat was in communication with three other boats by wireless; we watched the distress rockets sent off – they rose high in the air and burst.

No one seemed excited. Finally, as we stood by a collapsible boat lying on the deck and an emergency boat swinging from the davits was being filled, it was decided I should go. Mr Boxhall was trying to get the boat off, and called to the captain on the bridge, 'There's a boat coming up over there.' The captain said 'I want a megaphone.' Just before we got into the boat the captain called, 'How many of the crew are in that boat? Get out of there, every man of you'; and I can see a solid row of men, from bow to stern, crawl over on to the deck. We women then got in. I asked Mr Douglas to come with me, but he replied, 'No; I must be a gentleman,' turning away. I said, 'Try and get off with Mr Moore and Maj. Butt. They will surely make it.' Maj. Butt and Clarence Moore were standing together near us, also Mr Meyer, and I remember seeing Mr Ryerson's face in the crowd. There were many people about. I got into the boat and sat under the seats on the bottom, just under the tiller. Mr Boxhall had difficulty about getting the boat loose and called for a knife. We finally were launched. Mrs Appleton and a man from the steerage faced me. Mrs Appleton's sister was back to me, and on the seat with her, the officer. Mr Boxhall tried to have us count in order to find the number in the boat, but he did not succeed in getting any higher than 10, as so many did not speak English – I think there were 18 or 20. There was one other member of the crew. The rowing was very difficult, for no one knew how. I tried to steer, under Mr Boxhall's orders, and he put the lantern – an old one, with very little light in it – on a pole which I held up for some time. Mr Boxhall got away from the ship and we stopped for a time. Several times we stopped rowing to listen for the lapping of the water against the icebergs. In an incredibly short space of time, it seemed to me, the boat sank. I heard an explosion. I watched the boat go down, and the last picture to my mind is the immense mass of black against the starlit sky, and then – nothingness.

Mrs Appleton and some of the other women had been rowing and did row all of the time. Mr Boxhall had charge of the signal lights on the *Titanic*, and he had put in the emergency boat a tin of green lights, like rockets. These he commenced to send off at intervals, and very quickly we saw the lights of the *Carpathia*, the captain of which stated he saw our green lights 10 miles away, and, of course, steered directly to us, so we were the first boat to arrive at the *Carpathia*.

When we pulled alongside Mr Boxhall called out, 'Shut down your engines and take us aboard. I have only one sailor.' At this point I called out, 'The *Titanic* has gone down with everyone on board,' and Mr Boxhall told me to 'shut up.' This is not told in criticism; I think he was perfectly right. We climbed a rope ladder to the upper deck of the *Carpathia*. I at once asked the chief steward, who met us, to take the news to the captain. He said the officer was already with him.

The history of our wonderful treatment on the *Carpathia* is known to the world. It has been underestimated.

We reached the *Carpathia* at 4.10, and I believe by 10 o'clock all of the boats had been accounted for. We sailed away, leaving the *Californian* to cruise about the scene. We circled the point where the *Titanic* had gone down, and I saw nothing except quantities of cork, loose cork floating in the current, like a stream – nothing else.

In the afternoon I sent a brief Marconigram with the news that Mr Douglas was among the missing. I went myself to the purser several times every day, and others also made inquiries for me in regard to it, but it was not sent.

We heard many stories of the rescue from many sources. These I tried to keep in my mind clearly, as they seemed important.

Among them I will quote Mrs Ryerson, of Philadelphia. This story was told in the presence of Mrs Meyer, of New York, and others.

(Mrs Ryerson speaking.) 'Sunday afternoon Mr Ismay, whom I know very slightly, passed me on the deck. He showed me, in his brusque manner, a Marconigram, saying, "We have just had news that we are in the icebergs." "Of course, you will slow down," I said. "Oh, no"; he replied, "we will put on more boilers and get out of it."'

An Englishwoman, who was going to her sons in Dakota, told me: 'I was in a boat with 5 women and 50 men – they had been picked up from the London unemployed to fill out the crew. They would not row, told frightful stories to alarm the women, and when the *Carpathia* was sighted, said; "We are jolly lucky. No work to-night; nothing to do but smoke and yarn. Back in London next week with the unemployed."'

The history of the quartermaster's conduct was told by many women; his brutality is known. His inefficiency is shown by his asking 'Is that a buoy?' when they were out in the small boat on the ocean.

Maj. Peuchen came to me just before landing in New York with Mr Beattie, of the *London Times*. They asked me to repeat some things I had said, which I did. They took my address. Maj. Peuchen said, 'I have just been called up (I took this to mean before the officers of the *Titanic*) and asked what I meant by getting testimony and stirring up the passengers.' I replied, 'You have not answered my questions; I will not answer yours.'

All the women told of insufficient seamen to man the boats; all women rowed; some had to bail water from their boats. Mrs Smith was told to watch a cork in her boat, and if it came out to put her finger in place of it.

When we arrived in New York the crew of the *Titanic* was ordered to get off in the lifeboats before we could dock.

I sat in a deck chair and listened and looked. The unseamanlike way of going at their simple tasks without excitement showed me more plainly than anything I had seen or heard the inefficiency of the crew, and accounted, in some measure, for the number of the crew saved and the unfilled lifeboats. A passenger on the *Carpathia* also spoke to me of this.

Mr Lightoller and Mr Boxhall were extremely courteous and kind on board the *Carpathia*. I think them both capable seamen and gentlemen.

Mahala D. Douglas[174]

LUCY DUFF GORDON — First Class Passenger

Soon after the disaster, Lady Duff Gordon wrote a letter to her sister describing her experiences on the *Titanic*. The following fragmentary excerpt is all that survives:

... and we were so looking forward to a few days' rest before the frantic whirl of New York. The ship was an absolute marvel, Nell. The *Titanic* was surely the most beautiful ship that ever sailed. To think all that loveliness is now a watery hell. It is unbelievable. Our staterooms, divided by a short passageway, were small but truly beautiful. My cabin was all in pink with a lacy quilt and matching silk curtains and lampshades, a dainty gem of a place, and with all my photographs and flowers arranged, which our stewardess accomplished so well, it became my own little ocean-borne haven. I had as many of the things with me as could be fitted with ease into the room, but this dear stewardess, who was an Irish woman full of cheer, informed me otherwise and scolded me for taking up so much space with my 'fiddle-faddle,' as she called my travelling cases and boxes! I caught sight of her on the dear *Carpathia* the night we got into New York and was glad to know she was saved, though like all of us, she was obviously under a terrific strain. She seemed happy to see me as I approached and stood up and held out her hand affectionately. She said to me in her wonderful brogue, 'Ah, but Madame has lost all her glorious fluffs! What are we to do?' Fighting back the tears, I told her, 'We can buy more fluffs but can we mend our hearts?'

She replied, 'Oh, no milady, we none of us will be the same.'

Cosmo and I found we had a number of friends en route, Americans mostly, and we had a merry time visiting with...

(Several pages are apparently missing, before the following:)

... Franks rushed into my room in hysterics. The dear girl said she had seen the water coming along the corridor after her as she fled her room below. This shook me badly but Cosmo said to remain calm, that all was to be quite all right. But I felt at once we were in peril. Cosmo was so brave to try and keep us in good spirits, making rather a bad jest as to how unappetising we both looked in those sickly white life-preservers which two stewards were hooking round us. Oh, Nell we were so frightened. But we prayed for strength and felt the angels' reassurance that we were safe in God's hands.

Cosmo was in his Norfolk and went across the way to his room to collect his cap and gloves but came right back to take us on deck though we were but half-dressed ourselves. Franks wore only her nightclothes, a sweater, and a long woollen motor-coat, thrown on in haste, poor child. I was not much better arrayed. I took time only to fling over my nightdress a kimono dressing gown I'd been using as a wrap for my bath, but a meagre one I'm afraid, which I'd taken unfinished from the shop and had not had time to sew properly. It was a lovely pale lavender with touches of silvery mauve piped in black but as it was such a flimsy silk it was not much protection from the cold, as I soon discovered. I put on a heavy crepe scarf, the pretty turquoise one you admired, and tied it on as a turban which kept the wind out of my hair but alas did not warm my head!

Over all I wore the big squirrel coat which was ready at hand, but how I wish I'd chosen the sable! I could not bother about getting my jewels out so only brought away with me my little coral velveteen ring bag with a few odds and ends and bits. All the rest went down, dear, and yes, even the pearls! Oh, the loss of them and now the dreaded cost of repaying! It makes me go pale with rage when I think what a fool I was to take such a thing on a boat! The only real valuables I saved were not jewels but my beautiful pink velvet Yantorny mules with the pompon toes and ermine lining!

We went quickly out into the main passage and found at the end, gathered about the stairs, a great and noisy throng of people, everybody as ill at ease as ourselves, but putting brave faces on and doing a lot of silly chatting and laughing. We went past them and climbed the steps to the boat deck but there was such a crowd at the top we were obliged to wait some minutes while the queue filtered through. This was most aggravating and I was very near losing my temper at all the ribald fellows grouped about us, all American youths of course with their filthy humour. Quite insupportable lot.

Once ascended to the vestibule, we were for a moment in a mad crush before finding a place to stand in a corner out of the way. We could then look about us but noticed not a soul of our acquaintance, excepting Mrs Cavendish who was on the other side of the stairway leaning against the balustrade. I did not see her husband with her. I have wondered if they were separated in the crowd as you know he was lost. That poor woman. I tried to comfort her on the *Carpathia* later but she was inconsolable.

The three of us stood to the side keeping well out of the path of those going out on the deck, and we shivered awfully whenever the deck door opened. We were satisfied to stay put for the moment but as the crowd congregating in our vicinity grew ever more dense we finally followed others out into the chill night. We weren't speaking much to each other as the din of voices was such that it was difficult to hear our own conversation.

Outside we saw officers and other crewmen swarming over the lifeboats which had been uncovered and were being swung out and readied for lowering. This was startling to see. Although we had been warned by the stewards to be prepared for going away in a boat, it simply did not seem possible that all this was actually happening. We three walked down the deck a bit and found the gymnasium open and the room full of light and warmth. We came in and sat down a few minutes but on hearing an officer's call to the boats we stepped out again to watch the activity. We stood there quite some minutes as the officers called for women and children. Few seemed to want to brave the dark sea in an open boat and it was only after considerable coaxing that many went at all. A few men went into the boats as well to calm the ladies. It was the strangest scene to behold, people bundled up in odd clothes boarding lifeboats in the night.

Presently, a rocket, terribly loud and bright, was set off near the bridge and everybody lifted their heads to watch it shooting up, searing the night sky. It was an awesome spectacle, almost as if we were suddenly transported to some macabre fairground. The three of us kept clear of the boats and only observed the goings-on with a kind of nervous detachment. More rockets were fired. Shortly two of the boats nearest us were put over the side and we were just walking forward when a sailor ran up and tried to drag me away from Cosmo. Another had got hold of Franks who cried out to us. I pleaded with Cosmo not to let them take me away, to let us remain together. I told him I did not want to go without him. He relented and asked the men to release me. They were still going after poor Franks till she told them she was with us and would not go away alone and so they let her stay. This incident put us all in a frantic state but we did not say so till later, when we agreed that it was then, at that moment, that we recognised we were really in the most dreadful danger.

I clung to Cosmo and held onto Franks, as well. We were both shaking so, from the cold and fear. Directly before us we saw a boat – smaller than the rest – being made ready while the one beside us cast off. Almost all of those who had been standing near seemed to have gone in it or retreated up the deck, which was now angled noticeably towards the bows. We could see no one else round us and I felt the small boat was our chance to go away together. I asked Cosmo if we shouldn't try to get into it. He said, 'No, we must wait for orders.' But presently he thought better of it and asked the dear officers if we couldn't all get in. The officer was most kind and said, 'Please do.' And so we were each in turn hoisted – really that is the word for it – up over rather a high railing and then sort of plopped into ...[175]

(The remainder of the letter is missing.)

On 16 May 1912 Lady Duff Gordon wrote the following letter to Margot Asquith:

My dear Margot,

What a welcome your kind letter was to us.

After all the horror and confusion this last month has wrought, it is truly a wonderful relief to find ourselves among friends and family once more.

At last to have Esme with me and the children whom I thought I might never see again.

We do all undervalue our daily existence. But when that is threatened how sweet are the mundane things of life! Here in the house, the dreadful back stairs I wanted to pull down now seem quite lovely and I am only too glad to climb them again.

But, O Margot, the utter sorrow I feel for all the poor souls who cannot know the joy of a homecoming, whose dear ones are distracted with grief over their loss, is at times more than I can stand. The why of it all perplexes me so that I am not able quite to rest, which disturbs Cosmo exceedingly on my account as he is insistent that I should try and not think of it.

And yet he thinks of it all the while and shuts himself up in the library for hours on end, dear man, worrying and looking a fright when he emerges, he is so downcast.

Our suffering is made all the more acute as you well know by the vicious reports which are making the rounds of the Press and seem to be growing more outrageously vile by the day. Poor brave little Franks is here at my side, as ever, and her nearness is a comfort and a blessing. She will be with me tomorrow in the Court.

I am very much pleased and touched to learn that you intend coming and showing your support for us. I feel an enormous dread of the moment we shall take the box but there is nothing for it as we must defend ourselves against the atrocious lies being printed and which have caused us the greatest distress.

Knowing you are to be there, dear one, will soothe my nerves somewhat I trust, and I am indeed thankful for your special words of encouragement at this most trying time.

Fondest love,

Lucy[176]

ANNA ELIZABETH DYKER **Third Class Passenger**

Following the disaster, Anna Dyker's mother travelled to New York and appealed to the Women's Relief Committee for financial aid for her widowed daughter. Later Anna herself wrote the following letter to the Relief Committee:

> Dear Madam,
>
> When my dear mother arrived and told me the kindness which she had received in New York and that through your kindness she had received $300 and the clothes I wish to thank you, oh so much. Having lost my dear husband, I have lost everything.
>
> He had just been able to build a small house upon his wages as a trolley car conductor. This, as you understand, is mortgaged heavily and your gift in money enables me to retain it. As for my future support I trust God will help me, as I have suffered as much as I can.
>
> But I felt so happy in the good news which my mother had for me, and thank you most heartily and also for your kindness toward me.[177]

FRANK DYMOND **Crew (Fireman)**

While returning to England on board the *Lapland*, Mr Dymond wrote a letter to J. Rummage of Portsea. A general description of that letter's contents follows:

> Mr Dymond stated that the *Titanic* was travelling at about 22 knots when those on board heard a loud rasping sound like the scraping of a file. There were tons of ice on the deck after the collision. He was ordered into lifeboat 15 and, as there were no officers or sailors in the boat, he took charge of her. There were 68 people in the boat, 22 of whom were women, and five babies, some of whom had lost their parents. The passengers were ordered to put on lifebelts and go to the boat deck. Some put the belts on, and others did not. Had they done as they were told Mr Dymond thought that more people would have been saved.
>
> Dymond wrote in glowing terms of the crew, who he said were men and that England ought to be proud of them. There were only 71 firemen saved out of a total of 348. The *Titanic* broke in two, and her boilers blew up. The sound of the machinery as it ran out of her was plainly heard when she went down. The occupants of boat 15 rowed among the icebergs for six hours before they were picked up by the *Carpathia*.[178]

HENRY FRAUENTHAL **First Class Passenger**

In May 1912 Dr Frauenthal wrote the following account of his experiences on board the *Titanic*:

> Recalling the *Titanic* as I saw it from the tender just before going on board at Cherbourg, it is almost impossible to conceive that this magnificent vessel of 880 feet could have sunk. Up to the time of the accident, the trip had been ideal.
>
> On Sunday night, I retired at about ten o'clock, and my wife and I were sleeping soundly, when at about twelve o'clock, I was awakened by my brother pounding on my cabin door, and insisting upon my getting up. Thinking that I had overslept and was late, I asked what was the matter, and he said that something had happened to the boat. On going to the door, he informed me that he had overheard the captain informing Colonel Astor that something serious had occurred to the boat and advised that everyone put on life preservers, and they were lowering the lifeboats. When I went on the boat deck, there were a few people there, but no confusion, and I saw them lowering the boats. There seemed difficulty in filling the boats. I returned for my wife to my cabin, No.88, Deck C, and in passing Mr Widener, who was in No.80, Deck C, I informed him that I had learned the boat was in danger, but he said that it was ridiculous. This answer probably describes the mental state of nearly everyone on the boat, thinking that it was impossible for anything serious to happen to this paragon of modern ship architecture. I returned to my cabin, and insisted on my wife putting a life preserver on. We went on deck and got in the boat which was in charge of Third Officer Pitman. In this boat there were an equal number of men and women, thirty-four in all. The boat on the port side, which was lowered at the same time as ours, was sent off by order of Captain Smith with only twenty-two passengers, because at that time there were no more who were willing to trust themselves to the life boats.
>
> In the process of being lowered, several times we thought we would be thrown into the water. When nearing the water, it was discovered that the plug in the bottom of the boat had not been safely inserted, and this was attended to. Had this been overlooked, this lifeboat would have sunk as one of the others did, in which the plug was not inserted. After rowing a short distance, I inquired of Third Officer Pitman what had occurred in the boat, being under the impression that the trouble was with the machinery and we were likely to be blown up. I learned then for the first time that we had struck an iceberg. I asked when we would return to the *Titanic*, and he said within half an hour, as he thought there was no danger to the vessel and only as we observed one row of porthole lights after another disappearing below the water line did we begin to realise how serious the accident was. One of the sailors in our boat was on watch at the time the accident occurred and said that the iceberg was above the upper deck and through concussion several tons of ice were thrown on the upper deck. Pitman, the 3rd officer, who like myself was asleep, was not awakened by the accident. Those who were awake at the time said there was no concussion, but it seemed as if the boat scraped like a ferryboat going into the slip. Pitman was awakened by a sailor and

said he went down to see what had occurred and met some of the stokers coming out of the hold, saying that water was rushing in and driving them out. He then went on deck and aided in loading the other boats. He was ordered to take charge of the lifeboat in which I left the vessel, which I think was No.5.

There was no moon, but the stars in the sky were numerous and it made the surroundings appear as light as it would with a quarter moon. We rowed about a mile from the *Titanic*, believing that if she went down it would be a protection against the suction of the vessel. In the boat I was in, and in all the other lifeboats which I inspected as they were hoisted in the *Carpathia*, there was no compass, no lantern, no water and no food! The only light in any of the small boats was a lantern taken off by Fifth Officer Lowe, and his reason for taking it was, as he said, that he had been in two shipwrecks previously and realised its need. It was by the means of this light that the *Carpathia* was able to sight us, as they saw the light at a distance of ten miles. After daybreak it would have been difficult for the *Carpathia* to have detected us in the ice field we were in. The ocean surface during the whole night was as smooth as glass, nor was there any wind. The air was intensely cold, and nearly everyone suffered from the low temperature.

We watched the boat and timed her as she sank, which was about 2:20 a.m., according to the officer's watch. The time of the accident was about 10:45 p.m., showing that the boat remained afloat for only about three and a half hours.

One of the boats rowed up to us which had but twenty-seven passengers in it, and three men from our boat were transferred to this lifeboat.

When the vessel went down and for some time after, the cries of those who were on life preservers and floats were indescribable, and no one who heard these cries will ever forget them.

The *Carpathia* was in sight about 4:30 a.m., when all the small boats rowed towards her. We were taken on board at about six o'clock, being on the water just about 5½ hours. Some of the smaller boats did not arrive until nearly nine o'clock, after which we circled around for about three hours, hoping to pick up some of the shipwrecked. During the night we could see the large iceberg which we struck and several smaller ones, and I cannot see how so large a mass of ice could not have been seen in ample time by the lookout. At about 8 a.m. two big vessels arrived on the scene, and they were left on the ground to see if they could pick up any of the survivors. When day broke we saw about two miles away what seemed to be land, but which was a field of ice and which I since learned was 200 miles long. So had we missed the large iceberg, going at the rate of 21 or 22 knots an hour, we would have driven into the field of ice just ahead of us.

The passengers from the small boats were taken into the *Carpathia* by means of a pilot's ladder. For safety the women had a looped rope under their arms, and when they lost their footing on the rope ladder they were drawn on board the boat. Many did lose their footing on account of the nervous state they were in and the cold which made them stiff, and in being hauled on board received many bruises.

One cannot speak in too high praise of the arrangements for our reception on board the *Carpathia*. As each one got to the deck they were given a large hot drink of either hot water or hot tea or hot diluted brandy. If this did not warm them up, they were covered with blankets and additional drinks were given. By this means a reaction was brought about, and in place of being blue they became pink and moist, and out of the 705 survivors no case of bronchitis or pneumonia occurred to my knowledge, and the vessel came into port with a clean bill of health. Although all the papers were filled with the account of the large number of ill on board, it was not a fact. A certain number suffered from the exposure and from injuries and were taken to St Vincent's Hospital. A number of sprained ankles and Pott's fractures occurred from various causes. Owing to the fact that a number of women lost their husbands, a certain amount of nervous hysteria prevailed. This was intensified by the fact that on our trip to New York for four days, we were most of the time enveloped in fogs and everyone seemed to dread the recurrence of an accident.

About $6,000 was collected on the *Carpathia* from the survivors to meet the immediate needs of the *Titanic* passengers, of which $4,000 was afterwards given to the crew on the *Carpathia* in recognition of their services.

The large death list was due to the fact that the majority of the people did not know the nature and extent of the damage done to the boat, and a great number knew that the *Carpathia* had been in communication and that she was coming to the rescue. The fear of going into the small boats on account of the danger in case of a high sea, deterred many from entering. There was a general feeling that the boat could not possibly sink before some of the larger boats nearby would come to the rescue. This was particularly true as some of the people refused to depart shortly before the boat went down, thinking it safer than venturing in a small boat.[179]

MAY FUTRELLE **First Class Passenger**

After arriving in the United States, Mrs Futrelle wrote the following account of her *Titanic* experience:

> It seems to me like some horrible dream. I can't realise yet that my husband, 'My Jacques' and the hundreds of other brave men who with unexampled heroism stood back and gave up their lives that the women and children might be saved, are gone from us. Oh, it is all too terrible.
>
> Never shall I forget that sight. No words can express the despair of it all. One cannot adequately describe the sufferings of the women parted from their husbands with such frightful suddenness, the heroism of the men, the fortitude of the women, the high courage of the officers of the *Titanic*, and that dread last moment when the shrieks of the 1,600 dying men and women were sent across the waters in an appeal to those who had no power to save them. I shall never again look upon the ocean without thinking of that scene.

The world asks who is to blame? It is true there are lessons to be learned in the future from this great catastrophe which so effectively demonstrated the futility of human effort when pitted against the powers of nature. Man has reached the pinnacle of his genius in the construction of these ocean monsters, which it was confidently expected would defy successfully the dangers which lurk in the ocean.

In the briefest space of time, the elements, as if to show their scorn for his puny efforts, wrecked the ultimate product of man's genius in marine architecture. Death which hovers in various forms on the great ocean came with awful abruptness.

Men laughed at the idea of anything happening to the *Titanic*. It was mere idle speculation to think of such a thing, and why not, whoever feared drowning when seated in a luxurious library? What thought of death was there in the mind of man who enjoyed his after-dinner cigar in the big comfortable chairs of the smoking rooms? Why, it was as ridiculous to think of meeting death in the icy waters about us as to fear it in the beautiful swimming pool below decks or in the luxuriously appointed Turkish bath.

In the elegantly furnished drawing room, no premonitory shadow of death was present to cast a cold fear over the gaiety of the evening. It was a brilliant scene, women beautifully gowned, laughing and talking – the odour of flowers – ridiculous to think of danger. Why, it was just like being at some beautiful summer resort. There was not one chance in a million of an accident happening, they said.

But someone took that chance, there was no slacking of the speed as we went through the ice fields, for it was felt that no obstacle could stand in the path of this mighty leviathan of the seas.

Oh, I don't want to criticise, for they did their best, but why weren't there enough lifeboats for all?

Why were some men allowed in the boats and others kept out?

Why were the boats not manned by men who knew how to handle an oar?

Where was the system?

They did their best – the officers, poor, dear old Captain Smith – they were not to blame. The women and children were saved, but, I ask, where are the men? Why were they not given a chance to save their lives? Why were there not enough boats for them?

Why were they subjected to the fearful agony of parting from their wives? These are the questions which come to the lips of heartbroken women whose husbands are gone.

All that afternoon and in the evening, everyone was discussing the probability of arriving in New York on Wednesday. It was regarded as certain that the *Titanic* would make her trip in record time. We were not afraid of going so fast. We only knew of the speed by looking at the indicator.

The sea was so calm and the motion of the boat so slight that it was hardly noticeable.

The night was beautiful. The sea was placid and wonderful to look upon.

Countless stars were reflected in all their glory in watery depths which gave no hint of the treachery lurking in them. Phosphorescence gleamed upon the surface of the sea and reflected back its radiance from giant icebergs which were scattered over the face of the waters. There was not the slightest thought of danger in the minds of those who sat around the tables on the luxurious saloon after-deck.

It was a brilliant crowd. Jewels flashed from the gowns of the women. And oh, the dear women, how fondly they wore their latest Parisian gowns. It was the first time that most of them had an opportunity to display their newly acquired finery. The soft sweet odours of rare flowers pervaded the atmosphere. I remember at our table was a great bunch of American Beauty roses. The orchestra played popular music. It was a buoyant, oh, such a jolly crowd. It was a rare gathering of beautiful women and splendid men. There was that atmosphere of fellowship and delightful sociability which make the Sabbath dinner on board ship a delightful occasion.

The thought, as I glanced over the saloon, was that it would be hard to find gathered in one place a crowd which would better typify the highest type of American manhood and womanhood. I remember Jacques and Mr Harris discussing at our table the latest plays on the American stage. Everybody was so merry. We were all filled with the joy of living. We sat over dinner late that night.

I remember we discussed, among ourselves, a man sitting at a table across the cabin who was suspected of cheating at cards the night before. Card playing had been permitted on the boat for the first time. The men warned one another against this man, who they said was a professional gambler and who made a practice of fleecing ocean travellers. The men were sure that he had cheated, so sure, in fact, that they had agreed to keep him at a safe distance in the future. He sat in that great dining saloon, with a cold-blooded smile over his features as he gazed over the crowd. I remember this smile of his, which I saw as I looked towards him, when the men were discussing the incident of the card room, it struck me as the one discordant and harsh note in the jollity. News spreads quickly on board ship. The gambler was ostracised by all; even those who sat at his own table spoke to him only when the dictates of good breeding required that they should do so.

I remember that cold, calculating smile of his because hours afterwards his face still wore it when he cynically remarked that after all, he guessed there was something to the law of the 'survival of the fittest'. This cold-blooded crook had survived, while brave men and good men, men who served noble purposes in life, died. Was it the 'survival of the fittest?'

It was suggested that we take a bit of fresh air after dinner, and before retiring many of the passengers ventured out on the deck. I stepped out into the open to get one breath of fresh air, as I told Jacques, and to look upon the night before I retired.

There was a death chill in the air which sent a shudder through me and caused me to hurry back into the cheer and warmth of the cabin. The terrible chilliness affected all alike and a number of the men commented that we must be in the close vicinity of icebergs. No one had the slightest fear, however, for Mr Andrews, who had some part in the construction of the vessel, (he called it his baby) had laughingly assured us that at last man had constructed an unsinkable craft.

Before retiring, my husband complained of a slight headache. We had both gone to our staterooms. Nearly everyone on board had retired except the men who chattered over their cigars in the magnificent lounging room. There was the stillness which only comes with the sea. A faint tremor of the boat was the only thing that served to remind one that he was on the sea. Apart from this one might have imagined himself to have been in one of the magnificent hotels of New York City.

About 11:15 o'clock we felt a slight concussion. For a moment neither of us experienced any feeling of alarm. I asked Jacques what he thought of it.

'Oh, I guess it's nothing,' he said. 'We have simply bumped into a baby iceberg. If that's what it is, it's of no more importance than if the ship had struck a match.'

I couldn't help but feel alarmed, despite Jacques' confidence. A moment later there was the sound of scurrying feet in the halls which divided the staterooms. There was a babble of inquiring and anxious voices. I felt the ship quiver from bow to stern. It seemed to me that the ship lurched sideways from the force of a new impact. There was a grating noise. Neither of these blows to the ship had been sufficient to impress my husband with the belief that anything serious had happened. He was not inclined to investigate or even to make inquiries as to the nature of the disturbance. It was only when I had urged him to see what the trouble was that he dressed himself and went out to investigate.

Upon leaving our stateroom he encountered Mr Henry Harris, the theatrical magnate. Both told me to go across the hall into the stateroom occupied by Mrs Harris and to stay with her until they had returned. Mrs Harris was pale and frightened. Our fear was increased two-fold when we heard the harsh clanging of the great gong forward. The explanation of the reason for ringing the gong came to us in a flash. That very afternoon one of the officers had explained to us that this gong was only used as a signal for the closing of the water-tight compartments in case of emergency.

Mrs Harris was suffering from a broken arm, which she carried in a sling. I slashed her free and together we waited fear-struck and in silence for the return of our husbands. We had both dressed hurriedly. I had aided her in wrapping a heavy coat about her. It seemed but a few moments before our husbands returned and told us there was nothing to fear. I was faint with fright, but endeavoured to control myself.

At about the same time that our husbands came back to us an officer passed by. He spoke to Mr Harris in a low tone. I did not catch what he said, but there was something in his tone which frightened me. I don't know why. As the officer went on his way Mr Harris turned to us and said, 'I don't like the looks of things.'

Then we looked out of the cabin and saw people putting on life belts. None of them seemed greatly alarmed, but we thought it wise to follow their example. Both Jacques and Mr Harris tried to quiet our fears by joking with us about it. Their effort was not successful, however. Jacques and I returned to our stateroom. I asked him if he had his money with him, and he passed some laughing remark about not needing it. It's queer to think of the things one will do in a moment of great stress. I remember that I took a drink of water. I didn't think to take my valuables with me, not even the pearl necklace which I treasured so much and which was Jacques' last gift to me.

With our life jackets strapped in place we went into the saloon. Never shall I forget that picture of white-faced women clinging to their husbands. There was no panic and very little noise; the men were calm and possessed, with the women frightened but sustained by the examples set by their husbands.

The first rush of men with the fear of death in their faces came when a group of stokers climbed up from the hold and burst through the saloon, their grimy faces appearing wild and distracted in the brilliant light. The appearance of these stokers was the signal that the great heart of the ship had stopped beating – that the water had reached the engines.

In a moment we understood that the situation was desperate, that the compartments had refused to hold back the rush of the water. The black-faced group of men who poured from the vitals of the ship clustered together for a moment in one corner of the cabin.

At this moment the band was playing 'Alexander's Ragtime Band.' What a scene that was – the men of the first cabin, many of them still in evening clothes, with drawn, set faces, who but a few short minutes ago were in command of all the things of the world, now found themselves face to face with the spectre of death. Did they flinch? Not one. They were not the kind of men who quailed in the face of danger. Oh, their courage was superb! The stokers, for the most part, were fear-stricken. They looked across to the men of the first cabin and took courage from the example set them, however.

As for the women, perhaps their hearts did beat a little faster, perhaps there was a horrible fear in them, but they did not show it. Outwardly they were as calm as if they had come to attend a tea; that is, the majority were. I noticed that in this moment of stress, however, every woman on board was close to her husband.

As in the case of the stokers, their courage was buoyed up by the attitude of the men. There were intermittent bursts of feverish conversation in which the voices of the men could be heard, reassuring their loved ones. Most of the women in the first cabin had dressed hurriedly, many of them had not removed their evening gowns, others were half undressed and had thrown heavy coats over their dressing gowns.

I saw one woman barefooted, saw others in their stocking feet, some had on their hats, the latest creations from Paris, while others who had dressed at leisure and, prepared for an emergency, wore knitted wool caps. It was incongruous to see a woman in beautiful evening dress in her stocking feet. Apparently no one had thought the emergency serious enough to necessitate the gathering up of valuables.

We could not have been in the first cabin but a few moments when an officer came in and in quiet tones said, 'Ladies, you will please go to the promenade deck.' The first sign of hysteria on the part of the women came at this moment. A little Frenchwoman whose name I don't remember, began to weep in a frightened sort of way. Every woman in the cabin clasped her husband more tightly. This was the first moment that we were convinced that there was awful danger.

There was not a whisper from the men. They escorted their wives to the door leading out to the promenade deck with the same nonchalance which would have been displayed had they been escorting the women to a cloakroom. The women were ordered to go on deck 'A' on the promenade deck.

When we stepped out of the cabin, the officers said: 'Women and children will go to the promenade deck. The men will remain where they are.'

No man was supposed to be on the boat deck. This was the obvious requirement of the discipline which the officers attempted to put into force.

Oh, that was a terrible moment! It was awful, awful!

Each woman there kissed her husband. Men made an effort to still cheer further their wives by stating that the danger was not grave and that everybody would get off safely. No woman who went through that awful moment will ever forget the agony which came to her from the feeling that she might be separated from her husband forever.

I saw Mrs Straus clinging to her husband Isidor, the New York banker. I heard her say to an officer who was trying to induce her to get into a boat: 'No, we are too old, we will die together.'

Other husbands had great difficulty in persuading the women to leave them. Jacques stood there perfectly cool, saying: 'No, dear, I will follow you bye and bye.' I did not want to leave him, but he filled me with so much confidence that I obeyed and turned and walked onto the deck with an officer.

It was a pitiful spectacle that the great ship presented. Her back was broken in two: she was like a great worm that someone had stepped upon. I had no sooner reached the deck than she began to list to port; even then there was no panic, people simply couldn't believe that the *Titanic* could sink. One by one the women were seated, no hurry, no rush; in fact, there were only fifteen who went into that first boat. I heard the captain order the crew to lower away.

Every woman's eyes were turned towards the cabin, where the men stood. I could not make up my mind to leave my husband when I saw the lifeboat about to go down. I was afraid, the water looked so treacherous. I ran back, threw my arms around his neck and said, 'Jack, I don't want to leave you.'

'Oh, do be calm, dear,' he said, and he allowed me to stay with him for a while. He said there was no great hurry and that I might remain with him a few minutes. Oh, those few precious minutes were a lifetime! Jack just stood there with the men, with his arms about me, and I clung to him. We did not say much.

There were other women who did not wish to leave their husbands. After Jack had kissed me again and told me not to worry, that everything would be all right, he led me out to the main deck, but he never stepped on it, so conscientiously did he obey orders, so splendid was his bravery.

There were a few cowards who brushed by us in the crowd in an effort to secure places in the boats. Who they were I don't know, nor do I want to speak of them.

When I think of those poor, dear men – my own 'Jack,' Colonel Gracie, Mr Harris, Mr Hoyt – all of them, they followed orders to the last. They were men of calibre, who knew how to take orders as well as give them. For the second time I was on the promenade deck.

There was real alarm shown on the faces of the officers now, and the boats were being filled hurriedly. Again I saw a boat loaded away, and once again I turned back, not wishing to leave 'Jack.' I couldn't find him this time. I ran through the cabin with my heart full of fear, not with the fear of death but with fear of leaving my husband: filled with the agony the separation brought.

Finally I encountered him at the side, standing with an officer. When he saw me he said, 'This will never do; you must get into a boat.'

He took me on the starboard side and put me in boat No.14. I thought my heart would break at the thought of leaving him. He told me that I was only endangering his chances by staying, for he could get along himself in the water with a lifebelt, but he could not hold me up with him. He told me that he would cling on to one of the boats and be picked up.

I would never have left him, even then, but he whispered to me, 'Remember the children.'

The last I saw of my husband he was standing beside Colonel Astor. He had a cigarette in his mouth. As I watched him, he lighted a match and held it in his cupped hands before his face. By its light I could see his eyes roam anxiously out over the water. Then he dropped his head toward his hands and lighted his cigarette. I saw Colonel Astor turn toward Jacques and a second later Jacques handed the colonel his cigarette box. The colonel screened Jacques' hands with his own, and their faces stood out together as the match flared at the cigarette tip. I know those hands never trembled.

This was an act of bravado. Both men must have realised that they must die.

Just as I got placed in the boat, Mrs Hoyt got out. She brushed by the officers and I heard her say: 'Oh, I cannot go without my husband. Please let him come with me. Please do.'

The officers refused, but in kindly tones, telling her that it was impossible. The absolute rule was that only women and children were to be put in the boats. Our boat was lowered away, without being half filled. As it swung down the high sides I saw in the gleam of the light the men from the steerage who had rushed to the deck and were being held back by the officers with loaded revolvers.

There were only four first-class cabin women in my boat, three besides myself. Mrs Harris was with me. There were some women from the steerage and some men. I was absolutely stunned. The horror of it all just seemed to paralyse me. It was just like looking at a stage picture. The boat struck the water fairly and we did not ship a drop of water.

No sooner had we touched than the men started to row like mad, trying to get far enough away so as not to be carried under by the suction. I looked back, the *Titanic* was slowly sinking, port light after port light disappeared beneath the sea.

All around us were great icebergs. Coming from the warmth of the boat into the cold air was a shock, and the only way I can express the feeling was that it reminded me of a breath of air which comes from a refrigerator.

There was room in my boat for at least fifteen more people. I was sick at heart. The shock was so terrible that it left me almost numb. It seemed that I was subconsciously aware of the pitiful scenes enacted around me. I remember the feeling that it could not be true; that it was a dream: a play which I was looking upon. All about me the sea was so calm; the stars shone so brightly.

The ocean was aflame with the gleaming phosphorus which looked like a million little spirits of light dancing their way to the horizon. The icebergs looked like giant spectres, standing out dimly in the hideous night, waiting grimly to snatch the souls of the doomed men on board the *Titanic*. I hope I shall never again see an iceberg.

I was startled from my dazed condition by the cries of the men in my life boat. They could not unfasten the lashings.

'For God's sake,' I heard one ask, 'has no one a knife?'

Not a man in the boat carried a knife.

The men were in a frenzy of fear. The women sat like statues, arms outstretched and eyes turned toward the *Titanic*. All around were heard cries of 'Quick, now let's get away as far as possible when the *Titanic* sinks, she will suck us down if we don't.'

One great hulking fellow in the boat, frantic with fear, managed with superhuman strength to break the lashings. The men seized the oars, but they were perfectly helpless to handle them.

Their clumsiness verged on the grotesque. It was perfectly obvious to me that the crew was unfamiliar with handling of a boat.

They were not seamen, they were cooks and stewards. I asked one man why he was in the boat if he couldn't row. He replied in a tense, strained voice: 'I want to save my life just as much as you do yours.'

But I didn't care whether the life boat made any progress or not. As a matter of fact, it didn't. We could plainly see a group of men gathered in the stern. Rockets were still shooting into the air. We heard noises that sounded like pistol shots. This probably gave the impression that the officers were shooting the men who were attempting to force their way into the last collapsible life boat.

Lower and lower the *Titanic* sank into the sea. We prayed, oh how we prayed, during those few moments when the boat was settling.

We could see the last of the two collapsibles putting away from the steamer. The water by this time was so close to the upper deck that it was hardly necessary to lower the boat. I tried to shut my eyes, but I couldn't. There was a horrible fascination about it. Just before the lights went out we could see a group of men aft.

'Now, every man for himself,' shouted the officers, and some jumped.

Of a sudden the lights snapped out. There was a terrible creaking noise, the *Titanic* seemed to break in two. There was a tremendous explosion.

For a fraction of a second she arose in the air and was plainly visible in the light caused from the blowing up of the boilers.

She sank to the requiem of 'Nearer My God to Thee' played by the band. The great steamship then dived two miles to the bottom of the ocean. With her were the heroes, whose sacrifice made the lives of women and children possible and should give them everlasting place in the hearts of Americans.

Future generations can serve no higher standard of American manhood than was exemplified by our men who went down with the *Titanic*.

It seemed to me that I would die when the end came.

It was an inferno, the wails of the dying, the crying of women and children, the appeals for help from those who still lived and the bobbing corpses of men who had died from exposure or who were injured and bleeding from the effects of the explosion, was a vision of hell.

I was calm, I couldn't cry. I didn't want to. I felt that I was dead. A little Frenchwoman in the boat with me wailed and writhed in hysterics. The utmost confusion prevailed.

One of the collapsible lifeboats had overturned and thirty or more human beings fought for their lives in the icy waters.

It was an emergency which required a leader, and a leader with a cool head, desperate courage, and a knowledge of the sea. The emergency developed the man. It was Fifth Officer Lowe who was in charge of the boats. Without an instant's hesitation he directed the boat in which he was seated to the scene of the upset.

He shouted orders to all boats within earshot to move up near the spot where the *Titanic* sunk and pick up survivors.

He rescued many with his own hands. He seemed to have the power of instilling strength into the horror-stricken limbs of the boat crew and of urging them from struggling survivor to struggling survivor at top speed.

It is hard to conceive the horrible sights that were seen by the survivors in the boats who watched and attempted to assist the men who were struggling for their lives. The iridescence of the water illuminated the faces of the swimmers. I shall never forget the agony which contorted these faces. The faint light in which we saw them was green and sickly. They begged piteously for help in gasping, strangled voices.

Officer Lowe dragged every person he could reach into our boat. He would lean far over the side, get a hold on the swimmer and pull him straight into the boat. He must have been wonderfully strong. He was as wet as any of the ones he rescued because he pulled them up against his chest and then swung them inward.

The terror which had possessed the men in the lifeboats because of the belief they might be drawn down by the suction following the sinking of the *Titanic*, was found to be unwarranted.

We were not far from the *Titanic* when she went down, not so far but what we would have been greatly affected by suction had there been anywhere near as much as there usually is when a vessel sinks.

Within a few minutes Officer Lowe had the situation well in hand. He had picked up those who had tumbled out of the collapsible boat. He had issued orders to the other boats and they were rapidly picking up all the swimmers who had who had been able to keep their heads above water.

When the story of this great maritime disaster has been fully told, Fifth Officer Lowe will go down in the annals of the sea as one of the [unreadable] men.

My heart seemed to stop beating when I saw the *Titanic* sink. I did not cry. I was calm, stunned from the horror of it all.

From among the hundreds of men who were scattered about on the surface of the sea, I saw one whom I thought was my husband. I prayed as never before in my life.

The boat drew near and the man was hauled into it. It was not my husband. The man died as he was taken into the boat. The exposure was too much for him. His body lay for hours in the bottom of the boat, a ghastly reminder of the disaster.

My last hope was now gone, my prayers were unanswered. In shipping an oar, one of the men struck me on the head and for a few moments I was senseless. When I revived, we were a long distance from where the *Titanic* went down.

The men in the boat were laughing and talking, some of them were smoking.

The little Frenchwoman still sobbed hysterically. There were no lights on the boats except the first one.

The first boat which led the sad parade carried two green lights and the orders were to keep it in sight. There were no lights in our boat. Had there been a heavy sea our lifeboats would have surely been swamped, since the crew knew nothing whatever about the handling of the oars.

They admitted to me later that they were stewards. There was no compass on the boat and no water. It was discovered that there was no water aboard when the little Frenchwoman asked one of the men for a drink. A few biscuits were stored under one of the seats, but not more than enough for one meal.

Had there been any danger of the boat not being picked up for a few days some of the people surely would have died from thirst.

The crew did not seem to be greatly impressed with the terrible disaster. They knew that the S.O.S. signal had been sent out hours before and the chief subject of their conversation was the chances of being picked up by the *Californian* and the *Carpathia*.

In some of the boats near us women were obliged to take the oars.

Many of the women knew better how to handle the boat than the men who were put in charge. On one of the boats a man refused to take an oar. He was a coward. He shivered so with fright that he said that he could not hold an oar.

Another man held a small poodle dog in his arms and spoke to it as if it were a child. This was the kind of a man who would rather save a dog than a child. There are so many men and women who give more attention to dogs than human beings.

No one had any baggage. For the most part the women in the first cabin were warmly dressed. But the women in the steerage were, many of them, garbed in the thinnest clothes. They shivered in the cold air and their wails were frightful to hear. Many of them had lost their husbands and were clasping babies to their breasts.

One of the first cases of cowardice was brought to light when a man crawled from under one of the seats in one of the lifeboats an hour after the *Titanic* had sunk. This man had sneaked past the officers and had secreted himself without anybody having noticed it in the panic of the last moments.

When the boat was lowered to deck A, Mrs Candee stepped on the man, fell, and broke her ankle. She fell forward when she felt the squirming thing under her feet, but fainted with pain before it could be explained to the officers that there was a man hidden in the boat. In the panic it attracted no attention and the man escaped. I saw him afterwards on board the *Carpathia*. It was said that he was an Egyptian.

It seemed that we rowed for hours after the *Titanic* sank. For the most part the women were dry-eyed and silent. The men talked only of being rescued. We didn't care, for our hearts were near breaking when we thought of our men at the bottom of the sea.

With our extra wraps, we helped the poor wild-eyed steerage women to keep their babies warm. Many of the poor little things were almost naked.

It was a radiant dawn. The rising sun cast a pink reflection on the horizon. There was a long, dead swell on the sea. With the sun came the rescue ship, the *Carpathia*, with flag at half mast.

As we rowed up to the side the passengers gathered at the rail. The women passengers were waiting, ready with blankets and hot drinks. One by one we were hauled up the sides with a rope around our waists. Some of the women were nearly unconscious. Mrs Candee was suffering frightfully from her broken ankle. The face of the cowardly man who was responsible for it was livid. I really believe that he entertained a horrible fear that when the story became known the men on the *Carpathia* would kill him. In his mean mind he must have suffered the tortures of the damned. The women with babies and children were first put aboard the *Carpathia*.

Captain Rostron of the *Carpathia* directed the unloading of boats. He was very kind. Every woman was immediately helped to a blanket and given a hot drink and put to bed.

The passengers took the survivors to their staterooms. There was no distinction between the first cabin passengers and the women from the steerage. All were treated alike, with the same kindness and human sympathy. The women who had their husbands did everything in their power for us.

I noticed that many of the boats were not filled. In the first boats were many men, who explained that they had been ordered to get into the boat when the *Titanic* was struck. There were only fifteen people in our boat, in others there were sixty-five people. There were not enough staterooms for all and mattresses were laid on the floor of the main cabin. Captain Rostron circled around the spot where the *Titanic* was thought to have sunk, in the hope that he might recover some bodies, but there was not a vestige of wreck afterward on the sea, nothing but treacherous icebergs.

The boat went slowly and carefully.

The *Californian* arrived and signalled that she would also keep up the search for the bodies. Just before the *Carpathia* left the scene of the disaster, prayers were read for the dead. I shall never forget the scene. All joined in the prayers. The women wept so softly so that there was not a man on deck with dry eyes. We had been under way but a few hours when a deep fog set in. It was damp and miserable. It seemed as if the wrath of God was following the passengers of the *Titanic*.

In the days that followed we talked over our experiences. Many of the women were ill and hysterical. I saw poor Mrs Astor and I shall never forget her face. It was strained and white and wore an expression of almost hopelessness. She was very delicate and spent most of the time in her stateroom. From the time that we reached the *Carpathia* until we landed in New York, J. Bruce Ismay, managing director of the White Star Line, never put in an appearance in the cabin. There is no truth in the stories of his kindliness to the survivors. We never saw him. I was told that he had his meals served in his stateroom. Many of the passengers blamed him for the terrible disaster because it was said that it was he who urged that the *Titanic* be kept at high speed through the icefields in order that she might make a record.

We felt bitter at the thought that Mr Ismay and other men had escaped while our husbands had gone to their deaths like heroes, obeying the orders given to them by the officers of the *Titanic*. If the rule of the ocean is women and children first, then how is it that men got into the lifeboats when so many women went to their deaths?

Colonel Gracie, who was aboard and who was one of the gentlemen who held back to make way for the women and children, told us that when the last lifeboat had left the *Titanic* the officers had shouted: 'Now every man for himself.' This was the moment when the lights snapped out and the *Titanic* had begun to dip her nose for the final plunge to the bottom of the ocean.

Colonel Gracie, John B. Thayer and a man named Williams, all jumped at the same time. When the boilers exploded Colonel Gracie was thrown high into the air. When he struck the ocean again, half-stunned, he was hauled into a boat.

Mrs Thorn said that she saw my husband just before she left in one of the last boats [illegible], and he said to her, smilingly: 'See what the White Star Line has done to us?' He was just joking.

There was one young man, I won't mention his name, who said that he had got into the first boat with others. Why should men have been allowed in this boat with hundreds of women and children standing by? I have no fault to find with the officers of the *Titanic*. They did their best. There was only seven of them. But there was no system, none whatever, no thought of the saving of life should there be an accident.

All the first day I couldn't cry. The horror of the night was still before me. Next day I broke down and sobbed. It was a relief. One of the first men I saw on the *Carpathia* was the card crook. He wore the same cynical smile that he had on his face the night that he was pointed out to me in the dining saloon of the *Titanic*. He sat opposite me at the table. It was horrible to hear him talk. He said that it was a case of every man for himself, when the *Titanic* struck. He didn't seem to be horror-stricken in the least. What a heart that man must have.

The only consolation that we women had when we looked at men like him and some of the others was, that perhaps it was better after all that our husbands died like men rather than to have lived to be pointed as cowards. The women passengers on the *Carpathia* gave their clothes to us. Oh, they were so sympathetic. Many of the women from the *Titanic* had on silk gowns. Others were in kimonos. There were a few who only had on heavy coats over their night clothes. Some of the women had on beautiful jewels just as they had left the dining saloon. Many wore beautiful French hats. This was the incongruous part of it.

One of the first things I did was to send a wireless message to my sister. It never reached its destination. They said on the *Carpathia* that the wireless was out of order.

Everybody wanted to send a wireless. A ship's officer took our names the second day that we were out and they told us that they would be sent by wireless to New York so that it would be known who was saved. They also told us that the operator was just going to bed when the first S.O.S. was received from the *Titanic*.

Someone suggested that we have some music the first night that we were on the *Carpathia*. Mrs Harris, wife of the theatrical magnate, begged the musicians not to play. It would have driven us mad had they played. There was an awful storm the first night that we were on the *Carpathia*. None of us slept that night.

The next day there was a query received from the Associated Press asking why the names of the survivors had not been sent by wireless. The captain replied, but the messages were not sent for some reason or other.

Mrs Astor came into the cabin for a few minutes the next day, but she fainted and was obliged to return to her stateroom. For the remainder of the voyage she stayed in her stateroom under the care of a trained nurse. We pitied her because she is such a young girl. There were eleven brides on the boat who had lost their husbands on their honeymoons. Their grief was terrible to witness.

There was an incident on board the boat which made the women shudder. The day after we got on board Lord Duff Gordon lined up some of the stokers for a picture. He said they were such good fellows that he wanted to give them five pounds apiece, and to have a picture by which to remember them. As he lined up the black-faced stokers he said 'Now smile.' He asked them to smile when women all around him were breaking their hearts with grief.

Some of the women screamed when he asked the stokers to smile. They were of the men who escaped, but they did smile and Lord Duff Gordon too, as he took their pictures.

For two days the fog was very thick. The captain went along slowly and carefully. I don't believe he ever left the bridge. When we arrived at New York the customs officials were very kind.

The newspaper men, too, were very kind. They showed appreciation of the frightful strain that the women had been under and were very courteous. The beaming of flashlights from the windows of buildings outside of the police lines greeted us as we came off the dock to step into the waiting automobiles.

There was a great crowd of people gathered there. The scenes of grief on the dock as the survivors met their friends and relatives was heartbreaking.

Many of the women fainted and became hysterical and had to be carried to the automobiles.

There were a few women who laughed and joked about getting their pretty things from Paris through the customs officers and who were pleased to take advantage of the situation which allowed them to go through without examination.

I cried when I heard one of these women tell of getting her baggage through without examination. She asked Mrs Harris who I was and then said maliciously that the captain of the *Carpathia* had purposely sent his boat along slowly in the interests of the company and not because of the fog.

Colonel Gracie clasped both of my hands when we arrived at the dock, and said 'Cheer up, little girl, cheer up.' I told him I was so glad he was living, he was so good. I also thanked Mrs Cooper, who so kindly gave me her stateroom.

The heroism of the men who died that women and children might be saved is a story that cannot be told too often. It was wonderful, Godlike. The members of the band on board the *Titanic* also deserve a high place in the roll of honour.

Many of the passengers seemed to think that poor old Captain Smith was to blame, but I believe that he was acting under orders when he drove the ship at such speed through the icebergs. The *Titanic* was going through the water at a rate of over twenty-one knots an hour.

I have my own theory of the cause of the disaster. The iceberg that we struck stood about seventy-five feet from the surface of the water. It was like the Eiffel Tower, growing larger as it extended to the base.

When the Titanic struck it, going at full speed, the engines were not at first slowed down. The helm was swung to port apparently in the belief that the *Titanic* would graze the iceberg. There were two distinct horizontal shocks.

The tremendous force with which the *Titanic* struck the iceberg must have ripped her bottom open just as if it had been so much paper.

When the boat swerved to port, it simply served to open her up more. The compartments were useless even had they been closed, which I doubt, since most of them must have been ripped apart with the shock.

There was absolutely no system for the saving of life. When the boat struck most of the passengers put on the life belts because they saw the danger. They were not told to do so by the officers. There were only sixteen boats, not nearly enough. At least fifty life boats could have been swung on each of the decks without cramping the quarters.

It was simply a case of overconfidence in the powers of the *Titanic*. It was believed to be an unsinkable boat.

According to the statement of some of the men, they were ordered into the first boat although the rule of the sea is women and children first. Why should some of the men have been allowed in the boats and others kept out?

Some of the boats were filled and others were not.

The *Titanic* did not have a searchlight. I remember asking the captain the reason for this one day, and he said the darkness which followed a flash was very confusing and that it had been found impracticable to carry a search light. It seems to me, however, that a searchlight would have shown up the iceberg.

They were not prepared for death on the *Titanic*. We had talked about the possibility of collision several times, but the officers said that there would not be the slightest danger since the *Titanic* was unsinkable.

Some people said that just before boat went down there was a light like that carried by a fishing smack not far away. I do not believe this was so, however. I cannot account for so many men from the steerage on the promenade deck when so many of their women were lost. There were no rafts on the boat and there were two collapsible boats which were not used. I do not pretend to say who was to blame.

The lesson of this terrible disaster is that in the future all steamships should be equipped with enough life boats to take care of all on board in case the emergency should arise.

There was only one chance in a million of the *Titanic* sinking. This is one chance too many for any steamship company to take.

I hope that the laws in the future will provide against the possibility of such a frightful disaster that other women may be saved the horror of it, and that men heroes may not die needlessly.[180]

A few days later Mrs Futrelle wrote a second account of her *Titanic* experience:

My husband is dead because he preferred his duty to his life. He did right, and I must bear it. In times like that civilisation is gone; we are back in physical conditions. In those conditions women are the weaker, the less able to take care of themselves. Also, there is no time to make fine distinctions.

My husband, Jacques Futrelle, and his friend, Henry B. Harris, went down together. Now, suppose that there had been even a chance for just one of them to be saved. How would they have settled which one was to stay? I hope that Jacques would have said to Henry and Henry to Jacques, 'You go first.' But how could they have arrived at a decision?

But the difference between men and women, between those who are physically strong and will stand the better chance in a battle with the elements and those who are weak and will stand no chance, is broad and general. You can get it at once. That is the plain line of duty and nobility.

Understand, it is not a matter of sex, but just of the weak and the strong. Suppose that all the passengers had been men, but half of them invalids and half strong and well. By the law of chivalry it would have been the duty of the well men to save the invalids, just as it was the duty of our men on the *Titanic* to save us. And they did right to draw no distinction between their own class and other classes, between cabin and steerage. A woman is a woman, whether she is Mrs Astor, who has all the money and position that one could desire, or the poorest immigrant wife in the hold.

That many mediocre and useless women were saved and many able, useful men like Jacques were lost has nothing to do with the case. There is a terrible democracy about such a crisis. We have to act on the theory that all men are of equal value.

You understand, I think, how confused it all was; how little time there was to think and plan a course. Everything was done on instinct. And at no time until the very end did any of us rescued women fully understand what the men were doing. It was the flower of their heroism that, to keep us brave and increase our chances, they concealed their certainties from us. But they knew – long before they made their choice and parted with us forever – they had elected to die not only for their own women, but for every woman on board. Even if I disagreed with their point of view, should I mar their memories by saying that they were wrong?

Jacques and I sailed on the *Titanic* only accidentally. We had booked passage on the *Adriatic*. We were delayed and cancelled it. Then we decided to go on the *Mauretania*; but I had heard that the turbines of those fast boats made a disagreeable vibration. The *Titanic* was sailing on her maiden trip. We thought it a good adventure to go on her. The very afternoon before she started we made our decision, packed in a hurry, and just got on board. I remember that while we were throwing our last possessions into our bags I had a thought which made me faint for a second, and I expressed it to Jacques. I said:

'I'm a little afraid. This boat is new. She has never been tried out.' But he answered carelessly: 'Don't you ever worry about that. She'll never be so safe again as on this trip. They're out for a record in every way. Besides, those big boats are practically unsinkable.'

That reassured me; but at some later time either just before we sailed, or just afterward, I thought of the perils of the sea, as you always do before you sail, and asked: 'In case of trouble, whom do they save first?' And Jacques, still carelessly, said: 'They save the first-class passengers.' That's always used as an argument for sailing first-class instead of second. It is strange, now, to think that the real course of action, the one which he adopted instinctively, just like the others, never occurred to him then.

Because this was the *Titanic*'s maiden trip our departure was a great occasion. The wharves and the decks of the *Olympic* [*Oceanic*] and *New York*, which lay in port, were crowded with people, who had come to see us off. They cheered and saluted as we pulled out: our band played: a band from shore answered. Jacques and I stood by the rail nearest the *New York* as we got headway. Suddenly we saw the *New York* shiver and move; then her cable nearest us snapped, and the stump whipped back on deck, knocking over some people. I saw her begin to swing toward us. Jacques shouted: 'Hold fast for the shock!' I gripped the rail. She swung still nearer, and it seemed certain that we would collide; but just when her rail was about to touch ours she swung beyond our bows. I was only a little frightened. Jacques laughed and said: 'Well, she got that out of her system, anyway!' No one on board, it seemed, thought of being superstitious over the little incident. If we spoke of it at all we just joked about it. We never know our luck when it comes. It would have been so much better if the *New York* had wrecked us right there in port.

Then came the prettiest voyage I ever experienced. The ocean, all the way, was like an inland lake. Crowds came on the pier at Cherbourg, and at Queenstown even the peddlers who crowded about the ship with laces cheered us. The nights were so brilliant that you could see far ahead by starlight. We were very gay. No one was seasick, and we made a great occasion of the dinners. The women got out their new Parisian gowns, and the men all dressed.

On the second day Jacques and I went over the whole ship. I had heard from someone – I've forgotten who – that the *Titanic* had put to sea unfinished. I noticed that the Parisian Café men were fitting doors. Again I passed the warning by – thought nothing of it. The voyage had been so pleasant, the sea so smooth and beautiful, that I had no fears.

Just after we boarded we had met Mr and Mrs Harris, whom we had known before, and were delighted to find that they had a stateroom in the same entry with ours – amidships on the starboard side of C deck. We four were much together. On Saturday Mrs Harris fell and broke her collar-bone. After that I stayed with her a great deal. Someone had pointed out the Astors to us. Of course I, with every other woman on board, was curious about them. His height and her smart little figure would have made them noticeable in any circumstances. She was wearing a pretty ermine cap, and we used to spot it all over the ship, for they moved about among us very freely. They were all alone most of the time. Perhaps they would have been rather glad to scrape up a few acquaintances. I used to think so when I saw her glance up from her reading at every one who passed. But, of course, the rest of us felt that it would have been rather presumptuous to make the first move.

Sunday night came. We had started on the last leg of our trip; we were almost home and eager to see home sights and faces, as people are at the end of a foreign trip. The dinner was the most beautiful I ever saw. We remarked that we might have been in a hotel ashore for all the motion we felt. You had to look out of the portholes to realise that you were at sea. Once we turned and drank toasts to the next table. Not a person at that table was alive in the morning.

After dinner some of the passengers left the saloon for a turn about the deck. They came back reporting that it had turned freezing cold. I poked my nose out of doors to feel for myself. From a casual conversation I caught the one word, 'icebergs.'

The night was so beautiful and every one so gay that I wanted to sit up late; but a little after dinner Jacques was taken with a headache. I thought it best to go below with him. I saw him to bed and made him as comfortable as I could, and presently he fell asleep. I debated with myself over going back, decided that Jacques might need me, and ended by undressing. But I was so wide awake that instead of turning off the light I got out a novel and lay reading. Once or twice I nearly fell asleep over it, but as I was nearing the end I shook myself and went on reading.

I had fallen into another sleepy spell when I felt a shock and a kind of shiver of the ship. It was so slight that it did not disturb anything, but I sat up in bed. I heard the engines pounding below – reversing. For about twenty seconds, I should say, this pounding continued. Then followed another shock, scarcely heavier than the first. We had struck the submerged part of the berg; it had bounded away from us and bounced back to rip out the bottom of the *Titanic*.

When I sat up, only a little frightened, but still wondering what it all meant, there came the heavy clang of a gong – the signal to close the water-tight compartments. Of the meaning of that, too, I was perfectly ignorant. What frightened me more was a rush of feet on deck. It might be all right, I felt, but it seemed irregular somehow. I shook Jacques and woke him. He looked out of the door, walked into the passageway, and ended by saying that they had probably changed course for some reason, and that we had better go back to bed. He crawled into his berth again, but I could not compose myself. When the rushing of feet continued, Jacques also seemed nervous. He looked out of the door again just as Henry Harris came into the entry.

'What's happened?' he asked.

'Oh, nothing, I guess,' said Jacques, 'but I suppose we'd better get out and see what's doing.' As he and Harris started down the passage I ran over to Mrs Harris's cabin. The confusion on deck grew worse. We tried to reassure each other, but I, for one, was seized with a fit of trembling which I could not control. Just then a young man, a friend of the Harrises, came into their cabin where Mrs Harris and I were sitting. He was pale. I asked him to tell me what had happened. He said:

'I don't believe it's serious, but we seem to have brushed against an iceberg.'

Before this had fully sunk in, Jacques and Mr Harris were back. They said that they had heard the iceberg story, but that the officers had closed the water-tight compartments, had examined everything below and had reported that there was no danger.

There followed a time which I do not fully remember, except to recall that it was filled with growing terror which I managed to conceal. But next Mr Harris was talking to some man in the entry. I could not make out what the other man was saying, but I heard Mr Harris say: 'Really?' in a tone which I did not like at all. And when he came into the door he had gone pale.

'I think you'd better get over to your own cabin and dress,' he said. 'I don't like the looks of this very well.' And I had scarcely risen when I heard the sharp knocks in the corridor coming nearer and nearer. I opened the door. A steward in the opposite entry was calling:

'Every one put on life-preservers and come on deck.'

As I crossed the entry to our stateroom I saw men rushing down the passageway trying on life-preservers. With every moment the danger and my terror seemed to grow. But Jacques held me to my nerve by assuring me that he had looked into it and found it not serious; that going on deck was only a precaution. Sometimes I believed him and sometimes – I did not dare to think. At that very moment, I think, Jacques began to be a hero. From that time on he was sure of the worst and was facing what he had to do.

Yet we dressed carefully if swiftly, Jacques putting on all his clothes, even to his eyeglasses. I even fastened on the brooch which held my sailor suit at the throat, and my belt pins. I pulled on a pair of warm gloves, I threw on my fur coat, I took a blanket wrapper over my arm. I remember noticing my pretty dresses which I had bought abroad and thinking how little such things mattered now. In a drawer of the dresser lay my purse and a pearl necklace which we had got in Paris. I never thought of them, although the necklace was Jacques's last present to me. We did not even think of the manuscripts of four or five stories which we had finished abroad.

But I did remember one thing which seems odd now, although then it appealed to me as perfectly logical. I was getting prepared for everything but the worst. I had read of the tortures from thirst which shipwrecked people endured in open boats at sea. I took a big drink of water and offered one to Jacques, who looked at me curiously, as though wondering why I did that. He said that he had just taken a drink. Then we went out on deck. I saw that the people were wearing life preservers. I felt, rather than saw, that the ship was not riding the water as before, and I heard talk of the boats.

Then I broke down for a moment. Jacques comforted and encouraged me. We had come out close to the purser's cabin. To reassure me, he pointed to the daily bulletins and showed me that we had sighted seven ships that day. 'Someone will come to secure us, of course,' he said.

'But if we have to take to the boats we'll go together, won't we?' I asked.

'I suppose so,' he said. But he said it very low. He knew that there were not nearly enough lifeboats to go round. We mounted up toward the boat deck, for we had begun to hear the creak of davits and knew that they were already launching.

The boat deck on the *Titanic* was the highest of all. Next below that was A deck, and next B deck, and C deck, from which we started. On A deck were a number of men and women. We stopped, wondering why they had not gone toward the boats. And as we stood there an officer came among us calling:

'Women remain here. Men back to B deck.'

I had never thought of that before. It struck me all of a heap. But I remember Jacques telling me that it was only a formality, that the boats would stand by until they were sure that there was no danger, that the *Titanic* was the staunchest thing afloat and couldn't sink.

All about, I suppose, men were struggling in this way with their women, but I did not know it. I was sensible only to my own agony. They knew, those brave men, as my husband knew, that there was only the slightest chance in the world for them, and that this parting of which they were making so light was probably forever. Jacques had to put me gently away from him and commanded me to go before I got control of myself and released my hold. I had never disobeyed him in my life, and I did not now. But as he went down toward B deck with the rest of the men I ran after him, crying, until an officer stopped me.

I don't know what happened on the port side, but on the starboard side, where we were, they got all the men back on B deck before they drove us women up to the boat deck. They were filling the fourth boat as I came out, and the first thing I saw was Colonel Astor standing among the women. I wondered if he were saving his skin, if his influence had got him a place. I am sorry for that thought now – he himself explained a moment later. An officer stepped up to him and said: 'Only women are allowed in this boat.' Though the night was freezing cold, the perspiration was dripping from his face as he turned it toward the light.

'I know that perfectly well,' replied Colonel Astor. 'I am only making my wife comfortable. She is ill.' Then he stooped down, kissed her and jumped out on deck again. Before he left he asked: 'What is the number of this boat?' I suppose he wanted to identify her in case of rescue. They told him that it was Number 4; he nodded and started below. I didn't understand until later how he came to be on that deck at all. It appears that his wife had fainted when she learned that she must leave him, and he had got permission to help the nurse carry her. I have thought since that he was the most heroic of all. He had entered the place of safety and left it again voluntarily.

Then, as the officers moved to the next boat, I gave in all at once and went back to Jacques. The officer at the gangway must have left his post, for no one tried to stop me. There were still many women on Deck A. The men on Deck B stood strung along the rail smoking. I looked over them, sure that I would pick out Jacques by his great height. A match flared up and I saw that it was my husband giving a light to Colonel Astor. When I threw my arms around him he tried to scold me, but I said that there were many more boats and I couldn't leave him yet. I didn't fully understand as he did. There were moments still when I was almost overwhelmed with a terror which I could not reason away, and other moments when I believed what Jacques told me – that launching the boats was only a precaution against the unforeseen.

He took me forward, and for a long time – it may have been fifteen minutes – we walked and talked.

Like all the rest of the men, he was pale, but perfectly calm. In the time I stayed on that deck I never saw a sign of emotion nor heard a voice raised above a conversational tone. Yet they must have known, as I did not know, that they were all going to die. I cannot reiterate that too often. They knew they were dying for us, and they had the splendid manhood to conceal it from us so that we might have a better chance.

Jacques and I were silent or talked commonplace – he wouldn't let me begin on anything [illegible.] I asked him about his headache and he said that it was nearly gone. Once he talked about the beautiful night, pointing out the constellations and the phosphorescences on the water. Again he spoke about the chance of rescue – hopefully always and always without letting me know that he expected the *Titanic* to go down. When we touched on the boats he said that he would follow me, of course. However, once, as he looked down into the steerage where some of the women were making a noise, he said:

'Those are the poor devils that would get it in case anything should really happen.'

Again I had a terrible fright. I heard a hissing far below, a curious rushing sound such as I never heard before.

'Jacques, is that water pouring into the hold?' I cried.

'It's only escaping steam,' he replied.

Boats had been swinging past us all this time; and finally he straightened up from the rail and said: 'May, you must go now.' And almost at the same moment I heard someone calling:

'Any more women down there?' It was harder than it had been at first. As Jacques walked me to the ladder, I begged him again to let me stay, whatever happened.

'Certainly I'll come – just as soon as the women are taken care of,' he answered. 'Remember you have two children. You must think of them. Come, you're keeping people waiting. Don't you see you're spoiling my chances? They won't have me in a lifeboat until they've taken all the women.'

He said good-bye. An officer seized me by the shoulder crying: 'Come – you belong on deck!' There I had my first complete panic. I don't know what I did, but when we reached the deck the officer was carrying me.

The orchestra had come out on the boat deck, where there was a piano, at about the time when they launched the fourth boat. As we made our way across the deck they were playing 'Alexander's Ragtime Band' – to keep us moving, I suppose. Another officer picked me up and fairly threw me into the boat.

We settled on the water with hardly a splash. Then the men began calling for a knife. The oars were lashed, and they had forgotten to cut them loose before they launched. We bumped against the side. The men stood up and held us away with their hands. They must have found a knife among them, for a moment later they were shipping the oars. One of the men in shifting to the other side of the boat dropped his oar-blade on my head. In Jack's own words, in the very fact that they had put me off the vessel, I must have come to full realisation of the truth, for I remember thinking: 'This is the end of me, thank heaven!' I didn't seem to understand that a fatal blow on the head would stun me first – it shows my abnormal state of mind.

We rowed away very fast. I begged them to stand by, for I wanted to see Jacques again, but they said something about suction and we went on. At a safe distance we hove to. It may have been half a mile, it may have been less.

I never saw such a quiet, clear, beautiful night. It was dead calm, perfectly clear, brilliant with stars. The surface of the ocean was just heaving gently; there as not a ripple.

The *Titanic* still floated, the rows of lights indicating her decks. We watched numbly to see if she was going to stay up. We talked it over as impersonally as though it had been no affair of ours. We encouraged each other with false hopes, while our eyes told us that the rows of lights were getting nearer and nearer the water. Only when we saw those rows of lights beginning to get [illegible] did we give up hope and [illegible].

The rows of lights began to go out by sections, as though someone had gone along the boat turning off the control switches one by one. But the night was brilliant, and they were setting off rockets continually. We could still see her great hulk. She began to settle by the nose. Then came two dull explosions. We saw her break in two. The bow, which had been pointing downward, dipped, turned up again, writhed and sank with the stern – exactly as though one had stepped on a worm.

There we sat, dumb, moveless, we women, watching the execution of our heroic men.

I think we must have been a little crazy. Rather, I should say that we were exalted by the very greatness of the tragedy and its heroism. As the *Titanic* took her plunge, none made a sound. Then a little French woman began to scream in hysterics. It went through us like a knife, and I heard the voice of a sailor say:

'For heaven's sake make her shut up!' That was the only harsh word which we heard from those rough men that night; and he only expressed what we all felt. We had eighteen men and twelve women aboard and only four of the women were first cabin passengers. It seemed to me that we needed only ten or eleven men at most to man the boats. The rest were cooks, stewards or cabin attendants. One of the stewards, who relieved a sailor at the oar, couldn't row – his oar never touched the water. When I saw that, I asked, not in anger, but in a sort of wonder, 'Why is that man in this boat?' The Irish sailor, mistaking my meaning, I suppose, said: 'Madame, he wants to save his life as much as you do yours.'

About the rest of that night I can tell nothing consecutive. Mostly I prayed for Jacques's soul and my own – prepared myself for death. The men were always calling out that they saw the lights of a coming ship. I can't tell how often they were deceived by the green lights which Fourth Officer Boxhall was burning in his boat as a signal. These were always false alarms, and finally I paid no more attention to them. Toward morning I must have fallen into a heavy stupor which resembled sleep only on the surface – within my mind and soul were going on and on. Always I came back to the same thought – my husband had died heroically.

They must have sighted the *Carpathia*, and made sure of her, long before I realised it. When it did come home to me, I dared not look toward her. But I raised my head and perceived for the first time that dawn had broken – a beautiful pink dawn. And there, the cruellest, most wonderful sight I ever saw, were three great icebergs – one of them, doubtless, the murderer. From where we sat by the surface they appeared as tall as skyscrapers. The light made their spires and pinnacles glisten like rock quartz.

And among them, near and plain, was a steamer, approaching under full steam with her flag at half-mast. That flag, the sign that others were mourning with us – it touched me so that I was almost able to cry. She came nearer. I could see the people lining the rail to watch us. One of our passengers said, 'How glad they are to see us!' And a sailor answered, 'Not half so glad as we are to see them.'

But I said, and meant it, 'I'm not glad.' I had resigned myself to die. I had been through the preliminary agony, which is the worst; there was nothing left to fear.

As soon as we reached the deck of the *Carpathia* the stewardesses and women passengers came forward with hot blankets, which they wrapped around us. They took me into the salon and tried to give me some hot coffee, but I could not drink.

When I looked about me, I had a cruel shock. I had been taking it for granted that none of the male passengers was saved – only the women. But there stood Mr Hoyt, taking care of his wife. I managed to ask him why. He told me that he had gone down with the *Titanic* and had been picked up by the very boat which carried Mrs Hoyt. Then more and more men came in. I went through the salons and cabins with a dreadful hope in my soul. Jacques was not on board.

I asked how many boats were still out. They answered, 'Nine or ten.' Ours was the fifth boat picked up, because we had been rowing, just by accident, in the direction of the *Carpathia*. I made them let me get a place on the rail, and I watched two more boats come alongside. I kept thinking that every big man aboard was Jacques. Then they would come close and look at us, and I would see that I had been mistaken. I couldn't stand that strain any longer, so I went back to the salon and had the stewardess inform me when *Titanic* passengers were coming aboard; then I would watch them as they came over the rail. Even when I heard an officer say: 'This is the last of the *Titanic*'s boats,' I did not quite lose hope. Only when the *Carpathia* blew her whistle and started to move away did I give up.

I sat down in the cabin. I could not cry yet. The ship's orchestra came in and took their places by the piano. I think they were going to play a hymn. Mrs Harris cried, 'Please don't!' and they went away. But a more harrowing thing happened. A clergyman stood up among us and began to read the burial service from the Book of Common Prayer. This was right, I suppose. We widows had nothing left to cling to except religion – but the shock and finality of it were awful.

That day I heard Mrs Hoyt's story. She, like me and many other women, wanted to sink or swim with her husband. It appears that the officers always let the husbands decide that point. Straus was the only one who chose to let his wife stay. We had watched them on the boat and noticed that a sweetly affection[ate] old couple they were. He did the highest thing he knew to let her die in his arms, and it was sweet and beautiful according to his lights.

Now Mrs Hoyt, also, wanted to stay, but her husband would not let her make the sacrifice. He forced her into an early boat. Just as it was putting off she jumped out and returned to him. Finally, when the men from B deck had all been driven up by the water, when the boat deck itself was almost awash, and when they were launching the collapsible boat, Mr Hoyt and an officer threw her aboard. Mr Hoyt waited until he saw that she had cleared; then he jumped and swam – just before the *Titanic* blew up and sank.

That boat was in charge of a good officer. Finding that he had room for a few more people, he stood by when the *Titanic* plunged and began to pick men up from the wreckage on the surface. The last one they hauled aboard was so numb with cold that they hardly thought him alive at all. They laid him under the seats and called for wraps. Mrs Hoyt had thrown an extra coat over her arm. She passed it forward to him. Just as dawn was breaking he sat up, revived – and Mrs Hoyt recognised her husband!

Mrs Astor, the richest and most tenderly nourished of us all, the one who could have got most if she had cared to demand it, took her hardships with the rest. Her nurse had been rescued with her. They were in the last boat which the *Carpathia* took aboard, and by Mrs Astor's orders, I understand, the nurse asked for no special quarters. They were assigned to sleep on the floor of the library with some steerage and second cabin passengers. On the second afternoon she fainted and was very ill. Only then was she moved to a stateroom.

Again, as illustrating the different kinds of heroism, there was the fifth officer. I think his name is Lowe. He kept his head and courage after the plunge of the

Titanic, and stood by and picked up people until his boat had reached capacity. On the *Carpathia* he was always thinking of things to do for us. One day as we sat crying on deck he came up and said: 'You have all lost your husbands, haven't you?' And we answered 'Yes.'

'I hope you'll believe me,' he said, 'when I tell you that I would give my life now to bring any one of them back.' And I believed him. He did his duty – it didn't matter whether it was his duty to live for the rest of us or to die.

Mrs Harris brought me my only news from Jacques. She, like Mrs Hoyt, clung to her husband until they forced her into the last regular boat. By that time the steerage passengers had been driven to the boat deck. There were hardly any women among them. I think that there had been a mistake or confusion of orders below that someone had failed to send up the women. At any rate, after all the women were aboard there still remained a few places in the boat. Mrs Harris pleaded with the officer, saying:

'See, I have been injured. I need my husband to take care of me.'

Mr Harris made no move forward, but the steerage passengers, when they saw that there was a chance for a man to go with the boat, began crowding and shoving. The officer saw the situation – there was danger of a panic. He pointed his revolver toward them, fired twice in the air, and ordered the seamen to lower away. Something – perhaps it was one of the explosions – caused the sailors to stop lowering and abandon the davits when the boat was half-way down to the water. She dangled there, in danger of going down with the *Titanic*. They sat there calling, but no one responded at first; then, suddenly, the lowering was resumed. I like to think that the unknown people who saved them were Mr Harris and Mr Thorne and Jacques and the rest of our men.

Then the *Titanic* settled so fast that before they could push away the waves were breaking over the boat deck. There stood Jacques by the rail. With the water lapping his ankles, he gave Mrs Harris the last words I would ever hear from him – a great-hearted joke: 'See what good care the White Star Line takes of us!' he said.

It seemed that [I] somehow needed some news about how Jacques had died. One of the late boats, I heard, had picked up a large man – so large, in fact, that it took eight men to get him out of the water. When they laid him in the bottom of the boat, they saw that he was dead. He breathed his last in their arms. Then they threw the body overboard to make room for the others. I hoped this might be Jacques. If he was conscious when they pulled him aboard, he knew, perhaps, that he was rescued, which would be enough to ease his dying heart. I found the crew of that boat. They showed me a description of this man, but I saw that it could not be Jacques.

Afterward I heard about Colonel Gracie's experience, and had some one point him out to me. He had gone down with the ship, come up barely alive, managed to swim a little, and so reached a boat. He could tell me whether they suffered mentally as they were going down!

All that day I followed him at a distance, getting up courage to ask him. A dozen times I was on the very point of the question, but each time the fear that I would get the answer I didn't want drove me away. However, the next morning he passed the place where we women were crying and stopped to tell us how sorry he was. Then I asked. He said:

'No indeed. It was all quite ordinary. From the moment when the plunge came I thought only of keeping my mouth closed and trying to ride the waves. I was too busy with that to think of anything else. I'm sure that if I'd never come up I'd have no more suffering either mental or physical.'

After that I could let my heart die.[181]

JACOB GIBBONS — Crew (Saloon Steward)

After returning to England on the *Lapland* on 28 April, Mr Gibbons used the back of an old envelope to write the following letter to his family:

Plymouth
Sunday, 12.30

Dearest Mam,

Just a line, we have arrived here safe after our sad experience. I hope to be able to get home tomorrow and see you all, if they will let us leave. We are held here now to wait enquiry and are getting 2/6 a day and depart and go to Southampton tomorrow.

We had a lovely voyage home from New York. I don't feel any the worse for it. Our boat arrived about 9 o'clock here this morning.

Hope you are all well. You might send me a wire tomorrow early morning to say how you all are, in case I do not come. We don't know until the trip to Southampton tomorrow morning. I do not know what time that we have to leave. Send it to Southampton. I shall get it when we arrive. It's about seven hours from here to Southampton. We were treated well in New York and given all help. Overcoat and a pair of boots and things.

Dearest love to you all,
Daddy
XXXXXXXXX
Hope to see you soon.[182]

SAMUEL GOLDENBERG **First Class Passenger**

While the *Carpathia* was bound for New York, Mr Goldenberg chaired a committee of surviving passengers that composed a formal statement regarding the sinking of the *Titanic*; the statement was released to the press upon the *Carpathia*'s arrival in New York:

> We the undersigned surviving passengers from the steamship *Titanic*, in order to forestall any exaggerated statements, deem it our duty to give to the press a statement of facts which have come to our knowledge and which we believe to be true.
>
> On Sunday, April 14, at about 11:40 p.m. on a cold starlight night, in a smooth sea and with no moon, the ship struck an iceberg which had been reported to the bridge by lookouts but not early enough to avoid collision. Steps were taken to ascertain the damage and save passengers and ship. Orders were given to put on lifebelts and the boats were lowered. The ship sank about 2:20 a.m. Monday and the usual distress signals were sent out by wireless and rockets at intervals from the ship. Fortunately the wireless message was received by the Cunarder *Carpathia* at about 12 o'clock midnight and she arrived on the scene of the disaster about 4 a.m. Monday.
>
> The officers and crew of the steamship *Carpathia* had been preparing all night for the rescue and comfort of the survivors and the last mentioned were received on board with the most touching care and kindness, every attention being given, irrespective of class. The passengers, officers and crew gave up gladly their staterooms, clothing and comforts for our benefit. All honour to them.
>
> The English board of trade passenger certificate on board the *Titanic* showed approximately 3,500. The same certificate called for lifeboat accommodations for approximately 950 in the following boats: Fourteen lifeboats, two smaller boats and four collapsible boats. Life preservers were accessible and apparently in sufficient numbers for all on board.
>
> The approximate number of passengers carried at the time of the collision was: First class, 330; second class, 330; third class, 750. Total, 1,400. Officers and crew, 940. Grand total, 2,340. Of the foregoing about the following were rescued by the *Carpathia*: First class, 210; second class, 125; third class, 200; officers, 4; seamen, 39; stewards, 96; firemen, 71. Total, 210 of the crew. The total of about 745 saved was about 80 per cent of the maximum capacity of the lifeboats.
>
> We feel it our duty to call the attention of the public to what we consider the inadequate supply of life-saving appliances provided for on modern passenger steamships and recommend that immediate steps be taken to compel passenger steamers to carry sufficient boats to accommodate the maximum number of people carried on board. The following facts were observed and should be considered in this connection: The insufficiency of lifeboats, rafts, etc., lack of trained seamen to man the same (stokers, stewards etc. are not efficient boat handlers), not enough officers to carry out emergency orders on the bridge and superintend the launching and control of lifeboats: absence of searchlights.
>
> The board of trade rules allow for entirely too many people in each boat to permit the same to be properly handled. On the *Titanic*, the boat's deck was about

seventy-five feet above water and consequently the passengers were required to embark before lowering boats, thus endangering the operation and preventing the taking on of the maximum number the boat would hold. Boats at all times should be properly equipped with provisions, water, compasses, lights, etc. Life-saving boat drills should be more frequent and thoroughly carried out and officers should be armed at boat drills. Great reduction in speed in fog and ice as damage, if collision actually occurs, is liable to be less. In conclusion, we suggest that an international conference be called to recommend the passage of identical laws providing for the safety of all at sea and we urge the United States government to take the initiative as soon as possible.[183]

(The statement was signed by Samuel Goldenberg, chairman, and a committee of some twenty-five passengers.)

On 24 April Mr Goldenberg wrote the following letter in response to rumours that he had taken an article of luggage with him into one of the *Titanic*'s lifeboats:

New York
April 24, 1912

When I left the *Titanic* I was dressed in my pajamas, coat, trousers, dressing gown, raincoat and slippers (not shoes.) I had time to take two rugs with me, for my wife and for myself.

On reaching the *Carpathia* I was told that the barber had some toilet articles and other things to sell. I therefore made the necessary purchases of toothbrushes and other toilet articles, including shirt and collars; for my wife and myself a pair of shoes, &c. I then asked the barber if he had anything to put them into in the shape of a bag, and he sold me a brown canvas kit bag. On reaching New York I put all of the remaining things into this bag, and this is the bag that was mentioned in the *New York Times*. I state these facts simply for the purpose of not creating a wrong impression, as in common with all other passengers, I had no thought of saving any of my luggage at such a moment, and actually did not save any. — S. L. Goldenberg[184]

ARCHIBALD GRACIE — First Class Passenger

After the disaster Colonel Gracie wrote the following account of his experience on board the *Titanic*:

I am requested to give for *The Outlook*'s readers my personal account of what I saw and did in this horrible catastrophe of the *Titanic* on the night of April 14 when she was in collision with an iceberg off the banks of Newfoundland, latitude 41 degrees 46 minutes north, and longitude 50 degrees 14 minutes west.

I believe she was struck almost amidships by the iceberg and ripped her keel forward like a can-opener. The night was clear and the water smooth, and for this very reason, as I was told by old sailors of the *Carpathia*, it was the more difficult to distinguish the iceberg with no background on the horizon. The ship was proceeding, so far as I know, at the same pace she had been going on the day previous, and she was by no means rushing to make her best time, 24¾ knots an hour.

At the time of the collision I was asleep in my cabin and was awakened by the noise as of a collision with some object which I supposed to be a small boat! The jar amounted to nothing, certainly insufficient to shake me from my berth.

Jumping up, in accordance with habit, I glanced at the watch on my dresser, which showed twelve o'clock midnight exactly, though I had not set it by the ship's time in less than twenty-four hours. When I next looked at this watch, it was after I had been rescued aboard the *Carpathia*, when the works, filled with salt water, indicated twenty-two minutes past two o'clock. This I take to be the time when I went down with the ship, registering about two hours and twenty minutes as the interval of time between the collision and the sinking of the ship, and shows the reason why the ship sunk with so little suction after she had filled up to the bridge deck.

Hurriedly putting on underclothing, trousers, and an overcoat, I rushed up to the outer deck and soon learned that we had struck an iceberg, but, looking over the side, saw no indication of damage nor of any list to the ship. Some jocose friend there showed me some ice obtained on the deck and presented it to me as a memento to carry home. Presently, however, in the saloon deck I observed a slight list to the port side, to which I called the attention of my friend, Mr James Clinch Smith, of Smithtown, Long Island, but we thought best not to create any possible excitement by calling it to the attention of others. I returned to the cabin again and packed up all my belongings in three bags, so that if we had to leave the ship, or the baggage had to be removed the next day, I might not have to return to the cabin for that purpose.

Going on deck again, I met Mr Ismay with the ship's officer. Mr Ismay was smiling serenely and not in the slightest degree perturbed. Presently, however, I noticed people with life-preservers adjusted, which was said to be a mere provision of safety ordered by the captain. On deck at this time I observed the three ladies I had undertaken to look after at the outset of the voyage, never supposing that I would be called upon to do anything as serious as this; they had just returned from Paris by way of Southampton, having been with their sister, Lady Drummond, at the time of her death and funeral – Mrs E.D. Appleton, Mrs Cornell, and Mrs J.M. Brown, the latter from Boston, and the others from New York. They were accompanied by a young lady, Miss Evans. In years gone by this young lady had been warned by some fortune-teller to beware of water. This was the tale she told me now.

Looking out in the direction toward which the bow was pointing, we seemed to see a light, and concluded it was a steamship coming to our rescue summoned by the wireless. Colonel Astor also had come out on deck, and saw the light referred to. We can only suppose that this light was on a passing sailing ship which never came to our rescue.

Now followed the firing of sky-rockets and the assembling of the passengers together to be loaded on the boats on the boat deck. Moving towards the bow of the boat, the men were stopped from accompanying the ladies. About this time I went into the smoking room, and, as usual, I saw there seated around the table four good friends, Major Archibald Butt, military aide to President Taft and President Roosevelt, Mr Francis D, Millet, Clarence Moore of Washington, and Mr Ryerson of Philadelphia. They appeared oblivious of danger and were the only ones I saw in the room. It was at this time that I also heard the band play with the evident purpose of instilling courage and stopping confusion.

With Mr Clinch Smith I now took my station in the bow of the boat on the port side and helped in loading the boats at this side with the helpless women and children. I assisted a mother and babe to safety. I also helped Mrs Astor over the rail into the boat, and heard her husband request of the second officer that he be allowed to accompany her for protection.

'No, sir,' said the officer; 'no man must go on this boat.'

Colonel Astor bravely held his peace and gracefully accepted the painful situation, asking only for the boat's number in order that he might find his wife later.

And now so palpable was the list to starboard that the second officer ordered all passengers to the port side, but not before one had called for all the women on that side.

With Mr Smith I now made my way to the starboard side of the bow, and to my surprise found among other ladies there Mrs Brown and Miss Evans. 'Why have you not gone with your sisters?' I asked, but before her explanation was forthcoming I found that there was room for more women in the last boat going down on the port side of the bow. I rushed them back, and, seizing the two ladies by an arm, hurried them to a point where I was stopped by the crew from proceeding farther, the ladies alone being allowed to pass. Had I been able to accompany them, I would have assisted in lifting them over the rail. Little Miss Evans had made up her mind that she had to die because of the soothsayer's warning, and refused to leave the ship.

I went back to the starboard side again, and here I saw in close conversation Mr John B. Thayer, Vice-President of the Pennsylvania Railroad, and Mr George B. Widener, of Philadelphia. I never saw them again.

Now I helped the crew in adjusting the davits for lowering a boat which had been slid down from the bridge deck, but I had to make way for the crew, and here I heard two of them discussing conditions; and one said that we could not sink because of the compartments, which must keep us afloat. In five minutes the water from the deck below reached the boat deck on which we stood, and the sailors seemed not to have time to launch the boat; so Mr Smith and I decided to hurry toward the stern; but we had only gone a few paces when, to our amazement, we saw men and women in a solid mass come up from the decks below, steerage or second class perhaps, facing toward us. But even here there was no panic, though appalling death was evident in the near future.

At this point I may be permitted to make the statement that, from my personal viewpoint, at the bow of the ship as well as elsewhere I saw nothing but unexampled self-sacrifice and self-control and the greatest courage under the most harrowing circumstances.

Now it seemed our end had come, for we could not meet this mass in front of us. Mr Smith and I tried to jump to the bridge deck, but found it impossible. The waves at our heels now reached us, and just as the water was above my knees I jumped with the rising swell as I so often had done at the seashore, rose with the crest, and grasped the railings about the bridge deck; but alas! Poor Smith was separated from me and I never saw him again. Holding on as long as I could to the railing, I was at last compelled to let go, and was hurled around and around on my stomach on the deck where the funnels were. Then down I went into the waters below, drawn beneath by the suction.

Up to this time there certainly was no explosion, or else I would have heard it. And when the explosion occurred I must have been under the water, and it was through this cause (the explosion) that I was driven to the surface again. When I got to the surface, I struck out with all my might and struggled to keep my breath and not allow myself to be suffocated by the water.

How great as the depth to which I went I cannot say. Had it been of greater extent than twenty-five feet, undoubtedly the blood would have rushed from my nose and ears. My chief concern was to escape from being boiled, as I at this time expected the water to boil from the engines below.

When I reached the surface finally, there was nothing to be seen about me but a great field of wreckage of every sort and description. I learned later that one of the funnels had fallen from the ship before I reached the surface, and splashed its waves over young Mr Thayer and the second officer, who thought that the funnel would fall upon him.

My first efforts were devoted to getting towards a mass of wreckage consisting principally of a crate-shaped mass of wood, but when I saw a short distance beyond a boat upside down with men struggling on it, I struck out in that direction, took hold of one man's hand and lifted my legs over and secured a position thereon with members of the *Titanic*'s crew.

A man in front had sort of an oar with which he propelled our craft, while another in the stern seemed to have a plank for a similar purpose. At any rate, we pushed our way through the wreckage, and when the complement of men was about thirty we could not take a single one more on the boat. If we had, it would have collapsed. The men struggling in the water appealed for help, but we had to explain to them that to assist one would be to destroy us all. An unknown hero to whom we so explained said, 'All right, boys; good-by, and God bless you!'

All night long we lay upon this boat, the water frequently up to our waists. The Lord's Prayer was repeated over and over again in unison by us all. Towards dawn, in order to be seen better, we all stood up in column fashion two deep, and frequently shouted for help. But for anyone to have turned about to look back at that time would have meant almost certain destruction.

At dawn four of the *Titanic*'s boats appeared on our starboard side, and the second officer's whistle soon commanded to our relief two of the boats. It was a glad sight, and soon we were transferred to two larger boats. The one to which I was transferred was filled with upwards of sixty-five. If we had had to wait more than an hour in the water before entering the boat we would certainly have sunk. The second officer was the last to leave the capsized boat, and I helped to transfer a dead man into the large boat.

After long hours of suffering in the cold I at last was rowed with the rest to the sheltering arms of the hospitable *Carpathia*. Up the sides the women were lifted, and I clambered up a rope.[185]

HENRY HARPER — First Class Passenger

After the *Carpathia*'s arrival in New York, Mr Harper wrote the following account of his *Titanic* experience:

I was fast asleep when the *Titanic* struck, for I had been kept in my stateroom by tonsillitis ever since coming aboard the ship. Our stateroom was pretty well forward on the starboard side and was perhaps thirty feet or more above the water. I remember that the sea was quite smooth when we went to sleep. As to how fast the ship was going, I have no knowledge.

I am inclined to believe the statements of many passengers that the *Titanic* was going at the pace of twenty-three knots an hour when she ran over the submerged edge of the berg that ripped a long gash in her bottom and sank her. My first knowledge about it was that of being awakened by a grinding sound that seemed to come from far below our deck. It was not a loud crash; it was felt almost as much as heard. But years before I had been in a ship that ran over a reef and was sunk, and I remembered that the impact and thrill then were so slight that I thought we were simply running over a fishing smack that bumped and scraped under our keel. So the moment I was awakened by the noise and heard the same sort of sound I sat up in bed and looked out of the nearest port.

I saw an iceberg only a few feet away, apparently racing aft at high speed and crumbling as it went. I knew right away what that meant.

'Get dressed quickly,' I told my wife. 'We must go on deck.'

'Wait,' she replied. 'I'll ask Mrs ____ across the way if she has heard any word.'

'You haven't a moment for talk,' I insisted. 'Get dressed – at once.'

She dressed much faster than I did, for I was pretty weak from my sickness, and she hurried to the stateroom of the ship's doctor.

'I wish you'd speak to my husband,' she said. 'He insists upon going on deck, and he won't mind me.'

The doctor came in and ordered me to undress and go back to bed. He said he was sure there was nothing serious.

'Damn it, man,' I told him, 'this ship has hit an iceberg! How can you say there's nothing serious?'

I'm sorry now that I cussed him out, but it made me hot to hear him make little of such a grave danger.

'Well, stay here awhile,' he said, 'and I'll see what's up.' He was gone only a few moments and then popped his head in at my door.

'They tell me the trunks are floating around in the hold,' he said. 'You may as well go on deck.'

So I put on my overcoat and my wife put on her fur coat and we started up. I suppose this was a quarter of an hour after the ship struck, for we were completely dressed as if we were going ashore – shoes all laced up and tied, and all that sort of thing.

We walked very slowly up the steps of the big stairways, for I was pretty weak, and when we got to the next deck above I sat down on a lounge and rested five or six minutes. Then we climbed up to the next deck, and so on. At last we got up to the gymnasium, which was on the top deck, and I sat down beside my wife. Men and women were standing about in groups talking. I have heard some talk since about excitement, but I saw none then. Everybody seemed confident that the ship was all right. She certainly seemed all right. The engines had been stopped soon after we struck and by this time she had slowly lost headway and was standing still. The sea was quiet, a flat calm, but all the ship's lights were lit and there was not a suggestion of excitement anywhere. A few people were talking about the lifeboats, but they were laughed at.

'Lifeboats,' said a woman near me. 'What do they need of lifeboats? This ship could smash a hundred icebergs and not feel it. Ridiculous.'

After a little time, word was passed among the passengers that we'd better go back to bed.

'The ship will be delayed two hours,' the stewards said, 'and then go on to New York.'

At this a great many people went away from our neighbourhood. Whether they went back to bed or not I don't know, but I can't remember seeing their faces again. They dropped away a few at a time – casually drifted off. Funny thing to remember how they scattered here and there – two or three crossing over from one group to another and two or three going from that group to still another. They all seemed curious, not a bit anxious. The reassurance that the ship would be delayed only two hours seemed to satisfy the curiosity of most of them, though, and the crowds soon dwindled. However, there were still a few dozens of us left, in our neighbourhood, on the upper deck.

Perhaps a quarter of an hour later word was passed that we'd better put on life-preservers. Some people put on the lifebelts and others laughed at them. Then came a long wait. I was surprised that there was no officer in sight to direct people where to go or to warn them or reassure them. We were left to ourselves. It was rather like a stupid picnic where you don't know anybody and wonder how soon you can get away from such a boresome place. I couldn't help wondering what had become of all the fine sea discipline I had heard and read about so much. I said to myself: These steamship men are hotel-keepers rather than sailor-men. They hear there are icebergs ahead, and instead of swinging out of their way they simply turn on more steam as a hotel man would do with a cold wave coming, and then go plunging right into the iceberg. They hit an iceberg and then tell their guests they'd better go back to bed. I was pretty sore by that time, and I think anyone would be who knows anything about seafaring.

Not long after the passengers began telling one another that we were ordered to put on life-preservers, stewards came around our neighbourhood and began calling out: 'All women to go to the lower deck!' Some women went. Others were escorted down the companionway by their husbands. I take it that they all understood, as we certainly did, that the women were to be kept together there ready to be sent off in the first boats if it should become necessary to abandon the ship. My wife and I said nothing to each other, but simply sat still and waited.

Presently a number of stewards and other men of the ship's company began to fuss with the tackle of a couple of lifeboats near where we were on the upper deck. I say 'fuss' with them, but I might as well say 'make a mess of them'. They seemed quite unused to handling boat gear. They took away a section of the deck rail near each boat and then climbed into the boat and hoisted away on the falls so as to swing the boat clear on the davits and let her down so that the gunwale was flush with the deck. We passengers still remaining on the deck gathered around and watched the men at work. Very slowly, and stumbling here and there, the people began to get in. It was like stepping down, say, from this table to the chair alongside. We took a look at both boats. My wife thought the one farther off was better because there would be hardly a dozen people left to go in it after the big boat beside us was filled. I looked them both over, saw that the farther boat had no water-tight compartments in it while the one near had; so I said: 'No; let's take this. It will float longest.'

With that I handed my wife down into the nearer, bigger boat, and she comfortably seated herself on a thwart. Other women and other men climbed aboard. An old dragoman of mine who had come with me from Alexandria – because he wanted 'to see the country all the crazy Americans came from,' as he explained it – made his way into the unfamiliar boat and settled himself. He made himself quite at home. Four or five stokers or some such men came along and jumped into the boat at the forward end. The sailor who seemed to be in charge of the boat laughed a little.

'Huh!' he said: 'I suppose I ought to go and get my gun and stop this.' But he did not go and get any gun, and neither did he order the stokers out. Everybody seemed to take what was happening as a matter of course and there wasn't a word of comment.

I stepped in and sat down among the stokers. There was no one in sight on the decks. I had on my arm a little brown Pekinese spaniel we had picked up in Paris and named Sun Yat Sen in honour of his country's first President. The little dog kept very quiet. I found out, after boarding the *Carpathia*, that several dogs had been rescued in the same way in the early boats. There seemed to be lots of room, and nobody made any objection. The sailor who seemed to be in charge ordered, 'Lower away!' The gang at each end of the boat began to pay out the boat-falls, so that our life-boat went down, first by the head, then by the stern, in a series of jerks. Lower by machinery? Not an inch – so far as I saw. It was all done by hand, and very clumsily done. If there had been any sea running, I feel sure our boat would have been smashed against the ship's side. A boat that had descended fifteen or twenty feet was hailed by a man on the upper deck – a second-class passenger, an Australian going out to America to see his mother, it transpired later. He leaned out over the edge and called: 'Hey! Will you take me in that boat?'

'No,' said the man who seemed to be in charge.

'But you've lots of room in your boat,' the man on deck insisted.

'Yes,' replied the sailor, 'but we're too far down now for you to jump in. You'd hurt yourself.'

'Yes, but I can slide down the ropes,' the passenger answered.

'Very well. Come on,' the sailor agreed. Whereupon the crew ceased lowering, and the passenger twined arms and legs around the falls, slid down to the boat, said, 'Thanks,' and sat down. More lowering by fits and starts, and at last our boat was afloat. Then we had more trouble – they didn't know how to cast loose the tackle. They fussed and fiddled, and the life-boat grated up against the ship's black hull for minutes. Just imagine how we'd have been pounded to pieces if there had been any sort of sea running!

Somehow or other they got her clear at last, and the four men at the oars began to row. And such rowing! You've seen the young man who hires a boat on Central Park lake on Sunday and tries to show off? Well, about like that – skying the oar on every recover, burying the blade on the pull or missing it altogether. There was only one man in the four who knew how to row. The steering was worse. The four oarsmen paddled as briskly as they could, and our boat, with say, some forty people in it, began to move away from the ship, slowly but not surely. For the man at the tiller would pull it toward himself for a while and send her around to port, or push the tiller away and swerve her around to starboard.

'Ow!' he exclaimed; 'let's get on. There'll be a big wave when she goes under – ow! A terrible big wave! – so let's get out of her way!'

But the poor fellow was so anxious to escape from the neighbourhood of the *Titanic* that he kept steering in half-circles or worse. At last he headed the boat clear around so that her bow was pointed straight toward the ship. I couldn't stand that.

'Here!' I cried, 'do you want to run the ship down? I guess you may have steered with a wheel, but surely you've never handled a tiller. Shove the tiller the opposite to the way you want to go, and you'll be all right.'

He got her straightened out then, and our poor crew paddled very slowly away from the *Titanic*. I suppose by this time it must have been about one o'clock in the morning. There was a very little bit of the moon in the sky – the last quarter,

I suppose. The water was smooth as a lake, not a piece of ice anywhere except the big iceberg that had wrecked us, far astern; and at every stroke of the oars great glares of greenish-yellow phosphorescent light would swirl aft from the blades and drip in globules like fire from the oars as they swung forward. The phosphorescence was so brilliant that it almost dazzled us at first. I have never seen it so fine.

As we drew away from the *Titanic* she was brightly lighted as ever and not a sound came from her. I have heard since coming ashore about rioting and shooting, but throughout the whole incident I did not hear a shot fired or a loud voice. Of course, there may have been something like this as the later boats were loaded, but there was nothing like it in our vicinity. We seemed deserted on our part of the deck before launching our lifeboat, and I guess whatever violence there was happened on the lower deck to which the women were ordered some time before we left.

Nor did I see much of a list in the ship's body as I looked at her from the boat. She seemed a little down by the head, but as we moved away from her she looked like a great mountain of strength that would last forever. Her lights were all burning, as it seemed to us, and she made a wonderful picture. The air was so clear that we could see plainly such details as her rails and bits of the rigging standing out like lines in an engraving. We were lying off perhaps a quarter of a mile from her when I heard several bursts of cheering. I suppose that was when the people on board received the news by wireless that other ships were hurrying to the rescue.

After an hour or more – I had no way of seeing the exact time, but it seemed very long – the lights of the *Titanic* suddenly went out and we began to think her end could not be very far away. I have heard a lot of talk about explosions in the *Titanic*; that her boilers blew up and tore her body apart. I certainly heard nothing that sounded like an explosion. I did hear a great roar mingled with hissing coming from the direction of the ship. I supposed that this was caused by the sea-water rising in the hull high enough to put out the fires under the boilers. Water thus heated would hardly make boilers explode, I should think. No one in our boat said a word, but I feel sure the seriousness of the situation began to depress everybody. Very slowly the giant black hull began to diminish against the skyline. It was a frightful thing to feel that the ship was going, faster and faster, and that we could do nothing for the people on her. Not a sound came from the ship until the very last, and then there rose in the air a sort of wild maniacal chorus, a mingling of cries and yells in which I could distinguish voices of different tones. Many of the people, I fear, had gone mad as they felt the ship settle for her final plunge to the depths. No one gave any command, but our crew began to row as hard as they could away from the awful sounds, and then in the twinkling of an eye we were all alone on the dark sea. There was no talking in our boat, nothing but the rattling of the oars in the rowlocks. But the air still resounded with the long-drawn wail of agony that rose from the ship. These were the most awful moments in the whole experience. Bravery was shown by the people in every phase of the emergency; but flesh and blood could not withstand that gasping cry of horror as the sea rose to them. After a time our boat passed out of reach of the cry and we were alone indeed.

One sailor called to another: 'Did you put the plugs in the bottom of this boat before she was launched?'

'Well,' the other replied, meditating, 'I'm sure I put in one plug an' I hope I put in both, for I don't feel any water about our feet.'

Either the men didn't know where to look or they couldn't grope their way among the passengers to find out: but we found out later that both plugs were in place. After a long silence someone cried out that there was a green light dead ahead.

'Must be the starboard light of a fishing-smack,' another voice answered. I felt pretty sure it couldn't be, since very few fishermen will waste their money on kerosene for side-lights; but our crew made for the green light just the same. When we got a mile nearer to the light we found that it was the reflection of the stars shining on the side of an iceberg. A wind was blowing off the ice that seemed to bite as it struck us, it was so cold. No picture I have ever seen gives a fair idea of the size and the menace of a berg. This one looked fearful, and seemed to breathe out the threat of death. Nevertheless no one in our boat was frozen. We were all well wrapped up and we sat so close together that we kept one another comfortably warm. As the wind freshened up to what would be a good sailing breeze, the sea rose with it, and we began to pitch and roll.

They say it was a little before four o'clock in the morning when the *Carpathia* came in sight. Her lights looked very low and dim at first, but within a short time after we sighted her she came up near us and stopped. I remember thinking how tiny she looked, all picked out against the sky by her rows of lights, compared with the great bulk of the *Titanic* which we had seen all lighted up only a few hours before. Within a few minutes the sun began to show its edge above the horizon and soon rose clear of the sea. I never saw a finer sight than that ship which had raced through fifty miles of field ice and bergs to come to our rescue. I saw some of the bergs later, and they looked as big as the pyramids.

The little life-boats began racing toward the *Carpathia* as fast as their crews could row. They couldn't do much more than paddle, but soon they came alongside. Presently our boat came up to where they had a chair rigged to a whip and let down for our people, one by one. The third person to leave our boat – a woman of substantial size – was stepping forward to take her place in the chair when, to the utter amazement of everybody, another woman, clad only in night gown and kimono, sprang from nowhere and sat up on the floor of the boat.

'Look at that horrible woman!' she cried, pointing at the astonished lady in the chair. 'Horrible! She stepped on my stomach. Horrible creature!'

The unhappy woman in the kimono had been lying for all of the four hours on the floor of the life-boat, either unconscious or too frightened to speak. She was next up in the chair after her oppressor.

When it finally came my turn to go up I found myself hoisted aloft quickly. A pair of hands was thrust out to keep me from bumping my head against the ship as I ascended. At the deck one man seized me to hold me up, while another wrapped a blanket, warmed in advance, completely around me. A third man assisted me into a room where a cup of hot coffee and a big drink of brandy were served to me – the whole process from the moment of lifting me out of the chair taking about half a minute.

It seems to me now as if I should remember these details as long as I live. And, of course, all I saw and heard was a very small part of all the happenings of that awful night.[186]

IRENE HARRIS **First Class Passenger**

A day or two after the *Carpathia* arrived in New York, Mrs Harris wrote a letter to John Millet regarding the latter's father, Frank Millet, a victim of the *Titanic* disaster:

> He wore that same smile that he did all the way from Southampton. I remember well while I was in a lifeboat I looked back to the ill-fated ship and saw Mr Millet waving to some women in another boat. I could not mistake his genial smile. It was a sad farewell, but it was characteristic of the brave man.
>
> Mr Millet was with Maj. Butt and Col. Astor, helping them to lift women into the lifeboats. He was no less a real hero than they. He did more than his share in saving the women, and is one of the real heroes of the disaster.[187]

On 24 April Rene Harris wrote a letter to Clara Butt, the sister-in-law of victim Major Archibald Butt:

> April 24, 1912
>
> My dear Mrs Butt:
>
> In view of the fact that I am giving out a statement that I have heretofore had absolutely no interview with any paper, I want you to understand the [newspaper] statement I made regarding Major Butt.
>
> A messenger came to my home who claimed to be direct from the President, so to him I told the little I knew about the last few moments on the ship. I had no idea it would be put into print, but I am glad for your sake that you have been able to know the little that I know.
>
> I was the last rescued woman off the boat, having been put into a collapsible. I stayed with my husband until they forced me away from him, and in passing through the Captain's room I saw standing with the Captain on the bridge, Major Butt, the doctor and another gentleman who were talking very calmly together. The doctor stopped me to speak with me, as the day before he had attended me in the breaking of my arm when I slipped down the stairs, so that is how I came in such close touch with the Major.

> Although my heart bleeds with grief over the loss of my husband, I would a thousand times rather that he met his death as he did, standing up with those other brave men as did the Major, than that he had come off that boat with the feeling that he had not done his duty in obeying his superior officers. We may both be proud of our hero men.
>
> If I am a bit incoherent, it is because I am still suffering from the shock of seeing that boat go down when I was less than a hundred yards away from it. But some day, my dear Mrs Butt, I hope I may have the extreme pleasure of talking with you about it, so look me up if you ever come to New York, where I hope to continue the beautiful work that my husband has always done. It may interest you to know that we were partners for twelve years and a half, so you may appreciate how deep is my loss.
>
> This is the only communication of any kind I have made, but if it proves to be a source of any solace to you, I am re-paid.
>
> Sorrowfully yours
>
> Rene W. Harris
>
> P.S. I passed the bridge at 2:20 as someone mentioned the time, and the ship went down exactly at 2:30 according to one of the men in the collapsible.[188]

On 10 May, prior to the filing of the will of Henry B. Harris for probate, Mrs Harris signed the following affidavit regarding her husband's death aboard the *Titanic*:

> I left the steamer together with Mrs Thorne to enter a collapsible boat, which was the last boat to leave the steamer. At the time we both left to enter the boat my husband was standing on the deck of the *Titanic*. Within a few moments after we had struck the water, and while the *Titanic* was in full view, I saw it sink, and my husband was on the deck.
>
> Rene Harris[189]

On 11 May Mrs Harris described her *Titanic* experience for Ada Patterson, who transcribed the account for publication:

> One of the widows of the *Titanic* told me her story yesterday. Black-garbed, her right arm immovable in a plaster cast, her dark eyes staring with the same melancholy on the scenes she summoned as she looked upon the realities that night of April 14, Mrs Renee Harris lay on a couch in her drawing room. Upon the back of the couch rested a photograph of her husband, Henry B. Harris, who sank with the ship. On the piano opposite stood another photograph. Resting against it was a card that had accompanied one of his last gifts to her, a gift she cherished less than the inscription on it: 'To my only sweetheart on the twelfth anniversary of our wedding.'.
>
> 'I feel as though I had died and that my dear husband's spirit was in me and I was here to try to do what he would have done,' she said in a plaintive contralto voice, in this, her first interview. She looked at the easy, relaxed sitting figure and the pleasant face pictured in the frame on the piano. 'My boy,' she said as

though that picture was a person. 'My boy. His last words to me were "Goodbye sweetheart, I'll see you again."

I was one of the last to leave the *Titanic*. I didn't want to go. My husband kept me away from the rail of the boat.

"Don't look over, Renee," he warned me. "It will hurt your arm." So I did not know until I was tossed into the boat that we were even then only seven feet above water. We were sinking and he didn't want me to know it. "Take care of that woman. Her arm is broken," he called to the man, but they threw me into the boat anyway. I looked up at him and cried out, "Harry, won't you say goodbye to me?" And he spoke those words I have told you. They were the last I ever heard from him. Seven minutes after my husband kissed me and tossed a blanket after me into the boat, the *Titanic* sank.

With my face towards it I saw what looked like five long ribbons of light against a black shape. Behind this loomed something that even in the starlight looked like twin mountain peaks of snow. Silently one ribbon of light disappeared beneath the black waters, then another, then a third and a fourth. The last was on a line with the waters, and such a sound went up as will haunt one all one's life and into eternity. No one has heard anything so sad except those who have visited Jerusalem. In that city there is a wall which Jews are not permitted to pass to enter the city. There they come and mourn, and those cries of broken hearts are the only sounds in the world like those we heard when the *Titanic* went down.

I was in a collapsible boat. You understand what a collapsible boat is? It is of canvas and used for emergencies when the lifeboats give out.'

'Was Ismay on this boat?'

An eloquent silence, a flash of tragic black eyes, followed by, 'He was not.'

'The men on the boat were saying, "She's leaking. Look for a plug. Where's the plug?" "Cut a piece from the oar," I suggested. A woman at the end of the boat said, "Take my cap." But no one could find the hole in the boat. When the boat had sunk and the awful wails had ceased an Englishman, a passenger, said "Why are you looking for plugs? A collapsible boat has no plugs."

There were terror and chaos in the boat on the part of the quartermaster and crew. "Look out for the suction," they yelled. "Row for your lives." A woman took her place at the oars. When we had got farther away from the place where the *Titanic* sank a man was pulled into the boat. As he lay in the bottom of the boat he looked into the face of the woman who was rowing. "Jane," he said.

For a moment she stopped rowing. "Fred," she called and tossed him her shawl and went on rowing. It was her husband. The sea had given back the Hoyts to each other.

From the moment the *Titanic* sank I never spoke a word until the *Carpathia* picked us up. People came to me afterward and said, "How brave you were." I wasn't brave. I just sat there dumb thinking of the settling into the water of the big, black shape with ribbons of light and my thoughts followed one steady round. "How sad it was that I didn't stay with him! Why didn't I stay?" All but the mere shell of me died that night.

We had been drifting about an hour when out of the darkness came a voice – strong, ringing, youthful. "Anybody there?" The quartermaster answered. "All right, quartermaster," came the voice, "How many have you aboard?" "Nineteen." "How many can you take?" "Thirty." "All right, tie up to me."

A boat swung round in front of us and we tied fast. We started off with new strength. Now and then the young, strong voice rang back at us. "Everybody happy?" "You're tied fast, don't worry." "Morning's coming." At little intervals the voice would call, "Any boats around? Tie up to me." In a short while the young voice of the invisible commander was guiding a flotilla of open boats. Heretofore we had been drifting about, the people in every boat trying to keep the others away from it. Now there was union.

At last I heard the voice grow tense. "Courage!" it called. "We're coming. There's a boat ahead. It's almost under. Call out to them. We're coming. Every voice among you call. Say we're coming!" I couldn't speak. I opened my lips but no words came. But from ours came a strange mixed chorus, full of sadness and yet of help. "We're coming," it said.

Then we were nearly abreast the other. The boat had been pierced by a piece of wreckage. Its sides were within two inches of the surface. A woman and a dozen men were huddled close together. Some of them were in their night clothes. They stood in the icy water up to their waists. Their faces looked like those of famished wild animals. The voice that had commanded us had a stern tone. I saw a revolver pointed at the boat.

"The woman first," said the voice. "I will shoot the man who tries to get ahead." He swung her into the boat, a little woman dressed all in brown. She sank into the bottom of the boat like a drowned bird. The young officer still held the revolver pointed at the men in the sinking boat. "One man at a time," he warned. "Death to the man who makes a rush." So they were taken into the boat one at a time, and as the last was dragged in the other boat sank. With it went two stark figures. They were men who had died while drifting.

In the darkness the voice kept on cheering. "Tie fast." "Tie up to me," it would say. When the first light came we were in an orderly little fleet. Looking toward the spot from which the voice came I saw a young man of 6 feet 2, very slender and sinewy. His face was clear cut and of the fine British race. He had keen, deep set, merry black eyes. His cap was tilted boyishly on one side. He looked like a college boy out on an early morning lark.

It was his voice that told us there was a boat in sight. Over against the twin mountains of snow the sun rose just behind a ship.

"Call to her," said a voice from one of the boats.

"Wait for her to come after us. Don't go near the ice," warned another.

"I've taken command here," the voice that had cheered us through the night rang out sternly. "I intend to keep command because no one else seems to have sense enough to do it. Now, shut up. We will go to the boat. We can't expect her to come to us."

In a short time I was being hoisted over the side of the *Carpathia*. In my stateroom that afternoon I said, "Who's that boyish chap that took command?"

"It was Fifth Officer Lowe of the *Titanic*," someone told me. I sent for him and when he came to my door I said, "Mr Lowe, you are wonderful. I want to thank you. I have no money but when I get to New York I want to reward you." He pushed up his cap. "I will never take money for doing my duty," he said.

I made inquiries afterwards and learned he was Harold Godfrey Lowe, aged twenty-nine and a citizen of Perallt-Barmouth, North Wales. Since I have been in New York I have sent for him again and asked him to let me reward him. He flushed again and said, "Mrs Harris, you make me flush. I have only done my duty. I won't take a penny for that. I only hollered. Anybody can holler."

He could not be moved. Ismay found that out, for Lowe is the officer who said when Ismay tried to direct the filling and lowering of a lifeboat; told him to go – well, somewhere else.

I have told this story because if Great Britain had only such seamen there would be no such disasters. And this was the first transatlantic crossing. He is one hero of the survivors of the *Titanic*. He is a brave, splendid youth to whom Great Britain should reward with a promotion.'[190]

ESTHER HART **Second Class Passenger**

Following the disaster, Mrs Hart wrote the following account of her experience on the *Titanic*:

I can honestly say that from the moment the journey to Canada was mentioned, till the time we got aboard the *Titanic* I never contemplated with any other feelings but those of dread and uneasiness. It was all done in a hurry. My husband of late had not been successful in business and things looked like going from bad to worse.

He was a very clever carpenter and his chest of tools was considered to be as perfect and expensive as any carpenter could wish for. At any rate he valued them at £100. He was going out to start building with a Mr Wire at Winnipeg. Mr Wire has since written to me expressing his deep regret at Ben's untimely loss, and adding, 'There were five Winnipeg men lost on the *Titanic* and I might have been one of them.'

The idea seized on Ben's imagination. 'I'll go out to a new country,' he said, 'where I'll either sink or swim.' In fact, during the time prior to our leaving Ilford, the latter statement was always in his mouth. I little knew then how sadly prophetic it was to turn out for my poor dear.

I said at the commencement that I viewed the journey with dread and uneasiness, but in saying that I do not wish anyone to think that I ever imagined anything so dreadful would happen as did happen. You see I was leaving my father and mother when they were at fairly advanced age, and neither of them in the best of health and I knew that in saying goodbye, I was saying goodbye forever: but it has pleased God to take my husband and send me back to them. Then I was leaving all the friends I had known in Ilford for so many years: and lastly, I dreaded the sea: the idea of being on the sea at night was bad enough, but for six or seven, I could not contemplate it, it was a nightmare to me.

Well, we said all our 'Good-byes' and reached Southampton, and almost the first thing Ben did was take me to see the *Titanic*. He was always an enthusiastic in anything he was interested in: and he could not have been more enthusiastic over the *Titanic* had he been a part proprietor of it. 'There! old girl,' he said, 'there's a vessel for you! You're not afraid now.' I tried to share his confidence, but my heart quite failed me when we got aboard and I counted the number of boats there were. I said, 'Ben, we are carrying over 2,000 people and there are not enough boats for half of them if anything happens.' He laughed at my fears and said that beyond boat drills he did not expect the boats would come off the davits. But from that moment I made up my mind to one thing, till we were safe on land at New York. Nothing should ever persuade me to undress, and nothing did, although Ben at times got very cross with me. So each night I simply rested in my bunk, fully dressed and fully prepared. God knows why, for the worst.

We were fortunate in having some very nice people at our table. We were in parties of eight in the second saloon, and our party included a lady and gentleman from the Cape, Mr and Mrs Brown and their daughter, who were on their way to Vancouver. Mr Guggenheim's (a millionaire) chauffeur, (both Mr and Mrs Guggenheim and he were drowned), a lady named Mrs Mary Mack, whose body has since been recovered, and Mr Hart, myself, and baby.

Mr Brown and Ben got on capitally together. They were the exact opposite of each other. Mr Brown was a quiet, reserved man who scarcely ever spoke, and dadda was fond of talking and so they got on well, promenaded the deck together, had their mid-day 'Bass' together, and smoked their pipes together. Indeed, Mrs Brown said that she had never seen her husband 'take' to anyone like he had to my Ben.

Oh dear! Oh dear! To think that of the eight at the table, four were taken and four were left. I can see them bright, happy faces now as we sat round that table at meal times, talking of the future, they were all so confident, so looking forward to a new life in a new land, and well they found it, but in God's way, not theirs.

Now a very curious thing happened on the Saturday night. We had made splendid progress, and although I was still far from easy in my mind. I was as content as I could be off the land. I heard someone remark with glee that we were making a bee line for New York. I knew we were going at a tremendous speed, and it was the general talk – I cannot say what truth there was in it – that the Captain and others were 'on' something good if we broke the record.

But on the Saturday night I was resting in my bunk and my husband was sound asleep above me. Everything was quiet, except the throb of the screw and a strange straining and creaking of everything in the cabin, which I had noticed all the voyage. I may have just dozed off when I was awakened by a feeling as if some gigantic force had given the ship a mighty push behind. I could even hear the swirl of the waters which such a push to such a vessel would cause. I sat up, no doubt as to my being wide awake, again came the push and the swirl, and yet again a third time. For a few minutes I was dazed, frozen with terror of I know not what. Then I stood up and shook my husband who still sleeping soundly. 'Ben,' I said, 'Ben wake up, get up, something dreadful has happened or is going to happen.' He was a little cross, as a man naturally is when he is woke from a sound sleep by the ungrounded fears (as he thinks) of a woman, but he saw that I was upset, and so he got up and partly dressed, and went up on the hurricane deck, and soon returned and assured me that the sea was calm and that the ship was travelling smoothly.

The next morning at breakfast, he laughingly told our table about it, and said what he was going to do that (Sunday night) to keep me quiet. He was going to insist upon my having a strong glass of hot grog to make me sleep. Mr Brown explained the creaking and straining by saying that as it was a new vessel everything was settling down into its proper place. 'Why,' he said, 'when we get to New York, it's more than likely that a lot of the paint will have come away, a lot of the joints have started,' and so on. 'That's all very well,' I said, 'but what about those awful jerks one after the other?' That he could not explain, nor anybody else. I say it was a warning from God to me, for I think that perhaps I was the only one of the 2,000 odd about who went in daily and nightly dread of the unforeseen. But had I told it to those in authority! Would anyone have listened to a silly, weak woman's superstitious fears? Would they have gone one hair's breadth out of their course? Would they have ordered one revolution less per minute of the screw? So I could only do what women have had to do from the beginning, eat my heart out with fear and wait.

Now if I had known that just at this time of the year the icebergs get across the track of the Atlantic liners, a little incident which occurred on this Sunday would have sent me straight to the Captain, even if I'd have had to climb on to his bridge. But the simple things we ought to know we are never told. My husband was always a man who could bear extremes of heat and cold better than anyone I have ever met. All through those trying days of heat last year, when everyone else was melting and parched, he never once grumbled, but kept as cool as a cucumber. And the same with the cold. I have known him, when other people have been hanging over the fires, in and out of the house with his coat off, laughing at the poor shivering ones. And yet at midday on this fatal Sunday, he suddenly came up to baby and myself, and said rubbing his hands, 'How cold it has turned. I feel as if there was not a warm drop of blood in my body. Come and have a romp with daddy,' he said to baby, and together they went off and ran and romped on the hurricane deck.

We were in the iceberg region and the Almighty sent a warning to my husband – the man who was never cold before now shivered and shook like one stricken with ague.

But, beyond thinking it a curious thing, we took no heed.

And now, I come to a part of my story that I shrink from telling. Indeed, I think I have lingered over the first part because I dread relating the events of that awful night. I have read somewhere of people living a whole lifetime in a few hours. I know now that I have done so. To have gone through what I went through, to have suffered what I have suffered, to have seen what I have seen, to know what I know, and still to be alive, and above all – thank the Lord – to still preserve my reason, is a great and a growing marvel to me.

We had retired to our cabin about 10, and my husband, who thoroughly enjoyed the life aboard ship and drank his fill of the ozone (he could never get enough of it) was soon undressed and fast asleep in his bunk. My little Eva too was sound asleep, and I was sitting on my portmanteau with my head resting on the side of my bunk. And then all of a sudden there came the most awful sound I have ever heard in my life, a dreadful tearing and ripping sound – how any people were awake at the time can say they scarcely felt a shock I cannot understand – the sound of great masses of steel and iron being violently torn, rent and cut asunder.

I was on my feet in an instant, for I knew something dreadful had happened. I shook Ben, and he awoke. 'Daddy,' I said, 'get up at once. We have hit something I am sure and it's serious.' Poor dear Ben! He was partly asleep still, and he said, 'Oh woman, again! I really don't know what I shall do with you?' 'Ben,' I said, not loudly, but with a quiet insistence which influenced him far more, something has happened; go up on deck and find out what it is.' He went up in his nightshirt and bare feet; in a few moments he was back again. He said, 'All the men are at the lifeboats, it's only a lifeboat drill.' I said, 'They don't have lifeboat drills at 11 at night, I tell you something has happened, dress quickly and let us dress the baby.' So he hurriedly put on his pants and his overcoat, put his big motor coat over me and then dressed the sleeping little girl. Just then a stewardess, with whom I was on friendly terms came along and said she would soon find out all about it. She knew the Marconi operator and would ask him. So she went away and quickly came back saying that everything was all right. But I said, 'Everything is not all right, we have struck something and the water is coming in.' I think by this time Ben had realised, although he would not say so, that danger was ahead, for when he got up on 'B' deck, he turned away for a few moments, and said his Jewish prayers. The next few minutes were so crowded with events, so fraught with all that matters in this world – life to a few of us, death to the majority of us – that I have no coherent recollection of what happened.

I know that there was a cry of 'She's sinking.' I heard hoarse shouts of 'Women and children first,' and then from boat to boat we were hurried, only to be told 'already full'. Four boats we tried and at the fifth there was room. Eva was thrown in first, and I followed her. Just then, a man who had previously tried to get in, succeeded in doing so, but was ordered out, and the officer fired his revolver into the air to let everyone see it was loaded, and shouted out, 'Stand back! I say, stand back! The next man who puts his foot in this boat, I will shoot him down like a dog.' Ben, who had been doing what he could to help the women and children, said quietly, 'I'm not going in, but for God's sake look after my wife and child.' And little Eva called out to the officer with the revolver 'Don't shoot my daddy. You shan't shoot my daddy.' What an experience for a little child to go through!

At the age of seven to have passed through the valley of the shadow of death. I wonder if she will ever forget it? I know I shan't, if I live for a hundred years.

So that was the last I saw of my poor lost dear – no farewell kiss, no fond word, but in a moment he had gone and we were hanging over the sea, fifty or sixty feet above it, and then there were two or three horrible jerks as the boat was lowered from the davits and we were in the water, so crowded that we could scarcely move.

In the midst of all these stunning blows one despairing tact alone seized my thoughts: I knew, and a woman is never wrong in such matters, that I had seen the last of my Ben, and that I had lost the best and truest friend, the kindest and most thoughtful husband that ever woman had.

The officer in charge of our boat was standing on that raised part of it right at the end. We were all women and children aboard (at least I thought so then, but we were not, as I will presently tell you) and we were all crying and sobbing; and the officer said, not roughly, but I think with a kindly desire to keep our minds off the terrible time we had gone through. 'Don't cry, please don't cry. You'll have something else to do than cry; some of you will have to handle the oars. For God's sake stop crying. If I had not the responsibility of looking after you I would put a bullet through my brain.' So we got away from the ship for a safe distance, for there was no doubt now about her sinking. The front portion of her was pointing downwards and she appeared to be breaking in halves. Then with a mighty and tearing sob, as of some gigantic thing instinct with life, the front portion of her dived, for that is the only word I can use properly to describe it, dived into the sea, and the after part with a heavy list, also disappeared. And then a wonderful thing happened. Apart from the swirl of the water close to the vessel, caused by such a mass sinking, the sea was as smooth as glass; it seemed as if the Almighty, in order that as many should be saved as possible had with a merciful hand, smoothed and calmed the waters. For a few moments we could see everything that was happening, for, as the vessel sank, millions and millions of sparks flew up and lit everything around us. And in an instant the sea was alive with wreckage, with chairs, pillows, and rugs, benches, tables, cushions, and, strangely enough, black with an enormous mass of coffee beans. And the air was full of the awful and despairing cries of drowning men. And we were helpless to help, for we dared not go near them.

Our officer was busy shouting out till he was hoarse, 'Let all the boats keep as near together as possible. That's our only chance of being picked up. If we separate we are lost. Keep together.' An inky blackness now settled over us, and not a soul in our boat had a match; but the officer found in his pockets an electric torch, which he kept flashing, shouting out all the time, 'Keep together – it's our only chance.' The duty that the officer allotted to me was to bale the water out of the boat. While sitting there I had the impression that there was somebody near me who ought not to be there. So, when I could get my elbows free I put my hand down under the seat and touched a human form. It was a poor wretch of a man who had smuggled himself into the boat, and had sat there during all that awful time, under the seat in about six inches of water. When we got him out he was so stiff he could scarcely move.

It had got a little lighter now, and our officer had collected nearly all the boats together; and he called from one to the other, 'How many in yours – how many in yours?' and then he discovered that there was room in those other boats to put the whole of our fifty-five in, so we were transferred to them, and the officer now collected a few seaman in his now empty boat and rowed away to see what he could find. So, with proper management another fifty-five people could easily have been saved. I cannot understand why, in the midst of such terrible doings, these boats left the ship without their full number of passengers; fifty-five precious lives lost either through selfishness or carelessness, I know not which.

It was no easy matter for me to get from one boat to the other. I am no light weight at the best of times: but now I was weak from want of sleep, weak with the terror of the night, and laden with Ben's heavy motor coat. Eva had been handed in, and I shall never forget my feelings when I saw her leave, and found myself unable to get a footing on the boat she was in. At last I managed it, how I could not tell. Eva was suffering from a violent attack of vomiting: for, when they had thrown her into the first boat from the *Titanic* she had hit her stomach on the edge of the boat. And there the poor little thing was, and I could not get near her to wipe her mouth. So there we sat the weary night through until at eight in the morning, the *Carpathia* came on the scene. I always thought that these ship boats had to be provisioned beforehand, in view of possible accidents, but there was no water, nor were there biscuits in the boat. An oversight I suppose: but one fraught with terrible consequences had not the *Carpathia* arrived in good time.

Gradually the welcome dawn broke; and as the sun rose and we looked at where the sky and sea met, we saw one of the most wonderful sights that could be imagined. Right away there, stretching for miles and miles, there appeared what seemed to us, an enormous fleet of yachts, with their glistening sails all spread. As the sun grew brighter they seemed to sparkle with innumerable diamonds. They were icebergs; and, moving slowly and majestically along all by itself, a mile or so in length, in form like the pictures of Gibraltar I have seen, was the monster iceberg, the cause of all our trouble.

And now about 8 o'clock the *Carpathia* came into sight and we were all aboard by 8.30. I cannot say much of my life on board this vessel. It was no small matter for a ship to take on another 700 people, many of them but lightly clad, most of them ill, and all suffering severely from shock; all was done for us that could be done: but I could neither rest nor sleep. My little Eva was still suffering from her vomiting attack and I found my hands full in nursing her; but when at night she was asleep, I could do nothing but walk the corridor, up and down, up and down, and thinking, thinking all the time. So much did I walk about at night that the kind hearted sailors christened me The Lady of the Watch.

Well, eventually we arrived at New York. And what can I say of the kindness of the 'Women's Relief Committee', and the help they rendered us poor stranded souls. Kindness! that's but a poor word; and yet I can find no other for their intensely practical sympathy. No formulas, no questions. We had got to be helped and that quickly, and quickly they did it. In a short space of time with a speed that seemed incredible, there was a sufficiency of clothing for every destitute woman and child – my women readers will understand me when I say that everything a woman needed was there in abundance – from a blouse to a safety pin, underclothing, stays, stockings, garters, suspenders, hair pins, boots of all sizes, each pair with laces or a button hook in them as was necessary; I have never heard of such foresight. I have never experienced such real kindness. God bless the ladies of the 'Women's Relief Committee of New York', say I heartily and fervently. Why, Mrs Satterlee actually drove me in her beautiful car to the hotel where I was to stay pending my return to England, and wanted me to go to lunch with her in her house, but my heart was too full for that. She knew the reason and appreciated it like the lady she is. One touching little incident occurred before I sailed for home on the *Celtic*, and that was the receipt of a letter from little children in New Jersey. They had heard of my Eva and they sent her a dollar bill with a beautiful little letter. I don't think that bill will ever be changed; for both it and the letter will be framed.

There is but little to add. I returned on the *Celtic* with five other ladies from the *Titanic*, including Mrs Ada Clarke, of Southampton. We were treated with every kindness and consideration. A lady in the first saloon sent out word that whatever we wanted in the way of fruit or any other delicacies not included in our menu, we were to have.

And now I have only one object in life, and that is the future of my little Eva. My lost Ben had such dreams of her future; he meant to do such things for her; and, whatever money I get, apart from the bare cost of the necessities of life, shall be devoted to her up-bringing in such a way as shall realise, as far as my endeavours and finances can go, his wishes with regard to her.

Esther Hart
'Slinfold'
Chadwell Heath[191]

WALTER HAWKSFORD **First Class Passenger**

On 19 April Mr Hawksford wrote the following letter to his wife:

Hotel Astor New York
April 19th, 1912

Dear old Girl,

Here I am, you see, still alive and kicking, although we have had a pretty rough time of it. You will know almost as much as I do by now from the papers, so I will not enlarge on the horrors of it all.

We struck an iceberg about 12 o'clock on Sunday night. I was in bed at the time in that nice little cot you admired so much, just dozing off when I felt a bump and then a long grinding sound. I first got up and put my overcoat over my pajamas, then went out to see what had happened. We were not alarmed because everybody had such complete confidence in the ship, and when the ladies came out of the cabins we just laughed, and told them we had pushed an iceberg out of the way. About half an hour afterwards word was passed around to put on our life preservers, so I went to my cabin, slipped a suit on over my pajamas, overcoat and lifebelt, then had to go up to the boat deck.

You would hardly believe the calmness of everybody, not even a woman was panic-stricken. The men stood by while the women were quickly and methodically lowered into the boats with a few men in each boat to row. When it came to the last boat but one I was told to man the boat with four others, the rest were women, we were then lowered a distance of 90ft to the water and rowed about half a mile from the ship.

It was very cold but a beautiful night, starry, and the sea as smooth as glass. We watched her bow gradually getting lower, then about two o'clock all the lights went out, her stern rose in the air, and she slowly glided away. We raised our hats, bowed our heads, and nobody spoke for some minutes.

We remained in that boat for five hours. You cannot imagine the strange feeling of being in mid-Atlantic in a small rowing boat. Just as it was getting daylight we saw a rocket go up on the horizon and knew it would not be long before we were on another ship. We watched her slowly appear and then stop. You guess we did not wait any longer, it was the hardest and most difficult bit of rowing that I ever did. We rowed two or three miles and arrived on board at 5.45. They treated us royally on the *Carpathia*, but, of course, they could not provide proper sleeping accommodation for 700 extra passengers. I did not take my clothes off for four days and slept in the smoke room.

When we arrived at the river here we were met by a number of boats and followed by quite a procession, and directly it was known that I was at this hotel the place was besieged by reporters and I was chased all over the place. I must have shaken hands with hundreds of people until at last I slipped off to bed to get out of the way.

I shall rest here a few days and then decide my future movements. Everything, of course, is lost, but the company wired to our agent here to supply me with £100 and he called on me this morning. I learned he went to the docks last night in his car but somehow missed me. You never saw such a sight, it was almost impossible to get away through the mass of people. The thing that has troubled me most is the anxiety you must all have had. I am perfectly well and will write again next mail.

My love to you and the kiddies – and everybody.

Your loving husband,

Wall

P. S. I have had several cablegrams of congratulations from business houses.[192]

1. The *Titanic* awaits her passengers at Southampton. (Author's collection)

2. Olaus Abelseth, third class passenger: 'About half the ship was submerged when we jumped overboard. Sigurd held my hand.' (Author's collection)

3. Kornelia Andrews, first class passenger: 'Oh, it would have broken your heart to have seen them standing there so bravely and waving farewell to their wives and daughters.' (Courtesy of Don Lynch)

4. Elizabeth Allen, first class passenger: '... we could see her stern rising higher and higher until her lights began to go out.' (*St Louis Post Dispatch*)

5. Robert Bateman, second class passenger: 'Shall be home in about twelve days from this writing.' (Author's collection)

6. Karl Behr, first class passenger: 'The officer in charge of our boat, seeing the men swimming in the water, refused to go back...' (Author's collection)

7. Caroline Bonnell, first class passenger: 'Deck by deck we watched the lights go out as the boat dropped lower and lower into the sea.' (*Youngstown Vindicator*)

8. A rare photograph of the *Titanic* leaving Southampton. (Author's collection)

9. Margaret Brown, first class passenger: '...[Fifth Officer Lowe] stated that they saw to it that among those who were saved would not be any of the rich nabobs.' (Library of Congress)

10. Daniel Buckley, third class passenger: 'It would make the stones cry to hear those on board shrieking.' (Author's collection)

11. Archibald Butt, first class passenger: 'My ambition is to die leaving a name that will reflect credit on my family.' (Author's collection)

12. Lucile Carter, first class passenger: '...how wonderful you were through it all.' (*Denver Times*)

13. Sidney Collett, second class passenger: 'In the event of anything unforeseen happening to me in my journey to you, please open the enclosed letter...' (Library of Congress)

14. Eugene Daly, third class passenger: '... I saw the officer himself lying on the deck. They told me that he shot himself but I did not see him...' (Author's collection)

15. The Reading and Writing Room. Passengers undoubtedly wrote many letters and postcards in this room during the *Titanic*'s maiden voyage. (Author's collection)

16. The First Class Smoking Room. Many of the *Titanic*'s male passengers frequented this room to play cards and socialise with friends and acquaintances. (Author's collection)

17. Washington Dodge, first class passenger: '...the awful fact was born in upon me that many lives were perishing in those icy waters.' (*San Francisco Chronicle*)

18. Mahala Douglas, first class passenger: 'The engines stopped, then went on for a few moments, then stopped again.' (*Daily Graphic*)

19. May Futrelle, first class passenger: 'The night was beautiful. The sea was placid and wonderful to look upon.' (*National Magazine*)

20. Archibald Gracie, first class passenger: 'When I reached the surface finally, there was nothing to be seen about me but a great field of wreckage…' (*The Truth About the Titanic*)

21. Irene Harris, first class passenger: 'From the moment the *Titanic* sank I never spoke a word until the *Carpathia* picked us up.' (*Daily Graphic*)

22. Jessie Leitch, second class passenger: 'I remember Mr Harper saying, "It will be beautiful in the morning."' (Author's collection)

23. Charles Lightoller, second officer: 'At this moment the ship dived, and we were all in the water.' (*Illustrated London News*)

24. Lifeboats being lowered away from the sinking *Titanic*. (*Daily Graphic*)

25. Frank Millet, first class passenger: 'I thought I told you my ship was the *Titanic*. She has everything but taxicabs and theatres.' (*Literary Digest*)

26. George Rheims, first class passenger: '[The officer] gave us a military salute, then turned the revolver to his head and shot himself.' (Author's collection)

27. William Sloper, first class passenger: 'I could only think that I must be asleep and in an awful dream.' (*Daily Graphic*)

28. Edward Smith, captain: 'I leave [the *Olympic*] after another voyage and bring out *Titanic* on April 10 from Southampton.' (*Literary Digest*)

29. William Stead, first class passenger: 'I think I shall start for New York on the *Titanic*, which sails, if it can get coal enough, on April 10.' (*Literary Digest*)

30. The ‘unsinkable’ *Titanic* goes down. (*Daily Graphic*)

31. Marian Thayer, first class passenger: ‘Oh Mr Taft, is there any chance of seeing ... my husband ... here again in this life?’ (*Sinking of the Titanic*)

32. Eleanor Widener, first class passenger: 'Over two years have gone since I lost him, and I am no more reconciled than I was at first, and never will be again.' (*Sinking of the Titanic*)

33. Marie Young, first class passenger: 'In my thoughts I often lie again in my steamer chair and watch the passing throng on the *Titanic*'s promenade deck.' (*Richmond Times-Dispatch*)

34. Arthur Rostron, captain of the *Carpathia*. (Original photograph, author's collection)

35. The Cunard liner *Carpathia*. (Author's collection)

CLARA HAYS **First Class Passenger**

In order to counter false statements that had been attributed to her by newspaper reporters, Mrs Hays wrote the following statement on behalf of herself and her daughter, Mrs Thornton Davidson:

> We had retired to our cabins, but had not undressed when the crash came. Mr Hays and Mr Davidson were elsewhere on the steamer in company with Mr H. Markland Molson.
>
> Shortly after the *Titanic* ran into the iceberg we went on deck and Mr Hays and his son-in-law, Mr Davidson, went back to the cabins to get fur coats for us, as the night was very cold. All imagined that there was no immediate danger of the steamer sinking, and in spite of the fact that the boats were already being loaded it was thought to be the best course to pursue to remain with the ship.
>
> As the second last lifeboat was swung over the steamer's side Mr Hays informed me that he and Mr Davidson would wait until help came in the morning. They then wrapped warm coats about us and helped us, with our maid, into the boat.
>
> The last we saw of Mr Hays, Mr Davidson and Mr Molson they were standing on the deck waving to us in the boat, and as a further assurance Mr Hays called out that the *Titanic* was assuredly good for ten hours more, and by that time help would have surely arrived.
>
> The lights of the liner went out shortly after the smaller lifeboats were pulled some distance away, but neither of us saw her sink below the surface. Naturally we were greatly agitated, but although anxious for our husbands did not consider them in any imminent danger. We were huddled together in the bottom of the boat, but did not suffer any hardships from the exposure. This was due, of course, to the foresight of our husbands in insisting that we dress ourselves warmly.
>
> I don't know how many were in the lifeboat with us, but there was absolutely no confusion on board the *Titanic* as we were being helped into the lifeboats. It was not until Tuesday that we were definitely aware of the loss of our husbands. Although we are suffering greatly from the nervous shock experienced, we are doing our best to bear up under our great misfortune.[193]

(Mrs Hays also spoke in the highest terms of the gallantry of the officers and crew of the *Titanic*, and of the care and consideration of those on board the *Carpathia*.)

MARY HEWLETT — Second Class Passenger

While she was travelling back to England, Mrs Hewlett wrote the following letter in which she described her experiences on the *Titanic*:

> On Board The Cunard RMS *Laconia*
> May 30, 1912
>
> ... I did not feel the shock of the collision with the iceberg and no one called me. I awoke and finding the engines had stopped I got out of bed and looked into the alleyway and I saw the steward – he assured me that there was no danger and that I need not dress unless I liked – I went with the crowds and when I reached the top there were eight or ten stewards there who said I must get into a boat that was on the davits – but I begged not to go however they insisted. I was put into boat number 13 with about 50 people, mostly men of the unemployed class, stokers, stewards and cooks not one real seaman amongst them – no compass, lanterns or water – when the boat finally reached the water there was no one who understood how to release it from the ropes so we were there until a knife could be found and the ropes cut. I the meantime number 14 boat was descending on top of us and we had great difficulty in making them stop lowering that boat until we were free ...[194]

FREDERICK HOYT — First Class Passenger

Following the disaster, Mr Hoyt wrote a letter to fellow survivor Archibald Gracie which contained the following statement:

> I knew Captain Smith for over fifteen years. Our conversation that night amounted to little or nothing. I simply sympathised with him on the accident; but at that time, as I never expected to be saved, I did not want to bother him with questions, as I knew he had all he wanted to think of. He did suggest that I go down to A deck and see if there were not a boat alongside. This I did, and to my surprise saw the boat 'D' still hanging on the davits (there having been some delay in lowering her), and it occurred to me that if I swam out and waited for her to shove off they would pick me up, which is what happened.[195]

BRUCE ISMAY **First Class Passenger**

On 21 April Mr Ismay wrote the following note in reply to a query made by the *Washington Post* regarding the fate of victim Clarence Moore:

> Dear Sir:
> I am extremely sorry I am unable to give you any information in regard to Mr Clarence Moore.
> With deepest regret
> Yours sincerely,
> Bruce Ismay[196]

Also on 21 April, Mr Ismay wrote the following statement in reply to what he felt were unjust accusations that were being made against him in the press:

> When I appeared before the Senate Committee Friday morning I supposed the purpose of the inquiry was to ascertain the cause of the sinking of the *Titanic*, with a view to determining whether additional legislation was required to prevent the recurrence of so horrible a disaster.
>
> I welcomed such an inquiry and appeared voluntarily, without subpoena, and answered all questions put to me by the members of the committee to the best of my ability, with complete frankness and without reserve. I did not suppose the question of my personal conduct was the subject of the inquiry, although I was ready to tell everything I did on the night of the collision.
>
> As I have been subpoenaed to appear before the committee in Washington today, I should prefer to make no public statement out of respect for the committee, but I do not think that courtesy requires me to be silent in the face of the untrue statements made in some of the newspapers.
>
> When I went on board the *Titanic* at Southampton on April 10 it was my intention to return by her. I had no intention of remaining in the United States at that time. I came merely to observe the new vessel, as I had done in the case of other vessels of our lines.
>
> During the voyage I was a passenger and exercised no greater rights or privileges than any other passenger. I was not consulted by the commander about the ship, her course, speed, navigation, or her conduct at sea. All these matters were under the exclusive control of the Captain. I saw Captain Smith only casually, as other passengers did. I was never in his room; I was never on the bridge until after the accident; I did not sit at his table in the saloon; I had not visited the engine-room nor gone through the ship, and did not go, or attempt to go, to any part of the ship to which any other first-cabin passenger did not have access.
>
> It is absolutely and unqualifiedly false that I ever said that I wished that the *Titanic* should make a speed record or should increase her daily runs. I deny absolutely having said to any person that we would increase our speed in order to get out of the ice zone, or any words to that effect.

As I have already testified, at no time did the *Titanic*, during her voyage, attain her full speed. It was not expected that she would reach New York before Wednesday morning. If she had been pressed she could probably have arrived Tuesday evening.

The statement that the White Star Line would receive an additional sum of bounty, or otherwise, for attaining a certain speed, is absolutely untrue. The White Star Line receives from the British Government a fixed compensation of 70,000 pounds ($350,000) per annum for carrying the mails, without regard to the speed of any of its vessels, and no additional sum is paid on account of any increase in speed.

I was never consulted by Capt. Smith nor by any other person, nor did I ever make any suggestions whatsoever to any human being about the course of the ship. The *Titanic*, as I am informed, was on the southernmost westbound track of trans-Atlantic steamships. The tracks, or lanes, were designated many years ago by agreement of all the important steamship lines, and all captains of the White Star Line are required to navigate their vessels as closely as possible on these tracks, subject to the following instructions:

'Commanders must distinctly understand that the issue of these regulations does not in any way relieve them from responsibility for the safe and efficient navigation of their respective vessels, and they are also enjoined to remember that they must run no risk which might by any possibility result in accident to their ships. It is to be hoped that they will ever bear in mind that the safety of the lives and property entrusted to their care is the ruling principle that should govern them in the navigation of their vessels and that no supposed gain in expedition or saving of time on the voyage is to be purchased at the risk of accident. The company desires to maintain for its vessels a reputation for safety and only looks for such speed on the various voyages as is consistent with safe and prudent navigation.

Commanders are reminded that the steamers are, to a great extent, uninsured and that their own livelihood, as well as the company's success, depends upon immunity from accident; no precaution which insures safe navigation is to be considered excessive.'

The only information I ever received on the ship that other vessels had sighted ice was a wireless message from the *Baltic* which I have already testified to. This was handed to me by Capt. Smith without any remark as he was passing me on the passenger deck on the afternoon of Sunday, April 14. I read the telegram casually and put it in my pocket. At about 7:10 while I was sitting in the smoke room, Capt. Smith came in and asked me to give him the message received from the *Baltic* in order to post it for the information of the officers. I handed it to him and nothing further was said by either of us. I did not speak to any of the other officers on the subject.

If the information I had received had aroused any apprehension in my mind – which it did not – I should not have ventured to make any suggestion to a commander of Capt. Smith's experience. The responsibility for the navigation of the ship rested solely with him. It has been stated that Captain Smith and I were having a dinner part in one of the saloons from 7:30 to 10:30 Sunday night and that at the time of the collision Capt. Smith was sitting with me in the saloon.

Both of these statements are absolutely false. I did not dine with the captain nor did I see him during the evening of April 14. The doctor dined with me in the restaurant at 7:30 and I went directly to my state room and went to bed at about 10:30. I was asleep when the collision occurred. I felt a jar, went on into the passageway without dressing, met a steward, asked him what was the matter and he said he did not know. I returned to my room. I felt the ship slow down, put on an overcoat over my pajamas and went up on the bridge deck and on the bridge. I asked Capt. Smith what was the matter and he said we had struck ice. I asked him whether he thought it serious and he said he did. On returning to my room I met the chief engineer and asked him whether he thought serious and he said he thought it was.

I then returned to my room and put on a suit of clothes. I had been in my overcoat and pajamas up to this time. I then went back on the boat deck and heard Capt. Smith give the order to clear the boats. I helped in this work for nearly two hours as far as I can judge. Worked at the starboard boats, helping women and children into the boats and lowering them over the side. I did nothing with regard to the boats on the port side.

By that time every wooden lifeboat on the starboard had been lowered away, and I found that they were engaged in getting out the forward collapsible boat on the starboard side. I assisted in this work and all the women that were on this deck were helped into the boat. They were all, I think, third-class passengers. As the boat was going over the side Mr Carter, a passenger, and myself got in. At that time there was not a woman on the boat deck, nor any passenger of any class, so far as we could see or hear. The boat had between 35 and 40 in it, I should say, most of them women. There were perhaps four or five men and it was afterwards discovered that there were four Chinamen concealed under the thwarts in the bottom of the boat. The distance that the boat had to be lowered into the water was, I should estimate, about 20 feet.

Mr Carter and I did not get into the boat until after they had begun to lower it away. When the boat reached the water I helped row it, pushing the oar from me as I sat. This is the explanation of the fact that my back was to the sinking steamer. The boat would have accommodated certainly six or more passengers in addition if there had been any on the boat deck to go. These facts can be substantiated by W.E. Carter of Philadelphia, who got in at the same time that I did and was rowing the boat with me. I hope I need not say that neither Mr Carter nor myself would for one moment have thought of getting into the boat if there had been any women there to go into it, nor should I have done so if I had thought that by remaining on the ship I could have been of the slightest further assistance.

It is impossible for me to answer every false statement, rumour or invention that has appeared in the newspapers. I am prepared to answer any question that may be asked by the committee of the Senate or any other responsible person. I shall therefore make no further statement of this kind, except to explain the messages that I sent from the *Carpathia*. These messages have been completely misunderstood. An inference has been drawn from them that I was anxious to avoid the Senate committee's inquiry which it was intended to hold in New York. As a matter of fact when dispatching these messages I had not the slightest idea that any inquiry was contemplated and I had no information regarding it until the arrival of the *Carpathia* at the Cunard dock in New York on Thursday night when I was informed by Senators Smith and Newlands of the appointment of the special committee to hold the inquiry. The only purpose I had in sending these messages was to express my desire to have the crew returned to their homes in England for their own benefit at the earliest possible moment and I was also naturally anxious to return to my family but left the matter of my return entirely to our representatives in New York.

I deeply regret that I am compelled to make any personal statement when my whole thought is on the horror of the disaster. In building the *Titanic* it was the hope of my associates and myself that we had built a vessel which could not be destroyed by the perils of the sea or the dangers of navigation. The event has proved the futility of that hope. The present legal requirements have proved inadequate. They must be changed: but whether they are changed or not, this awful experience has taught the steamship owners of the world that too much reliance has been placed in water-tight compartments and on wireless telegraphy, and that they must equip every vessel with lifeboats and rafts sufficient to provide for every soul on board and sufficient men to handle them.[197]

On 25 April Mr Ismay wrote the following letter to J.B. Millet, the brother of victim Frank Millet:

The New Willard
Washington, Wed., April 25th, 1912

My dear Mr Millet:

For your very kind letter please accept very sincere thanks. I regret extremely I had not the pleasure of meeting your brother and am therefore unable to give you any information in regard to him. May I take this opportunity of expressing my deep sympathy with you in the loss you have sustained, and I would also like to say that I am not in any way responsible for the truly dreadful disaster which God knows, if it had been possible, I would have done anything in the world to avert. We had the finest ship in the world, and appointed as her commander a man in whom we had absolute confidence. Why people try to make me responsible for the horrible disaster I cannot imagine. The last week has been a horrible nightmare to me, and I cannot yet realise the *Titanic* has gone. I can only hope God will give me strength to see the matter out to the end. I am having a truly awful time. I would again express my most heartfelt thanks for your kindness in writing me.

Yours very sincerely,

Bruce Ismay (Please forgive pencil.)[198]

On 31 May Mr Ismay sent the following letter to the widow of *Titanic* victim Thomas Andrews:

30 James Street
Liverpool, 31st May, 1912

Dear Mrs Andrews,

Forgive me for intruding upon your grief, but I feel I must send you a line to convey my most deep and sincere sympathy with you in the terrible loss you have suffered. It is impossible for me to express in words all I feel, or make you realise how truly sorry I am for your, or how my heart goes out to you. I knew your husband for many years, and had the highest regard for him, and looked upon him as a true friend.

No one who had the pleasure of knowing him could fail to realise and appreciate his numerous good qualities and he will be sadly missed in his profession.

Nobody did more for the White Star Line, or was more loyal to its interests than your good husband, and I always placed the utmost reliance on his judgment.

If we miss him and feel his loss so keenly, what your feelings must be I cannot think. Words at such a time are useless, but I could not help writing to you to tell you how truly deeply I feel for you in your grief and sorrow.

Yours sincerely,

Bruce Ismay[199]

MARIE JERWAN **Second Class Passenger**

In May 1912 Mrs Jerwan wrote the following letter to her sister in Mont-de-Couvet, France:

How can I thank you all for your sympathy! I do it with all my heart, for all the people who took part in my distress. I was so happy, my dear sister, to receive your good letter that reassured me of the arrival of my telegrams. I imagined your anxiety and could not wait to let you know that I was, thank God, among those rescued. Forgive me for not writing to you sooner. You must have often been disappointed at the mailman's arrival. I was so ill and especially nervous, that it was impossible to focus my ideas. Several times I began a letter unable to finish it.

Fortunately I feel better now, yet each night I still have terrible nightmares; I see the scene unrolling again and I stay in a semi-sleep unable to believe in the reality that I have returned to the house. Then I become frightened; in the street, in the tram, everywhere, it seems to me that I am in danger. I suppose that all shipwrecks are the same way. Oh! That night leaves you a horrible impression, however it is not comparable with the moments spent by those who, as us, had the right to be saved, but stayed in the waves.

To tell you about the welcome of all my parents and friends is unnecessary. For three days they believed I was lost, for I was still on the list of missing persons. At first Armin could not really believe that I was truly there. Likewise, all the city was excited. There was only one word, one thought: the *Titanic*.

Now, I believe, that to give you a narration a little bit more complete, I want to transport myself for several minutes to this unfortunate *Titanic* which swallowed up so many victims with itself.

It was about 6:00 in the evening, Wednesday, the 10th of April, when the small tugboat took us aboard. I will never forget its majestic entry to the ship at Cherbourg. Each one of us experienced a certain sensation. Our small tugboat seemed like nothing in front of the superb ship.

The sea was calm and beautiful. Everything seemed to smile at us and to tell us 'Bon Voyage.'

I did not get the cabin that I asked for, but instead I was given one that was very comfortable on the upper deck, which I shared with Mrs Balls. In this way we were very well off.

This same evening I went to bed early, and it was not until the next morning that I met my roommate. Mrs Balls was taking a trip with her brother, Mr Bateman, a very respected minister in Florida whose purpose was to go to London to get his sister and take her to his home. I spent a great deal of my time with them; we took walks together. As I have told you, life on board the ship is very gay, especially when the sea is calm. The weather was exceptional, superb for the season. Therefore there were few illnesses.

We had at our disposal three walking decks, and a very large, well-arranged lounge where there were concerts twice a day.

The dining room was very large and well decorated. For table-mates I had a Frenchman, Mr Malachard, who was coming to New York for business. Mr Malachard had his cabin next to ours and occupied it with two other gentlemen, one of which was a French engineer. We often had a moment of conversation with them in French after dinner or in the lounge, whereas, with Mrs Balls and Mr Bateman, we spoke English.

The trip was one of the most beautiful of the season. The passengers prepared for a concert on Monday; the profits were for poor shipwrecked sailors. We did not suspect then that we ourselves would be shipwrecked.

Sunday morning there was Protestant worship in the dining saloon and a Catholic worship in the lounge. Mrs Balls and Mr Bateman did not want to go up on the deck in the afternoon, finding it too cold, so I went alone. I walked about an hour and as Mr Malachard was there also, we discussed religion, he having been Catholic. We were so absorbed in our conversation that we did not see the French engineer arrive. An amusing coincidence: he said to us in watching the rescue boats that were suspended near us, 'I am sure that if it were necessary to put these boats in the sea, the ropes would be too short. In my opinion, if I had to go in one of these boats, I would prefer to be swallowed up with the ship.' We were so surprised at that thought, made so unexpectedly, that Mr Malachard could not stop himself from asking what was wrong with him. 'Oh, nothing. It was just an idea.' Then he added, 'Don't you want to go down and get a cup of tea? How can you stay on the deck; it's so cold?' As a matter of fact, in spite of the sunshine, the air was icy.

In the evening, as usual, there was a concert in the lounge until 8:15, then a worship in the dining saloon. We sang several hymns, after which the minister finished with a beautiful prayer, asking God to protect forever this beautiful ship. He prayed also for all those who had perished in the sea. We were far from suspecting that two hours later this minister and his wife would be victims themselves of that dreadful ocean.

After having a cup of coffee and several rolls, I returned to Mrs Balls and her brother in the lounge where we chatted for several minutes more. Then I went to look at the time on the clock in order to set back my watch 50 minutes to have the correct time the next day. Mr Bateman did the same thing. It was, I suppose, the last time that he wound his watch, poor Mr Bateman. As it was 10:30, we wished him good night, Mrs Balls and I, then we went up to go to bed.

Maybe all these details seem childish to you, but for me all these memories are dear, and I hope that they will interest you equally.

Not being able to sleep, I started to read. It was a quarter till midnight when a big shock was felt which shook all the boat. I thought it was an explosion of one of the engines, for an instant later the machines stopped. A chill ran all through my body. I did not dare breathe for several minutes. I called Mrs Balls who woke up without knowing too much about what happened. I told her, 'The engines are no longer running.' I got up in haste, hurriedly got dressed, then went in the hall for information. I saw several men coming and going, then finally learned that the ship had run into an iceberg, but there was no danger.

I returned to my cabin and reported that news to Mrs Balls who was resting in her bed. However, I did not feel reassured. I got dressed and went up on the deck where I found several people, for the most part men who were going and coming, and again an officer told me: 'That there was no danger, that one could go back to bed.' Instead of that, I went up on the deck and went all the way to the front, where I saw sailors getting into boats at the top of the deck.

From that time I was certain of our hazardous position. For a minute I felt faint, but soon I regained my composure.

I went back to my cabin and met Mr Malachard and his friends in the hall, who did not believe we were in imminent danger. When I told the engineer that we were sinking in the front, he started to laugh, claiming that it was only a figment of my imagination because the boat was no longer running.

I returned, therefore, to my cabin and told Mrs Balls: 'Get up and get dressed quickly. We are sinking.' I should have thought about getting dressed myself, not having done so sufficiently. I put on the clothes that I had in my hand, and took my watch that was under my pillow, and which is actually all my fortune with my rings. The rest was destroyed because we could not take anything, and I did not even have my little wallet. And if we had been warned ahead, we could have taken in our pockets the money and jewellery of value. It was only an hour after the collision that the order was given: 'Everyone on the deck with lifejackets.' It was for that reason that so many women and children did not have the time to get dressed, most of them having gone back to sleep.

Mr Bateman came knocking at our door and gave us the life-jackets that were above the dresser. We did not even know where they were. Mrs Balls and her brother went up on deck. Most of the lifeboats were already in the water when I arrived there. Most of the women were crying. There were faces completely discomposed, however there was no panic in spite of the terrible situation. I searched everywhere for Mrs Balls, but in vain. There was such a large crowd on the deck that it was impossible to find her, and I suppose that she had already disembarked. An instant later I heard someone calling me. It was Mr Malachard and his friends. He attached my lifejacket, and taking me by the arm said: 'Stay with us, we will take care of you.' I was so happy to no longer be alone, for I felt uncourageous. That returned me to myself a little. We were on the deck B. An officer told us to get up on deck A by the sailor's ladder. Everything was going well, but at the moment of clearing the hand railing, I lost my footing and fell on the deck. I sprained my foot, but I did not pay attention to it.

The officers cried: 'Women and children in the boats, men in the back.' Mr Malachard himself came to put me in the boat, then he withdrew. To this day I ask myself how I would have escaped without his help, for I really was not myself, and it was the moment to make a decision, as it was the second to last boat that was being filled. I admired the men at this moment. They conducted themselves like real heroes, and the officers did their duty. They were even sometimes cruel. There were, as a matter of fact, terribly distressing scenes when the poor women had to separate from their husbands. I could then consider myself privileged not to have to undergo that awful heartbreak.

So many mothers separated from their children; it is an unforgettable picture. There were almost 30 of us in the boat, and I always hoped that our friends could get on it, but a child of eight months was put on whose mother they would not let enter. She begged them to give her her child, but the officer was firm, and he seemed to us cruel. He told her: 'You will rejoin your child. Go to the following boat.'

Then they let us go. Mr Malachard and his friends yelled good-bye and waved, after which they went toward the other boat. It was, alas, their last good-bye. I did not see them again. Poor friend of one day. They were for me really admirable, and I will be eternally grateful to them. God did not permit them to be saved.

As the *Titanic* was very high, it seemed that the boat was hastening into nothingness, and just before touching the water the sailors let go of the ropes, more on one side than the other. The boat was therefore so slanted that we cried out in distress. Finally we were able to regain our balance and reached the water. They cut the ropes and six men who were part of the group started to row.

We can be very grateful to God for this really miraculous rescue, for if the sea had been rough, none of us would have escaped that terrible catastrophe. We had an absolutely calm sea. Never have I seen the ocean so tranquil; not a wave. It was so startling, that sheet of water, without a sound around us, a sky admirably starry, but without a moon, and we could see the ship gradually sinking. At this moment the bow was completely under water. We were all silent, incapable of articulating a word. The sight will remain forever engraved in our memory. When the boat was at some distance, they assured us that the bottom was good and dry. It was, happily, for I learned later that certain boats leaked. They searched again for a lantern, but in vain. There were none. Imagine these boats without light, running the risk of colliding with one another, or of coming upon ice, without food, drinkable water, and in the middle of a frozen ocean. We understood our terrible situation, and we did not have much hope. I projected myself into thoughts of all those who are dear to me, and said good-bye to all of them. Then by a fervent prayer, we united to ask God for his protection. Many other prayers came out in that horrible night toward the throne of God. How many who did not believe in anything rediscovered the faith of their childhood. The last passenger of our boat, the little baby, cried pitifully. He was hardly dressed. One of the men wrapped him in his overcoat, I put him on my knees as comfortably as possible, and he was consoled. We went further and further from the *Titanic* for we feared that in going down, it would sink us too.

Little by little the lights disappeared one after another, until we could see only a black mass. The bow was already submerged. We still heard the musicians of the ship playing the beautiful hymn: 'Nearer My God to Thee,' to which we joined in with all our heart. What heroism to stay that way at their post to give courage to those who were going to die, in playing this song, so beautiful and so solemn.

A few minutes later a loud noise was heard when the water penetrated the boilers, but without an explosion, in spite of what certain people said. The mechanics all stayed at their posts right to the time that they verified that their job was finished. The ship broke apart. The stern was all that was left which stood up several minutes like a sail, and all was finished and disappeared forever in the deadly gulf.

It was a terrible, unforgettable moment. One would have preferred to be able to plug up his ears in order not to hear the indescribable outcries uttered by more than a thousand unfortunates for whom there was no more hope of help. I felt my blood freezing in my veins, and it was then that we understood how really privileged we were. Up until the last minute we had thought everyone would be saved, for the rumour circulated on the ship that wireless telegraphy signalled the approach of a rescue ship. A little more than an hour passed from the minute when the *Titanic* crashed into the floating glacier until the time when I got into the lifeboat, and about three quarters of an hour later all was finished.

And to say that the terrible catastrophe is the work of several crazy ideas (as is noted in the record of the *Olympic*): Each one blames the captain and Ismay who knew very well that we were going at a speed much too great, and especially as other ships had signalled [the presence of] icebergs. We were in a field of ice and we were going at a speed of 21 to 22 knots an hour. Then we had only 18 lifeboats, out of which one turned over with 60 men. Another could not be used, therefore there were only 16 in total. It was ridiculous for a ship of that size.

Not having any compass in the boat, we strayed under the protection of God, and after everything had disappeared, we let our boat go at will in the water, having only the stars for our guide. From time to time the sailor burned a piece of rope in order to make signals to other boats. Fortunately one of the men had some matches with him, and it's thanks to his foresight that we could signal the other unfortunate companions. The sailor who drove us was an older man. He told us that during the 45 years of his career as a sailor, it was the second time that he was the witness of an accident. The first was on the *Olympic* coming from America to Europe. This ship was also driven by Captain Smith. Although the accident was of little importance, it necessitated repairs, and it was the cause of the delay that had obliged me to take the *Titanic* and not the *Olympic*.

Our sailor then enlisted on the *Titanic* thinking to be more safe on this boat, which was so highly praised. He hardly suspected that he would have an accident even more terrible still, and that he would owe his safety to the Divine protection. Oh! What a night my dears! An unforgettable night! It is impossible that you could understand our anguish. Several hours passed troubled by false hopes, for from time to time someone claimed to have seen the light of a mast; a light which was none other than a star appearing on the horizon.

Finally to the great joy of each one of us, dawn arrived, but the wind rose and we feared a storm. Little by little, the stars disappeared and we saw three big black masses. At first we believed we saw boats coming to our aid, but it was two large icebergs which stood up like mountains. In any other circumstances we would have admired the sunrise on the glaciers. It was splendid, these beams of fire reflected on that large sheet of water which the wind was agitating rhythmically. It was a very awe inspiring sight.

All of a sudden the sailor told us: 'I see the light of a mast.' We had been so often mistaken that we could not believe it. However the light became more and more distinct, and we soon distinguished the *Carpathia* which really was coming to our aid. We regained courage and attempted to approach it. It was 7:30 in the morning when we were taken aboard the *Carpathia*. We were overcome with cold; fear and anguish paralysed us. The children were put in sacks and hoisted up by pulleys (one by one) and then they did the same for us. They tied us with a rope around our bodies, then they hoisted us up one after another. At the arrival on deck they wrapped us in blankets and served us hot coffee with liquor. They rubbed our limbs to revive our circulation. When I could move, I looked for my acquaintances. What a pitiful sight! Women cried, looking for their husbands, others for their children. Oh! Then I thanked God for being alone, for if Armin had been with me, we would have probably been separated forever. A very painful scene took place at this moment. A poor woman who had become crazed called her child: 'Baby! Baby!' They brought her one. She seized it in her arms at the risk of suffocating it. The doctor and other people had every difficulty in getting it away from her. A few minutes later, the poor creature died. A large number of people had lost half their minds.

I was on the deck when the last boat was collected, and I was so happy to find Mrs Balls on it. She was incapable of walking, but after a good massage she felt better. I looked everywhere for her brother, Mr Bateman, but in vain. Mrs Balls told me that after having left me, they looked for me on the deck without being able to see me. She ended up entering one of the last boats. Her brother threw her the silk handkerchief that he had around his neck, telling her 'Good-bye. Have confidence that if we do not meet again, we will meet in Heaven.' It was his last words. Then he left to hunt for me, but I did not see him again, poor Mr Bateman. I lately received several words from Mrs Balls who wrote me that the body of her brother had been found and transported to Florida where he had been buried a month ago.

Mrs Balls found herself in a boat that leaked. There were 70 women and only one man to row, so they continued to row somehow or other themselves. The officer who had loaded them on the boat left them to go with a sailor to the aid of some poor unfortunates who were floating after the *Titanic* had sunk. He saved about thirty of them. Honour to that officer who risked his life for those poor unfortunates.

At daybreak these 70 exhausted women were happily gathered up and towed by another boat, for I don't know what would have become of us, Mrs Balls told me.

I could tell you many other things, if I could do so in person ...

When the *Carpathia* came to our rescue, it was en route for Italy and did not hesitate for a minute, even though 60 miles away, to come to collect 789 shipwrecked people. It did its best to accommodate each one of us, for it was a small ship compared to the *Titanic*. Everyone on board was really good to us. They put down covers everywhere to sleep. Up until my arrival in New York I slept on the floor of the kitchen without undressing (which is what everyone did.)

Monday morning we saw two whales. Can you imagine if we had seen them from the life boat!

The following night we had a terrible storm, dreadful bolts of thunder followed by a strong wind. We were no longer alive. It seemed to us that at any moment we would be sunk again. We had fog almost all the time. I believe that if the trip had lasted a few more days, I would have lost my mind. I was so afraid; my nerves were so sick that even now I am still not yet recovered.

To tell you my joy when I saw the lights of New York is indescribable, but the arrival was not as joyful as had been my departure at Mont-de-Couvet.

At that time there were also heartbreaking scenes. How many people who counted on the arrival of their friends did not see them again.

So to say to you that I thank God for His protection, and that I thank Him for having saved all my friends would be unnecessary.

Although my health is strongly shaken, I am happy to be with my family and to send you my affection from New York.[200]

CHARLES JOUGHIN — Crew (Chief Baker)

After the *Carpathia* arrived in New York, Mr Joughin jotted down the following brief note regarding his experiences:

> I remained on board until the *Titanic* began to sink. Then I jumped. I had a life preserver on.
>
> The water was bitter cold. I began swimming vigorously, knowing that if I did not get far away from the liner before she sank the suction would draw me under and there would be no hope.
>
> This vigorous swimming kept me from giving in. I kept swimming until everything became a blur to me. Several times I lost consciousness. Finally one of the lifeboats picked me up. Afterward I discovered that I had been in the water for an hour and a half.[201]

NORA KEANE — Second Class Passenger

After arriving in New York, Miss Keane dictated the following account to her brother Dennis, who wrote it down and telegraphed it to their home town newspaper:

> It was terrible! I can hardly tell how it happened. We were asleep when we struck the ice.
>
> The ship was going – I don't know how fast – but when it struck it broke and the front end of the ship pointed down.
>
> The lights soon went out. Before they did we started to the deck. They had boats ready then and the officers stood besides and let only women and children in. Men, enough to work the boats, were let go.
>
> We had few clothes on. Only what we did gather up. The night was cold, but at first we didn't mind it much. People cried and acted nearly crazy. Some broke down – men, I mean. Some of the women fainted, but the officers made them put them in the boats anyhow.
>
> I was not among the first people to go into the boats. Some women said they wouldn't go without their husbands. Some of these men were let go along. I think the sky was clear, but there was a mist near the water.
>
> Everything was awful. Men called out orders to the men with the boats. The officers worked right with them. I left the ship in a boat filled full of women and a few men. I don't know what happened then, for we couldn't always see the ship. Then we were picked up; I don't know how long after we left.
>
> Some shots were fired on the ship. People said men had been shot. I don't know who they were. The officers didn't come with the boats. Only men to handle them.

It was fearful to hear the people. Some of them were quiet, but most were almost wild. Some of us prayed, but the men worked. The officers watched after everything and would not let men in before women.

I think some of them jumped into the sea.

On the *Carpathia* everyone cared for us well. We were given attention by the officers and the passengers. Clothes for the women and men were given to everyone who needed them.

It is so awful I cannot think of all that happened.[202]

On 15 May Miss Keane wrote the following letter to fellow survivor Edwina Troutt:

May 15, 1912
Harrisburg, Pa.

My Dear Miss Troutt,

It is with the greatest of pleasure I received your note yesterday. I was just writing you [illegible] directory to try New York or New Jersey for Auburndale as I could see no state you put. Oh you dear girl I will remember you and the kindness you showed me while in our stateroom by helping me with some clothing and then straight jacket [lifebelt] which they reminded me of as you helped me on with it. For all my distress at the time I actually felt as if I would [not] have presence of mind to find the top deck had it not been for the officer who came to our room and ordered us up on the top deck there was others who did not get that word of command to go up there. I met a royal reception when I came to Harrisburg that Friday night in the 7.10 train there was about 3 or 4 hundred people waiting to see me & had all Hbg going [illegible] as if I was the only one from here on that ill fated ship they had me well advertised with my picture on every paper. I often thought of you dear girl if you had my change you would have made lots of money to relate your experience. I did not or could I stand any Irish excitement my nerves was all unstrung and it made them worse on account of all the people coming and crying or even get a chance to congratulate me I have had so many letters of congratulations from people whom I never spoke too my two brothers meet me in Hbg with two automobiles which was presented to them for use to bring the party of us who met me in N York 5 brothers and their wives though they came to meet me and herd my name amongst the survivors they still was not sure till they had me in their arms as we left you on the pier they went and cabled to mother she got that on Friday they did not let her no anything about till they could tell her of my safety they were as bad home as they were here of my safety. Just imagine one paper here had me lost the papers treated my people and myself fine & am going to put my [illegible] in this week what did you do or how have you made out I had a letter from that priest though I did not get to see him [illegible].

Ps write with lots of love from Nora Keane[203]

EDWIN KIMBALL **First Class Passenger**

After arriving in New York, Mr Kimball wrote the following letter to his nephew, C.P. Kimball of Chicago:

> On Sunday evening I had gone down from the smoking-room to my stateroom and removed my coat and was standing in the middle of the room when the ship struck the iceberg. It seemed to me like scraping and tearing, more than a shock. It was on the starboard side of the ship under our room, and the ice came in our port hole.
>
> After assuring Mrs Kimball that it was simply an iceberg and that was probably had scraped it, and as the ship did not seem to slacken her speed, I stepped in the companionway and spoke to some friends who were located in the same section.
>
> I then went on deck to see whether I could see the iceberg; there were very few people out around the ship, and the stewards and officers were assuring everybody that everything was all right and advising all to return to bed, which many of them probably did.
>
> I came back to our stateroom, which was near the stairway which went down to the deck below to the squash courts and mailroom. At that time I saw a mail clerk go down the stairs, and when he came up he had one mail bag in his hands and was wet to the knees. I asked him about how bad it was. He seemed very serious and said it was pretty bad and that he would advise the women to dress, as they might have to go on deck, and it would be cold.
>
> We instructed the other women in our party to dress and everyone else in our corridor, including a number of women who were travelling alone. Mrs Kimball already had started dressing, and I told her to dress warmly, as we probably would be on deck for some time. I put on a sweater and a heavy ulster.
>
> We than started out, feeling that everything was all right. After we had gone a few steps a young lady of our party came back from the upper deck and we asked her what was going on up there. She said the order had been given to put on the life belts. We returned to our staterooms, which were only a few feet away, got our life belts and notified all the women in the corridor to do the same and come with us. None of us knew how to put on the belts, but I saw an officer in the companionway and he showed us how to put them on, telling us that there was no danger and that everything would be all right.
>
> When we arrived upon the deck only a few people were there. As it was about seventy-five feet from the boat deck to the water, the officers were having great difficulty in getting the people to go into the lifeboats, assuring them at the same time that it would not be a long while before they probably would be back on the big boat. The first boat that went was not more than two-thirds full, and the officers said we would have to do something to get the people started.[204]

(Mr Kimball assisted his wife and other ladies into one of the lifeboats, and an officer then pushed him into the same boat as it was being lowered.)

BERTHA LEHMANN **Second Class Passenger**

In later years Miss Lehmann wrote the following account of her *Titanic* experience for publication in her home town newspaper:

> It was a beautiful, warm spring day, April 8, 1912, when, happy and carefree I said goodbye to my dear mother and sister, all my friends and schoolmates. My father went with me as far as Basel. I remember well when I left an old lady asked me what I would do if the boat would sink, and I told her that the boat could not sink. And if it would, there would always be a piece of wood that I could hang on to. How little did I know that would actually happen in less than a week.
>
> The cherry and apple blossoms made the orchards look like they were covered with snow. It was Easter Monday and all the people in Bern, Switzerland, my home, were out to tell me goodbye.
>
> I'll never forget while walking down to the depot, where I was to take the train, my father said, 'Bertha, every time you come along with me I have some sort of bad luck, and I feel now like something is going to happen to you.' I told him that nothing could happen to me and there would be lots of people that I could talk to because, at that time, I could speak very good French. And should anything happen to me they would find it out right away. It was hard for dad to let me go, as I had a sister and brother already in Iowa. Father was taking a train to work, and as his train left before mine we had to say goodbye before my train left. Tears nearly came into my eyes, and as I was determined to be brave and not cry when the time came, I did not cry. Dad kissed me goodbye and said, 'I suppose I will never see you again.'
>
> I left Basel about midnight and got to Paris about 6 o'clock Tuesday morning. Arriving there I went to a hotel and breakfasted. After that we went to a house where they inspected our trunks. We were not allowed to take any tobacco with us on the boat. After we had our things checked we took a train to Cherbourg, France. We arrived there about midnight, where we went to a hotel and rested until 3 o'clock the next afternoon. When I say we I don't mean that I had anybody else with me because I was alone.
>
> We were then taken aboard a small steamer. This was to take us to the *Titanic*. The *Titanic* was so far out on the ocean that it took us from three in the afternoon until sundown to get out there. After we got on the *Titanic* we could just barely make out the shoreline of France.
>
> It sure surprised me how big the *Titanic* really was. It was 882 feet long. Thinking back now the small boat looked like a mosquito in comparison and the *Titanic* like a cow. The people on it called it the 'floating palace.' There were faster boats then but the *Titanic* was built for comfort and safety and not for speed. I had been in many beautiful hotels in Europe and in America but I have never seen anything quite as beautiful as this boat. I had a cabin by myself on the right side of the boat, and it was on the outside so I had a port hole. I travelled second class but it was nicer than I had expected. The stewards were extremely courteous.

They also had stewardesses on the boat so that when lady passengers got sick they could be looked after by ladies rather than men. The boat was equipped with, shall I say, a small hospital. They also had doctors and nurses.

The first two days I was sea-sick. I stayed below all the time until Saturday. I came up and found that I was to sit at a table with two little boys and their father. On the other side was a young married couple. I learned to know these boys because they could speak French. Sunday their father came and asked me to stay with them while he played a game of cards. The boys' mother was still in England. They were separated and the father wanted the boys and so did the mother. The father had, in reality, kidnapped the boys and thought that he could keep them if he got them to America.

Sunday night I went to the library to write some letters to mail after I got to New York. When I had finished my letters I went below. Almost all of the people were English and as I could not speak English I did not want to stay up there and listen to something I could not understand. I had brought along lots of Swiss and French reading material so I went to read.

I read until I got sleepy and then I turned the light off. I went to a very light sleep and it seemed all at once that I was on a train and it was grinding to a very sudden stop. The first thing that entered into my mind was that we were in New York. I sat up first and then got out of bed and walked over to the lounge that was right under the port hole and looked out. It seemed that there were lights outside. I think now it must have been either the stars or else the reflection of the lights of the *Titanic* on the iceberg we had just hit.

I heard the two ladies come into their room that was next to me. Their voices sounded as though they were very excited. Although I couldn't understand a word they were saying, I knew something had happened. They left their cabin, and then I thought that I really should get dressed and find out the reason for stopping in the middle of the night, because I knew then that we were no longer moving. I dressed and went up on deck. I saw a French musician that I had met talking to another lady. She went away and then I asked him what was wrong. He just told me that we would have to go on another boat to get to New York and that I should go down and get my coat.

I went, and when I came back he put a life belt on me and took me to another deck. He said to a couple of officers that here was another lady. As I was standing there waiting my turn to get in the lifeboat I could see and hear women crying and hanging on the arms of loved ones. There were some ladies there that did not want to go because their husbands could not go. Then came my turn.

The lifeboats had been lowered to the deck level. I was taken out there and then, as I stepped into the life boat, it was dark and, of course, the inside of the boat was lower than the deck, I fell. I thought for a moment that I was going to fall right into the water, but I hit the bottom of the boat. I don't remember if I was hurt or not. I guess I forgot about it in the excitement.

I was not frightened or excited at first at all. I suppose the only reason I wasn't was that I did not realise what had happened. When the boat had been partly filled I saw two men jump from the deck into the life boat and hide behind their wives' skirts. One of them was found, but the other one got away.

Then the time came to let the lifeboat into the water. As we went down the ropes did not work right or something, and one side of the boat was much lower than the other. We all had to scramble to the higher side of the boat to keep it from tipping over. After we had it sitting straight in the water there was no knife to cut the ropes. Everyone was asked if they had a knife, and at last a man found one in his pocket. After the ropes were cut the men bent to their task of rowing. Incidentally, the only men allowed on the boats were the ones that had to row.

We were not very far from the boat and could still hear people crying and yelling to one another. All at once there were three loud reports, they sounded something like a very loud crash of thunder when it strikes very close to you. We all looked at the *Titanic*. It had broken apart! The front part of the boat went under first. The helm of the front half sank and then the middle.

The last part of the boat was still above the water. The broken part of the last half of the boat sank slowly into the water and then the stern. That was the last of the ship that could not sink. The work of many men destroyed, and along with that the lives of 1,600 men, women and children. All was silent for a while, and then the people that was taken under from the suction of the boat came up again. And, of course, those that had life belts on stayed up. We could hear them yelling and screaming for help. As we rowed farther and farther away the cries were lost in the distance between us and the boat.

That night was the longest one I ever put in in my life. It seemed that it would never be dawn. Sometime during the night we met a capsized life boat with three men on the bottom of it. They were wet and cold. We picked them up, and that made us even more crowded. We still rowed on and on. Would morning ever come?

We saw a growing light on the horizon. It was really getting daylight. When it was almost daylight we then came upon another lifeboat. It had only a few men in it, and as our boat was crowded some of us stepped from our boat into the other one. Both of the boats went on again, but in the course of time we drifted apart.

It must have been about 7: [illegible] when we first sighted a boat, the *Carpathia*. No one knows how glad we were to see it. It was about 8:30 when we were finally taken on to the *Carpathia*.

The crew of the *Carpathia* put down a sort of basket in which we had to sit and be pulled, one by one, to the deck. We were taken into the dining room and given a blanket and a cup of coffee. The *Carpathia* was overloaded, and somebody threw the ice out to make up for the extra weight. From Sunday night until Thursday night the ones that were rescued did not have a bed to sleep on. We had to sit up all the time and did not get a chance to take our clothing off.

On Thursday night we saw the lights of New York. Everyone was on deck. At last all was ready for us to go down the gang plank to New York. When we got off the *Carpathia* we were taken to a hospital. We had to stay there from Thursday until Monday while everything was checked and double checked.

There seemed to be no end to the questions we had to answer. At last I was able to go to Iowa.

That is my story, and I can assure you that I never want to experience anything like it again.[205]

JESSIE LEITCH **Second Class Passenger**

After the *Carpathia* arrived in New York, Miss Leitch prepared the following brief statement about her experiences on board the *Titanic*:

About midnight Mr Harper, the Rev. Dr John Harper, came to my stateroom and told me that the vessel had struck an iceberg. While I was dressing he went to learn further particulars and returned to say that orders had been given to put on the lifebelts. I did so. Picking up Nana, his daughter, in his arms he took her up to the deck. There the women were ordered to the upper deck. I had to climb a vertical iron ladder, and Mr Harper brought Nana after me up the ladder and the men at the top lifted her up to me again.

There was no opportunity for a farewell and, in fact, even then we did not realise the danger, as we were assured again and again that the vessel could not sink, that the *Olympic* would be alongside at any minute and that the women and children were to be put into the boats first and the men to follow and that there were boats sufficient for all. Our boat was well manned and it was the eleventh to leave the vessel.

After about half an hour the *Titanic* went down. We were about a mile away, but even then I hoped and expected that Mr Harper was in one of the other boats, many of which reached the *Carpathia* before ours did. How eagerly I looked for his face on the deck as we approached that vessel, but when all the boat-loads had come aboard I feared the worst.

The last day we spent on the *Titanic* was Sunday. Mr Harper asked me to read the chapter at our morning family prayers and later we went to the Sunday morning services. The day was quietly but pleasantly spent and when Nana and I went to look for Mr Harper at about 6 o'clock to go to dinner, I found him earnestly talking to a young Englishman whom he was seeking to lead to Christ. That evening before we retired we went on deck, and there was still a glint of red in the west.

I remember Mr Harper saying, 'It will be beautiful in the morning.'

We then went down to the staterooms. He read from the bible and prayed, and so he left us.[206]

CHARLES LIGHTOLLER **Crew (Second Officer)**

On 24 April 1912 Second Officer Lightoller wrote the following letter to the widow of First Officer William Murdoch:

Hotel Continental,
Washington.
April 24th, 1912.

Dear Mrs Murdoch,

I am writing on behalf of the surviving officers to express our deep sympathy in this, your awful loss. Words cannot convey our feelings, much less a letter.

I deeply regret that I missed communicating with you by last mail to refute the reports that were spread in the newspapers. I was practically the last man, and certainly the last officer, to see Mr Murdoch. He was then endeavouring to launch the starboard forward collapsible boat. I had already got mine from off the top of our quarters. You will understand when I say that I was working the port side of the ship, and Mr Murdoch was principally engaged on the starboard side of the ship, filling and launching the boats. Having got my boat down off the top of the house, and there being no time to open it, I left it and ran across to the starboard side, still on top of the quarters. I was then practically looking down on your husband and his men. He was working hard, personally assisting, overhauling the forward boat's fall. At this moment the ship dived, and we were all in the water. Other reports as to the ending are absolutely false. Mr Murdoch died like a man, doing his duty.

Call on us without hesitation for anything we can do for you.

Yours very sincerely,
(Signed)
C.H. Lightoller, 2d Officer
G. Groves Boxhall, 4th Officer
H.J. Pitman, 3d Officer
H.G. Lowe, 5th Officer[207]

Second Officer Lightoller also wrote the following account for publication in the *Christian Science Journal*:

It is difficult to tell of the experience which follows, but the student of Christian Science will readily see in it that acceptance of the truth made the overcoming of fear possible, even as in the case of disease, and that divine Principle is to be relied upon at all times.

While the *Titanic* was sinking, and during the whole time I was working at the boats, I held to the truth, thereby eliminating all fear. I do not pretend that any man can go down on a ship at midnight, in mid-Atlantic, and succeed in eliminating fear, without hard work. It was hard work, and yet the very conditions which existed on the port side were in themselves a demonstration of the workings of Truth, for not the slightest hitch occurred, and all boats were got away, the last one, which was a flat-bottomed collapsible, floating off the deck. Now it is proverbial that the last thing a sailor will think of is a lifebelt; certainly no thought had entered my head of my own lifebelt, and I was far too busy at the boats to leave them, even had I thought of it. And this is how I came to obtain my belt.

Murdoch had been appointed chief, I was first and Blair was second officer; in that rank we had joined the *Titanic* in Belfast. Shortly before we sailed from Southampton, Wilde, who was formerly chief of the *Olympic*, and who was to have been given command of another of the White Star steamers, which, owing to the coal strike and other reasons was laid up, was sent for the time being to the *Titanic* as chief, Murdoch ranking back to first, myself to second, and Blair standing out for the voyage. Now it will be seen why it was that Wilde, on wanting some articles which were received by the first officer in Belfast, came to me. I took him into the first officer's room and showed him where they were, and was on my way back on deck again when I heard Wilde say, 'I am going to put on my lifebelt.' At that precise moment I was passing my own room door, facing which is a wardrobe, and on the top of this was my own lifebelt. On hearing Wilde's remark, I instinctively looked into the room, reached for the belt, and put it on.

I now resumed my work at the boats, finally calling for men to follow me up on top of the officers' quarters to cut adrift the last boat, which was stowed there. This boat we had not time even to open up, so just hove her down to the deck from which we had launched the others. As I saw her slide over the edge of the quarters I turned and ran across the deck to the other side of the ship to see if anything further could be done. Looking down I could see that all material work was finished, so from where I was on top of the quarters and above the bridge, I faced forward and walked into the water. The sudden immersion in this penetratingly cold water for a few seconds overcame all thought, and I struck out blindly for the crow's-nest which is on the foremast and was at that time just above the water. In a couple of seconds I realised that the crow's-nest and all other material help was of the same value, and almost immediately I found myself drawn with great force against the grating covering the mouth of the forward blower, a huge ventilator leading down to the forward stoke-hold. In this position I went below the surface with the ship.

I want to emphasise strongly this point, that as soon as I collected my thoughts after taking to the water, I remember saying to myself, 'Now, I'll see how much I have learned from Christian Science.' A doubt never entered my mind as to the possibility of my surviving; in other words, of the ability of the divine power to save me. I think I can conscientiously say that with this thought all fear left me, and I commenced again to realise the truth of being. It was at this moment that I was drawn into the water, still realising the truth, and while I was below the surface these words from the 91st Psalm came to me so distinctly that I seemed to realise their full import: 'He shall give his angels charge over thee.' Immediately, I think, I was thrown away from the blower, and came up to find a piece of wood in my hand which seemed to be attached to the top of the funnel by a wire.

I remained still, while the water rushed past me carrying the people with it away from me. A second time I went down, still holding fast to the truth, and again came to the surface. My piece of wood was gone, but alongside me was the flat-bottomed collapsible boat which I had thrown down on the other side of the ship. This I laid hold of, but made no attempt to board it.

I want it to be understood that during this time in the water the fact came calmly and clearly that there was a divine power which could be utilised in a practical manner, and also it seemed perfectly natural to rely on this power with the spiritual understanding which is so often spoken of in the Bible, and which is explained in 'Science and Health with Key to the Scriptures' by Mrs Eddy. Now, with the sinking of a great ship like the *Titanic*, there was also the fear of suction to overcome, and at this time the forward funnel fell, throwing the boat, myself, and other survivors about twenty feet clear of the ship, so that of suction we felt nothing.

About thirty of us floated the remainder of the night on the upturned boat, and I could not overcome the intense cold experienced, yet when a man handed me a bottle of something that smelt somewhat like essence of peppermint, the thought of material means was nothing short of repulsive, and needless to say, it was not taken. At daybreak we found two lifeboats floating nearby, into which we were taken. I was the last member of the *Titanic* to board the *Carpathia*, and after interviewing her captain, discarded my wet clothes in favour of a bunk, in which I remained for about half an hour, and was not in bunk or bed again till we arrived in New York. Reaction or effects from the immersion – which I was confidently assured would take place – there were none; and though surprise has been expressed by very many, it only goes to prove that 'with God all things are possible.'

Lieut. C.H. Lightoller, R.N.R. [208]

WILLIAM LINDSAY **Crew (Fireman)**

After arriving in New York, Mr Lindsay sent the following letter to his brother in Pennsylvania:

I expect you have heard before now about the *Titanic* going down, but thank God we got picked up all right. I don't know how mother and wife feel about it, but I do hope that they have heard by now that we are safe, what few there are of us. There were about 60 firemen and trimmers saved out of 400. Stewart Palmer and Charles Newman were drowned. Fred Palmer was saved. He picked us up in his boat. I was on the ship till the water came up to the funnel and got away on a raft. There were 30 of us on it. Oh, but the sight was awful. I shall never forget it, for she broke in three pieces. I only hope that the wife and mother know by now, for the company sent a cable for us. They ought to get that on Saturday. Well, Jack, I feel too upset to write more, so will close. Write home as soon as you can.[209]

HAROLD LOWE **Crew (Fifth Officer)**

After arriving in New York, Mr Lowe gave the following sworn deposition to the British consulate:

My name is Harold Godfrey Lowe. My home is Penrallt, Barmouth, England. I will be 29 years old the autumn of this year.

I joined the *Titanic* at Belfast in the capacity of fifth officer on the 29th of March, 1912. I hold an ordinary master's certificate of competency, issued by the British Board of Trade about 4 years ago, and the number I cannot at the present moment remember.

While the ship was at Belfast, lying fast alongside the wharf, at the direction of Mr Murdoch, who was then chief officer, I in company with Mr Moody, the sixth officer, inspected all the lifeboats, emergency boats and collapsible boats on the starboard side, together with their equipment.

On the starboard side there were seven lifeboats, one emergency boat and two collapsibles. The seven lifeboats rested on chocks under the davits with the falls attached. The emergency boat was hanging outboard on falls from davits. One of the collapsibles was resting on the deck that held the davits that held the emergency boat, and the other collapsible was directly opposite this and on top of the officers' quarters.

There was a set and a half of oars in each lifeboat. In each of the lifeboats there were a mast, sail rigging, and tarpaulin bag to hold the same. There were a double set of thole pins and one veering rowlock. There were a rudder and tiller and a rudderrope, a painter, a sea anchor, bailers and breakers. There were two water breakers in each of the lifeboats, and one in the emergency boats. One bread tank in each of the lifeboats and in the emergency boats. I do not remember whether there were any bread tanks in the collapsibles. I do not remember whether there was any water in the water breakers when I inspected them in Belfast; and there was no bread in the bread tanks and water breakers as I saw in the *Carpathia* subsequently after the accident did contain bread and water.

I cannot remember having seen any lanterns in the lifeboats when I inspected them in Belfast. I do not know of my own knowledge whether there were any lifeboat lanterns on board the ship. After the lifeboats had been taken on board the *Carpathia*, I remember having seen some lanterns taken from some of the boats, but which I cannot remember, nor how many.

There were no lifebuoys on board. There were life belts placed in every room on board.

On the trials the *Titanic* behaved splendidly and manoeuvred very well.

We sailed from Belfast on the 1st, and got to Southampton about the 3rd. While the ship was lying alongside the dock at Southampton the whole deck department was mustered, and two of the lifeboats on the starboard side were manned and lowered away, I myself taking charge of one and the sixth taking charge of the other. This is the only time that I saw a boat drill take place on the *Titanic*.

After leaving Queenstown, Mr Murdoch, the first officer, made out a boat list, stationing the men at their different positions at the boats, and there was an emergency boat list made out as well. I cannot say definitely whether either or both of these lists were posted in the forecastle. I do not now remember to what boat I had been assigned to on this list. The general boat list passed through my hands in being sent to the captain for approval. I glanced at this list casually, and remember from this glance that there were three seamen assigned to some of the boats and four to others.

We left Southampton at about 12:05 p.m. on Wednesday April 10th, and arrived at Cherbourg in the same evening. We sailed for Queenstown from Cherbourg the same evening, and arrived at Queenstown about 2:30 the same afternoon.

All went well from Queenstown until Sunday, April 14th. We had fine clear weather and smooth sea.

During my watch on deck from 6 to 8 I noticed that a chit had been placed on the officers' chart room table. There was written on the chit the word 'Ice' and the position underneath. I cannot remember what the position of the ice was. So far as I can remember, I figured it out roughly mentally and found that we would not come within the limits of the ice regions during my watch.

At the beginning of each watch the junior officer relieving the deck immediately ring up the engine room and get the revolutions for the last watch. I did this several times during the voyage, and the highest number of revolutions which I remember being reported to me from the engine room was about 74. During my watch from 6 to 8 the engine room telegraph indicated full speed ahead. The night was fine and clear, bright overhead and dark on the water; calm wind and sea. I did not particularly notice that it was very cold during the watch on deck. As near as I can remember, the barometer during the watch would be about 29.80. I went below at 8 o'clock, undressed, turned in, and went to sleep.

The next thing I remember was hearing voices. It must have been just about midnight. I half woke up; I was not fully awake; and I listened; and after listening a while I got up and opened the door and looked out on the deck, and saw passengers with lifebelts on and the crew clearing away the boats. I dressed and went to the starboard side, and assisted in getting over No.7 lifeboat on the starboard side. I cannot remember whether all the seamen on the starboard side were engaged in working No.7 lifeboat. I know that we worked the lifeboats one by one, and that before we proceeded to No.5 lifeboat some men had cut off the covers. I cannot say definitely, or give any estimate for, the number of seamen on this side of the ship at this time.

We succeeded in lowering No.7 after having filled it with women and children and placed four men in it as well for a crew. I do not know whether these four men were seamen, or firemen, or stewards, or what they were.

Then I proceeded to No.5 lifeboat and loaded it in a similar fashion, and then No.3 and then the emergency boat, placing women and children in each of them until all the women and children on that side of the deck had gone. In No.3 and the emergency boat we put men as well as women. The ship at this time was tipping rather badly, but she had no list that I noticed.

I then proceeded to port side, and found Sixth Officer Moody filling boat No.16 with women and children. I then carried on with filling No.14 with women and children. No.12 was also filled with women and children. I stated to Moody that I had seen five boats go away without a responsible person in them, meaning by this an officer. And I asked him who was it to be, him or I, to go in the boat. He said 'You go. I will get away in some other boat.'

I went in No.14. That was the last boat I was loading. Boat Nos. 16, 14 and 12 were loaded much about the same time.

I saw no confusion whatever, either in handling, loading, or lowering of either the boats on the starboard or port side.

I took two boats away with me; that is, excluding my own. I was in boat 14. I took them to a distance of about 150 yards from the ship. I then returned and escorted another boat to the other two boats. I then returned again to the ship and escorted a collapsible to the other three boats. I then made all the boats make fast to each other fore and aft, and also made them all set their masts ready for an emergency, such as wind. I then tied my own boat at the head of the string of boats.

The ship by this time [was] settling down rapidly by the head, and sank in about 20 minutes. The lights were burning up to 5 minutes before the stern disappeared. I did not hear anything that I should call explosions. A kind of distant smothered rumblings. I thought at the time it was produced by the sinking of the ship.

As I was putting over the starboard emergency boat somebody mentioned something about a ship on the port bow. I glanced in that direction and saw a steamer showing her red light about 5 miles to the northward of us.

At this time Fourth Officer Boxhall was firing off signals of distress, and we also Morsed to the ship by electric Morse lamps on the bridge.

When I had got these boats tied together I still saw these [lights] in the same position, and shortly afterwards she seemed to alter her position and open her green. I knew a few minutes afterwards all the lights went out, and I did not see any more lights until I saw the lights of the *Carpathia*.

The cries of the drowning people had very much subsided, and I thought it safe to venture in amongst them; and to do this I had to transfer all my 58 passengers from my boat into the other 4 boats; and then went away with an empty boat with just a boat's crew and no passengers. I searched the wreck thoroughly and found four persons, three of whom survived, and one died on board my boat.

During this time I was under sail, and as I was sailing away from the wreckage, I saw the collapsible which was in my charge, and I sailed down to her and took her in tow. She was in a pretty bad condition, because a breeze had sprung up and there was some sea, and she was somewhat overcrowded because I transferred my passengers. Whilst I was towing this collapsible boat, which had been pierced by wreckage and was settling fast; and I sailed down to her and took off approximately 20 men and 1 woman. I then made away for the *Carpathia*, and we were picked up by her.

In the morning, I saw a number of male bodies floating about. They all had lifebelts on. I did not see a single female body.

The wreckage that was floating about consisted of tables, chairs, blankets, settees, and other wood furniture.

There were no compasses on any of the lifeboats, as far as I can say.

As boat 14, of which I had charge, was being lowered two dark complexioned men tried to jump into the boat. One of them succeeded, and I threw him out; and then, to prevent any repetition of the occurrence, I fired my revolver in the air as I passed each deck.

Signed and sworn to the British Consulate General, New York this ... [unspecified] day of May 1912 before me ... [unspecified][210]

On 14 March 1913 Mr Lowe wrote the following letter to fellow survivor Selina Rogers:

S.S. *Gothic*, Durban, S. A.
Mar. 14th/13

Dear Miss Rogers,

Your very welcome letter to hand, (it has followed me all round the world) for which, very many thanks. I have since been twice to Australia & back to England, so you will see that I have not quite been standing still.

Several survivors of the *Titanic* have written letters to me, but I fancy they have been too glowing, anyway I suppose it is from their hearts, although I did not do much on that awful night, & my only hope is, that I or any other person that went through it, will not witness or go through another similar experience again.

Again thanking you for your very kind & thoughtful letter -

I remain
Yours Sincerely,
H.G. Lowe
3rd Officer[211]

THURE LUNDSTRÖM **Third Class Passenger**

Following the disaster, Mr Lundström wrote the following letter to his family:

The trip from South Hampton [*sic*] was so wonderful that one barely had an inkling that one was on the ocean. On that Sunday night, the liner hit an iceberg and sank after two and a half hours.

> We were all sleeping good when the ship hit, but awakened immediately ... I followed my friends to the second class deck where they should get into the lifeboats. Surely I thought them saved as they obtained spaces in the boats. I myself along with my 18-year-old Albin Klasen went back to the third class deck to wait for the end.

(During the wait Mr Lundström did what he could to help others find lifebelts. He came across a group of ten or fifteen young men who were very frightened and said, 'Let's pray.' He led them in prayer.)

> All the lifeboats were gone as I stood on the third class deck praying. A calmness filled my soul as only a person could feel that has left themselves in God's hand. I didn't feel any fear about death. I prayed that God's will for my life would be done and that if it was meant for me to live He would show me a way to be rescued.

(Lundström then lowered himself down a rope into the sea.)

> I didn't swim long before I was taken on one of the lifeboats, where I stood, soaking wet for over four hours in water.

(The lifeboat was already carrying several dead bodies, and the rest of the night was spent bailing water out of the craft to keep it from sinking.)

> After 20 minutes after I had been rescued the big liner sank taking several hundred with it to the deep. This was a huge catastrophic drama playing before my eyes.[212]

PIERRE MARÉCHAL — First Class Passenger

The following account was written and signed by survivors Pierre Maréchal, Alfred Omont and Paul Chevré, and its text was cabled to France for publication in that country:

> We were quietly playing auction bridge with Mr Smith, of Philadelphia, when we heard a violent noise similar to that produced by screw racing. We were startled and looked at one another under the impression that a serious accident had happened. We did not, however, think for a moment of a catastrophe, but through the portholes we saw ice rubbing against the ship's sides. We rushed on the deck and saw that the *Titanic* had a tremendous list. There was everywhere a momentary panic, but it speedily subsided. To the inquiries of a lady one of the ship's officers caustically replied 'Don't be afraid. We are only cutting a whale in two.'

Confidence was quickly restored, all being convinced that the *Titanic* could not founder. Captain Smith, nevertheless, appeared nervous. He came down on deck, chewing a toothpick. 'Let everyone,' he said, 'put on a lifebelt. It is more prudent.' Then he ordered the boats to be got out. The band continued to play popular airs in order to reassure the passengers. Nobody wanted to go in the boats, everyone saying 'What's the use? and firmly believing that there was no risk in remaining on board. In these circumstances some of the boats went away with few passengers. We saw boats with only about 15 passengers in them. Disregarding the advice of the officers, many of the passengers continued to cling to the ship.

When our boats had rowed about half a mile from the vessel the spectacle was quite fairylike. The *Titanic*, which was illuminated from stem to stern, was perfectly stationary, like some fantastic piece of stage scenery. The night was clear and the sea perfectly smooth, but it was intensely cold.

Presently the gigantic ship began to sink by the bows, and then those who had remained on board realised to the full the horror of their situation. Suddenly the lights went out, and an immense clamour filled the air in one supreme cry for help. Little by little the *Titanic* settled down, and for three hours cries of anguish were heard like some vast choir singing a death song. At moments cries of terror were lulled, and we thought that it was all over, but the next instant they were renewed in still keener accents of despair. As for us, we did nothing but row, row, row to escape from the obsession of heartrending death cries. One by one the voices were stilled.

Strange to say, the *Titanic* sank without noise, and contrary to expectations the suction was very feeble. There was a great backwash, and that was all. In the final spasm the stern of the leviathan stood up in the air, and then the vessel finally disappeared, completely lost.

In our little boat we were frozen with cold, having left the ship without overcoats or rugs. We shouted from time to time to attract the attention of the other boats, but obtained no reply. With the same object a German baron who was with us fired off all the cartridges in his revolver. This agonising suspense lasted for many hours, until at last the *Carpathia* appeared. We shouted 'Hurrah,' and all the boats scattered on the sea made towards her. For us it was like coming back to life.

A particularly painful episode occurred on board the *Titanic* after all the boats had left. Some of the passengers who had remained on the ship, realising too late that she was lost, tried to launch a collapsible boat which they had great difficulty in getting into shape. Nevertheless, they succeeded in lowering it, and some fifty got into it. The frail skiff was soon half full of water and the occupants one after the other either drowned or perished with the cold, the bodies of those who died being thrown out. Out of the original fifty only fifteen were picked up by the *Carpathia*, on board which we joined them.

We cannot praise too highly the conduct of the officers and men of the *Carpathia*. All her passengers gave up their cabins to the rescued women and sick, and we were received with every possible kindness. Similarly, we heard sorrowful tribute to the brave dead of the *Titanic*. Colonel Astor and others were admirable in their heroism, and the crew fulfilled with sublime self-sacrifice all the dictates of humanity. Much useless sacrifice of life would have been avoided, but for the blind faith in the unsinkableness of the ship and if all the places in the boats had been taken in time.

What have we saved from the wreck. Omont has a hairbrush, Marechal a book ('Sherlock Holmes'), and Chevré nothing. We all three send to our families resurrection greetings, and it is with immense joy that we cry from this side of the Atlantic '*à bientôt*'.[213]

CATHERINE MCCARTHY — Third Class Passenger

After arriving in the United States, Miss McCarthy wrote the following letter to her father in Ireland:

> About twelve o'clock on Sunday night Roger Tobin called us to get up, but told us not to be frightened, as there was no danger. To make sure, however, of our safety, he told us to get lifebelts. There were three of us in the room – Katie Peters, Katie Connolly, and myself. When Roger Tobin called us I wanted them to come up on deck, but they would not come. They appeared to think that there was no danger. That was the last I saw of them. I then left the room, and on going out I met a man from Dungarvan, who took me up to the second class boat deck, where they were putting out the boats. I was put into one boat, but was taken out of it again as it was too full. I was in the last boat to leave the ship, and was the second last person put into it. This was a short time before the ship went down. We were only just out of the way when the ship split in two and sank. We remained in the boat all night until near eight o'clock next morning, when we were rescued by the *Carpathia*. Our boat was so full I thought it would go down every moment, and one of the boats capsized when we were leaving the sinking ship. I did not, however, feel at all frightened, and did not fully realise the danger and the full nature of the awful tragedy until I was safe on board the *Carpathia*. When we were put on board the *Carpathia* we were immediately given restoratives and put to bed. I slept for an hour and then got up, feeling all right. When we landed in New York on Thursday night at eleven o'clock we were met by a number of Sisters of Charity nurses, who took us up to St Vincent's Hospital, where we were treated with the greatest kindness.[214]

JAMES MCGOUGH First Class Passenger

On 1 May 1912 Mr McGough made the following affidavit for the Senate *Titanic* inquiry:

I, James R. McGough, do depose and say that I was a passenger on the steamship *Titanic* on Sunday, April 14, 1912, the time of the disaster; that I live in Philadelphia, Pa.; that I am 36 years of age; and I hereby make the following statement:

I was awakened at 11.40 p.m., ship time; my stateroom was on the starboard side – deck E – and was shared with me by Mr Flynn, a buyer for Gimbel Bros., New York, at Thirty-third and Broadway. Soon after leaving our stateroom we came in contact with the second dining-room steward, Mr Dodd, in the companionway, of whom we asked the question, 'Is there any danger?' and he answered, 'Not in the least,' and suggested that we go back to bed, which we did not, however, do.

It was our intention to go up on the promenade deck, but before doing so I rapped on the door of the stateroom opposite mine, which was occupied by a lady, and suggested to her that she had better get up at once and dress as there was apparently something wrong.

Mr Flynn and I then ascended to promenade deck A, and after being up there about 10 minutes were notified to put on life preservers as a matter of precaution. We then had to go all the way from promenade deck back to our stateroom, which was on E deck. After procuring our life preservers we went back again to the top deck, and after reaching there discovered that orders had been given to launch the lifeboats, and that they were already being launched at that time.

They called for the women and children to board the boats first. Both women and men, however, hesitated, and did not feel inclined to get into the small boats, thinking the larger boat was the safer. I had my back turned looking in the opposite direction at that time and was caught by the shoulder by one of the officers, who gave me a push, saying, 'Here, you are a big fellow; get into the boat.'

Our boat was launched with 28 people; we, however, transferred 5 from one of the other boats after we were out in the ocean, which was some time after the ship went down.

When our lifeboats left the vessel, we were directed to row away a short distance from the large boat, feeling it would be but a short time until we would be taken back on the *Titanic*. We then rested on our oars; but after realising that the *Titanic* was really sinking, we rowed away for about half a mile, being afraid that the suction would draw us down.

Although there were several of us wanted drinking water, it was unknown to us that there was a tank of water and also some crackers in our boat, having no light on our boat; and we did not discover this fact – that is, as to the tank of water – until after reaching the *Carpathia*.

The following questions are asked by Mr O'Donnell:

Q. Do you know anything about the wireless?

A. No.

Q. Did you see the captain at any time after being awakened?

A. No.

Q. Did you see any neglect of duty by the crew at the offset?
A. No; they were all calm and apparently well disciplined: there was no panic at all.
Q. Have you any complaint to make in regards to the officers or crew?
A. No.
Q. Did you see any other ships or lights?
A. I saw lights, but was told they were from our own life-saving boats.
Q. Did you hear any guns or revolvers fired
A. No.
Q. Which side of the ship were you on?
A. Starboard side.
Q. Did you see any one drunk, or drinking, on the *Titanic* during your voyage?
A. I saw no one drunk.
Q. How fast was the *Titanic* going at the time of the accident?
A. I do not know.
Q. Did you see Mr Ismay at any time after you awakened?
A. No.
Q. Did you see any ice?
A. Not until the next morning, as I had gone bed at 10 o'clock and was asleep.
Q. Did you hear any groans or moaning after you got into the lifeboat?
A. Yes.
Q. Do you think if the crew on the lifeboat had gone back they could have picked up some of the passengers who were in the water?
A. I could not say; but some of the women passengers objected to our making the effort.
Q. Did the captain or officers tell the steward to call the passengers on one side only, and what was the purpose?
A. I do not know.
Q. State further anything else you know?
A. The above is a complete statement from the time of the accident until the time I got on board the *Carpathia*.
Q. Were you fully dressed?
A. I was fully dressed.

It is hereby certified that the within statement is true and correct, to the best of my knowledge and belief.

James R. McGough[215]

WILLIAM MELLORS **Second Class Passenger**

On 9 May 1912 Mr Mellors wrote the following letter to Dorothy Ockenden:

May 9, 1912
Richmond County Country Club, N.Y.

Dear Dorothy,

I was so pleased to receive your letter and to find you had not forgotten me. I had intended writing to you before but I was ashamed of my writing. You see I have no feeling yet from my knuckles to the tips of my fingers owing to having been frozen in the water, and so having heard from you I have got to write. I can assured you I felt it rather keenly when you left on the Thursday evening without saying good-bye. Well I am glad to say I am getting along fairly well considering the experience I had on the *Titanic*. I did not take any notice of the slight shock caused by the collision. I was asleep at the time it happened, and I just turned over and went to sleep again, about ten minutes later the young chap who shared my cabin with me, came and began to yell out that the ship had struck an iceberg and he thought we were going down. I really thought he was joking and told him so, but was soon convinced of the fact by hearing people running about and shouting on the deck and the engines being stopped. I soon dressed and got up on deck, to find crowds up there putting on lifebelts and I had about 15 mins hard work tying the women's belts on. It was an awful sight to see the men's faces when the last boat went off. At this time it was almost impossible to walk on the deck without you caught hold of something owing to the ship heeling right over. We were trying to fix up a collapsible boat when she gave the first signs of going under. There seemed to be a tremble run through the whole of the ship and the next thing we heard were loud reports inside which I think were the water-tight doors giving way and before you could say Jack Robinson there seemed to be mountains of water rushing through the doors, and I was swept away from where I was right against the collapsible boat, and I simply clung on for all I was worth, whilst all this was going on she was going under water and it seemed as if thousands of men were dragging me under with her, when suddenly her (the forward) nose on which I was seemed to suddenly rise from underneath the water and I and a few more that were close by cut the ropes that held the boat to the falls (davits). There was suddenly an explosion and I found myself whizzing through the water at an awful pace, having been blown away by the explosion. When I came to my senses a few minutes after I looked round and suddenly saw the ship part in the middle with the stern standing several hundred feet out of the water, at this time I was trying to swim away from her, but could not get more than a few yards away and I had as much as I could do to hold myself up from being dragged down with her. But the suction was not so great as I imagined it would be. After she had gone the sight that met one's eyes was terrible. There were great masses of wreckage with hundreds of human beings fighting amongst hundreds of dead bodies for their lives. I had been swimming for about 5 mins when a woman caught hold of my coat collar and begged me to save her life. Well Dorothy I felt that I was doomed and the least I could do was to try to keep both of us afloat. I had been holding her up for about (as far as I could tell) for about 20 minutes when I noticed my hands began to become as swollen as if I had a pair of miniature boxing gloves on and

I began to lose my grip of the woman who was almost dead and she must have noticed the fact herself for she began to struggle like a madman and clutched me round the throat with the strength of a man. It was then I noticed she had no lifebelt on and I found she was dragging me under the water with her. I had the most awful fight for life under water as I shall never forget, but eventually I broke away from her and rose at once to the surface. I was so done up with the want of breath that I thought my lungs were affected through holding my breath so long but it did not take so long as it does to tell it. I had not been swimming for long when I was caught hold of by the leg and found a seaman was holding on to me, I tried to kick him off but found my legs were becoming numbed and he held on to me like a leech. I struck at him but he only laughed and began to try to pull me under water. I managed to get hold of him by the hair of his head and push his head under the water. He became almost insensible and I got my feet clear of his hands and when he came to the surface he began to try and swim alongside of me but I managed to keep clear of him. I suddenly heard a most awful sound like a rattle and he threw up his arms and I knew he was dead. I shall never forget it for I am sure he went mad. I had been swimming for about 1 hour altogether when I saw an object a little way off which turned out to be a collapsible boat with about 20 or thirty people clinging to it, I managed after a hard struggle to get on this and found that the sides were broken away and that she was well under water. After a time I saw some of the people gradually dropping down dead one at the time and we had to push their bodies off to keep the raft afloat. Every now and again we were all thrown into the water owing to the boat capsizing and when we climbed back I noticed there were less climbed on. We suddenly noticed lights on the horizon which turned out to be the *Carpathia* and suddenly she turned round and went out of sight and we thought she had picked the other boats up and missed us. There were then several of our own boats in the distance and we were calling them for about two hours and they answered us back by flashing a green light and blowing whistles but would not put back to save us. There was then only ten or twelve of us left on the raft alive and there were five or six laying dead on the bottom. By this time I had become exhausted and had to let a man I had been holding up fall to the bottom of the raft but he was saved.

Eventually we were picked up and taken to the *Carpathia*. Having been in the water for about six hours and only about ten or twelve saved from 30 to 40 people hanging on the raft. I have since been rather bad through having been frozen from the hips downwards and my hands were the same. So Dorothy I have told you in a nutshell my experience on the *Titanic*. I hope you will forgive this writing as I am almost asleep on the pen; well I can scarcely hold it. The doctor thinks I shall get the feeling back to my hands etc. as time goes on. Will you kindly thank Miss Davy for her letter and tell her I will write as soon as I can. I am awfully busy writing letters now.

Well Dorothy you are the first to hear my story in England. I hope you are getting along well and also given up whistling. I must now close hoping to hear from you by return of mail.

With kind regards. I remain

Yours sincerely
William J. Mellors
P.S. Remember me to Miss Gravestock, I do not know her new name and also excuse this rotten writing.[216]

KARL MIDTSJØ **Third Class Passenger**

On 19 April Mr Midtsjø wrote the following letter to his brother in Norway:

New York 19/4

Dear brother

I have now come to New York, and am now in a hospital. We have been given lodging here by some higher authorities. You mustn't think I am ill, but they probably didn't have any other place for us, I imagine. I had a lucky escape with the *Titanic* affair. Only a fraction came from it alive. I can't really say I was afraid at all, and then not more than about 100 3rd class passengers, 210 of the crew, and the rest first and second class were saved. But some millionaires also went down the drain, as I have also heard. I have lost everything I had, clothes and money, so I don't have anything other than what I am wearing at the moment. Yes, it is no fun being in a little boat in the Atlantic Ocean. Because it was just about in the middle of the Atlantic. We lay in the lifeboats and thought now it is their turn, soon it is ours. Yes, it isn't a joke when such a big vessel is sinking. When the rockets were fired it was serious. It was a starry night and the stars shone there just like they do at home and then there was a four day voyage with a steamer to land, yes that is a whole day's story, but I will content myself with saying only a few words. We are being treated as earls and looked upon as unnatural people and there are plenty of those who want to help us. I am thus in the best of health and haven't suffered from the disaster. Then you become rather serious when you see something so terrible. I still imagine I am hearing the cries of distress.

And someone was shot when they tried to force their way up into the boats.

But there is at least something I cannot forget, a whole lot who bent their knees on deck and prayed to God, but there was no one who made fun of them then, even though there had been dancing and card playing the whole way and one felt as safe on board as on land. And then she sank in a couple of hours. Give my love to father and all my nearest. Send the letter home when you have read it, because I haven't got time to write to anybody else.

Karl[217]

DAISY MINAHAN **First Class Passenger**

On 13 May 1912 Miss Minahan made the following deposition for the Senate *Titanic* inquiry:

> Daisy Minahan, being first duly sworn, upon oath deposes and says: I was asleep in stateroom C-78; I was awakened by the crying of a woman in the passageway. I roused my brother and his wife, and we began at once to dress. No one came to give us warning. We spent five minutes in dressing and went on deck to the port side. The frightful slant of the deck toward the bow of the boat gave us our first thought of danger.
>
> An officer came and commanded all women to follow, and he led us to the boat deck on the starboard side. He told us there was no danger, but to get into a lifeboat as a precaution only. After making three attempts to get into boats, we succeeded in getting into lifeboat No.14. The crowd surging around the boats was getting unruly.
>
> Officers were yelling and cursing at men to stand back and let the women get into the boats. In going from one lifeboat to another we stumbled over huge piles of bread lying on the deck.
>
> When the lifeboat was filled there were no seamen to man it. The officer in command of No.14 called for volunteers in the crowd who could row. Six men offered to go. At times when we were being lowered we were at an angle of 45 degrees and expected to be thrown into the sea. As we reached the level of each deck men jumped into the boat until the officer threatened to shoot the next man who jumped. We landed in the sea and rowed to a safe distance from the sinking ship. The officer counted our number and found us to be 48. The officer commanded everyone to feel in the bottom of the boat for a light. We found none. Nor was there bread or water in the boat. The officer, whose name I learned afterwards to be Lowe, was continually making remarks such as, 'A good song to sing would be 'Throw Out the Life Line' and 'I think the best thing for you women to do is to take a nap.'
>
> The *Titanic* was fast sinking. After she went down the cries were horrible. This was at 2:20 a.m. by a man's watch who stood next to me. At this time three other boats and ours kept together by being tied to each other. The cries continued to come over the water. Some of the women implored Officer Lowe, of No.14, to divide his passengers among the three other boats and go back to rescue. His first answer to those requests was, 'You ought to be damn glad you are here and have got your own life.' After some time he was persuaded to do as he was asked. As I came up to him to be transferred to the other boat he said, 'Jump, God damn you, jump.' I had showed no hesitancy and was waiting only my turn. He had been so blasphemous during the two hours we were in his boat that the women at my end of the boat all thought he was under the influence of liquor. Then he took all of the men who had rowed No.14, together with the men from the other boats, and went back to the scene of the wreck. We were left with a steward and a stoker to row our boat, which was crowded. The steward did his best, but the stoker refused

at first to row, but finally helped two women, who were the only ones pulling on that side. It was just 4 o'clock when we sighted the *Carpathia*, and we were three hours getting to her. On the *Carpathia* we were treated with every kindness and given every comfort possible.

A stewardess who had been saved told me that after the *Titanic* left Southampton that there were a number of carpenters working to put the doors of the air-tight compartments in working order. They had great difficulty in making them respond, and one of them remarked that they would be of little use in case of accident, because it took so long to make them work.

Daisy Minahan[218]

On 11 May Miss Minahan wrote the following letter to Senator William Alden Smith at the Senate inquiry:

Hon. Wm. Alden Smith
Washington, D.C.

Dear Sir:

I have given you my observations and experiences after the disaster, but want to tell you of what occurred on Sunday night, April 14.

My brother, his wife, and myself went to the café for dinner at about 7:15 p.m. (ship's time). When we entered there was a dinner party already dining, consisting of perhaps a dozen men and three women. Capt. Smith was a guest, as also were Mr and Mrs Widener, Mr and Mrs Blair [Thayer], and Maj. Butt. Capt. Smith was continuously with his party from the time we entered until between 9:25 and 9:45, when he bid the women good night and left. I know this time positively, for at 9:25 my brother suggested my going to bed. We waited for one more piece of the orchestra, and it was between 9:25 and 9:45 (the time we departed), that Capt. Smith left.

Sitting within a few feet of this party were also Sir Cosmo and Lady Duff-Gordon, a Mrs Meyers, of New York, and Mrs Smith, of Virginia. Mr and Mrs Harris also were dining in the café at the same time.

I had read testimony before your committee stating that Capt. Smith had talked to an officer on the bridge from 8:45 to 9:25. This is positively untrue, as he was having coffee with these people during this time. I was seated so close to them that I could hear bits of their conversation.

Yours,
Daisy Minahan[219]

PHILLIP MOCK **First Class Passenger**

Following the disaster, Mr Mock wrote the following letter to fellow survivor Archibald Gracie:

> No.11 carried the largest number of passengers of any boat – about sixty-five. There were only two first-cabin passengers in the boat besides my sister, Mrs Schabert, and myself. The remainder were second-class or stewards and stewardesses. I last saw the ship with her stern high in the air going down. After the noise I saw a huge column of black smoke slightly lighter than the sky rising high into the sky and then flattening out at the top like a mushroom.
>
> I at no time saw any panic and not much confusion. I can positively assert this as I was near every boat lowered on the starboard side up to the time No.11 was lowered. With the exception of some stokers who pushed their way into No.3 or No.5, I saw no man or woman force entry into a lifeboat. One of these was No.13 going down, before we touched the water.[220]

WALTER NICHOLS **Crew (Assistant Saloon Steward)**

After the *Carpathia* reached New York on the evening of 18 April, Mr Nichols dictated the following account to his sister, Mrs James Openshaw, who wrote it down for publication:

> I've been a sailor for twenty years, and I've crossed about 300 times, but this!
>
> We left Southampton on Wednesday, April 10, with fine weather. Everything aboard was ship shape. We got to Cherbourg at about six that night and took on a lot of people there, though not quite so many as we took on at Southampton, counting steerage and all. We only stopped for a little at Queenstown, leaving there between 2 and 2:30 on Thursday afternoon. Our first day's run was 488 knots. This was counting from the time we left Queenstown until 12 o'clock on Friday. From Friday noon to Saturday noon she ran 544 knots, and the next day 546. She wasn't trying for a record because she was a new ship, and this was her first trip.
>
> All day Sunday it was very cold, although the weather was fine. There was ice all around us. There were services on board that day, in the first and second cabins. I was busy with my work and didn't go. Sunday night was my night off, and I went to bed at about 10 o'clock. I got off at 9, but I fooled around for a couple of hours before I turned in. I didn't go on deck. On a big boat like that a man working inside doesn't go on deck often. Sometimes you don't get a peep at the water for days at a time. It's just like working in a big hotel. But I knew that it was mighty cold outside and I knew what the reason was, too. I've crossed

enough to know that when it gets cold like that at this season it's because there's icebergs around. And if we fellows down below knew it I guess the navigating officers knew it, too.

My bunk was amidships on deck E, the main thoroughfare of the boat. There are still two decks below that, F and G. At 11:40 I was awakened by feeling a bit of a vibration. The ship went on for a bit and then the engines stopped. Nobody was frightened and some of the men in the room with me didn't want to trouble to get up to look out and see what had happened. I put on my coat and took a run out to look. It was all black outside and I couldn't see anything except that there was some ice on the deck forward.

Half of the men went back to bed. Nobody believed anything could be wrong. They had such faith in the ship. Everybody believed in her.

It was bitter cold outside, and I was glad enough to get back into the cabin where I bunked. It's located not far from the engine room – the engine rooms are just behind and below us – and within a few minutes of the time we struck I could hear the engineers passing along the order to close the watertight doors. One man would tell it to the next and he would pass it on to someone else.

Well, as I say, some of the men went back to bed. I stayed up and sat around talking with some of the fellows for I should say three-quarters of an hour after the collision, when the second steward in charge of our cabin came in and gave us orders to report up on deck. That meant that we were to report to the positions assigned to us in the lifeboat drill. My place was with lifeboat No.15. So I went up on deck A, where the lifeboats are. On my way up I noticed some of the passengers about, but no one seemed to be worried or excited. I passed by the gymnasium on my way. Inside were a number of passengers amusing themselves. One man was riding the bicycle, one of those exercise machines, and another was punching the bag.

No.15, my boat, was the after boat on the starboard side. All the odd numbered boats are on one side of the ship and the even numbered boats on the other. There were ten of us to man the boat, which is a big one, holding about seventy to eighty persons. When I got on deck it was still dark, but I could hear the wireless machine sputter. I didn't see any icebergs or anything. Up on deck A, which is the boat deck, there were only the boat crews. At least that is all I could see. I saw them working away at Boat No.11 and Boat No.13. When I looked down I saw that several of the boats were already in the water. The ship was brightly lit and I could see the boats, with people in them, floating about in the reflection of the light from the ship.

The officer in charge of the boats on that part of the deck had a revolver in his hand. He gave his orders quietly and we didn't realise even then that anything serious was the matter. The ship was down in the water a little forward but you couldn't notice it much from where I was.

We stood in line waiting for orders while boats 11 and 13 were swung out on the davits and lowered. The crews would make them ready and get into them. Then they would lower them to deck B, where the passengers were. The boats are held by three ropes, one on either end and one in the middle. They are cut loose by knocking out a block in the centre after she is in the water.

I guess we waited for some minutes while they were getting the two other boats away. They were mighty careful not to let one boat go before the other had got clear. It's a drop of some ninety or a hundred feet from the boat deck to the water, and they had to look sharp to keep one boat from fouling the other.

After we got in our boat and were waiting to be lowered to deck B I heard the band playing. I was looking sharp after what I was doing and I don't remember what they played. I could just hear a sort of confused sound of the instruments, enough to know that they were playing. Someone told me afterward that the last piece they played was 'Nearer, My God, to Thee.' They didn't have a chance, poor devils. They were cooped up in one of the reception rooms, and they were drowned like rats, every one of them.

Altogether it took us about twenty minutes to fill our lifeboat and get away. There was no confusion and no rush. On deck B, where we loaded the passengers, First Officer Murdoch was in charge. He saw to the giving of the orders to the men that handled the boats. The order was to take women only, and the officers kept saying, 'We can only take women. No man is allowed to get in.'

But no one seemed particularly anxious to get in. The officer kept on talking to the women, sort of urging them. 'Come, now,' he'd say. 'Get in or we'll have to leave you behind. The boat's going to leave and we can't wait for you.' Several women stepped back as they saw the boat and refused to leave their men folks when they saw that they would have to go alone. One woman stepped up to the rail against which we were holding the boat, looked into it and then stepped back as though she didn't like it. I saw Colonel Astor kiss his wife good-bye. I knew him because he had been pointed out to me in the saloon. I didn't know any of the rest.

All the time we were there the officer kept talking quiet like, urging women to get in. He didn't say anything about danger. I guess he didn't want to have any rush and he just talked, quiet like, and kept sort of joking them along, telling them to hurry or they'd be left, and things like that. But they all seemed to think that the ship was a better place to be than in a lifeboat. Many of the boats weren't full. We only had about fifty people in ours. Some of the men passengers had to urge the women to go, and some of the women whose men folks didn't happen to be close to them refused to go.

Our boat was one of the last to get away. We held on until we were sure No.13 was clear. Then we dropped to the water. None of us was excited and some of the men seemed to take it as a sort of little excursion in the boat. None of us had any idea that the *Titanic* would sink. We knew that the *Olympic* was on the way to us and we expected that she would come in the morning to pick up the boats and to take off the people that were left on the *Titanic*.

As soon as we struck the water we started to pull away from the ship, so as not to foul against her side. As soon as we got a little distance off I could see that she was down a good deal by the head because the propeller was sticking half way out of the water. When we were a couple of hundred yards away from the ship I saw two flashes and heard two revolver shots coming from near the bridge. All the boats had been lowered and I didn't know what the shots meant. By this time it must have been about 1 o'clock in the morning and the lights were still going on the main part of the ship. The other boats were all about us and we kept shouting to one another to keep close together. After we left the ship about four other boats got away. I kept pulling away at my oar and we rowed around just to keep warm. The women we had on board were huddled down in the centre of the boat. Some of them were standing, but most of them were squatting down.

We saw the ship gradually settling down at the bow, until the forepart of the ship wasn't visible. Part of the time the band was still playing and we could hear the wireless. About an hour after we left her the fore part of the boat was going under and that was the first time we realised that she was going to sink. Because up to this time the men in the boat had taken the whole thing as a sort of holiday.

The ship sank slowly and steadily and then we heard a little explosion that must have been the first boiler. After that the lights began to go out in different parts of the ship. Then came a big explosion. We could see a mass of black smoke. The boat seemed to lift right up out of the water and tilt up on end, and then seemed to break and drop back. For one moment she was right up in the air standing on her nose.

That's when the people left on board went into the water. There were 1,500 to 1,700 left on the ship and most of them were thrown into the water by this explosion. Then a horrible shriek went up, cries for help and weird shouts. You can imagine what it was like, 1,500 of them. If you've ever been around when they were feeding a kennel of dogs, that's the only thing I can think of that it sounded like – and that kept up for half an hour, growing fainter and fainter as the minutes passed. There was no other sound – just the crying of the people.

The ship quietly sank out of sight without a sound. We could see black spots of wreckage and hundreds of people struggling in the water. Some of the boats were near enough to help and pull some of the people in. One of the women in our boat wanted us to go back, but we wouldn't do it. Had we got in among that crowd struggling in the water it might have meant the end of us. With twenty of them grabbing the boat on one side it would have swamped us in a minute. It was awful, but there was nothing to do but wait. I won't forget those shrieks. The women in our boat crouched down and murmured. No one spoke. For half an hour we could hear those cries for help. Some of those left on the boat had managed to get on bits of wreckage. Some were on rafts so loaded down that they were partly under water. Some of the women in our boat started to move around. We had to keep them quiet, for with their shifting about we might have gone over.

Gradually those voices died away, and in something like half an hour everything was quiet and dark. We could see the other boats drifting about and kept close to them. Every now and then we passed a body floating on the water.

Just as it was getting light, a few hours later, I don't know just how many, we saw the lights of the *Carpathia*. We hadn't suffered any, because we kept warm by rowing. Every man that was saved was in one of the boats. The cold water killed the others. No one could stand the water for six or seven hours. Every one of the bodies had on a lifebelt. We didn't try to pick them up; what was the use? We had all we could tend to with the living without bothering about the dead ones. The women in our boat didn't see the bodies. They were too far down in the bottom of the boat. They kept talking quietly, just as though they were still on the ship.

In some of the boats, I heard later, there was a lot of weeping, but not in ours. I guess those must have been Continentals. The women in our boat were mostly English stock, and they're a braver sort. The kind makes a big difference.

By the time we started to row toward the *Carpathia* – we didn't know it was she until later; we thought it was the *Olympic* – it was getting light enough so we could look about us. Then, for the first time, we saw that there were big icebergs all about us. We counted fifteen of sixteen big bergs. They loomed up through the light, which wasn't strong yet, like sailing craft, and they were shaped like schooner sails, too. In all my sailing I've never seen so many icebergs in one place. A little further off was a big ice floe; I guess it must have been ten to fifteen miles long. There was a cold, freezing wind blowing toward us from this shoal.

When we got up to the *Carpathia* they were all ready for us. The men climbed on board up a rope ladder. The women were hoisted up in a bo'sun's chair and the children were put in sacks.

After we got on board and the strain was over I felt weak for the first time. [illegible] ... a lot of the women became hysterical. The people on the *Carpathia* were surprised that there were so few of us left. They had expected to pick up everybody. If they had I guess there wouldn't have been room enough on board to stand up. The passengers were distributed all about and we were told to bunk wherever we could. After the *Carpathia* had got us all on board from the lifeboats she started to cruise about. Bodies were floating all around and bits of wreckage. I saw chairs, cushions and pillows floating on the water. The *Californian* came along a short time after we were on board the *Carpathia*. The *Carpathia* cruised among the wreckage until 9 or 10 o'clock. We didn't pick up anyone. All those that were alive were in the boats. And several of the men in the boats that had been fished up out of the water were dead. They dropped them over the side a little later. Nobody could have lived long in that cold water.

On board the *Carpathia* things were pretty crowded. The passengers were put wherever there was room in the steerage and anywhere. The *Titanic* crew waited on the *Titanic* passengers. Many of the women stayed in their rooms during the whole trip. I heard that Mr Ismay stayed in his cabin all the time. I didn't see him. Orders came to us that no news of any kind was to be given out. The captain handled all the news that was received or sent out. The first thing some of the passengers tried to do after getting on the *Carpathia* was to send wireless messages telling their people they were safe, but they weren't allowed to do it.

They kept asking questions, but they weren't told anything. These were the orders: Don't give any information. I suppose a lot of the *Titanic*'s passengers on the *Carpathia* knew less about the accident than anyone else. They took all our names soon after we got aboard. But a lot of them were never sent ashore. My name wasn't sent in and my sister Ruth didn't know I was safe until I went to see her at 16 East Eleventh street, where she is working. My brother Frank came down to the boat to see if I was there, but he missed me.

Whatever news may have come to the ship we didn't know anything about it. All the news went to the captain through the Marconi man. We were a sorry looking lot on the *Carpathia*. You wouldn't have known them to be the same people that were on the *Titanic*. All the clothes anyone had were those they wore in the boats. Some of the women only had on their nightdresses and their outer coats which they put on when they came up on deck. A lot of the men, like myself, threw on their clothes over their pajamas. I'm still wearing mine.

After we got on board the *Carpathia* we heard all sorts of experiences that others had had. I was told of one woman who took off her coat and insisted on giving it to a man who had been pulled out of the water into one of the boats. One man who was saved had jumped down 150 feet into the water from the stern of the ship just after the explosion. The baker, who was also picked up by a boat, jumped from one of the top decks into the water just before the big explosion.

As to the cause of the accident, I think someone must have been careless. There was no excuse for their not seeing the berg. We who were below knew there were icebergs about and the officers of the ship must have known of it. The collision must have torn out the bottom of the ship beyond the first line of watertight bulkhead doors. She must have had hundreds of tons of water in her forward part to make her propellers stick up out of the water the way they did.

There were a lot of life rafts aboard the *Titanic* that were not used. If the people on board had only realised that. Some of the men did throw the life rafts into the water and jumped in after them. Then they climbed up on them and some of them were afterwards picked up by the small boats.

All the engineers were drowned – thirty-two or thirty-six of them. Not one was saved. The Marconi man who was saved was hurt about the legs. They had to carry him to the wireless room on the *Carpathia*, but he worked most of the time. Some of the men picked up by the boats died after they got on board the *Carpathia*. I think there were three or four. They were buried on Monday. The *Carpathia* didn't meet any ships until we were off Sandy Hook this afternoon. Then we were met by a couple of newspaper tugs. But orders were given to allow no communication and a couple of bo'suns manned the rail to see that the order was carried out. I was surprised the way they let us through. No quarantine stop and no bother with the customs. I didn't expect that they would let us members of the crew off the ship. But I just walked off and no one interfered with me. Now I guess I'll have to start in [last few words are illegible].[221]

PATRICK O'KEEFE **Third Class Passenger**

A week after arriving in New York, Mr O'Keefe wrote a letter to his father in Ireland describing a premonition he had experienced before boarding the *Titanic* at Queenstown:

> I dreamt myself she was going down before I left Queenstown, and I thought to sell my passage note for £7.00, but then I thought if I went back to Waterford again the boys would be laughing at me. I lost everything I had on the *Titanic*, but thank God, my life was spared.[222]

HELEN OSTBY **First Class Passenger**

In the years following the disaster, Miss Ostby dictated the following account of her experiences on board the *Titanic*:

> While in Nice we heard that the *Titanic* was about to make her maiden voyage. We talked it over, decided it would be interesting to go on her, and obtained reservations.
>
> We went up to Paris and while there we met two acquaintances, Mr and Mrs Frank Warren of Portland, Oregon, whom we had met in Egypt, and who also had reservations on the *Titanic*.
>
> On the 10th of April we took the boat train to Cherbourg. The *Titanic* remained out in the harbour, lighted and beautiful in the night. We boarded her from a tender.
>
> We spent the first few days exploring the ship, or should I say, the areas reserved for passengers in the first class. There were great distinctions and the different classes were kept apart. Mostly, we just wandered around between meals, enjoying the luxury and newness of it all. We always travelled on the White Star Line, so we could compare the *Titanic* with other ships of the company.
>
> The first few days were fairly mild, but by Sunday it had begun to get quite chilly. On Sunday the speed of the ship seemed to pick up, too.
>
> Late Sunday morning, as I was sitting on deck, Captain Edward Smith was talking nearby to a few passengers when a steward came out and handed him a message. Captain Smith looked at it, but then continued talking for a while with the passengers. I have always felt this might have been one of the several messages received that day warning of ice ahead.
>
> Sunday was always fairly quiet on a liner. In those days they didn't have all of the ready-made entertainment they have today. In those days you got on board simply to cross the Atlantic. My father and I chatted about the great welcome New York would probably give the *Titanic*.

There was the usual Sunday evening concert by the ship's orchestra in the main lounge, and after that nearly everybody retired early to their cabins.

I had just dropped off to sleep when I was awakened by a jar that felt about as it would if you were in a car that scraped the side of a tree. I sat up straight in bed, trying to make out what had happened. It seemed completely silent for a minute or two. The engines were cut off. The corridors were quiet until one began to hear doors open and voices speaking. The first voice I heard was a woman asking the steward what had happened. He replied calmly, 'Everything will be all right.'

I got out of bed. I pulled on some of my clothes, but not too many, because for some reason it occurred to me that I didn't want to have too many on if I had to be in the water. It was just something that flashed through my mind, although I had no real hint, even, that the ship was in danger. At that time, the possibility of the ship sinking was unthinkable. I put on a dress, coat and shoes.

Then, of course, the passengers began to gather in the corridors one by one, trying to get some information. My father came out of his stateroom across the corridor. It was very quiet, as when a train stops in a station and you can hear everyone's voice. You could see anxious looking faces, people with outlandish clothes and women in curlers. People had thrown on anything just to cover themselves.

We all just wandered around the corridors, which were on an upper deck. People were calm. They were very calm. There was no panic, but they were wondering what it was and trying to get news, and really not thinking there was anything too serious. We soon learned that the ship had hit an iceberg, but nobody knew how much damage had been done. This was the first we had heard that ice might have been ahead of the ship.

It was a good part of an hour before the stewards came and told us to put our lifejackets on and go up to the boat deck. Everybody went back to their cabins to get their lifejackets. They were very awkward to get on, since there had been no boat drill and nobody even thought of trying on the lifejackets, but the stewards were very helpful in getting us into them.

The order to put on the lifejackets was the first inkling we had that something was seriously wrong. Many people thought we would just be going off in the lifeboats for a short time, as a precaution, then would probably come back to the ship. The idea had been talked up so long ahead of time that the *Titanic* was unsinkable, it was hard to get it out of people's minds.

With the Warrens, we went up to the boat deck by the main staircase. I remember seeing Captain Smith and one or two other officers coming down it, to explore the ship and see what damage had been done. The officers looked very sober. They didn't stop to talk to the passengers at all.

When we got out on the boat deck, the noise of the ship blowing off steam from all four funnels was a deafening roar. You could hardly hear anyone speak to you.

The boats were being gotten ready, and the word came that women and children should get into them. The men stood back to await their turn. That was the last we saw of my father and Mr Warren.

Mrs Warren was helped into the boat, and I followed her. It was a very unpleasant feeling stepping into that boat because, although it was level with the boat deck, it was swung out over the water so there was a little gap between it and the side of the ship. An officer and two sailors manned the lifeboat, and just as it was about to be lowered two men from among the passengers were allowed to jump in.

It was also very unpleasant being lowered down to the water. Once below the boat deck, there were no lights so that it was difficult for the men on deck, who were letting the boat down by ropes, to keep it level. First one end would dip down, then the other, and the people in the boat would shout to them to level it off.

By the time we were lowered to the water, the *Titanic* had begun very noticeably to go down by the head. The stars were out, but it was pitch dark. The sea was calm. As we pulled away, we could see the lights of the ship, and the lighted forward portholes gradually disappearing.

Our boat had more than forty people in it. As we were sitting there watching, the first of about eight distress rockets went off, so high in the sky that they startled everyone. Everybody began to talk in the dark and wonder whether our ship had been able to send off any wireless messages.

Up until that time, things had gone on very calmly. There had been no panic. But at the very end, we could see and hear that the people on board were realising there was no place to go.

As the ship began to stand on end, we heard a big rumbling, rattling noise as if everything was being torn from its moorings inside the ship. All of a sudden that stopped, and she stood on end very quietly for a minute, then went down like an arrow.

Personally, I didn't see any people in the water, but we could hear voices and the sound still rings in my ears when I think of it. It was quiet after a while, and we got next to another lifeboat and tied to it. About four of our people got into the other boat, which had fewer people.

Mrs Warren and I were sitting side by side. It was very cold, and you couldn't move around. It was crowded, and if you sat still on a little bit of wood seat, your legs became stiff from the cold. I can't stress the cold too much when you are sitting in a cramped boat.

Everybody was looking and hoping to see the lights of a ship. The women – I can't remember and children in our boat – were naturally concerned about what happened to the men who had had to stay behind. That was the worst part of it. Of course, there are always some people who complain about losing jewellery and clothing and, of course, some complained about the cold. One woman was seasick and didn't feel happy for that reason.

When somebody happened to mention jewellery she had left behind, I remembered for the first time that I had lost a diamond bar pin, given to me by my father, which was still pinned to my nightgown on board ship. I hadn't given it a thought, and when I was reminded, it didn't matter.

The only lights we saw until almost dawn were one or two green flares held briefly in one of the lifeboats, and later we saw a light come up over the horizon.

We learned subsequently it was a rocket from the *Carpathia*. Our boat had no provisions of any kind. Somebody in our boat lighted a match, but in the middle of the Atlantic it was not very useful.

Just before dawn we saw the masthead lights of the *Carpathia*, but we didn't know whether she was really coming toward us. It was a beautiful dawn and sunrise, beautiful. And it was then we realised there was ice around us. There were big bergs and small ones, a few miles away, and beyond them a field of pack ice as far as you could see, to the north and west. We thought the berg we had hit had perhaps been the only one in the area. As it turned out, if the *Titanic* hadn't hit that one, it probably would have hit another.

As dawn came, we could see the *Carpathia* was heading toward us. Then people began to feel a little happier about the situation. The *Carpathia* stopped one or two miles away and let the scattered lifeboats come to her. With day, the sea got a little choppier, and there was quite a bit of swell by the time we reached her side. I was so stiff that when they put a rope pilot's ladder over the side I couldn't climb it. They slung over a rope hitch like a bo'sun chair. I sat in it, held on to the rope and was hauled up.

On deck, steamer blankets were put around our shoulders. They took us to the dining room, where very hot tea and coffee were ready. It took me some time to stop shivering. We were all sort of dazed.

After they took our names, Mrs Warren and I and most of us went back to the rail of the *Carpathia*, hoping we would see someone in the following lifeboats. Until the last one arrived there was always hope.[223]

ERNST PERSSON — Third Class Passenger

After arriving in New York, Mr Persson wrote the following letter to his family in Sweden:

Beloved Parents, Wife, and Children,

My beloved, you have probably heard about the terrible catastrophe which struck us, and what a night I've experienced since I last wrote you.

Probably you have received the letter I wrote from England and the telegram which I sent at my arrival. We departed Southampton at the 10th and everybody was happy and content every day for food, and everything was the best we could wish for, but then the terrible night came. They woke us up at 12 a.m. and told us to enter the afterdeck because we hit an iceberg. Nobody believed there was any danger, the boat was unsinkable as they said. At that time nobody was worried until they started to send down the lifeboats. Then there was panic, and everybody who wanted to jump into the lifeboats without permission was shot.

Women and children first; men had to save themselves as they could. When Elna and I came up all the lifeboats were crowded, so no rescue was possible. We stood together all the time, so we agreed to accompany each other into the deep. But as the boat sank and the water started pouring over the deck there was a terrible sight and scuffle, and that separated us.

Then I heard Elna say, 'Tell Wilhelm and my parents and brothers and sisters if you get rescued.' I didn't see her again because we were all washed overboard. When I entered the water, I sank several metres below the surface. Floating up again, I had a roof of wreckage over my head, and hung on for a good while. But then the ship began to sink, so I had to leave the wreckage and try to swim away. Otherwise, I would have been dragged into the depths once again. As I floated and swam around, I saw how people in the water tried to save themselves in an overloaded boat, but when they hung on to the sides, the boat overturned with the keel upward, and all drowned. I saw how some people climbed up on it, so I swam to it, and was taken up. Only Italians were on this boat, and it was so crowded that it floated nearly one metre below the water. There I had to lie for six hours with the water up to my shoulders. Then we were taken up in a lifeboat that rowed us to the big boat that had come to rescue us.

You cannot imagine how it was as thousands of people lay in the water crying for help and no help was available. But don't grieve too deeply my beloved. We can thank God that any of us got rescued among so many thousands of people who lost their lives. Tears are shed all over the world over this catastrophe. But surely it is awful to think that Elna and little Telma no longer exist. I don't know how it will be to come to Wilhelm because I don't believe that she got rescued. There are so many in the hospitals, but I have not seen her name in the newspaper although all rescued are registered. Some of us Swedes are staying at this hotel. As you can see, we were photographed by all newspapers, movie theatres and all bookshops. We were well received when we arrived. Three of us had no caps or overcoats, and we were let in first and got dressed from top to toe and received 15 dollars, because I had not a single penny when I disembarked.

Now we can stay at this hotel where we get good food and nice rooms, free of charge. All societies and theatres collect money for us, so we [will] probably get more money after a while. So don't worry about me. I feel well though I feared that I would not be able to withstand the [cold ocean] 'bath'. My whole body was stiff when I came up. On the boat that rescued us, we were bedded down and could rest two days. Then we had to get up and try to dry our clothes because nobody cared to help us with that. We didn't arrive in New York until Thursday night and the disaster occurred on Sunday night. So you can imagine how far we were from land. The boat rescuing us was a real pigsty. It was a boat travelling to Italy with only swarthy passengers. So then you can understand how it was. But we were satisfied to be out of the water.

I have posted a card to Aunt Anna. I got her address from Elna by chance. Otherwise, I would not have known where to go because I had no other. Well, now my beloved, I have given you a brief report about what happened. You will get more information later on because it is impossible to put any more of these sheets in the envelope, and I don't have any other paper. I hope you are all healthy and don't grieve too much so that you become ill from it. I will find work and save money because I will probably come home again. I will not expose my beloved wife and children to the same voyage that I went on. So farewell for a while. I shall write as soon as I arrive in Chicago. You will then get my address, so I can hear from you. My warm greetings and solace to you my beloved in Sweden from your castaway son, husband, and father of our small boys.

Ernst,

I cannot describe in words how awful everything was. You have to try to imagine it – the last moment I saw my dear sister stand there with little Thelma tightly in her arms.

I wish I could send you a paper with our photographs, but all are sold out, and we cannot take the ones they have here. I am pictured almost full size in one paper – the best photograph I've seen of myself. You, my dear wife, got to be with me in the water. Yours was the only photograph I had, and it stayed fast in my pocket. The first I did when I was on a dry surface, I took it out and looked at it. I began to cry, but then I thought that you smiled at me, and I became calm.[224]

ALICE PHILLIPS — Second Class Passenger

Following the disaster, Miss Phillips wrote a letter to Miss May Williams in which she described her experiences on the *Titanic*:

My Dear May,

I expect you have read of the awful wreck of the *Titanic*, and have seen my name in the list of survivors? I expect you have. Oh! I cannot tell you how dreadful it was! My darling father has perished in the wreck, and I feel almost out of my mind with grief. You know how good he was to me, so you can imagine just what I feel like. It seems almost too hard to bear, dear.

I cannot give you a full account of everything that happened. It would take too long to tell, but I will try to describe something of it. I had gone to bed on the Sunday night, but was not asleep. About a quarter to twelve we felt an awful crash – when the boat struck an iceberg – and was nearly rocked out of bed. Soon after I heard the engines stop. I rung up the steward to enquire what had happened, and he said it was nothing serious, and that we could go to sleep. I did not feel satisfied. Father came to my cabin, and asked if I would care to go on deck with him; so I did. We had not been there long when someone said: 'All on deck with lifebelts on.'

I cannot tell you, dear, how I felt in that moment! Dad and I got our belts on, and I went on deck again, and then all the women and children were put into the lifeboats and lowered. I saw my dear father for the last time in this world, and I almost felt I would have liked to die with him. To see that boat sinking, and to know he was there was too terrible to think of. After drifting around for nine hours, almost frozen with the intense cold, we were rescued by the *Carpathia*.

I cannot tell you the joy we felt when we were safely on the boat. We had hot coffee and brandy, which warmed us. We were sleeping in the smoke-room on the floor or anywhere, and were only too thankful to do so! We reached New York on Thursday evening, and my uncle was there to meet me. I cannot tell you how pleased I was to see him. We stayed at the Strand Hotel for the night, and the next day a lady, who is named Mrs Longstaffe, came and enquired for me, and took us to her home for the day, and provided me with some clothes. I lost everything I possessed, and had not a penny to call my own. I cannot forget the awful cries of those poor people who perished. It was simply awful![225]

BERK PICKARD **Third Class Passenger**

After the *Carpathia* reached New York, Mr Pickard made the following statement to the Senate *Titanic* inquiry:

Berk Pickard; No.229, Hebrew Immigrant Society. At the time I took passage on the *Titanic* I came from London. I am 32 years old. I am a leather worker; a bag maker. I was born in Russia, in Warsaw. My name was Berk Trembisky. I was for a long time in France and I assumed a French name. As regards private business, I am Pickard.

I was one of the third-class passengers on the *Titanic*. My cabin was No.10 in the steerage, at the stern. I first knew of the collision when it happened, about 10 minutes to 12. We had all been asleep, and all of a sudden we perceived a shock. We did not hear such a very terrible shock, but we knew something was wrong, and we jumped out of bed and we dressed ourselves and went out, and we could not get back again. I wanted to go back to get my things but I could not. The stewards would not allow us to go back. They made us all go forward on the deck. There were no doors locked to prevent us from going back. I did not take much notice of it, and I went to the deck. The other passengers started in arguing. One said that it was dangerous and the other said that it was not; one said white and the other said black. Instead of arguing with those people, I instantly went to the highest spot.

I said to myself that if the ship had to sink, I should be one of the last. That was my first idea, which was the best. I went and I found the door. There are always a few steps from this third class, with a movable door, and it is marked there that second-class passengers have no right to penetrate there. I found this door open so that I could go into the second class, where I did not find any people, only a few that climbed on the ladder and went into the first class, which I did. I found there only a few men and about two ladies. They had been putting them into lifeboats and as no women were there, we men sprang in the boat. We had only one woman and another young girl. There were two women. They just stood in front of me. We were lowered down, and when I was lowered down I saw the whole ship, as big as she was, the right side a little bit sinking, and I was far from imagining that it was the beginning of the end. When I was going away from the ship, of course I was rather frightened; I was sorry at not being on the ship, and I said to the seaman, 'I would rather be on the ship.' He was laughing at me, and he said, 'Do you not see we are sinking?' I was rather excited, and I said, 'It is fortunate that now the sea is nice, but perhaps in five minutes we will be turned over.' So I was in the boat until 5 o'clock in the morning.

In regard to the ship, I saw the ship very quickly started sinking, and one rail went under and then another, until in a half an hour, from my point of view, the ship sank altogether.

The steerage passengers, so far as I could see, were not prevented from getting up to the upper decks by anybody, or by closed doors, or anything else. While I was on the ship no one realised the real danger, not even the stewards. If the stewards knew, they were calm. It was their duty to try to make us believe there was nothing serious. Nobody was prevented from going up. They tried to keep us quiet. They said, 'Nothing serious is the matter.' Perhaps they did not know themselves. I did not realise it, the whole time, even to the last moment. Of course, I would never believe such a thing could happen.

The lifeboat I got into was an ordinary lifeboat. I do not know what number it was; I am sorry to say I did not look at it. There was some seaman in charge of it, who belonged to the ship. What kind of employment the seamen were in I do not know, but they belonged to the ship.

The only warning given to the steerage passengers after the collision was that we were ordered to take our life belts and go to the deck. There was no water in the steerage when I left.

That is all I know about it. I was one of the first to go. Of course, if I had stayed until a little bit later, I would have seen a little bit more. I was one of the luckiest ones, I think.[226]

LILY POTTER **First Class Passenger**

Following the disaster, Mrs Potter wrote the following letter to fellow survivor Archibald Gracie:

> There was no panic. Everyone seemed more stunned than anything else ... We watched for upwards of two hours the gradual sinking of the ship – first one row of light and then another disappearing at shorter and shorter intervals, with the

bow well bent in the water, as though ready for a dive. After the lights went out, some ten minutes before the end, she was like some great living thing who made a last superhuman effort to right herself and then, failing, dove bow forward to the unfathomable depths below.

We did not row except to get away from the suction of the sinking ship, but remained lashed to another boat until the *Carpathia* came in sight just before dawn.[227]

JANE QUICK **Status: Survivor**

On 25 April Mrs Quick wrote the following letter to her mother in England:

334 Brooklyn Avenue
Detroit
Michigan
April 25th, 1912

My darling Mother,

I hope this will find you quite well. I know how anxious and worried you must have felt when you heard about the wreck of the *Titanic*. I sent you a cablegram as soon as I arrived at New York. Now dear mother, I have been through a terrible a time as you must know, but I thank God that I was able to save the dear children and also myself. I will just tell you how it all happened. I had put the children to bed and went to bed myself at 9 o'clock on the Sunday. I was sound asleep when the accident happened. I did not feel the boat strike, a lady passenger knocked at my cabin door and told me to get up as there was something the matter, then the steward came and told us to put on our lifebelts and go up to the deck at once. Well, dear mother, you can just imagine how I felt. It was about half past eleven. I knew there was not time to dress, so I put on a few things to myself also to Winnie. I took Phyllis out of bed and put a shawl around her and went up on deck. A man took the baby from me and another put the lifebelts around us, then we had to climb an iron ladder to get to the lifeboats. Winnie was screaming nearly all the time, but Phyllis was asleep. The sailors put the children into the boat and I got in after them, then we had to be lowered from the top of the *Titanic* into the water. It was a terrible sight to see the husbands and wives saying good-bye to each other, as the men had to stand back for the women and children to [be] saved first. When we were about ¾ of a mile away from the *Titanic* I looked back and saw the boat sinking fast. The lights went out one after another, the machinery broke and, dear Mother that was my worst time when I heard the cries of those who were drowning. We were in the lifeboats about five or six hours. It was bitterly cold, as we were simply right among the icebergs. When morning came we saw the iceberg which we had struck. Well dear Mother, when we saw the lights of the *Carpathia* [it] was a welcome sight to us all. When we got alongside of her the children had to be taken up the side of the vessel in bags and I had to sit in a swing and be hauled up. My hands were nearly frozen, but I managed to catch hold of the rope, and after a time I found I was on the *Carpathia*. We were given hot drinks and a little clothing. When we were in the lifeboat Winnie said, 'I know we shall be saved, mamma, because I have asked God.' Fred was at New York to meet us. He was nearly wild with worry and excitement. We had to stay in New York one night, as it was after ten o'clock when we landed. The next day we had to go by train to Detroit. We caught the six o'clock train on Friday the 19th and we got to Detroit about half past two the next day. Mr and Mrs Parker and the young man that Fred used to lodge with was there to meet us. They are very kind indeed to one. Ever since I landed in New York I have been worried out of life & with the news-paper men as they were anxious to get my story to put in the paper. Now darling Mother, I expect you will be surprised to hear that I am appearing at the National Theater and telling the public how I was saved from a horrible death from the *Titanic*. I have to appear eight or nine times a day from the morning until half past ten at night. You will be frightened to hear I shall be paid about 400 dollars or eighty pounds in English money for one week, but I can assure you it takes a lot of nerve to speak to hundreds of people every time. This is my third day, and I shall not be sorry when the week is over. Winnie and Phyllis send their darling Grandma lots of love and kisses. They have very bad colds and coughing with their exposure in the lifeboat, but Fred has got medicine for them and we are rubbing their chest every night with turpentine and fresh lard. It is a splendid thing. When I write next time I am going to send you a nice little present out of my own money, also the money for the clubs. I am glad to tell you I have kept up remarkably well, in fact I am a marvel to myself, for if I had given in we should all have been drowned, but I thank God that he gave me the strength to save myself and also the dear children. Now I hope you are looking after yourself and not worrying about us, as we are alright now. So now I will conclude with all my love to my darling Mother. Good-bye for the time and God bless you. I am writing this at the theatre.

xxxxxxxx
Jeannie.
Dear Mother, will you go up and tell James Quick our address is
334 Brooklyn Avenue
Detroit
Michigan
U.S. America[228]

LILLIAN RENOUF — Second Class Passenger

On 16 May the widowed Mrs Renouf wrote the following letter to fellow survivor Lilian Bentham:

Thurs 16. 1912

My dear Lilian

In answer to your most welcome letter of last week was, so glad to hear from you but sorry to hear you had been ill with your back. I do hope you are all right again. Well dear as for myself I don't get on like I would like to but dear I am so Broken hearted I can't help it – I do miss my dear husband and Brothers and Bert [Denbury].

Don't forget to write again to me dear my Cough is not better yet.[229]

GEORGE RHEIMS — First Class Passenger

On 19 April Mr Rheims wrote the following letter to his wife Mary:

... I dined with Joe Sunday evening and went up to my cabin to go to sleep around 11:00 P.M. I felt, being in the front part of the ship, a strong shock and heard a noise that sounded like steam escaping, it was dreadful. I thought we had an accident in the engine. After one fourth of an hour there was an announcement informing us that we had collided with an iceberg but that there was no danger and we should all go back to sleep!!! Since I noticed that the ship wasn't listing I thought nothing of it. Soon after Joe came to join me and we stayed together until the end. Around 11:30 all passengers left their cabins. The ship tilted more and more. An officer came to tell us to put on our life jackets. You can well imagine how this news affected me!

I went down to my cabin to put on some warm clothing and my life jacket. Joe did the same and rejoined me on the boat's deck, where by now a crowd of people gathered. We started lowering the lifeboats down in the ocean – 16 lifeboats for [a ship that held] 3,000 people. The men were forbidden to use the lifeboats. A few men – traitors – did not hesitate to jump into the lifeboats just the same. In general the people's attitude was admirable. It took one and a half hours for all 16 lifeboats to be lowered. A few of them were only half full. As the last lifeboat was leaving I saw an officer kill a man with one gun shot. The man was trying to climb aboard that last lifeboat. Since there was nothing left to do, the officer told us, 'Gentlemen, each man for himself, goodbye.' He gave us a military salute, then turned the revolver to his head and shot himself. This was a man!!!

We were about 1,500 people left on board without any means of escape. It was death for us all. I cannot convey how calm everyone was. We said goodbye to all our friends and everyone prepared himself to die properly. Joe took both my hands and said, 'George, if you survive look after my babies. If I live you will not have to worry about Mary.' I then left him for one minute to go back to my cabin and find your photograph, then went up to join Joe on the deck. We then undressed, keeping on only our underwear. I did not lose one second of composure and had decided to jump overboard to save myself by swimming. I cannot describe the unbelievable things I saw at that moment. Suddenly the ship started nose-diving and I was thrown to the deck by an explosion. I found myself entangled in chairs and ropes. I was able to free myself. Joe wanted to go back in the rear of the ship. I told him it would mean death and that he should follow me. He told me that he could not swim well enough. Then I took my momentum [a running leap] and jumped overboard. The fall seemed endless, then suddenly icy cold and a long plunge down into the ocean. When I came up again I started swimming vigorously to get away from the ship fearing that I would be dragged down with it. It was frightfully cold. Suddenly I saw the *Titanic* going straight down with horrible explosions and piercing screams. All the passengers were pressed against the railing like flies. There was a big whirlpool swirling movement, then silence. Suddenly there were pitiful pleas that I will never forget. It was all those who were able to float crying for help. It was atrociously grim, mysterious – supernatural. This lasted for half an hour, then all was quiet. The poor people went down.

I swam alone in the night, when at a distance I noticed a raft, half sunk and filled with men. It took me I suppose 15 minutes to reach it. At first they refused to let me come aboard, but I was able to persuade them after all. I stood up on the raft. We were about 20 men and women, with icy water up to our thighs. We had to balance ourselves to avoid capsizing. I stayed six hours in my underwear, shaking with cold. Twice I thought of throwing myself into the ocean and each time the thought of you held me back. I regained courage and resumed – I don't know how – my efforts to stay on the raft. What a horrible night! We had to push back about 10 poor people who wanted to climb aboard. We were filled to the limit. During the night eight people died from cold or desperation. I am sparing you the details for they are too frightful. I had the pleasure to be able to save a poor man, father of nine children, who asked me to give him a picture of myself with a dedication fit for the King of England. At 8:00 in the morning a lifeboat from the *Titanic* came to pick us up and took us aboard the *Carpathia*. They took marvellous care of us.

I had some trouble walking, my feet being frostbitten. Here I am settled at Harry's and I think that a little rest of a few days will do me a lot of good.

I affirm that I am a little tired. You must not hold it against me for ending this letter so abruptly.[230]

ELIZABETH ROBERT — First Class Passenger

After the *Carpathia* arrived in New York, Mrs Robert wrote the following brief account for publication:

> I had retired for the night. The crash of the ship against the iceberg was so violent I was thrown out of my berth. I did not realise what had happened. I managed to get on a few clothes when we heard the shouts of men and the screams of women.
>
> I will never forget those cries. I rushed out of my cabin and was swept along by the rush of passengers. But in a few seconds it seemed that something like order was being restored. At least men were shouting orders and, remarkable as it may seem, people seemed to obey them.
>
> Since we have been saved we recall that the men did all in their power to help the weak first. Of course, there were mad struggles, but I do not know who could be blamed.
>
> I was trampled upon, pushed and shoved. There was a dear, grey-haired woman by my side. She kept praying and telling us to try and take our time. I recall that she seemed to talk in a whisper, but we seemed to hear and understand her, even in the midst of all the excitement.
>
> We were told that we must get in the boats. I have no idea when I was lowered over the side, or what boat I was put in, but I recall some of the officers were actually polite, and some of the men passengers were saying, 'Be careful, Madame. Step right along. There is no danger. Be calm.'
>
> I was lowered in a boat and was ordered into a seat. I did not have the slightest idea what time it was. I did not even try to guess. I was more than half numb with the cold.
>
> I doubt if many of the passengers realised that we floated around on that ice-covered ocean for hours.
>
> We did not seem to think about being saved. I have heard some of the passengers tell, on the *Carpathia* during the last few days, how they thought we had been a week in the boat. But to me it is much like a blank period in my life.
>
> I recall the shout of joy that was given when we sighted our rescuing steamer. I was told that it was after 8 o'clock in the morning when we boarded the ship. I do not know. Once on the ship everything possible was done for us.[231]

EDWARD RYAN **Third Class Passenger**

After arriving in New York, Mr Ryan wrote the following letter to his parents in Ireland:

Dearest Father and Mother,

I had a terrible experience. I shall never forget it. You will see all about it in the papers which I'll send on to you. I was the last man to jump into the last boat. I stood on the *Titanic* and kept cool, although she was sinking fast. She had gone down about forty feet by now. The last boat was about being rowed away when I thought in a second if I could only pass out I'd be all right. I had a towel round my neck. I just threw this over my head and left it hang at the back. I wore my waterproof overcoat. I then walked very stiff past the officers, who had declared they'd shoot the first man that dare pass out. They didn't notice me. They thought I was a woman. I grasped a girl who was standing by in despair, and jumped with her thirty feet into the boat. An Italian and myself rowed away as fast as we could, and soon after the great liner sank. We were for seven long hours in the boat, and were nearly dead for want of a drink. I attribute my safety to Almighty God. We were treated fine on the *Carpathia* and landed in New York on Thursday. I was released from St Vincent's Hospital on Saturday, hale and hearty, even without having got a cold, and went on to Troy on Sunday. I'll tell you more of my experience in my next letter.[232]

EMILY RYERSON **First Class Passenger**

On 9 May Mrs Ryerson submitted the following deposition to the Senate *Titanic* inquiry:

Emily Borie Ryerson, being duly sworn, deposes and says: I reside in the city of Chicago, Ill. I was a passenger on the steamship *Titanic* on April 14, 1912. At the time of collision I was awake and heard the engines stop, but felt no jar. My husband was asleep, so I rang and asked the steward, Bishop, what was the matter. He said, 'There is talk of an iceberg, ma'am, and they have stopped, not to run into it.' I told him to keep me informed if there were any orders. It was bitterly cold, so I put on a warm wrapper and looked out the window (we were in the large cabins on the B deck, very far aft) and saw the stars shining and a calm sea, but heard no noise. It was 12 o'clock. After about 10 minutes I went out in the corridor, and saw far off people hurrying on deck. A passenger ran by and called out, 'Put on your life belts and come up on the boat deck.' I said, 'Where did you get those orders?' He said, 'From the captain.' I went back then and told Miss Bowen and my daughter, who were in the next room, to dress immediately, roused my husband and the two younger children, who were in a room on the other side, and then remembered my maid, who had a room near us. Her door was locked and I had some difficulty in waking her. By this time my husband was fully dressed, and we could hear the noise of feet tramping on the deck overhead. He was quite calm and cheerful and helped me put the life belts on the children and on my maid. I was paralysed with fear of not all getting on deck together in time, as there were seven of us. I would not let my younger daughter dress, but she only put on a fur coat, as I did over her nightgown. My husband cautioned us all to keep together, and we went up to A deck, where we found quite a group of people we knew. Everyone had on a life belt, and they all were very quiet and self-possessed.

We stood about there for quite a long time – fully half an hour, I should say. I know my maid ran down to the cabin and got some of my clothes. Then we were ordered to the boat deck. I only remember the second steward at the head of the stairs, who told us where to go. My chief thought and that of everyone else was, I know, not to make a fuss and to do as we were told. My husband joked with some of the women he knew, and I heard him say, 'Don't you hear the band playing?' I begged him to let me stay with him, but he said, 'You must obey orders. When they say, "Women and children to the boats" you must go when your turn comes. I'll stay with John Thayer. We will be all right. You take a boat going to New York.' This referred to the belief that there was a circle of ships around waiting. The *Olympic*, the *Baltic*, were some of the names I heard. All this time we could hear the rockets going up – signals of distress. Again, we were ordered down to A deck, which was partly enclosed. We saw people getting into boats, but waited our turn. There was a rough sort of steps constructed to get up to the window. My boy, Jack, was with me. An officer at the window said, 'That boy can't go.' My husband stepped forward and said, 'Of course, that boy goes with his mother; he is only 13.' So they let him pass. They also said, 'No more boys.' I turned and kissed my husband, and as we left he and the other men I knew – Mr Thayer, Mr Widener, and others – were all standing there together very quietly. The decks were lighted, and as you went through the window it was as if you stepped out into the dark. We were flung into the boats. There were two men – an officer inside and a sailor outside – to help us. I fell on top of the women who were already in the boat, and scrambled to the bow with my eldest daughter. Miss Bowen and my boy were in the stern and my second daughter was in the middle of the boat with my maid. Mrs Thayer, Mrs Widener, Mrs Astor, and Miss Eustis were the only others I knew in our boat.

Presently an officer called out from the upper deck, 'How many women are there in that boat?' Someone answered, 'Twenty-four.' 'That's enough; lower away.'

The ropes seemed to stick at one end and the boat tipped, someone called for a knife, but it was not needed until we got into the water, as it was but a short distance, and I then realised for the first time how far the ship had sunk. The deck we left was only about 20 feet from the sea. I could see all the portholes open and water washing in, and the decks still lighted. Then they called out, 'How many seamen have you,' and they answered one. 'That is not enough,' said the officer, 'I will send you another,' and he sent a sailor down the rope. In a few minutes after several other men not sailors came down the ropes over the davits and dropped into our boat. The order was given to pull away, then they rowed off – the sailors, the women, anyone – but made little progress; there was a confusion of orders; we rowed toward the stern, someone shouted something about a gangway, and no one seemed to know what to do. Barrels and chairs were being thrown overboard. Then suddenly, when we still seemed very near, we saw the ship was sinking rapidly. I was in the bow of the boat with my daughter and turned to see the great ship take a plunge toward the bow, the two forward funnels seemed to lean and then she seemed to break in half as if cut with a knife, and as the bow went under the lights went out; the stern stood up for several minutes, black against the stars, and then that, too, plunged down, and there was no sound for what seemed like hours, and then began the cries for help of people drowning all around us, which seemed to go on forever. Someone called out, 'Pull for your lives, or you'll be sucked under,' and everyone that could rowed like mad. I could see my younger daughter and Mrs Thayer and Mrs Astor rowing, but there seemed to be no suction. Then we turned to pick up some of those in the water. Some of the women protested, but others persisted, and we dragged in six or seven men; the men we rescued were principally stokers, stewards, sailors, etc., and were so chilled and frozen already they could hardly move. Two of them died in the stern later and many were raving and moaning and delirious most of the time. We had no lights or compass. There were several babies in the boat, but there was no milk or water. (I believe these were all stowed away somewhere, but no one knew where, and as the bottom of the boat was full of water and the boat full of people it was very difficult to find anything.)

After the *Titanic* sank we saw no lights, and no one seemed to know what direction to take. Lowe, the officer in charge of the boat, had called out earlier for all to tie together, so we now heard his whistle, and as soon as we could make out the other boats in the dark, five of us were tied together, and we drifted about without rowing, as the sea was calm, waiting for the dawn. It was very cold, and soon a breeze sprang up, and it was hard to keep our heavy boat bow on; but as the cries died down we could see dimly what seemed to be a raft with about 20 men standing on it, back to back. It was the overturned boat; and as the sailors on our boat said we could still carry 8 or 10 more people, we called for another boat to volunteer and go to rescue them. So we two cut loose our painters and between us got all the men off. They were nearly gone and could not have held out much longer. Then, when the sun rose we saw the *Carpathia* standing up about 5 miles away, and for the first time saw the icebergs all around us. The *Carpathia* steamed toward us until it was full daylight; then she stopped and began picking up boats, and we got on board about 8 o'clock. Very soon after we got on board they took a complete list of the names of all survivors. The kindness and the efficiency of all the arrangements on the *Carpathia* for our comfort can never be too highly praised.

The foregoing affidavit is made at the request of William Alden Smith, chairman of the Senate investigating committee, in relation of the *Titanic* disaster.

Emily Borie Ryerson[233]

ADOLPHE SAALFELD **First Class Passenger**

After arriving in New York, Mr Saalfeld typed up the following account of his experiences on the *Titanic*:

> In smoking room on Sunday night 11.45 – slight jar felt which for a moment made us think some breakage machinery, but soon engines stopped and stepping from verandah café iceberg plainly seen and felt. Most people abed. Boat absolutely quiet even.
>
> 5 minutes later, going boat deck, noticed very slight list – coming A Deck saw boats being lowered and noticed general reluctance people going into them. Then I saw a few men and women go into a boat and I followed and when lowered pushed off, and rowed some distance fearing suction in case *Titanic* sinking – All expected to go back after damage patched up, but as we drifted away gradually, saw *Titanic* sink lower and lower and finally lights on her went out, and others in my boat said that they saw her disappear. Our boat was then nearly 2 miles away but pitiful cries could be plainly heard.[234]

JULIUS SAP **Third Class Passenger**

Following the disaster, Mr Sap wrote the following letter to his family in Belgium:

> Detroit, Michigan,
> 28 April 1912
>
> The day was almost broken when everybody came on the boat. The first and the second class passengers were up on the deck earlier than usual. Yes, it was a Sunday, a really festive day. Everyone was happy. Even our small number of Belgians were together and satisfied. There was music from the morning until the evening and the ship was beautifully joyous when we went to our rooms; the third class always had to go down earlier. I don't know what happened while I was sleeping. Around 12 PM I felt cold water coming into my bed, I was suddenly completely awake, I took my clothes and a lifebelt. I ran to the other Belgians who were sleeping a bit higher. When I surprised them in their sleep, they couldn't believe my words when I told them that I thought the ship was sinking.
>
> When we arrived on the deck, we saw that half of the boat had already sunk and that the people that were still on board were up on the keel [stern?]. The cry for help was deafening and heart-rending. Hundreds of people were swimming in the cold water crying for help to God and to the Holy Mary to be saved from a horrible death. They jumped into the sea one after the other without knowing what to hold on to. The people of Swevezeelde remained together and helped each other up the

keel [stern?], with the help of the flagpole, where the flag was still attached. Every lifeboat had already left and none of us had been offered an opportunity to save ourselves. As we couldn't get any help, we tried to do something ourselves. We will never forget the last words of Emelie Vandemoortele, wife of Julius Plancke.

Hanging on to the hair of her husband, she shouted at me: 'Don't struggle any longer, let death come and God will welcome us in Heaven.' And then the words of Augusta Van der Plancke! Our last moments had come. The poor girl held my hand and asked me to save her. I couldn't hold back my tears. There, in front of me, there was a child that put every hope and trust in me. But unfortunately I was powerless and couldn't help or save her. Blood filled my head: I became indifferent. I pushed myself away and jumped into the sea. Hundreds of people seemed to be around me. I swam to a boat and was able to get in. A sweet voice talked to me; a rough hand grabbed me by my hair and I was rescued! A raw voice shouted several times: 'Let up!' What did it mean? I tried to climb into the boat. There was a shot. Thank God! I was not hit. I heard again this sweet voice that reminded me of my mother's. This time I understood what she wanted to say. This good lady was talking to a small girl who held my hand to make sure that I didn't sink in the deep. A little later, I was in the boat; some men tried to throw me out, but the women covered me with their clothes and I lay covered for 8 hours in the bottom of the boat, thanks to my well-doers. The day broke; I was allowed to show myself. I took a last look at the *Titanic*. And an unforgettable play appeared in front of my eyes; I watched on my knees and with upraised hands; I saw the people from my village pray, and a sorrowful song played.

There was a terrible explosion. The shock threw me in the water to swim. I awoke like out of a dream and I couldn't see anything else but corpses floating in the water. I thought: am I going to lose my senses? I prayed to God for help and a new feeling made my power stronger.

There was a shot; what I saw: a person fall from a boat into the sea. What cruelty does Faith still have in store for me? But the ones who saved me talked to me; I couldn't understand them. I fell on my knees. I thanked them while big tears were rolling on my face. The son of one of my rescuers died in a boat after having floated for some hours!...

Alphonse Warnez, a Belgian 3rd class passenger, works in a car factory in Detroit now, together with his brother, whom he had already thought to be dead. When the big ship sank, he was driven from the lifeboat with a revolver; he jumped into the sea and tried three times to get into another lifeboat, but he was pushed away every time. His fingers are still in pieces because of the hits he got. Finally he found another lifeboat and a young lady helped him to get aboard, in spite of the others hitting him.

Julius Sap[235]

JOSEPH SCARROTT **Crew (Able Bodied Seaman)**

In May 1912 Mr Scarrott wrote the following account of the *Titanic* disaster:

The night of April 14, 1912 will never be forgotten. It was a beautiful starlight night, no wind, and the sea was as calm as a lake, but the air was very cold. Everybody was in good spirits and everything throughout the ship was going smoothly.

All of a sudden she crashed into an iceberg, which shook the giant liner from stem to stern. The shock of the collision was not so great as one would expect considering the size of the iceberg and the speed the ship was going, which was about 22½ knots an hour.

I was underneath the forecastle enjoying a smoke at the time. It happened about twenty minutes to twelve o'clock. The shaking of the ship seemed as though the engines had suddenly been reversed to full speed astern.

Those of the crew who were asleep in their bunks turned out, and we all rushed on deck to see what was the matter. We found the ship had struck an iceberg as there was a large quantity of ice and snow on the starboard side of the fore deck. We did not think it very serious so went below again cursing the iceberg for disturbing us.

We had no sooner got below when the boatswain called all hands on deck to uncover and turn all the boats out ready for lowering. We did not think then there was anything serious. The general idea of the crew was that we were going to get the boats ready in case of emergency, and the sooner we got the job done the quicker we should get below again.

The port side boats were got ready first, and then the starboard ones. As the work proceeded passengers were coming on deck with lifebelts on.

Then we realised the situation.

Every man went to his station. There was no panic, everybody was cool, and when the boats were ready the usual order was given, 'Women and children first.' That order was carried out without any class distinction whatever.

In some cases we had to force women into the boats as they would not leave their husbands. The men stood back to allow the women to pass, except in one or two cases where men tried to rush, but they were very soon stopped. This occurred at the boat I was in charge of – No.14. About half-a-dozen foreigners tried to jump in before I had my complement of women and children, but I drove them back with the boat's tiller.

Shortly afterwards the fifth officer, Mr Lowe, came and took charge of the boat. I told him what had happened. He drew his revolver and fired two shots between the boat and the ship's side into the water as a warning to any further attempts of that sort.

When our boat was lowered we had fifty-four women, four children, one sailor, one window-cleaner, two firemen, three stewards, and one officer; total, sixty-six souls.

When the boat was in the water we rowed clear of the ship. We then saw four other boats well clear and fairly well filled with women and children. We went to them and found none of them had an officer in charge. So the fifth officer took charge of the lot, ordering them to keep with him.

The ship sank shortly afterwards, I should say about 2:20 a.m. on the 15th, which would be two hours and forty minutes after she struck. The sight of that grand ship going down will never be forgotten. She slowly went down bow first with a slight list to starboard until the water reached the bridge, then she went quicker. When the third funnel had nearly disappeared I heard four explosions, which I took to be the bursting of the boilers. The ship was right up on end then.

Suddenly she broke in two between the third and fourth funnel. The after part of the ship came down on the water in its normal position and seemed as if it was going to remain afloat, but it only remained a minute or two and then sank. The lights were burning right up till she broke in two.

The cries from the poor souls struggling in the water sounded terrible in the stillness of the night. It seemed to go through you like a knife.

Our officer then ordered all the boats under his charge to row towards where the ship went down to see if we could pick up anybody. Some of our boats picked up a few. I cannot say how many. After that we tied all our boats together so as to form a large object on the water which would be seen quicker than a single boat by a passing vessel.

We divided the passengers of our boat amongst the other four, and then taking one man from each boat so as to make a crew we rowed away amongst the wreckage as we heard cries for help coming from that direction.

When we got to it the sight we saw was awful. We were amongst hundreds of dead bodies floating in lifebelts. We could only see four alive. The first one we picked up was a male passenger. He died shortly after we got him in the boat. After a hard struggle we managed to get the other three. One of these we saw kneeling as if in prayer upon what appeared to be part of a staircase. He was only about twenty yards away from us but it took us half-an-hour to push our boat through the wreckage and bodies to get to him; even then we could not get very close so we put out an oar for him to get hold of and so pulled him to the boat.

All the bodies we saw seemed as if they had perished with the cold as their limbs were all cramped up. As we left that awful scene we gave way to tears. It was enough to break the stoutest heart.

Just then we sighted the lights of a steamer, which proved to be the steamship *Carpathia* of the Cunard line. What a relief that was. We then made sail and went back to our other boats.

By this time day was just beginning to dawn. We then saw we were surrounded with icebergs and field ice. Some of the fields of ice were from sixteen to twenty miles long.

On our way back we saw one of our collapsible boats waterlogged; there were about eighteen persons on it, so we went and took them off. We left two dead bodies on it, and we were told two others had died and had fallen off.

All of our boats then proceeded towards the *Carpathia*. She had stopped right over where our ship had gone down. She had got our wireless message for assistance.

When we got alongside we were got aboard as soon as possible. We found some survivors had already been picked up. Everything was in readiness for us – dry clothes, blankets, beds, hot coffee, spirits, etc.; everything to comfort us. The last of the survivors was got aboard about 8:30 a.m.

The dead bodies that were in some of the boats were taken aboard and after identification were given a proper burial. They were two male passengers, one fireman, and one able seaman.

We steamed about in the vicinity for a few hours in the hope of finding some more survivors, but did not find any. During that time wives were enquiring for husbands, sisters for brothers, and children for their parents, but many a sad face told the result.

The *Carpathia* was bound from New York to Gibraltar, but the captain decided to return to New York with us. We arrived there about nine p.m. on Thursday, the 18th. We had good weather during the trip, but it was a sad journey.

A list of the survivors was taken as soon as we had left the scene of the disaster.

On arrival at New York everything possible was ready for our immediate assistance – clothing, money, medical aid, and good accommodation, in fact, I think it would have been impossible for the people of America to have treated us better.

Before closing this narrative, I must say that the passengers when they were in the boats, especially the women, were brave and assisted the handling of the boats a great deal.

Thank God the weather was fine or I do not think there would have been one soul left to tell the tale.

J. Scarrott[236]

IMANITA SHELLEY — First Class Passenger

On 15 May Mrs Shelley made the following deposition for the Senate *Titanic* inquiry:

Mrs Imanita Shelley, of lawful age, being first duly sworn as regards the *Titanic* disaster, on her oath deposes and says:

That her mother, Mrs Lutie Davis Parrish, of Woodford County, Ky., and herself embarked on the White Star steamship *Titanic* at Southampton, England, upon the 10th day of April, 1912, having purchased the best second-class accommodation sold by said company.

That instead of being assigned to the accommodation purchased, were taken to a small cabin many decks down in the ship, which was so small that it could only be called a cell. It was impossible to open a regulation steamer trunk in said cabin. It was impossible for a third person to enter said cabin unless both occupants first of all crawled into their bunks.

That the stewardess was sent to the chief purser demanding transfer to accommodation purchased. That he replied he could do nothing until the boat had left Queenstown, Ireland, when he would check up all tickets and find out if there was any mistake.

That after leaving Queenstown Mrs L.D. Parrish made 11 trips herself to the purser asking for transfer, only to be put off with promises. That at 9 o'clock p.m., no one having come to make them to better quarters, Mrs Shelley wrote a note to the purser to the effect that she had paid for the best second-class accommodation on the ship and had the receipts to prove it; that she was very ill and, owing to the freezing cold of the cabin, was in great danger; that if he, the purser, refused to act she, Mrs Shelley, would appeal to the captain; that if neither would act she realised she would have to wait until reaching America for redress, but most assuredly would claim damages if she lived to reach her native land.

That the result of this letter was the arrival of four stewards to carry her to the room paid for, who offered apology after apology.

That the stewardess, on being asked what the purser had said on reading the note, replied: 'He asked first if you were really so very sick, to which I answered there was no doubt about that. Then the purser asked me if there was such a cabin on board the *Titanic*, where a cabin trunk could not be opened; to which I replied in the affirmative. I also told him that the cabin was entirely too small for two women, and that two men could not hardly fit in; that it was impossible for myself or the steward to enter the cabin and to wait upon the occupants unless both of them first climbed into their berths. The purser then told me that he would have to act at once, or the company would get into trouble.'

That after being transferred to this new cabin the second-class physician, Dr Simpson, called from three to four times a day; that he feared the attack of tonsillitis brought on by the chill would become diphtheretic and ordered Mrs Shelley to remain in her cabin.

That this cabin, though large and roomy, was not furnished in the comfortable manner as the same accommodation procured on the Cunard and other lines; that it looked in a half-finished condition; that this room was just as cold as the cell from which we had just been removed, and on asking the steward to have the heat turned on, he answered that it was impossible, as the heating system for the second-class cabins refused to work. That of all the second-class cabins, only three – the three first cabins to be reached by the heat- had any heat at all, and that the heat was so intense there that the occupants had complained to the purser, who had ordered the heat shut off entirely; consequently the rooms were like ice houses all of the voyage, and Mrs L.D. Parrish, when not waiting on her sick daughter, was obliged to go to bed to keep warm.

That afterwards, when on board the *Carpathia*, Mrs Shelley took pains to inquire of steerage passengers as to whether or not they had heat in the steerage of the *Titanic* and received the answer that there was the same trouble with their heating plant, too.

That although the servants on board were most willing, they had a hard time to do their work; that the stewardess could not even get a tray to serve Mrs Shelley's meals and had to bring the plates and dishes one at a time in her hands, making the service very slow and annoying. The food, though good and plentiful, was ruined by this trouble in serving. That although both steward and stewardess appealed time and time again to the heads of their departments, no relief was obtained: there seemed to be no organisation at all.

That in the ladies toilet room only part of the fixtures had been installed, some of the said fixtures being still in crates.

That in the early evening of the night of the accident the temperature had fallen considerably, so that all on board realised we were in the ice belt. There were rumours of wireless messages from other ships warning of icebergs close at hand. It was also reported that certain first-class passengers had asked if the ship was to show down whilst going through the ice belts and had been told by the captain that, on the contrary, the ship would be speeded through.

That at the moment of the collision we were awakened out of sleep by the shock, and especially by the stopping of the engines.

That excited voices were heard outside in the passage, saying that an iceberg had been run into. That after continued ringing of the steward bell a steward, but not the regular one, came and insisted that all was well and for all passengers to go back to bed. Afterwards, on board the *Carpathia*, a first-cabin passenger, a Mme Baxter, of Montreal, Canada, told Mrs Shelley that she had sent her son to the captain at the time of the collision to find out what to do. That her son had found the captain in a card game, and he had laughingly assured him that there was no danger and to advise his mother to go back to bed.

That about three-quarters of an hour after returning to their berths a steward came running down the passage bursting open the cabin doors and calling 'All on deck with life belts on.' That this steward brought Mrs Parrish and Mrs Shelley each a life belt and showed them how to tie them on. That they were told to go up to the top deck, the boat deck. That as Mrs Shelley was very weak, it took several minutes to reach the upper deck. That Mr and Mrs Isidor Straus, who had known of Mrs Shelley being so ill, met them on the way and helped them to the upper deck, where they found a chair for her and made her sit down.

That owing to the great number of persons on the deck Mrs Shelley was not able to see anything of the handling of boats except the one she herself was placed in. There was practically no excitement on the part of anyone during this time, the majority seeming to think that the big boat could not sink altogether, and that it was better to stay on the steamer than trust to the lifeboats. After sitting in the chair for about five minutes one of the sailors ran to Mrs Shelley and implored her to get in the lifeboat that was then being launched. He informed Mrs Shelley that it was the last boat on the ship, and that unless she got into this one she would have to take her chances on the steamer, and that as she had been so sick she ought to take to the boat and make sure. Mrs Straus advised taking to the boats, and, pushing her mother toward the sailor, Mrs Shelley made for the davits where the boat hung. It was found impossible to swing the davits in, which left a space of between 4 and 5 feet between the edge of the deck and the suspended boat. The sailor picked up Mrs Parrish and threw her bodily into the boat.

Mrs Shelley jumped and landed safely. That two men of the ship's crew manned this boat at the time of launching, one of whom said he was a stoker and the other a ship's baker. That at the time of launching these were the only men in the boat. That at the time of lowering the boat it seemed to be as full of passengers as the seating capacity called for, but owing to the excitement no thought of numbers entered Mrs Shelley's head. The boat appeared to be filled with as many as could get in without overcrowding, all of them women and children, with the exception of the two mentioned above.

That on trying to lower the boat the tackle refused to work and it took considerable time, about 15 minutes, it is believed, to reach the water. That on reaching the water the casting-off apparatus would not work and the ropes had to be cut.

That just as they reached the water a crazed Italian jumped from the deck into the lifeboat, landing on Mrs Parrish, severely bruising her right side and leg. This gave them one extra man.

After cutting loose from the ship the orders were to pull out toward the other boats and get as far away from the probable suction which would ensue if the steamer should sink. Orders were also given to keep in sight of the green light of the ship's boat which had been sent out ahead to look for help. That on reaching a distance of about 100 yards from the *Titanic* a loud explosion or noise was heard, followed closely by another, and the sinking of the big vessel began.

Throughout the entire period from the striking of the icebergs and taking to the boats the ship's crew behaved in an ideal manner. Not a man tried to get into a boat unless ordered to, and many were seen to strip off their clothing and wrap around the women and children who came up half clad from their beds. Mrs Shelley feels confident that she speaks the truth when she says that with the exception of those few men ordered to man the boats all other sailors saved had gone down with the ship and were miraculously saved afterwards. Mrs Shelley says that no crew could have behaved in a more perfect manner and that they proved themselves men in every sense of the word. That after the sinking of the ship the boat they were in picked up several struggling in the water and were fortunate enough to rescue 30 sailors who had gone down with the ship, but who had been miraculously blown out of the water after one of the explosions and been thrown near a derelict collapsible boat to which they had managed to cling. That after taking all those men on board the boat was so full that many feared they would sink, and it was suggested that some of the other boats should take some of these rescued ones on board; but they refused, for fear of sinking.

Mrs Shelley states that she does not know what the official number of her lifeboat was, nor the official numbers of the boats finally rescued by the *Carpathia*: that on conversing with members of the crew and other survivors on board the *Carpathia* it was told Mrs Shelley that 13 boats had been picked up; that the first boat to be picked up by the *Carpathia* was what was called the signal boat – the one with the green light – which all followed as a guide and which had been picked up about 3 or half past 3 in the morning; that the boat Mrs Shelley was in was picked up shortly after 8 o'clock in the morning.

That as to equipment of the lifeboats there was none in her boat except four oars and a mast, which latter was useless; there was no water nor any food; that there was neither compass nor binnacle light nor any kind of lantern; that on questioning occupants of other lifeboats they told her the same story – lack of food, water, compass, and lights, and that several boats had no oars or only two or three.

That one of that *Titanic*'s crew who was saved told that no positions had been assigned to any of the crew in regard to lifeboat service, as is the rule, and that that was one of the reasons of the confusion in assigning men to manage the lifeboats when the accident did occur.

That right after the *Titanic* began to sink a steamer was sighted about 2 miles away, and all were cheered up; as it was figured that they would all be picked up inside an hour or so; that, however, their hopes were blighted when the steamer's lights suddenly disappeared. Further deponent saith not.

Mrs Imanita Shelley[237]

Following the disaster, Mrs Shelley wrote the following letter to Edith Harper, the secretary of victim William T. Stead:

My Dear Miss Harper,

Your letter received and I hasten to grant your request. I was only on deck a short time, until Mother and I took to the lifeboat.

Your beloved Chief, together with Mr and Mrs Straus, attracted attention even in that awful hour, on account of their superhuman composure and divine work. When we, the last lifeboat left, and they could do no more, he stood alone, at the edge of the deck, near the stern, in silence and what seemed to me a prayerful attitude, or one of profound meditation. You ask if he wore a life-belt. Alas! no, they were too scarce.

My last glimpse of the *Titanic* showed him standing in the same attitude and place.

Many thanks for the heather and forwarding my letter to Julia from whom I hope to hear shortly. When in America you will ever find a cordial welcome awaiting you, or any member of Mr Stead's family, where ever we may be. My husband and I send our very kindest regards to them and yourself and wish Julia's Bureau Library the greatest success.

Very sincerely,

Imanita Shelley[238]

ELIZABETH SHUTE — First Class Passenger

Following the disaster, Miss Shute wrote the following account of her experience on the *Titanic*:

Such a biting cold air poured into my stateroom that I could not sleep, and the air had a strange odour, as if it came from a clammy cave. I had noticed that same odour in the ice cave on the Eiger glacier. It all came back to me so vividly that I could not sleep, but lay in my berth until the cabin grew so very cold that I got up and turned on my electric stove. It threw a cheerful red glow around, and the room was soon comfortable; but I lay waiting. I have always loved both day and night on shipboard, and am never fearful of anything, but now I was nervous about the icy air.

Suddenly a queer quivering ran under me, apparently the whole length of the ship. Startled by the very strangeness of the shivering motion, I sprang to the floor. With too perfect a trust in that mighty vessel I again lay down. Someone knocked at my door, and the voice of a friend [Edith Graham] said: 'Come quickly to my cabin; an iceberg has just passed our window; I know we have just struck one.'

No confusion, no noise of any kind, one could believe no danger imminent. Our stewardess came and said she could learn nothing. Looking out into the companionway I saw heads appearing asking questions from half-closed doors. All sepulchrally still; no excitement. I sat down again. My friend was by this time dressed; still her daughter and I talked on, Margaret pretending to eat a sandwich. Her hand shook so that the bread kept parting company from the chicken. Then I saw she was frightened, and for the first time I was too, but why get dressed, as no one had given the slightest hint of any possible danger? An officer's cap passed the door. I asked: 'Is there an accident or danger of any kind?' 'None, so far as I know,' was his courteous answer, spoken quietly and most kindly. This same officer then entered a cabin a little distance down the companionway and, by this time distrustful of everything, I listened intently, and distinctly heard, 'We can keep the water out for a while.' Then, and not until then, did I realise the horror of an accident at sea. Now it was too late to dress; no time for a waist, but a coat and skirt were soon on; slippers were quicker than shoes; the stewardess put on our life-preservers, and we were just ready when Mr Roebling came to tell us he would take us to our friend's mother, who was waiting above.

We passed by the palm room, where two short hours before we had listened to a beautiful concert, just as one might sit in one's own home. With never a realising sense of being on the ocean, why should not one forget? – no motion, no noise of machinery, nothing suggestive of a ship. Happy, laughing men and women constantly passing up and down those broad, strong staircases, and the music went on and the ship went on – nearer and nearer to its end. So short a life, so horrible a death for that great, great ship. What is a more stupendous work than a ship! The almost human pieces of machinery, yet a helpless child, powerless in its struggle with an almighty sea, and the great boat sank, fragile as a rowboat.

How different are those staircases now! No laughing throng, but on either side stand quietly, bravely, the stewards, all equipped with the white, ghostly life-preservers. Always the thing one tries not to see even crossing a ferry. Now only pale faces, each form strapped about with those white bars. So gruesome a scene. We passed on. The awful good-byes. The quiet look of hope in the brave men's eyes as the wives were put into the lifeboats. Nothing escaped one at this fearful moment. We left from the Sun Deck, seventy-five feet above the water. Mr Case and Mr Roebling, brave American men, saw us to the lifeboat, made no effort to save themselves, but stepped back on deck. Later they went to an honoured grave.

Our lifeboat, with thirty-six in it, began lowering to the sea. This was done amid the greatest confusion. Rough seamen all giving different orders. No officer aboard. As only one side of the ropes worked, the lifeboat at one time was in such a position that it seemed we must capsize in mid-air. At last the ropes worked together, and we drew nearer and nearer the black, oily water. The first touch of our lifeboat on that black sea came to me as a last good-bye to life, and so we put off – a tiny boat on a great sea – rowed away from what had been a safe home for five days. The first wish on the part of all was to stay near the *Titanic*. We all felt so much safer near the ship. Surely such a vessel could not sink. I thought the danger must be exaggerated, and we could all be taken aboard again. But surely the outline of that great, good ship was growing less. The bow of the boat was getting black. Light after light was disappearing, and now those rough seamen put to their oars and we were told to hunt under the seats, any place, anywhere, for a lantern, a light of any kind. Every place was empty. There was no water – no stimulant of any kind. Not a biscuit – nothing to keep us alive had we drifted long. Had no good *Carpathia*, with its splendid Captain Rostron, its orderly crew, come to our rescue we must all have perished. Our men knew nothing about the position of the stars, hardly how to pull together. Two oars were soon overboard. The men's hands were too cold to hold on. We stopped while they beat their hands and arms, then started on again. A sea, calm as a pond, kept our boat steady, and now that mammoth ship is fast, fast disappearing. Only one tiny light is left – a powerless little spark, a lantern fastened to the mast. Fascinated, I watched that black outline until the end. Then across the water swept that awful wail, the cry of those drowning people. In my ears I heard: 'She's gone, lads; row like hell or we'll get the devil of a swell.' And the horror, the helpless horror, the worst of all – need it have been?

To-day the question is being asked, 'Would the *Titanic* disaster be so discussed had it not been for the great wealth gathered there?' It surely would be, for at a time like this wealth counts for nothing, but man's philanthropy, man's brains, man's heroism, count forever. So many men that stood for the making of a great nation, morally and politically, were swept away by the sinking of that big ship. That is why, day after day, the world goes on asking the why of it all. Had a kind Providence a guiding hand in this? Did our nation need so mighty a stroke to prove that man had grown too self-reliant, too sure of his own power over God's sea? God's part was the saving of the few souls on that calmest of oceans on that fearful night. Man's part was the pushing of the good ship, pushing against all reason, to save what? – a few hours and lose a thousand souls – to have the largest of ships arrive in port even a few hours sooner than anticipated. Risk all, but push, push on, on. The icebergs could be avoided. Surely man's experience ought to have lent aid, but just so surely it did not.

In years past a tendency to live more simply away from pomp and display led to the founding of our American nation. Now what are we demanding today? Those same needless luxuries. If they were not demanded they would not be supplied. Gymnasiums, swimming pools, tea rooms, had better give way to make peace for the necessary number of lifeboats; lifeboats for the crew, also, who helped pilot the good ship across the sea.

Sitting by me in the lifeboat were a mother and daughter (Mrs Hays and Mrs Davidson). The mother had left a husband on the *Titanic*, and the daughter a father and husband, and while we were near the other boats those two stricken women would call out a name and ask, 'Are you there?' 'No,' would come back the awful answer, but these brave women never lost courage, forgot their own sorrow, telling me to sit close to them to keep warm. Now I began to wish for the warm velvet suit I left hanging in my cabin. I had thought of it for a minute, and then had quickly thrown on a lighter weight skirt. I knew the heavier one would make the life-preserver less useful. Had I only known how calm the ocean was that night, I would have felt that death was not so sure, and would have dressed for life rather than for the end. The life-preservers helped to keep us warm, but the night was bitter cold, and it grew colder and colder, and just before dawn, the coldest, darkest hour of all, no help seemed possible. As we put off from the *Titanic* never was a sky more brilliant, never have I seen so many falling stars. All tended to make those distress rockets that were sent up from the sinking ship look so small, so dull and futile. The brilliancy of the sky only intensified the blackness of the water, our utter loneliness on the sea. The other boats had drifted away from us; we must wait now for dawn and what the day was to bring us we dare not even hope. To see if I could not make the night seem shorter, I tried to imagine myself again in Japan. We had made two strange night departures there, and I was unafraid, and this Atlantic now was calmer than the Inland sea had been at that time. This helped a while, but my hands were freezing cold, and I had to give up pretending and think of the dawn that must soon come.

Two rough looking men had jumped into our boat as we were about to lower, and they kept striking matches, lighting cigars, until I feared we would have no matches left and might need them, so I asked them not to use any more, but they kept on. I do not know what they looked like. It was too dark to really distinguish features clearly, and when the dawn brought the light it brought something so wonderful with it no one looked at anything else or anyone else. Someone asked: 'What time is it?' Matches were still left; one was struck. Four o clock! Where had the hours of the night gone? Yes, dawn would soon be here; and it came, so surely, so strong with cheer. The stars slowly disappeared, and in their place came the faint pink glow of another day. Then I heard, 'A light, a ship.' I could not, would not, look while there was a bit of doubt, but kept my eyes away. All night long I had heard, 'A light!' Each time it proved to be one of our other lifeboats, someone lighting a piece of paper, anything they could find to burn, and now I could not believe. Someone found a newspaper; it was lighted and held up. Then I looked and saw a ship. A ship bright with lights; strong and steady she waited, and we were to be saved. A straw hat was offered (Mrs Davidson's); it would burn longer. That same ship that had come to save us might run us down. But no; she is still. The two, the ship and the dawn, came together, a living painting. White was the vessel, but whiter still were those horribly beautiful icebergs, and as we drew nearer and nearer that good ship we drew nearer to those mountains of ice. As far as the eye could reach they rose. Each one more fantastically chiselled than its neighbour. The floe glistened like a never-ending meadow covered with new-fallen snow. Those same white mountains, marvellous in their purity, had made of the just ended night one of the blackest the sea has ever known. And near them stood the ship which had come in such quick response to the *Titanic*'s call for help. The man who works over hours is always the worth-while kind, and the Marconi operator awaiting a belated message had heard the poor ship's call for help, and we few out of so many were saved.

From the *Carpathia* a rope forming a tiny swing was lowered into our lifeboat, and one by one we were drawn into safety. The lady pulled up just ahead of me was very large, and I felt myself being jerked fearfully, when I heard someone say: 'Careful, fellers; she's a lightweight.' I bumped and bumped against the side of the ship until I felt like a bag of meal. My hands were so cold I could hardly hold on to the rope, and I was fearful of letting go. Again I heard: 'Steady, fellers; not so fast!' I felt I should let go and bounce out of the ropes; I hardly think that would have been possible, but I felt so at the time. At last I found myself at an opening of some kind and there a kind doctor wrapped me in a warm rug and led me to the dining room, where warm stimulants were given us immediately and everything possible was done for us all. Lifeboats kept coming in, and heart-rending was the sight as widow after widow was brought aboard. Each hoped some lifeboat ahead of hers might have brought her husband safely to this waiting vessel. But always no.

I was still so cold that I had to get a towel and tie it around my waist. Then I went back to the dining-room and found dear little Louis, the French baby, lying alone; his cold, bare feet had become unwrapped. I put a hot water bottle against this very beautiful boy. He smiled his thanks. Knowing how much better I felt after taking the hot stimulant, I tried to get others to take something; but often they just shook their heads and said, 'Oh, I can't.'

Towards night we remembered we had nothing – no comb, brush, nothing of any kind – so we went to the barber-shop. The barber always has everything, but now he had only a few toothbrushes left. I bought a cloth cap of doubtful style; and felt like a walking orphan asylum, but very glad to have anything to cover my head. There were also a few showy silk handkerchiefs left. On the corner of each was embroidered in scarlet, 'From a friend.' These we bought and we were now fitted out for our three remaining days at sea.

Patiently through the dismal, foggy days we lived, waiting for land and possible news of the lost. For the brave American man, a heart full of gratitude, too deep for words, send out a thanksgiving. That such men are born, live and die for others is a cause for deep gratitude. What country could have shown such men as belong to our American manhood? Thank God for them and for their noble death.[239]

MARY SLOAN **Crew (Stewardess)**

On 27 April 1912, while she and the *Titanic*'s surviving crew were returning to England on the *Lapland*, Miss Sloan wrote the following letter to her sister:

S.S. *Lapland*, April 27th, 1912

My dear Maggie,

I expect you will be glad to hear from me once more and to know I am still in the land of the living. Did you manage to keep the news from Mother? I trust she is well.

Well, we are now nearing England in the *Lapland*. They are very good to us here, and we have had a lovely passage home. About that dreadful night, I won't go into details now, I shall tell you all when I see you. I hope you got the cablegram alright. I shall never forget Mr Shannon's friends in New York. They, I mean Mrs M'Williams, came on board the *Lapland* on Friday morning accompanied by a Mr Robb, president of the telephone in N.Y. Mr Robb sent off the cable, and Mrs M'Williams took me to Brooklyn, gave me money and clothes. Mr and Mrs Robb came at night, and Mr Robb made me take a 10 dollar bill. Young Mr Bryand a 5 dollar bill. Did you ever hear of such kindness from strangers? Of course I took them on condition I would pay them back again. You must write to them and thank them, as I will also. The ladies of New York Relief Committee came on board the *Lapland* with changes of underclothing, but I was at Brooklyn. You will be glad to know that dreadful night I never lost my head once. When she struck at a quarter to twelve and the engines stopped I knew very well something was wrong. Doctor Simpson came and told me the mails were afloat. I knew things were pretty bad. He brought Miss Marsden and I into his room and gave us a little whiskey and water. I laughed and asked him if he thought we needed it, and he said we should. Miss Marsden was crying, and he was cross with her. He asked me if I was afraid, I replied I was not. He said, 'Well-spoken – like a true Ulster girl.' He had to hurry away to see if there was anyone hurt. We helped him on with his greatcoat, I never saw him again. I felt better after, then I saw our dear old Dr O'Loughlin. I asked him to tell me the worst, he said, 'Child, things are very bad.' I indeed got a lifebelt and got on deck. I went round my rooms to see if my passengers were all up and to see if they had lifebelts on. Poor Mr Andrews came along, I read in his face all I wanted to know.

He saw me knocking at some of the passengers' doors, he said 'that was right,' also told me to see that they had lifebelts on and to get one for myself and go on deck. He was a brave man. Last time I saw and heard him was about an hour later helping to get the women and children into the boats, imploring them not to hesitate, but to go when asked as there was no time to be lost, so Mr Andrews met his fate like a true hero realising his great danger, and gave up his life to save the women and children of the *Titanic*. They will find it hard to replace him, and I myself am terribly cut up about him. I was talking to him on the Friday night previous as he was going into dinner. The dear old doctor was waiting for him on the stair landing, and calling him by his Christian name Tommy. Mr Andrews seemed loth to go, he wanted to talk about home, he was telling me his father was ill and Mrs A. was not so well. I was congratulating him on the beauty and perfection of the ship. He said the part he did not like was that the *Titanic* was taking us further away from home every hour. I looked at him and his face struck me at the time as having a very sad expression. He is one of the many who can be ill spared.

Well, I got away from all the others and intended to go back to my room for some of my jewellery, but I had not time at the last. I went on deck the second time, one of our little bell boys recognised me, and pointing to a crowded boat said, 'Miss Sloan, that's your boat No. [illegible].' I said child how do you know, I will wait for another, so it pushed off without me. I was still standing when I saw Captain Smith getting excited, passengers would not have noticed, I did. I knew then we were soon going, the distress rockets were then going every minute, so I thought if anyone asked me again to go I should do so, there was then a big crush from behind me. At last they realised their danger, so I was pushed into the boat. I believe it was one of the last ones to leave. We had scarcely got clear when she began sinking rapidly. The rest is too awful to write about. We were in the boats all night. I took a turn to row. The women said I encouraged them, I was pleased. We picked up 30 men standing on an upturned boat, among them was one of our officers Mr Lightoller, who then took charge until the *Carpathia* picked us up about 7 in the morning. I only hope I shall never have a like experience again. Mr Lightoller paid me the compliment of saying I was a sailor.

We are arriving about midnight on Sunday night. I don't know what the White Star people are going to do with us, I shall wait and see. I have lost everything. I will stay in Marland Terrace so you can write me there. Should love to see you all and talk to you. We are arriving on the *Lapland*. I think I told you this before. Trusting this will find you all safe and well.

Your loving sister,

May

Give my love to Mrs Brown, Millie and Joe. Let Lizzie read this as the paper is short here.[240]

While on board the *Lapland*, Miss Sloan wrote another letter describing her memories of victim Thomas Andrews:

> ... I was proud of him. He came from home and he made you feel on the ship that all was right. It was good to hear his laugh and have him near you. If anything went wrong it was always to Mr Andrews one went. Even when a fan stuck in a stateroom, one would say, 'Wait for Mr Andrews, he'll soon see to it,' and you would find him settling even the little quarrels that arose between ourselves. Nothing came amiss to him, nothing at all. And he was always the same, a nod and a smile or a hearty word whenever he saw you and no matter what he was at.
>
> ... I was talking to him on the Friday night as he was going in to dinner. The dear old Doctor was waiting for him on the stair-landing, and calling him by his Christian name, Tommy. Mr Andrews seemed loth to go, he wanted to talk about home; he was telling me his father was ill and Mrs Andrews not so well. I was congratulating him on the beauty and perfection of the ship; he said the part he did not like was that the Titanic was taking us further away from home every hour. I looked at him and his face struck me as having a very sad expression.

Miss Sloan also saw Andrews on Sunday evening:

> I saw him go to dinner. He was in good spirits, and I thought he looked splendid.

After the collision, Andrews came up from investigating the damage and met Miss Sloan. He instructed her to have her passengers dress and assemble on the boat deck with their lifebelts. She scrutinised his face:

> ... which had a look as though he were heart broken.

As the last boats were filled, Andrews spoke to some female passengers:

> Ladies, you must get in at once. There is not a minute to lose. You cannot pick and choose your boat. Don't hesitate. Get in, get in!

Then, upon seeing Miss Sloan:

> Don't hesitate! There's not a moment to lose. Get in![241]

MARY ELOISE SMITH — First Class Passenger

On 20 May Mrs Smith made the following deposition for the Senate *Titanic* inquiry:

> At 7.30 p.m., as usual, my husband and I went to dinner in the café. There was a dinner party going on, given by Mr Ismay to the captain and various other people on board ship. This was a usual occurrence of the evening, so we paid no attention

to it. The dinner did not seem to be particularly gay; while they had various wines to drink, I am positive none were intoxicated at a quarter of 9 o'clock, when we left the dining room. There was a coffee room directly outside of the café, in which people sat and listened to the music and drank coffee and cordials after dinner. My husband was with some friends just outside of what is known as the Parisian Café. I stayed up until 10.30, and then went to bed. I passed through the coffee room, and Mr Ismay and his party were still there. The reason I am positive about the different time is because I asked my husband at the three intervals what time it was. I went to bed, and my husband joined his friends. I was asleep when the crash came. It did not awaken me enough to frighten me; in fact, I went back to sleep again. Then I awakened again, because it seemed that the boat had stopped. About that time my husband came into the room. Still I was not frightened, but thought he had come in to go to bed. I asked him why the boat had stopped, and, in a leisurely manner, he said; 'We are in the north and have struck an iceberg: It does not amount to anything, but probably delay us a day getting into New York. However, as a matter of form, the captain has ordered all ladies on deck.' That frightened me a little, but after being reassured there was no danger I took plenty of time in dressing – putting on all my heavy clothing, high shoes, and two coats, as well as a warm knit hood.

While I dressed, my husband and I talked of landing, not mentioning the iceberg. I started out, putting on my life preserver, when we met a steward, who was on his way to tell us to put on life preservers and come on deck. However, I returned to the room with the intention of bringing my jewellery, but my husband said not to delay with such trifles. However, I picked up two rings and went on deck. After getting to the top deck, the ladies were ordered on Deck A without our husbands. I refused to go; but, after being told by three or four officers, my husband insisted, and, along with another lady, we went down. After staying there some time with nothing seemingly going on, someone called upstairs saying they could not be lowered from that deck, for the reason it was enclosed in glass. That seemed to be the first time the officers and captain had thought of that, and hastened to order us all on the top deck again. There was some delay in getting lifeboats down: in fact, we had plenty of time to sit in the gymnasium and chat with another gentleman and his wife. I kept asking my husband if I could remain with him rather than go in a lifeboat. He promised me I could. There was no commotion, no panic, and no one seemed to be particularly frightened; in fact, most of the people seemed interested in the unusual occurrence, many having crossed 50 and 60 times. However, I noticed my husband was busy talking to any officer whom he came in contact with; still I had not the least suspicion of the scarcity of lifeboats, or I never should have left my husband.

When the first boat was lowered from the left-hand side I refused to get in, and they did not urge me particularly; in the second boat they kept calling for one more lady to fill it, and my husband insisted that I get in it, my friend having gotten in. I refused unless he would go with me. In the meantime Capt. Smith was standing with a megaphone on deck. I approached him and told him I was alone, and asked if my husband might be allowed to go in the boat with me. He ignored me personally, but shouted again through his megaphone, 'Women and children first.' My husband said, 'Never mind, captain, about that; I will see that she gets in the boat.' He then said, 'I never expected to ask you to obey, but this is one time you must; it is only a matter of form to have women and children first. The boat is thoroughly equipped, and everyone on her will be saved.' I asked him if that was absolutely honest, and he said, 'Yes.' I felt some better then, because I had absolute confidence in what he said. He kissed me good-by and placed me in the lifeboat with the assistance of an officer. As the boat was being lowered he yelled from the deck, 'Keep your hands in your pockets; it is very cold weather.' That was the last I saw of him, and now I remember the many husbands that turned their backs as that small boat was lowered, the women blissfully innocent of their husbands' peril, and said good-by with the expectation of seeing them within the next hour or two. By that time our interest was centred on the lowering of the lifeboat, which occurred to me – although I know very little about it – to be a very poor way to lower one. The end I was in was almost straight up, while the lower end came near touching the water. Our seaman said, himself, at the time, that he did not know how to get the rope down, and asked for a knife. Some person in the boat happened to have a knife – a lady, I think – who gave it to him. He cut the rope, and we were about to hit bottom when someone spoke of the plug. After a few minutes' excitement to find something to stop up the hole in the bottom of the boat where the plug is, we reached the water all right. The captain looked over to see us, I suppose, or something of the kind, and noticed there was only one man in the boat. Maj. Peuchen, of Canada, was then swung out to us as an experienced seaman. There was a small light on the horizon that we were told to row toward. Some people seemed to think it was a fishing smack or small boat of some description. However, we seemed to get no nearer the longer we rowed, and I am of the opinion it was a star.

Many people in our boat said they saw two lights. I could not until I had looked a long time; I think it was the way our eyes focused, and probably the hope for another boat. I do not believe it was anything but a star. There were but 24 people in our boat – they are supposed to hold 50. During the night they looked for water and crackers and a compass, but they found none that night. We were some distance away when the *Titanic* went down. We watched with sorrow, and heard the many cries for help and pitied the captain, because we knew he would have to stay with his ship. The cries we heard I thought were seamen, or possibly steerage, who had overslept, it not occurring to me for a moment that my husband and my friends were not saved. It was bitterly cold, but I did not seem to mind it particularly. I was trying to locate my husband in all the boats that were near us. The night was beautiful; everything seemed to be with us in that respect, and a very calm sea. The icebergs on the horizon were all watched with interest; some seemed to be as tall as mountains, and reminded me of the pictures I had studied in geography. Then there were flat ones, round ones also. I am not exactly sure what time, but think it was between 5 and 5.30 when we sighted the *Carpathia*. Our seaman suggested we drift and let them pick us up; however, the women refused and rowed toward it. Our seaman was Hichens, who refused to row, but sat on the end of the boat wrapped in a blanket that one of the women had given him. I am not of the opinion that he was intoxicated, but a lazy, uncouth man, who had no respect for the ladies, and who was a thorough coward. We made no attempt to return to the sinking *Titanic*, because we supposed it was thoroughly equipped. Such a thought never entered my head. Nothing of the sort was mentioned in the boat, having left the ship so early we were innocent of the poor equipment that we now know of. The sea had started to get fairly rough by the time we were taken on the *Carpathia*, and we were quite cold and glad for the shelter and protection.

I have every praise for the *Carpathia*'s captain and its crew, as well as the passengers aboard. They were kindness itself to each and every one of us, regardless of position we occupied on boat. One lady very kindly gave me her berth, and I was as comfortable as can be expected under the circumstances until we arrived in New York. The ship's doctors were particularly nice to us. I knew many women who slept on the floor in the smoking room while Mr Ismay occupied the best room on the *Carpathia*, being in the centre of the boat, with every attention, and a sign on the door, 'Please do not knock.' There were other men who were miraculously saved, and barely injured, sleeping on the engine-room floor, and such places as that, as the ship was very crowded. The discipline coming into New York was excellent. We were carefully looked after in every way with the exception of a marconigram I sent from the *Carpathia* on Monday morning, April 15, to my friends. Knowing of their anxiety, I borrowed money from a gentleman and took this marconigram myself and asked the operator to send it for me, and he promised he would. However, it was not received. Had it been sent, it would have spared my family, as well as Mr Smith's, the terrible anxiety which they went through for four days. This is the only complaint I have to make against the *Carpathia*. They did tell me they were near enough to land to send it, but would send it through other steamers, as they were cabling the list of the rescued that way. He also said it was not necessary to pay him, because the White Star Line was responsible. I insisted, however, because I thought that probably the money might have some weight with them, as the whole thing seemed to have been a monied accident.

Mrs Lucian P. Smith[242]

JULIA SMYTH — Third Class Passenger

Miss Smyth wrote the following letter to her mother shortly after the disaster (spelling as in original):

My Dear Mother

I suppose you thought you would never here tell of me again when the ship sank. I suppose youse were in a terribl fret. but if any of you see they site that we all had to go through your faces would never be seen again. I cannot always be explain of it for I am sick and tired of it talking of it all the time.

Well mother I am not feeling so lonesome now because I have a good place for the start. I am learning everything. it is so hard to get a first class place but I got it. but there is nothing but work. no matter where you go every one say I am the luckeys one that ever struk New York to get in because there is not a job to be got in the office. these people go to the country from the Summer. Nora Glean and me is left in the house for the Summer. we will be do in nothing the holl Summer. I can have a good rest. I hope youse have all the work done home and not last. hope youse have Lary McCoonarty again. tell him for me I will send him what will give him a good wash down for the Summer. I am so very lucky to be on the land of the living atall. every says to me I was not on the Titinice atall I look so good. every say I must get good times in the old Ireland. I suppose I would look if I never got much. I was pretty shuck coming over. I was sick all the time on the ship. I nearly fell into big sea when I was going up they ladder to the carpatin that morning I got wake. I was a few steps up, I fell back again but I said to myself I might as well strive and get in. everyone for themselves that moment life or death. I am sure there is not one in Pottle boys or girls would make the fight I made. there was thousand before me and Katie jumped ought into the boat. only my legs was long I would never made it. everyone seems very nice to me. Bridget Ballasty bought me a nice waist. Bridget the neighbour bought me a lovely present. I saw all from home. James told me that a lot of people went from home. he never told me there names. tell him write and tell me. I'm finished cleaning resting all evening. write me soon. pray for me mama.

XX

Julia

I get oatmeal sturboat in the morning to ate. tell the cricket I was asking for him. is the gang in Pottle again.

346 Lexington Ave

this is my adres. America is no jock. Ireland is the place for everyone that can stay home. I am sure Henry crys the day he ever left Pottle.[243]

JOHN PILLSBURY SNYDER **First Class Passenger**

On 24 April Mr Snyder wrote the following letter to his father:

Minneapolis, Minn.
April 24, 1912

Dear Father,

Here we are again both safe and sound, thankful and glad to be home. You perhaps have not heard of the way we reached safety. I can't tell you all about it because that would take a very long time and would fill a book.

I can only tell you that I have a mighty fine wife and she is the one you must thank – besides our Lord – for my being able to write this letter. If it hadn't been for Nelle I am sure that I never would be here now. She is the one who urged me to get up when I wanted to go back to bed.

We were both asleep when the boat hit. I don't know whether the bump woke me up or I woke when Nelle spoke to me. At any rate she made me get up and go out to the companionway to see what was going on. I went out three times before we decided to get up and get dressed.

When we reached the top deck only a few people were about and we all were told to go down and put on our lifebelts. We did it at once thinking it was only a precaution. When we got back on the top deck again we saw they were getting the lifeboats ready. As soon as they were ready, they told the people to get into them. Nearly everybody stepped back from in front of us and as a result we were almost the very first people placed in the lifeboat. Only a very few people were on deck at that time and they thought it much safer to stay on the big boat than to try the lifeboat. When we had rowed some distance away from the *Titanic*, we realised, seeing the different rows of portholes getting less and less – three rows, then two rows, and finally the bow went under – that the finest boat in the world was doomed.

We hit between 11:40 and 11:50 at night and the *Titanic* sank at 2:22 in the morning.

We spent some anxious hours in the lifeboat and finally sighted the *Carpathia*, between 4 and 5:30. We rowed to meet her and at 5:30 we felt better. You can't imagine how we felt, and I am sure the Lord had his guiding hand over Nelle's and my head.

We both were entirely dressed. Nelle had on every stitch of clothing of her winter suit, a sweater, her long steamer coat, mink furs, winter hat, light shoes, etc. I had on my suit, a sweater, winter overcoat, shoes. In fact, we both were as comfortably dressed as possible.

Uncle Ed, Mabel and Charlie Williams, Aunt Edith and Uncle Victor, all met us in New York. Many of my Hotchkiss classmates were also there.

Nelle got weighed yesterday and showed a gain of 20 pounds since we got married. Pretty good, hey!

I hope you get this letter and I sure will be glad to see you home. Home looks mighty good to me.

With heaps of love to all,
from
Nelle and John[244]

AMY STANLEY **Third Class Passenger**

On 20 April Miss Stanley wrote the following letter to her parents in New York:

Dear Father and Mother,

I have had a terrible experience, one that I shall never forget as long as I live. I seemed to have a presentiment that something would happen to the boat I was going to sail on. I enjoyed the first part of the voyage immensely. I had not been sea-sick all the voyage. I am now only suffering from shock and exposure to intense cold, with scarcity of clothing. I was writing a postcard the night that the boat struck the iceberg. It was about 11.30 p.m. I got out of bed and put my coat on and went out on deck and asked the steward what was the matter. He told me it was only the engines stopped, and ordered all the women back to bed. But I did not go. I shared a cabin with an American lady and child. I assisted them to dress, and then we went up on deck. We tried to reach the boats. Then I saw two fellows (whom we met at meals, the only men we made real friends of) coming towards us, who assisted us over the railings into the lifeboat. As we were being lowered a man about 16 stone jumped into the boat almost on top of me. I heard a pistol fired – I believe it was done to frighten the men from rushing the boat. This man's excuse was that he came because of his baby. When we rowed off the child must have died had I not attended to it.

We were rowing for several hours. I seemed to have extra strength that night to keep up my nerves, for I even made them laugh when I told them we had escaped vaccination, for we were all to have been vaccinated that day (meaning the Monday). I will say no more of that awful row, except that I was able to fix the rope round the women for them to be pulled up on the *Carpathia* while the men steadied the boat – the women seemed quite stupefied – yet when I was safe myself, I was the first to break down. The sight on board was awful, with raving women – barely six women were saved who could say they had not lost a relative. Oh! the widows the *Titanic* has made! The last three days have been terrible. I attended to a woman who was picked up on a raft with four men. The latter died, but she lived. She has lost two sons on the *Titanic*. Their cabin was next to mine. She was the last woman I spoke to on the ship's deck. I am staying in a Woman's League Hotel, but I am quite well, and these people are fitting me up with clothes. I have telegraphed to Grace but have not yet received a reply. I long now to be with her. I will not write again until I am safe in Newhaven. Don't you think I have been lucky throughout?

I remain your loving Daughter

Amy

P.S. I nearly lost the boat at Southampton.[245]

ANNIE STENGEL — First Class Passenger

Following the disaster, Mrs Stengel wrote the following letter to fellow survivor Archibald Gracie:

> As I stepped into the lifeboat an officer in charge said: 'No more; the boat is full.' My husband stepped back, obeying the order. As the boat was being lowered, four men deliberately jumped into it. One of them was a Hebrew doctor – another was his brother. This was done at the risk of the lives of all of us in the boat. The two companions of this man who did this were the ones who were later transferred to boat No.7, to which we were tied. He weighed about 250 pounds and wore two life preservers. These men who jumped in struck me and a little child. I was rendered unconscious and two of my ribs were very badly dislocated. With this exception there was absolutely no confusion and no disorder in the loading of our boat.[246]

MARTHA STEPHENSON — First Class Passenger

Following the disaster, Mrs Stephenson wrote the following account of how she and Elizabeth Eustis survived the sinking of the *Titanic*:

> Sunday morning, April 14, 1912, was a beautiful clear day, high wind and cold. Elizabeth and I wrote letters before service, remarking at the service that they did not sing the hymn 'For Those in Peril On the Sea.' Then read the chart and noticed we had made a run of five hundred and forty-seven miles. After lunch we spoke to Penrose, our room steward, about the run and he said it was nothing to what we would do on Monday, when they expected to do five hundred and eighty.
>
> We spent our afternoon reading, had tea on deck, then went to see the restaurant before going down. McElroy, the purser, was walking on the boat deck when we took our last walk before dinner. We had a delicious dinner with souvenir menus, our steward bringing us many views of the ship. We spent our evening in the reception room listening to a fine musical program, many whom we knew sitting about us. About nine-thirty we went up to the lounge, a most beautiful room with open fire. I, having finished all my books, got the library steward to lend me Sir Ernest Shackleton's book of the South Pole and I spent half an hour looking at pictures of icebergs and ice fields, little realising that I should ever see similar ones. At ten o'clock we started down to bed and on our deck D found Mr and Mrs Thayer, with whom we sat until quarter of eleven talking of our wonderful trip. We then said good night and turned in, I remarking to Elizabeth that we had but two more nights, and neither of us had had one bit of discomfort from seasickness.

I was sound asleep when at quarter before twelve I was awakened by a terrible jar with ripping and cutting noise which lasted a few moments. We both were much frightened, sitting up in our beds and turning on the electricity. Our door was on the hook and we soon heard voices in the hall so that Elizabeth put on her wrapper, slippers and cap and ran out. I was bitterly cold, and, shivering from fright and cold, sat undecided as to what to do. Our steward came down to close the port and I asked him if the order had been given to close all the ports, but he said 'No, it's only cold, go to bed; it's nothing at all.' Before Elizabeth returned I decided to get dressed as I had seen a gentleman in one of the rooms opposite pull his shoes in from the passageway. When she came in she told of many people outside half-dressed, one woman having a thin white pigtail down her back and a feather hat; also that some man was fastened in his inside room unable to open his door. He was much worried, calling for help, and young Williams put his shoulder to the panels and broke it in. The steward was most indignant and threatened to have him arrested for defacing the beautiful ship.

I had my shoes nearly buttoned, and she said 'Why, Martha, are you dressing?' and I said I should feel much safer with my clothes on and could go to bed later if all was right. She then decided to dress also. We did not hurry, and dressed fully as if for breakfast, putting on our burglar pockets containing our letters of credit and money. I determined also to do my hair and put on a lined waist and old winter suit as it was so cold. While Elizabeth was doing her hair the ship suddenly settled, frightening me very much, and I urged her not to take pains but to hurry.

Just as I was wholly dressed and she hooking her waist Mr Thayer appeared at our door, which we had opened, and said he was very glad that we had dressed. He thought there was no danger, but we had struck ice and there was much on deck and he urged us to come up and see it, saying we would find him and Mrs Thayer on the deck. I put on my fur coat over everything and Elizabeth said she thought she would wear her watch, which reminded me that mine was hanging by the bureau and I quickly put it on. I took my glasses and small change purse, also a clean handkerchief and was dressed as if for breakfast. We then left our room, leaving the electric lights on, also the electric heater so it would be warm on our return. We closed the door and started down the long passageway and up the stairs.

On the next deck we met the Thayer family, who seemed to be waiting for us, and started up to go on the deck when a steward called 'All back to staterooms for life preservers.' We turned around and I cannot remember that we ran, but we walked quickly to our rooms and Elizabeth climbed up, pulling down two life preservers from off the top of her closet. We said then we felt it must be serious if they had ordered the lifebelts, and we were much frightened though very quiet. We again went up the stairs, with our life preservers in our hands and once more joined the Thayer family. We quietly read the notices of 'inside front' and 'inside back' and put them on over our heads, Elizabeth tying mine and I tying hers. We put ours on over our heavy coats. After our life preservers were on, Mrs Thayer suggested getting Jack's coat, and Elizabeth and I followed to the steward's room, and when Mrs Thayer took the coat we each took our steamer rugs, not knowing why, but simply that we were there.

My mind is a blank as to a trip we took to the boat deck, when I distinctly remember being beside the gymnasium on starboard side and seeing Mr Ismay come out, noting the fact that he had dressed hurriedly, as his pajamas were below his trousers. After getting our rugs we were in the companionway of A deck when order came for women and children to boat deck and men to starboard side.

Elizabeth and I took each other's hands, not to be separated in the crowd, and all went on deck, we following close to Mrs Thayer and her maid and going up narrow iron stairs to the forward boat deck which, on the *Titanic*, was the captain's bridge.

At the top of the stairs we found Captain Smith looking much worried, and anxiously waiting to get down after we got up. The ship listed heavily to port just then. As we leaned against the walls of the officers' quarters rockets were being fired over our heads, which was most alarming, as we fully realised if the *Titanic* had used her wireless to ill effect and was sending rockets it must be serious. Shortly after that the order came from the head dining saloon steward to go down to the A deck, when Mrs Thayer remarked, 'Tell us where to go and we will follow. You ordered us up here and now you are taking us back,' and he said 'Follow me.'

On reaching the A deck we could see, for the decks were lighted by electricity, that a boat was lowered parallel to the windows; those were opened, and a steamer chair put under the rail for us to step on. The ship had listed badly by that time and the boat hung far out from the side so that some of the men said, 'No woman could step across that space.' A call was made for a ladder on one of the lower decks, but before it ever got there we were all in the boat. Whether they had drawn the boat over with boathooks nearer the side I do not know, but the space we easily jumped with the help of two men in the boat. The only gentleman I remember seeing at all was Colonel Astor, who was stepping through the window just in front of me when the crew said, 'Step back, sir; no men in this boat.' He remarked that he wanted to take care of his wife, but on being told again that no men could go, he called 'Goodbye' and said he would follow in another boat, asking the number of our boat, which they said was 'No.4.' In going through the window I was obliged to throw back the steamer rug, for, with my fur coat and huge cork life preserver, I was very clumsy. Later we found the stewards or crew had thrown the steamer rugs into the boat, and they did good service, Elizabeth's around a baby thinly clad, and mine for a poor member of the crew pulled in from the sea.

Our boat I think took off every woman on the deck at that time and was the last on the port side to be lowered. Only one man went down with us; the boat was lowered slowly, first at the bow, then at the stern, and very carefully. When near the water the man gave the order to 'Let her go,' but we all called 'Not yet, it's a long way to the water.' On reaching the water they called from the deck to know who was in command, and a man answered 'The quartermaster.' They then said 'Who else?' and he said 'I am alone.' Then they said 'We will send you two more men,' and shortly a boatswain and common sailor came down over the davit ropes into the boat. When we reached the sea we found the ship badly listed, her nose well in so that there was water to the D deck, which we could plainly see as the boat was lighted and the ports on D deck were square instead of round. No lights could be found in our boat and the men had great difficulty in casting off the blocks as they did not know how they worked. My fear here was great, as she seemed to be going faster and faster and I dreaded lest we be drawn in before we could cast off.

When we finally were ready to move on the order was called from the deck to go to the stern hatch and take off some men. There was no hatch open and we could see no men, but our crew obeyed orders, much to our alarm, for they were throwing wreckage over and we could hear a cracking noise resembling china breaking, which we learned later was the cracking of the boiler plates. We implored the men to pull away from the ship, but they refused, and we pulled three men into the boat who had dropped off the ship and were swimming toward us. One man was drunk and had a bottle of brandy in his pocket which the quartermaster promptly threw overboard and the drunk was thrown into the bottom of the boat and a blanket thrown over him. After getting in these three men they told how fast she was going and we all implored them to pull for our lives to get out from the suction when she should go down. The lights on the ship burned till just before she went. When the call came that she was going I covered my face and then heard someone call, 'She's broken.' After what seemed a long time I turned my head only to see the stern almost perpendicular in the air so that the full outline of the blades of the propeller showed above the water. She then gave her final plunge and the air was filled with cries. We rowed back and pulled in five more men from the sea. Their suffering from the icy water was intense and two men who had been pulled into the stern afterwards died, but we kept their bodies with us until we reached the *Carpathia*, when they were taken aboard and Monday afternoon given a decent burial with three others.

After rescuing our men we found several life boats near us and an order was given to tie together, which we obeyed. It did not seem as if we were together long when one boat said they could rescue more could they get rid of some of the women and children aboard, and those were put into our boat. Soon after cries of 'Ship ahoy' and a long low moan came to us and an officer in command of one of the boats ordered us to follow him. We felt we were already too crowded to go, but the other three boats refused to stir, and our men, with quartermaster and boatswain in command, followed the officer and we pulled over to what proved to be an overturned boat crowded with men. We had to approach it very cautiously, fearing our wash would sweep them off. We could take only a few and they had to come very cautiously. The other boat took most of the men and we then rowed away, the cries soon ceasing.

The sea was smooth and the night brilliant with more stars than I had ever seen. We could see the outline of several bergs and scanned the horizon hoping to see the light of some vessel. Occasionally a green light showed, which proved to be on the emergency boat, and our men all recognised it as such. We all prayed for dawn, and there was no conversation, everyone being so awed by the disaster and bitterly cold. We found ourselves in the boat with Mrs Arthur Ryerson, her boy, two daughters, governess and maid; Mrs John Thayer and maid, Mrs Widener and maid, Mrs Astor, her trained nurse and maid, Mrs Carter, her two children and maid, Mrs Cumings, and Mrs Walter Clark of Los Angeles, with many from second and third cabin besides the eight men whom we had pulled in from the sea. By a strange coincidence Mrs Cumings discovered that the man whom she pulled in was her own bedroom steward. By this time our women, Mrs Thayer and Mrs Cumings, were helping two of the half-drowned sailors pull on the oars, as the boat was tremendously heavy.

With the dawn came the wind and before long quite a sea was running. Just before daylight on the horizon we saw what we felt sure must be the lights of a ship. The quartermaster was a long time in admitting that we were right, urging that it was the moon, but we insisted and they then said it might be the *Carpathia* as they had been told before leaving the *Titanic* that she was coming to us. For a long time after daylight we were in great wreckage from the *Titanic*, principally steamer chairs and a few white pilasters. Before leaving the *Titanic* they had been breaking off planks and throwing seats from the upper deck which we realised were thrown over for people to float on. We felt we could never reach the *Carpathia* when we found she had stopped, and afterwards when we asked why she didn't come closer we were told that some of the early boats which put off from the starboard side reached her a little after four, while it was after six when we drew under the side of the open hatch.

It had been a long, trying row in the heavy sea and impossible to keep bow on to reach the ship. We stood in great danger of being swamped many times and Captain Rostron, who watched us come up, said he doubted if we could have lived an hour longer in that high sea. Our boat had considerable water in the centre, due to the leakage and also the water brought in by the eight men from their clothing. They had bailed her constantly in order to relieve the weight. Two of the women near us were dying seasick, but the babies with us slept most of the night in their mothers' arms. The boatswain's chair was slung down the side and there were also rope ladders. Only few, however, of the men were able to go up the ladders. Mail bags were dropped down in which the babies and little children were placed and hoisted up. We were told to throw off our life preservers and then placed in a boatswain's chair and hoisted to the open hatch where ready arms pulled us in; warm blankets waited those in need and brandy offered to everybody. We were shown at once to the saloon, where hot coffee and sandwiches were being served. We asked anxiously for the men and nothing had been heard of any of them excepting Mr Carter, who was already on the *Carpathia* with Mr Ismay, they having gone off together in a lifeboat. Watching the other boats come in we found Jack Thayer who, it seems, was on the overturned boat, but got into the other boat and not ours. He had lost his father after the women left and could not find him. He picked up young Long of Springfield and with him decided to jump as the ship went down. After being sucked under twice he swam for the overturned boat, was pushed back into the water three times, finally finding a place and sitting there till rescued. He never saw young Long after they slid over the side.

The *Carpathia* was small and so crowded. We fortunately found friends on the ship who took us to their stateroom, letting us do our hair and wash our faces and hands. At about nine o'clock or later we had a regular breakfast. From the deck of the *Carpathia* we scanned the sea and such fields of ice only Shackleton's book the night before had shown me. The entire horizon for the complete circle had bergs stationed like sentinels.

The *Californian* came up to us at about eight o'clock and stood so close that the wireless could not be used, but for nearly an hour they wig-wagged and used the semaphore and finally the *Carpathia*'s captain steamed away with the feeling that all boats were accounted for and the *Californian* had promised to stand by with the hope of rescuing any people then living. But we felt sure that Captain Rostron believed that he had everybody.

No one will ever know the kindness and consideration shown us by passengers and crew of the *Carpathia*. Stewards and stewardesses worked without sleep and were indefatigable trying to give help and comfort to the rescued. Passengers gave up staterooms and everybody took someone in where they had a vacant berth or sofa. The barber shop was soon sold out. Elizabeth secured a small comb, tooth paste, nail file, sponges and wash cloths, also a buttonhook. The purser was able to give us a small inside room with four berths that had only been used as a dressing room for many years. However, we slept there very comfortably and took Mrs Cumings and Mrs Astor's maid for the other two berths. We lived on deck as there was no place on the ship to sit.

Two days the sun shone, then came fearful weather with fog and thunder storm so that at times it seemed as if the Lord had intended us all to go. Captain Rostron was more than thoughtful, knowing how our nerves had already been under great strain. The fog horn was blown only when absolutely necessary and as soon as it lightened the least bit it was promptly stopped.

Our meals were remarkable. Of course, the saloon was set up always twice and sometimes three times for people to go, and while we had no appetites still the menu was the same as on all ocean steamers. Broth and tea were served on deck every day. The few of the rescued stewards from the *Titanic* gladly worked in the dining-room. The stewardesses, however, were not asked to help. We found our woman, Mrs Pritchard, was saved, but Penrose, our steward, I never saw after he told me to go back to bed, that it was nothing, and I am confident that his belief after thirty years at sea, that nothing could sink the *Titanic*, made him stick close to the decks.

When we reached the Ambrose Channel Lightship the pilot boat was bearing down on us. Also two tugs bearing large signs of *New York Tribune* and *New York World*. Then began such a scene as I never hope to witness. In the small pilot boat with the pilot in some way a reporter had secreted himself and when the boat came alongside the rope ladder this man fought with the sailors to get aboard. It was most exciting as Captain Rostron stood on the bridge with the megaphone ordering the men not to allow anyone but the pilot to come aboard and the two sailors who were trying hard to keep their small rowboat from being crushed against our side had at the same time to overcome this reporter and throw him back into the bottom of the boat. The tugs then began their rush. One of them struck us such a blow on the side that she jarred the whole ship and frightened us badly. The men on board the tugs were screaming through megaphones, asking names and asking for stories, offering large prices for any story that would be written and passed over to them. The captain, with the pilot on the bridge, soon got under way again and fortunately we left those tugs far behind.

Our stop at quarantine was very short. Dinner was served, but no one had any appetite. When we got up the North River small boats were as thick as bees. At the foot of the Cunard pier we stopped and a large lighter came alongside from the White Star Company to take off the fourteen lifeboats which Captain Rostron had taken aboard in case of accident to the *Carpathia*. While standing, a small newspaper tug which was under us caused us some amusement. A sudden rush of water frightened us, but on inquiry we discovered Captain Rostron had turned the hose on her and she was scurrying off at full speed and I trust the men were well soaked. We were soon off at the pier and among the earliest to leave the ship, as we had been on the deck all the way up and the gangplank was put on right beside us so we only had a few steps to walk.

The family were all close to us and we quickly got away, all going first to the Pennsylvania station, where I left with George, Helen, Ned, Jim Boyd and Dr Christie. Elizabeth went with Tracy, Martha, Arthur, Mary and Angie to the Belmont, where they spent the night, going to Boston the next day. A special train was run to Philadelphia and we left at North Philadelphia, where Joseph met us with the motor and we got to Haverford a little after three in the morning.[247]

MARTHA STONE **First Class Passenger**

After arriving at the Hotel Wolcott in New York, Mrs Stone dictated the following account to Evelyn Campbell:

Only the mercy of God saved the passengers who escaped from the Titanic. If the sea had not been like glass every boat would have been swamped as it went over the side, so inefficiently were they handled.

I do not want to speak ill of the dead, and I will say nothing of any rumours that I may have heard. I can only speak from my own personal experience that terrible night, and because of it I feel that I must sound a note of warning to the many men and women who will cross the sea in the future.

I had gone to bed when the crash came, but I was not asleep. It was not a terrific crash at all. I have travelled extensively, and it was no worse than is often caused by some trivial accident to the machinery.

I knew we were in the vicinity of icebergs, and so I slipped on a kimono over my night dress, put on slippers and went out of my stateroom into the corridor, where I found other people similarly attired.

I spoke to a ship's officer standing near my door and asked him if we had not run into an iceberg.

'Yes,' he answered, 'but there is no danger. Go back to bed and go to sleep.'

All this time the steam was blowing off with a terrible noise, and I asked him why they were doing it.

'We have stopped to see what damage is done, but there is not the slightest danger,' he reiterated.

I was not quite convinced, but it was cold in the corridor, so after a little discussion the woman in the cabin opposite mine, who also had come into the corridor, decided to go back to bed, and we did so.

If I had gone to sleep I should not be here.

Not a single warning was given in the part of the ship in which I was. No one came to tell us. No bell was rung, no horn was sounded. We could have died like rats in a trap for all the warning we received.

Now remember, I can only speak of what occurred in my own part of the ship. Whether other passengers were warned I do not know. I am only telling you of what I myself experienced.

The blowing of steam went on interminably. It got on my nerves at last and I resolved to get up and investigate for myself. I called my maid and she dressed me completely, and then started to dress herself. She had only partially clothed herself when the daughter of the woman opposite came flying down the corridor, crying, 'Get on your life-preservers quickly. They say we must get in the boats.'

My maid and I took all the warm wraps we could carry and, taking the life-preservers in our hands, hurried to the deck.

Nobody appeared to be very much alarmed. The sailors were getting down the lifeboats, but there seemed to be no head or system to the arrangements.

Some lifeboats held 22, some held 50. They were let down in so haphazard a fashion and tilted so alarmingly that if the sea had not been the smoothest I ever saw we certainly should all have been upset.

I do not know what happened after I left the steamer. I went in the second boat that put off, but while I was there there was not the slightest evidence of either panic or cowardice.

The behaviour of the women was a revelation to me. I have always imagined that the majority of women in a crisis like that would be hysterical and hard to manage, but every woman on that deck was as calm and controlled as if she were waiting to take her seat at a dinner table instead of a lifeboat which had to be lowered 70 feet to the water, and the men acted in the same calm manner.

Captain Smith had said, 'Women and children first,' and the men put their wives and daughters and sisters in the boats and then stood back and helped other women to get in.

I do not think anybody thought for a moment that the ship could sink. The crew must have known, but the passengers certainly did not.

I know that this was the reason why many husbands and wives were separated.

The women did not want to leave their husbands, but I think that many of them felt as I did that they were simply going asked to go away for a time that they might not be in the way and in order to avoid any possible risk and that we would soon return.

There was terrible mismanagement in the loading of the boats. For instance, in the second boat in which I was stationed there were but 20 women and two men. Eighteen more lives could have been saved, and we sorely needed more men to row.

One of the men steered, the other managed the other end, while six women, three on a side rowed the boat. My part was to take care that the plug in the bottom of the boat did not come out.

I stood on it for seven hours while another woman about my age, for the same number of hours, waved the solitary lantern which had been handed down to us as we cut loose from the ship.

There were no provisions, no lights, no way of bailing out the icy waters which came in when the boats were launched. I was told that Mrs Astor was one of the women who stood for hours with the icy water nearly to her knees.

Our boat did not have very much water, but if there had been we had not so much as a tin cup with which to throw it out. The state of our solitary lantern was a fair sample of conditions. It went out as soon as it was handed to us and we were given no matches.

Finally one of the women discovered that she had three or four matches, and after a long struggle we succeeded in getting the wick up and lighted it.

[*I realised that the Titanic was doomed*] as soon as we were in the boat. Captain Smith called to the sailors to get away. One of the two men in the boat turned to the women seated at the oars and said excitedly: 'You must row for your lives. If we are not a half mile away in 20 minutes, we will be sucked down with the ship.'

And row for life those women did.

I did not hear any [*explosion*], but that does not prove there was none. Remember, I was in one of the first boats and much farther away from the ship than the boats which got away later.

I heard no explosion, no shots, saw no panic of steerage passengers, nor the heroic quelling of maddened men by Major Butt. But all these things could well have been without my knowledge.

Two things I did hear – I think I will hear them all my life. I heard the screams of the people when the *Titanic* finally sank, and I heard the hymn which those brave musicians played until the very last minute. They must have played till the water rose to their instruments and silenced them forever.

To us, watching a half mile off, the *Titanic* seemed to sink to her grave as gently as a baby would slip into slumber in his mother's arms. The water kept creeping higher, the lights went out one by one, the music sounded fainter and fainter, until at last the waves covered forever the ship that 'could not sink.'

But those cries! They rang out after the ship went down as the people drowned in the vortex of her going, and they were answered by the moans of the bereft women in the boats, who realised at last that the brave smiles with which their husbands and brothers and fathers had bidden them goodbye were the last which they were ever to see of their dear ones.

No words can describe the physical suffering which some of the women endured. Some of us, who had dressed and brought warm wraps, were able to withstand that terrible, intense icy breath which only is felt in the vicinity of large masses of ice. But some of the women, misled by that criminal lack of sufficient warning, had only evening gowns and thin satin slippers. It is a wonder to me how they ever survived.

If anything could have alleviated the misery it would have been the princely treatment we received upon the *Carpathia*. Captain, officers, stewards, crew and passengers all vied in lavishing all their stores of possessions and kindness upon us. I had brought some money in my clothing, and to one of the cabin boys, who had been especially attentive, I gave a tip. He drew back as if hurt. 'I don't want to take your money,' he said. 'I am afraid you won't have enough to get home on.'

On the *Carpathia*, too, I witnessed a most wonderful instance of the power of a woman's soul to rise above her suffering. We knew that many of the passengers had lost all their possessions and were in desperate need, so we organised a committee for their relief.

Every one of the woman so terribly bereaved put aside her grief in plans for her sisters in want. We raised $10,000 in those days on the *Carpathia*, and some of the hardest workers were women whose hearts were breaking.

[*'Was the ship going at full speed when she struck the iceberg?'*]

She certainly was not travelling any slower than she had been at any time.

[*'And the lesson of it all?'*]

People who travel must demand safety in travel, and accept nothing less than the best appliances, the most efficient handling of those appliances. We get just what we demand.[248]

ELMER TAYLOR — First Class Passenger

Following the disaster, Mr Taylor wrote a letter to his cousin, Mr Noble. The letter said that Taylor and his wife were in bed at the time of the collision, which was merely a grinding sensation. Mr Taylor insisted that his wife dress warmly, and they then went out into the companionway. Taylor knocked at the door of his business partner, Lambert Williams, but Williams called out that he didn't think the alarm was worth his getting out of bed. Mr and Mrs Taylor went up to the boat deck, where Mrs Taylor entered the 'second lifeboat'. After the boat had been lowered a few feet, Mr Taylor and another man were ordered to fill two vacant seats in the boat. Taylor's letter continued:

We were indeed fortunate to escape with our lives, but I feel so sad at the loss of my partner in business, Lambert Williams. Of our little party at the table of only six, two are among the missing. While we lost all we had, I feel I have gained everything and feel as thankful to have come through such an experience without the slightest difficulty.[249]

(Mr Taylor added that he would never be able to forget the horrible things he saw and heard after the *Titanic* went down.)

JOHN THAYER JR — First Class Passenger

On the afternoon of 20 April Mr Thayer dictated the following account of his experiences on board the *Titanic*:

> Father was in bed, and mother and myself were about to get into bed. There was no great shock. I was on my feet at the time, and I do not think it was enough to throw anyone down. I put on an overcoat and rushed up on 'A' deck on the port side. I saw nothing there. I then went forward to the bow to see if I could see any signs of ice. The only ice I saw was on the Well deck. I could not see very far ahead, having just come out of a brightly lighted room. I then went down to our room and my father and mother came on deck with me, to the starboard side of 'A' deck. We could not see anything there. Father thought he saw small pieces of ice floating around, but I could not see any myself. There was no big berg.
>
> We walked around to the port side and the ship had then a fair list to port. We stayed there looking over the side for about five minutes. The list seemed very slowly to be increasing. We then went down to our rooms on 'C' deck. All of us dressed quickly, putting on all our clothes. We all put on life preservers, including the maid and over these we put our overcoats. Then we hurried up on deck and walked around, looking out at different places until the women were all ordered to collect on the Port side. Father and I said good-bye to mother at the top of the stairs on 'A' deck. She and the maid went right out on 'A' deck on the port side and we went to the starboard side.
>
> As at this time we had no idea the boat would sink, we walked around 'A' deck and then went to 'B' deck.
>
> Then we thought we would go back to see if mother had gotten off safely, and went to the port side of 'A' deck. We met the chief steward of the main dining saloon and he told us that mother had not yet taken a boat, and he took us to her. Father and mother went ahead and I followed. They went down to 'B' deck, and a crowd got in front of me and I was not able to catch them, and lost sight of them. As soon as I could get through the crowd I tried to find them on 'B' deck, but without success. That is the last time I saw my father.
>
> This was about one-half an hour before she sank. I then went to the starboard side, thinking that father and mother must have gotten off in a boat. All of this

time I was with a fellow named Milton C. Long of New York, whom I had just met that evening.

On the starboard side the boats were getting away quickly. Some boats were already off in a distance. We thought of getting into one of the boats, the last boat to go on the forward part of the starboard side, but there seemed to be such a crowd around I thought it unwise to make any attempt to get into it. He and I stood by the davits of one of the boats that had left. I did not notice anybody that I knew, except Mr Lindley [Lindeberg-Lind], whom I had also just met that evening. I lost sight of him in a few minutes. Long and I then stood by the rail just a little aft of the Captain's bridge.

The list to the port had been growing greater all the time. About this time the people began jumping from the stern. I thought of jumping myself, but was afraid of being stunned on hitting the water. Three times I made up my mind to jump out and slide down the davit ropes and try to make the boats that were lying off from the ship, but each time Long got hold of me and told me to wait awhile. He then sat down and I stood up waiting to see what would happen. Even then we thought she might possibly stay afloat.

I got a sight on a rope between the davits and a star and noticed that she was gradually sinking. About this time she straightened up on an even keel and started to go down fairly fast at an angle of about thirty degrees. As she started to sink we left the davits and went back and stood by the rail about even with the second funnel. Long and myself said good-bye to each other and jumped up on the rail. He put his legs over and held on a minute and asked me if I was coming. I told him I would be with him in a minute. He did not jump clear, but slid down the side of the ship. I never saw him again. About five seconds after he jumped I jumped out, feet first. I was clear of the ship, went down, and as I came up I was pushed away from the ship by some force. I came up facing the ship and one of the funnels seemed to be lifted off and fell towards me about fifteen yards away with a mass of sparks and steam coming out of it. I saw the ship in a sort of a red glare, and it seemed to me that she broke in two just in front of the third funnel. At this time I was sucked down, and as I came up I was pushed out again and twisted around by a large wave, coming up in the midst of a great deal of small wreckage. As I pushed it from around my head my hand touched the cork fender of an overturned life boat. I looked up and saw some men on the top and asked them to give me a hand. One of them, who was a stoker, helped me up. In a short time the bottom was covered with about 25 or 30 men.

When I got on this I was facing the ship. The stern then seemed to rise in the air and stopped at about an angle of 60 degrees. It seemed to hold there for a time and then with a hissing sound it shot right down out of sight with people jumping from the stern. The stern either pivoted around towards our boat, or we were sucked toward it, and as we only had one oar we could not keep away. There did not seem to be very much suction and most of us managed to stay on the bottom of our boat.

We were then right in the midst of fairly large wreckage, with people swimming all around us. The sea was very calm and we kept the boat pretty steady, but every now and then a wave would wash over it.

The assistant wireless operator was right next to me, holding on to me and kneeling in the water. We all sang a hymn and said the Lord's Prayer and then waited for dawn to come. As often as we saw the other boats in the distance we would yell 'Ship Ahoy!' but they could not distinguish our cries from any of the others so we all gave it up thinking it useless. It was very cold and none of us were able to move around to keep warm, the water washing over her almost all the time.

Towards dawn the wind sprang up, roughening up the water and making it difficult to keep the boat balanced. The wireless man raised our hopes a great deal by telling us that the *Carpathia* would be up in about three hours. About three-thirty or four o'clock some men on our boat on the bow sighted her mast lights. I could not see them as I was sitting down with a man kneeling on my leg. He finally got up and I stood up.

We had the second officer, Mr Lightoller on board. He had an officer's whistle and whistled for the boats in the distance to come up and take us off. It took about an hour and a half for the boats to draw near. Two boats came up. The first took half and the other took the balance including myself. We had great difficulty about this time in balancing the boat as the men would lean too far, but we were all taken aboard the already crowded boats and in about half or three quarters of an hour later we were picked up by the *Carpathia*.

I have noticed Second Officer Lightoller's statement that J.B. Thayer was on our overturned boat, which would give the impression that it was father, when he really meant it was I, as he only learned my name in a subsequent conversation on the *Carpathia* and did not know I was 'Junior'.[250]

MARIAN THAYER **First Class Passenger**

On 21 April the widowed Mrs Thayer wrote the following letter to President William Howard Taft regarding the death of Taft's aide-de-camp, Major Archibald Butt:

Dear Mr Taft,

In my own grief I think often of yours and feel I must write to tell you how I spent that last Sunday evening with Major Butt – for we all cherish news of last hours – and we spoke much of you.

How devoted he was to you and what a lovely noble man he was!

We were dining in the restaurant with the poor Wideners & from the moment we met never moved from each other for the rest of the evening.

Never before have I come in such close contact immediately with anyone. He felt the same & we both marvelled at the time at the strangeness of such a thing, for we both realised it while actually opening our innermost thoughts to each other.

He told me much about his mother and their letters, his sister-in-law, you, and someone else he loved but that I do not [Theodore Roosevelt].

He spoke with deep enthusiasm of leaving his mark and memorial of truth to the world with those letters which should be published after he had gone.

He made an engagement for the next afternoon as I was going to teach him a method of control of the nerves through which I had just been with a noted Swiss doctor knowing it would be a very wonderful thing for him if he could get hold of it for he was very nervous & did not know how he was going to stand the rushing life he was returning to, and we were going to work so hard over it the rest of the time on board.

He said I was just like his mother and opened his heart to me & it was as though we had known each other well for years.

It was the strangest sensation and felt as tho' a veil was blown aside for those few hours eliminating distance between two who had known each other always well long, long before and had just found each other again – I believe it.

Otherwise we could not have met just then and talked as we did.

That night about 12:10 I saw him again and for the last time.

As Mr Thayer, my son, and I had come from dressing in our staterooms & were standing in the hall near the door he came towards us with a strange unseeing look on his face. I caught hold of his coat and said, 'Major Butt, Major Butt, where are you going? Come with me' & he replied 'I have something to do first but will come then' and went in the direction of the staterooms & I said to myself, 'He has gone for his letters.'

And what of those letters? He told me he had had duplicates made of all. Did he mean while he was abroad and that he had them all with him or are they safe with someone in Washington? I must hear.

Oh Mr Taft, is there any chance of seeing either my husband or him here again in this life? My reason tells me no but how can we give up all hope until some days yet go past of this cruel torture.

Oh how he loved you and how frightfully you will miss his care – such a true, devoted, close more-than-friend.

I am sorry for you.

My brief deep knowledge of that lovely personality (I cannot call him acquaintance) is very, very strong & strange to look back upon, and as I say we both at the time remarked and greatly marvelled at it.

It was meant to be for some reason & I am compelled to write you.

Believe me, with the deepest sympathy and grief,

Sincerely,

Marian L.M. Thayer

P.S. Today is my husband's fiftieth birthday. Oh he is young to go and leave us he so loved.

April 21st, 1912[251]

EDWINA TROUTT **Second Class Passenger**

After arriving in New York on 18 April, Miss Troutt wrote the following entry in her diary:

> Thursday, April 18: Terrible screams were heard when I arrived in New York after a terrible thunder & fog-bound journey. Claimed at the dock by Cousin Jenny & Cousin Jim. Sent cable to John Pollins. Automobile waiting with Cousin Grace & clothing remarkable courage of Cousin Jim driving thru the dense crowds of anxious spectators, reached 23rd St. ferry at 10-15 p.m. Caught train for Upper Montclair at 10-25, reached Bellevue Avenue at 11-15 p.m. Had a splendid hot bath & a remarkably comfortable bed. Slept soundly until morn.[252]

On 19 April Miss Troutt wrote a letter to her friend Annie Webbers:

> Belview Avenue
> Upper Montclair
> New Jersey
>
> My dear Annie,
>
> Here am I quite cosy and comfortable as Jennie can make me.
>
> We had a very thrilling time, all having gone to bed, some sleeping heavily, others just gone off, when we heard an unnatural noise, also the sudden ceasing of the vibration, the engines being stopped. I was in a stateroom with 2 others. I being the youngest said: 'Wait and I will see what's the matter,' so having put on my dressing gown, I entered the corridor & only to find it all quiet. I & a few more passengers a little anxious, we were all told to go back to our beds as she had only struck an iceberg. We were all satisfied that it was only slight and were surprised to hear 'All passengers put your lifebelts on and go up on top deck.' We just had the presence of mind to recall what a cold night it was & slip on all warm clothing we could. It was just 1 o'clock when I entered the boat and [illegible] to 5 when we were picked up by the S.S. *Carpathia*. It was a beautiful starlight night. I saved a little baby & we had to keep singing and shouting that being the only signal of our peril. The lifeboats were without light, compass or time ... We were so glad when the break of day came. The conduct of Passengers, Officers and Crew and bandsmen were too magnificent to describe. I saw no panic but read in every paper of them. The *Titanic* sank in eyes of all and with thousands of souls on deck, the band playing 'The Land of Hope' and 'Nearer My God to Thee.' It all seems a dream to me still, altho I saw it and was there. I lost everything & I believe everybody was penniless.
>
> We saw the icebergs everywhere, and we were surrounded by a big ice field. Our lifebelts kept our bodies warm but our limbs were nearly frozen.
>
> The seas were very calm, which was in our favour. The most terrible part of it all was the separation of men and wives and to see room in some of the life boats, and yet the hundreds just waiting for the sea to swallow them up on board the liner.

Trusting this is clear to you & with [illegible] and my love to all enquiring friends and hoping you and Leo Charles are well.

From yours lovingly,

Winnie[253]

Miss Troutt also continued writing her diary entries on 19 April:

Friday 19. *Montclair Times* reporter called me on telephone for descriptive evidence. Cousin Jenny had a whole outfit of new clothes from Macy's Store & a purse of money. Slept most of the day suffering slightly from cold & nerves. Sent letters to [illegible] Buffalo, N.Y. & Annie Webber & Elsie ...

Monday. Called at White Star line for advice, given letter of introduction to relief fund. Advised to send in claim later on. Address given of Miss S. Webber. Had lunch at City. Did shopping returning to Montclair at 3 p.m. All New York in mourning, flags to be seen half mast every where. Dinner in Orange ...

Tuesday April 30. Went to New York City. J.K. tried [illegible] on Fanny. Had lunch at 6 W 50. Spent the afternoon with Jenny Crawford & Nellie Conway returned home 10.00 Got ticket for Auburndale from White Star Line ...

Wednesday May 1. Jenny & I were advised to call at Red X Society regarding the *Titanic* survivors. $100.00. Called at Fanny's met Carrie & Beatrice had invitation to Brooklyn sat evening to dinner.[254]

On 15 May Miss Troutt wrote a letter to a friend in England:

Auburndale
Mass.

Rev & Dear Father Sweeney,

In my Mother's letter she states that you called & made very kind enquiries as to my safety. I thank you very much indeed, and also for the prayers you have said for me.

On the boat there were 3 Priests. The English Priest was an Oxford man also a convert. He celebrated Holy Mass every morning & on Saturday heard confessions. The last I saw of him was at 1 o'clock, he was very reconciled to his fate, & was just gathering the men around him.

The whole affair is too terrible to dwell upon. The only thing that I can do is to pray for the lost souls.

Requiem Masses were celebrated in every Church in the United States for the Heroes of the *Titanic*. Elsie was very pleased that I was saved & we are very happy together. She also has a beautiful son for whom I shall be God Mother next Sunday I believe.

I am getting over the experience of the disaster.

Thanking you for all past kindnesses & hoping you are keeping well.

From Yours Very Sincerely,

Edwina C. Troutt

S.A.G.

May 15th, 1912[255]

On 5 June Miss Troutt wrote the following letter to the widow of *Titanic* victim Jacob Milling:

June 5th, 12
22 Riverside Street
Auburndale
Mass. USA

My very dear Mrs Milling,

Your letter reached me today. Yes, I am the girl in question. Mr Milling dined at my table also 4 (four) other men & two women. All the men are lost & we 3 in all women were saved. Your Husband told me at Queenstown that he felt he had known me for years & had written to you about me. He also I believe sent a letter from Cherbourg & when he was in mid ocean was going to send a wireless. He was very much taken up with the *Titanic*, it being such a beautiful steady ship & many times said, 'My wife has gone with me to Scotland & various places. I wish she was here, this is a beautiful trip.'

All day Saturday he was wanting to send the wireless & told me he had to wait until we were in communication with Cape Race, & Sunday at the dinner table he told me, in these words: 'I have managed to send a wireless today to my wife. We are now right in the middle of the ocean. Just think of it, my wife will have my message & I am miles away.'

Sunday was a very cold day & the evening was spent in prayer & reading. Mr Milling, Mr Andrew & myself were in the Library talking over various things. He went to bed about 10:30 & at 10:55 I heard the ship make a stumbling noise, enough to wake me. (I was sound asleep.) In my state room were two other women & I being the younger suggested them remaining in bed & I would see if there was anything the matter. I met only a few curious women & Mr Andrew. I tried to find out what was the matter, & the officer told me, 'It's only an iceberg. You must go back to your stateroom or you'll catch cold.'

I went to the state room & told my companions everything would be alright. It's only an iceberg. I would go up on boat deck & try & get fuller particulars. I saw them lower one lifeboat with no one in it & noticed the men were also uncovering another. I then realised that something was the matter. I at once went to the state rooms of all my friends & told them to dress in case we were called up. Then I met Mr Milling & he said 'What is the trouble, Miss Troutt? What does it all mean?' I said, 'A very sad parting for all of us. This ship is going to sink.' (Mr Andrew laughed at me & said impossible.)

Your husband caught hold of my two hands & said, 'Don't worry I am sorry that such a thing has happened, but I sent the wireless to day & we are in communication with several vessels & we will all be saved, though parted, but I won't go back home on so big a ship.'

No thought was given to letters. I left Mr Milling talking with several men. Mr Andrew & I then went looking for other friends & so many of them couldn't do anything for themselves so we helped them with their life preservers & it was after 1 o'clock when I was pushed into the lifeboat. It was so dark I couldn't see a soul I knew. I have regretted so many times that I hadn't the presence of mind to ask the men if they had any letters for me to mail as your Husband & Mr Andrew wrote letters every morning. He was most devoted to you & showed me your picture with the two children. All passengers thought he was my Father. I cannot express my sympathy upon your very great loss as I know even in so short a time Mr Milling to be a devoted Husband & Father. Trusting this letter will be satisfactory & that yourself & children are bearing up through your very great bereavement. God Bless you.

Yours very sincerely,

Edwina Celia Troutt

I did not know his body was found until your letter reached me & I have watched for his name.

Finished June 10th[256]

ELLEN WALCROFT — Second Class Passenger

On 23 April Miss Walcroft wrote the following letter to her home town newspaper:

Sir, I am sending the account of my journey on the *Titanic* thinking that it will interest those at Maidenhead whom I know.

I left Maidenhead on April 9th, stayed in London and caught the special train to Southampton at 8:30 on the morning of April 10th. My sister and a friend saw me off. After a splendid quick run we arrived at Southampton Dock Station at 10:15.

Looking through the window I saw the largest ship I had ever seen, the sun was shining on it and it was magnificent, everyone was going over the ship and it was greatly admired. The bell rang and all the visitors left the ship. Then we ... started to the hand waving of thousands of people.

We left the docks. We did not know about the near collision we had until we arrived this side. We arrived at Cherbourg at 5 o'clock and at Queenstown on Thursday morning; we had a perfect trip.

On the Sunday night we went to our stateroom about 10:30. We had not been asleep long when suddenly a crash came and I was nearly thrown out of my berth. I woke my friend, Miss Clear Cameron, who did not hear anything unusual and then I heard the noise of footsteps along the corridor. I waited very anxiously to hear what was the matter because the engines had stopped.

Immediately the Steward came down and said 'Go back to your beds. No danger!' but I heard whispering of icebergs and then suddenly we heard very loud hammering as if they were closing heavy iron doors. Five minutes after the steward came down and said 'Go back to your beds! no danger!' Oh what a relief, but a few minutes later he came in and said 'Will you dress and go on deck with your lifebelts on as quickly as possible, it's only a precaution.' My friend and I dressed. There were full instructions how to put the lifebelts on in the stateroom, but we were too nervous to stop to read them.

People were going up on deck so we both went, carrying our belts from E deck. A man took the lifebelts from us and put them over our heads and tied them on. The order was for women and children to go on the lower deck but there was such a lot he told some to go up on the boat deck, so we went.

We walked round, thinking there was no hurry when suddenly rockets went up! We then began to realise the danger we were in. Boats were lowered, there was room for two more in boat 14 which I think was the last but three to leave the ship.

Immediately the order was given to lower the boats we began to descend. There were 58 women and children but only about three to row when going down. There was no man in charge and 5th Officer Harold Lowe jumped on our boat and gave the orders. Some men in the Steerage were going to spring in and he threatened them with his revolver to shoot the first, knowing that another one would buckle up the lifeboat. He shot twice, but only at the side, so that the men, who were panic-stricken in the steerage should know it was loaded and that he meant what he said. When from below the shouting 'Stop lowering No.14' was heard, we were being dropped onto a lifeboat, they could not get away from the side of the ship.

At last they did so the men lowered our boat. One side worked better than the other and the ropes on one side did not act so the officer gave the order to cut the ropes and the boat fell some distance and then we got safely away from the ship's side. It was a lovely starlight night, but not light enough for us to see who were in the boats. The officer told the men to lay on their oars, so as to be handy later on. We did not seem to be long on the water.

We could see the ship gradually going down, but all the lights were on, when suddenly two terrible explosions took place. The ship seemed to go forward and then split in the middle and then there were two more explosions that seemed from underneath the water. No more could be seen of that grand ship; all was silent for a moment and then the cries of 1600 men. All were crying for help; it was terrible.

I should think the cries must have lasted two hours, or even more and then the day dawned and we could see about six large icebergs. Each looked as large as a house and all the time the cries of the drowning were getting fainter. Then Officer Lowe wanted to go back to the rescue, but the women begged him not to go. He got about four boats together and distributed his passengers amongst them as many as he possibly could and then went back to the rescue. I believe they rescued six alive from that raft; the others had all died from exposure, as it was intensely cold.

The boat I got in was No.10. There had been six picked up but one man was mad. He shook the boat and we were afraid it would capsize. Two men revived but they were terribly frozen and two were dead and fell into the water at the bottom of the boat.

Several times we thought we saw the lights of a ship, but no. Then we saw the lights of the *Carpathia*. We tried to shout for joy but it was a poor noise.

My friend, Miss Clear Cameron, took an oar and the sea was getting much rougher and several of the passengers were very sick. By this time the cries of the drowning had ceased and the men rowed as quickly as possible. We wondered if ever we should get to it; our boat had about two feet of water in it, although we bailed out all the time. Every wave we thought would swamp us and the wreckage was sailing down right in our course. We got safely over that but when the boat was so deep in the water we were pulled back to lie at the end of the boat. Oh, that last hour's row with hope in sight!

When we got to the *Carpathia* we were helped up with ropes. The kindness of the Officers and crew we shall never forget. They took us all along to the saloon and gave us neat brandy. The women were brought in screaming on account of children they had lost. Some of the children got separated from their parents and others looked after them.

Those we had said good-night to on the *Titanic* on the Sunday evening we shook hands with on the Monday at a quarter to seven, that was the time we were picked up by the *Carpathia*, thanking God for our safety. All the boats were not in, so we went up on deck and watched the others coming up. Quite near the *Carpathia* were quite large icebergs and ice about 12 miles long, broken ice, it was a most imposing sight. I went to the wireless operator, who was very kind and promised if possible, to get a wireless through to tell Mother I was saved, but he was unable to do so, having so much to do.

The men on the *Carpathia* had the message from the *Titanic* to say it was sinking and the Captain had every member of the crew up at one o'clock to prepare for all the survivors of the *Titanic*. No one could have been kinder. We tried to sleep that night on the tables in the saloon but it thundered and lightened all night. How thankful we were that it was not the previous night! We were so glad when the news came that the Captain was going to New York! We had fog and rain nearly all the way until we got to Sandy Hook, when the Pilot and several more steamers came out to meet us.

When we arrived at New York it was about 8 o'clock and the steamers all round were making flash-light photographs of the *Carpathia* and passengers and the reporters kept shouting at us for news. When we arrived at the pier we did not know that we should be allowed off the ship, but the gangway was put up, and having no customs to go through, having lost everything, we were allowed ashore.

There were gentlemen from the Stock Exchange, Sisters-of-Mercy and ladies to meet us. We felt very dazed and strange.

They took us and gave us necessary clothes and then I met my brother, and very glad I was. They took us to a cab and we were 'Flash-lighted' going along; 70,000 people were waiting, roped off, to see us.

How glad we were to get to my sister and have a wash and go to bed again.

Everyone is very kind to us. There were 36 women saved whose husbands were left on the *Titanic*. It was fearfully sad when they knew their husbands had gone.

They had hoped to meet them in New York. When they were told that no more had been picked up they were in a terrible state.

How much more fortunate were my friend and I than so many other poor things!

Yours faithfully,
Nellie Walcroft
Mamaroneck, New York.
April 23rd, 1912[257]

ROBERTHA WATT **Second Class Passenger**

In 1914 Miss Watt wrote the following account of her *Titanic* experience for her school newspaper:

As April 15 comes around once more, it brings to our memory the greatest marine disaster the world has ever known, the sinking of the *Titanic* in mid-ocean on that day of 1912.

As the great ship drew away from the wharf, on April 10, on her ill-fated voyage, she broke the cable of the *Philadelphia*, and almost had a collision with her, which caused many superstitious people to think that this meant a bad voyage, which at that time we did not believe.

Up until Sunday the weather was beautiful, but on Sunday it became very cold and we quickened our speed to twenty knots an hour. In the evening we sang hymns in the dining room until nearly 11 o'clock. Then about 12 o'clock a huge iceberg struck the ship, tearing open the bottom and exposing the boilers to the icy waters. I was then sleeping and was, therefore, not fortunate enough to see the huge blue iceberg, which was the height of the funnels. About 1 o'clock I was awakened and put on my coat and life belt and went on deck. As the elevator was not running, the people were crowding up the stairway.

The master-at-arms stood with a pistol in his hand, threatening to shoot steerage passenger men who attempted to come up the second cabin stairway.

On reaching the top deck we met some friends, who told us that the eight first-class boats had gone off.

The port side of the ship was very crowded, so we went around to the starboard side, and there we heard a call, 'All women and children this way.' We went and got into boat No.9, which was the tenth to leave.

There was a gentleman friend of ours who came into the boat with us, but was immediately put out, and we were then lowered with only about forty-five people in the boat, which would have help ninety people, and yet we could not wait to take another man in, as they feared the steerage passenger men might charge the boats.

We had neither compass, light, matches, nor water and were out quite a long time before we could find the rudder.

As the *Titanic* gradually sank down by her bow, the lights went out row after row, and then we heard many pistol shots and could see people running hopelessly up and down the decks. We did not hear the band play 'Nearer, My God to Thee' but a friend who left the ship when it broke told us that the minister and his wife, who had conducted the hymns in the evening, suggested that they should play a hymn.

Then about 2 o'clock we heard the boilers burst and then she broke in two and slid into the water, leaving nothing to be seen. We were left entirely alone and in the dark, except for the stars.

The water was wonderfully calm, not even a ripple on it, except when the ship went down, and even then it was not very rough. It would really have been a lovely midnight sail had we known what was going to happen to us next and also been prepared for the intense cold. We had just to drift around till dawn, occasionally flickering a gentleman's cigar-lighter to let the other boats see where we were. Then, about 4 o'clock, we observed a light and, as we came closer, we saw that it was a ship, but feared that we would be crushed by an iceberg before it reached us, as there were many surrounding us. One of the most beautiful scenes was that of one of the boats passing between two huge icebergs. The sun was rising in the east and shining on the ice, thus making it glitter like silver, and the boat seemed like a tiny black speck in comparison with the icebergs.

When we got alongside the *Carpathia*, a rope was fixed around our waists and we climbed up a rope ladder. On board we got all the blankets we required and hot drinks. Then we watched the other boats come in and one raft landed with seven people, three of whom survived that night. This raft had left the *Titanic* with about fifty men and one woman, and all that survived was the woman, a young boy of about eighteen, and an old man. All three were practically frozen when brought on board, as they had been nearly eight hours in the water. About 4 o'clock in the afternoon the *California* came and stayed, watching for anyone else that might still be around, thus letting us start for New York.

The *Carpathia* was a great change from the luxuries of the *Titanic*, but we had learned to be thankful for small mercies. In the following days nothing eventful happened, only a few electric storms and fogs. We landed in New York about 9 o'clock in the evening.[258]

AUGUST WEIKMAN **Crew (Barber)**

On 24 April 1912 Mr Weikman made the following deposition for the Senate *Titanic* inquiry:

> I certify that my occupation on the *Titanic* was known as the saloon barber. I was sitting in my barber shop on Sunday night, April 14, 1912, at 11:40 p.m., when the collision occurred. I went forward to the steerage on 'G' deck and saw one of the baggage-masters, and he told me that water was coming in in the baggage room on the deck below. I think the baggageman's name was Bessant. I then went upstairs and met Mr Andrews, the 'builder', and he was giving instructions to get the steerage passengers 'on deck'. I proceeded along 'E' deck to my room on 'C' deck. I went on the main deck and saw some ice laying there. Orders were given, 'All hands to man the lifeboats, also to put on life belts.' Who gave the orders? Mr Dodd, second steward.
>
> I helped to launch the boats, and there seemed to be a shortage of women. When I was on 'E' deck I met the captain returning from 'G' deck, who had been there with Mr Andrews, and the captain was on the bridge at that time. I did not think there was any danger. What happened after the orders were given? Instructions were given to get the passengers into life belts and get on deck from all the staterooms. Did you see Mr Ismay? Yes. I saw Mr Ismay helping to load the boats. Did you see him get in a boat? Yes; he got in along with Mr Carter, because there were no women in the vicinity of the boat. This boat was the last to leave, to the best of my knowledge. He was ordered into the boat by the officer in charge. I think that Mr Ismay was justified in getting in that boat at that time.
>
> I was proceeding to launch the next boat when the ship suddenly sank at the bow and there was a rush of water that washed me overboard, and therefore the boat was not launched by human hands. The men were trying to pull up the sides when the rush of water came, and that was the last moment it was possible to launch any more boats, because the ship was at an angle that it was impossible for anybody to remain on deck. State further what you know about the case. After I was washed overboard I started to swim, when there was a pile of ropes fell upon me, and I managed to get clear of these and started to swim for some dark object in the water. It was dark. This was about 1:50 a.m. toward the stern. How do you know it was 1:50 a.m.? Because my watch was stopped at that time by the water. Did you hear any noise? Yes; I was about 15 feet away from the ship when I heard a second explosion. What caused the explosion? I think the boilers blew up about in the middle of the ship. The explosion blew me along with a wall of water toward the dark object I was swimming to, which proved to be a bundle of deck chairs, which I managed to climb on. While on the chairs I heard terrible groans and cries coming from people in the water. Was it possible to help them? No; it was not. The lifeboats were too far away. Do you think if the lifeboats were nearer they could render any assistance? Yes; had the lifeboats remained close to the *Titanic* they could have taken 10 to 15 or maybe 20 more passengers to each boat. There was a great number of people killed by the explosion, and there

was a great number that managed to get far enough away that the explosion did not injure them, and these are the people that I think could have been saved had the lifeboats been closer. Did you see the ship go down? I mean the *Titanic*. Yes; I was afloat on some chairs about 100 feet away, looking toward the ship. I seen her sink. Did you feel any suction? No; but there was some waves come toward me caused by the ship going down, and not enough to knock me off of the chairs. How many lifeboats were there on the *Titanic*? About 18 or 20 and four collapsible boats, and the best equipment possible to put on a ship. Do you think there was enough lifeboats? No. Do you know anything about the water-tight doors? Yes; she had self-closing doors of the latest type, and they all worked, to the best of my knowledge. How fast was she going when she struck the iceberg? I think about 20 knots per hour. I was told by Mr Ismay that she was limited to 75 revolutions several days before.

A.H. Weikman[259]

ELEANOR WIDENER — **First Class Passenger**

On 29 May the widowed Mrs Widener made the following deposition for the Senate *Titanic* inquiry:

> I was a passenger with my husband, George D. Widener, and my son, Harry Widener, on the steamship *Titanic* of the White Star Line on her voyage from Southampton on the 10th day of April, 1912. On the night of Sunday, the 14th of April, 1912, my husband and I gave a dinner at which Capt. Smith was present. Capt. Smith drank absolutely no wine or intoxicating liquor of any kind whatever at the dinner.[260]

In July 1914, during the construction of Harvard University's Harry Elkins Widener Memorial Library, Mrs Widener wrote the following letter to A.S.W. Rosenbach, a bookseller and close friend of her late son, victim Harry Widener, regarding the deposition of Harry's personal collection of rare books:

> When the library is finished I want all the books installed here. Then I will feel happiness and know I have done as my dear boy wished. Over two years have gone since I lost him, and I am no more reconciled than I was at first, and never will be again. All joy of living left me on April 15, 1912. Forgive me for writing you like this, but you loved Harry, and can understand my sorrow.[261]

RICHARD WILLIAMS **First Class Passenger**

After one of the *Titanic*'s collapsible Engelhardt lifeboats was recovered by the *Oceanic* in May 1912, Mr Williams wrote a letter to fellow survivor Archibald Gracie describing his own survival on board that same collapsible:

> I was not under water very long, and as soon as I came to the top I threw off the big fur coat. I also threw off my shoes. About twenty yards away I saw something floating. I swam to it and found it to be a collapsible boat. I hung on to it and after a while got aboard and stood up in the middle of it. The water was up to my waist. About thirty of us clung to it. When Officer Lowe's boat picked us up eleven of us were still alive; all the rest were dead from cold. My fur coat was found attached to this Engelhardt boat 'A' by the *Oceanic*, and also a cane marked 'C. Williams.' This gave rise to the story that my father's body was in this boat, but this as you see, is not so. How the cane got there I do not know.[262]

(Note: the notion that a cane was found in Collapsible A was due to a newspaper error.)

MARION WRIGHT **Second Class Passenger**

After her marriage to Arthur Woolcott, the former Marion Wright sent the following letter to the mother of victim Dr Alfred Pain:

> Cottage Grove,
> Oregon, U.S.A., May 28
>
> Dear Mrs Pain,
>
> I have been wanting so much to write you for some time, but I didn't know your address until a few days ago, when I got a letter from Miss Elsie Richards, written from Devonshire, in which she asked me to write her all I could about your dear son, Dr Alfred Pain. She also gave me your address, so now I feel I must do my duty, painful though it is. How your poor heart must be torn to lose him as you have, in all his prime, and in such perfect health. We did not get acquainted till the Friday after we sailed, so, though I only knew him for three days, yet I felt he was a friend. He said I was the first lady he had spoken to. I had noticed him before. He seemed so good getting up games for the young fellows on board. We had several meals together and he told me how much he enjoyed his stay in England. On the Sunday I asked him to come to the service in the second class saloon. He did, and again in the evening came with a number of others to sing hymns in the dining room, and himself chose one or two. I believe he especially asked for 'Abide With Me, Fast Falls the Eventide.' Afterwards we had supper with

one or two other people who had been singing with us, and then retired to our berths. About 12.30 a.m., when I had been on deck already for some time, your son came up, properly dressed, and with his lifebelt on. I could see he was looking for someone, and after a while he found me, and said: 'I have been trying to find you for some time.' I asked him if he thought there was any great danger, and he assured me there could not be. We stood for some time on the starboard, watching them lower boats. There were hundreds of women on that side, and your son suddenly said: 'I think we had better go round the other side; there aren't so many people there.' We did so, and scarcely had we got round when the cry came, 'Any more ladies, this way!' Your son said, 'You had better run.' I did so, and he followed and put me in the lifeboat. It is such a grief to me that I didn't say goodbye to him, but I thought, as everyone else did, that we would go back to the *Titanic* before very long. But when we got out on the sea we could see the boat gradually sinking, deck after deck, and oh! how much we hoped all would be saved ere she went down. But when the awful news came to us that only 700 were saved, and those were with us on the *Carpathia*, how grieved I felt and how I wished your son had been among that 700. It all seems so sad and overwhelming. My mind will never forget it, as long as I live. I trust just these few lines may comfort the heart of Dr Pain's sorrow-stricken mother, is the prayer of yours, with much sympathy,

Marion Woolcott[263]

MARIE YOUNG — First Class Passenger

On 10 May 1912 Miss Young wrote the following letter to President Taft regarding the death of his aide-de-camp, Major Archibald Butt:

10th May
Briarcliff Lodge
Briarcliff Manor, New York
President William H. Taft,

Dear Mr President,

I have read an account of the Memorial Service in Washington recently, in honour of Major Archibald Butt, at which service the Secretary of War alluded to a farewell conversation, supposed to have taken place between Major Butt and myself. Had such a conversation taken place, I should not have delayed one hour in giving you every detail of the last hours of your special aide & friend.

Although a Washingtonian, I did not know Major Butt, having been in deep mourning for several years. The alleged 'interview' is entirely an invention, by some officious reporter; who thereby brought much distress to many of

Major Butt's near relatives and friends – for while they wrote me, of what a comfort the story was to them, I had to tell them it was untrue, as no such deception could be carried through.

They wrote me that through Mr Sloan's kindness, they obtained my address – and I immediately wrote Mr Sloan that there was no truth in this newspaper story.

When I last saw Major Butt, he was walking on deck, with Mr Clarence Moore, on Sunday afternoon.

With deep regret that I could not be his messenger to you,

Believe me,

Very sincerely yours,

(Miss) Marie G. Young[264]

In October 1912 Miss Young wrote the following account of her experience on the *Titanic*:

Six months have elapsed since the *Titanic* – the most splendid of all passenger ships – sank in the North Atlantic Ocean, in sight of fifteen boat loads of survivors, numbering less than a third of the passengers and crew who had embarked at her three ports of call.

Perhaps no two survivors would answer alike the question, 'What is your most poignant memory of the fatal voyage, and of its fifth and final night?'

A panorama of incidents passes before the mind – trivial events ordinarily, but rendered tragic because of the death of many who sailed on the *Titanic*, but who never heard the eager roll-call of the *Carpathia*. What became of the merry group of boys who were beside me, in the telegraph office at the dock at Cherbourg, hurrying off last messages to friends on shore?

Who can forget the cruel change in the faces of those who had waved gay farewells as the tender left the French harbour, and ere they again sighted land, had yielded up all that made life beautiful to them? Figures, faces and even varying facial expressions are remembered of those who, though strangers, were fellow-passengers, beloved of many ashore to whom even our fading impressions and slight knowledge would be a consolation, should the paths of our lives ever cross.

In my thoughts I often lie again in my steamer chair, and watch the passing throng on the *Titanic*'s promenade deck. After the usual excitement of buying lace from the Irish girls who came aboard at Queenstown, was over, the routine of life on deck was established.

Two famous men passed many times every day in a vigorous constitutional, one talking always – as rapidly as he walked – the other a good and smiling listener.

Babies and nurses, dear old couples, solitary men, passed sunlit hours of those spring days on deck, while the *Titanic* swept on to the scene of the disaster; approaching what might not have been so much a sinister fate awaiting her, as it was an opportunity for her commander and the President of the White Star Line, to prove true seamanship and their great discretion in the presence of reported and recognised peril.

It so happened that I took an unusual interest in some of the men below decks, for I had talked often with the carpenter and the printer, in having extra crates and labels made for the fancy French poultry we were bringing home, and I saw a little of the ship's life, in my daily visits to the gaily crowing roosters, and to the hens, who laid eggs busily, undismayed by the novelty and commotion of their surroundings.

I had seen the cooks before their great cauldrons of porcelain, and the bakers turning out the huge loaves of bread, a hamper of which was later brought on deck to supply the life boats.

In accepting some gold coins, the ship's carpenter said, 'It is such good luck to receive gold on a first voyage!' Yet he was the first of the *Titanic*'s martyrs, who, in sounding the ship just after the iceberg was struck, sank and was lost in the inward rushing sea that engulfed him.

Who can imagine the earthly purgatory of anguish endured by Captain Smith, during the pitifully short time vouchsafed him to prepare for death – whose claim upon him he, more than all others, must acknowledge?

Who exchanged a last word with any of the joyous bridal couples, to whom each day at sea had brought a deeper glow of happiness? Expectant, they stood at the threshold of earthly life, yet they passed together that night through the gates of Eternity, to a fairer day than that which dawned for those left to face an unknown fate.

What scenes were enacted to immortalise forever the engineers who kept the ship lighted and afloat, giving a last chance of escape to passengers and even officers. How can we ever realise what it meant to find courage to reject the thought of beloved dependents on shore, and to face death in stoke-hold and engine room?

The 'greater love' that lays down life that another may live burned in many a heart in the *Titanic*'s list of dead, and those who survive owe them a debt, only to be acknowledged and wiped out by a flawless record of lives nobly lived, because so cruelly bought.

Vivid and endless are the impressions of that great night. They remain as closely folded in the brain as the shock of the discharge of guns, the cries of the drowning and the sobs of the broken-hearted.

Clearest of all is the remembrance of the eighteen self-controlled women in our boat (number 8), four of whom had parted, bitterly protesting, from their husbands.

In those hours spent face to face with the solemn thoughts of trials still to undergo before possible rescue, it was inspiring to see that these Twentieth Century women were, in mentality and physique, worthy descendants of their ancestors, who had faced other dire peril in Colonial and Revolutionary periods.

Women rowed all night, others in the bow waved the lantern high in air as a signal to the ship toward whose light our boat crept slowly till dawn, with only a young girl at the tiller to keep the boat headed straight in spite of the jerky, uneven rowing.

Treasured above all else was the electric light in the handle of a cane belonging to Mrs J. Stuart White, who waved it regularly while counting strokes for the haphazard crew. The assurance that its light would burn continuously for thirty hours helped comfort many minds aghast at the possibility of another night to be endured before rescue. We had no knowledge of wireless response to the *Titanic*'s frantic calls for help, nor of the glorious rush through the sea of ice which was bringing near the fearless little *Carpathia*.

If we, the survivors, spent a night of exhausting struggle, of emotion, and of prayer, what of the Captain, the crew, and the awakening passengers of the rescue ship?

Nevertheless, we turn to a brighter side of the picture, for hope must have filled all the hearts of those who turned back so promptly at the first distress signal.

The United States Senate investigation brought to the world's notice a document containing Captain Rostron's written orders to his officers and crew, a copy of which should be framed on every ship as a model of perfect organisation in time of stress.

No detail of careful preparation was omitted.

All the reading world knows now that, after answering the *Titanic*'s wireless appeal, Captain Rostron put an additional officer on the *Carpathia*'s bridge, doubled his lookouts in the crow's nest, and called out an extra fire room force.

But of his final and complete preparations, enough cannot be said. His three physicians – English, Italian and Hungarian – were detailed to look after the different classes of rescued passengers; his life boats were supplied with food, medicine and blankets, and they were ready to lower as soon as he should approach the wreck, which alas! He was indeed never to see.

He ordered his own crew to be fed and fortified for the coming hours of strain, and they promised their brave commander to show the world of what stuff the British seaman is made.

His own steerage passengers were placed in close quarters, and their natural excitement quieted by a few judicious words. And these given instances of careful forethought are but a few, remembered at random, and only a suggestion of the great work accomplished by Captain Rostron in the cause of humanity.

When the *Carpathia* reached the scene of the disaster, finding fifteen boats, some only half filled, the survivors of the tragedy that had been enacted between the setting and the rising sun were lifted on board, with pity and tenderness almost divine in their gentleness.

The details of the shipwreck, its perils, horrors and racking uncertainties, have filled the magazines and newspapers. But of the wonderful, unique days that followed, little has been said.

Many of the survivors were dazed by the paralysing events of the night – the shock of the collision and the terror of the realisation that their only chance for life was in escaping in the life boats. The perilous descent into the boats, their ignorant handling, the immediate sinking of the *Titanic*, the heartrending cries of the dying, the night spent adrift on the bitterly cold sea, and finally the hazardous ascent in the boatswain's seat from life boat to the *Carpathia*'s gangway, were all experiences to haunt and tax the most stoical.

For those who had lost members of their families, friends or servants, it was a bitter moment when, at ten o'clock on Monday morning, April 15, Captain Rostron steamed away from the scene of the wreck, leaving two tardy and cruelly negligent steamers to watch the scene of the greatest maritime tragedy.

The day was cold, but brilliant. All morning the *Carpathia* passed a field of ice, forty miles in length, and extending northward as far as eye could see.

After food and blankets had been distributed amongst the survivors, their names were carefully noted; then the weary task began, lasting for days, of sending them by wireless to an awe-stricken, listening, longing world. The *Carpathia*'s own exhausted operator was relieved by the equally worn-out second operator [Harold Bride] from the *Titanic*, who had been lifted more dead than alive from the ocean.

Meanwhile, the *Carpathia*'s sympathetic passengers were sharing rooms and clothing with those rescued; every possible berth was assigned, and all available space in the library and dining saloon used for sleeping quarters. Mattresses were laid on the dining tables, and at night old and young 'made up' beds on the library floors, a most informal proceeding consisting of spreading a folded steamer rug on the floor, with a second rug to sleep under, and perhaps, if one had luck, a sofa cushion for pillow.

Such beds were smilingly and uncomplainingly occupied. One bright old lady, who slept thus beside her sister's bed on a bench, called it the 'lower berth in the *Carpathia* Pullman!'

No such makeshift, however, for the President of the White Star Line – hidden in the English physician's comfortable room, he voyaged to New York, as heedlessly indifferent to the discomfort of his Company's passengers as he had been to the deadly peril that had menaced them. Richer, far, in experience were those who mingled freely in that ship's company.

There were lessons to be learned in every hour of that voyage. Who could ever forget the splendid work of one young girl, whose father was a missionary? After giving garments of her own to many survivors, she collected more clothing to supply further needs – she cut out dresses for the many forlorn babies, and spent days ministering to the terrified emigrants in the steerage.

Cruel indeed was the plight of these foreigners; many of them were young mothers, with wailing babies who refused food – widowed, penniless, ignorant of the language of an unknown country, they faced the New World. But, indeed, the wind was truly tempered to these shorn lambs, for North and South, East and West were gathering together a golden store for their needs on landing and for their future assistance.

The last three days of the voyage were taxing because rain kept the passengers crowded in the library, the wail of the fog-horn sounding continually, strained overwrought nerves, as the *Carpathia* steered cautiously and slowly toward New York, with her doubly precious freight of human souls.

Many were the experiences and tales of adventures on sea and land exchanged in those penned-in, irksome hours; hot and bitter were the denunciations of the criminal neglect of those whose authority could and should have averted the disaster.

Inevitable were the collections and disagreements over loving cups and votes of thanks, to be presented to the embarrassed, bashful, but truly heroic Captain.

Fire Island! Ambrose Channel! Welcoming sirens of hundreds of tugs, newspaper boats, steamers and yachts! And the lights of New York!

Hardly were the many telegrams from our friends handed to us before we neared the Cunard docks; never was homecoming so sweet as on that immortal night of nights, when again the world waited, hushed, for the coming epic of abysmal horror, of consuming, unending grief, and of sublime heroism.

Even now one must doubt whether the terrible lesson to be learned from such an appalling tragedy has been given due consideration by those who govern the courses of the ocean liners. One reads of steamers again venturing over the northerly course and reporting ice in sight. The captains of the best patronised lines state they would have followed Captain Smith's route under similar conditions, apparently preferring insane speeding among icebergs to taking a more southerly course.

Almost from the time of the world's creation, men have 'gone down to the sea in ships'. Human intelligence has laboured long to conquer the elements, and today inventive genius seems to triumph over all that vexed the soul and brain of the sturdy adventurers who discovered our land. But man can never be Omnipotent. An unsinkable ship will never cross the sea. Granting that the *Titanic* was a triumph of construction and appointments, even she could not trespass upon a law of nature and survive.

Helplessly that beautiful and gallant ship struggled to escape from the hand of God, but was only an atom in the Hold of inexorable justice.

Majestically she sailed; but bowed, broken and crouching, she sank slowly beneath the conquering ocean; a hidden memorial shaft to the unburied dead she carried with her, and to the incredible wickedness of man, until the coming of the day when 'there shall be no more sea'.[265]

Passenger and Crew Biographies

Note: passengers' ages at the time of the voyage are included in parentheses after their names.

KAREN ABELSETH **Status: Survivor**

Karen Abelseth (16) lived with her widowed father and six brothers and sisters on their farm in Sondmore, Norway. Karen was supposed to graduate from school in June 1912, but an opportunity arose for her to join her older sister, Ann Marie, who had emigrated to Inglewood, California in 1909. Miss Abelseth was allowed to take her school examinations early, and she then travelled to Southampton with family friend Olaus Abelseth, who was returning to America and who had agreed to look after Karen during her journey. Karen and Olaus booked their passages as steerage passengers on board the *Titanic*.

OLAUS ABELSETH — Status: Survivor

Olaus Abelseth (25) grew up with his seven brothers and sisters on the family farm in Ørskog, Norway. In 1903 Olaus emigrated to America and became a farm hand in North Dakota, eventually securing his own homestead in South Dakota.

By 1911 Abelseth had accumulated enough money to visit his family in Norway, and he made the trip back to his homeland in the autumn of that year. In the spring of 1912, Mr Abelseth prepared to return to the United States, and a number of friends and relatives decided to accompany him to the New World; these were Sigurd Moen (his brother-in-law), Peter Søholt (his cousin), Adolf Humblen, Anna Salkjelsvik and Karen Abelseth. The small party of Norwegians travelled together to Southampton and booked steerage passages on board the *Titanic*.

ELIZABETH ALLEN — Status: Survivor

Elizabeth Allen (29) was born on 1 October 1882 in St Louis, Missouri, she and her sister Clara being the daughters of George and Lydia Allen. George Allen was a judge and formerly lived in Pittsfield, Massachusetts, and Elizabeth spent part of her childhood in that city.

In January 1912 Elizabeth travelled to England to finalise the plans for her autumn marriage to Dr James Mennell, a London physician; she resided at 4 South Terrace in Littlehampton. Elizabeth Allen purchased her trousseau in Paris but left her treasures there in readiness for her anticipated return to the City of Light later that summer. Miss Allen's wedding preparations were ably guided by her aunt, Elizabeth Robert (43), who was accompanied by her daughter Georgette Madill (16) and her maid Emilie Kreuchen (29).

By April 1912 Elizabeth Allen was ready to return to St Louis to arrange for the shipment of her personal belongings to England, and she, Mrs Robert, Miss Madill and Miss Kreuchen made arrangements to return to the United States on the maiden voyage of the *Titanic*. On 10 April the four travellers took the train to Southampton, boarded the *Titanic* as first class passengers and proceeded to deposit $25,000 worth of valuables with the ship's purser.

EDGAR ANDREW — Status: Victim

Edgar Andrew (17) was born in the province of Cordoba, Argentina on 28 March 1895 and was one of eight children of Samuel and Annie Andrew (English immigrants who had settled in Argentina in the 1870s). Samuel was the administrator of a large farm in Cordoba and sent each of his children, as they grew older, to England to permit them to know their relatives there.

Edgar's father passed away in 1906, and in 1911 it became Edgar's turn to leave the nest. Instead of sailing to England, however, the young man travelled to the United States to visit his brother Silvano, who was living and working there. Silvano then arranged for Edgar to enrol in a school in Bournemouth, England and periodically sent his younger brother money to support his education.

In 1912 Edgar received a letter from Silvano inviting him to return to the United States to attend his wedding on 27 April 1912; Silvano also asked Edgar to go to work for a company belonging to his fiancée. Eager to comply with his elder brother's wishes, Edgar arranged to sail on board the *Oceanic* on 17 April; when the coal strike forced cancellation of that voyage, however, Edgar transferred his booking to a second class passage on the brand new *Titanic*.

Edgar's altered travel plans created a problem, though, because his close friend Josefina ('Josey') Cowan had written him a letter from Argentina saying that she would be visiting England shortly after the *Titanic*'s sailing date and expressing the hope that she could spend time with Edgar while she was there. As much as Edgar wished to see Josey, he knew that his brother's wedding date could not be postponed, and it was for that reason that he boarded the *Titanic* at Southampton on 10 April.

KORNELIA ANDREWS — Status: Survivor

Kornelia Andrews (62) was born in Hudson, New York on 12 August 1849. She, her three sisters and her brother Robert were the children of Robert and Matilda Andrews. Kornelia's grandfather, the Revd Jacob Fonda, had been pastor of the Dutch Reformed Church at Linlithgo from 1842 to 1847, and her grandmother, Cornelia Scudder, was the sister of the Revd John Scudder, a noted missionary.

Miss Andrews spent a number of years working in her father's law office and was very helpful to him in preparing his cases. Upon her father's death Miss Andrews devoted herself to her mother's welfare.

Kornelia Andrews had a reputation for kindness and generosity and was devoted to her church as well as to her community's social and charity functions. In 1902 Miss Andrews became secretary of the Board of Trustees of the Hudson City Hospital, and she was still serving in that capacity in 1912.

In April 1912 Miss Andrews was in England with her sister Anna Hogeboom (51) and their niece Gretchen Longley (21). The three ladies made plans to return home to Hudson, and on 10 April they travelled to Southampton and boarded the *Titanic* as first class passengers.

THOMAS ANDREWS — Status: Victim

Thomas Andrews Jr was born in Comber, Ireland on 7 February 1873, a son of the Right Hon. Thomas Andrews and Eliza Pirrie; he was also a nephew of Lord Pirrie, principal owner of Harland & Wolff (the builders of the *Titanic*).

In 1884 Andrews entered the Royal Academical Institution, but at the age of 16 he left school and entered Harland & Wolff shipbuilders as a premium apprentice, gradually working his way up through various departments. He eventually became the managing director of Harland & Wolff in charge of designing, and was familiar with every detail of the construction of the firm's ships. In 1901 Andrews became a member of the Institution of Naval Architects.

On 24 June 1908 Thomas Andrews married Helen Reilly Barbour; and two years later a daughter, Elizabeth, was born to the young couple.

Thomas Andrews made a point of sailing with a team of mechanics on the maiden voyages of the *Adriatic*, *Oceanic* and *Olympic* in order to observe their operation and recommend improvements to future vessels slated to be built by his firm. It was for this reason that Andrews planned to sail on *Titanic*'s maiden voyage to America, and the 39-year-old executive left his wife and daughter in Belfast while he accompanied the vessel first to Southampton and, later, out onto the vast expanse of the North Atlantic.

RAMON ARTAGAVEYTIA — Status: Victim

Ramon Artagaveytia (71) was born in Montevideo in July 1840. On 24 December 1871 he was one of only sixty-five passengers who survived the burning and sinking of the ship *America* off the coast of Uruguay, a traumatic event that caused him to have nightmares for the rest of his life.

In 1905 Mr Artagaveytia took over a farm in Argentina, and in 1912 he was still living there when he made a decision to travel to Berlin to visit his nephew. After concluding his visit to Germany, Mr Artagaveytia decided to visit the United States before returning to Argentina, and he travelled to Cherbourg to board the *Titanic* as one of her first class passengers.

ALGERNON BARKWORTH — Status: Survivor

Algernon Barkworth (47) was born in 1864 and became a pipe-smoking Justice of the Peace who lived at Tranby House, Hessle, East Yorkshire. Mr Barkworth was a bit of a sportsman, and in April 1912 he decided to make his first voyage across the ocean, partly as a holiday and partly because he wished to sail on the largest ship in the world. He therefore booked a first class passage on the *Titanic* and boarded the great vessel at Southampton on 10 April.

ROBERT BATEMAN — Status: Victim

Robert Bateman (51) was born on 14 October 1860 while his parents, Charles and Hester Bateman, were on a visit to the United States. The first few months of Bateman's life were spent in East Baltimore, Maryland, after which the family re-crossed the Atlantic to their home in Bristol, where Charles earned his living as a builder.

Robert Bateman married Emily Hall in 1880, and the first two of the couple's seven children were born in England. When Bateman completed his education in 1881 he entered the Baptist ministry and emigrated to Toronto, Ontario to begin his life's work. After spending several years in Toronto, Revd Bateman went to Dallas, Texas, to continue his ministry.

When Revd Bateman's mother passed away in Bristol his father emigrated to Baltimore, Maryland. Revd Bateman soon decided to make his own home in Baltimore and moved there with his family. He worked among the city's poor for several years and helped establish the Union Mission, a home for men. The mission was later turned over to the Woman's Christian Temperance Union.

Revd Bateman's father died while Bateman was head of the Union Mission and was buried in Baltimore. Bateman then moved to Knoxville, Tennessee, where he took charge of Rescue Mission, a home for men similar to the one he had established in Baltimore. Five years later Revd Bateman returned to Baltimore and took charge of a church there. He remained in Baltimore for two years and then moved with his family to Jacksonville, Florida.

Revd Bateman enjoyed working among the poorer classes and tried to relieve the plight of Jacksonville's needy citizens. For several years he conducted his mission work in a building on the corner of Bay Street and Bridge Street, but he eventually arranged for a new mission house to be built on Monroe Street. One hot day he was working alongside the men who were building the new Central City Mission when his wife asked, 'Robert, why don't you give this sort of work up and go back to the pastorate?' Bateman replied, 'Wife, I had rather have my mission than the best church in America.'

Revd Bateman was a thirty-second degree Mason and began making preparations to take his thirty-third degree. In addition to being a member of the Damascus Commandery, Knights Templar, Bateman was also a member of Solomon Lodge No.20 and the Order of the Eastern Star, No.15.

On 21 February 1912 Revd Bateman sailed to England on the *Olympic* for the purpose of paying his first visit to his mother's grave in Bristol. He wrote several letters to his son Ernest describing his pleasant trip and expressing the wish that the rest of the family could be in England with him. Bateman wrote that his own health was greatly improved, that he was anxious to return home and that he was planning for greater church work during the coming summer.

Revd Bateman proved to be very popular in Bristol and preached a fair number of sermons while he was there. His cheerful demeanour impressed everyone who came to know him, and a relative noted that Bateman enjoyed singing to himself whenever he found himself with some free time between his many sermons.

On 2 April 1912 a friend took Revd Bateman to Muller's Orphanage in Bristol; the two men gave the facility a thorough inspection, and Bateman was delighted with the way the orphanage was being run.

When the time approached for Revd Bateman to return to the United States, his sister-in-law Ada Ball (36) expressed a desire to accompany him to Jacksonville to see her sister; Bateman was glad to have company on the voyage home and purchased two second class passages to the United States. In discussing the upcoming voyage with his nephew, Revd Bateman told the young man, 'Tom, if I go to the bottom I shall not be there; I shall be up yonder. Think of it.'

On the morning of their departure from Bristol, Ada Ball was awakened by the strains of music. When she asked Revd Bateman where the music was coming from, Bateman told her to come and see. Crowds of well-wishers had assembled in front of the house, and a band was playing many different selections of music. The crowd cheered Revd Bateman when he came outside, and a number of men wept openly when he bade farewell to the many friends who had gathered to see him off.

When their train arrived in London, Revd Bateman and Ada Ball were met by a friend who had come to see them off. The man gave Bateman his photograph as a remembrance, and Bateman put the photograph in the back of his watch case and told his friend, 'John, where that goes, I will go, and where I go that will go.'

The boat train departed for Southampton, and upon its arrival in that port city Revd Bateman found that he had been followed there by a young man who said that he intended to accompany the two travellers to the ship. The man's wife had told him that they could not spare the money for train fare, so he had ridden his bicycle half the necessary distance in order to see Bateman off on his voyage to America.

And so it was that on 10 April 1912 the Revd Robert Bateman and his sister-in-law, Ada Ball, arrived at the White Star dock and boarded the new liner *Titanic* as second class passengers.

EDWARD BEANE — Status: Survivor

Edward Beane (32) was born on 19 November 1879 in Norwich, and was the son of George and Mary Beane.

Edward Beane had a sweetheart named Ethel Clarke (19), and around 1906 the two young people made long-term plans to be married. Edward and Ethel began saving their money toward that goal, and Edward thought about leaving his sweetheart in England and emigrating to the United States so that he could earn more money. Mr Beane followed through on this plan and emigrated to Rochester, New York, where he obtained a job as a bricklayer.

Edward Beane stayed in close contact with Ethel Clarke, and during the next several years he made several trips back to Norwich to see her. By 1912 Edward and Ethel had been able to save $500 between them, and they decided it was finally time for them to be married. Edward returned to Norwich, and he and Ethel were married there during March (one source says the ceremony occurred on 7 April). The young couple then made plans to travel to Rochester, New York to the new home that Edward had prepared there for Ethel. Mr and Mrs Beane packed up their sixty-five wedding presents and travelled to Southampton, where on 10 April they boarded the new White Star liner *Titanic* as second class passengers.

ETHEL BEANE — Status: Survivor

Ethel Clarke (19) was born in Norwich, England on 15 November 1892 and eventually became a maid in a Norwich household. She was betrothed to Edward Beane (32), a bricklayer who was living in Rochester, New York but who returned to Norwich to marry her.

Ethel and Edward had saved their money for six years in order to be able to start their married life in America without any financial worries. They were married in Norwich in March 1912 (one source says 7 April) and then booked second class passages to America on the *Titanic*, boarding on 10 April at Southampton.

HENRY BEAUCHAMP **Status: Victim**

In April 1912 Henry Beauchamp (28) and his wife were living in London. After encountering various difficulties in his life, Beauchamp decided to relocate to Toronto, Ontario and made plans to travel to Canada alone and establish himself there before sending for his wife.

Mr Beauchamp travelled to Southampton and, along with fellow passenger Percival Sharp (27) he boarded the *Titanic* as a second class passenger on 10 April.

NELLIE BECKER **Status: Survivor**

Nellie Baumgardner (35) was born on 19 June 1876 in Springfield, Ohio and attended Wittenburg College, where she met her future husband, Allen Becker. After Nellie and Allen both graduated from Wittenburg in 1896, Allen spent two years at Hamma Divinity School studying for the ministry. A manpower shortage caused the Board of Foreign Missions of the Lutheran Church to ask Allen to go to India as a missionary, and he readily agreed to go; he and Nellie were married on 20 September 1898 and left for India on 7 November.

Conditions in India were so alien to Nellie Becker's experience that she soon suffered a nervous breakdown. She also found herself expecting a child; her daughter Ruth was born on 28 October 1899 and was the first white child born in the city of Guntur.

By 1904 Nellie's nervous condition has deteriorated to the point where Revd Becker was granted a furlough to bring his wife and little Ruth back to the United States. Revd Becker was assigned to a Lutheran Church in Lima, Ohio, and the familiar surroundings and ministrations of family and friends caused Nellie's health to improve greatly. In March 1905 she gave birth to a second child, a son whom they named Luther.

In December 1905 the Beckers returned to India, where Revd Becker was put in charge of the mission's orphanage. Various illnesses soon plagued the family, though, and Luther contracted tetanus and passed away on 7 February 1907. Almost immediately Mrs Becker became pregnant again, and on 28 December her daughter Marion was born. A fourth child, Richard, was born on 26 June 1910.

Richard Becker did not thrive in India's subtropical climate, and his health deteriorated to the point where his life was in danger. It was decided that the family would return to Benton Harbor, Michigan as soon as possible, but Revd Becker, who was also ill, was unable to obtain another furlough in time to sail with his family.

He therefore packed up the family's household possessions, and on 7 March 1912 he saw his wife and children off on the first leg of their trip to the United States.

Nellie Becker and her children sailed to England, where they stayed in London and saw the sights until the time came for them to leave for America. On 10 April Nellie herded her three children onto the boat train at Waterloo, and they travelled to Southampton and boarded the *Titanic* as second class passengers.

RUTH BECKER — Status: Survivor

Ruth Becker (12) was born on 28 October 1899 in Guntur, India. Her father, the Revd Allen Becker (39) was a missionary who hailed from Berrien Center, Michigan, and her mother Nellie (35) was originally from Springfield, Ohio.

Ruth's childhood was exotic compared to those of her American contemporaries, and encounters with monkeys, lizards, cobras and scorpions were everyday occurrences to the little girl. The stress of living in such an exotic world took its toll on Ruth's mother, though, and Nellie Becker's mental health deteriorated to the point where in 1904 Ruth's father obtained a leave of absence and took his family to visit Nellie's relatives in Ohio. Ruth was introduced to her mother's family for the first time, but the relatives were unable to understand much of what the little girl said due to the fact that she spoke only Telegu, an Indian dialect understood only by her parents.

In March 1905 Ruth's brother Luther was born, and in December 1905 she and her family returned to India, where her father was put in charge of an orphanage. Ruth's brother Luther eventually contracted tetanus and passed away in February 1907, but the following December her mother had a baby daughter named Marion. Ruth's brother, Richard, was born in June 1910.

When Richard Becker became so ill that his life was in jeopardy, it was decided that the family would return to Revd Becker's home in Benton Harbor, Michigan as soon as possible. Revd Becker, who was also ill, was unable to gain permission in time to sail with his family, so he remained in India while his family sailed alone on the first leg of their trip to the United States.

Ruth Becker sailed to England with her mother and siblings, and they stayed in London and saw the sights until the time came for them to leave for America. On 10 April 1912 Ruth, Marion, Richard and Nellie Becker boarded the boat train at Waterloo, which took them to Southampton and their departure on the *Titanic*.

RICHARD AND SARAH BECKWITH — Status: Survivors

Richard Beckwith (37) was born on 9 November 1874 and lived in Hartford, Connecticut until 1904, at which time he moved to Columbus, Ohio. It was there that Mr Beckwith married widow Sarah 'Sallie' Newsom (46), *née* Monypeny, who was born in Columbus on 21 September 1865. She and her brother Peris were the children of William Monypeny and were cousins of Ohio's Governor Harmon. Sallie had two children by her first marriage to Logan Newsom – a son named William and a daughter named Helen.

Mr and Mrs Beckwith eventually decided to discontinue their full-time residency in Columbus and began spending part of each year in New York. They also maintained a summer home at Squam Lake near Sandwich, New Hampshire.

The Beckwiths spent a great deal of their time travelling, and in February 1912 they decided to take Sallie's daughter Helen Newsom on a pleasure trip to Europe (this being the Beckwiths' attempt to get Helen away from the attentions of tennis star Karl Behr, an admirer who was six years Helen's senior). The Beckwiths and Helen Newsom sailed from New York on the White Star liner *Cedric*, and while on board that vessel they made the acquaintance of future *Titanic* passenger William Sloper. (They also met Karl Behr, who had secretly arranged to sail to Italy on the same vessel as his sweetheart.)

The Beckwiths and Miss Newsom spent the next two months in Italy, and in April they travelled to England on the first leg of their return to the States. On 10 April Richard and Sallie Beckwith and Helen Newsom boarded the *Titanic* in Southampton as first class passengers – little knowing that they were destined to 'accidentally' meet Karl Behr again when he boarded the great vessel at Cherbourg.

LAWRENCE BEESLEY — Status: Survivor

Lawrence Beesley (34) was born on 31 December 1877 in Wirksworth, Derbyshire, England and was one of eight children belonging to Henry and Annie Beesley.

Lawrence Beesley was educated at Derby School and later entered Gonville and Caius College at Cambridge University. On 17 June 1901, while still an undergraduate, Mr Beesley married Miss Gertrude Macbeth.

In due time Lawrence Beesley graduated from Cambridge, and in 1902 he became a teacher at Wirksworth Grammar School. On 15 October 1903 Lawrence and Gertrude Beesley had a son whom they named Alec.

In 1904 Mr Beesley left Wirksworth Grammar School and became a member of the faculty of Dulwich College, where he taught science. Two years later young Mr Beesley was widowed when his wife Gertrude passed away after suffering a heart attack.

Lawrence Beesley had developed an interest in the Christian Science movement in 1905, and in 1906 he seems to have formally joined the movement. In 1909 Mr Beesley gave up his teaching job at Dulwich and devoted himself entirely to the promotion of Christian Science.

In 1912 Mr Beesley made plans to travel to America in order to visit his brother as well as to study Christian Science in New York, Boston and later on in the west. Mr Beesley booked his passage on the first steamer that was convenient to his travel plans; the young man made arrangements to stay at the Cornell Club in New York City, and on 10 April he boarded the new White Star liner *Titanic* as she prepared to leave Southampton on the first leg of her maiden voyage.

KARL BEHR **Status: Survivor**

Karl Behr (26) was born on 30 May 1885 in Brooklyn, New York; he, his sister and his brother Frederick were the children of Grace and Herman Behr, Mr Behr being the owner of a sandpaper company.

Karl Behr showed a decided aptitude for tennis at a very early age. The 14-year-old Behr won the men's singles title at a New Jersey club where the family summered. As a student at Lawrenceville School Behr won the United States Lawn Tennis Association's interscholastic singles in 1903, and the following year he enrolled at Yale University.

In addition to attending his classes at Yale, Karl Behr became known as an excellent golfer and played on the college hockey team as well; he also exhibited a reputation as being one of the best tennis players in the country, winning the intercollegiate doubles in 1904. Behr graduated from Yale University in 1906.

After graduation, Mr Behr worked in his father's business and played tournament tennis. In 1907 the USLTA ranked Behr as the number 3 player in the country, and he played on the U.S. tennis team that was sent to England to compete for the Davis Cup; that same year Behr and a partner were the runners-up in the Wimbledon men's doubles championship.

Karl Behr continued to play tennis competitively even after he entered Columbia Law School, where he earned a degree in 1910. After being admitted to the Bar, Behr went to Australia as part of the American tennis team, and he was also one of the strongest contenders at the national tennis championship in Newport during the summer of 1911.

By 1912 Karl Behr was living in New York City; his law office was located at 40 Wall Street, while his residence was at 777 Madison Avenue. Mr Behr was also a member of the Crescent Athletic Club.

Some time prior to 1912 Mr Behr had made the acquaintance of Miss Helen Newsom, a college friend of his younger sister. Despite being six years her senior, Mr Behr had been courting Miss Newsom despite the disapproval of her mother and stepfather, Mr and Mrs Richard Beckwith of Columbus, Ohio.

At the beginning of March 1912 Mr and Mrs Beckwith arranged for Miss Newsom to accompany them on a pleasure trip to the Mediterranean in an attempt to divert her attention from Karl Behr. Mr Behr was not easily discouraged, however, and he made arrangements to take his own separate trip to the Mediterranean, booking his passage on the *Cedric* just as had Mr and Mrs Beckwith, Miss Newsom and their acquaintances, Mr and Mrs Edwin Kimball.

Six weeks later, after having discreetly 'shadowed' Miss Newsom across Europe, Karl Behr learned that she and the Beckwiths would be returning to the United States on board the new White Star liner *Titanic*. Mr and Mrs Beckwith and Miss Newsom rejoined their old acquaintances Mr and Mrs Kimball in boarding the *Titanic* at Southampton on 10 April, while Karl Behr affected an 'accidental' reunion with the family when he boarded the great liner as a first class passenger when she touched at Cherbourg on the evening of 10 April.

JAKOB BIRNBAUM **Status: Victim**

Jakob Birnbaum (25) was born in Krakow, Poland on 24 May 1887; Jakob and his four brothers and four sisters were the children of diamond cutter Joachim Birnbaum Sr and his wife Theophile. Sometime between 1903 and 1909 Joachim Birnbaum and his family moved to Antwerp, where they lived at 11 Memlingstraat.

After completing their schooling, Jakob Birnbaum and his brothers Michael and Leopold became diamond merchants like their father, but Jakob soon decided to enlarge the scope of his family's business ventures by leaving Antwerp and emigrating to the United States. On 26 June 1909 Jakob boarded the Red Star liner *Kroonland* and sailed to New York, where he established the jewellery firm of J. Birnbaum & Co. Jakob's brother Michael followed his example and became a diamond importer operating out of Boston, New York and Antwerp.

In 1911 Jakob Birnbaum left his New York office and moved to San Francisco, intending to make the latter city his headquarters. In January 1912 the young bachelor sailed for England on the first leg of a European buying trip, and he carried with him some diamonds which fellow jeweller David Zaslave, of Waterbury, Connecticut, had asked him to match with European stones of the same size and quality.

During the voyage to England Mr Birnbaum shared a cabin with a Canadian gentleman named Charles Alford and his young son, Willie. Birnbaum and Willie soon became fast friends, and the jeweller promised the boy that he would soon send him some Belgian coins with holes in their centres as a souvenir of their new friendship.

After completing his business in England, Jakob Birnbaum travelled to Europe on the second leg of his buying trip. When his gem purchases were finally concluded and the time came for him to return home, Mr Birnbaum booked passage from Antwerp to New York on board the steamer *Lapland*. The coal strike interfered with Birnbaum's travel plans, however, and his family in Antwerp asked him to delay his departure until after Passover; these two considerations convinced Birnbaum to abide by his family's wishes and delay his departure from Antwerp, and he eventually cabled his firm in San Francisco that he expected to return to America on board the new White Star liner *Titanic*.

On 10 April 1912 Jakob Birnbaum arrived in Cherbourg carrying the jewellery that he had purchased in Antwerp and also carrying the consignment of diamonds that he had acquired for his friend David Zaslave. That same evening the Cherbourg tender carried Mr Birnbaum out into the harbour to where the *Titanic* was taking on passengers and mail, and he boarded the great vessel as a first class passenger.

CAROLINE BONNELL **Status: Survivor**

Caroline Bonnell (30) was born on 3 April 1882 in Chicago, Illinois; she and her brother Hugh were the children of John and Emily Bonnell of Youngstown, Ohio.

Caroline attended a fashionable school for girls in New York and, after graduation, accompanied Colonel George Wick (her mother's cousin), his wife Mary and his daughter Mary Natalie Wick on a pleasure trip to Europe. On the outward voyage Caroline and the Wicks became acquainted with fellow passengers Washington Roebling and Stephen Blackwell, and after arriving in Europe the combined party toured a portion of France together.

In April 1912 Caroline Bonnell and the Wick family made arrangements to return to the United States, and Caroline's aunt, Elizabeth Bonnell of London, arranged to travel to America with her relatives. It so happened that Caroline's uncle was scheduled to sail for England on the *Olympic* at the same time that Caroline and her relatives would be at sea, and it was arranged for Caroline to send him a wireless message as soon as possible during her own voyage.

On 10 April 1912 Caroline Bonnell, Colonel and Mrs Wick, their daughter Natalie and their friends Washington Roebling and Stephen Blackwell all boarded the *Titanic* in Southampton as first class passengers.

ELIZABETH BONNELL — Status: Survivor

Elizabeth ('Lily') Bonnell (58) lived in Birkdale, Lancashire, where she was involved in setting up and running the Birkdale and Southport children's nursery.

In the spring of 1912 Miss Bonnell felt that she would like to see her brother, William F. Bonnell, who resided in Cleveland, Ohio. Miss Bonnell decided to travel to Youngstown, Ohio with her niece Caroline Bonnell and with Mr and Mrs George Wick (to whom she was related by marriage). Miss Bonnell booked a stateroom for herself on the brand new *Titanic*, and on 10 April she and her relatives boarded the great vessel at Southampton as first class passengers.

ROGER BRICOUX — Status: Victim

Roger Bricoux (20) was born in Cosne-sur-Loire, France on 1 June 1891. Mr Bricoux made his living as a cellist and, until the end of 1911, was living at 5 Place du Lion d'Or in Lille, France while his parents made their home in Monaco. In 1912 Bricoux made an unannounced trip to England and obtained a job as a musician on board the passenger liners that sailed from that country.

In February 1912 Mr Bricoux began undergoing a paid two-month trial period during which his employers evaluated his performance in order to decide if they wanted to retain him in a permanent capacity. Bricoux was assigned to the Cunard liner *Carpathia*, and on 10 February he was excited when his vessel left England bound for a number of exotic foreign ports, including Tangiers, Alexandria and Constantinople. While on board the *Carpathia*, Mr Bricoux made the acquaintance of a fellow shipboard musician, pianist Ronald Brailey (24).

On 17 March the *Carpathia* arrived at Gibraltar, where Mr Bricoux took a tour of the city, even though he was worried by recent news that his father was seriously ill. Later, when the *Carpathia* arrived in New York, Bricoux was transferred to the *Mauretania* and accompanied that vessel to Liverpool.

From Liverpool Roger Bricoux travelled down to Southampton to join the next vessel that was scheduled to utilise his talents as a professional musician. Upon arriving in Southampton, Mr Bricoux became an official member of the *Titanic*'s orchestra, and – along with his friend Ronald Brailey – he boarded the big liner on the morning of 10 April.

HAROLD BRIDE **Status: Survivor**

Harold Bride (22) was born on 11 January 1890 in Nunhead, London; Harold, his brothers Frank, Arthur, Edwin and their sister Marie were the children of Arthur and Mary Ann Bride. In 1901 the Bride family lived at 58 Ravensborne Avenue, Beckenham in a house which they named 'Crofton's', and Harold attended Roan School in Greenwich followed by the Beckenham Secondary School.

In 1910 Harold Bride's budding enthusiasm for wireless telegraphy led him to erect a wireless antenna in the back yard of his family's home. Around November of that same year, Bride enrolled at the British School of Telegraphy in Clapham Road, and on 28 June 1911 he obtained his radial telegraphy certificate; his sending and receiving rate was recorded as being 22 words per minute, and his knowledge of the rules was described as 'very good'. Bride's wireless licence was issued on 29 June 1911.

Despite his fascination with wireless telegraphy, Harold Bride's thoughts were not dominated by that subject to the exclusion of everything else; at some point during this period Bride became engaged to Mabel Ludlow, a nurse who lived and worked in East Grinstead. After obtaining his wireless licence, Harold Bride joined the Marconi Co. and went to sea, serving twice as first operator on board the *Haverford* during her crossings to Philadelphia. Bride then sailed twice to New York as second operator on the *Lusitania*, and this was followed by three trips to Brazil as first operator on board the *Lanfranc* and the *Anselm*. In 1912 the Marconi Co. issued Bride a transfer and assigned him to serve as second operator on board the brand new *Titanic*.

Harold Bride joined the *Titanic* at Belfast and served on board her during her sea trials on 2 April as well as during her delivery trip to Southampton the next day. Bride left the *Titanic* at Southampton on 3 April and did not return to her until 11:30 p.m. on the evening of 9 April; he was still on board the great White Star liner when she began her maiden voyage from Southampton at noon on 10 April.

HARRY BRISTOW **Status: Victim**

Harry Bristow (38) was born near East Looe in Cornwall on 26 April 1873 and was the son of John and Mary Ann Bristow. Harry married Ethel Elliott, and the couple had two children, Vivian John Henry and Philip, and they lived in Shortlands, Kent.

In 1912 Harry Bristow made plans to begin working on the big liners that were based in Southampton, and on 9 April he signed on to the brand new *Titanic* to serve as a first class steward. He was serving in that capacity on the new *Titanic* when that vessel departed on her maiden voyage on 10 April.

AMELIA BROWN **Status: Survivor**

Amelia ('Mildred') Brown (18) was born in London on 18 August 1893 and worked as a cook. She lived at 152 Abbey Road.

In early 1912 Miss Brown was hired by Mr and Mrs Hudson Allison to work as a cook at their new home in Canada. On 10 April Mildred Brown joined Hudson Allison (30), Bessie Allison (25), Helen Allison (2), Hudson Allison (11 months), maid Sarah Daniels (33), nurse Alice Cleaver (22) and chauffeur George Swane (26) in boarding the *Titanic* at Southampton; Miss Brown and Mr Swane travelled as second class passengers, while the remaining members of the party travelled in first class.

EDITH BROWN **Status: Survivor**

Thomas Brown (60) was a prosperous South African hotelier whose first wife predeceased him after bearing him two sons and two daughters (one of whom was Mrs W. Bosman of Cape Town). Mr Brown eventually remarried, and he and his wife Elizabeth (40), moved to Worcester, Cape Colony, South Africa, where they purchased the Masonic Hotel; the couple made their home in that establishment, and it was there that their daughter Edith was born on 27 October 1896. (A second daughter died of diphtheria at the age of 8.)

Thomas Brown remained the owner of the Masonic Hotel for eight years, and he raised the hotel's reputation and saw it prosper during the Boer War. Around 1902 Mr Brown sold the hotel to Mr J. Carroll for £12,000 and moved with his family to the suburbs of Cape Town. There Mr Brown invested in various cottage properties and purchased interests in several hotels at Bloemfontein, Colesburg, Johannesburg and the 'Mountain View' in Cape Town.

Elizabeth Brown had a sister in Seattle, Washington, and toward the end of 1911 Thomas Brown decided to take his wife and daughter to Seattle and set up in business there. After making that decision, Mr Brown disposed of all of the family's South African assets except for some shares in the Western Wine and Brandy Co., which he retained as a reminder of Worcester and all of the people he had known there.

Thomas Brown insured the family's belongings for the first leg of the coming trip, and in February 1912 he, Elizabeth and Edith left Cape Town and sailed to England, where they took up temporary residence in a London hotel. Mr Brown utilised the next few weeks in purchasing hotel equipment to take with him to America, but he did not think it necessary to insure that equipment or the family's belongings for the second leg of their trip to America; his decision to economise might have stemmed from the fact that he and his family were scheduled to sail to New York on board the new, reportedly unsinkable *Titanic*.

On 10 April the Browns travelled to Southampton, but as they walked through the big gates leading to the White Star Pier Mr Brown suddenly turned away from the gate and his face went white. He put off Elizabeth's anxious inquiries as to what was the matter, but he later confided to her that he had experienced a ghastly feeling that 'something was going to happen'. Despite his nameless fear, Mr Brown, his wife

Elizabeth and their daughter Edith walked up the gangplank and boarded the *Titanic* as second class passengers.

MARGARET BROWN **Status: Survivor**

Margaret Tobin (44) was born on 18 July 1867 and, along with her two brothers, her sister Helen and two half-sisters, lived with her parents John and Johanna Tobin in Hannibal, Missouri, where John worked as a manual labourer at the Hannibal Gas Works. Margaret was schooled in the home of her aunt and, at the age of 13, she went to work at Garth's tobacco factory.

In 1886 one of Margaret's brothers sent her enough money to join him in Leadville, Colorado, and Margaret worked there as her brother's housekeeper before getting a job at the dry goods firm of Daniels, Fisher and Smith. That same year Margaret met James Joseph Brown, shift manager at the Maid and Henriette Mine, and the young couple were married on 1 September 1886.

Margaret Brown was determined to improve her education and took lessons in reading, literature and music. On 30 August 1887 she gave birth to her son Lawrence, and on 1 July 1889 her second child Catherine (known as Helen) was born.

In 1893 James Brown was appointed superintendent of all the properties held by the Ibex Mining Co., and his technical ingenuity led to the successful mining of gold from the previously-barren 'Little Jonny' mine. This success brought wealth and recognition to the Brown family, and Margaret was able to make her debut in the Denver social register when she and her family moved to that city in 1894.

The Browns were prominent in Denver social and business circles for the next few years, and Margaret discovered that she enjoyed travelling and learning foreign languages. When James's health began to decline, however, he and Margaret moved to Ireland for a year and arranged for their children to be schooled in Paris.

When the Brown family returned to Colorado in 1900, Margaret began taking classes at Carnegie Institute. She also took an active role in improving Denver civic life and helped found the Denver Woman's Club, an organisation which promoted education, suffrage, and human rights in the United States. Margaret also raised funds to build St Joseph's Hospital and worked with Judge Ben Lindsey in his campaign to help needy children and establish the first Juvenile Court in the country.

Marital relations between Margaret and her husband began to deteriorate during this period, and she and James were separated on 10 August 1909. Margaret continued to travel, however, and in 1910 she attended the coronation of King George V.

In early 1912 Margaret and her daughter Helen made plans to travel abroad, and on 25 January they accompanied the John Jacob Astor party to North Africa and Egypt. On their return trip the travellers spent a few days in Rome, and Margaret purchased four cases of pictures and some models of the ruins of Rome that she intended to bring back to the Denver Art Museum.

When the Astor party arrived in Paris, Margaret received a disturbing cablegram from her son Lawrence telling her that her infant grandson was ill. Although Helen Brown decided to remain in Paris with friends, Margaret was determined to see her little grandson and decided to return to America immediately; along with the Astors, Margaret Brown booked a first class passage on the brand new *Titanic* and boarded the great liner at Cherbourg on the evening of 10 April.

DAGMAR BRYHL **Status: Survivor**

Dagmar Bryhl (20) was born on 2 October 1891 and was the daughter of Mr and Mrs Gustaf Gottfried Lustig of Skara, Sweden. Mr Lustig was Skara's stationmaster, and Dagmar lived with her parents along with her four sisters and three brothers. She was well educated and could speak French and German fluently as well as write English.

In late 1911 or early 1912 Dagmar became engaged to her sweetheart Ingvar Enander (21).

Dagmar's uncle, Oscar Lustig, lived in Rockford, Illinois, and it is said that Dagmar agreed to visit her uncle in order to please her father. She made arrangements to travel to America along with Ingvar and her brother Kurt Bryhl (26). Dagmar and Ingvar planned to be married a few months after they arrived in Rockford, and they even entertained the possibility of remaining in the United States if they both liked it there.

Dagmar, Ingvar and Kurt left Skara, Sweden on 3 April 1912 and headed for Southampton. Ingvar had given his fiancée a watch sometime prior to her departure, and Dagmar was wearing the watch on a chain around her neck when she and her friends boarded the *Titanic* as second class passengers on 10 April.

DANIEL BUCKLEY **Status: Survivor**

Daniel Buckley (21) was born on September 28, 1890 and lived in Kingwilliamstown, County Cork.

When Mr Buckley and his friends Patrick O'Connor, Patrick O'Connell and Michael Linehan decided to emigrate to New York, they booked their passages together in the *Titanic*'s steerage section and travelled to Queenstown to board the great vessel on 11 April.

JEREMIAH BURKE **Status: Victim**

Jeremiah Burke (19) was born in England to William and Catherine Burke and grew up with his six siblings on the family farm in Glanmire, County Cork.

In 1912 Burke and his cousin Nora Hegarty decided to emigrate to America, and Burke made arrangements to live at the home of his sister, Mrs Michael Burns, of Charlestown, Massachusetts. Burke and Miss Hegarty originally planned to sail on *Cretic*, but the coal strike delayed her sailing a considerable period, and the local White Star agent advised them to wait and cross on the new *Titanic*. Mr Burke and Miss Hegarty booked their passage in the *Titanic*'s steerage section, and they boarded the great vessel when she touched at Queenstown on 11 April.

EWART BURR — Status: Victim

Ewart Burr (29) was born in Bristol and eventually moved to Southampton to make his living as a steward on board the big passenger ships based in that city.

Mr Burr and his wife Ethel were married in 1910 and lived in Victoria Road in the Woolston area of Southampton with their infant son Cecil.

Ewart Burr served on board the White Star liner *Oceanic* before signing onto the brand new *Titanic* as a first class steward; it was in that capacity that he sailed on the great liner when she left Southampton on 10 April 1912.

KATE BUSS — Status: Survivor

Kate Buss (36), the daughter of Mr and Mrs James Buss, was born in 1875 at Milton, Sittingbourne, Kent. She had four sisters and two brothers and lived in Halling, where she worked at a grocer's shop that was owned by one of her brothers.

Kate's fiancé, Samuel G. Willis, also of Sittingbourne, emigrated to San Diego, California, and in 1912 Kate made plans to join him there, where they were to be married. Wishing to arrive in the U.S. in April in order to avoid a May wedding (a superstition), Miss Buss packed up her trousseau, wedding presents and household effects, booked a second class passage on the *Titanic* and boarded the great vessel at Southampton on 10 April.

ARCHIBALD BUTT — Status: Victim

Archibald Butt (46) was born on 26 September 1865. Archie, his sister Mary Ann and his brothers Lewis, Edward and John were the children of Joshua and Pamela Butt of Augusta, Georgia.

Archie Butt's early schooling took place in Augusta, but when his father passed away in 1879 the 14-year-old boy was forced to leave the Summerville Academy and seek employment in order to support his family. Three years later Butt's mother and a generous family friend found the financial means to enrol him in the preparatory department at the University of the South at Sewanee, Tennessee.

Archie Butt entered the University in 1882, and upon graduation he obtained a job at a life insurance company in Augusta, Georgia. Around January 1890 he travelled to Louisville, Kentucky with the idea of becoming a newspaper man, and he was soon the youngest reporter on the *Courier-Journal*'s staff and was assigned to police work. Archie remained at the *Courier-Journal* until 1893, at which point he returned to Georgia to work for the *Macon Telegraph*. Butt stayed at the *Telegraph* for slightly more than a year, after which he went to Washington, D.C. and served as a correspondent for several Southern newspapers.

Archie's outstanding newspaper work enabled him to make the acquaintance of many important men, and this led to Major Matt Ransom choosing him to be his secretary and attaché when President Cleveland sent Ransom to Mexico City as ambassador.

Within a year Archie returned to Washington, but when hostilities commenced at the outbreak of the Spanish-American War, he decided to enter military service. On 2 January 1900 Butt's friend, Adjutant General Henry Corbin, secured a commission for him as Assistant Quartermaster in the Volunteer Service with the rank of captain. Captain Butt's first tour of duty was in the Philippines, where he soon became head of the army's transportation department in Manila.

During this period Archie became good friends with William Howard Taft, the Civil Governor of the Philippines, and on 7 January 1901 Taft wrote to the Secretary of War recommending Butt for an appointment as captain and assistant quartermaster in the United States regular army. This recommendation was acted upon, and on 2 February 1901 Captain Butt was promoted to Quartermaster, his volunteer rank being converted to a full commission as a captain in the regular army. Captain Archibald Butt served in the Philippines until June 1903, at which point he returned to the United States and was appointed Depot Quartermaster at Washington, D.C. the following year.

Archie remained Washington's Depot Quartermaster until September 1906, at which point, at the conclusion of the revolution in Cuba, General Funston took Butt to that country in order to establish a base of supplies for the army of pacification. Captain Butt served as Depot Quartermaster at Havana from September 1906 until 1908, at which point he returned to Washington, D.C. In June 1908 President Roosevelt summoned Captain Butt to the White House and appointed him as his military aide-de-camp, utilising him that same day at a formal reception. Captain Butt afterwards went to the Army and Navy Club and told his friend Lieutenant Victor Blue, 'Old boy, it is mighty tiresome, but I believe I am going to like it.'

The year 1908 was a hectic but exciting year for Captain Butt. In addition to advising the President on military and social matters, Butt found that he was also called upon to accompany the President during rock climbing excursions, horse-galloping sessions, swimming outings, tennis matches and other physical activities of the outdoors-minded Chief Executive. Archie Butt's sterling personal qualities very quickly made him a valued friend and trusted confidant of President Roosevelt.

The year 1908 proved to be a year of mixed blessings for Archie Butt, since his mother Pamela – to whom he was very devoted – was seriously ill. In the belief that exposure to sea air might help to improve her health, Archie took his mother to Europe and left her at the home of his brother Edward. Pamela Butt passed away not long after Archie returned alone to the States, and a few months later he personally placed his beloved mother's ashes in the ground of her native soil in Augusta, Georgia.

Captain Butt served as President Roosevelt's aide-de-camp until March 1909. When William Howard Taft was elected president on 4 March, Taft asked his old friend Archie Butt to stay on at the White House as his own military aide-de-camp. President Taft was quickly reminded of how much value he placed on Captain Butt's friendship, and Butt soon became as highly esteemed an advisor to Taft as he had been to Roosevelt. In March 1911 Taft promoted Captain Butt to the rank of Major.

As the Taft administration wore on, however, the President's political policies slowly began to veer away from the course that had been steered by his predecessor, Theodore Roosevelt. A schism formed between the two friends, and this split became more and more serious – and vocal – as the 1912 presidential election approached. Eventually,

Roosevelt publicly expressed his intention to displace President Taft and secure the Republican party's nomination for the presidency.

Archie Butt found himself in an impossible position; Taft and Roosevelt were both his close friends, and Butt was distressed by his divided loyalties and felt enormous pressure at being caught in the middle of their conflict. In late 1911 Archie began suffering from 'toxine poisoning' while travelling out west with President Taft, and by February 1912 he had lost twenty pounds and was feeling so poorly that he placed himself under the care of a physician.

Artist Frank Millet shared a house and living expenses with Major Butt, and Millet could see the enormous strain that his friend was labouring under and realised that Major Butt was badly in need of rest. Millet induced President Taft to grant Archie a six-week leave of absence, and in March 1912 Archie and Millet sailed to Europe together and spent time together in the city of Rome. Major Butt also enjoyed making sightseeing trips through the city, and at one point he joined the immense crowd that was gathered before the Quirinal Palace and saw Italy's King Victor Immanuel on the same day that an assassination attempt was made against the monarch. Butt later spent another day in Gibraltar with his friend Fred Carpenter.

President Taft had written letters of introduction to various Italian dignitaries on behalf of Major Butt, and these letters enabled Butt to see Cardinal Merry del Val (the Vatican Secretary of State) on 19 March; this visit was followed by an audience with Pope Pius X on 21 March, and the Pope gave Major Butt a personal letter written in French to deliver to President Taft. Several days after his visit with the pontiff, Major Butt went to the Quirinal for a private audience with King Victor Immanuel, to whom he was presented by the American Ambassador, Thomas O'Brien.

Archie had begun experiencing a premonition of approaching danger even before he left Washington, D.C., and it appears that his presentiments continued throughout his entire stay in Italy. Despite the fact that his presentiments of impending danger continued unabated, Archie seems to have felt that, by booking his passage home on the *Titanic*, he would thereby be able to avoid the last possible source of potential danger that his trip might present. When Major Butt dined with Baron Carlo Allotti, the Italian Minister to Mexico, he told the Baron that his holiday had been very pleasant, but that he wanted to get back to America in a hurry in order to be of service to President Taft during his campaign for re-election. 'I'll get to Washington in time,' said the major, 'because I am fortunate enough to have a reservation on the new *Titanic*. When I step aboard the *Titanic*, I shall feel absolutely safe. You know she is unsinkable.'

On 30 March Major Butt left his friend Frank Millet in Rome and made a brief trip to Basel and Berlin before meeting his niece, Arrington, in Paris. Archie and Arrington left Paris together and travelled to the coast, where they crossed the Channel to England; the two travellers were bound for the city of Chester with the intention of spending Easter with his brother Edward at the latter's farm.

Archie Butt spent four wonderful April days visiting Edward and his family in Chester, and he was noticeably sad when he finally said goodbye and travelled to London. Archie Butt spent two days in London at the home of his cousin and her husband, the Baron and Baroness Rosenkrantz. Major Butt's presentiments of impending tragedy seem to have been intensifying steadily, and the Baroness could see that her normally cheerful cousin was in a noticeably depressed and sad state of mind; Archie repeatedly spoke of death and told his hosts that he felt he did not have much longer to live. Archie concluded his final evening in England by confiding to the Rosenkrantzes that he had left all of his private diaries to his friend Mrs Cloman for publication after his death.

On the morning of 10 April the Baron and Baroness Rosenkrantz drove Archie Butt to the boat train, and they could not help but notice that he was still in a very depressed and distracted state of mind. The Major took his final leave of his cousin and her husband, and – referring to the Scottish branch of his family – he left his hosts with some very disturbing words of farewell: 'We Robertsons,' he said, 'never live long.' Archie then took the boat train to Southampton, where he boarded the *Titanic* as a first class passenger.

JACK BUTTERWORTH — Status: Victim

Jack Butterworth (23) was born in Manchester, England and in 1912 was living at 270 Priory Road, Southampton. He served as a crewman on board the *New York* before signing onto the *Titanic* as a first class steward on 4 April 1912. Six days later, on the morning of 10 April, Mr Butterworth boarded the *Titanic* for the last time prior to the commencement of the great vessel's maiden voyage.

ALBERT AND SYLVIA CALDWELL — Status: Survivors

Albert Caldwell (26) was born on 8 September 1885 to William and Fannie Caldwell. Sylvia Harbaugh (28) was born on 23 July 1883 in Pittsburgh, Pennsylvania and was the daughter of Chambers and Sylvia Harbaugh. Albert and Sylvia (of Colorado Springs, Colorado) graduated from Park College in 1909 and were married in September of that year.

Shortly after their marriage Albert and Sylvia Caldwell left their home in Washington and sailed to Bangkok, Siam (now Thailand). Here Albert became a missionary and teacher at the Christian High School, representing the Jane Hayes McFarland memorial fund of the Washington Presbyterian churches.

On 10 June 1911 the Caldwell's son Alden was born. Sylvia's health was not the best, however, and the following year the young couple was permitted to take the automatic year-long furlough that was granted every five years due to Siam's unhealthy climate.

After sailing from Bangkok, the Caldwells' vessel made an intermediate stop in the harbour at Naples, where Albert and Sylvia happened to notice the Cunard liner *Carpathia* at the dock, the American flag (the vessel's next destination) flying on her foremast. It was while they were in Naples that the Caldwells first heard about the *Titanic*, and, since the timing of that vessel's maiden voyage coincided with their own travel plans, they decided to sail on her to America when the time came.

Albert and Sylvia Caldwell and their infant son spent a couple of weeks sightseeing in Rome, Venice, Lucerne and Paris. They then sailed to England, and while in London they booked second class passages for the *Titanic*'s maiden voyage. Albert, Sylvia and little Alden were on board the big passenger liner when she pulled away from the Southampton Docks on 10 April.

LUCILE CARTER **Status: Survivor**

Lucile Polk was born on 8 October 1875 in Baltimore, Maryland and was the daughter of Mr and Mrs W. Stewart Polk. Miss Polk was a direct descendant of President James K. Polk and was reportedly 'a belle' of Baltimore at the time of her social debut.

In 1896 Miss Polk married William Carter (36), a wealthy Philadelphia sportsman and frequenter of Newport. The couple's daughter Lucile was born 20 October 1898 in Philadelphia, and their son William Carter II was born on 14 September 1900.

By 1911 the Carter family was living in Bryn Mawr, Pennsylvania, but during that year the family travelled to England, where Mr Carter spent several months hunting in the Melton Mowbray area and playing polo while his children attended school. In late March the Carters made reservations to return to the United States on board the *Olympic*, but they apparently changed their minds and transferred their passages to the *Titanic*. On 10 April Mr and Mrs Carter, their children Lucile (13), William (11), maid Augusta Serraplan (30), and manservant Alexander Cairns boarded the *Titanic* at Southampton as first class passengers, while the family's chauffeur Charles Aldworth (30) boarded the vessel as a second class passenger. The Carters also had with them two dogs – an Airedale and a King Charles spaniel.

ELEANOR CASSEBEER **Status: Survivor**

Eleanor Genevieve Fosdick (36) was born on 11 November 1875. Miss Fosdick, her sister and her brother Yale were the children of Dr and Mrs William Fosdick of LaPorte, Indiana.

Genevieve Fosdick married Dr Henry Cassebeer, a wealthy New York physician, and the couple lived in New York City.

Around January 1912 Mrs Cassebeer made her tenth crossing of the Atlantic Ocean in order to visit her brother Yale, who lived in France. She spent considerable time in Paris.

Mrs Cassebeer had not originally intended to return to the United States in April, but she received word that her husband was in rather delicate health in New York and that her presence there was desirable. Mrs Cassebeer therefore purchased a first class passage on the first available steamer, and she wrote a letter to her sister in Spencer, Iowa saying that she would be travelling on the new White Star liner *Titanic* and that she would be boarding the steamer at Cherbourg. On the evening of 10 April 1912, Mrs Cassebeer followed through on the travel plans that she had confided to her sister.

NORMAN CHAMBERS — Status: Survivor

Norman Chambers (27) was born on 27 April 1884 in Olean, New York and was the son of James and Jeanette Chambers. Norman, who was an athletic young man, spent many of his early years abroad with his parents, since James Chambers held consular positions in Russia and also had charge of the business of the Standard Oil Co. in that part of the world.

Norman Chambers graduated from Cornell University as a Master of Engineering, and he later married Bertha Griggs (32) of Ithaca, New York. Bertha's mother was Dr Elam Griggs, the leading woman physician of Ithaca.

Norman Chambers was a well-to-do mechanical engineer, and he and his wife lived at 111 Broadway in New York City. Chambers was employed by a tool company located on East 44th Street; the company also had headquarters in Buenos Aires, however, and around 1909 Mr Chambers was sent to South America to work at that office, which was mainly concerned with the planing of machinery.

In the spring of 1912 Norman and Ethel Chambers began making plans to return to the United States; they sailed to England and arrived in Southampton on 5 April on board the steamer *Aragon*. After spending the next five days in England, Mr and Mrs Chambers boarded the *Titanic* as first class passengers on the final leg of their journey to New York.

JOHN AND SARAH CHAPMAN — Status: Victims

John Chapman (36), of St Neot, Cornwall, was the son of James and Isabella Chapman and was one of five children. John started out life farming with his father, but in 1906 he emigrated to Canada and eventually moved to Spokane, Washington to work as a cemetery worker.

In late 1911 Mr Chapman wanted his fiancée Sarah Elizabeth Lawrie (28) to join him in America to be married, but her family refused to allow it. John therefore returned to Cornwall, England, where he married Sarah in December of that year. The two newlyweds decided to emigrate to the United States and live near Sarah's brother in Wisconsin, so in April 1912 they travelled to Southampton and booked their passage to America as second class passengers on the *Titanic*.

JOSEPH CHAPMAN — Status: Survivor

Joseph Chapman (32) was born in Southampton on December 10, 1879 and was the son of railway porter William Chapman and his wife Eliza. In 1881 the family was living at 49 Kent Street in Portsea in Portsmouth, but when Joseph grew up he moved to 31 Belleview Road in Southampton and began working on the passenger liners that served British ports.

In September 1911 Mr Chapman was working as a second class plate steward on board the *Olympic* when the big liner collided with the cruiser HMS *Hawke*, and on

4 April 1912 signed onto the *Titanic* in as a second class boot steward. He was on board that great vessel when she departed Southampton on 10 April.

GLADYS CHERRY **Status: Survivor**

Gladys Cherry (30) was born on 27 August 1881, lived in London and was the cousin of the Earl of Rothes.

In 1912 the Earl of Rothes went to Pasadena, California to investigate a fruit farm investment there, and in April of that year his wife, the Countess of Rothes, decided to meet her husband in California. Miss Cherry had a childhood friend living in southern California, so she made plans to accompany the Countess to America in order to visit her friend. Miss Cherry and the Countess booked first class passages on the *Titanic* and boarded her at Southampton on 10 April.

CHARLES CLARKE **Status: Victim**

Charles Valentine Clarke (29), of Cosham, Hampshire, was the second son of Mr and Mrs Harry Clarke. His wife Ada (28) was the third daughter of Mr and Mrs Wingfield of Southampton. The Clarkes' home was called 'Sea View', and Charles helped at his father's business, Park Dairy.

Charles and Ada had been married for four years when, in 1912, they made plans to emigrate to San Francisco to join Mrs Clarke's sister and brother-in-law. Charles and Ada left Cosham on 6 April and headed for Southampton, where they were booked as second class passengers on the *Titanic*.

GERSHON COHEN **Status: Survivor**

Gershon Cohen was born in 1893 in Whitechapel, London, and in 1912 he was an 18-year-old, out-of-work printer. Cohen decided to seek his fortune in America, so he borrowed the equivalent of $32 and booked a steerage passage on the *Adriatic*. His father travelled with him to Southampton to say farewell, but upon their arrival there Cohen learned that the coal strike had forced the cancellation of the *Adriatic*'s voyage; his steerage passage was therefore transferred to the brand new *Titanic*, and he boarded the big liner on 10 April.

REGINALD COLERIDGE **Status: Victim**

Reginald Charles Coleridge (29) was adopted by the Revd A.C. Crossfield of Huntingdon. Reginald and his father had arranged for a joint holiday trip to Niagara Falls and other places, but they could not get away together, so they made plans to meet in Detroit,

Michigan. Revd Crossfield sailed on the *Corsican*, while Reginald made arrangements to sail later as a second class passenger on the *Titanic*.

SIDNEY COLLETT — Status: Survivor

Sidney Stuart Collett (25) was born on 8 January 1887 in North London and was a son of Revd and Mrs Mawbey Ernest Collett. When Sidney was 18 years old his family began to leave England in a piecemeal fashion; this process began with his brother Thomas, who moved to Syracuse, New York in 1904. Another of Sidney's brothers emigrated to Ontario, while a third brother, Frederick, went to Shanghai to work for the General Electric Co.

In 1910 Sidney's parents emigrated to Port Byron, New York. His three sisters, Lillian, Daisy and Violet, followed shortly thereafter and made arrangements to attend college in Rochester, New York.

By 1912 the only two members of the Collett family who remained in England were Sidney and his brother Ernest, but Sidney had travel plans of his own and began making arrangements to attend William Jewell College, a theological seminary in Liberty, Missouri. In April Mr Collett arranged to take passage to America on board the *St Louis*, but the coal strike forced cancellation of that voyage. Collett then tried to book passage on the *Philadelphia*, but the same thing happened and that vessel's voyage was cancelled as well. Mr Collett was pleased, however, when he found that he could obtain a second class passage on the *Titanic* for the same fare that he had intended to spend on the *Philadelphia*. He therefore purchased his ticket and made arrangements for his family's personal library, important family papers and a considerable amount of money to be taken with him aboard the brand new liner.

On 9 April 1912 Mr Collett purchased a brand new walking stick in London as a last souvenir of England. The next day he travelled to Southampton, where he promised relatives of fellow passengers Kate Buss (36) and Marion Wright (26) that he would conduct the two ladies safely to America. Mr Collett then stepped on board the *Titanic* as a second class passenger.

CHARLOTTE COLLYER (Survivor) and HARVEY COLLYER (Victim)

Charlotte Tate (31) was the daughter of Mr and Mrs Allen Tate of Elm Villa, Leatherhead. Harvey Collyer (31) and his twin brother Walter were born in West Horsley, Surrey on 26 November 1880 and were the sons of George and Ellen Collyer. Harvey had three brothers (William, George and Eugene) as well as two sisters named Nellie and Fanny. Miss Tate married Harvey Collyer, who worked as a van man for Messrs Mould, Ironmongers, and was also a popular member of the Leatherhead Young Men's Institute. In 1904 the couple had a daughter whom they named Marjorie.

Charlotte Collyer worked for the Revd S.N. Sedgwick, who around 1908 moved from Leatherhead to Bishopstoke. The Collyers followed Revd Sedgwick to Bishopstoke, and

Mr Collyer bought a small store there and became a clerk and sexton at Bishopstoke Parish Church. Harvey was also in charge of the church's 'chime' of bells, and he and Charlotte enjoyed helping in the performance of the rector's operettas.

A few years earlier some family friends had bought a fruit farm in Idaho, and these friends wrote to Harvey and Charlotte praising the profits and good climate and urging them to join them there. The Collyers originally had no plans to do so, but in 1911 Mrs Collyer contracted tuberculosis, so she and Harvey decided to take the plunge and join their friends in America. Mr Collyer sold his store and planned to buy a half-interest in a 10-acre apple orchard in Payette, Idaho.

The day before the Collyers left for Southampton to board the steamer New York, some friends escorted them to the local churchyard, climbed into the church belfry and chimed a selection of songs for them as a last farewell. It took more than an hour to do so, and Mr Collyer was very pleased with this gesture of friendship.

The next day Harvey Collyer put his family's life savings into $5,000 worth of banknotes, which he put into a wallet inside his jacket before he and his family left for Southampton. Upon their arrival in that port city, the Collyers learned that, due to the coal strike, their second class passage on the *New York* had been transferred to the brand new *Titanic*. Harvey, Charlotte and little Marjorie boarded the great White Star liner on 10 April; in the ship's hold were the few personal possessions that the family had kept after the sale of their home – which meant that every possession in the world that the Collyers owned was on board the *Titanic* with them.

SELINA ROGERS COOK — Status: Survivor

Selina Rogers (22) was born on 6 April 1890 in Oxford and grew up there. In 1912 she worked as a nurse and was also a newlywed, her husband being named Arthur Cook.

Mrs Cook made plans to travel to Boston to pay a visit to her mother, who was an assistant to a coachman's wife. The young woman said goodbye to her new husband and booked passage on the *Titanic*, boarding her at Southampton on 10 April.

MARY COUTTS — Status: Survivor

Mary 'Minnie' Treanor (36) was born in Ireland. She married William Coutts, a jewellery engraver, and the couple eventually had two sons, William (11) and Neville (3). The family lived in Islington, London.

Around June 1911 William Coutts left his wife and children in England and travelled to New York in order to prepare a new home for them. In February 1912 Mr Coutts sent money to his family so that they could join him in the States, but Minnie decided to remain in England for a while longer to save more money so that the family could make a better start in America.

In April Mrs Coutts booked a steamship passage to America for herself and her two sons; when the sailing of that vessel was cancelled due to the coal strike, she, William and Neville were transferred to the brand new *Titanic*, which they boarded as steerage passengers at Southampton on 10 April.

LAURA CRIBB — Status: Survivor

Laura Cribb (16) was born in Newark, New Jersey on 24 July 1895 and was the daughter of John and Bessie Cribb. Laura's two brothers were named Ernest and Frank, and her sister was named Ellen.

John Cribb made his living as a butler in prominent homes around New York. For several years he was an assistant steward on several vessels at the Essex Club of Newark, and he was employed in a similar capacity on the yacht *Helenita* owned by financier Frank Gould. Mr Cribb later became the butler at the home of Herbert Ballantine.

In 1902 John Cribb's wife and children are reported to have been living in Bournemouth while Mr Cribb earned his living in the United States. John Cribb frequently travelled between England and America in order to see his family, and he is said to have crossed the Atlantic twenty-two times, his daughter Laura having accompanied him on nine of those crossings.

In 1911 John Cribb was the butler at the home of E.S. Repello of 841 Madison Avenue in New York. In September of that year Mr Cribb went to England to join his family.

In 1912 Laura Cribb was an assistant at J.E. Beale's Fancy Fair in Bournemouth. She was also connected with Sunday school work at the Parkstone Congregational Church, where she was a member of the choir and where her father was a sidesman.

It was John Cribb's intention to take his family to the United States in 1912 and establish a permanent home for them in America. In April of that year Mr Cribb and his daughter Laura made plans to travel to New York to set up housekeeping before sending for the rest of the family, and 10 April found them in Southampton, where they boarded the *Titanic* as steerage passengers on what was intended to be Mr Cribb's twenty-third crossing of the Atlantic Ocean.

CATHERINE CROSBY — Status: Survivor

Catherine Halstead (64) was born on 26 October 1847 in Waterloo, New York, and was the daughter of Mr and Mrs J.Y. Halstead.

On 18 April 1868 Catherine Halstead married Civil War veteran Edward Crosby, and the young couple set up home in Michigan. The Crosbys had three children, Martha (*b*.1870), Harriette (*b*.1872) and Frederick (*b*.1881).

Edward Crosby spent his early married life trying out a variety of different jobs, including working for the Lake Shore and Michigan Southern Railway Co. For a brief period of time Crosby was engaged in the manufacturing of brick in Kansas City, Missouri, but in 1869 he returned to Michigan and worked as a lumber driver at Whitehall. In 1871 the Crosbys moved to Muskegon, where Edward became superintendent of the Muskegon Boom Co.

In 1880 Catherine and Edward Crosby faced a family tragedy when their daughter Martha died from appendicitis. Despite this sad event, however, the Crosbys forced themselves to go on, and they continued to save their money in order to ensure their family's prosperity.

The day finally came when Edward Crosby had enough money to buy a small tugboat, which he put to use in the towing of logs. This business venture eventually expanded into a prosperous contracting business, and in 1881 Edward founded the E.G. Crosby Co., which operated a line of tugs and barges and which also engaged in the building of piers and drydocks. As head of the company, Captain Crosby supervised the construction of most of the government piers on the eastern shore of Lake Michigan as well as several breakwaters on the Wisconsin shoreline.

Captain Crosby became impressed with the possibilities of freight transportation across Lake Michigan, and he joined with several other businessmen and purchased the steamer *Nyack*, which went into the freight and passenger service between Milwaukee and Chicago. The *Nyack* was soon joined by the *Fremont*, and the Grand Trunk Railroad awarded Crosby a contract to operate a service between Milwaukee, Grand Haven and Muskegon.

In 1892 the Crosbys' daughter Harriette got married and moved with her husband to Detroit. In the meantime, Captain Crosby continued to enlarge his fleet of ships, and in 1896 he purchased the steamer *Wisconsin*, which he re-christened the *Naomi*. The *Naomi* burned not long after Captain Crosby acquired her, and she was towed into port badly damaged; Crosby borrowed $100,000 and rebuilt the vessel, which he later renamed the *E.G. Crosby*.

In 1897 the Crosbys moved to Milwaukee, Wisconsin to be closer to the centre of their transport business. Catherine Crosby was very family oriented, however, and she missed her daughter Harriette very much. In order to be nearer to Harriette, Catherine is said to have made an attempt to break up her daughter's marriage; the lonely mother's efforts apparently succeeded, because Harriette's marriage came to an end and she moved to Milwaukee to live with her parents even though she missed her husband dreadfully.

In 1903 Captain Crosby founded the Crosby Transportation Co., and by 1910 he had purchased two additional steamers, the *Conestoga* and the *May Graham*, in order to augment his company's fleet. Crosby's company had suffered at least one loss during this same time period, however, when one of its steamers, the *Moran*, was crushed in the ice and went down in Lake Michigan.

In Milwaukee, Harriette Crosby became friends with a young woman named Lilly Brand, and in 1910 the two ladies travelled to Paris to study music. While in Paris Harriette engaged in an affair with a married man, and in May 1911 she found herself expecting a child. Later in her pregnancy, Harriette's paramour sent her to London, and in the closing months of 1911 Catherine and Edward Crosby joined their daughter in London to be with her during her time of trouble. (Mr and Mrs Crosby did not tell anyone – even their son Fred – about Harriette's pregnancy, and they advised their friends and relatives that they were going to Europe on a pleasure trip.)

On 11 February 1912 Harriette gave birth to a daughter, whom she named Andree. Within a month, however, Harriette surprised her parents with the news that she wanted to leave Andree with a private nurse in England and accompany her parents to the United States. Catherine and Edward Crosby agreed to this proposition, and Edward bought steamship tickets for himself, his wife and daughter.

At that point Captain Crosby ran into Charles Hays, a family friend and business associate who happened to be holidaying with his wife in England. Mr Hays convinced Crosby to cancel his family's current steamship reservations and transfer them to the new White Star liner *Titanic*, upon which Hays and his wife planned to travel to America. Captain Crosby agreed to do so, and he wired friends and relatives in Milwaukee to say that he and his wife would be sailing to New York on the maiden voyage of the *Titanic* and that they would be bringing Harriette home with them.

Several weeks prior to the *Titanic*'s sailing, one of Captain Crosby's own steamships, the *Conestoga*, narrowly escaped being crushed in the ice in Lake Michigan. It is unknown if the Crosbys were aware of this near disaster when they boarded the *Titanic* as first class passengers at Southampton on the morning of 10 April.

CHARLES DAHL — Status: Survivor

Karl Dahl (45) was born on 22 July 1866 in Finnmarkens, Norway and was one of eight children of Nordmand and Marcelie Dahl.

In 1892 Karl Dahl emigrated to Adelaide to work as a joiner. He became a naturalised Australian citizen and anglicised his Christian name to Charles.

In 1912 Charles Dahl started on a journey to visit his old homeland of Norway, but after arriving in England he decided to change his plans and travel to Fingal, North Dakota, where his mother was then living. Mr Dahl therefore journeyed to Southampton and booked a steerage passage to America on the brand new *Titanic*; he was carrying a wallet containing his entire life's savings when he boarded the great vessel on 10 April.

EUGENE DALY — Status: Survivor

Eugene Daly (29) of Athlone, Ireland, was born on 23 January 1883. The young man saved for fourteen years in order to accumulate the £98 that he intended to take with him when he finally emigrated to the United States. Mr Daly planned to take up residence in Boston, Massachusetts, and on 11 April 1912 he carried his bagpipes and luggage aboard the *Titanic* as one of her steerage passengers when the great liner touched at Queenstown.

MARGARET DALY — Status: Survivor

Margaret Daly (30) was the daughter of Bridget Daly of Upper Irishtown, Athlone. Miss Daly emigrated to the United States, but she returned to Ireland in 1910 to spend some time with her mother and sister.

In April 1912 Miss Daly made arrangements to travel to the home of John Daly, a policeman who resided at 356 East 157th Street in New York. On 11 April 1912, along with her cousin Eugene Daly, Miss Daly boarded the *Titanic* at Queenstown as a steerage passenger.

CHARLES DAVIES — Status: Victim

Charles Henry Davies was a 21-year-old from Cornwall, who was living in Lyndhurst. In April 1912 he travelled to Southampton along with Percy Deacon (18), Ambrose Hood (21), William Dibden (18) and three brothers named Hickman – Leonard (34), Lewis (32) and Stanley (21). Mr Davies and his friends boarded the *Titanic* on 10 April as second class passengers.

ELIZABETH DAVIES — Status: Survivor

Elizabeth Agnes Friggens (48) was born on 23 November 1863 in Ludgvan, Cornwall, she and her three brothers and three sisters being the children of John and Elizabeth Friggens.

In 1881 Agnes was a dressmaker living in Penzance. She eventually married Richard Nicholls, and the young couple lived in Nancledra near the quarry where Mr Nicholls worked as a stonemason. Mr and Mrs Nicholls had three children – John, Mary and Joseph, the latter of whom was born on 24 July 1892.

Richard Nicholls passed away around 1900, and Agnes moved with her children to live near relatives in St Ives, Cornwall. She later married a man named John Davies, and the family relocated to Cardiff, Wales, where another son, John, was born on 31 July 1903. When Agnes's husband John passed away in 1910, Agnes once again moved to St Ives with her children.

Agnes Davies' son Richard eventually emigrated to Houghton, Michigan, and it wasn't long before Agnes decided to follow Richard and his wife to America. Agnes sold all of her belongings in St Ives and purchased three second class tickets to America on the White Star liner *Titanic*; Agnes Davies, her young son John (8) and her older son Joseph Nicholls (19) then travelled to Southampton and, along with family friend Maude Sincock (20), they boarded the new 'unsinkable' luxury liner on 10 April.

MARY DAVISON — Status: Survivor

Mary Fink (34) was born on 19 February 1878 and was the daughter of Mr and Mrs John Fink of Cleveland, Ohio.

Miss Fink married Thomas Davison (32), an Englishman from Liverpool, and the young couple made their home in Chippenham, Wiltshire.

In 1908 Thomas and Mary Davison visited Mary's parents in Cleveland and decided that they would return to America in a few years and make their permanent home there. In 1912 the young couple decided that it was time for them to make their move, and they began to make their preparations to leave England.

The Davisons originally intended to sail to America very early in 1912, but they decided to postpone their plans so that they could enjoy the novelty of sailing on the maiden voyage of the brand new *Titanic*. It was as steerage passengers that Thomas and Mary Davison boarded the great vessel at Southampton on 10 April.

EVA GEORGETTA DEAN — Status: Survivor

Eva 'Ettie' Light (32) was born on 18 May 1879. Ettie eventually married Bertram Dean (25) and in 1912 she and her husband lived in Southampton with their two children, son Bertram (2) and daughter Elizabeth Gladys (7 weeks).

In 1912 the Deans made plans to visit Ettie's brother in Hume, Missouri, where they planned to purchase a farm and settle down. Bertram and Ettie sold their pub in Southampton and used every penny of their life savings to purchase gold bars to take with them to America; the Deans were carrying everything they owned when they boarded the *Titanic* as steerage passengers on 10 April.

THEODOOR DE MULDER — Status: Survivor

Theodoor de Mulder (30) was born in Nederhasselt, Belgium on 15 September 1881. He was the son of Francis and Maria-Theresia de Mulder, and the family lived together in Aspelare.

On 11 April 1907 Mr de Mulder married Jeanette D'Hondt, and by 1912 the couple had three children whom they named Gilbert, Jean and Cyriel.

Theodoor de Mulder made his living as a farmer, but times were hard in Belgium and he had to support his wife's elderly parents as well as his own family. Theodoor decided to emigrate to Toronto in search of a higher-paying job and a better way of life. Just one month before his scheduled departure, though, the de Mulders' youngest child, Cyriel, passed away before reaching his first birthday.

Despite this tragedy, in April 1912 Mr de Mulder travelled to Antwerp, where he boarded a ship to Harwich and then travelled to Southampton by train. On 10 April Theodoor de Mulder boarded the White Star liner *Titanic* as a third class passenger to begin the next stage of his journey to the New World.

VERA DICK — Status: Survivor

Vera Gillespie (17) was born in Calgary, Alberta on 12 June 1894 and was the daughter of Frederick and Anne Gillespie. On 31 May 1911 Vera married Albert Dick (31), a Calgary builder and real estate developer, and, while their new home was being built, the newlyweds went abroad with the intention of making a honeymoon tour around the world.

While they were in Egypt the honeymooners suddenly decided to curtail their honeymoon trip and return to the United States, and they cabled for reservations on the new White Star liner *Titanic*. Mr and Mrs Dick then travelled to London, where they purchased furniture and shipped it to Canada to furnish their new home, and on 10 April they took the boat train to Southampton and boarded the *Titanic* as first class passengers.

WASHINGTON DODGE — Status: Survivor

Washington Dodge (52) was born on 3 June 1859 in Sonora, Tuolumne County, California, he and his sister Adelaide being the children of Mark and Eliza Dodge. When Mark Dodge died in 1866, Washington and his mother and sister were left to face the world alone.

Washington Dodge spent his early years in Tuolumne County and later attended the Boys High School in San Francisco. In 1881 Dodge enrolled at the University of California, and in 1884 he graduated from the university with a degree in medicine.

Dr Dodge established a private medical practice in San Francisco, and the practice's prosperity soon made him one of the leading physicians in the city. Dodge became a faculty member in the University of California's medical department, and he also served in various capacities at a number of local hospitals.

Dr Dodge married Alice Shepard on 11 February 1891, and the young couple's son Henry was born on 29 November of that same year.

Despite the success of his medical practice, Washington Dodge was deeply interested in politics, and he decided to give up medicine and run for public office. In 1896 Dr Dodge was elected as a member of the Phelan Board of Supervisors in San Francisco; after the expiration of his two-year term in 1898, Dodge was elected as the City Tax Assessor for the Port of San Francisco, an office he held for the next fourteen years.

All was not well with the Dodge marriage, though, and Washington and Alice Dodge were divorced in 1902. Dr Dodge married for the second time on 17 April 1906, his second wife being Ruth Fontaine, the widow of a French sugar magnate. The new Mrs Dodge had a daughter, Vida Fontaine, who would later attend school in San Mateo. However, Dr and Mrs Dodge soon had a son of their own, Washington Dodge Jr, who was born on September 23, 1907. The Dodge family made their home at 2129 Laguna Street in San Francisco.

In 1908 Dr Dodge was working on an automobile in his garage when he had a narrow escape from disaster; when Dodge lit a match to enable him to see underneath the car, the accumulated gas fumes inside the garage ignited and severely seared his face and head.

In February 1912 Dr and Mrs Dodge and their son Washington Jr (4) sailed to Europe on the White Star liner *Olympic* for a brief holiday. The main purpose of Dodge's trip, however, was to enable him to undergo treatment by a medical specialist in Paris for a blood condition he was suffering from.

Dr Dodge intended to retire from the Assessorship upon his return to San Francisco and accept an appointment as first vice president of the Anglo-California and London-Paris National Bank. It was with that intention in mind that Dr Dodge, his wife Ruth and their young son Washington Jr travelled to Southampton, where they boarded the White Star liner *Titanic* as first class passengers on 10 April.

MAHALA DOUGLAS **Status: Survivor**

Mahala Dutton (48) was born on 26 January 1864, she and her sister being daughters of Rollin and Sophia Dutton. The family lived in Cedar Rapids, Iowa.

In 1906 Mahala Dutton married widower Walter Douglas, a Cedar Rapids native and a director of the Quaker Oats Co. (which had been co-founded by his father). Mr Douglas also had an interest in the Douglas & Co. starch works.

George C. Douglas (one of Walter Douglas's two sons by his previous marriage) had a child named George B. Douglas. This grandchild was a great favourite of Walter and Mahala Douglas, and Walter used to have the time of his life romping with the little boy.

In 1911 Walter Douglas retired at the age of 50. He and Mahala moved to Minneapolis, where they became prominent in society and built a palatial summer home called 'Walden' at Lake Minnetonka.

In 1912 Walter and Mahala Douglas went to Europe on a pleasure trip, intending to search for furnishings for their new home. In April they made arrangements to return home to the United States on the *Titanic*. The Douglases and their French maid Berthe Leroy (27) were at Southampton Docks on 10 April when the time came for them to board the great vessel to begin their journey home.

LUCY DUFF GORDON **Status: Survivor**

Lucy Sutherland (48) was born in London on 13 June 1863, she and her sister Elinor (later author Elinor Glyn) being the daughters of Douglas and Elinor Sutherland. Douglas Sutherland died when the girls were still babies, and they were raised by their mother on their grandparents' ranch in Canada.

In 1884, at the age of 21, Lucy married wine merchant James Wallace, and the couple had one child, Esme, later Countess of Halsbury. Lucy and James were divorced in 1890, however, and Lucy was forced to start a dressmaking business to support herself and her daughter. The clothing she designed quickly became very popular, and her shop prospered under the trade name 'Lucile' in London's Hanover Square. By 1897, when the firm was incorporated as Lucile Ltd, it had become a major force in the British fashion industry.

Lucy's lack of confidence in her own financial acumen inspired her to become business partners with Scottish landowner Sir Cosmo Duff Gordon, the fifth baronet of Halkin, to whom she became engaged. In 1900 Lucy became Lady Duff Gordon when she and Sir Cosmo were married in Venice, and in 1906 the couple took up residence at 22 Lennox Gardens, Knightsbridge.

In 1910 Lucy Duff Gordon opened a branch of Lucile Ltd at 17 West 36th Street in New York City. A second branch of Lucile Ltd opened in Paris in 1911.

As 'Lucile', Lucy Duff Gordon became one of the most influential couturieres of the Edwardian era. She was particularly famous for her lingerie designs, for training the first professional fashion models and for introducing the first runway style shows. Her clientele represented European royalty, American high society and the entertainment world. In addition to her work as a designer, Lucy was a leading fashion journalist, being a correspondent for William Randolph Hearst's powerful news syndicate.

In 1912 Lucy Duff Gordon began making arrangements to move her New York showrooms from West 36th Street to larger facilities on West 57th Street, with a new studio and workrooms on Fifth Avenue. When the time came for her to sign the new lease in April, however, she and Sir Cosmo were in France and needed to sail to America on the first available ship; they therefore booked passage for themselves and Lucy's secretary Laura Francatelli ('Franks') on the new White Star liner *Titanic*; the three travellers boarded the great vessel at Cherbourg on the evening of 10 April.

ANNA ELIZABETH DYKER — Status: Survivor

Anna Anderson (22) was born on 24 November 1889 and was one of three children of Mr and Mrs Carl Anderson of West Haven, Connecticut. Anna's two brothers were named William and F.C. Anderson.

In 1912 Anna was a recent newlywed, her new husband being a 23-year-old trolley car conductor named Adolf ('Ned') Dyker; the young couple set up housekeeping in a small house in West Haven.

It wasn't long before tragedy intruded itself into the lives of Mr and Mrs Dyker. Word reached them that Ned's father in Stockholm had fallen seriously ill and was not expected to live, so Ned and Anna decided to mortgage their small home for the fourth time in order to raise money to sail to Sweden to visit Ned's father. The Dykers travelled to Stockholm and managed to arrive there shortly before Ned's father passed away, where they remained in order to attend the funeral.

Eventually the time came for Ned and Anna Dyker to return home to Connecticut, and they travelled to Southampton in order to connect with the ship on which they had booked a steerage passage to America; it was on 10 April 1912 that the young couple walked up the gangway and set foot on the *Titanic*, the newest addition to the White Star Line's prestigious fleet of passenger liners.

FRANCIS DYMOND — Status: Survivor

Frank Dymond (36) was apparently born in 1876 in Poole, Dorset, and was the son of William and Catherine Dymond. He married Mary Jane Lisle on 10 May 1898.

Mr Dymond served in the Royal Navy from 1897 to 1904. He was a stoker on board the HMS *Hermione* during the Boxer Rebellion in China, and he later served on board a number of other naval warships. After leaving the Royal Navy, Frank Dymond became a stoker in England's merchant navy and served in the boiler rooms of many British vessels, including the Cunard liner *Mauretania*.

In April 1912 Frank and Mary Dymond lived at 2 Farmer's Court in Southampton. Frank had last served as a fireman on board the White Star liner *Teutonic* before the opportunity presented itself for him to transfer to the *Titanic*. On 6 April Mr Dymond signed onto the brand new liner as a fireman, and at noon on 10 April he was on board her when she left Southampton Docks on the first leg of her maiden voyage.

ALBERT ERVINE **Status: Victim**

Albert Ervine (18) was born on 2 August 1893 in Belfast, where his mother still lived in 1912. Early that year Ervine worked on the SS *Maloja*, and he later became one of the Harland & Wolff staff assigned to evaluate the *Titanic*'s performance and correct any malfunctions that might occur during that vessel's maiden voyage.

Mr Ervine was on board the *Titanic* on 2–3 April during her trip from Belfast to Southampton, and it was in the latter city that he again boarded the great vessel for the commencement of her maiden voyage on 10 April.

THOMAS EVERETT **Status: Victim**

Thomas Everett was born in Bedminster, near Bristol, and, by the time he was 39, was living in Bristol with his wife Fanny and three children (Everett, Harry, aged 11 and Harold, aged 6). For the previous eighteen years Mr Everett had been employed fairly regularly as a crane operator for a coal agent; since there was no work in the yard for about three weeks prior to the coal strike, however, he decided to try his fortune in America.

Frederick Shellard, who was visiting Bristol from New York, promised to help Thomas Everett obtain a factory job in Troy, New York if he emigrated there, so Everett made plans to settle in Troy and then send for his wife and children later.

Thomas Everett and Fred Shellard both bought steerage tickets to travel on the *Titanic*'s maiden voyage, and they boarded the great vessel in Southampton on 10 April.

ERNEST FARRENDEN **Status: Victim**

Ernest John Farrenden (22) was the youngest son of Mr and Mrs W. Farrenden, confectioners and bakers of Emsworth, near Portsmouth.

Mr Farrenden was in service of White Star Line for some time, and he worked in the ships' kitchens as a confectioner. His first voyage was to the Mediterranean on board the *Romanic*, and he completed several voyages on that vessel before transferring to the *Olympic*. During Farrenden's second voyage on the *Olympic* the big liner collided with the cruiser *Hawke*. Farrenden was superstitious of the *Olympic* and told mother that none of crew liked working on her, and at the conclusion of his third voyage on board *Olympic* the young man was happy to be transferred to the *Titanic*.

Ernest Farrenden came home to visit his mother on Easter Sunday in 1912, and he left again the next day to join the *Titanic*.

LAURA FRANCATELLI — Status: Survivor

Laura Francatelli (32) was born in Lambeth, London in 1880. She and her sisters Elizabeth and Jessie were the children of maître d'hôtel Charles Francatelli and his wife Elizabeth.

In 1912 Miss Francatelli worked as a secretary for Lucy Duff Gordon, an American fashion designer whose husband was Sir Cosmo Duff Gordon, Scottish landowner and fifth baronet of Halkin.

In April 1912 the Duff Gordons and Miss Francatelli were in France when Lucy Duff Gordon received word that business concerns required her immediate return to the United States. The Duff Gordons purchased passages home on the first available ship, and on the evening of 10 April they and Miss Francatelli arrived in Cherbourg and boarded the White Star liner *Titanic* as first class passengers.

THOMAS FRANKLIN — Status: Victim

Thomas Franklin (37), a resident of London, boarded the *Titanic* at Southampton on 10 April as a first class passenger.

HENRY FRAUENTHAL — Status: Survivor

Henry Frauenthal (49) was born on 13 March 1863 in Wilkes-Barre, Pennsylvania and was the son of merchant Samuel Frauenthal and his wife Henrietta, both of whom had come to the United States from Germany. Henry had three brothers named Hermann, Isaac and Isidor, and his two sisters were named Carrie and Rose.

After graduating from high school in Wilkes-Barre, Henry Frauenthal studied analytical chemistry at Lehigh University and also played on the college's first American football team. After graduating in 1888, Mr Frauenthal studied medicine at New York's Bellevue Hospital Medical College, receiving his medical credentials in 1890. Dr Frauenthal then became a clinical assistant to Dr Lewis Sayre, a famed orthopaedic surgeon, and worked in that capacity until 1901, when he set up his own private practice.

Dr Frauenthal had a great interest in joint diseases and infantile paralysis, and in 1905 he and his brother Hermann founded the Jewish Hospital for Deformities and Joint Diseases at 558 Lexington Avenue in New York City. The hospital had a dispensary and beds for seven patients, and its stated mission was the 'bringing relief through care to orthopaedic problems of children'.

The clinic proved to be very successful, and in 1906 Dr Frauenthal expanded the facility by taking over a brownstone building at 1919 Madison Avenue in upper Manhattan. Within six months the clinic was doing so well that it expanded into the brownstone building situated next door, and by the end of the year Dr Frauenthal had treated 1,212 patients. The clinic was enlarged once again in 1908 and changed its name to the Hospital for Deformities and Joint Diseases; the facility was very successful and brought great prosperity to Dr Frauenthal, whose residence was at 783 Lexington Avenue.

Dr Henry Frauenthal was a member of the Electro-Therapeutic Association (which, among other things, investigated the therapeutic uses of electricity as a medical treatment), and at the organisation's annual meeting in September 1908 he presented a paper on a topic he had long been interested in: 'Anterior Poliomyelitis'.

On 26 March 1912 Dr Frauenthal was in Nice when he married Clara Heinsheimer of New York City. 10 April found the honeymooners in Southampton, where they boarded the brand new *Titanic* as first class passengers. Mr and Mrs Frauenthal were also looking forward to Henry's brother Isaac joining them on board the *Titanic* when the vessel touched at Cherbourg that same evening.

MARGARETHA FROLICHER-STEHLI — Status: Survivor

Margaretha Stehli (48) was born in Solothurn, Switzerland and was the daughter of Emil Stehli-Hirt, a silk manufacturer. In 1885 Margaretha married Maximilian Frolicher (60), a wealthy Zurich silk manufacturer and importer who was (along with his cousin) a joint owner of a silk mill in Rossmore, Pennsylvania.

In April 1912 the Frolichers planned to take a trip abroad as a reward for their daughter Hedwig's (22) fine performance in college. They booked first class passages to America on the *Titanic*, and boarded the great liner at Cherbourg on the evening of 10 April.

HEDWIG MARGARITHA FROLICHER — Status: Survivor

Hedwig Frolicher was born in Zurich, Switzerland and lived there with her parents, Maximilian and Margaretha Frolicher-Stehli. Hedwig graduated from university early in 1912, and in April of that year her parents planned to take her on a trip abroad as a reward for her fine academic performance, the family boarding *Titanic* at Cherbourg.

JACQUES FUTRELLE (Victim) and LILLIE MAY FUTRELLE (Survivor)

Jacques Futrelle (37) was born in Atlanta, Georgia, on 9 April 1875 and was the son of Wiley and Linnie Futrelle. Jacques' father was an instructor at an Atlanta preparatory college. Lily May Peel (35), the daughter of Mr and Mrs D.G. Peel of Atlanta, Georgia, was born on 26 May 1876. She and her brother John grew up in the family home at 56 West 4th Street.

As a schoolboy Jacques worked at a local printing shop, and at the age of eighteen he became an aide to the business manager of the *Atlanta Constitution*. In 1894 Futrelle went to work for the *Boston Post*, but he soon became homesick and returned to Atlanta to work for the *Atlanta Journal*, where he set up the paper's first sports department.

In July 1895 Jacques Futrelle married Lillie May Peel at her parents' home in Atlanta. The newlyweds moved to New York and set up housekeeping at 71 Irving Place in Gramercy Park, and Jacques became the telegraph editor at the *New York Herald*. The young couple's daughter Virginia was born in 1897, and their son John (Jacques Jr) followed in 1898.

In 1898 Jacques Futrelle was kept so busy at the newspaper during the Spanish-American War that – despite his height of 6ft 4in and his massive 18-stone build – the unremitting strain began to affect his health to the point of exhaustion; at the conclusion of hostilities, Jacques and May left New York and went to stay at the cottage of Jacques' sister Alberta in Scituate, Massachusetts so that Jacques could recover his health. Jacques and May enjoyed Scituate so much that they later built a home, 'Stepping Stones', there.

Jacques and May Futrelle next moved to Richmond, Virginia, where Jacques did a bit of newspaper work and also spent two years working as a theatrical manager, where he wrote, directed and acted. In 1904 the Futrelles moved to Cambridge, Massachusetts, where Jacques went to work on the editorial staff of the *Boston American*.

In 1905 Jacques Futrelle began writing short stories for the *Boston American*, and his delight in Conan Doyle's Sherlock Holmes stories led him to write a tale called 'The Great Suit Case Mystery' in which Holmes investigated an actual murder that took place in Boston that same year. Futrelle's story, which was serialised in the 5–8 October issues of the *American*, enabled Sherlock Holmes to arrive at the correct identity of the guilty parties several weeks before the real-life Boston police arrested them.

It was while he was at the *Boston American* that Jacques Futrelle also wrote his first mystery detective story featuring the fictional Professor Van Dusen, aka 'The Thinking Machine'. This story was serialised in the *Boston American* on 30 October 1905.

In 1906 Jacques Futrelle left the newspaper business and became a freelance writer, devoting his attention to novels. He published a novel titled *The Chase of the Golden Plate* in which Professor Van Dusen made his first appearance in book form; this was followed by an entire book of Van Dusen stories that was titled *The Thinking Machine*. In 1907 Professor Van Dusen reappeared in a second book of mystery stories called *The Thinking Machine on the Case*.

Jacques Futrelle wrote many other short stories for various newspapers and periodicals of the day, and these included a few detective stories featuring protagonists other than Professor Van Dusen. In 1908 Futrelle published a novel called *The Simple Case of Susan*, which was a sentimental romance about confused identities. Two mystery novels followed in 1909, *The Diamond Master* and *Elusive Isobel*. Futrelle's political novel *The High Hand* appeared in 1911, and he also completed work on *Blind Man's Bluff* and *My Lady's Garter*, the latter of which was a tale of burglary, impersonation and detection. May Futrelle was herself a successful writer of short stories, but she eventually decided to apply herself to writing a full length novel. The end result, *The Secretary of Frivolous Affairs*, was published in 1911 and was Mrs Futrelle's first long work.

In January 1912 Jacques and May Futrelle decided to travel to Europe to try and expand the European market for Jacques' stories and books. The Futrelles left their two children in the States; John, 15, was a student at Marist College, while 16-year-old Virginia was enrolled at the Convent of Notre Dame in Baltimore.

Jacques and May Futrelle spent the early months of 1912 in Italy. As spring approached, however, they began anticipating the prospect of spending the summer in Scituate, where they were popular members of the local 'Author's Colony'.

The Futrelles originally booked their passage to America on the *Adriatic*, but they were delayed in their travels and were forced to cancel their reservations. Next they considered travelling on the *Mauretania*, but May had heard stories about the ship's excessive vibration, so they decided against it. After arriving in England, the Futrelles heard about the *Titanic*'s upcoming maiden voyage and decided it would be a novel experience to sail on the brand new White Star liner.

While they were in London at the end of March 1912, Jacques and May Futrelle decided to send powers of attorney to May's brother, John Peel of Atlanta, for the administration of their estates should anything befall them during their travels. The Futrelles also gave John Peel specific instructions as to the future care of their children.

It so happened that 9 April 1912 was Jacques Futrelle's 37th birthday, and that night the Futrelles' friends gathered in London to celebrate the occasion and give the travellers a big send-off. The party lasted until 3 a.m., so – instead of going to bed – Jacques and May Futrelle hurriedly packed their bags and made arrangements to make the trip to Southampton in time to board the *Titanic*.

It was rumoured that Jacques Futrelle had six unpublished Thinking Machine stories in his possession when he and May boarded the *Titanic* as first class passengers on the morning of 10 April.

ARTHUR GEE — Status: Victim

Arthur Gee (47) was born in Manchester and after completing his education he moved to Russia to work for a calico printing company. In the early months of 1912 Mr Gee, his wife Edith and their four children returned to England and moved to St Annes, Lancashire.

Arthur Gee represented Messrs Whitehead, Sumner, Harker & Co., a Manchester machinery exporter, and in April 1912 he was scheduled to make a business trip to Mexico (after which he was contemplating retiring). Mr Gee intended to sail from Liverpool, but he readily agreed with a suggestion that he transfer to the brand new *Titanic*.

When the time came for Arthur Gee to leave for Southampton, the family dog (which was normally devoted solely to the children) followed his cab to the train station and jumped about him in such a demonstrative fashion that he commented to a friend on the strangeness of the incident; Mr Gee felt it remarkable that the dog seemed to sense that he was going on a long voyage.

On 10 April 1912 Arthur Gee commenced the first leg of his business trip when he stepped on board the White Star liner *Titanic* at Southampton.

JACOB GIBBONS — Status: Survivor

Jacob Gibbons (36) was born on 10 October 1875 in Charminster, Dorset. Mr Gibbons and his wife and five children lived at 'Harbour View', a guest house in Studland, Dorset, whose guests included author Virginia Woolf and Major-General Robert Baden-Powell, the founder of the Boy Scout movement.

In the spring of 1912 Jacob Gibbons was suffering from peritonitis, and his physician thought that exposure to sea air might help to improve his condition. Mr Gibbons decided to give this prescription a try, and in April 1912 he arranged to take his very first sea voyage by signing onto the *Titanic* as a saloon steward. On 10 April 1912 Jacob Gibbons was on board the big liner when she cast off her moorings and pulled away from Southampton Docks on the first leg of her maiden voyage.

DOROTHY GIBSON — Status: Survivor

Dorothy Brown (22) was born in Hoboken, New Jersey on17 May 1889 and was the daughter of John and Pauline Brown. After Mr Brown's unexpected death, Pauline Brown married Leonard Gibson, who adopted Dorothy and gave her his surname.

After completing her schooling Dorothy Gibson became a model, and she soon became known as the original 'Harrison Fisher Girl' when that well-known illustrator chose her as the subject for many of his artistic renderings.

In 1911 Miss Gibson received an offer to work as a film actress for the Éclair Motion Pictures Co., and it wasn't long before she became romantically involved with the company's owner, Jules Brulatour.

During the early months of 1912 Miss Gibson completed work on a film called *The Easter Bonnet*, and on 17 March she and her mother sailed to Europe for a brief holiday. In early April the two travellers were in Genoa when Dorothy received a cable from her employer asking her to return to the United States, so she and her mother travelled to Paris and purchased two first class passages on the new White Star liner *Titanic*. Dorothy Gibson and Pauline Gibson (45) boarded the ship at Cherbourg on the evening of 10 April 1912.

SAMUEL GOLDENBERG — Status: Survivor

Samuel Goldenberg (47) was born on 8 September 1864 and was one of four directors of the importing firm of Goldenberg Bros & Co. of 109 Fifth Avenue and 18th Street in New York City. The firm was one of largest lace importing firms in the United States.

Samuel Goldenberg and his wife Nella lived in New York until 1905, at which time they moved to France and took up residence in Nice. The Goldenbergs made business trips to New York several times each year, however, and while in the city they lived at the Hotel Savoy.

Samuel and Nella Goldenberg were both prominent dog fanciers; Mr Goldenberg was President of the 'Canine d'Savoie' and owned many valuable show dogs.

In April 1912 Samuel and Nella Goldenberg were coming from Berlin to New York City to attend the French Bull Dog Club of America's show on 20 April (at which Mr Goldenberg was to be a judge). On the evening of 10 April the Goldenbergs boarded the *Titanic* at Cherbourg as first class passengers.

ARCHIBALD GRACIE IV — Status: Survivor

Archibald Gracie IV (54) was born on 15 January 1858 in Mobile, Alabama and was the son of Archibald Gracie III and his wife, the former Josephine Mayo. The Gracies were an old and well known Southern family, Archibald's grandfather having given his life fighting for the Confederacy during the Civil War. The Gracies also had solid roots in New York and Washington, D.C.

Archibald Gracie received his schooling at St Paul's Academy in Concord, New Hampshire and then attended West Point; the young man's record at the prestigious military academy was less than exemplary, however, and he failed to graduate. Gracie later joined the New York National Guard and eventually attained the rank of Colonel.

Archibald Gracie married Constance Schack, the New York-born daughter of a former minister from Denmark to the United States. Constance was an accomplished linguist and pianist, was active in New York society and was known for her philanthropy. Constance and Archibald eventually had four children; two daughters died very young, but their eldest surviving daughter, Constance, was born around 1891, and another daughter, Edith, was born around 1894.

The early years of the new century found the Gracies living at 1527 16th Street NW in Washington, D.C. Tragedy was soon to strike the family, however, for on 6 June 1903, while in Paris, Mrs Gracie witnessed the death of her 12-year-old daughter Constance in a lift accident. The following year Colonel Gracie developed diabetes.

The independently wealthy Colonel Gracie was very history minded, and in 1904 he began researching the Battle of Chickamauga, a Civil War battle in which his grandfather had taken part. The end result of Gracie's research was a book titled *The Truth About Chickamauga*, which was published in late 1911.

The many years of working on his Civil War book project had greatly fatigued Colonel Gracie, so in the spring of 1912 he decided to take a trip to England in order to recuperate. Gracie intended to do some research there for an article on the War of 1812 that he had already begun working on, but it is said that he was also suffering from some health problems that he hoped his trip abroad would help to improve.

In mid-March 1912 Archibald Gracie sailed to England alone on the White Star liner *Oceanic*. After arriving in London, Gracie went to Westminster Abbey to return thanks for his safe arrival in England. The following Sunday he went to St Margaret's to pray, and on Easter Sunday he went to St Paul's, where his ancestor, John Rogers, had once been a cleric. Interspersed between these religious pilgrimages were intensive bouts of archival research for the historical article that Gracie was working on.

When the time came for Archibald Gracie to return home to the States, he booked a first class passage on the new White Star liner *Titanic* and boarded the great vessel at Southampton on 10 April.

GEORGE GRAHAM — Status: Victim

George Graham (39) was born on 11 June 1873, and he and his six brothers lived with their parents on a farm near St Mary's, Ontario.

At the age of 17, Mr Graham began working as a hardware clerk in St Mary's; he soon landed another job in Galt, but in 1903 he moved to Toronto and went to work for the local T. Eaton Co. department store.

In 1905 George Graham married Edith Jackson, and the young couple was active in the local Methodist Church. When Eaton's opened another store in Winnipeg, Manitoba the following year, George was asked to move his family there so that he could take charge of the store's crockery and fine china division. Mr Graham eventually became the Winnipeg store's head buyer, and he and Edith made their home at 31 Dundurn Place.

In 1908 the Grahams' son John was born, but the little boy passed away in January 1911; when Edith suffered a miscarriage shortly thereafter, the combined emotional shock of these two traumatic events took a heavy toll on the young woman. When the time came for George Graham to leave home for his annual buying trip in the spring of 1912, he was reluctant to leave his ailing wife alone but was nevertheless obligated to fulfil his business commitment to Eaton's. Mr Graham therefore made arrangements for Edith to stay at her parents' home in Harriston while he was abroad.

George Graham travelled abroad to England, Belgium and Austria and completed his buying arrangements there. Eager to return to his wife in Canada, Mr Graham then booked a first class passage on the White Star liner *Titanic* and boarded the great vessel at Cherbourg on the evening of 10 April.

ANNA HAMALAINEN — Status: Survivor

John Hamalainen came to the United States from Finland around 1907 and settled in Hartford, Connecticut, where he met and married his wife Anna (23), who was also a Finn.

In August 1911 Anna and the couple's 5-month-old baby Wiljo (William) went back to Finland to visit Anna's parents. In September of that year John moved to Detroit, Michigan and got a job at the Wilson Body Co.

On 2 April 1912 Anna wrote a letter to John saying that she would be returning home on the *Titanic* and that she would be bringing a young friend, Martta Hiltunen (18) to work as her maid. On 10 April Anna Hamalainen, her infant son Wiljo and Martta Hiltunen boarded the *Titanic* in Southampton as second class passengers.

HENRY HARPER — Status: Survivor

Henry Harper (48) was born on 11 March 1864 in New York City, he and his sisters Maria and Josephine being the children of Joseph and Abigail Harper. Joseph Harper managed Harper & Brothers, a venerable publishing firm that was established by his father and three uncles in 1812. Sadly, Abigail Harper passed away not long after her son Henry was born.

Henry Harper attended Columbia University and belonged to the University, Century, and Columbia Clubs; he was also a member of the Delta Phi fraternity. After his graduation in 1888, Mr Harper became a director and member of Harper & Brothers.

It was probably in the late 1880s or early 1890s that Henry Harper married Myra Haxtun (49), the daughter of Benjamin and Susan Haxtun of New York.

In 1893 the stock market plunged, starting the 'Panic of '93', culminating in a dramatic crash on 27 June. The resulting economic depression hit the publishing business very hard, and in 1894 Joseph Harper retired from Harper & Brothers and was succeeded by his son Henry.

Harper & Brothers revised its editorial policies in an attempt to stop the declining circulation of its periodicals, but these attempts were unsuccessful and, from 1894 through 1896, the revenues from the company's periodicals continued to decline with the depression. In order to remain in business, Harper & Brothers terminated the Harper partnership, and on 16 November 1896 the firm was reorganised as a stock company. The corporation issued $2 million in stock and $3 million in bonds, and over the next three years Harper & Brothers borrowed $850,000 from J.P. Morgan & Co.

In 1899 the firm of Harper & Brothers found itself unable to meet interest payments on its loans from J.P. Morgan, and the company was once again reorganised; in June of that year Doubleday & McClure officially took over Harper & Brothers. Rather than accept further loans from J.P. Morgan, Harper & Brothers declared bankruptcy on 4 December 1899 and went into receivership; the firm discontinued publishing several of its literature-oriented periodicals and concentrated instead on making *Harper's Weekly* a successful magazine.

Henry Harper remained at Harper & Brothers throughout this period and had a desk in the company's offices, but he gradually had less and less to do with the actual management of the business. A lover of outdoor life, Mr Harper was an amateur naturalist and was active in the work of preserving the Adirondack forests from the depredations of loggers. The fact that Henry and Myra Harper were childless also enabled them to spend about six months every year travelling abroad.

Around 1902 Mr Harper had a narrow escape during one of his globetrotting forays when the ship in which he was travelling collided with an iceberg off the coast of Newfoundland.

In February 1912 Henry and Myra Harper left New York and sailed abroad on a tour of Egypt and Europe. While in Alexandria, Henry hired Hamad Hassab (27) to serve as interpreter, guide and manservant; later, in Paris, the Harpers purchased a Pekingese dog that they named Sun Yat-Sen. When the time came for them to return to the United States, Henry and Myra Harper, Hamad Hassab and Sun Yat-Sen took the boat train from Paris to Cherbourg, where they boarded the tender that took them out to where the White Star liner *Titanic* was waiting to receive them as first class passengers.

JOHN HARPER **Status: Victim**

John Harper (39) was a native of Houston, Scotland and worked in the carpet fields at Glenpatrick, and also at McLaurin's Paper Mills in Milliken Park. Harper eventually moved to Kilbarchan and later entered into mission work.

Revd Harper operated missions in Johnstone and Bridge of Weir, and for a short time was associated with the Memorial Hall in Kilbarchan. While engaged there he was persuaded by the Revd E.A. Carter, founder of the Baptist Pioneer Mission, to take up evangelistic work. Revd Harper was stationed in Plantation District, Glasgow as pastor of the Paisley Road Baptist church, and he had the pleasure of seeing his congregation grow from sixteen to 500.

Revd Harper married Annie Bell, and in January 1906 a daughter, Anna Jessie Speirs Harper, was born to them in Govan. Mrs Harper died in childbirth, however, and Revd Harper's niece, Miss Jessie Leitch, moved into the Harper household to help care for little 'Nan'.

Revd Harper eventually became pastor of the Walworth Road Baptist church, London. From December 1911 to January 1912 Revd Harper conducted a series of revival meetings at the Moody church in Chicago, Illinois, and the meetings were so popular that he was asked to return and repeat them. Harper made all the arrangements to do so and booked second class passages to America for himself, little Nan (6) and Miss Leitch (29), and the three travellers were on board the White Star liner *Titanic* when the great vessel left Southampton on 10 April.

IRENE HARRIS **Status: Survivor**

Irene 'Rene' Wallach (35) was born on 15 June 1876 and was the daughter of Mr and Mrs Samuel Wallach of Washington.

After leaving school, Rene Wallach moved to Boston, Massachusetts, where she obtained a day job as a legal secretary while she attended law school at night. Miss Wallach eventually met theatrical manager Henry Harris, and she started reading plays for him and even attended rehearsals of his plays. Romance blossomed between the two, and Rene Wallach and Henry Harris were married on 22 October 1898. Rene thereafter devoted herself to assisting her husband in his dealings with writers, actors and producers; she was very good at it, too, for her husband once told her, 'You are a better businessman than I am.'

In 1901 Henry Harris became business manager for the Frohman, Harris and Rich companies and was so successful at it that Miss Amelia Bingham hired him as her business manager in 'The Climbers'. Harris's success was steady after that, and he and Rene were soon able to shift their base of operations to New York.

In 1903 Mr Harris and a partner built New York's Hudson Theater on West 44th Street, and he later became the theatre's sole owner. In 1905 Harris produced the hit play *The Lion and the Mouse*, which was wildly successful, and he then negotiated for the purchase of the Hackett Theater on West 42nd Street. By 1908 Mr Harris had six stars under contract and eleven plays on tour.

In February 1912 Henry and Rene Harris sailed to England to arrange for the production of various British plays in the United States and also to arrange for the appearance of American actress Frances Starr in England. After completing their business Mr and Mrs Harris ran into an old theatrical friend named John 'Jack' Baumann (60), who was down on his luck; Mr Harris kindly arranged for Mr Baumann to accompany him and Rene back to New York.

On 10 April Henry and Rene Harris boarded the *Titanic* at Southampton as first class passengers, and they looked forward to seeing Mr Baumann again when he joined the *Titanic* at Cherbourg that evening.

ESTHER HART Status: Survivor

Esther Bloomfield (48) was born on 13 May 1863. She married at the age of 18, but her married life was very unhappy and she was physically abused by her husband. Esther bore nine children, but none of them survived more than a few months; when Esther was widowed in her early thirties, she returned home to live with her parents and vowed never to marry again.

Several years later Esther's father contacted a local builder to construct a new house in Chadwell Heath. The builder was Benjamin Hart (49), and Ben was immediately attracted to Esther Bloomfield. Despite Esther's previous marital experiences, she and Benjamin were married in 1900 and lived in the London suburb of Seven Kings, where their daughter Eva was born on 31 January 1905.

By the time 1911 arrived, the building business had gone into a slump in England and there were no renters for the homes that Benjamin built. When a friend returned from Canada and told of the prosperity to be found in that country, Benjamin Hart decided to emigrate to Winnipeg, Canada and go into the construction business there with his friend.

Esther Hart was very uneasy about her husband's decision to take her and little Eva to Canada, and she made no secret of her apprehension. Despite Benjamin's constant queries about why she was uneasy, Esther couldn't really give him a meaningful answer.

Benjamin Hart decided to travel to Canada via New York so that he could visit his sister, whom he hadn't seen for many years, after which he and his family could travel to Canada by train. Benjamin booked passage on the *Philadelphia* and was in process of selling the family house when the coal strike suddenly disrupted their travel plans by forcing the cancellation of the *Philadelphia*'s voyage. When Benjamin pressed the shipping company for an alternate means of transportation, the company arranged for the Harts to travel to America as second class passengers on the White Star liner *Titanic*.

Upon hearing this news, Esther Hart's anxieties finally seemed to crystallise, and she was convinced that she now knew the reason for her strange unease about the upcoming trip. Esther felt that the *Titanic*'s reputation for unsinkability was 'flying in the face of the Almighty' and that the ship would never complete her maiden voyage.

Despite Esther's fears, Benjamin completed the arrangements for his family's emigration, and on 10 April 1912 he, Esther and Eva boarded the *Titanic* at Southampton as second class passengers.

WALLACE HARTLEY **Status: Victim**

Wallace Hartley (33) was the son of Albion and Elizabeth Hartley of 92 Greenfield Road in Colne, Lancashire. He was born on 2 June 1878, his elder sister having been born the previous year. (He is reported to have had a brother and at least one other sister as well.)

As a youth Wallace Hartley was a chorister at the Bethel Independent Methodist chapel in Colne, where his father was a choirmaster for twenty-five years. In the mid-1890s the Hartley family moved to Dewsbury, West Yorkshire, where Wallace's father became an insurance superintendent for the Refuge Assurance Co.

Wallace Hartley attended the George Street Wesleyan School in Dewsbury and developed an interest in music and in playing the violin. After leaving school Hartley became a bank clerk, but his musical ability soon landed him a position as violinist at the Harrogate Kursaal; he later became leader of the orchestra at Bridlington and also toured with the Carl Rosa and the Moody-Manners opera companies.

Eventually Wallace Hartley went to work for the Cunard Steamship Co. and made at least eighty transatlantic crossings as bandmaster on board the *Mauretania* and *Lusitania*. By 1912, however, the young man was engaged to be married and had every intention of leaving his seagoing life for a shore-bound position. Hartley's father had even spent several years' worth of his own savings to purchase two valuable violins for his son in the hope that Hartley's use of the two instruments would enable him to help his brother and sisters financially.

In the spring of 1912 the musical director of the White Star and Cunard steamship lines asked Wallace Hartley to postpone his departure from the nautical world and become bandmaster of the *Titanic* during that vessel's maiden voyage; Mr Hartley accepted this prestigious appointment and made plans to begin another crossing of the Atlantic Ocean.

A friend once asked Wallace Hartley what he would do if he ever found himself on a sinking ship. Hartley replied, 'I don't think I could do better than play "O God, Our Help in Ages Past" or "Nearer, My God, to Thee".' It wasn't long after making this statement that Wallace Hartley had a chance to act on his beliefs; his two valuable, uninsured violins were with him when he boarded the *Titanic* at Southampton on 10 April.

WALTER HAWKSFORD **Status: Survivor**

Walter Hawksford (45) was born in London on 30 January 1867, he and his brothers Nicholas, Albert and Thomas being the sons of Nicholas and Annie Hawksford. Walter married his wife Edith around 1898, and the couple had three children, Walter, Mabel and Edith. By 1912 Walter and his family were living at 'Tanjore', Lower Ham Road, Kingston upon Thames, and Walter made his living working for Schweppes.

In April 1912 Walter's employer scheduled him to make a business trip to the United States and Canada, and he booked his passage as a first class passenger on the *Titanic*. Walter's wife Edith was scheduled to accompany him on the trip, but the sister in Canada with whom she was planning to stay became ill, so Mr Hawksford left his wife in Kingston and travelled to Southampton, where he boarded the *Titanic* as a first class passenger.

CLARA HAYS **Status: Survivor**

Clara Gregg (52) was born on 13 October 1859 in St Louis, Missouri and was the youngest daughter of Mr and Mrs William Gregg of 3013 Pine Street. Clara had one sister and a brother named Norris.

On 13 October 1881 – her 21st birthday – Clara Gregg married Charles Hays, the general manager of the Missouri Pacific Railroad in St Louis. The couple had three daughters, one of whom, Orian, was born on 18 November 1884.

Charles Hays' railway career was one long, steady success story, and he and Clara eventually moved to Montreal, Canada, where Charles became general manager of the Grand Trunk Railroad and soon turned it into a world class operation. In 1909 Mr Hays became president of the Grand Trunk through the direction of King Edward of England.

In the spring of 1912 Mr and Mrs Hays made a business trip to England; they were accompanied by their daughter Orian and her husband Thornton Davidson, Mrs Hays' maid Anne Pereault and Mr Hays' private secretary Mr Vivian Payne.

After concluding his business in London, Charles and Clara Hays spent two weeks relaxing in Kent while the Davidsons travelled to Paris. On the morning of 10 April 1912 Mr and Mrs Hays, Miss Pereault and Mr Payne arrived in Southampton and boarded the *Titanic* as first class passengers in order to return to the United States. Charles and Clara looked forward to seeing Orian and her husband again when they boarded the *Titanic* at Cherbourg at 6 p.m. on that same evening.

MARY HEWLETT **Status: Survivor**

Mary Kingcome was born on 8 July 1855 in Bristol and was the daughter of John and Rosa Kingcome. In 1875 Mary married Frederick Hewlett, a draper, and they resided in the Clifton area of the city with their children Francis, Rosa, Florence and Philip.

Mary's husband Fred passed away sometime before 1912, and Mary moved to Lucknow, India to live with her son Philip. In the spring of 1912 Mary returned to England to visit her daughter Florence in Brondesbury, Middlesex, and she then made plans to travel to Rapid City, South Dakota to visit her son Francis and his family. Mrs Hewlett travelled to London, and on 10 April she took the boat train to Southampton and boarded the *Titanic* as a second class passenger.

SAMUEL HOCKING **Status: Victim**

Samuel James Hocking (36) was born in Devon in 1876, one of four sons of William and Elizabeth Hocking.

By 1910 Mr Hocking made his living as a confectioner, and he, his wife Ada and their children Dorothy and Frank lived at 3 Fore Street in Devonport, Devon.

In 1912 Samuel Hocking made plans to emigrate to the United States, where his wife and children would join him in Connecticut later. On 10 April 1912 Mr Hocking boarded the *Titanic* at Southampton as a second class passenger.

HENRY P. HODGES — Status: Victim

Henry Hodges was a highly respected musical instrument dealer who lived with his wife and eight children in Southampton. Hodges was 50 years old and was a member of the Southampton Town Council.

In April 1912 Mr Hodges decided to go to Boston to visit relatives, and he booked a second class passage from Southampton to New York on the new White Star liner *Titanic*.

ELLEN HOWARD — Status: Victim

Ellen Truelove Howard (60) lived in Swindon with her husband Benjamin (63), who, after working for the Great Western Railway for thirty-nine years, retired in May 1908 as foreman of the Line's bolt shop. The couple's two sons, Herbert and Frederick, also worked for the Great Western for a time, but both sons had decided to emigrate to Idaho some years earlier in order to start new lives.

By 1912 Ellen and Benjamin missed Herbert and Frederick terribly, so they decided to travel to Idaho to visit their two sons. On 10 April the Howards boarded the *Titanic* in Southampton as second class passengers.

FREDERICK HOYT — Status: Survivor

Frederick Hoyt (38) was born in Stamford, Connecticut on 15 September 1873; he, his brothers William and Joseph and their sister Frances were the children of Joseph and Susan Hoyt, who operated a farm near Stamford.

Mr Hoyt graduated from the Sheffield Scientific School of Yale University in 1895. An avid yachtsman, Hoyt became a member of the Larchmont Yacht Club on 28 June 1899 and served as rear-commodore of the club from 1901 to 1904. Mr Hoyt was also a member of the New York Yacht Club, owned three well-known racing yachts and helped crew the *Atlantic* when that vessel won the Kaiser's Cup in a race from the United States to Spain.

In 1906 Frederick Hoyt married Jane Forby, and by 1912 the couple was living at 36 West 35th Street in New York City, where Hoyt worked as a stock broker.

In the spring of 1912 Fred and Jane Hoyt (31) found themselves in England on a combined business trip and holiday. When the time came for them to return to the United States, they booked two first class passages on the White Star liner *Titanic*, which they boarded at Southampton on the morning of 10 April.

JOSEPH BRUCE ISMAY **Status: Survivor**

Bruce Ismay (49) was born in Liverpool, England on 12 December 1862, the eldest son of Thomas Henry Ismay, who was head of the firm of Ismay, Imrie & Co. of Liverpool, the founders of the White Star Line. Ismay was educated at Elstree and at Harrow before going straight into apprenticeship at his father's firm. He began crossing the Atlantic during his youth and by 1912 was said to hold the record for the number of crossings from Europe to America.

After a full apprenticeship at Liverpool, Bruce Ismay went to New York and spent several years there as agent of the recently formed White Star Line. In 1888 he married Julia Florence Schieffelin of New York, and they eventually had two sons and two daughters.

In 1890 Mr Ismay and his family returned to England, where Ismay became a full partner in the firm of Ismay, Imrie & Co. On the death of his father in 1899, Mr Ismay was made chairman and managing director of the White Star Line, and on 23 February 1904 he was elected president of the International Mercantile Marine Co.

Bruce Ismay enjoyed shooting, motoring and golf, and he also made it a habit to sail on the maiden voyage of every Atlantic liner launched since his connection with his late father's firm. On 10 April 1912 Mr Ismay boarded the *Titanic* at Southampton in order to continue his long-standing tradition of sailing on the maiden voyage of the line's newest ships.

MARIE JERWAN **Status: Survivor**

Marie Thuillard (23) was born on 28 May 1888 and, along with her sister, was raised in Mont-de-Couvet in Switzerland. Miss Thuillard was a fluent speaker of both French and English.

In 1909 Miss Thuillard emigrated to the United States and made her home in New York City. In July 1910 she married Armin Jerwan, a proofreader for a New York publisher, and the young couple lived at 227 West 145th Street.

In the spring of 1912 Marie Jerwan travelled back to Switzerland to visit her relatives in Mont-de-Couvet. When the time came for her to return home she travelled to Cherbourg, where she boarded the brand new *Titanic* when that vessel arrived on the evening of 10 April.

JAKOB JOHANSSON **Status: Victim**

Jakob Alfred Johansson was born in Nykarleby, Finland on 11 June 1877. He was one of nine children and lived with his parents on small farm called Bonas.

Mr Johansson emigrated to the United States in 1896 at the age of 19 and became a timber worker in Washington state. Before long he moved to Idaho to work in the mines, and later went to Alaska. Sometime during this period he met his wife-to-be, Anna Louisa Andersson, who came from the same area of Finland as he did. They were married in Olympia, Washington on 2 December 1901.

The Johanssons eventually went to Alaska with Jakob's brother, cousin and some friends in order to work in the gold fields. Anna served as cook for the men, and during that period she and Jakob had two children, John (1905) and Susanna (1907).

The Johanssons succeeded in finding gold, became prosperous and decided to return to Finland. They went there in 1908 and bought a farm in their home village, where their second son, Anders, was born in 1909. The family's money evaporated quickly, however, and they decided to return to America. Jakob sold his farm to his brother Edvard in 1911 and intended to use the money to buy land in California.

Jakob Johansson arranged to sail to America alone, intending to send for his family later. Johansson booked his passage on the *Philadelphia*, but due to the coal strike he was transferred to the *Titanic*. He boarded the great vessel in Southampton as one of her steerage passengers.

ANDREW AND ELIZABETH JOHNSTON — Status: Victims

Andrew Johnston (35) was born on 14 May 1876 and was the son of William Johnston (clerk of the school board, Newmachar, Aberdeenshire) and his wife Catherine. Andrew and his three brothers and two sisters were educated in Newmachar, and Andrew then became a plumber. He eventually met Elizabeth Watson (34), and the two were married in 1902.

Andrew's work caused him and his wife to do a bit of travelling in England, and the young couple's son, William, was born there in 1903; a daughter, Catherine, arrived in 1905.

In 1912 the Johnstons were living at 6 Newton Place, London when they decided to leave England and travel to New London, Connecticut, where Eliza's brother, William Watson, lived. Andrew and Eliza arranged to travel with Mrs Margaret Ford (Eliza's sister), Mrs Ford's four children and a friend named Alice Harknett. The nine members of the Johnston party booked their passages on the *Titanic* as steerage passengers and boarded the great vessel on 10 April at Southampton.

CHARLES JOUGHIN — Status: Survivor

Charles Joughin (32) was born on 3 August 1879 in Liverpool, England. He had one brother and a sister who later married and emigrated with her husband to Chicago, Illinois.

Mr Joughin first went to sea at the age of 11. Around 1897 he began working as a baker on board vessels of the White Star Line, and he continued to serve in that capacity for the next fifteen years. Joughin eventually rose to the position of chief baker and served in that capacity on board the *Olympic*.

Charles Joughin married Louisa Woodward; the couple, their son and their daughter Agnes lived in Elmhurst, Leighton Road, Southampton.

In the closing days of March 1912 Charles Joughin wrote a letter to his brother-in-law in Chicago saying he had been transferred from the *Olympic* to the *Titanic*. On

2 April Mr Joughin helped crew the *Titanic* during her delivery trip from Belfast to Southampton, and it was as her Chief Baker that he boarded the great liner on 10 April at the commencement of the vessel's maiden voyage.

HENRY FORBES JULIAN — Status: Victim

Henry Forbes Julian, the son of Henry and Maria Julian of Cork, was born on 9 May 1861. The family moved to Bolton, Lancashire, about 1869.

As a youth Julian was interested in engineering and mechanical pursuits and took part in the works his father had established. He attended Owens College, Manchester, where his interest in metallurgy was first kindled. Upon graduation, his chosen field enabled him to travel widely throughout the world.

From 1886 to 1893 Julian was a constituent for the mines at Barberton, Johannesburg, and Kimberley in South Africa, superintending the opening of mines and the erection and operation of mills and reduction plants there. From 1893, as technical advisor on mining and metallurgical matters to the Deutsche Gold und Silber Scheide-Anstalt in Frankfurt, he conducted extensive researches which provided the basis for improvements in the recovery of precious metals from ores.

In 1896 Julian's health began to fail, and a London physician advised him to abstain from his research activities for several years and move to some quiet place by the sea. He moved to Shaldon in Devon, where he provided a home for his father and sisters. In 1902 he moved to Torquay, and in October of that year married Hester Pengelly, a girl who shared his interest in science and travel.

In 1904 Julian was the joint author of *Cyaniding Gold and Silver Ores*, a standard work on the subject. In 1906 he became a consulting engineer to Charles Butters & Co., and was a member of the General Committee of the British Association and a contributor to the work of the Chemical Section. Julian travelled frequently to the U.S. and Canada on behalf of the Butters Co., his wife often accompanying him.

In the early months of 1912 Henry Julian was working in London when his employer requested that he make a business trip to America for them. Besides his regular work for the firm, Julian was also preparing a small book for them titled *Slime Filtration and Cyaniding*; this latter project forced Julian to remain in England a few days longer than he had anticipated, and he consequently made arrangements to travel to America as a first class passenger on the *Titanic*, which he boarded at Southampton on 10 April.

NORA KEANE — Status: Survivor

Nora Keane (46) was born in 1866 in Limerick and was brought up there along with her five brothers and one sister. By 1911 all seven siblings had emigrated to Harrisburg, Pennsylvania, where Nora lived and worked with one of her brothers.

Early in December 1911 Nora left Harrisburg to spend Christmas with her mother in Limerick, this being Nora's third trip across the Atlantic. The young woman intended to return to Harrisburg in March 1912 but decided to spend Easter with her mother and then return home afterwards. Nora's brother Michael wrote and urged her to return home in April on the brand new *Titanic*; Nora replied that travelling on an older, well-tried ship might be safer, but Michael finally persuaded her to book a second class passage on the new White Star liner. Nora Keane boarded the great vessel at Queenstown on 11 April.

EDWARD KENT **Status: Victim**

Edward Kent (58) was born on 19 February 1854 in Bangor, Maine. He, his brother William and his sister Charlotte were the children of Henry and Harriet Kent (of the family who part-owned Buffalo, New York's Flint and Kent Department Store).

Edward Kent graduated from Briggs Classical School in Buffalo and then attended the Sheffield Scientific School at Yale. After graduation Mr Kent travelled to Europe and studied architecture at L'École des Beaux Arts in Paris before continuing his studies in England. He later practised in Chicago as a partner of Joseph Lyman Silsbee before coming to Buffalo, New York in the late 1880s. Along with his brother William (who was also an architect), Edward founded the architectural firm of Kent, Jardeen and Kent, with offices at 1088 Ellicott Square.

Edward Kent designed a number of well-known Buffalo business buildings including his family's department store on Main Street, the Chemical 5 Fire Hall, the Unitarian church and the Temple Beth Zion. Mr Kent was the chief consulting engineer for the Toronto Board of Trade Building in Buffalo, and he also designed the homes of many prominent families from the area, including the home of S. Douglas Cornell (the Cornell Mansion).

One of Mr Kent's most ambitious undertakings was the designing of the New Kent House at Lakewood on Chautaqua Lake. Built in 1880, this 150-room hotel boasted a dining room that could seat 800, a Turkish bath and even a lift.

Edward Kent fought for passage of a state law requiring the licensing of architects for the protection of clients from 'unscrupulous bilkers'. He was instrumental in the formation of the Buffalo Association of Architects, and in 1893, 1894 and 1902 he was elected president of the Buffalo chapter of the American Institute of Architects (which absorbed the earlier organisation). In 1908 Mr Kent was the organisation's delegate to an international conference in Berlin.

Edward Kent lived at the Buffalo Club and was contemplating retirement when he planned one more trip to Europe in February 1912. His journey was more for pleasure than for professional reasons, and he spent several weeks renewing old acquaintances in England. Later he moved on to the Riviera and then to Egypt, where he stayed on for his health.

Mr Kent purposely delayed his trip home so that he could travel on the brand new *Titanic* (which he had planned to do from the outset of his journey). Upon arriving in Cherbourg, Mr Kent was introduced by mutual friends to fellow passenger Mrs Helen Candee and promised to look after Mrs Candee during their voyage back to the States.

Mr Kent wrote to friends in Buffalo telling them that he was about to sail on the *Titanic*. After writing a letter to the Buffalo Club asking that his quarters at the club be made ready for his return, he also wrote a letter of introduction for a British army officer who was about to pay his first visit to Buffalo, New York.

At 6 p.m. on the evening of 10 April, Edward Kent and Mrs Helen Candee joined the rest of the *Titanic*'s passengers in boarding the tender that was to take them out to where the great vessel was waiting for them in the outer harbour.

EDWIN KIMBALL — Status: Survivor

Edwin Kimball was born on 9 March 1870, in Atlanta, Georgia and was the son of Edwin and Emma Kimball. The family eventually moved to Boston, where the younger Edwin married Susan Parsons and lived at 859 Beacon Street. Edwin eventually succeeded his father as president of the Hallet & Davis Piano Co.

During the winter of 1911 Mr Kimball and his wife felt the need for a relaxing holiday, so on 6 March 1912 they sailed from New York on the *Cedric* en route for the Mediterranean, where they intended to take a rest. The Kimballs toured Italy, Switzerland, France and England, and at some point during their travels they began contemplating returning home on the *Titanic* with their friends Mr and Mrs Richard Beckwith, Mrs Beckwith's daughter Helen Newsom and the latter's friend Karl Behr.

Mr and Mrs Kimball did indeed book first class passages on the *Titanic*, and they boarded the great liner at Southampton on 10 April.

JULIETTE LAROCHE — Status: Survivor

Joseph Laroche was born in Haiti on 26 May 1886. In 1901, at the age of 15, he left Haiti and travelled to Beauvais, France, where he hoped to enrol in the local school to study engineering.

While visiting nearby Villejuif, Joseph met Miss Juliette Lafargue; Juliette was born on 20 October 1889 and was the daughter of widower Monsieur Lafargue, a wine seller of the town. Juliette and Joseph were married in March 1908 after Joseph graduated and received his degree. The couple's daughter Simonne was born on 19 February 1909; a second daughter, Louise, was born prematurely on 2 July 1910 and suffered many subsequent medical problems.

Racial discrimination against black people prevented Joseph Laroche from obtaining a high-paying job in France. Since the family needed more money to cope with Louise's medical bills, Joseph decided to return to Haiti to find a better paid engineering job, the move being planned for 1913. However, in March 1912 Juliette discovered that she was expecting another child, so she and Joseph decided to leave for Haiti before her pregnancy became too far advanced for travel. Joseph's mother in Haiti bought them steamship tickets on the *France* as a welcome present, but the shipping line's strict policy regarding children caused them to transfer their booking and obtain second class tickets on the *Titanic*. On 10 April the Laroche family took the train from Paris to Cherbourg and boarded the new liner later that evening.

ALICE LEADER — Status: Victim

Alice Farnham (49) was born on 10 May 1862 in New York City and was the daughter of Reuben and Frances Farnham. She had at least one sister and one brother.

Alice eventually became a physician and married Dr John Leader of Lewiston, Maine, and the husband and wife medical team worked together at a practice in New York City. The Leaders were childless when John Leader passed away, and Alice maintained her medical practice while making her home at 340 West 118th Street.

At the beginning of 1912 Dr Leader and her friend Mrs Joel Swift (46) decided to sail to Europe on a pleasure trip. After three months of travelling abroad, on 1 April Dr Leader wrote a letter to her sister-in-law Nellie Leader saying that she intended to sail for home on the *Titanic* on 10 April. Dr Leader and Mrs Swift decided to share a first class cabin on the new White Star liner and boarded the great vessel at Southampton on 10 April.

BERTHA LEHMANN — Status: Survivor

Bertha Lehmann (17) was born in Berne, Switzerland on 31 March 1895, and she, her brother and two sisters were the children of Mr and Mrs Johann Lehmann-Kupferschmied.

In 1912 Bertha decided to emigrate to the United States to live with her married sister Marie at her home six miles east of Central City, Iowa. Whereas Bertha originally planned to sail for America on 4 May, however, she spontaneously decided to change her plans and sail in April instead in order to surprise her sister with an early arrival.

On 8 April 1912 Bertha Lehmann bade her mother, sister, relatives and friends goodbye and walked down to the local train station with her father. During their walk her father said, 'Bertha, every time you come along with me I have some sort of bad luck, and I feel now like something is going to happen to you.' Bertha reassured her father and said that, if anything should go wrong, her fluency in French and German would ensure that there would be plenty of people whom she could ask for help. Bertha's father kissed his youngest daughter goodbye and said, 'I suppose I will never see you again.'

In due course Bertha Lehmann's train arrived safely in Basel; Bertha departed Basel by another train at around midnight and arrived in Paris at around 6 a.m. on 9 April. At that point Bertha went to a local hotel and ate breakfast, after which she went to a customs facility where her trunk (which contained the sum total of her personal possessions) was inspected for contraband. Bertha then took a train to Cherbourg and arrived there at around midnight, at which point she booked a hotel room and rested until 3 p.m. on the afternoon of 10 April.

After journeying down to Cherbourg harbour, Bertha was taken aboard a White Star tender and was ferried out toward the great vessel that was to carry her to America; at about 6:30 p.m. on 10 April Bertha Lehmann and her fellow passengers walked up the tender's gangplank and boarded the *Titanic*, on which Bertha had booked a second class passage to the New World.

JESSIE LEITCH **Status: Survivor**

Jessie Leitch (31) was apparently born around 1881, and she and her brother Alexander were raised by their parents in Renfrewshire. Miss Leitch was later trained as a nurse in William Quarries Homes.

Jessie Leitch's uncle, the Revd John Harper, married Annie Bell in 1906, and a daughter, Annie Jessie Speirs Harper, was born to the couple. When Mrs Harper passed away in 1909, Jessie Leitch moved into the Harper household to help care for her uncle's young daughter 'Nan'.

Revd John Harper eventually became pastor of the Walworth Road Baptist church in London. During the winter of 1911/12 Harper travelled to Chicago, Illinois to conduct a series of revival meetings at the Moody church, and his efforts proved to be so popular that he was asked to return to Chicago that same Spring.

On 10 April 1912 Jessie Leitch, her little cousin Nan and the Revd John Harper began the first leg of their trip to America when they boarded *Titanic* at Southampton as second class passengers.

BERTHE LEROY **Status: Survivor**

Berthe Leroy (27) and her twin sister Marthe were born on 10 August 1884 in Hersin-Coupigny, France. The two girls and their brothers Leon, Jules and Samuel were the children of coal miner Jules Leroy and his wife Marie-Adeline.

Berthe Leroy was only four years old when her father passed away in 1888. The young girl's subsequent schooling was irregular, and while still in her early teens she was taught how to sew by the Sisters of Charity.

Miss Leroy left home around 1903 and travelled to Paris, where she went to work as a maid in the home of a well-to-do family living in the Avenue du Bois.

Among the frequent visitors to the home of Miss Leroy's employers were Walter and Mahala Douglas of Cedar Rapids, Iowa; Mr Douglas was a wealthy director of the Quaker Oats Co., and he and his wife spent a great deal of their time travelling abroad. In 1910 Mrs Douglas asked Miss Leroy if she would like to come to America to become Mrs Douglas's maid and travelling companion and help her increase her fluency in the French language. Miss Leroy eagerly agreed to this proposal, and for the next two years she worked in the Douglas household and accompanied her employers on a number of trips throughout the United States and various foreign countries. Miss Leroy spoke very little English, but she was a conscientious worker and was a great favourite with Mrs Douglas.

In 1911 Walter Douglas retired at the age of 50, and he, his wife and Miss Leroy moved to Minneapolis, Minnesota. The Douglases soon became prominent in Minneapolis society, and they built a palatial summer home called 'Walden' on Lake Minnetonka.

In January 1912 the Douglases and Miss Leroy left Minneapolis on a three-month pleasure trip to Europe in order to search for furnishings for their new home. In April Mr Douglas decided that he would like to return to the United States in time to celebrate his 51st birthday at home in Minneapolis on 21 April, and he booked three first class passages to New York on the new White Star liner *Titanic*; the Douglases and Miss Leroy boarded the great vessel at Cherbourg on the evening of 10 April.

CHARLES LIGHTOLLER **Status: Survivor**

Charles Lightoller (38) was born in Chorley, Lancashire on 30 March 1874. He went to sea at the age of 13 on board the barque *Primrose Hill*. His second voyage, on board the *Holt Hill* in 1889, ended in shipwreck, but Lightoller and most of the crew were picked up alive after spending eight days adrift in the Indian Ocean.

Lightoller was serving as third officer on board the *Knight of St Michael* when her cargo of coal caught fire. Lightoller's efforts to extinguish the flames resulted in his being promoted to second officer.

In 1895 Lightoller obtained his accreditation as first officer, and he began his career in steamships by going to work for Elder Dempster's African Royal Mail Service. He spent three years sailing up and down the West African coast and came close to succumbing to a bad case of malaria.

In 1898 Lightoller briefly left the sea and prospected for gold in the Yukon, worked as a cowboy in Alberta and eventually found his way back to England as a crewman on board a cattle boat.

In January 1900 Charles Lightoller joined the White Star Line and served as fourth officer on board the *Medic* on the Australia run. After being transferred to the Atlantic run for a while, Lightoller returned to the Australia run, which is where he met and married his wife Sylvia.

Charles Lightoller soon transferred back to White Star's Atlantic run, where he served on the *Majestic* before being promoted to third officer on the *Oceanic* in 1907. He eventually made second and first officer on that vessel, and in 1912 he was assigned to the brand new *Titanic* as her first officer. A last minute administrative shuffle resulted in Lightoller's temporary demotion to second officer, however, and it was in that capacity that Charles Lightoller stepped on board the *Titanic* in Southampton on 10 April.

WILLIAM CHARLES LINDSAY **Status: Survivor**

William Lindsay (31) was born on 9 November 1881 in Bedminster near Bristol. He was the eldest son of John and Alice Lindsay, his younger brother being named John and his sister Mabel.

Mr Lindsay saw service in the British army in South Africa, but around 1904 he decided to make his living at sea by working as a fireman on board the big passenger liners that sailed from British ports. It was in Southampton that Lindsay met a young woman named Harriet Maria Gates, and the young couple married on 20 September 1910 in the parish church of St Mary's in Southampton.

Mr and Mrs Lindsay set up home at 12 Coleman Street, but they eventually moved to 37 Grove Street in the Chapel area of Southampton. In 1912 the Lindsays were living at 3 Coleman Street, and by April of that year Harriet was two months along in her first pregnancy.

William Lindsay worked on board the White Star liner *Olympic* before signing papers to transfer to the boiler rooms of the *Titanic*; Lindsay was on board the brand new liner when she left Southampton Docks at noon on 10 April.

MARY LINES — Status: Survivor

Mary Lines (16) was born on 27 July 1895 in Mt Vernon, New York and was the daughter of Dr Ernest and Elizabeth Lines. Mary and her parents lived in New York until 1900, after which the Lines family moved to France, where Dr Lines represented the New York Life Insurance Co. as its chief medical examiner for Europe. Mary Lines was educated in Italy and France, and lived with her parents at 111 Quai d'Orsay in Paris.

In April 1912 Dr and Mrs Lines and Mary made plans to return to the United States to attend the graduation of Mary's brother from Dartmouth College. At the last moment, however, the press of business caused Dr Lines to remain in Paris, so his wife and daughter were forced to make the trip without him.

On 10 April Elizabeth and Mary Lines arrived in Cherbourg, and at 6 p.m. that evening they rode the tender out to where the White Star liner *Titanic* was waiting to take them on as first class passengers.

HAROLD LOWE — Status: Survivor

Harold Lowe (29) was born in Wales on 21 November 1882. In 1896 he ran away to sea and served on seven schooners before graduating to square-rigged sailing vessels and, eventually, to steamers. Lowe helped crew West African coasters for five years before joining the White Star Line around January 1911.

Mr Lowe served on White Star's Australian run as third officer on the *Belgic* and *Tropic* before his superiors gave his career a boost by assigning him to the *Titanic*. It was as the *Titanic*'s fifth officer that Lowe stepped on board the new liner at Southampton on 10 April.

OLGA LUNDIN — Status: Survivor

Olga Lundin (23) was born in Svaneryd, Sweden on 9 January 1889 and was the daughter of Gustafva Lundin.

By 1911 Miss Lundin was working as a cook in the United States and was engaged to marry Nils Johansson, a machinist who lived in Chicago. In late 1911 Miss Lundin, her brother-in-law Carl Jonsson and Mr Johansson returned to Sweden to visit their families. In the spring of 1912 the three travellers prepared to return to the States and were joined by Albert Augustsson and Pal Andreasson, who planned to accompany them to Illinois. The five Swedes travelled to Copenhagen, Denmark and boarded a ship for Hull, where they took a train to Southampton. On 10 April Miss Lundin, Mr Johansson and their three friends boarded the *Titanic* as third class passengers.

THURE LUNDSTRÖM **Status: Survivor**

Thure Lundström (32) was born on 8 March 1880 in Gislof, Sweden. In 1900 Mr Lundström emigrated to the United States, and he spent the interval between 1905 and 1911 in China. He returned to Sweden just prior to the Boxer Rebellion, and in 1912 he arranged to travel to Los Angeles, California with his fiancée, Elina Olsson (31). It was at Southampton on 10 April that Mr Lundström and Miss Olsson boarded the *Titanic* as steerage passengers.

PIERRE MARÉCHAL **Status: Survivor**

Pierre Maréchal (28) lived in Paris and was the son of a vice-admiral in the French navy.

Mr Maréchal was an aviator who did a great deal of flying in France. In 1912 he made plans to travel to the United States in order to sign a contract to fly the Curtiss hydroplane in Europe.

On the evening of 10 April 1912 Mr Maréchal, with his monocle firmly in place, boarded the tender at Cherbourg and was conveyed out to the waiting *Titanic*, which he boarded as a first class passenger.

CATHERINE MCCARTHY **Status: Survivor**

Catherine McCarthy (24) was born in 1887 in Ballygurtin, Tipperary, and she, her sister Mary and her brother Patrick were the children of farmer Patrick McCarthy. Miss McCarthy made her living as a domestic servant.

In 1912 Katie McCarthy decided to follow her brother and sister to the United States; along with her friends Kate Connolly (35), Kate Peters (26) and Roger Tobin (20), Miss McCarthy arranged to travel to New Jersey as a steerage passenger on board the *Titanic*; she boarded the great vessel when it touched at Queenstown on 11 April.

GEORGE MCGOUGH **Status: Survivor**

George 'Paddy' McGough (25) was born in Duncannon, County Wexford. His mother was still living in 1912, and he and his wife lived in St George's Street in Southampton. Mr McGough was an able bodied seaman who had spent the past twenty-five years at sea, being shipwrecked several times during that period.

George McGough served on board the Hermione before signing on as a *Titanic* crewman on 6 April 1912. On 10 April Mr McGough left his wife in Southampton and stepped on board the new White Star liner to serve as an able bodied seaman during her maiden voyage.

JAMES MCGOUGH **Status: Survivor**

James McGough (35) was born in Mandistown, County Meath, on 4 July 1876, he and his brothers Philip, Thomas and Andrew being the sons of Thomas and Catherine McGough. While James was still a boy he and his family emigrated to the United States and established a home in Philadelphia, Pennsylvania.

By 1912 James McGough was married and supported his wife Mary by working as a buyer for the clothing firm Strawbridge & Clothier; McGough supplemented his income by working as a buyer for the toy department at Gimbel Brothers' Department Store.

In March 1912 James McGough, in company with fellow buyers John Flynn (36) and Edward Calderhead (42), went to Europe on a buying trip for Gimbel's. By early April the three men had concluded their business and were ready to return to the United States; in company with another buyer named Spencer Silverthorne (35), James McGough and his friends Flynn and Calderhead booked first class passages to America on the White Star liner *Titanic*. The four men were on board the great liner when she left Southampton at noon on 10 April.

MARION MEANWELL **Status: Victim**

Mary Ann Ogden was born on 9 December 1848 in Lancashire and was the daughter of John and Ann Ogden. Mary grew up to be a milliner and married Thomas Meanwell, and the couple had three children – a son named Walter and twin girls named Margaret and Annie.

Thomas Meanwell left his family after the death of his daughter Annie, and, when Mary's son Walter went to live with her parents, Mary and her daughter Margaret lived alone. By 1881 Mary and her daughter were living at Horton in Bradford, where Mary (who was now known as Marion Meanwell) made her living as a milliner.

Margaret Meanwell eventually moved out of her mother's home and went to America, where she married, had two children and worked as a ballet dancer in a circus. When Margaret's husband died in 1912, Marion Meanwell resolved to travel to America to help her daughter raise her two children. Marion booked her passage on the White Star liner *Majestic*, but the coal strike forced her to transfer to the brand new *Titanic*, which she boarded at Southampton as a third class passenger on 10 April.

WILLIAM MELLORS — Status: Survivor

William Mellors (18) was born on 14 January 1894 in London, and he and his brother Henry lived with their parents William and Harriet Mellors. Harriet moved to Motcombe with her two sons while her husband (who was a soldier) was serving in South Africa during the Boer War, but, when William was invalided home in 1902, the family settled in London. In 1903 the couple had a daughter whom they named Violet.

Because her husband's war wounds prevented him from working, Harriet and her son William obtained jobs in order to support the family. In 1911 young William Mellors began serving as a valet to Sir Frederick Schuster in London, but by 1912 he was planning to emigrate to New York and work at the Richmond County Country Club on Staten Island. On 10 April William Mellors travelled from London to Southampton and boarded the *Titanic* as a second class passenger.

KARL MIDTSJO — Status: Victim

Karl Midtsjo (21) was born on 4 August 1890 to Johannes and Marie Midtsjo who, with their other seven children, lived in Krakstad, Norway. The Midtsjos made their living on the family farm.

Karl's mother passed away in 1900, and his father remarried several years later. In 1904 Karl obtained a job as a carpenter; his income did not go far in such a large family, though, so he decided to emigrate to Chicago, Illinois to try and find a better-paying job. On 3 April 1912 Midtsjo travelled to Hull and from there on to Southampton, where he boarded the *Titanic* as a steerage passenger on 10 April.

FRANCIS MILLET — Status: Victim

Francis Davis Millet (65) was born in Mattapoisett, Massachusetts on 3 November 1846, a son of Asa and Huldah Millet. Frank and his two brothers and two sisters were raised on the family farm near East Bridgewater.

In July 1864, during the American Civil War, Frank Millet enlisted as a private in the 60th Massachusetts Volunteer Regiment; he served as a drummer until 30 November of that year, at which time he was honourably discharged.

After the war Mr Millet entered Harvard College; he developed a strong interest in painting during his second year, and in 1869 he graduated with a Master of Arts degree in modern languages and literature; Mr Millet obtained an additional degree in 1872.

After leaving college Frank Millet joined the staff of the *Boston Daily Advertiser*; he eventually became the local editor of the *Boston Courier* and, later, of the *Boston Saturday Evening Gazette*. Millet retained his interest in painting, however, and his first artistic endeavour was to decorate the Eagle Cotton Gin in Bridgewater, to help a friend who had the commission. He also studied lithography with D.C. Fabronius, which enabled him to earn enough money to travel to Europe to continue his artistic studies.

In 1871 Mr Millet entered the Royal Academy at Antwerp; at the close of his first year there he received the prize of excellence in the antique class, and the following year he received the prize of excellence in painting; Millet was publicly crowned by the King in recognition of his outstanding accomplishment.

In 1873 Frank Millet went to the Vienna Exposition as secretary to the Commissioner for the State of Massachusetts. At the close of the Exposition he travelled through Hungary, Turkey, Greece and Italy and spent the winter of 1873/74 in Rome. Travelling on to Venice, Millet spent a year in that Italian city and painted his first picture there in 1876.

Returning to Boston later that same year, Mr Millet represented the *Boston Advertiser* as a correspondent at the Philadelphia Centennial Exhibition. He helped to decorate the interior of Trinity church in Boston, and he also painted a portrait of Mark Twain.

Early in 1877 Frank Millet went to Paris, and in May of that year he travelled to Turkey to cover the Russian side of the Russo-Turkish War for the *New York Herald* and to act as special artist for the *London Graphic*. Millet's hard rides on horseback to post his dispatches taught him a lot about the lay of the land, and he once broke military etiquette by revealing to Russian officers the location of a ford unknown to them. The ensuing Russian attack on the Turkish flank was successful, and Millet's contribution to the victory was later acknowledged when a Russian general presented him with the Cross of St Stanislaus; Millet was later awarded the Cross of St Anne for valuable and exceptional service to the Russian government, and he also received the Iron Cross of Romania.

At the conclusion of the war in the spring of 1878, Frank Millet returned to France by way of Sicily. He painted in Paris until the following spring and also served as a member of the fine arts jury at the Paris exposition.

On 11 March 1879 Frank Millet married Boston's Elizabeth (Lily) Greely Merrill in Paris; Lily was the attractive, intelligent sister of one of Frank's Harvard classmates, and Augustus Saint-Gaudens and Mark Twain were the witnesses at their marriage.

Frank and Lily Millet settled in Boston, Massachusetts for a time before eventually moving to New York. The couple eventually had three children, Kate, Laurence and John, and the two boys eventually attended Harvard like their father.

Frank Millet continued to travel widely abroad, and in 1881 he made a trip through Denmark, Sweden and North Germany on behalf of Harper & Brothers publishers. Millet painted in England for a season or two, and in 1884 he, his wife and children settled at Broadway in Worcestershire. Mr Millet, in company with E.A. Abbey, John Singer Sargent and Alfred Parsons, formed a Bohemian art colony in the village and produced many worthwhile works there. Frank Millet usually spent his summers painting in his Broadway studio, and he and his family spent the winters in New York and Washington, D.C.

In 1885 Frank Millet made a trip through all of the United States and its territories as well as Mexico. In 1887 Millet was commissioned by *Harper's Monthly* to write and illustrate an article about the Russo-Turkish war titled 'Campaigning With the Cossacks', and he also published his own translation of Tolstoy's *Sebastopol* that same year.

In 1891 Frank Millet made a 1,700-mile canoe trip down the full length of the Danube for Harper & Brothers. Millet then published a series of articles for *Harper's Weekly* about his trip, and in 1893 these articles were turned into a book titled, *The Danube, from the Black Forest to the Black Sea.* He also published a series of popular short stories.

Frank Millet was made director of decorations for the Columbian Exposition in 1893; he ended up as the Exposition's master of ceremonies and brought the fair to a brilliant end despite the concurrent financial panic that was gripping the country.

In 1894 Mr Millet went to England and remained there until 1896, at which point he made a trip through Algeria, Tunisia, Tripoli and Sicily. In 1898 Millet went to Manila as the special war correspondent for *The Times*, and he also represented *Harper's Weekly* and the *New York Sun*; the following year Millet's war-related correspondence was turned into a book titled *The Expedition to the Philippines*.

In the autumn of 1899 Frank Millet travelled through Japan, China, Burma and India before returning to England, and the following year he had charge of the decoration of the United States Government Pavilion at the Paris Exposition of 1900. Following his return to the States, Mr Millet painted historical murals for the Minnesota and Wisconsin capitols and the Boston Custom House.

In 1905 Frank Millet made a trip through Yellowstone Park, Alaska and British Columbia. In 1906 he was commissioned to do the interior paintings and decoration in the new Custom House at Baltimore, Maryland, and in 1907 he was appointed chairman of a committee to advise the National Gallery of Art on guidelines for the selection of works of art to be acquired.

In August 1908 Frank Millet went to England, France, Italy and Germany in the interests of the Commission to the Tokyo Exposition. After being made a chevalier of the Legion of Honour in France, Millet then proceeded to Japan by way of the Siberian railway. There he was received by the Emperor and Empress of Japan and was awarded the first class Order of the Sacred Treasure.

After concluding his business in Japan, Frank Millet went to China and travelled widely in that country. From there he proceeded to Seoul before travelling once again to Tokyo and finally returning to Washington. Frank Millet designed seven medals for the United States Army; these included the medals for veterans of the Civil War, American Indian Wars, Chinese Expedition, Spanish War and the Philippine insurrection. Mr Millet also designed a merit medal for the enlisted men of the United States Army and was also in charge of the production of the Panama Canal medal.

During the winter of 1908/09 Frank Millet painted thirteen large interior panels for the Cleveland Trust Co. in Cleveland, Ohio, and in June 1909 the United States Treasury Department commissioned him to decorate the Federal Building, also in Cleveland.

Frank Millet was the creative spirit behind the American Federation of Arts and of the National Commission of Arts, which was created in 1910. In 1911 Mr Millet reluctantly accepted the directorship of the American Academy in Rome at a time when the academy was undergoing an internal crisis, he travelled to Rome and completed a reorganisation of the academy, returning to Washington, D.C. in January 1912.

In February 1912 Mr Millet was making plans to return to Rome when he noticed that his friend Archibald Butt, military aide to President Taft, was looking tired and ill. Millet spoke with President Taft and succeeded in convincing him to ask Major Butt to accompany Millet to Rome in order to recuperate, after which Butt would be able to do some sightseeing on the continent. On 2 March 1912 Millet and Butt sailed for Europe together on the steamer *Berlin*.

During his stay in Rome Frank Millet devoted much of his attention to the American Academy and also spent time making sketches for the murals he was to paint in the new library at New Bedford, Massachusetts. Mr Millet asked fellow artist and sculptor Frank Chamberlin if he would like to return to Washington with him to take over his Washington studio and carry out his New Bedford mural commission; Mr Chamberlin, was busy sculpting his figure of *The Cup Bearer*, though, and he was forced to decline Millet's invitation.

When the time came for him to return to the United States, Frank Millet travelled to Cherbourg to board the *Titanic*, upon which he had booked a first class passage. On the evening of 10 April, as the tender carried him out to the great White Star liner, Mr Millet was undoubtedly looking forward to rejoining his friend Archie Butt, who had boarded the *Titanic* at Southampton earlier that same day.

DAISY MINAHAN — Status: Survivor

Daisy Minahan (33) was born on 9 January 1879 and was the youngest daughter of William and Mary Minahan of Fond du Lac, Wisconsin. She was the youngest sister of brothers Robert, John, William and Victor Minahan.

Daisy Minahan was a teacher of handicapped children in Fond du Lac, but in 1909 she was forced to retire from teaching after she contracted tuberculosis. She lived with the family of her brother Robert, who was a physician and who could help to take care of her.

In January 1912 Daisy's brother William (another physician) planned to take his wife Lillian on a European holiday, and it was arranged for Daisy to accompany them on the trip. On 12 January the Minahans stopped in Washington, D.C. to do some sightseeing, and they visited the house where President Lincoln died in 1865.

On 22 January the Minahans sailed for Naples on the steamship *Berlin*, with intermediate sightseeing stops before they began travelling through Italy and France. The pace of the family's wanderings was intended to be very leisurely, with Daisy's fragile health always being uppermost in William's mind. In a letter home William Minahan wrote that he and Lillian always accommodated Daisy's schedule for rest, fresh air and exercise.

When March arrived, however, Daisy Minahan began to have serious health problems while she, William and Lillian were in Paris. On the evening of 2 March William Minahan performed an appendectomy on Daisy at the American Hospital in nearby Neuilly.

After Daisy had recovered somewhat from her operation, the Minahans began thinking about returning home to the United States. On 21 March, however, William's steamship reservations were cancelled due to the coal strike; as a consequence of this, William, Lillian and Daisy Minahan changed their travel arrangements and boarded the *Titanic* as first class passengers when the great vessel arrived at Queenstown on 11 April 1912.

PHILLIP MOCK — Status: Survivor

Phillip Mock (30) was born in New York City on 16 August 1881, he and his sister Emma being the children of Richard and Emma Mock, who had immigrated to the United States from Germany. The Mock family later moved to Derby, Connecticut.

Phillip Mock attended Sewanee University and studied art in Europe, where he developed an interest in the painting of miniatures. Mock fought for the United States during the Spanish-American War and eventually returned to Derby, where he earned his living as a banker.

In the spring of 1912 Phillip Mock was in Hamburg, Germany visiting his sister Emma, who had married German diplomat Paul Schabert but whose marriage was in serious difficulty. Indeed, Mr Schabert was in the United States at that time, preparing to initiate divorce proceedings against Emma, and Phillip planned to accompany his sister to the United States so that she could attempt to reconcile with her husband.

Phillip Mock and his sister Emma Schabert (35) booked first class passages for themselves on the brand new *Titanic*, and they boarded the great liner at Cherbourg on the evening of 10 April.

CLARENCE MOORE — Status: Victim

Clarence Moore (47) was born on 1 March 1865 in Clarksville, West Virginia. He was a member of the Washington, D.C. brokerage firm of W.B. Hibbs & Co. and had an annual income of $25,000. Mr Moore also had an interest in a farm and ranch in Montgomery County, Maryland and in real estate at Leesburg, Virginia.

For many years Clarence Moore was the master of hounds at Washington, D.C.'s exclusive Chevy Chase Hunt Club, and he was regarded as one of the foremost fox hunters in America.

Clarence Moore married Mabelle Swift, a daughter of meat packer Edward Swift of Chicago, and the couple had five children. The Moores lived at 1746 Massachusetts Avenue NW in Washington, D.C., which is where Mrs Moore always stayed when her husband was abroad on business. During the summer months the family resided at their home 'Swiftmore' on the North Shore near Lynn, Massachusetts, their home being one of the area's showplaces.

In early March 1912 Clarence Moore went to Europe, one purpose of his trip being to purchase fifty pairs of foxhounds drawn from the best packs in the north of England; these dogs were to be used in hunts around Washington D.C. and in the Loudoun hunt at Leesburg, Virginia, where Mr Moore had been appointed as master for a term of three years.

Once his business in England was concluded, Mr Moore travelled to the port city of Southampton, where he boarded the *Titanic* as a first class passenger on 10 April.

THOMAS MUDD **Status: Victim**

Thomas Mudd (16) was from Huntingfield, Suffolk, and lived with his family at 157 Mortlake Road.

Thomas was the youngest of Thomas and Elizabeth Mudd's thirteen children and, as times were hard, it was decided that the young man should emigrate to the United States and live with his brothers James and George, who were prospering in that country. James and George Mudd sent a steamer ticket to their younger brother, and on 10 April 1912 Thomas Mudd boarded the *Titanic* at Southampton as a second class passenger.

BERTHA MULVIHILL **Status: Survivor**

Bertha Mulvihill (25) was born in Coosan, County Westmeath, on 10 September 1886. She eventually emigrated to the United States to be near her married sister, Mrs Edward Norton of Providence, Rhode Island, and by 1912 she was engaged to be married to Edward Noon of Providence.

In the early months of 1912 Miss Mulvihill returned to Ireland to attend a wedding in Athlone. When the time came for her to return to Providence, the young woman bought a steerage ticket and travelled to Queenstown to board the *Titanic* when the vessel arrived there on 11 April.

MICHEL NAVRATIL **Status: Victim**

Michel Navratil (32) was born in Szered, Slovakia in 1880. Mr Navratil later moved to Hungary before settling in Nice in 1902, where he became a tailor's cutter.

Michel Navratil was in London when he met Marcelle Caretto, a young woman who had been born in Buenos Aires. Michel and Marcelle were married in London on 26 May 1907, and they then moved to Cannes and later to Nice. Michel continued to work as a tailor's cutter, while Marcelle set up a small shop in Nice and soon had a good trade. The young couple's son Michel was born on 12 June 1908, and his little brother Edmond followed on 5 March 1910. The two boys were cared for by a nurse from Marseille.

By 1911 the Navratils' marital harmony was in trouble. Marcelle's parents are said to have disapproved of their daughter's marriage and are reported to have done their best to break it up. In addition to this, Michel – who was of a jealous disposition – eventually suspected Marcelle of having an affair. The couple argued, and around November 1911 Michel and Marcelle Navratil separated, after which Marcelle instituted divorce proceedings against her husband.

In March 1912 Michel Navratil began mentioning to various friends that he would like to avoid the impending divorce proceedings and take his two sons to the United

States. On 5 April Mr Navratil was permitted to take charge of Michel and Edmond for the Easter weekend, but on 7 April he and the two little boys suddenly dropped out of sight.

Several days after Michel Navratil's disappearance Marcelle received a letter from him that had been sent from Pressburg, Hungary, where Michel had formerly lived. The letter stated that Michel had taken the two children and that Marcelle would never see them again. Despite the letter's Hungarian postmark, Marcelle suspected that Michel had actually had a Hungarian friend forward the letter to her, since Michel was a deserter from the Austrian army and probably would not have dared to return to a country that was at that time part of the Austro-Hungarian Empire. Mrs Navratil couldn't help but recall how her husband had often told her that he would like to go to the United States and start a dressmaking establishment there.

Michel Navratil and his two little boys arrived in Monte Carlo, where Mr Navratil went to the local office of Cook's, the travel agent, and purchased three steamship tickets to America. He purchased the tickets using the alias 'Louis Hoffman' (which was the name of one of his friends in Nice).

From Monte Carlo Michel Navratil took his two little boys to England, where they stayed at London's Charing Cross Hotel. From London they travelled to Southampton, where, on 10 April, they boarded the *Titanic* as second class passengers.

WALTER NICHOLS — Status: Survivor

Walter Nichols (35) was born on 10 May 1876 in an English village called Whitley. He and his three sisters were the children of the late George Joseph Nichols, who for many years had been the coachman to Lord Knutsford. Walter's mother had also been in Lord Knutsford's service.

Walter Nichols spent his youth in the village of Whitley, where he was known as an excellent cricketer. He became a steward on the P&O Line's passenger liners when he was eighteen years old, and he travelled all over world in the service of the line. Mr Nichols was such a good worker that he eventually achieved the position of second saloon steward on passenger liners belonging to the American Line, and by 1912 he had crossed the Atlantic Ocean about three hundred times.

Walter Nichols married a Miss Sheath, who had grown up in Ripley and made her living as a stewardess on the passenger liners that sailed out of Southampton. Mr and Mrs Nichols, their two children and Walter's mother had lived at 40 Kent Road in Southampton, but by April 1912 they were living at 16 Kent Road.

Walter Nichols had last served as a steward on board the American liner *St Paul*, but while waiting for an appointment on another American liner he received an offer of a posting as assistant saloon steward on the White Star liner *Titanic*. Mr Nichols accepted the appointment, knowing that he would be able to rejoin his old ship the *New York* before she began her next voyage. Walter Nichols was on board the *Titanic* when she pulled away from the Southampton Docks at noon on 10 April.

ELIZABETH NYE **Status: Survivor**

Elizabeth Rammell (29) was born on 27 May 1882 in Folkestone, Kent, and was the daughter of Thomas and Elizabeth Rammell.

On 26 December 1904 Elizabeth married Edward Nye, but in 1906 their only child, a daughter named Maisie, died at the age of 9 months. The young couple later immigrated to New York City, but on 22 May 1911 Edward passed away and left Elizabeth completely alone.

Elizabeth Nye worked for the Salvation Army at their New York headquarters, but after her husband died she took a leave of absence and returned to England to visit her parents. She was scheduled to return to the United States on board the *Philadelphia*, but when that vessel's sailing was cancelled due to the coal strike Elizabeth's booking was transferred to a second class berth on the *Titanic*. On 10 April 1912 Mrs Nye walked up the gangplank and boarded the great vessel as she lay at the White Star Dock in Southampton.

PATRICK O'KEEFE **Status: Survivor**

Patrick O'Keefe (21) was born on 15 July 1890 and was the son of John and Catherine O'Keefe. Patrick made his living as a porter in County Waterford but decided to emigrate to New York City; he therefore booked a steerage passage on the *Titanic* and boarded her at Queenstown when she touched there on 11 April 1912.

HENRY OLSEN **Status: Victim**

Henry Olsen was born on 22 March 1884 in Trondheim, Norway and was the illegitimate son of Ole Rorosgaard and Eva Söderholm. A few years after Henry's birth his mother emigrated to the United States and left her son behind, so Henry was brought up by foster parents in Norway.

In the early 1900s Olsen signed on as a crewman on a local steamer, and around 1907 he met Larsine ('Sina') Olsen in Bergen. The two young people fell in love, but Olsen's job demanded that they temporarily conduct most of their love affair via love letters.

In the autumn of 1908 Henry Olsen was called up for his National Service at the naval base in Horten, and while serving on the warship *Eidsvoll* he travelled to Hamburg and a number of other places he had never visited before.

On 14 August 1909 Olsen and Sina were married in Bergen and purchased a home there. On 18 November their daughter Mathilde was born, followed by Solveig on 24 September 1911.

Mr Olsen worked at Bergen's Engineering Workshop during the day and attended an engineering school at night. In March 1912 Olsen passed his engineering exam and quickly obtained a job on a small New York-based vessel named the *Edda*. On 10 April 1912 in Southampton, Henry Olsen boarded the *Titanic* as a steerage passenger in company with Albert Andersen (33) and Johan Holten (28), two fellow Norwegians who intended to join Olsen as crewmen on the *Edda*.

HELENE OSTBY — Status: Survivor

Helene Ostby (22) was born in Providence, Rhode Island on 30 November 1889, she and her siblings Harold, Erling, Ralph and Raymond being the children of Engelhart and Elizabeth Ostby. Helene's mother passed away on 26 November 1899 at the age of 45, and her father and grandmother took over the raising of the younger children until the grandmother's own death in December 1902.

Helene's father was a jeweller who often travelled to Europe on business, and in 1906 he began taking Helene with him on his business trips. Father and daughter visited Norway (Engelhart's homeland) in 1907, and in January 1912 they sailed to Europe on holiday and travelled to Egypt and Southern Europe. While they were in Nice they decided that it would be interesting to return to the United States on the maiden voyage of the *Titanic*, and when they journeyed to Paris they encountered Frank and Anna Warren, with whom they had become acquainted in Egypt and who had also made arrangements to sail on the *Titanic*.

On 10 April Helene and her father Engelhart Ostby travelled to Cherbourg and boarded the *Titanic* when she touched there that evening.

ERNST PERSSON — Status: Survivor

Ernst Persson (25) was born in Sweden on 29 July 1886 and worked in Stockholm as a janitor and chauffeur. When Persson's married sister Elna Ström (29) and her daughter Selma (2) returned from the United States to Sweden to visit their family, Ernst decided that he would emigrate to the United States and made plans to accompany his sister and little niece back to their home in Indiana Harbor, Indiana. When the time came to do so, Mr Persson, Elna and the young Selma travelled to Southampton and boarded the *Titanic* as steerage passengers on 10 April.

ARTHUR PEUCHEN — Status: Survivor

Arthur Peuchen (52) was born in Montreal, Quebec, on 18 April 1859, he and his sister being the children of Godfrey and Eliza Peuchen.

Mr Peuchen was educated in Montreal, but he and his family moved to Toronto in 1871. He married Margaret Thompson in 1893, and the couple eventually had a son and daughter. Soon Peuchen joined the Queen's Own Rifles, and by 1904 he had been promoted to the rank of Major and was second in command under Sir Henry Pellatt. Major Peuchen was the discoverer of a method of extracting valuable chemicals such as acetic acid, acetone and wood alcohol from scrap hardwood left on the forest floors by Canada's lumbermen. In 1897 Peuchen created and became president of the Standard Chemical Co. in order to exploit his discovery, and he soon became rich as well as influential. His mansion on Lake Simcoe was known as 'Woodlands', and his estate boasted tennis courts, a bowling green, a private golf course and a horse named 'C.O.' (for 'Commanding Officer').

Major Peuchen owned his own yacht and was an avid racer of large sailing boats. He had a boathouse on Ashbridges Bay and was eventually made a Vice Commodore of the Royal Canadian Yacht Club situated on Centre Island.

Major Arthur Peuchen often travelled abroad on business, and April 1912 found him in Southampton on the last major leg of his trip home to Canada. Peuchen was being considered for promotion to Lieutenant Colonel of his battalion of the Queen's Own Rifles in Toronto, but he was probably not thinking about that possibility when he booked a first class passage on board the new White Star liner *Titanic* and boarded the great liner on 10 April.

ALICE PHILLIPS **Status: Survivor**

Alice Phillips (21) was born on January 26, 1891 and was the only child of Escott Robert and Hannah Phillips. The family lived in Ilfracombe, Devon, where Alice grew up and completed her schooling.

Alice's mother taught at Medford, near Newbury Post, but when she passed away in August 1911 Robert Phillips decided to sell the family home and emigrate to America, where his brother William lived in New Brighton, Pennsylvania. Mr Phillips made arrangements to sail on the *Philadelphia*, but the coal strike caused that sailing to be cancelled and forced a change of travel plans. On 10 April Escott and Alice Phillips boarded the *Titanic* at Southampton as second class passengers.

BERK PICKARD **Status: Survivor**

Berk Trembisky (32) was born around 1880 in Warsaw, a city which – at that time – was in Russia.

For many years Mr Trembisky lived in France, where he eventually took the French surname Pickard. By 1912 Mr Pickard was living in London, where he made his living as a maker of leather bags.

In April 1912 Berk Pickard made plans to travel to San Francisco, California, and on 10 April he arrived in Southampton and boarded the White Star liner *Titanic* to begin the first leg of his trip to America's west coast.

LILY POTTER **Status: Survivor**

Lily Wilson (56) was born on 15 August 1855 in Young's Prairie, Cass County, Michigan and was the daughter of Seth and Martha Wilson. The family relocated to Philadelphia in 1870.

On 17 October 1876 Lily Wilson married Thomas Potter, president of Thomas Potter Sons & Co., Inc., a manufacturer of linoleum. The well-to-do young couple set up home in Chestnut Hill, Philadelphia and eventually had three children: Thomas (*b*.1877), Wilson (*b*.1880) and Olive (*b*.1888).

Thomas Potter was eventually appointed as an aide to Pennsylvania's Governor James Beaver, and in 1889 he performed sterling service in providing relief to the victims of the Johnstown Flood. Lily Potter took an interest in her husband's relief work and provided funding for a nurse to help combat the effects of typhoid fever among the flood victims.

Thomas and Lily Potter's eldest son, Thomas, passed away on 2 December 1894. In 1910 their daughter Olive married J. Boulton Earnshaw, but later that same year, on 2 December, the same date as his son, Thomas Potter passed away and left Lily and her children alone.

The marriage of Boulton and Olive Earnshaw proved to be troubled almost from the very start, and by 1911 Olive had filed for divorce from her husband. Lily Potter was concerned about Olive's frame of mind and arranged to take her daughter on a tour of Europe and the Holy Land to try and take her mind off of her troubles. Lily also arranged for Margaret Hays (a school friend of Olive's) to accompany them during their travels, and Margaret brought along her pet Pomeranian dog as an added diversion.

Mrs Potter, Mrs Earnshaw (23) and Miss Hays (24) toured Italy, Palestine and Turkey together, and in April 1912 they travelled to Cherbourg in order to return to the United States on board a brand new passenger liner that Mrs Potter had heard about. On 10 April the three ladies boarded the *Titanic* as first class passengers.

ALFRED PUGH — Status: Survivor

Alfred Pugh (20) was born in Hampshire and lived at 72 Orchard Lane in Southampton, where he and his brothers Percy (31) and Samuel made their living working on British passenger liners. Alfred served on board the *Oceanic*, and on 6 April1912 he signed onto the *Titanic* to serve as a third class steward.

On 10 April Alfred and his brother Percy (who had signed on as a leading fireman) boarded the *Titanic* at Southampton, their brother Samuel having walked off of the ship in the belief that it was unlucky for three brothers to serve on board the same vessel.

JANE QUICK — Second Class Passenger

Frederick Quick was a plasterer who worked with his father in Plymouth. Fred married Jane ('Jeannie') Richards in 1902 when she was 22 years old. The couple had two daughters, Winnifred (born on 23 January 1904) and Phyllis (born on 27 July 1909).

The Quick family lived in England until 1910, at which point Fred heard of the good life that could be had in America if a man applied himself. Deciding to start over in a new country, Fred made arrangements to travel alone and establish a home for his family in Detroit, Michigan. In the meantime, Mrs Quick and the children continued to live with her mother in Plymouth until Fred felt sufficiently established and financially able to send for them.

In the spring of 1912, Mrs Quick got her two girls ready to travel and packed several trunks with all the family's possessions: heirlooms, wearing apparel, blankets and a three-year supply of bedding. Soon after booking their passage to America, Mrs Quick was notified that their intended steamer's sailing had been cancelled due to the coal strike and that her bookings had been transferred to a new and bigger ship that was scheduled to sail on 10 April. Mrs Quick was unhappy with this arrangement and made another trip to the shipping office to complain to the young man behind the counter, 'I don't want to sail on a new ship, I want one that has been tried and true and tested.'

After being assured that nothing would happen to the new ship, Mrs Quick resigned herself to the revised travel arrangements and returned home. On sailing day she, Winnifred (8) and Phyllis (2) said goodbye to their relatives in Plymouth and took the train to Southampton, where they boarded *Titanic*, the vessel that would soon reunite them with husband and father.

LILLIAN RENOUF — Status: Survivor

Lillian Jeffreys (30) and her brothers Clifford (24), Ernest (22) and Fred were the children of Mr and Mrs William Jeffreys of Roslyn, Guernsey.

Lillian Jeffreys married Peter Renouf (35), the son of William and Martha Renouf of Half Way, Guernsey. Peter and Lillian emigrated to the United States in 1907 (one report says 1910) and made their home in an apartment at 21b Florida Street in Elizabeth, New Jersey. Peter continued to practise his trade as a carpenter, and he and Lillian were members of Elizabeth's Grace Episcopal church. Peter was also active at the Hawthorne Athletic Club and was a member in good standing of the Brothers of the Order of the Sons of St George.

On 9 December 1911, following the death of Lillian's mother in Guernsey, Peter and Lillian Renouf sailed back to England and returned to Guernsey for a short holiday. The Renoufs spent Christmas with Mrs Falla, a relative who lived in Half Way, and they remained there as her guests until the time came for them to return home in April.

Lillian Renouf's brothers, Clifford and Ernest, decided that they would like to see America for themselves, and they arranged to accompany Lillian and Peter to New Jersey; three friends of the family, Herbert Denbury (25), Emily Rugg (21), and Lawrence Gavey (26) expressed a similar interest in accompanying the Renoufs to New Jersey (Mr Gavey having previously lived in Elizabeth for five years, establishing a reputation as an excellent amateur American football player). The entire Renouf party therefore booked their passages on the steamship *Philadelphia*; when the coal strike forced the cancellation of that vessel's sailing, however, the party's bookings were transferred to second class cabins on the new White Star liner *Titanic*.

And so it was that Peter and Lillian Renouf, Ernest and Clifford Jeffreys, Lawrence Gavey, Herbert Denbury and Emily Rugg all boarded the *Titanic* at Southampton on 10 April for the commencement of her maiden voyage.

GEORGE RHEIMS Status: Survivor

George Rheims (36) was a New York City importer who was travelling to that city with his brother-in-law Joseph Loring (30). The two men booked their passages to America on the *Titanic* and boarded the great vessel at Cherbourg on the evening of 10 April.

EMILE RICHARD Status: Victim

Emile Richard (23) was born in St Jean d'Angeleys, France on 24 August 1888 and was the son of P.H. Richard.

In the spring of 1912 Emile completed his compulsory service in the French army, and his father celebrated his son's separation from the service by providing him with funds for a holiday trip to Montreal. It was planned that, upon his return home, Emile would join his father in operating the family's distillery business.

Emile Richard commenced the first leg of his trip to Canada by travelling to Cherbourg, and on the evening of 10 April 1912 he boarded the White Star liner *Titanic* as a second class passenger.

ELIZABETH ROBERT Status: Survivor

Elizabeth McMillan (43) was born on 5 August 1868 in Alleghany, Pennsylvania and was the daughter of John and Elizabeth McMillan.

Elizabeth married Judge George A. Madill in 1895, and the newlyweds resided in St Louis, Missouri. Their daughter Georgette (16) was born on 15 March 1896.

Judge Madill had for many years been one of the leading lawyers of St Louis, and he was the first president of the Union Trust Co. and was still its president at time of his death in December 1901. Upon her father's death Georgette Madill was reckoned to be the wealthiest heiress in St Louis, and a court order was issued granting her an annual allowance of $7,500 for her use as 'pin money'.

In 1904 Elizabeth Madill married another lawyer, Edward S. Robert. Mr Robert's health slowly deteriorated over the years, however, and he eventually left his wife and stepdaughter in St Louis while he went abroad seeking treatment; Robert was still in Europe when he passed away in December 1911.

The death of her second husband took a heavy toll on Elizabeth Robert, who herself was suffering from a chronic illness. Mrs Robert and her daughter Georgette therefore decided to do some travelling in an attempt to put their troubles behind them, and they left their home at 1110 Lindell Boulevard and sailed to Europe early in 1912.

While the ladies were in Europe, Georgette Madill began to feel ill and eventually underwent an operation for appendicitis. Mrs Robert and Georgette decided to return home to St Louis to recuperate, and they made plans to sail with Mrs Robert's niece Elizabeth Allen (29), who wished to spend a few months in America before returning to England in June to marry Dr James Mennell, a London physician.

The three ladies made arrangements to return to England on board the *Baltic* on 6 June, and, along with her maid Emilie Kreuchen (29), Mrs Robert, Miss Madill and Miss Allen went to Southampton and boarded the *Titanic* as first class passengers on 10 April.

WILLIAM ROGERS — Status: Victim

William Rogers (29) was a miner who lived in Pontardawe, South Wales. On 10 April 1912 Mr Rogers and his friend Evan Davies (22) travelled to Southampton, where they boarded the *Titanic* as third class passengers.

RICHARD ROUSE — Status: Victim

Richard Rouse (53) lived in Sittingbourne, Kent with his wife Charity and 8-year-old daughter Gladys. An older daughter, Harriet, married George Maylum and emigrated to Cleveland, Ohio.

Richard Rouse earned his living as a coal miner, but a coal strike during the winter of 1911/12 took away his livelihood. For a time Mr Rouse attempted to earn money as a bricklayer, slaughterhouse worker and railwayman, but none of these jobs enabled him to earn enough money to support his family. In order to increase the family's income, Charity Rouse began doing day work by taking in the neighbours' washing and cleaning their homes. Harriet Maylum also did her part to help her parents and enclosed regular financial contributions along with her weekly letters.

Eventually Richard and Charity Rouse decided that their prospects would be brighter in the United States than they were in England, so they made plans for Richard to emigrate to America and establish himself financially before sending for Charity and Gladys. Charity began to sell off many of the family's belongings in order to raise money for Richard's trip, and their daughter Harriet obtained a job for him in Cleveland and sent him $38 for a steamship passage to America. Richard Rouse used the money to purchase a third class passage on the new White Star liner *Titanic*.

In early April 1912 Richard Rouse took Charity and Gladys to Southampton to see the ship on which he would be travelling to the United States. When Charity saw the great vessel lying at the White Star dock, however, she experienced sudden misgivings about the upcoming voyage.

'Dick, that ship is too big,' declared Charity. 'I have a bad feeling it will never reach America. Don't go.'

'Charity, don't worry,' replied Richard reassuringly. 'It's a brand new ship, and besides they say it's unsinkable.'

On 10 April 1912 Richard Rouse was on board the *Titanic* when she left Southampton on the first leg of her maiden voyage.

EDWARD RYAN **Status: Survivor**

Edward Ryan (24) was born on 28 January 1888 and was the youngest son of Daniel Ryan of Ballinareen, County Tipperary. Ryan worked in Dublin as an engineer and saved money to purchase a steamship ticket to visit his sister, Mrs Bridget Walsh, in Troy, New York. Ryan hoped to find work as an engineer in New York City, and on 11 April 1912 he boarded the *Titanic* as a steerage passenger at Queenstown in the hope of fulfilling his lifelong dream.

EMILY RYERSON **Status: Survivor**

Emily Borie (48) was born on 10 August 1863 in Philadelphia, Pennsylvania and was the third child of John and Susan Borie. Emily had three sisters named Elizabeth, Sophie and Emily, and her four brothers were named Adolph, John Jr, Syliffe and Henry.

When Emily Borie eventually became engaged to Arthur Ryerson (who was thirteen years her senior), her sisters were appalled. 'You aren't going to marry that old man, are you?' they asked Emily one day while she was washing dishes. Emily's reply was short and to the point: 'You don't think I'm gonna do THIS the rest of my life!'

Arthur Ryerson and Emily Borie were married on 31 January 1889 in Philadelphia, Pennsylvania, and the couple eventually had five children: Susan (*b.*1890), Arthur Jr (*b.*1891), Emily (*b.*1893), Ellen (*b.*1895) and John (*b.*1898).

Emily's new husband, Arthur Ryerson (61), had been born on 12 January 1851 in Chicago, Illinois and was the son of Joseph Ryerson, founder of the city's Joseph T. Ryerson Steel Co. Arthur and his siblings Edward, Josephine and Eleanor were baptised in the old St James's church, and later in his life Arthur served there as a vestryman.

As a young man Arthur Ryerson was proficient in mountain climbing, and throughout his life he continued to be devoted to outdoor sports. Mr Ryerson prepared for college at private schools, and he attended Yale University, graduating in 1871. Ryerson then took courses in the law schools of Chicago University and Columbia College in New York, receiving the degree of Bachelor of Law from each institution. Mr Ryerson was then admitted to the bar in Illinois and practised law in Chicago; he was a member of one of the city's leading law firms until 1900, at which point he decided to leave the practice of law to others and devote his energies to other interests.

Arthur Ryerson was a deeply religious man, and in his satchel and in the cabin of his yacht he always kept his personal prayer book as well as copies of *Thomas à Kempis*, *St Augustine's Confessions* and *In Memoriam*. Mr Ryerson took an active part in church and charitable work, and he founded, funded and maintained the Mission Chapel of St John the Evangelist located on Chicago's poor West Side; Ryerson loved that chapel very much.

For many years Mr Ryerson was a member of the vestry of St James's church in Chicago and represented it frequently in the Diocesan Conventions. He served as delegate to four triennial conventions of the Protestant Episcopal Church in the United States, and for eighteen years he was a member of its General Board of Missions. Mr Ryerson was connected with Chicago's St Luke's Hospital for twenty years and served it faithfully as trustee and president; it was largely due to Mr Ryerson's managerial efforts that the hospital got out of debt and was guided back down the road to prosperity.

Emily and Arthur Ryerson and their children had always made a point of summering at Bar Harbor in Maine, arriving there in their yacht from New York. After leaving Chicago in 1900, however, the Ryersons made their summer home at 'Ringwood', a stuccoed house and huge estate situated on the north shore of Otsego Lake in Cooperstown, New York. The interior of 'Ringwood' boasted ceiling beams and wall panelling of dark oak, as well as enormous fireplaces. Emily Ryerson filled her family's summer home with furnishings gathered from all over the world. The estate contained a number of separate homes on its grounds and also had its own stables, kennels and beehives from which to harvest fresh honey. Mr Ryerson was well able to afford these luxuries, as his financial worth was eventually estimated to be somewhere around $5 million.

In 1903 the Ryerson family took a trip to Europe, sailing for Liverpool on 2 December on board the White Star liner *Cedric*; two unnamed manservants accompanied the family during their travels abroad.

In addition to their summer home in Cooperstown, the Ryerson family also maintained a home at Gray's Lane in Haverford, Pennsylvania. Arthur Ryerson kept up an active interest in the intellectual life of the country, and he continued to devote his energies to pious and charitable works, becoming a member of the General Board of Episcopal Missions in Philadelphia.

During the early months of 1912 Emily and Arthur Ryerson decided to close their house at Haverford and take three of their children, Suzette (21), Emily (18) and John (13) on a holiday to Europe. Another daughter, 17-year-old Ellen, a student at St Timothy's School in Catonville, Maryland, was to remain in the States, as was her 21-year-old brother Arthur Jr, who was now in his first year at Yale. Mr and Mrs Ryerson, their three children, Grace Bowen (John Ryerson's governess and tutor) and Victorine Chaudanson (Mrs Ryerson's maid) duly sailed to Europe on the *Olympic* in February 1912.

On 8 April 1912 tragedy struck the Ryerson family when Arthur Ryerson Jr and his college friend, John Hoffman, were killed when Hoffman's car ran off the road in Pennsylvania and struck a telephone pole. Mr and Mrs Ryerson were in Paris when they received the news of their son's death, and Mr Ryerson made arrangements for himself and his family to obtain first class passages on the earliest possible steamer back to New York.

On the evening of 10 April 1912 Arthur and Emily Ryerson, their children Susan, Emily and John, Grace Bowen (45) and Victorine Chaudanson (36) were in Cherbourg when the *Titanic* touched there to pick up mail and receive passengers who were intending to travel to the United States of America.

ADOLPHE SAALFELD **Status: Survivor**

Adolphe Saalfeld (47) was born in Germany in 1865, and in 1912 he and his wife Gertrude were living in Manchester, England. Mr Saalfeld was head of the wholesale chemists firm Sparks, White & Co. of London.

In April 1912 Mr Saalfeld planned a pleasure trip to North America, where he hoped to visit friends in Montreal, see Niagara Falls and then travel to Chicago before finally returning home to England in May. Mr Saalfeld commenced the first leg of his journey by booking a first class passage on the *Titanic* and boarding the great vessel at Southampton on 10 April.

STELLA SAGE **Status: Victim**

Stella Sage (20) was born in 1891 and lived in Peterborough with her parents, Mr and Mrs John Sage, and her five brothers and three sisters. John Sage was a grocer, and Stella made her living as a dressmaker.

In 1911 John Sage and his son George emigrated to Canada and went to work for the Canadian Pacific Railway. Their jobs enabled them to visit Florida, where they fell in love with the climate and countryside. John Sage purchased some land there to start a fruit farm, and he and his son returned home to England to fetch the rest of the family. All were excited about the prospect of emigrating to the United States except Stella, who, as the eldest child, had established many friendships in Peterborough. Stella agreed to accompany the family on the condition that her father pay for her return if she didn't like America. The eleven members of the Sage family booked their passage in the *Titanic*'s steerage section and boarded the great vessel at Southampton on 10 April.

ANNA SALKJELSVIK **Status: Survivor**

Anna Salkjelsvik (21) was born on 30 October 1890 in Skodje, Norway. She decided to emigrate to Proctor, Minnesota, and, along with fellow Norwegians Karen Abelseth (16), Olaus Abelseth (25), Sigurd Moen (27), Peter Søholt (19) and Adolph Humblen (42), she travelled to Southampton and boarded the *Titanic* as a steerage passenger on 10 April.

JULIUS SAP **Status: Survivor**

Julius Sap (25) was born in Rek, near Zwevezele, Belgium and was the third of eight children born to Constant and Melanie Sap. Julius grew to young manhood in Rek and worked as a clerk at the flax works at Aime Prince.

The Sap family lived near the Zomerweg Café, an establishment where young Julius frequently spent time as a customer. One evening in 1911 Julius was seated in the café when some nearby men began brawling over a woman. When Julius intervened on the woman's behalf, one of the men drew a knife. Julius drew his own knife in self defence, and during the ensuing scuffle he stabbed his antagonist in an attempt to wound him just severely enough to force him to stop fighting. The injured man bled copiously, though, and the police were forced to take Julius briefly into custody, although he was soon allowed to return home.

The legal action against Julius that resulted from this fight dragged on and on, and Julius became worried even though he was convinced he was in the right. In April 1912, after talking things over with his father, it was decided that Julius would emigrate to the United States and work as a harvester in the sugar beet industry near Detroit, Michigan.

Julius Sap left home and travelled to Antwerp, where he booked passage on a ship to Harwich, England and then took the train to Southampton. On 10 April 1912 Mr Sap boarded the new White Star liner *Titanic* as a third class passenger to begin the final stage of his journey to America.

JOSEPH SCARROTT **Status: Survivor**

Joseph Scarrott (33) was born in Portsmouth on 25 April 1878. In 1912 he lived at 36 Albert Road in Southampton and made his living as an able bodied seaman on the passenger liners that sailed from British ports.

Mr Scarrott served on board the *Kildonan Castle* before transferring to the *Titanic*, and on the morning of 10 April 1912 he made preparations to join the big liner on her maiden voyage. Scarrott felt an odd reluctance to sail on the *Titanic*, though, and it was only after debating the matter with himself that he finally decided to make the voyage.

When the time came for him to walk down to the docks, Mr Scarrott kissed his sister and said, 'Goodbye.' The sister called him back to her doorstep and asked him why he had said 'goodbye' instead of his usual, 'So long, see you again soon.' Scarrott hadn't noticed his own departure from his usual routine, and the matter stuck in his mind as he walked down to the Docks. Joseph Scarrott was serving as an able bodied seaman on board the *Titanic* when the great vessel pulled away from Southampton Docks at noon on 10 April.

EMMA SCHABERT **Status: Survivor**

Emma Mock (35) was born on 23 May 1876 in New York City, she and her brother Philip being the children of German immigrants Richard and Emma Mock. Emma and Philip were both educated in Europe.

Emma Mock married Rufus Blake of Derby, Connecticut, but she was widowed when Mr Blake passed away. In 1894 Emma married a second time, this time to Paul Schabert, a wealthy landowner from Hamburg. Mr Schabert was a captain in the German army and was also a veteran of the Sino-Japanese war, and he and Emma eventually had two children, daughter Beatrice and son Kyrill.

By 1912 Mr and Mrs Schabert seem to have grown apart, and Paul left Emma in Germany and travelled alone to Reno, Nevada to gain a six-month residency there in order to file a suit for divorce. While in Reno, Mr Schabert retained Cole Harwood as his attorney.

In April 1912 Emma Schabert made plans to follow her husband to the United States, and her brother Phillip Mock agreed to accompany her. The two booked first class passages on board the brand new *Titanic*, and they boarded the great liner when she touched at Cherbourg at 6 p.m. on 10 April.

IMANITA SHELLEY **Status: Survivor**

Imanita Parrish (25) was the daughter of Mrs Lucinda Parrish (59) of Woodford, Kentucky. Miss Parrish married accountant William Shelley, and the young couple made their home in Deer Lodge, Montana.

In 1912 Imanita Shelley suffered from a severe illness, and she and her mother travelled to England so that Imanita could convalesce and regain her strength. When she finally felt well enough to return home, Mrs Shelley and Mrs Parrish purchased second class tickets on the *Titanic* and boarded her at Southampton on 10 April.

ELIZABETH SHUTE **Status: Survivor**

Elizabeth Shute (40) was born on 30 April 1871 in Newburgh, New York. She was an unmarried French teacher who was employed by Mrs William T. Graham (59) as an instructor and governess for her daughter Margaret (19).

In January 1912 the three ladies sailed for Europe on board the *Cedric*, and on 10 April, homeward bound, they boarded the *Titanic* in Southampton as first class passengers.

MAUDE SINCOCK **Status: Survivor**

Maude Sincock (20) was born on 17 April 1891 in Toronto, and was the daughter of Frank and Melinda Sincock. Frank was originally from Cornwall and decided to return there with his family, and it was in St Ives in the county that Maude and her two brothers and sisters grew up.

A few years prior to 1912 one of Maude's uncles emigrated to Hancock, Michigan and became prosperous in real estate and other business ventures, and Frank Sincock decided to follow his brother to America and made plans to bring his family there a few at a time as money permitted. In September 1911 Frank and one of Maude's elder sisters went to Hancock, where Frank went to work for the Quincey Mining Co. Maude's turn came in 1912, and the young woman made arrangements to sail for America in April of that year. Her original sailing was cancelled because of the coal strike, however, and Maude was transferred to the *Titanic* as a second class passenger. Along with her friends Mr and Mrs William Lahtinen (35 and 26), Lyyli Silven (17), Elizabeth Davies (48) and the latter's sons John Davies (8) and Joseph Nicholls (19), Maude boarded the new White Star liner at Southampton on 10 April.

MARY SLOAN **Status: Survivor**

Mary Sloan (28) was born in Belfast in 1884 and lived with her brother and sister at 1 Kerrsland Terrace, Knock in the city. Earning her living as a White Star stewardess, Miss Sloan was on board the *Olympic* at the time of her collision with the cruiser *Hawke*. In April 1912 she was transferred to the *Titanic* and signed onto the great vessel at Southampton on 10 April.

WILLIAM SLOPER **Status: Survivor**

William Sloper (28) was born on 13 December 1883 and was the son of Andrew and Ella Sloper of New Britain, Connecticut. Andrew Sloper was a former United States Senator and was president of the First National Bank of New Britain.

William Sloper finished school and in the autumn of 1902 went to work at the New Britain National Bank. In April 1904 Mr Sloper sailed to Europe on the *Cedric*, his three-month trip to Europe having been financed by his father. In February 1905 Sloper's grandmother, uncle and father financed his second, five-month-long trip to Europe, but from that point on Mr Sloper's successful financial investments enabled him to pay for his own holidays.

In February 1910 William Sloper was forced to leave the New Britain National Bank because of a physical disability; Mr Sloper's health problem was corrected by an operation that he underwent two years later.

In January 1912 William Sloper and his friend Howard Humphrey sailed to Egypt on a holiday, stopping in Algiers, Monte Carlo and Athens along the way. When Mr Humphrey suddenly received word that he must leave Cairo and to go to Paris on business, Mr Sloper thought he would have to continue his travels alone. As luck would have it, he then encountered the Frank Stiles family, whom he had previously met while sailing to Europe in January. Sloper and the Stiles family spent the next six weeks sightseeing in Egypt via train and river steamer on the Nile.

During his stay at Shepheard's Hotel in Cairo, William Sloper encountered Mr and Mrs Mark Fortune (64 and 60) and their four children, Ethel (28), Alice (24), Mabel (23) and Charles (19), who, like the Stiles family, had been Sloper's fellow passengers on his January voyage. While Mr Sloper was seated with the Fortunes on the hotel's terrace, an Indian soothsayer gave Alice Fortune a chilling warning: 'You are in danger every time you travel on the sea, for I see you adrift on the ocean in an open boat. You will lose everything but your life. You will be saved but others will be lost.' This warning put the rest of the Fortune family in a pensive mood, so they paid the fortune teller and sent him on his way.

Early in March 1912 William Sloper sailed from Alexandria to Naples, and from there he took another steamer to Europe. Sloper spent two weeks in Nice before travelling to Paris, where he spent an additional two weeks; at that point Mr Sloper crossed the Channel to England and arrived in London on 1 April.

William Sloper intended to return to the United States on board the *Mauretania*, but on 8 April he again ran into the Fortune family, this time at London's Carlton Hotel. Alice Fortune convinced Mr Sloper to cancel his booking on the *Mauretania* and travel with her and her family on board the White Star liner *Titanic*. When Sloper went ahead and did as she asked, however, he was surprised at the girl's reaction to his altered travel arrangements: 'I am sorry you did it,' Alice admitted. 'Don't you remember that fortune teller last winter on the terrace at Shepheard's Hotel? You have forgotten that I am a dangerous person to travel with.'

William Sloper placed no stock in fortune tellers, however, and on 10 April he joined the Fortune family at London's Waterloo station to board the boat train to Southampton. Upon their arrival in the port city, Mr Sloper and all six members of the Fortune family stepped on board the *Titanic* as first class passengers.

EDWARD J. SMITH — Status: Victim

Edward J. Smith (62) was born in Hanley, Staffordshire on 27 January 1850 and was the son of Edward and Catherine Smith. In 1869 Smith went to sea on the *Senator Weber*, an American clipper, and served as an apprentice. In 1876 he was aboard the square rigger *Lizzie Fennel* as fourth officer, and by 1880 had risen to the rank of fourth officer of the White Star liner *Celtic*.

On 13 January 1887 Edward Smith married Sarah Pennington at St Oswald's church in Winwick, near Warrington, but eventually the couple moved to Southampton.

In 1887 Smith secured his first command as captain of the *Republic* before later transferring to the *Baltic*. Later he took command of the *Cufic*, *Runic*, the old *Adriatic*, *Celtic*, *Britannic* and the *Oceanic* in the late 1880s.

While Captain Smith was commander of the *Oceanic* he held regular weekly fire drills and boat drills for the crew, insisting that the crew must always be prepared for something he was hopeful would never happen. Although Smith was a disciplinarian, his crewmen found him easy to get along with as long as they did their duty.

The only mishap to the *Oceanic* while under Smith's command occurred while the vessel was cautiously exiting the harbour of Honolulu. The usual soundings were being taken when suddenly there were two slight but distinct bumps as her keel struck a coral reef. Apparently no damage was done to the vessel's hull, and the *Oceanic* continued on into deep water without incident.

Captain Smith commanded the *Coptic* in the Australian trade before moving on to the *Germanic* and later transferring to the *Majestic* in 1894. In 1898 Smith and his wife were blessed with a little daughter whom they named Helen. When the Boer War broke out the following year Captain Smith, who was a commander in the Royal Naval Reserves, was placed in command of troop transports that were bound for the Transvaal.

Captain Smith assumed command of the *Baltic* in 1904. He had the reputation of being a very careful commander and was known to be on the *Baltic*'s bridge for two days at a time during a foggy spell. Smith was always willing to hurry to the bridge whether he was on duty or off, and was known to leave his dinner table if he thought he was needed on the bridge.

Captain Smith never drank (at least while at sea) and would not stand for any of his crew drinking, either; he would immediately discharge any crewman he heard of who took a drink on board his ship. (Smith's bedroom steward on the *Baltic* later said that he never found any kind of liquor in Smith's room.) Despite Smith's diligence and concern for safety on the *Baltic*, however, his bedroom steward later told of an incident that came close to putting an irreparable blot on Captain Smith's record.

Late one evening, after a particularly long day, the steward in charge of the *Baltic*'s smoking room locked that room up for the night and commenced his routine fire inspection elsewhere on the ship. When the steward returned to the smoking room he was so tired that he sat down and, nodding his head for a moment, fell asleep. At that point a tiny flame that had apparently been smouldering in the room during his absence suddenly began to flare up, but the exhausted steward did not awaken. A sailor at work on the deck outside happened to notice a wisp of smoke, and upon investigation he saw flames inside the locked smoking room. He awakened a few of his mates, broke into the smoking room and succeeded in putting the fire out. It was estimated that, had the flames burned just ten minutes more, they would have been out of control. Captain Smith's bedroom steward said that the above near-catastrophe was kept quiet by the *Baltic*'s crew, and the general public never got so much as a hint that the incident had ever taken place.

Captain Smith continued to serve the White Star Line with quiet efficiency, and his rise in rank was commensurate with the safe, routine nature of his command. In 1907, when he brought the new *Adriatic* to New York on her maiden voyage, he is reported to have said, 'When anyone asks me how I can best describe my experiences of nearly forty years at sea, I merely say uneventful... I will say that I cannot imagine any condition which would cause a ship to founder. I cannot conceive of any vital disaster happening to this vessel. Modern shipbuilding has gone beyond that.'

Not long afterwards, though, a friend of Captain Smith's pointed out to him that the *Adriatic* had insufficient lifeboats for everyone on board, and he asked Smith what would happen if the *Adriatic* were to strike a concealed reef, or ice, and was badly damaged. Captain Smith's reply was short and to the point: 'Some of us would go to the bottom with her.'

Captain Smith was in command of the *Olympic* when she was rammed by the British cruiser *Hawke* on 20 September 1911, an accident which forced the *Olympic* to return to Southampton for repairs. On a subsequent crossing of the *Olympic*, Smith became involved in a discussion with several passengers concerning the recent collision:

'Anyhow,' Smith declared, 'the *Olympic* is unsinkable, and the *Titanic* will be the same when she is put into commission. Why, either of these vessels could be cut in halves and each half would remain afloat indefinitely. The non-sinkable vessel has been reached in these two wonderful craft. I venture to add that even if the engines and boilers of these vessels were to fall through their bottoms, the vessels would remain afloat.'

In February 1912 the *Olympic* threw a propeller blade at sea but was able to complete her journey under her own steam. The White Star Line did not lose confidence in Captain Smith, though, and he was subsequently given command of the new *Titanic*. Smith, who was a Mason, earned an annual salary of £1,250.

While he was in New York on the night before he took the *Olympic* back to England to assume command of the *Titanic*, Captain Smith told his friends Mr and Mrs W.P. Willie that he had utter confidence in the *Titanic*'s safety. Smith said that it was impossible for the *Titanic* to sink, and that her appearance on the Atlantic marked a high point of safety and comfort in the evolution of ocean travel.

On 10 April 1912 Captain Smith stepped aboard the *Titanic* as her commander and left his wife Eleanor and 14-year-old daughter Helen at their home in Southampton.

MARY SMITH — Status: Survivor

Mary Eloise Hughes (18) was born on 7 August 1893 and was one of two daughters of Congressman and Mrs James A. Hughes of Huntington, West Virginia.

In late 1911 or early 1912 Miss Hughes debuted in Washington, D.C., and on 8 February 1912 she was married to Lucian Smith (24) at the Central Christian church in Huntington. Mr Smith was a wealthy young man from Morgantown, West Virginia, and his marriage to Eloise Hughes was one of the year's great social functions.

Lucian and Eloise Smith honeymooned abroad and spent at least part of their travels sightseeing in Egypt. When Eloise discovered that she was pregnant, she and her husband decided to return home so that their first child could be born in the United States. Lucian and Eloise Smith travelled to Cherbourg, and on the evening of 10 April 1912 they boarded the tender and were shuttled out to the *Titanic* to join her as first class passengers.

RICHARD SMITH — Status: Victim

Richard William Smith, a resident of Streatham, Surrey, was connected with a large tea-importing firm in London and was manager of the American business of Messrs Reinachs, Nephew & Co. Mr Smith was a well-known judge of tea and made numerous trips to the United States, where he had many friends in the tea business.

In April 1912 Richard Smith prepared to make yet another business trip to America, and on 10 April he travelled to Southampton to board the *Titanic* as a first class passenger.

JULIA SMYTH — Status: Survivor

Julia Smyth (17) was born on 4 July 1894 in Dublin and lived with her parents in Kilcoghy, County Cavan. She decided to emigrate to New York City, and on 11 April 1912 she boarded the *Titanic* at Queenstown as a steerage passenger.

JOHN SNYDER — Status: Survivor

John Pillsbury Snyder (24) was born on 8 January 1888 in Minneapolis, Minnesota and was the son of Fred Snyder and Susan Pillsbury. His maternal grandfather, flour magnate John Sargent Pillsbury, was an ex-governor of Minnesota.

In February 1912 Mr Snyder married Nelle Stevenson (23), daughter of T.W. Stevenson of Minneapolis. The young couple spent their honeymoon touring the Holy Land, and they were homeward bound when they booked first class passages on the *Titanic* and boarded the new liner at Southampton on 10 April.

MARGARETTA SPEDDEN — Status: Survivor

Margaretta ('Daisy') Stone (39) was born on 19 November 1872 in Morristown, New Jersey. On 9 June 1891 she graduated from the Ogontz School for Young Ladies in Ogontz, Pennsylvania; Miss Stone attended the graduation ceremony even though she was ill with German measles, but she paid the price by spending the next three days in the school infirmary.

During the decade known as the 'Gay Nineties' Daisy and her family took several trips to the southern United States and one trip to California; they divided the remainder of their time between Morristown and New York, where Daisy pursued her musical studies.

Daisy Stone and her family attended the Chicago World's Fair in 1893, and while there Daisy met several old friends from her school days. One day Daisy and her sister Emma were driving in a carriage to a friend's house for lunch when their carriage rounded a corner and accidentally fell in with the Princess Eulalie of Spain's procession. The two girls were pleased to be mistaken for part of the royal entourage and happily bowed right and left in response to the cheers and greetings of the crowds of bystanders.

The twentieth century opened with Daisy Stone becoming engaged to Frederick Spedden (45), a New York banker whom she married in June 1900. The young couple immediately began to travel and took three Mediterranean cruises besides spending two winters in Madeira.

Frederick and Daisy Spedden's son Robert Douglas (6) was born on Daisy's birthday, 19 November 1905, and the family made its home at Wee Wah Lodge in Tuxedo Park, New York.

In 1911 Mr and Mrs Spedden decided to take a European holiday, and they and their son embarked on the Cunard liner *Caronia*. Travelling with the Spedden family were Mrs Spedden's maid Helen Wilson (31) and Douglas's nanny, Elizabeth Burns (41). The family spent the winter of 1911/12 in Algiers, Tunis before travelling to Monte Carlo and finally to Paris.

In April 1912 the Speddens made first class reservations to return to the United States on board the *Titanic*, and on the evening of 10 April Frederick, Daisy and Douglas Spedden, Helen Wilson and Elizabeth Burns boarded the tender that was to take them out to the huge White Star liner that awaited them in the outer harbour.

AMY STANLEY — Status: Survivor

Amy Stanley (24) was born on 4 January 1888 to Thomas and Eliza Stanley and was the only daughter among their five children. The family lived in Ledwell, Oxfordshire, before moving to Wolvercote, and Thomas Stanley began working there as a 'Farm Sherrif' while simultaneously operating a grocery store in Green Road.

Amy may have spent her early years helping in the family grocery business, but eventually she apprenticed herself to Oxford dressmaker Harold Brown in Woodstock Road. Later she left home to work at a couple of different business establishments before finally going into domestic service in Wallington, Surrey.

In 1912 Miss Stanley made preparations to emigrate to New Haven, Connecticut, where she had obtained a position as a children's maid. She originally intended to sail early in the spring, but the coal strike interfered with her plans and forced her to obtain a third class passage on board the new *Titanic*. Miss Stanley purchased her ticket jointly with 21-year-old Edward Roland Stanley (who was bound for Cleveland, Ohio), and the two Stanleys boarded the *Titanic* in Southampton on 10 April.

WILLIAM T. STEAD — Status: Victim

William Thomas Stead was born in Embleton, England on 5 July 1849, the second of nine children of the Revd William and Isabella Stead, the Revd Stead being a Congregationalist minister at Howdon-on-Tyne, near Newcastle.

William Stead was schooled at Silcoates (Wakefield), where he took pride in his distinction of being 'the boy with the hardest shins'. He was taken from school at 14 to be apprenticed in a merchant's office at Newcastle, and he stayed there for seven years, rising to the position of salaried clerk.

William Stead went to the *Northern Echo* newspaper in 1871, where he became its editor. He married Emma Lucy Wilson in 1873, and the couple's first son was born in 1874, followed by other sons and daughters.

In 1880 William Stead attended his first séance and developed a strong interest in the paranormal. He later became a prominent proponent of spiritualism.

Mr Stead took over as assistant editor of the *Pall Mall Gazette* in 1880, and in 1883 he became its editor. Between 1883 and 1890 Stead revolutionised Fleet Street by introducing the concept of the interview, pictorial illustrations in newspapers, and the gossip column. In 1885 he crusaded against child slavery and prostitution, and later became a crusader for world peace.

In 1890 Mr Stead resigned his editorship of the *Pall Mall Gazette* and founded the *Review of Reviews*. He also travelled to Russia and talked with the Tsar, which led to the Peace Conference at The Hague. For this endeavour Stead was nominated for the Nobel Peace Prize in 1901.

Mr Stead's eldest son died in 1907, which intensified his long-standing interest in spiritualism. In 1911 Stead went to Constantinople in an attempt to promote peace in the Balkans.

In April 1912 William Thomas Stead made plans to sail to America to speak on the topic of world peace to a gathering of the Men and Religion Forward movement at Carnegie Hall. Mr Stead accordingly made arrangements to board the *Titanic* at Southampton as one of her first class passengers.

ANNIE AND CHARLES STENGEL — Status: Survivors

Annie Morris (44) was born in New York on 2 May 1867 and was the daughter of Charles and Amanda Morris. Annie's three brothers were named Frank, Joseph and Edward, and her sister was named Emma. Charles Stengel (54) was born on 19 November 1857 in Newark, New Jersey and was the son of Jacob and Elizabeth Stengel.

Annie Morris married Charles Stengel, who, in company with his business partner Martin Rothschild, owned and operated the firm of Stengel & Rothschild, manufacturer of leather clothing. The Stengels eventually had three children named Evan, Raymond and Inez, and the family lived at 1075 South Broad Street in Newark.

In the spring of 1912, after concluding a month-long European holiday, Charles and Annie Stengel booked passages for their return voyage to America. Travelling with the Stengels were Charles's business partner Martin Rothschild (46) and his wife Elizabeth (54), and the four voyagers took the train to Cherbourg and boarded the brand new *Titanic* on the evening of 10 April.

MARTHA STEPHENSON — Status: Survivor

Martha Eustis (52) was born on 13 March 1860 in Boston, Massachusetts, her sister Elizabeth (54) having been born two years earlier on 1 March 1858. The two girls, along with their sisters Eleanor and Mary and brothers Henry and Joseph, were the children of William and Martha Eustis.

On 10 October 1883 Martha Eustis married Walter Stephenson. The young couple settled in Haverford, Pennsylvania, and had three children whom they named George, Martha and Helen. Walter Stephenson passed away on 11 March 1901 and left Martha a widow.

In 1906 Mrs Stephenson was staying at San Francisco's St Francis Hotel when she survived the great earthquake that destroyed that coastal California city.

In the spring of 1912 Martha Stephenson and her sister Elizabeth Eustis took a pleasure trip to the Mediterranean. When the time came for them to return home, they booked two first class passages on the new White Star liner *Titanic* and boarded the great vessel at Cherbourg on the evening of 10 April.

MARTHA STONE — Status: Survivor

Martha Stevens (62) was born on 29 January 1850 in Boston, Massachusetts. After her first husband, John Harrington, passed away, Martha married Captain George Stone, the multimillionaire president of the Cincinnati Bell Telephone Co.

Mr and Mrs Stone resided in luxury in Cincinnati, Ohio, but when George Stone passed away in 1901, the twice-widowed but wealthy Martha moved to New York and took up residence in the Plaza Hotel.

By 1912 Martha Stone had greying hair and was a confirmed traveller. April of that year found Martha and her French maid, Amelia Icard (38) in England, where they were making plans to board a steamer to return to the States. On 10 April Martha Stone and Amelia Icard were in Southampton when they walked up the gangplank and stepped on board the brand new *Titanic* as first class passengers.

ROSALIE STRAUS — Status: Victim

Rosalie Ida Blun (63) was born on 6 February 1849. In 1871 Miss Blun married Isidor Straus (67), and the young couple eventually had six children. Mr and Mrs Straus shared the same birthday (although separated by four years) and were almost inseparable. On the rare occasions when they spent time apart, they wrote to each other every day.

Isidor Straus took a large part in forming and directing the New York importing firm of L. Straus & Sons. In 1874 Isidor and his brother Nathan became associated with R.H. Macy & Co.; Isidor became a partner in 1888, and by 1896 had acquired ownership of the firm.

Isidor Straus held a congressional seat for New York State between 1895 and 1897 and aided in drafting non-protectionist tariff legislation. Mr and Mrs Straus later devoted their time and attention to philanthropy and reform.

In early 1912 Ida and Isidor Straus were wintering at Cap Martin. Mr Straus was investigating the currency question in Europe for the purpose of deriving information that would help the United States reform its own currency.

The Strauses then travelled to the Holy Land, and in April they spent some time in Jerusalem. During their stay there Mr Straus was unwell, so Ida Straus visited the poor Jewish quarter by herself and was distressed by the misery and squalor she saw there. Mrs Straus told her husband what she had seen and suggested that they ought to do something to relieve such misery. Mr Straus accordingly made arrangements for a soup kitchen to be opened to which he would guarantee future funds.

On 4 April 1912 Mr and Mrs Straus were luncheon guests of Ambassador and Mrs Whitelaw Reid at the American Embassy in London. When the time came for them to return home to America the Strauses travelled to Southampton, and, along with Isidor's manservant John Farthing (over 50) and Ida's maid Ellen Bird (31), they boarded the *Titanic* as first class passengers on 10 April.

EMIL TAUSSIG — Status: Victim

Emil Taussig (52) was born in Austria in June 1859. He emigrated to the United States where he became President of the West Disinfecting Co., manufacturing chemists of New York City. The company was located at 2 East 42nd Street, while the San Francisco branch was located at 53 Taylor Street.

Mr Taussig's wife Tillie (39) was the daughter of Hermann Mandelbaum of 1229 Park Avenue. Emil and Tillie's daughter Ruth (18) was born on 25 November 1893, and the Taussig family lived at 777 West End Avenue.

In 1912 the Taussigs travelled to England so that Mr Taussig could establish a branch office of his company in London. When it came time for them to return home, Mr and Mrs Taussig and their daughter Ruth travelled to Southampton, where they boarded the *Titanic* as first class passengers.

ELMER TAYLOR — Status: Survivor

Elmer Taylor (48) married Juliet Wright (49), and the young couple originally resided in Smyrna, Delaware. Along with Fletcher Lambert Williams, Taylor was co-owner of the Mono Service Co., a firm that manufactured paper cups.

Mr Taylor frequently made business trips abroad, and he and his wife were in London during the spring of 1912. The Taylors planned to spend the coming summer in East Orange, New Jersey, and they booked first class passages on the *Titanic* and boarded her at Southampton on 10 April.

JOHN B. THAYER III — Status: Survivor

John 'Jack' B. Thayer III (17) was born on 24 December 1894; Jack, his younger brother Frederick and his younger sisters Margaret and Pauline were the children of John (49) and Marian (39) Thayer of Haverford, Pennsylvania.

In 1894 Jack Thayer's father was employed by the Pennsylvania Railroad as its assistant general freight agent in Philadelphia. Mr Thayer's advancement in the business was steady, however, and by 1912 he had become the company's Second Vice President.

Young Jack Thayer attended school in England, but upon his graduation in early 1912 his father planned for him to return to the United States to attend Princeton. In March, John and Marian Thayer and Mrs Thayer's maid Margaret Fleming travelled to England to retrieve young Jack, after which the family did a little travelling on the Continent. The end of March found the Thayers in Berlin, Germany as guests of the American Consul General, but the time was fast approaching for the family to return to America. 10 April found John, Marian and Jack Thayer and Miss Fleming in Cherbourg, where the four travellers boarded the *Titanic* that evening as first class passengers.

MARIAN THAYER — Status: Survivor

Marian Morris (39) was born in Haverford, Pennsylvania on 9 November 1872 and was the daughter of Frederick and Elizabeth Morris.

Miss Morris married John B. Thayer II (49) some time prior to 1894. Mr Thayer was an avid cricketer, and he and his new wife up residence in Mr Thayer's home, 'Redwood', which was situated just behind the Merion Cricket Club. The Thayers eventually had four children: John B. (III), Frederick, Margaret and Pauline.

John B. Thayer was an employee of the Pennsylvania Railroad Co. and served as the division freight agent of the Northern Central Railway. On 1 December 1894 Mr Thayer was promoted to the position of assistant general freight agent, and on 10 March 1897 he became general freight agent in charge of through traffic. In 1899 Thayer became general freight agent of the Pennsylvania railway as well as of several subsidiary companies.

On 1 June 1903 John Thayer was appointed as the company's fifth vice-president in charge of traffic; Mr Thayer's advancement continued steadily after that, and on 3 March 1911 he was appointed second vice-president of the Pennsylvania Railroad.

In March 1912 John and Marian Thayer and Mrs Thayer's maid Margaret Fleming travelled to England to meet their son Jack (17), who had completed his schooling there and was ready to return home. From there they travelled in Europe before joining the *Titanic* at Cherbourg.

EDWINA TROUTT — Status: Survivor

Edwina Troutt (27) was born in Bath on 8 July 1884 and was one of four surviving children of Edwin Troutt (a brewer) and his wife Elizabeth. Edwina was a sickly child, and in 1900 a severe bout of illness permanently collapsed one of her lungs. She survived that affliction, though, and that very same year went to work teaching at a nursery school.

In 1901 Miss Troutt was awarded a three-year scholarship at a technical school. Her teaching job forced her to study for her classes at night, and her eyesight began to suffer from the strain of reading by gaslight. Edwina's father urged her to give up her studies before her eyesight failed completely, and she complied with his wishes and went to work for her brother-in-law, a tobacconist.

By 1907 Edwina was tired of her current job and decided to emigrate to America to start a new life. She crossed the Atlantic on the *Arabic* and went to work in New York as a waitress. This job did not agree with her, however, and she soon went to work for the wife of a minister and, later, worked in the household of the president of Williams College in Williamstown, Massachusetts.

In 1911 Miss Troutt decided she could not face another New England winter and returned to her family in Bath. By the spring of 1912, however, her younger sister (who had also moved to Massachusetts) had had her first baby, and it was decided that Edwina should help her sister to care for the child. Edwina booked passage on the *Oceanic*, which was scheduled to sail on 13 April, but the coal strike forced the cancellation of that voyage. Edwina Troutt's second class passage to America was therefore transferred to the *Titanic*, and she boarded that vessel in Southampton on 10 April.

ELLEN WALCROFT **Status: Victim**

Ellen 'Nellie' Walcroft (35) was born in Maidenhead, Berkshire on 9 December 1875 and was the daughter of John and Rebecca Walcroft. The Walcrofts had another daughter, Lucy, as well as two sons, Fred and Walter.

Nellie Walcroft worked as a cook in a Dulwich household, but in 1912 she decided she could make a better life by emigrating to the United States and joining her sister in Mamaroneck, New York. Nellie and her friend Clear Cameron (35) booked their passages to America, but the coal strike forced the cancellation of their original sailing and caused them to transfer their bookings to second class berths on the *Titanic*. Miss Walcroft and Miss Cameron boarded the new White Star liner at Southampton on 10 April.

ELIZABETH AND ROBERTHA WATT **Status: Survivors**

Elizabeth 'Bessie' Milne (40) resided in Aberdeen, Scotland with an uncle, Mr Shanks, who for many years was in charge of that city's blind asylum on Huntly Street. When her uncle obtained a similar position in Inverness and moved his family to that city, Bessie accompanied her relatives there. After her marriage to architect James Watt, Bessie once again made her home in Aberdeen, where she and her husband were members of the Belmont Congregational church. Their daughter Robertha ('Bertha') was born in 1899.

In the autumn of 1911 James Watt went to Portland, Oregon to start a business, and by the spring of 1912 he was ready for his wife and their daughter Bertha (12) to join him in America. Mrs Watt and Bertha booked their passage on the *New York*, but the sailing was cancelled due to the coal strike. The Watts were staying with relatives in London while waiting to sail, and Bertha's uncle obtained second class passages for mother and daughter on board the *Titanic*. Mrs Watt and her daughter took the train from London to Southampton and boarded the new White Star liner on 10 April.

AUGUST WEIKMAN **Status: Survivor**

August Weikman (51) was born in Philadelphia, Pennsylvania around 1861. Mr Weikman married a Miss Henricks, and the couple eventually lived in Palmyra, New Jersey with their three children.

Around 1878 Mr Weikman went to work for the White Star Line and began serving as a barber on board the Line's passenger vessels; after receiving a promotion around 1892, Weikman assumed the duties of barber for the Line's first class passengers. Mr Weikman saved his money, and he eventually became one of Palmyra's largest property owners, numbering among his holdings a large chicken farm.

In September 1911 August Weikman was serving under Captain Edward J. Smith on board the White Star liner *Olympic* when that vessel was rammed by the British cruiser HMS *Hawke*. Six months later Weikman was able to boast of having crossed the Atlantic

705 times during his long career, and in April 1912 his seniority with the White Star Line enabled him to be transferred to the brand new *Titanic* as her chief barber.

Mr Weikman signed the *Titanic*'s articles at Southampton on 6 April, and four days later he was on board the big liner when she left that port city on the first leg of her maiden voyage.

ELEANOR WIDENER — Status: Survivor

Eleanor Elkins (50) was born on 21 September 1861 in Philadelphia, Pennsylvania; Eleanor and her siblings George, William, Ida and Nellie were the children of William and Maria Elkins, members of a wealthy Philadelphia family that had originally amassed its fortune in traction lines.

On 1 November 1883 Eleanor Elkins, who had developed into a great beauty, became the wife of George Widener (50), the son of Peter A.B. Widener, a fabulously wealthy Philadelphian who was a director of the International Mercantile Marine (the parent company of the White Star Line). George Widener, a prominent Philadelphia financier, served as his father's chief advisor in financial matters, owned a local streetcar business and was also the president of Cheltenham Township.

Although George Widener was keenly interested in horses and was a regular exhibitor at horse shows, the young man also had a philanthropic side and was the benefactor of the Widener Memorial School, a facility located at the junction of York Road and Olney Avenue that had been founded by his father; Mr Widener frequently visited the facility, which housed ninety-eight children ranging from 4–18 years of age.

Eleanor Widener had her own interests and enjoyed collecting silver and porcelains. She was also said to possess one of the finest collections of jewels in the world, these having been gifts from her husband. One of Mrs Widener's strings of pearls was said to be worth $250,000.

Eleanor Widener also encouraged the collecting instincts of her son Harry, a Harvard undergraduate who had developed an interest in rare books. In January 1906 Mrs Widener purchased $20,000 worth of colour-plate books for her son, and upon Harry's graduation from Harvard in 1907 she provided him with money to purchase a rare first folio by William Shakespeare.

Around 1911–12 George and Eleanor Widener began making plans to construct a new and spacious villa in Newport, a home which they intended to name 'Miramar'. The Wideners designed the villa themselves and enjoyed purchasing the contents of a number of old French homes with which to furnish the rooms of their new abode.

There was additional excitement in the future for George and Eleanor Widener, because their daughter Eleanor was planning to be married on 19 June 1912. The Wideners made plans to travel to Paris in the spring of 1912 so that Eleanor could assist her daughter in purchasing her trousseau. Harry Widener made plans to accompany his parents and sister to Europe so that he could haunt the Continent's rare book shops in search of additional treasures for his collection.

When the time came for the family to sail to Europe, young Eleanor decided to remain in the United States instead of accompanying her parents and brother on their travels. Mr and Mrs Widener acquiesced to their daughter's wishes, and in February 1912 they and their son Harry (27) sailed to England on the *Mauretania* without her. The three Wideners were accompanied by Mr Widener's valet, Edwin Keeping (32) and Mrs Widener's maid, Amalie Geiger (35), arriving in England on 19 March.

George Widener spent part of his trip inspecting several of his business interests, and on 21 March 1912, at the opening of the London Museum by King George, Eleanor Widener presented thirty silver plates to the museum, these items having once been the property of Nell Gwyn.

While he was in London, Harry Widener made a point of visiting the establishments of Bernard Quaritch and Maggs Brothers, two rare book dealers with whom he intended to do business. Harry Widener also attended several London book auctions in his search for treasures, but he was unsuccessful in obtaining a Shakespeare quarto containing a presentation inscription to Ben Jonson; however, young Widener did manage to acquire a number of desirable items like Thackeray's copy of Cowper and Boswell's *Life of Johnson* presented by the biographer to Sir Joshua Reynolds.

During the first week of April 1912 Harry Widener sent an enthusiastic letter to a fellow bibliophile in the United States telling his friend that he would soon be able to see the rare books that Harry had purchased; Harry Widener also mentioned that he and his parents would be sailing home on the new White Star liner *Titanic* the following week.

One of the books that Harry Widener was able to acquire for his collection was a rare copy of the second edition of Bacon's *Essaies* (1598). When Widener called in at Bernard Quaritch's book shop in order to say goodbye to his friend, the young bibliophile took the *Essaies* out of his pocket and laughingly told Mr Quaritch, 'If I am shipwrecked you will know that this will be on me.'

Mr and Mrs Widener were said to have spent time in Paris and at Cap Martin in France, but – if that was the case – Mr Widener appears to have left his wife and two servants in France and returned to London to rejoin his son Harry. On 10 April 1912 George and Harry Widener boarded the *Titanic* as first class passengers at Southampton and were looking forward to being reunited with Mrs Widener and the servants when the ship touched at Cherbourg that same evening.

RICHARD WILLIAMS **Status: Survivor**

Richard Norris Williams II was born in Geneva on 29 January 1891 and was the son of Charles and Lydia Williams. Charles had been born in the United States in 1860; originally a Philadelphia lawyer and a great-grandson of Benjamin Franklin, he and Lydia Biddle White were married in 1885 in Scranton, Pennsylvania but later moved to Switzerland. Their son Richard was educated in that country, where he became fluent in French and German as well as English. Richard and his parents were not isolated from their relatives in America, however, and they travelled to the United States at least once prior to 1912 in order to visit family members and do a little travelling around the country.

Richard's father Charles had a strong interest in lawn tennis and felt that all countries where lawn tennis was played should be joined together in one single federation in order to ensure the uniformity of the sport and its rules. Charles first proposed the idea to the Secretary of the Swiss Tennis Association and asked him to find ways and means to bring this idea to fruition, which eventually resulted in the formation of the International Lawn Tennis Federation.

Richard Williams was barely into his teens when he began competing in European tennis tournaments; the talented young athlete won the singles Championship of Switzerland in 1911 and the French indoor singles championship the following year.

In 1912 it was Richard's intention to spend a full summer on the U.S. tennis tour as well as take the Harvard University entrance exams. He and his father originally planned to sail for the U.S. in March, but they were forced to postpone their journey when Richard came down with the measles. After his son's recovery, Charles Williams booked their passages to America on board the White Star liner *Titanic*, and he and Richard left Geneva on the evening of 8 April and arrived in Paris the next morning. Father and son spent the afternoon of 9 April at the Tennis Club de Paris and occupied their evening by viewing a German operetta called *The Count of Luxembourg*.

The next morning, having initially been directed to the wrong train station, Charles and Richard endured a wild taxi ride through the streets of Paris and arrived at the correct station just in time to board the boat train to Cherbourg. The trip to the port city was very pleasant, and Richard enjoyed seeing the well-known tennis player Karl Behr (26) seated nearby in the same railway carriage.

After arriving at Cherbourg, Richard and Charles joined the other passengers in boarding the tender and travelled out into the outer harbour to await the coming of the White Star Line's newest passenger liner; the *Titanic* arrived in the harbour at around 6 p.m., and Richard and his father walked across the gangway and boarded the great vessel to begin their voyage back to America.

HUGH WOOLNER **Status: Survivor**

Hugh Woolner (45) was the son of the late Thomas Woolner RA, a distinguished English sculptor. Hugh was born in 1867 and was a Cambridge oarsman during his university career. In 1912 he apparently resided at Crooms Hill, Greenwich, and also had a residence at Salisbury House. His adopted daughter married the 16th Earl of Buchan.

Hugh Woolner boarded the *Titanic* at Southampton on 10 April 1912.

FREDERICK WRIGHT **Status: Victim**

Fred Wright (24) was born in 1888 in Great Billing, Northamptonshire. As a young man he always showed a great interest in sports and in 1905 he was appointed squash racquets marker at the Bath Club in London. (In the meantime, Wright's sister Ida continued to live at home with their father.)

In 1911 Fred joined the White Star Line in time to sail as the racquet court attendant on *Olympic*'s 13 June maiden voyage. He remained on the *Olympic* in that capacity until he returned to Southampton on 8 April 1912 to fill the same job on board the *Titanic*.

In Southampton Fred stayed with Herbert Cave, a first class steward who was also scheduled to serve on board the *Titanic*; Fred Wright and Herbert Cave both joined the *Titanic* on 10 April and were on board the great vessel when she sailed at noon.

MARION WRIGHT — Status: Survivor

Marion Wright (26) was born on 26 May 1885 and lived on the family farm in Yeovil, Somerset with her father, stepmother and three stepsisters.

Arthur Woolcott, a friend from Miss Wright's schooldays, had previously emigrated to the United States to take up residence in Cottage Grove, Oregon, and in 1911 the 32-year-old Woolcott returned to England to visit his home town. The young man's former acquaintance with Miss Wright blossomed into romance, and when he returned to the United States it was understood that Marion would soon follow him there so that they could be married. In April 1912 Miss Wright travelled to Southampton and boarded the White Star liner *Titanic* as a second class passenger.

MARIE YOUNG — Status: Survivor

Marie Young (36) was born in Georgetown, District of Columbia on 3 January 1876 and was a daughter of Samuel and Margaret Wilson Young. Miss Young was convent-educated, spent her childhood in Washington, D.C. and graduated from Acadia University in Canada. Miss Young became a music instructor in Washington, D.C. and was eventually giving sixty-eight piano lessons per week. Among her students were Ethel, Quentin and Archie Roosevelt, the children of President Theodore Roosevelt.

After enduring the strain of her mother's death, Miss Young went to Atlantic City to recuperate and there met Mrs J. Stuart White, a wealthy New York widow who befriended her and eventually asked her to come to New York, live with her in her sumptuous apartment in the Waldorf Astoria and serve as her travelling companion.

In the spring of 1912 Miss Young and Mrs White were travelling in France, where Mrs White purchased a $5,000 trousseau for Miss Young's forthcoming marriage. Sadly, Miss Young then received word that her fiancé in the United States had passed away.

In April it became time for Miss Young and Mrs White to return to the United States, and Miss Young was apparently making plans to return to her home town of Georgetown. On the evening of 10 April Miss Young and Mrs White boarded the tender at Cherbourg and were ferried out to the *Titanic*, the vessel on which they had booked two first class passages to America.

Notes

1. *Toronto Star*, 16 April 1912
2. Shan Bullock, *Thomas Andrews: Shipbuilder*
3. Courtesy of Olivier Mendez
4. Courtesy of Olivier Mendez
5. Courtesy of the Titanic Historical Society and Titanic Museum
6. William H. Taft papers, Library of Congress
7. *Decatur Review*, 22 April 1912
8. William H. Taft papers, Library of Congress
9. *Syracuse Post-Standard*, 22 April 1912
10. Unknown Ohio newspaper
11. *Syracuse Post-Standard*, 18 April 1912
12. *New York American*, 29 April 1912
13. Hester Julian, *Memorials of Henry Forbes Julian*
14. Courtesy of Brian Ticehurst
15. Courtesy of the G.W. Blunt White Library
16. George Behe, *Titanic: Psychic Forewarnings of a Tragedy*
17. *Charlotte Daily Observer*, 25 April 1912
18. *Daily Express*, 16 April 1912
19. *The Irish Times*, 16 April 1912
20. National Archives
21. Shan Bullock, *Thomas Andrews: Shipbuilder*
22. Courtesy of the *Daily Telegraph*, 3 November 1997
23. *Evening Metropolis*, 23 April 1912, courtesy of John Cowart
24. Courtesy of *The Times*, 21 November 1998
25. Courtesy of Robert Burr
26. Courtesy of Brian Ticehurst
27. *Hampshire Post*, 19 April 1912
28. *The RMS* Titanic *and Her Cancellation*
29. Courtesy of Lynne Farr
30. Courtesy of Tony Probst
31. *Salford Reporter*, 23 May 1912, courtesy of Geoff Whitfield
32. Courtesy of Tony Probst

33 Courtesy of the *Southern Evening Echo*, 9 December 1952
34 Courtesy of the *Southern Evening Echo*, 9 December 1952
35 Hester Julian, *Memorials of Henry Forbes Julian*
36 Courtesy of Lynne Farr
37 Courtesy of Olivier Mendez
38 Courtesy of Olivier Mendez
39 Courtesy of Gladys Weaver
40 Courtesy of Patrick Bogue, Onslows auctioneers
41 Courtesy of Patrick Bogue, Onslows auctioneers
42 Courtesy of Steve Miller
43 Courtesy of Patrick Bogue, Onslows auctioneers
44 Courtesy of the Titanic Historical Society and Titanic Museum
45 *Portland Oregonian*, courtesy of Melissa McClone
46 Courtesy of Quincy Williams
47 *Posdata*, courtesy of Hermann Söldner and Daniel Klistorner
48 Courtesy of Steve Maynard
49 Courtesy of the Alford family
50 Courtesy of Eric Porch
51 *East Kent Gazette*, 4 May 1912
52 Courtesy of Brian Ticehurst
53 Courtesy of Sheila Pearce
54 Courtesy of Sheila Pearce
55 Courtesy of Vera Jones and Julia Collyer
56 Courtesy of the Titanic Historical Society and Titanic Museum
57 Courtesy of Ken Marschall
58 *St Louis Post Dispatch*, 26 April 1912 and *Belfast Telegraph*, 24 April 1912
59 *Bristol Evening News*, 16 April 1912
60 *Hampshire Post*, 19 April 1912
61 Brigitte Schwartzenbach, courtesy of Don Lynch
62 Courtesy of the Titanic Historical Society and Titanic Museum
63 Courtesy of Patrick Bogue, Onslows auctioneers
64 Courtesy of the *Daily Telegraph*, 21 July 1981 (from Elizabeth Jean Martin)
65 Courtesy of Patrick Bogue, Onslows auctioneers
66 Courtesy of Kalman Tanito
67 Courtesy of Patrick Bogue, Onslows auctioneers
68 Hester Julian, *Memorials of Henry Forbes Julian*
69 Courtesy of the Titanic Historical Society and Titanic Museum
70 Courtesy of Olivier Mendez
71 Courtesy of *The Titanic Chronicler*
72 Courtesy of Cecily Pilgrim, Stella Clarke and Prudence Morris
73 Courtesy of Patrick Bogue, Onslows auctioneers
74 Courtesy of Per Kristian Sebak
75 Courtesy of Carl Sagan
76 Courtesy of Patrick Bogue, Onslows auctioneers, Nelson Arnstein and Don Lynch

77 *The Sage Family of Peterborough*, courtesy of Geoff Whitfield
78 Courtesy of Per Kristian Sebak
79 Courtesy of the *Eastern Daily Press*, 29 August 2001
80 Courtesy of Patrick Bogue, Onslows auctioneers
81 Estelle Stead, *My Father*
82 Estelle Stead, *My Father*
83 Edith Harper, *Stead the Man*
84 Courtesy of the Titanic Historical Society and Titanic Museum
85 *Belfast Evening Telegraph*, 15 April 1912
86 Courtesy of Patrick Bogue, Onslows auctioneers
87 Courtesy of Patrick Bogue, Onslows auctioneers
88 *New York Times*, 20 April 1912
89 *East Kent Gazette*, 4 May 1912
90 Courtesy of Kalman Tanito
91 *Cork Examiner* and *Irish Echo*
92 *East Kent Gazette*, 4 May 1912
93 Courtesy of Kalman Tanito
94 Courtesy of Eva Hart
95 Courtesy of Kalman Tanito
96 National Archives
97 Courtesy of Patrick Bogue, Onslows auctioneers
98 *Madras Mail*, 22 May 1912, courtesy of Don Lynch
99 *East Kent Gazette*, 4 May 1912
100 *Philadelphia Evening Bulletin*, 20 April 1912
101 Courtesy of Henry Hoyt, Helen H. Hoyt, Richard N. Hall II and Henry I. Hall
102 Courtesy of Kalman Tanito
103 *Folkestone Herald*, 4 May 1912
104 Courtesy of the Titanic Historical Society and Titanic Museum
105 *Bath Chronicle*, 4 May 1912
106 *Portland Oregonian*, 24 April 1912, courtesy of Melissa McClone
107 *Hudson Evening Register*, 20 April 1912
108 *Eastern Daily Press*, 1 May 1912
109 Courtesy of the Merseyside Maritime Museum
110 Courtesy of the *Cork Examiner*
111 *East Kent Gazette*, 4 May 1912
112 John Robertson, courtesy of Don Lynch
113 Hester Julian, *Memorials of Henry Forbes Julian*, and the *Atlantic Daily Bulletin*
114 *Westmeath Independent*, courtesy of Don Lynch
115 *St Ives Western Echo*, 4 May 1912
116 *Bath Chronicle*, 4 May 1912
117 Courtesy of Don Lynch
118 *Newark Advocate*, 20 April 1912
119 *New York Evening Journal*, 19 April 1912
120 *Toronto World*, 19 April 1912
121 *The Times*, 20 April 1912, courtesy of Dinah Quilter and Pat Cook

122 *Cork Constitution*, 13 May 1912
123 Hester Julian, *Memorials of Henry Forbes Julian*, and the *Atlantic Daily Bulletin*
124 Courtesy of the Titanic Historical Society and Titanic Museum
125 *New York Evening Journal*, 19 April 1912
126 Brigitte Schwartzenbach, courtesy of Don Lynch
127 *Karjalan Sanomat*, courtesy of Kalman Tanito
128 *Toronto World*, 20 April 1912
129 Courtesy of Paddy O'Sullivan and Noel Ray
130 Kyrill Schabert, courtesy of Don Lynch
131 *Hartford Times*, 19 April 1912
132 *Diario de Noticias*, courtesy of Michael Goss
133 *New York Sun*, 19 April 1912
134 *Washington Post*, 21 April 1912
135 National Archives
136 *Sondmoorsposten*, 28 May 1912
137 Translation courtesy of Per Kristian Sebak
138 Archibald Gracie, *The Truth About the* Titanic
139 *St Nicholas Magazine*, 1913
140 *Canton Evening Repository*, 19 April 1912
141 *New York Times*, 29 April 1912
142 *New York Times*, 8 May 1912
143 *Christian Science Sentinel*, 20 December 1912, courtesy of the Christian Science Publishing Co.
144 Courtesy of Dinah Quilter and Pat Cook
145 *Brooklyn Daily Eagle*, 19 April 1912
146 *Decatur Review*, 19 April 1912
147 Senate *Titanic* Investigation
148 Courtesy of the Merseyside Maritime Museum
149 *Newport Herald*, 28 and 29 May 1912
150 *Rockford Republic*, 1912 (date unknown)
151 *East Kent Gazette*, 4 May 1912
152 *The Park Alumniad*, May 1912, courtesy of Don Lynch
153 Sylvia Caldwell, *Women of the* Titanic *Disaster*
154 Courtesy of Malcolm Cheape
155 *Binghampton Press*, 29 April 1912
156 *Lawrenceville Alumni Bulletin*, October 1912, courtesy of Daniel Klistorner
157 Courtesy of Sybil Lane and Don Lynch
158 Hester Julian, *Memorials of Henry Forbes Julian*
159 *London Observer*, 26 May 1912
160 *Moody Church Bulletin*, 1912 (date unknown)
161 Vera Jones, courtesy of Geoff Whitfield
162 *Washington Post Semi-Monthly Magazine*, 26 May 1912
163 *Washington Post Semi-Monthly Magazine*, 14 July 1912
164 *Islington Daily Gazette & North London Tribune*, 9 May 1912
165 Senate *Titanic* investigation

166 *Manitoba Free Press*, 29 April 1912
167 *Westmeath Independent*, 1912 (date unknown)
168 *Cork Examiner* 1912 (date unknown)
169 *Westmeath Independent*, 1912 (date unknown)
170 *Handelsblad van Antwerpen*, 23 May 1912
171 *Washington Post*, 19 April 1912
172 Washington Dodge, *The Loss of the Titanic*
173 *Los Angeles Times*, 21 April 1912
174 Senate *Titanic* inquiry
175 Lady Flavia Anderson, courtesy of Randy Bigham
176 Lady Clair Lindsay, courtesy of Randy Bigham
177 *New Haven Register*, 1912 (date unknown)
178 *Hampshire Telegraph*, 3 May 1912
179 'My Experience in the Wreck of the *Titanic*', *American Medicine*, May 1912, courtesy of Eric Sauder
180 *Seattle Daily Times*, 22 and 23 April 1912
181 *Philadelphia Evening Bulletin*, April (possibly 29 April) 1912
182 Courtesy of Susan and Rebecca Stares
183 *Houghton Mining Gazette*, 19 April 1912
184 *New York Times*, 25 April 1912
185 *The Outlook*, 27 April 1912, courtesy of Randy Bigham
186 *Harper's Weekly*, 27 April 1912
187 *Boston Herald*, 23 April 1912
188 Archibald Butt scrapbooks, Georgia Archives
189 *New York Times*, 11 May 1912
190 *New York Evening Journal*, 11 May 1912
191 *Ilford Graphic*, 10 May 1912
192 Courtesy of the *Atlantic Daily Bulletin*
193 *Providence Evening Bulletin*, 20 April 1912
194 Courtesy of Patrick Bogue, Onslows auctioneers
195 Archibald Gracie, *The Truth About the Titanic*
196 *Washington Post*, 22 April 1912
197 *Berkshire Evening Eagle*, 22 April 1912
198 'Frank Millet: A Versatile American' by Hilda Millet Booth and John Parsons Millet, courtesy of the Smithsonian Archive of American Art.
199 Shan Bullock, *Thomas Andrews, Shipbuilder*
200 Courtesy of Don Lynch
201 *New York Evening Journal*, 19 April 1912
202 *Harrisburg Patriot*, 19 April 1912
203 Courtesy of Don Lynch
204 *Chicago Evening Post*, 23 April 1912
205 *Brainerd Daily Dispatch*, 2 December 1937
206 *Los Angeles Times*, 21 April 1912
207 *Dumfries & Galloway Standard*, 11 May 1912
208 *Christian Science Journal*, October 1912

209 *Johnstown Tribune*, 22 April 1912
210 Courtesy of John Creamer
211 Courtesy of the Titanic Historical Society and Titanic Museum
212 *Grant's Pass Daily Courier* (date unknown)
213 *Manchester Guardian*, 20 April 1912
214 *Cork Examiner*, 11 May 1912, courtesy of Delia Mahoney
215 Senate *Titanic* inquiry
216 Courtesy of Brian Ticehurst
217 Øyvind Sollie and Tone Bunæs, courtesy of Per Kristian Sebak
218 Senate *Titanic* inquiry
219 Senate *Titanic* inquiry
220 Archibald Gracie, *The Truth About the Titanic*
221 *Brooklyn Daily Eagle*, 19 April 1912
222 *Waterford News* (date unknown), courtesy of Arne Mjåland
223 Courtesy of the *Rhode Island Sunday Magazine*, 15 April 1962
224 Courtesy of Gerald Pearson and Patti Pearson-Kotz
225 *North Devon Journal*, 25 April 1912
226 Senate *Titanic* inquiry
227 Archibald Gracie, *The Truth About the Titanic*
228 Courtesy of Linda Messenger and Trudy Ransome
229 Courtesy of Craig Sopin
230 Richard de Roussy de Sales, courtesy of Rustie Brown
231 *St Louis Times*, 19 April 1912
232 *Cork Examiner*, 6 May 1912
233 Senate *Titanic* inquiry
234 Courtesy of Patrick Bogue, Onslows auctioneers
235 *Gazette van Brugge*, 25 May 1912
236 *Sphere*, 25 May 1912
237 Senate *Titanic* inquiry
238 Edith Harper, *Stead the Man*
239 Archibald Gracie, *The Truth About the Titanic*
240 Richard Faber, courtesy of Don Lynch
241 Shan Bullock, *Thomas Andrews, Shipbuilder*
242 Senate *Titanic* inquiry
243 Unknown 1912 newspaper, courtesy of Rebecca Rah
244 Courtesy of Steve Miller
245 *Oxford Times*, 18 May 1912
246 Archibald Gracie, *The Truth About the Titanic*
247 Martha Stephenson and Elizabeth Eustis, *The Titanic – Our Story*, courtesy of Christina Gorch and Jacque Gorch
248 *Cincinnati Enquirer*, 20 April 1912
249 *Camden Daily Chronicle*, 16 May 1912
250 Memo from the office of the first vice-president, Pennsylvania Lines West of Pittsburgh, George Behe collection
251 William H. Taft papers, Library of Congress

252 Courtesy of Don Lynch
253 Courtesy of Don Lynch
254 Courtesy of Don Lynch
255 Courtesy of Don Lynch
256 Courtesy of Don Lynch
257 *Maidenhead Advertiser*, 29 April 1912, courtesy of Pat Cook
258 *The Spectrum*, April 1914, courtesy of Roy Kristiansen
259 Senate *Titanic* inquiry
260 Senate *Titanic* inquiry
261 Courtesy of the Rosenbach Museum and Library
262 Archibald Gracie, *The Truth About the Titanic*
263 Dr Alfred Pain memorial pamphlet, courtesy of Don Lynch
264 William H. Taft papers, Library of Congress
265 *National Magazine*, October 1912

INDEX

Abelseth, Karen 139–40, 407, 481
Abelseth, Olaus 141, 409, 481
Aldworth, Charles 189, 427
Allen, Elizabeth 141–2, 408, 477–8
Allison, Bessie 94, 420
Allison, Helen 420
Allison, Hudson 94, 169, 420
Allison, Hudson Trevor 420
Allison, Loraine 94
Andersen, Albert 473
Anderson, Harry 190–1
Andreasson, Pal 86, 462
Andrew, Edgar 392–3, 408–9
Andrews, Kornelia 91–3, 103–5, 409
Andrews, Thomas 17–18, 31, 191–2, 249, 300–1, 367–9, 398, 409–10
Appleton, Charlotte 238–39, 274
Artagaveytia, Ramon 45–6, 410
Asquith, Margot 243
Astor, John Jacob 92, 104, 122, 124, 155, 163, 245, 253, 263, 265–6, 275, 283, 323, 334, 378, 421–2
Astor, Madeleine 92, 104–5, 122, 124, 130, 163, 165, 258–9, 261, 263, 269, 275, 334, 352–3, 380–1, 384
Augustsson, Albert 86, 462

Ball, Ada 302–4, 306–7, 411–2
Barr, Captain 129
Bateman, Robert 32, 302–4, 306–7, 410–12
Baumann, John 450
Baxter, Helene 360
Baxter, Quigg 360
Beane, Edward 93, 105–6, 412
Beane, Ethel 93, 105–6, 412–13
Beauchamp, Henry 47, 413
Becker, Nellie 79–80, 142–4, 413–14
Becker, Richard 79–80, 142–4, 413–14
Becker, Ruth 79–80, 142–4, 413–14
Beckwith, Richard 144–5, 160–1, 414–16, 458
Beckwith, Sarah 144–5, 160–1, 414–16, 458
Beesley, Lawrence 106–12, 145–60, 226, 235, 415
Behr, Karl 144, 160–1, 198, 415–16, 458, 497
Bessant, Edward 398
Bird, Ellen 491
Birnbaum, Jakob 47, 417
Björnström-Steffanson, Mauritz 130–2
Blackwell, Stephen 419
Blair, David 316
Bonnell, Caroline 48, 162–5, 417–18
Bonnell, Elizabeth 48, 162–5, 418
Bowen, Grace 351–2, 480
Boxhall, Joseph 142, 238–40, 268, 315, 320
Bradford, Wallace 231
Bradley, Bridget 113
Brewe, Arthur 171
Bricoux, Roger 18–19, 418–19
Bride, Harold 166–9, 405, 419

Bristow, Harry 19, 419
Brown, Amelia 93–4, 169, 420
Brown, Caroline 274–5
Brown, Edith 12, 32, 288, 420–1
Brown, Elizabeth 288, 420–1
Brown, Margaret 170–80, 421–2
Brown, Thomas 288–9, 420–1
Bryhl, Dagmar 180–1, 422
Bryhl, Kurt 422
Buckley, Daniel 95, 113, 422
Bucknell, Emma 171–2
Burke, Jeremiah 73, 422
Burns, Elizabeth 129, 488
Burr, Ewart 33, 423
Buss, Kate 33–4, 48–50, 69–70, 74, 81–3, 95–6, 181–4, 198–9, 423
Butt, Archibald 20, 92, 275, 283, 388–9, 401–2, 423–6
Butt, Clara 283
Butterworth, Jack 50–1, 426
Byles, Thomas 208

Cairns, Alexander 427
Calderhead, Edward 179, 464
Caldwell, Albert 96–7, 184–5, 226–7, 426–7
Caldwell, Alden 96–7, 184–5, 226, 426–7
Caldwell, Sylvia 96–7, 184–9, 226, 426–7
Cameron, Clear 393, 395, 494
Candee, Helen 130–2, 257–8
Carter, Lillian 81, 155–6
Carter, Lucile 189–90, 380, 427
Carter, Lucile (Miss) 380
Carter, Revd Ernest 81, 155–6, 449
Carter, William 189, 234, 238, 299, 380, 398
Carter, William Jr 380
Cassebeer, Eleanor 190–92, 427
Cave, Herbert 498
Cavendish, Julia 99, 242
Chambers, Ethel 192–8, 428
Chambers, Norman 192–8, 428
Chapman, John and Sarah 51, 56, 428
Chapman, Joseph 198–9, 428–9
Chaudanson, Victorine 480
Cherry, Gladys 97–9, 114, 199–200, 429
Chevré, Paul 322, 324
Clark, Virginia 380
Clark, Walter 380
Clarke, Ada 293
Clarke, Charles 34, 429
Cleaver, Alice 420
Cloman, Flora 426
Cohen, Gershon 115, 429
Coleridge, Reginald 35, 429–30
Collett, Sidney 20–1, 49, 200–1, 430
Collyer, Charlotte 12, 51–2, 201–11, 430–1
Collyer, Harvey 51–2, 201–11, 430–1
Collyer, Marjorie 51–2, 186, 201–11, 430–1
Connolly, Kate 324, 463
Cook, Selina 52, 321, 431
Cooper, Mrs Colin 260
Cornell, Malvina 142, 274
Cottam, Harold 168
Coutts, Mary 211–3, 431–2
Coutts, Neville 211–3
Coutts, William 211–3
Cribb, John 116–17, 432
Cribb, Laura 116–17, 432
Crosby, Catherine 213–15, 432–4
Crosby, Edward 213–15, 432–4
Crosby, Harriette 432–4
Cumings, Florence 380–1

Dahl, Charles 215–17, 434
Daly, Eugene 217–18, 434
Daly, Margaret 218, 434–5
Daniels, Sarah 94, 420
Davidson, Orian 295, 365–6, 452
Davidson, Thornton 295, 452
Davies, Charles 35, 435
Davies, Elizabeth 484
Davies, Evan 478
Davies, John 484
Davison, Mary 21, 435–6
Davison, Thomas 435–6
Deacon, Percy 435
Dean, Bertram 436
Dean, Eva 52, 436
Denbury, Herbert 348, 476
Dibden, William 435
Dick, Albert 220–1, 436–7
Dick, Vera 220–1, 436–7
Dodd, George 325, 398

Dodge, Ruth 221–36, 437
Dodge, Washington 221–36, 437
Dodge, Washington Jr 221–36, 437
Douglas, Mahala 237–40, 438
Douglas, Walter 237–40, 438
Duff Gordon, Cosmo 238, 240–3, 259, 331, 438–9
Duff Gordon, Lucy 240–3, 331, 438–9
Dulles, William 126
Dyker, Anna 244, 439
Dymond, Francis 244, 439–40

Earnshaw, Olive 475
Eddy, Mary Baker 156–7, 159, 317
Enander, Ingvar 422
Ervine, Albert 53, 440
Eustis, Elizabeth 352, 376, 490
Evans, Edith 274–5
Everett, Thomas 53, 440

Farrenden, Ernest 54, 440
Farthing, John 491
Fenwick, James 159
Fleming, Margaret 492–3
Flynn, John 325, 464
Fortune, Alice 484–5
Fortune, Charles 484–5
Fortune, Ethel 484–5
Fortune, Mabel 484–5
Fortune, Mark 484–5
Fortune, Mary 484–5
Francatelli, Laura 439, 441
Franklin, Thomas 35, 441
Frauenthal, Henry 245–7, 441–2
Frauenthal, Isaac 441–2
Frolicher, Hedwig 54, 117–18, 442
Frolicher-Stehli, Margaretha 54, 117–18, 442
Frolicher-Stehli, Maximilian 54, 117–18, 442
Futrelle, Jacques 21, 247–71, 442–4
Futrelle, Lillie May 21, 247–71, 442–4

Gavey, Lawrence 476
Gee, Arthur 36, 444
Geiger, Amalie 498
Gibbons, Jacob 271, 445
Gibson, Dorothy 123–7
Gibson, Pauline 123–7
Goldenberg, Nella 272–3, 445–6
Goldenberg, Samuel 272–3, 445–6
Gracie, Archibald 21–2, 130, 141, 253, 258, 260, 270, 273–7, 296, 332, 345, 376, 400, 446
Graham, Edith 363
Graham, George 36–7, 447
Guggenheim, Benjamin 288

Hamalainen, Anna 119, 447
Hamalainen, Wiljo 119, 447
Harknett, Alice 455
Harmer, Abraham 165
Harper, Anna 55, 314, 449, 460
Harper, Edith 64, 362
Harper, Henry 277–83, 447–8
Harper, John 55, 200–1, 314, 449, 460
Harper, Myra 277–83, 449
Harris, Henry 249–50, 253, 261, 263–4, 269–70, 283–4, 331, 449–50
Harris, Irene 249–50, 253, 259–60, 263–4, 269–70, 283–4, 287, 331, 449–50
Hart, Benjamin 75–6, 287–93, 450
Hart, Esther 75–6, 287–93, 450
Hart, Eva 75–6, 287–93, 450
Hartley, Wallace 56, 451
Hassab, Hamad 448,
Hawksford, Walter 293–4, 451–2
Hays, Charles 295, 434, 452
Hays, Clara 295, 365, 452
Hays, Margaret 475
Hegarty, Nora 422
Hewlett, Mary 296, 452
Hichens, Robert 223, 371
Hickman, Leonard 435
Hickman, Lewis 435
Hickman, Stanley 435
Hilles, Charles 20
Hiltunen, Martta 447
Hocking, Samuel 56–7, 452–3
Hodges, Henry 37, 453
Hogeboom, Anna 409
Holten, Johan 473
Hoyt, Frederick 253, 268, 269–70, 285, 296, 453
Hoyt, Jane 253, 269–70, 285, 296, 453

Hoyt, William 126, 165
Humblen, Adolf 139–40, 408, 481

Icard, Amelia 491
Immanuel, King Victor 425
Immigration, Commissioner of 137
Ismay, Bruce 121, 130, 144–6, 151–2, 161, 163, 189, 191–2, 206, 226, 234, 237–9, 258, 274, 285, 287, 297–301, 305, 326, 336, 369, 372, 378, 380, 398–9, 403, 454

Jeffreys, Clifford 476
Jeffreys, Ernest 476
Jerwan, Marie 301–7, 454
Johansson, Jakob 57, 71, 74, 76, 454–5
Johansson, Nils 86, 462, 463
Johnson, A. 78
Johnston, Andrew 57, 455
Johnston, Elizabeth 57, 455
Jones, Thomas 200
Jonsson, Carl 86, 462
Joughin, Charles 308, 455–6
Julian, Henry 22, 38, 57–8, 456

Keane, Nora 308–9, 456–7
Keeping, Edwin 496
Kenyon, Frederick 83
Kimball, Edwin 310, 416, 458
Kimball, Gertrude 310, 416, 458
Kirkwood, John 15
Klasen, Albin 322
Knapp, J.J. 77–8
Kreuchen, Emilie 408, 478

Lahtinen, Anna 484
Lahtinen, William 484
Lambert-Williams, Fletcher 492
Laroche, Joseph 58–9, 458
Laroche, Juliette 58–9, 458
Laroche, Louise 58–9, 458
Laroche, Simonne 58–9, 458
Leader, Alice 83–4, 459
Lehmann, Bertha 311, 459
Leitch, Jessie 314, 449, 460
Leroy, Berthe 59, 438, 460–61
Lightoller, Charles 119, 145–6, 151–2, 157, 197, 222, 240, 315–17, 368, 388, 461
Lindsay, William 317–18, 461–2
Linehan, Michael 113, 422
Lines, Elizabeth 84–5, 462
Lines, Mary 84–5, 462
Long, Milton 387
Longley, Gretchen 409
Loring, Joseph 477
Lowe, Harold 12, 180, 205–7, 209–10, 227, 246, 255, 256, 269, 287, 315, 318–21, 330, 353, 356, 394, 400, 462
Lundin, Olga 85–6, 462–3
Lundström, Thure 321–2, 463
Lyons, William 165

Mack, Mary 288
Madill, Georgette 142, 408, 477–8
Malachard, Noel 302–4
Marconi, Guglielmo 111, 168
Maréchal, Pierre 322–4, 463
Marsden, Evelyn 367
Mauro, Philip 105
Mayne, Berthe 172
McCarthy, Catherine 324, 463
McGough, James 325–6
Meanwell, Marion 59, 464
Mellors, William 327–9, 465
Meyer, Edgar 238
Meyer, Leila 239, 331
Middleton, Alfred 53
Millet, Francis 20, 60, 275, 283, 300, 425, 465–8
Millet, John 300
Minahan, Daisy 330–1, 468
Minahan, Lillian 330–1, 468
Minahan, William 330–1, 468
Mock, Phillip 120, 332, 469, 482–3
Molson, Harry 295
Moody, James 318, 320
Moore, Clarence 220, 238, 275, 297, 402, 469
Mudd, Thomas 38, 61, 470
de Mulder, Theodoor 218–19, 436
Mulvihill, Bertha 99–100, 217–18, 470
Murdoch, William 12, 149, 190, 205–6, 222, 225, 315–6, 318–19

Nagel, Charles 137
Newman, Charles 317
Newsom, Helen 160, 414–16, 458
Nicholls, Joseph 484
Nichols, Walter 332–7, 471
Norman, Robert 26
Nye, Elizabeth 86–8, 472

O'Connell, Patrick 113, 422
O'Connor, Patrick 422
O'Keefe, Patrick 338, 472
O'Leary, Hanora 113
Olsen, Henry 61, 472–3
Olsson, Elina 463
Omont, Alfred 322, 324
Ostby, Engelhart 338, 473
Ostby, Helene 338, 473

Pain, Alfred 400–1
Palmer, Fred 317
Palmer, Stewart 317
Parrish, Lutie 358–61, 483
Parsons, Alfred 60, 466
Payne, Vivian 452
Penrose, John 376, 381
Pereault, Anne 452
Persson, Ernst 341–3, 473
Peters, Katie 324, 463
Peuchen, Arthur 119, 240, 371, 473–4
Phillips, Alice 23, 343–4, 474
Phillips, Escott 23, 343–4
Phillips, John 166–9
Pickard, Berk 344–5, 474
Pirrie, Lord 16, 18, 409,
Pitman, Herbert 157, 191, 195–6, 245, 315
Pius X, Pope 425
Potter, Lily 345–6, 474–5
Pritchard, Alice 381
Pugh, Alfred 120, 475

Quick, Fred 346–7, 475–6
Quick, Jane 346–7, 475–6
Quick, Phyllis 346–7, 475–6
Quick, Winifred 346–7, 475–6

Renouf, Lillian 348, 476
Renouf, Peter 348, 476
Rheims, George 12, 348–9, 477
Richard, Emile 39, 477
Riordan, Hannah 113
Robert, Elizabeth 142, 350, 408, 477–8
Roebling, Washington 363–4, 418
Rogers, William 62, 478
Roosevelt, Theodore 275, 389, 424–5, 498
Rosenkrantz, Baroness 425–6
Rostron, Arthur 151, 165, 236, 257, 364, 380–2, 404–5
Rothes, Countess 33, 200, 429
Rothschild, Elizabeth 490
Rothschild, Martin 490
Rouse, Richard 39, 478
Rugg, Emily 476
Ryan, Edward 351, 479
Ryerson, Arthur 238, 275, 351–3
Ryerson, Emily 152, 237–9, 275, 351–3, 379, 479–80
Ryerson, John 351–3
Ryerson, Suzette 351–3

Saalfeld, Adolphe 39–40, 62, 354, 481
Sage, John 481
Sage, Stella 63, 481
Salkjelsvik, Anna 63, 408, 481
Sap, Julius 354–5, 481–2
Scarrott, Joseph 356–8, 482
Schabert, Emma 120–2, 332, 469, 482–3
Sharp, Percival 413
Shellard, Fred 440
Shelley, Imanita 358–62, 483
Shine, Ellen 113
Shute, Elizabeth 88, 363–7, 483
Silven, Lyyli 484
Silverthorne, Spencer 464
Simonius-Blumer, Alfons 117–18
Simpson, John 359, 367
Sincock, Maude 100, 435, 483–4
Sloan, Mary 367–9, 484
Sloper, William 122–7, 415, 484–5
Smith, Edward 23, 29, 87, 134–5, 143, 150–2, 161, 166–8, 209, 217, 220, 225, 232, 245, 248, 260, 296–9 306, 322, 331, 338–9, 368, 370, 378, 383–4, 399, 403, 406, 485–7

Smith, James Clinch 130, 274–6
Smith, Lucian 322, 372
Smith, Mary Eloise 240, 331, 369–72, 487
Smith, Richard 63, 487
Smyth, Julia 372–3, 487
Snyder, John 41, 373–4, 488
Snyder, Nelle 373–4
Søholt, Peter 481
Spedden, Frederick 128–30, 488
Spedden, Margaretta 128–30, 488
Spedden, Robert 128–30, 488
Stanley, Amy 375, 489
Stanley, Edward 489
Stead, William 23–4, 41, 64, 362, 489–90
Stengel, Annie 376, 490
Stengel, Charles 376, 490
Stephenson, Martha 376–82, 490
Stone, Martha 382–5, 490–1
Straus, Isidor 42, 132, 155, 252, 269, 360, 362, 491
Straus, Rosalie 42, 132, 252, 269, 360, 362, 491
Strom, Elna 473
Swane, George 93, 420
Swift, Margaret 135, 459

Taft, Mrs Henry 20
Taft, William Howard 20, 92, 275, 388–9, 401, 424–5, 467
Taussig, Emil 24, 491–2
Taussig, Ruth 491–2
Taussig, Tillie 491–2
Taylor, Elmer 213, 215, 385–6, 492
Taylor, Juliet 385–6, 492
Thayer III, John 179, 276, 377, 380, 386–8, 492–3
Thayer, John B. 92, 104, 258, 275, 331, 352, 376–7, 386–9, 492–3
Thayer, Marian 190, 331, 352–3, 376–8, 380, 386–9, 492–3
Thorne, Gertrude 270, 284
Tobin, Roger 324, 463
Townley, Ernest 25–7
Troutt, Edwina 64–5, 89, 100–1, 309, 390–3, 493

United States Hydrographic Office 77–8
Unknown newspaper correspondents 28
Unknown passengers 65–6
Unknown Southampton resident 67

Val, Cardinal Merry del 425
Villiers, Madame de 172

Walcroft, Ellen 393–6, 494
Warnez, Alphonse 355
Warren, Anna 338–41, 473
Warren, Frank 338–41, 473
Watt, Elizabeth 42, 89–90, 396–7, 494
Watt, Robertha 42, 89–90, 396–7, 494
Weikman, August 398–9, 494–5
White Star Line 10, 20, 23, 29–30, 145, 151–3, 177, 189, 258, 270, 298, 301, 338, 372, 391, 399, 402, 405, 439–40, 454–5 461–2, 486–7, 494–5, 497
White, Percival 84
White, Richard 84
Wick, George 48, 162–5
Wick, Mary 162–5
Wick, Natalie 162–5
Widener, Eleanor 238, 331, 380, 388, 399, 495–6
Widener, George 234, 238, 245, 275, 331, 352, 388, 399, 495–6
Widener, Harry 399, 495–6
Wilde, Henry 316
Williams, Charles 43, 496–7
Williams, Fletcher Lambert 385, 492
Williams, Richard 43, 258, 377, 400, 496–7
Williams, William 137
Wilson, Helen 488
Woolner, Hugh 130–3, 497
Wright, Frederick 67, 497–8
Wright, Marion 49, 89, 183, 400–1, 430, 498

Young, Marie 134–7, 401–6, 498